Pattern/ Principle	Description
Information Expert	A general principle of object design and responsibility assignment? Assign a responsibility to the information expert—the class that has the information necessary to fulfill the responsibility.
Creator	Who creates? (Note that Factory is a common alternate solution.) Assign class B the responsibility to create an instance of class A if one of these is true: 1. B contains A 4. B records A 2. B aggregates A 5. B closely uses A 3. B has the initializing data for A
Controller	What first object beyond the UI layer receives and coordinates ("controls") a system operation? Assign the responsibility to an object representing one of these choices: 1. Represents the overall "system," a "root object," a device that the software is running within, or a major subsystem (these are all variations of a *facade controller*). 2. Represents a use case scenario within which the system operation occurs (a use-case or *session controller*)
Low Coupling (evaluative)	How to reduce the impact of change? Assign responsibilities so that (unnecessary) coupling remains low. Use this principle to evaluate alternatives.
High Cohesion (evaluative)	How to keep objects focused, understandable, and manageable, and as a side-effect, support Low Coupling? Assign responsibilities so that cohesion remains high. Use this to evaluate alternatives.
Polymorphism	Who is responsible when behavior varies by type? When related alternatives or behaviors vary by type (class), assign responsibility for the behavior—using polymorphic operations—to the types for which the behavior varies.
Pure Fabrication	Who is responsible when you are desperate, and do not want to violate high cohesion and low coupling? Assign a highly cohesive set of responsibilities to an artificial or convenience "behavior" class that does not represent a problem domain concept—something made up, in order to support high cohesion, low coupling, and reuse.
Indirection	How to assign responsibilities to avoid direct coupling? Assign the responsibility to an intermediate object to mediate between other components or services, so that they are not directly coupled.
Protected Variations	How to assign responsibilities to objects, subsystems, and systems so that the variations or instability in these elements do not have an undesirable impact on other elements? Identify points of predicted variation or instability; assign responsibilities to create a stable "interface" around them.

"This edition contains Larman's usual accurate and thoughtful writing. It is a very good book made even better."

—**Alistair Cockburn**, author, *Writing Effective Use Cases* and *Surviving OO Projects*

"People often ask me which is the best book to introduce them to the world of OO design. Ever since I came across it *Applying UML and Patterns* has been my unreserved choice."

—**Martin Fowler**, author, *UML Distilled* and *Refactoring*

"This book makes learning UML enjoyable and pragmatic by incrementally introducing it as an intuitive language for specifying the artifacts of object analysis and design. It is a well written introduction to UML and object methods by an expert practitioner."

—**Cris Kobryn**, Chair of the UML Revision Task Force and UML 2.0 Working Group

"Too few people have a knack for explaining things. Fewer still have a handle on software analysis and design. Craig Larman has both."

—**John Vlissides**, author, *Design Patterns* and *Pattern Hatching*

APPLYING UML AND PATTERNS

THIRD EDITION

APPLYING UML AND PATTERNS

AN INTRODUCTION TO OBJECT-ORIENTED ANALYSIS AND DESIGN AND ITERATIVE DEVELOPMENT

THIRD EDITION

CRAIG LARMAN

Prentice Hall PTR
Upper Saddle River, NJ 07458
www.phptr.com

Publisher: John Wait
Editor in Chief: Don O'Hagan
Acquisitions Editor: Paul Petralia
Marketing Manager: Chris Guzikowski
Managing Editor: John Fuller
Project Editor: Julie Nahil
Manufacturing Buyer: Carol Melville

The publisher offers excellent discounts on this book when ordered in quantity for bulk purchases or special sales, which may include electronic versions and/or custom covers and content particular to your business, training goals, marketing focus, and branding interests. For more information, please contact:

U. S. Corporate and Government Sales
(800) 382-3419
corpsales@pearsontechgroup.com

For sales outside the U. S., please contact:

International Sales
international@pearsoned.com

Visit us on the Web: www.phptr.com

Library of Congress Cataloging-in-Publication Data:

Larman, Craig.
    Applying UML and patterns: an introduction to object-oriented analysis and design and
    iterative development / Craig Larman.— 3rd ed.
        p. cm.
    Includes bibliographical references and index.
    ISBN 0-13-148906-2 (alk. paper)
    1. Object-oriented methods (Computer science) 2. UML (Computer science) 3. System
analysis. 4. System design. I. Title.

QA76.9.O35 L37 2004
005.1'17--dc22   2004057647

Quote acknowledgments:

Paul Erdos: From "The Man Who Only Loved Numbers" by Paul Hoffman.
H.G. Wells: Used by permission of A.P. Watt Ltd. On behalf of the Executors of the Estate of H.G. Wells.

ISBN 0-13-148906-2
Text printed in the United States on recycled paper at Courier in Westford, Massachusetts
Fourth printing, June 2005

For Julie, Haley, and Hannah

Thanks for the love and support.

CONTENTS AT A GLANCE

CONTENTS BY MAJOR TOPICS

This book introduces a topic incrementally, spread out over chapters as the case studies unfold. That's useful, but it introduces a problem: How can you find most material on a major subject (e.g., OO Design)? The Index is one solution, but fine-grained; this listing provides another.

TABLE OF CONTENTS

FOREWORD

Programming is fun, but developing quality software is hard. In between the nice ideas, the requirements or the "vision," and a working software product, there is much more than programming. Analysis and design, defining how to solve the problem, what to program, capturing this design in ways that are easy to communicate, to review, to implement, and to evolve is what lies at the core of this book. This is what you will learn.

The Unified Modeling Language (UML) has become the universally-accepted language for software design blueprints. UML is the visual language used to convey design ideas throughout this book, which emphasizes how developers really apply frequently used UML elements, rather than obscure features of the language.

The importance of patterns in crafting complex systems has long been recognized in other disciplines. Software design patterns are what allow us to describe design fragments, and reuse design ideas, helping developers leverage the expertise of others. Patterns give a name and form to abstract heuristics, rules and best practices of object-oriented techniques. No reasonable engineer wants to start from a blank slate, and this book offers a palette of readily usable design patterns.

But software design looks a bit dry and mysterious when not presented in the context of a software engineering process. And on this topic, I am delighted that for his new edition, Craig Larman has chosen to embrace and introduce the Unified Process, showing how it can be applied in a relatively simple and low-ceremony way. By presenting the case study in an iterative, risk-driven, architecture-centric process, Craig's advice has realistic context; he exposes the dynamics of what really happens in software development, and shows the external forces at play. The design activities are connected to other tasks, and they no longer appear as a purely cerebral activity of systematic transformations or creative intuition. And Craig and I are convinced of the benefits of iterative development, which you will see abundantly illustrated throughout.

So for me, this book has the right mix of ingredients. You will learn a systematic method to do Object-Oriented Analysis and Design (OOA/D) from a great teacher, a brilliant methodologist, and an "OO guru" who has taught it to thousands around the world. Craig describes the method in the context of the Unified Process. He gradually presents more sophisticated design patterns—this will make the book very handy when you are faced with real-world design challenges. And he uses the most widely accepted notation.

I'm honored to have had the opportunity to work directly with the author of this major book. I enjoyed reading the first edition, and was delighted when he asked me to review the draft of his new edition. We met several times and exchanged many e-mails. I have learned much from Craig, even about our own process work on the Unified Process and how to improve it and position it in various organizational contexts. I am certain that you will learn a lot, too, in reading this book, even if you are already familiar with OOA/D. And, like me, you will find yourself going back to it, to refresh your memory, or to gain further insights from Craig's explanations and experience.

Happy reading!

Philippe Kruchten
Professor of Software Engineering, University of British Columbia

formerly,
Rational Fellow and Director of Process Development for the RUP
Rational Software
Vancouver, British Columbia

PREFACE

Thank you for reading this book! If I can answer a question, or for consulting or coaching a team (in OOA/D, UML, modeling, iterative and agile methods) please contact me at www.craiglarman.com.

This is a practical introduction to object-oriented analysis and design (OOA/D), and to related aspects of iterative development. I am grateful that the previous editions were extremely popular worldwide. I sincerely thank all the readers!

Here is how the book will benefit you.

design well

First, the use of object technology is widespread, so mastery of OOA/D is critical for you to succeed in the software world.

learn a process roadmap

Second, if you are new to OOA/D, you're understandably challenged about how to proceed; this book presents a well-defined iterative roadmap—an agile approach to the Unified Process—so that you can move in a step-by-step process from requirements to code.

learn UML for modeling

Third, the Unified Modeling Language (UML) has emerged as the standard notation for modeling, so it's useful to be able to apply it skillfully.

learn design patterns

Fourth, design patterns communicate the "best practice" idioms OO design experts apply. You will learn to apply design patterns, including the popular "gang-of-four" patterns, and the GRASP patterns. Learning and applying patterns will accelerate your mastery of analysis and design.

learn from experience

Fifth, the structure and emphasis in this book are based on years of experience in education and mentoring thousands of people in the art of OOA/D. It reflects that experience by providing a refined, proven, and efficient approach to learning the subject, so your investment in reading and learning is optimized.

learn from a realistic study

Sixth, it exhaustively examines two case studies—to realistically illustrate the entire OOA/D process, and goes deeply into thorny details of the problem.

design to code, with TDD & refactoring

Seventh, it shows how to map object design artifacts to code in Java. It also introduces test-driven development and refactor.

layered architecture

Eighth, it explains how to design a layered architecture and relate the UI layer to domain and technical services layers.

design frameworks

Finally, it shows you how to design an OO framework and applies this to the creation of a framework for persistent storage in a database.

Educator and Web Resources

You may find related articles of interest at www.craiglarman.com.

Hundreds, if not thousands, of teachers use the book worldwide; it's been translated into at least ten languages. At my website there are a variety of educator resources, including all the book figures organized into Microsoft PowerPoint presentations, sample OOA/D PowerPoint presentations, and more. If you're an educator, please contact me for resources.

I am collecting material from existing educators using the book, to share with other educators. **If you have anything to share, please contact me**.

Intended Audience—an Introduction!

This book is an *introduction* to OOA/D, related requirements analysis, and to iterative development with the Unified Process as a sample process; it is not meant as an advanced text. It is for the following audience:

- Developers and students with some experience in OO programming, but who are new—or relatively new—to OOA/D.

- Students in computer science or software engineering courses studying object technology.

- Those with some familiarity in OOA/D who want to learn the UML notation, apply patterns, or who want to deepen their analysis and design skills.

Prerequisites

Some prerequisites are assumed—and necessary—to benefit from this book:

- Knowledge and experience in an object-oriented programming language such as Java, C#, C++, or Python.

- Knowledge of fundamental OO concepts, such as class, instance, interface, polymorphism, encapsulation, and inheritance.

Fundamental OO concepts are not defined.

Java Examples, But ...

In general, the book presents code examples in Java due to its widespread familiarity. However, the ideas presented are applicable to most—if not all—object-oriented technologies, including C#, Python, and so on.

Book Organization

The overall strategy in the organization of this book is that analysis and design topics are introduced in an order similar to that of a software development project running across an "inception" phase (a Unified Process term) followed by three iterations (see Figure P.1).

1. The inception phase chapters introduce the basics of requirements analysis.

2. Iteration 1 introduces fundamental OOA/D and how to assign responsibilities to objects.

3. Iteration 2 focuses on object design, especially on introducing some high-use "design patterns."

4. Iteration 3 introduces a variety of subjects, such as architectural analysis and framework design.

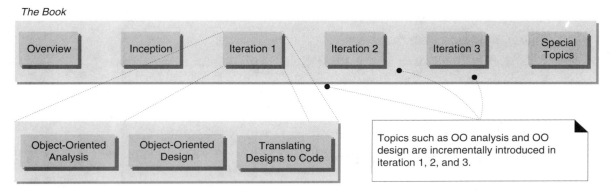

Figure P.1. The organization of the book follows that of a development project.

About the Author

Craig Larman serves as chief scientist for Valtech, an international consulting and skills transfer company with divisions in Europe, Asia, and North America. He is also author of the best-selling software engineering and iterative, agile development text *Agile and Iterative Development: A Manager's Guide*. He travels worldwide, from Indiana to India, coaching development teams and managers.

Since the mid 1980s, Craig has helped thousands of developers to apply OOA/D, skillful modeling with the UML, and to adopt iterative development practices.

After a failed career as a wandering street musician, he built systems in APL, PL/I, and CICS in the 1970s. Starting in the early 1980s—after a full recovery—he became interested in artificial intelligence (having little of his own) and built knowledge systems with Lisp machines, Lisp, Prolog, and Smalltalk. He's also worked in organizations that build business systems in Java, .NET, C++, and Smalltalk. He plays bad lead guitar in his very part-time band, the *Changing Requirements* (it used to be called the *Requirements*, but some band members changed...).

He holds a B.S. and M.S. in computer science from beautiful Simon Fraser University in Vancouver, Canada.

Contact

Craig can be reached at craig@craiglarman.com and www.craiglarman.com. He welcomes questions from readers and educators, and speaking, mentoring, and consulting enquiries.

Enhancements to the Previous Edition

While retaining the same core as the prior edition, this edition is refined in many ways, including:

- UML 2
- A second case study
- More tips on iterative and evolutionary development combined with OOA/D
- Rewritten with new learning aids and graphics for easier study
- New college-educator teaching resources
- Agile Modeling, Test-Driven Development, and refactoring
- More on process modeling with UML activity diagrams
- Guidance on applying the UP in a light, agile spirit, complementary with other iterative methods such as XP and Scrum
- Applying the UML to documenting architectures
- A new chapter on evolutionary requirements
- Refinement of the use case chapters, using the very popular approach of [Cockburn01]

Acknowledgments

First, thanks to my friends and colleagues at Valtech, world-class object developers and iterative development experts, who in some way contributed to, supported, or reviewed the book, including Chris Tarr, Tim Snyder, Curtis Hite, Celso Gonzalez, Pascal Roques, Ken DeLong, Brett Schuchert, Ashley Johnson, Chris Jones, Thomas Liou, Darryl Gebert, and many more than I can name.

To Philippe Kruchten for writing the foreword, reviewing, and helping in many ways.

To Martin Fowler and Alistair Cockburn for many insightful discussions on process and design, quotes, and reviews.

To Oystein Haugen, Cris Kobryn, Jim Rumbaugh, and Bran Selic for reviewing the UML 2 material.

To John Vlissides and Cris Kobryn for the kind quotes.

To Chelsea Systems and John Gray for help with some requirements inspired by their Java technology ChelseaStore POS system.

To Pete Coad and Dave Astels for their input.

Many thanks to the other reviewers, including Steve Adolph, Bruce Anderson, Len Bass, Gary K. Evans, Al Goerner, Luke Hohmann, Eric Lefebvre, David Nunn, and Robert J. White.

Thanks to Paul Becker at Prentice-Hall for believing the first edition would be a worthwhile project, and to Paul Petralia for shepherding the later ones.

Finally, a special thanks to Graham Glass for opening a door.

Typographical Conventions

This is a **new term** in a sentence. This is a *Class* or *method* name in a sentence. This is an author reference [Bob67].

Production Notes

The manuscript was created with Adobe FrameMaker. All drawings were done with Microsoft Visio. The body font is New Century Schoolbook. The final print images were generated as PDF using Adobe Acrobat Distiller, from PostScript generated by the Adobe Universal driver. The UML wall sketch photos were cleaned up with ClearBoard for whiteboard photos.

PART 1 INTRODUCTION

OBJECT-ORIENTED ANALYSIS AND DESIGN

*Le temps est un grand professeur, mais
malheureusement il tue tous ses élèves
(Time is a great teacher, but unfortunately it kills all its pupils.)*

—Hector Berlioz

Objectives

- Describe the book goals and scope.
- Define object-oriented analysis and design (OOA/D).
- Illustrate a brief OOA/D example.
- Overview UML and visual agile modeling.

1.1 What Will You Learn? Is it Useful?

What does it mean to have a good object design? This book is a tool to help developers and students learn core skills in object-oriented analysis and design (OOA/D). These skills are essential for the creation of well-designed, robust, and maintainable software using OO technologies and languages such as Java or C#.

What's Next? This chapter introduces the book goals and OOA/D. The next introduces iterative and evolutionary development, which shapes how OOA/D is presented in this book. The case studies are evolved across three iterations.

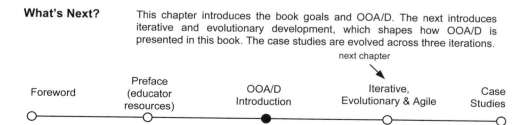

The proverb "owning a hammer doesn't make one an architect" is especially true with respect to object technology. Knowing an object-oriented language (such as Java) is a necessary but insufficient first step to create object systems. Knowing how to "think in objects" is critical!

This is an introduction to OOA/D while applying the Unified Modeling Language (UML) and patterns. And, to iterative development, using an agile approach to the Unified Process as an example iterative process. It is *not* meant as an advanced text; it emphasizes mastery of the fundamentals, such as how to assign responsibilities to objects, frequently used UML notation, and common design patterns. At the same time, mostly in later chapters, the material progresses to some intermediate-level topics, such as framework design and architectural analysis.

UML vs. Thinking in Objects

The book is not just about UML. The **UML** is a standard diagramming notation. Common notation is useful, but there are more important OO things to learn—especially, how to think in objects. The UML is not OOA/D or a method, it is just diagramming notation. It's useless to learn UML and perhaps a UML CASE tool, but not really know how to create an excellent OO design, or evaluate and improve an existing one. This is the hard and important skill. Consequently, this book is an introduction to object design.

Yet, we need a language for OOA/D and "software blueprints," both as a tool of thought and as a form of communication. Therefore, this book explores how to *apply* the UML in the service of doing OOA/D, and covers frequently used UML.

OOD: Principles and Patterns

How should **responsibilities** be allocated to classes of objects? How should objects collaborate? What classes should do what? These are critical questions in the design of a system, and this book teaches the classic OO design metaphor: **responsibility-driven design**. Also, certain tried-and-true solutions to design problems can be (and have been) expressed as best-practice principles, heuristics, or **patterns**—named problem-solution formulas that codify exemplary design principles. This book, by teaching how to *apply* patterns or principles, supports quicker learning and skillful use of these fundamental object design idioms.

Case Studies

This introduction to OOA/D is illustrated in some **ongoing case studies** that are followed throughout the book, going deep enough into the analysis and design so that some of the gory details of what must be considered and solved in a realistic problem are considered, and solved.

Use Cases

OOD (and all software design) is strongly related to the prerequisite activity of **requirements analysis**, which often includes writing **use cases**. Therefore, the case study begins with an introduction to these topics, even though they are not specifically object-oriented.

Iterative Development, Agile Modeling, and an Agile UP

Given many possible activities from requirements through to implementation, how should a developer or team proceed? Requirements analysis and OOA/D needs to be presented and practiced in the context of some development process. In this case, an **agile** (light, flexible) approach to the well-known **Unified Process** (UP) is used as the *sample* **iterative development process** within which these topics are introduced. However, the analysis and design topics that are covered are common to many approaches, and learning them in the context of an agile UP does not invalidate their applicability to other methods, such as Scrum, Feature-Driven Development, Lean Development, Crystal Methods, and so on.

In conclusion, this book helps a student or developer:

- Apply principles and patterns to create better object designs.

- Iteratively follow a set of common activities in analysis and design, based on an agile approach to the UP as an example.

- Create frequently used diagrams in the UML notation.

It illustrates this in the context of long-running case studies that evolve over several iterations.

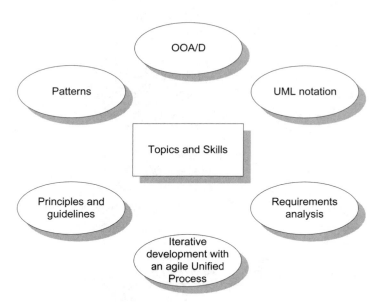

Figure 1.1 Topics and skills covered.

Many Other Skills Are Important!

This isn't the *Compleate Booke of Software*; it's primarily an introduction to OOA/D, UML, and iterative development, while touching on related subjects. Building software involves myriad other skills and steps; for example, usability engineering, user interface design, and database design are critical to success.

1.2 The Most Important Learning Goal?

There are many possible activities and artifacts in introductory OOA/D, and a wealth of principles and guidelines. Suppose we must choose a single practical skill from all the topics discussed here—a "desert island" skill. What would it be?

> A critical ability in OO development is to
> skillfully assign responsibilities to software objects.

Why? Because it is one activity that must be performed—either while drawing a UML diagram or programming—and it strongly influences the robustness, maintainability, and reusability of software components.

Of course, there are other important skills in OOA/D, but *responsibility assignment* is emphasized in this introduction because it tends to be a challenging skill to master (with many "degrees of freedom" or alternatives), and yet is vitally important. On a real project, a developer might not have the opportunity to perform any other modeling activities—the "rush to code" development process. Yet even in this situation, assigning responsibilities is inevitable.

Consequently, the design steps in this book emphasize principles of responsibility assignment.

> Nine fundamental principles in object design and responsibility assignment are presented and applied. They are organized in a learning aid called **GRASP** of principles with names such as *Information Expert* and *Creator*.

1.3 What is Analysis and Design?

Analysis emphasizes an *investigation* of the problem and requirements, rather than a solution. For example, if a new online trading system is desired, how will it be used? What are its functions?

"Analysis" is a broad term, best qualified, as in *requirements analysis* (an investigation of the requirements) or *object-oriented analysis* (an investigation of the domain objects).

Design emphasizes a *conceptual solution* (in software and hardware) that fulfills the requirements, rather than its implementation. For example, a description of a database schema and software objects. Design ideas often exclude low-level or "obvious" details—obvious to the intended consumers. Ultimately, designs can be implemented, and the implementation (such as code) expresses the true and complete realized design.

As with analysis, the term is best qualified, as in *object-oriented design* or *database design*.

Useful analysis and design have been summarized in the phrase *do the right thing (analysis), and do the thing right (design)*.

1.4 What is Object-Oriented Analysis and Design?

During **object-oriented analysis** there is an emphasis on finding and describing the objects—or concepts—in the problem domain. For example, in the case of the flight information system, some of the concepts include *Plane, Flight,* and *Pilot*.

During **object-oriented design** (or simply, object design) there is an emphasis on defining software objects and how they collaborate to fulfill the requirements. For example, a *Plane* software object may have a *tailNumber* attribute and a *getFlightHistory* method (see Figure 1.2).

Finally, during implementation or object-oriented programming, design objects are implemented, such as a *Plane* class in Java.

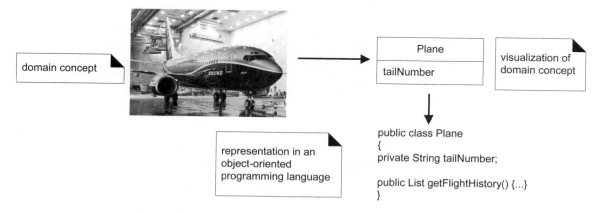

Figure 1.2 Object-orientation emphasizes representation of objects.

1.5 A Short Example

Before diving into the details of iterative development, requirements analysis, UML, and OOA/D, this section presents a bird's-eye view of a few key steps and diagrams, using a simple example—a "dice game" in which software simulates a player rolling two dice. If the total is seven, they win; otherwise, they lose.

Define Use Cases

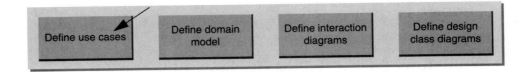

Requirements analysis may include stories or scenarios of how people use the application; these can be written as **use cases**.

Use cases are not an object-oriented artifact—they are simply written stories. However, they are a popular tool in requirements analysis. For example, here is a brief version of the *Play a Dice Game* use case:

> **Play a Dice Game**: Player requests to roll the dice. System presents results: If the dice face value totals seven, player wins; otherwise, player loses.

Define a Domain Model

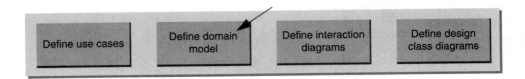

Object-oriented analysis is concerned with creating a description of the domain from the perspective of objects. There is an identification of the concepts, attributes, and associations that are considered noteworthy.

The result can be expressed in a **domain model** that shows the *noteworthy* domain concepts or objects.

For example, a partial domain model is shown in Figure 1.3.

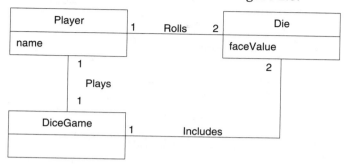

Figure 1.3 Partial domain model of the dice game.

This model illustrates the noteworthy concepts *Player*, *Die,* and *DiceGame*, with their associations and attributes.

Note that a domain model is not a description of software objects; it is a visualization of the concepts or mental models of a real-world domain. Thus, it has also been called a **conceptual object model**.

Assign Object Responsibilities and Draw Interaction Diagrams

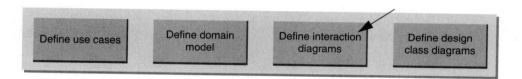

Object-oriented design is concerned with defining software objects—their responsibilities and collaborations. A common notation to illustrate these collaborations is the **sequence diagram** (a kind of UML interaction diagram). It shows the flow of messages between software objects, and thus the invocation of methods.

For example, the sequence diagram in Figure 1.4 illustrates an OO software design, by sending messages to instances of the *DiceGame* and *Die* classes. Note this illustrates a common real-world way the UML is applied: by sketching on a whiteboard.

Notice that although in the real world a *player* rolls the dice, in the software design the *DiceGame* object "rolls" the dice (that is, sends messages to *Die* objects). Software object designs and programs do take some inspiration from real-world domains, but they are *not* direct models or simulations of the real world.

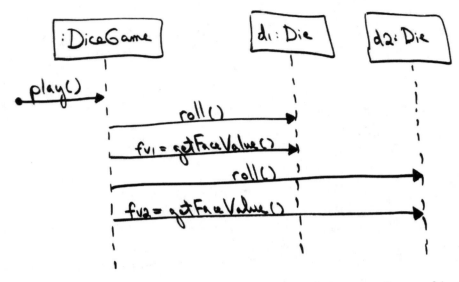

Figure 1.4 Sequence diagram illustrating messages between software objects.

Define Design Class Diagrams

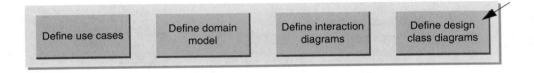

In addition to a *dynamic* view of collaborating objects shown in interaction diagrams, a *static* view of the class definitions is usefully shown with a **design class diagram**. This illustrates the attributes and methods of the classes.

For example, in the dice game, an inspection of the sequence diagram leads to the partial design class diagram shown in Figure 1.5. Since a *play* message is sent to a *DiceGame* object, the *DiceGame* class requires a *play* method, while class *Die* requires a *roll* and *getFaceValue* method.

In contrast to the domain model showing real-world classes, this diagram shows software classes.

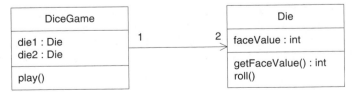

Figure 1.5 Partial design class diagram.

Notice that although this design class diagram is not the same as the domain model, some class names and content are similar. In this way, OO designs and languages can support a **lower representational gap** between the software components and our mental models of a domain. That improves comprehension.

Summary

The dice game is a simple problem, presented to focus on a few steps and artifacts in analysis and design. To keep the introduction simple, not all the illustrated UML notation was explained. Future chapters explore analysis and design and these artifacts in closer detail.

1.6   What is the UML?

To quote:

> The Unified Modeling Language is a visual language for specifying, constructing and documenting the artifacts of systems [OMG03a].

The word *visual* in the definition is a key point—the UML is the de facto standard *diagramming notation* for drawing or presenting pictures (with some text) related to software—primarily OO software.

This book doesn't cover all minute aspects of the UML, a large body of notation. It focuses on frequently used diagrams, the most commonly used features within those, and core notation that is unlikely to change in future UML versions.

The UML defines various **UML profiles** that specialize subsets of the notation for common subject areas, such as diagramming Enterprise JavaBeans (with the *UML EJB profile*).

At a deeper level—primarily of interest to **Model Driven Architecture** (MDA) CASE tool vendors—underlying the UML notation is the **UML meta-model** that describes the semantics of the modeling elements. It isn't something a developer needs to learn.

Three Ways to Apply UML

In [Fowler03] three ways people apply UML are introduced:

- **UML as sketch**—Informal and incomplete diagrams (often hand sketched on whiteboards) created to explore difficult parts of the problem or solution space, exploiting the power of visual languages.

- **UML as blueprint**—Relatively detailed design diagrams used either for 1) reverse engineering to visualize and better understanding existing code in UML diagrams, or for 2) code generation (forward engineering).

UML and "Silver Bullet" Thinking

There is a well-known paper from 1986 titled "No Silver Bullet" by Dr. Frederick Brooks, also published in his classic book *Mythical Man-Month* (20th anniversary edition). Recommended reading! An essential point is that it's a fundamental mistake (so far, endlessly repeated) to believe there is some special tool or technique in software that will make a dramatic order-of-magnitude difference in productivity, defect reduction, reliability, or simplicity. *And tools don't compensate for design ignorance.*

Yet, you will hear claims—usually from tool vendors—that drawing UML diagrams will make things much better; or, that Model Driven Architecture (MDA) tools based on UML will be the breakthrough silver bullet.

Reality-check time. The UML is simply a standard diagramming notation—boxes, lines, etc. Visual modeling with a common notation can be a great aid, but it is hardly as important as knowing how to design and think in objects. Such design knowledge is a very different and more important skill, and is not mastered by learning UML notation or using a CASE or MDA tool. A person not having good OO design and programming skills who draws UML is just drawing bad designs. I suggest the article *Death by UML Fever* [Bell04] (endorsed by the UML creator Grady Booch) for more on this subject, and also *What UML Is and Isn't* [Larman04].

Therefore, this book is an introduction to OOA/D and *applying* the UML to support skillful OO design.

❍ If reverse engineering, a UML tool reads the source or binaries and generates (typically) UML package, class, and sequence diagrams. These "blueprints" can help the reader understand the big-picture elements, structure, and collaborations.

❍ Before programming, some detailed diagrams can provide guidance for code generation (e.g., in Java), either manually or automatically with a tool. It's common that the diagrams are used for some code, and other code is filled in by a developer while coding (perhaps also applying UML sketching).

■ **UML as programming language**—Complete executable specification of a software system in UML. Executable code will be automatically generated, but is not normally seen or modified by developers; one works only in the UML "programming language." This use of UML requires a practical way to diagram all behavior or logic (probably using interaction or state diagrams), and is still under development in terms of theory, tool robustness and usability.

agile modeling
p. 30

Agile modeling emphasizes *UML as sketch*; this is a common way to apply the UML, often with a high return on the investment of time (which is typically short). UML tools can be useful, but I encourage people to also consider an agile modeling approach to applying UML.

Three Perspectives to Apply UML

The UML describes raw diagram types, such as class diagrams and sequence diagrams. It does not superimpose a modeling perspective on these. For example, the same UML class diagram notation can be used to draw pictures of concepts in the real world or software classes in Java.

This insight was emphasized in the Syntropy object-oriented method [CD94]. That is, the same notation may be used for three perspectives and types of models (Figure 1.6):

1. **Conceptual perspective**—the diagrams are interpreted as describing things in a situation of the real world or domain of interest.

2. **Specification (software) perspective**—the diagrams (using the same notation as in the conceptual perspective) describe software abstractions or components with specifications and interfaces, but no commitment to a particular implementation (for example, not specifically a class in C# or Java).

3. **Implementation (software) perspective**—the diagrams describe software implementations in a particular technology (such as Java).

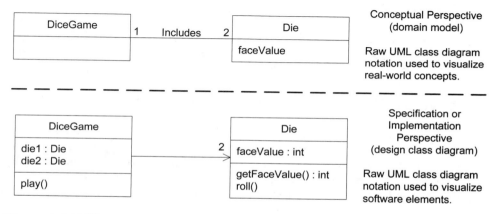

Figure 1.6 Different perspectives with UML.

We've already seen an example of this in Figure 1.3 and Figure 1.5, where the same UML class diagram notation is used to visualize a domain model and a design model.

In practice, the specification perspective (deferring the target technology, such as Java versus .NET) is seldom used for design; most software-oriented UML diagramming assumes an implementation perspective.

The Meaning of "Class" in Different Perspectives

In the raw UML, the rectangular boxes shown in Figure 1.6 are called **classes**, but this term encompasses a variety of phenomena—physical things, abstract concepts, software things, events, and so forth.[1]

A method superimposes alternative terminology on top of the raw UML. For example, in the UP, when the UML boxes are drawn in the Domain Model, they are called **domain concepts** or **conceptual classes**; the Domain Model shows a conceptual perspective. In the UP, when UML boxes are drawn in the Design Model, they are called **design classes**; the Design Model shows a specification or implementation perspective, as desired by the modeler.

To keep things clear, this book will use class-related terms consistent with the UML and the UP, as follows:

- **Conceptual class**—real-world concept or thing. A conceptual or essential perspective. The UP Domain Model contains conceptual classes.

- **Software class**—a class representing a specification or implementation perspective of a software component, regardless of the process or method.

- **Implementation class**—a class implemented in a specific OO language such as Java.

UML 1 and UML 2

Towards the end of 2004 a major new release of the UML emerged, UML 2. This text is based on UML 2; indeed, the notation used here was carefully reviewed with key members of the UML 2 specification team.

Why Won't We See Much UML for a Few Chapters?

This is not primarily a UML notation book, but one that explores the larger picture of applying the UML, patterns, and an iterative process in the context of OOA/D and related requirements analysis. OOA/D is normally preceded by requirements analysis. Therefore, the initial chapters introduce the important topics of use cases and requirements analysis, which are then followed by chapters on OOA/D and more UML details.

1.7 Visual Modeling is a Good Thing

At the risk of stating the blindingly obvious, drawing or reading UML implies we are working more visually, exploiting our brain's strength to quickly grasp symbols, units, and relationships in (predominantly) 2D box-and-line notations.

This old, simple idea is often lost among all the UML details and tools. It shouldn't be! Diagrams help us see or explore more of the big picture and relationships between analysis or software elements, while allowing us to ignore or hide uninteresting details. That's the simple and essential value of the UML—or any diagramming language.

---

1. A UML class is a special case of the general UML model element **classifier**—something with structural features and/or behavior, including classes, actors, interfaces, and use cases.

1.8   History

The history of OOA/D has many branches, and this brief synopsis can't do justice to all the contributors. The 1960s and 1970s saw the emergence of OO programming languages, such as Simula and Smalltalk, with key contributors such as Kristen Nygaard and especially Alan Kay, the visionary computer scientist who founded Smalltalk. Kay coined the terms *object-oriented programming* and *personal computing,* and helped pull together the ideas of the modern PC while at Xerox PARC.[2]

But OOA/D was informal through that period, and it wasn't until 1982 that OOD emerged as a topic in its own right. This milestone came when Grady Booch (also a UML founder) wrote the first paper titled *Object-Oriented Design*, probably coining the term [Booch82]. Many other well-known OOA/D pioneers developed their ideas during the 1980s: Kent Beck, Peter Coad, Don Firesmith, Ivar Jacobson (a UML founder), Steve Mellor, Bertrand Meyer, Jim Rumbaugh (a UML founder), and Rebecca Wirfs-Brock, among others. Meyer published one of the early influential books, *Object-Oriented Software Construction,* in 1988. And Mellor and Schlaer published *Object-Oriented Systems Analysis*, coining the term *object-oriented analysis*, in the same year. Peter Coad created a complete OOA/D method in the late 1980s and published, in 1990 and 1991, the twin volumes *Object-Oriented Analysis* and *Object-Oriented Design*. Also in 1990, Wirfs-Brock and others described the responsibility-driven design approach to OOD in their popular *Designing Object-Oriented Software*. In 1991 two very popular OOA/D books were published. One described the OMT method, *Object-Oriented Modeling and Design*, by Rumbaugh et al. The other described the Booch method, *Object-Oriented Design with Applications*. In 1992, Jacobson published the popular *Object-Oriented Software Engineering*, which promoted not only OOA/D, but use cases for requirements.

The UML started as an effort by Booch and Rumbaugh in 1994 not only to create a common notation, but to combine their two methods—the Booch and OMT methods. Thus, the first public draft of what today is the UML was presented as the *Unified Method*. They were soon joined at Rational Corporation by Ivar Jacobson, the creator of the Objectory method, and as a group came to be known as the *three amigos*. It was at this point that they decided to reduce the scope of their effort, and focus on a common diagramming notation—the UML—rather than a common method. This was not only a de-scoping effort; the Object Management Group (OMG, an industry standards body for OO-related standards)

---

2. Kay started work on OO and the PC in the 1960s, while a graduate student. In December 1979—at the prompting of Apple's great Jef Raskin (the lead creator of the Mac)—Steve Jobs, co-founder and CEO of Apple, visited Alan Kay and research teams (including Dan Ingalls, the implementor of Kay's vision) at Xerox PARC for a demo of the Smalltalk personal computer. Stunned by what he saw—a graphical UI of bit-mapped overlapping windows, OO programming, and networked PCs—he returned to Apple with a new vision (the one Raskin hoped for), and the Apple Lisa and Macintosh were born.

was convinced by various tool vendors that an open standard was needed. Thus, the process opened up, and an OMG task force chaired by Mary Loomis and Jim Odell organized the initial effort leading to UML 1.0 in 1997. Many others contributed to the UML, perhaps most notably Cris Kobryn, a leader in its ongoing refinement.

The UML has emerged as the de facto and de jure standard diagramming notation for object-oriented modeling, and has continued to be refined in new OMG UML versions, available at www.omg.org or www.uml.org.

1.9 Recommended Resources

Various OOA/D texts are recommended in later chapters, in relation to specific subjects, such as OO design. The books in the history section are all worth study—and still applicable regarding their core advice.

A very readable and popular summary of essential UML notation is *UML Distilled* by Martin Fowler. Highly recommended; Fowler has written many useful books, with a practical and "agile" attitude.

For a detailed discussion of UML notation, *The Unified Modeling Language Reference Manual* by Rumbaugh is worthwhile. Note that this text isn't meant for learning how to do object modeling or OOA/D—it's a UML notation reference.

For the definitive description of the current version of the UML, see the on-line *UML Infrastructure Specification* and *UML Superstructure Specification* at www.uml.org or www.omg.org.

Visual UML modeling in an agile modeling spirit is described in *Agile Modeling* by Scott Ambler. See also www.agilemodeling.com.

There is a large collection of links to OOA/D methods at www.cetus-links.org and www.iturls.com (the large English "Software Engineering" subsection, rather than the Chinese section).

There are many books on software patterns, but the seminal classic is *Design Patterns* by Gamma, Helm, Johnson, and Vlissides. It is truly required reading for those studying object design. However, it is not an introductory text and is best read after one is comfortable with the fundamentals of object design and programming. See also www.hillside.net and www.iturls.com (the English "Software Engineering" subsection) for links to many pattern sites.

ITERATIVE, EVOLUTIONARY, AND AGILE

You should use iterative development only on projects that you want to succeed.

—Martin Fowler

Objectives

- Provide motivation for the content and order of the book.
- Define an iterative and agile process.
- Define fundamental concepts in the Unified Process.

Introduction

Iterative development lies at the heart of how OOA/D is best practiced and is presented in this book. Agile practices such as Agile Modeling are key to applying the UML in an effective way. This chapter introduces these subjects, and the Unified Process as a relatively popular *sample* iterative method.

What's Next?
Having introduced OOA/D, this chapter explores iterative development. The next introduces the case studies that are evolved throughout the book, across three iterations.

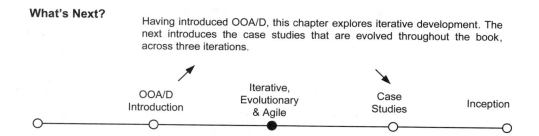

Iterative and evolutionary development—contrasted with a sequential or "waterfall" lifecycle—involves early programming and testing of a partial system, in repeating cycles. It also normally assumes development starts before all the requirements are defined in detail; feedback is used to clarify and improve the evolving specifications.

We rely on short quick development steps, feedback, and adaptation to clarify the requirements and design. To contrast, waterfall values promoted big upfront speculative requirements and design steps before programming. Consistently, success/failure studies show that the waterfall is strongly associated with the highest failure rates for software projects and was historically promoted due to belief or hearsay rather than statistically significant evidence. Research demonstrates that iterative methods are associated with higher success and productivity rates, and lower defect levels.

2.1   What is the UP? Are Other Methods Complementary?

A **software development process** describes an approach to building, deploying, and possibly maintaining software. The **Unified Process** [JBR99] has emerged as a popular *iterative* software development process for building object-oriented systems. In particular, the **Rational Unified Process** or **RUP** [Kruchten00], a detailed refinement of the Unified Process, has been widely adopted.

Because the Unified Process (UP) is a relatively popular iterative process for projects using OOA/D, and because some process must be used to introduce the subject, the UP shapes the book's structure. Also, since the UP is common and promotes widely recognized best practices, it's useful for industry professionals to know it, and students entering the workforce to be aware of it.

test-driven development and refactoring p. 385

The UP is very flexible and open, and encourages including skillful practices from other iterative methods, such as from **Extreme Programming (XP)**, **Scrum**, and so forth. For example, XP's **test-driven development**, **refactoring** and **continuous integration** practices can fit within a UP project. So can Scrum's common project room ("war room") and daily Scrum meeting practice. Introducing the UP is not meant to downplay the value of these other methods—quite the opposite. In my consulting work, I encourage clients to understand and adopt a blend of useful techniques from several methods, rather than a dogmatic "my method is better than your method" mentality.

The UP combines commonly accepted best practices, such as an iterative lifecycle and risk-driven development, into a cohesive and well-documented process description.

To summarize, this chapter includes an introduction to the UP for three reasons:

1. The UP is an *iterative* process. Iterative development influences how this

book introduces OOA/D, and how it is best practiced.

2. UP practices provide an example *structure* for how to do—and thus how to explain—OOA/D. That structure shapes the book structure.

3. The UP is flexible, and can be applied in a lightweight and *agile* approach that includes practices from other agile methods (such as XP or Scrum)—more on this later.

This book presents an introduction to an agile approach to the UP, but not complete coverage. It emphasizes common ideas and artifacts related to an introduction to OOA/D and requirements analysis.

What If I Don't Care About the UP?

The UP is used as an *example* process within which to explore iterative and evolutionary requirements analysis and OOA/D, since it's necessary to introduce the subject in the context of some process.

But the central ideas of this book—how to think and design with objects, apply UML, use design patterns, agile modeling, evolutionary requirements analysis, writing use cases, and so forth—are independent of any particular process, and apply to many modern iterative, evolutionary, and agile methods, such as Scrum, Lean Development, DSDM, Feature-Driven Development, Adaptive Software Development, and more.

2.2 What is Iterative and Evolutionary Development?

A key practice in both the UP and most other modern methods is **iterative development**. In this lifecycle approach, development is organized into a series of short, fixed-length (for example, three-week) mini-projects called **iterations**; the outcome of each is a tested, integrated, and executable *partial* system. Each iteration includes its own requirements analysis, design, implementation, and testing activities.

The iterative lifecycle is based on the successive enlargement and refinement of a system through multiple iterations, with cyclic feedback and adaptation as core drivers to converge upon a suitable system. The system grows incrementally over time, iteration by iteration, and thus this approach is also known as **iterative and incremental development** (see Figure 2.1). Because feedback and adaptation evolve the specifications and design, it is also known as **iterative and evolutionary development**.

Early iterative process ideas were known as spiral development and evolutionary development [Boehm88, Gilb88].

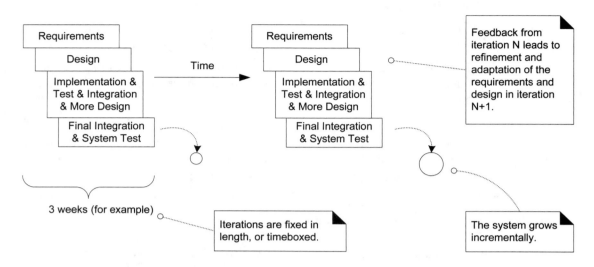

Figure 2.1 Iterative and evolutionary development.

Example

As an example (not a recipe), in a three-week iteration early in the project, perhaps one hour Monday morning is spent in a kickoff meeting with the team clarifying the tasks and goals of the iteration. Meanwhile, one person reverse-engineers the last iteration's code into UML diagrams (via a CASE tool), and prints and displays noteworthy diagrams. The team spends the remainder of Monday at whiteboards, working in pairs while agile modeling, sketching rough UML diagrams captured on digital cameras, and writing some pseudocode and design notes. The remaining days are spent on implementation, testing (unit, acceptance, usability, ...), further design, integration, and daily builds of the partial system. Other activities include demonstrations and evaluations with stakeholders, and planning for the next iteration.

Notice in this example that there is neither a rush to code, nor a long drawn-out design step that attempts to perfect all details of the design before programming. A "little" forethought regarding the design with visual modeling using rough and fast UML drawings is done; perhaps a half or full day by developers doing design work UML sketching in pairs at whiteboards.

The result of each iteration is an executable but incomplete system; it is not ready to deliver into production. The system may not be eligible for production deployment until after many iterations; for example, 10 or 15 iterations.

The output of an iteration is *not* an experimental or throw-away prototype, and iterative development is not prototyping. Rather, the output is a production-grade subset of the final system.

How to Handle Change on an Iterative Project?

The subtitle of one book that discusses iterative development is *Embrace Change* [Beck00]. This phrase is evocative of a key attitude of iterative development: Rather than fighting the inevitable change that occurs in software development by trying (unsuccessfully) to fully and correctly specify, freeze, and "sign off" on a frozen requirement set and design before implementation (in a "waterfall" process), iterative and evolutionary development is based on an attitude of embracing change and adaptation as unavoidable and indeed essential drivers.

This is not to say that iterative development and the UP encourage an uncontrolled and reactive "feature creep"-driven process. Subsequent chapters explore how the UP balances the need—on the one hand—to agree upon and stabilize a set of requirements, with—on the other hand—the reality of changing requirements, as stakeholders clarify their vision or the marketplace changes.

Each iteration involves choosing a small subset of the requirements, and quickly designing, implementing, and testing. In early iterations the choice of requirements and design may not be exactly what is ultimately desired. But the act of swiftly taking a small step, before all requirements are finalized, or the entire design is speculatively defined, leads to rapid feedback—feedback from the users, developers, and tests (such as load and usability tests).

And this early feedback is worth its weight in gold; rather than *speculating* on the complete, correct requirements or design, the team mines the feedback from realistic building and testing something for crucial practical insight and an opportunity to modify or adapt understanding of the requirements or design. End-users have a chance to quickly see a partial system and say, "Yes, that's what I asked for, but now that I try it, what I really want is something slightly different."[1] This "yes...but" process is not a sign of failure; rather, early and frequent structured cycles of "yes...buts" are a skillful way to make progress and discover what is of real value to the stakeholders. Yet this is not an endorsement of chaotic and reactive development in which developers continually change direction—a middle way is possible.

In addition to requirements clarification, activities such as load testing will prove if the partial design and implementation are on the right path, or if in the next iteration, a change in the core architecture is required. Better to resolve and *prove* the risky and critical design decisions early rather than late—and iterative development provides the mechanism for this.

Consequently, work proceeds through a series of structured build-feedback-adapt cycles. Not surprisingly, in early iterations the deviation from the "true

---

1. Or more likely, "You didn't understand what I wanted!"

path" of the system (in terms of its final requirements and design) will be larger than in later iterations. Over time, the system converges towards this path, as illustrated in Figure 2.2.

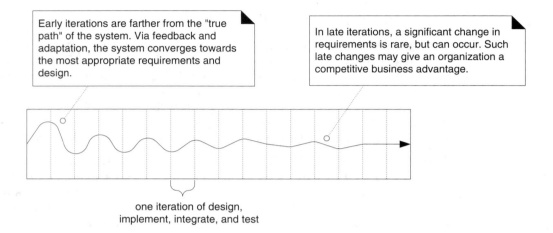

Early iterations are farther from the "true path" of the system. Via feedback and adaptation, the system converges towards the most appropriate requirements and design.

In late iterations, a significant change in requirements is rare, but can occur. Such late changes may give an organization a competitive business advantage.

one iteration of design, implement, integrate, and test

Figure 2.2 Iterative feedback and evolution leads towards the desired system. The requirements and design instability lowers over time.

Are There Benefits to Iterative Development?

Yes. Benefits include:

- less project failure, better productivity, and lower defect rates; shown by research into iterative and evolutionary methods

- early rather than late mitigation of high risks (technical, requirements, objectives, usability, and so forth)

- early visible progress

- early feedback, user engagement, and adaptation, leading to a refined system that more closely meets the real needs of the stakeholders

- managed complexity; the team is not overwhelmed by "analysis paralysis" or very long and complex steps

- the learning within an iteration can be methodically used to improve the development process itself, iteration by iteration

How Long Should an Iteration Be? What is Iteration Timeboxing?

Most iterative methods recommend an iteration length between two and six weeks. Small steps, rapid feedback, and adaptation are central ideas in iterative development; long iterations subvert the core motivation for iterative development and increase project risk. In only one week it is often difficult to complete sufficient work to get meaningful throughput and feedback; more than six weeks, and the complexity becomes rather overwhelming, and feedback is delayed. A very long timeboxed iteration misses the point of iterative development. Short is good.

A key idea is that iterations are **timeboxed**, or fixed in length. For example, if the next iteration is chosen to be three weeks long, then the partial system *must* be integrated, tested, and stabilized by the scheduled date—date slippage is illegal. If it seems that it will be difficult to meet the deadline, the recommended response is to de-scope—remove tasks or requirements from the iteration, and include them in a future iteration, rather than slip the completion date.

2.3 What About the Waterfall Lifecycle?

In a **waterfall** (or sequential) lifecycle process there is an attempt to define (in detail) all or most of the requirements before programming. And often, to create a thorough design (or set of models) before programming. Likewise, an attempt to define a "reliable" plan or schedule near the start—not that it will be.

Warning: Superimposing Waterfall on Iterative

If you find yourself on an "iterative" project where most of the requirements are written before development begins, or there is an attempt to create many thorough and detailed specifications or UML models and designs before programming, know that waterfall thinking has unfortunately afflicted the project. It is not a healthy iterative or UP project, regardless of claims.

---

feature use research p. 56

Research (collected from many sources and summarized in [Larman03] and [LB03]) now shows conclusively that the 1960s and 1970s-era advice to apply the waterfall was—ironically—a poor practice for most software projects, rather than a skillful approach. It is strongly associated with high rates of failure, lower productivity, and higher defect rates (than iterative projects). On average, 45% of the features in waterfall requirements are never used, and early waterfall schedules and estimates vary up to 400% from the final actuals.

In hindsight, we now know that waterfall advice was based on *speculation* and *hearsay*, rather than evidence-based practices. In contrast, iterative and evolutionary practices are backed by evidence—studies show they are less failure prone, and associated with better productivity and defect rates.

Guideline: Don't Let Waterfall Thinking Invade an Iterative or UP Project

I need to emphasize that "waterfall thinking" often incorrectly still invades a so-called iterative or UP project. Ideas such as "let's write all the use cases before starting to program" or "let's do many detailed OO models in UML before starting to program" are examples of unhealthy waterfall thinking incorrectly superimposed on the UP. The creators of the UP cite this misunderstanding—big up-front analysis and modeling—as a key reason for its failed adoption [KL01].

Why is the Waterfall so Failure-Prone?

There isn't one simple answer to why the waterfall is so failure-prone, but it is strongly related to a key false assumption underlying many failed software projects—that the specifications are predictable and stable and can be correctly defined at the start, with low change rates. This turns out to be far from accurate—and a costly misunderstanding. A study by Boehm and Papaccio showed that a typical software project experienced a 25% change in requirements [BP88]. And this trend was corroborated in another major study of thousands of software projects, with change rates that go even higher—35% to 50% for large projects—as illustrated in Figure 2.3 [Jones97].

These are *extremely* high change rates. What this data shows—as any experienced developer or manager is painfully aware—is that software development is (on average) a domain of high change and instability—also known as the domain of **new product development**. Software is not usually a domain of predictable or mass manufacturing—low-change areas where it is possible and efficient to define all the stable specifications and reliable plans near the start.

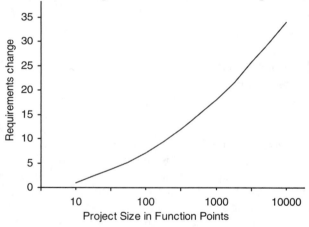

Figure 2.3 Percentage of change on software projects of varying sizes.

Thus, any analysis, modeling, development, or management practice based on the assumption that things are long-term stable (i.e., the waterfall) is fundamentally flawed. *Change* is the constant on software projects. Iterative and evolutionary methods assume and embrace change and adaptation of *partial and evolving* specifications, models, and plans based on feedback.

The Need for Feedback and Adaptation

In complex, changing systems (such as most software projects) feedback and adaptation are key ingredients for success.

- Feedback from early development, programmers trying to read specifications, and client demos to refine the requirements.

- Feedback from tests and developers to refine the design or models.

- Feedback from the progress of the team tackling early features to refine the schedule and estimates.

- Feedback from the client and marketplace to re-prioritize the features to tackle in the next iteration.

2.4   How to do Iterative and Evolutionary Analysis and Design?

This introduction may have given the impression that there is no value in analysis and design before programming, but that is a misunderstanding as extreme as thinking that "complete" up-front analysis is skillful. There is a middle way. Here's a short *example* (not a recipe) of how it can work on a well-run UP project. This assumes there will ultimately be 20 iterations on the project before delivery:

1. Before iteration-1, hold the first timeboxed requirements workshop, such as exactly two days. Business and development people (including the chief architect) are present.

    ○ On the morning of day one, do high-level requirements analysis, such as identifying just the names of the use cases and features, and key non-functional requirements. The analysis will not be perfect.

    ○ Ask the chief architect and business people to pick 10% from this high-level list (such as 10% of the 30 use case names) that have a blending of these three qualities: 1) architecturally significant (if implemented, we are forced to design, build, and test the core architecture), 2) high business value (features business really cares about), and 3) high risk (such as "be able to handle 500 concurrent transactions"). Perhaps three use cases are thus identified: UC2, UC11, UC14.

    ○ For the remaining 1.5 days, do intensive detailed analysis of the functional and non-functional requirements for these three use cases. When finished, 10% are deeply analyzed, and 90% are only high-level.

2. Before iteration-1, hold an iteration planning meeting in which a subset from UC2, UC11, and UC14 are chosen to design, build, and test within a specified time (for example, four-week timeboxed iteration). Note that not

all of these three use cases can be built in iteration-1, as they will contain too much work. After choosing the specific subset goals, break them down into a set of more detailed iteration tasks, with help from the development team.

3. Do iteration-1 over three or four weeks (pick the timebox, and stick to it).

   ○ On the first two days, developers and others do modeling and design work in pairs, sketching UML-ish diagrams at many whiteboards (along with sketching other kinds of models) in a common war room, coached and guided by the chief architect.

   ○ Then the developers take off their "modeling hats" and put on their "programming hats." They start programming, testing, and integrating their work continuously over the remaining weeks, using the modeling sketches as a starting point of inspiration, knowing that the models are partial and often vague.

   ○ Much testing occurs: unit, acceptance, load, usability, and so forth.

   ○ One week before the end, ask the team if the original iteration goals can be met; if not, de-scope the iteration, putting secondary goals back on the "to do" list.

   ○ On Tuesday of the last week there's a code freeze; all code must be checked in, integrated, and tested to create the iteration baseline.

   ○ On Wednesday morning, demo the partial system to external stakeholders, to show early visible progress. Feedback is requested.

4. Do the second requirements workshop near the end of iteration-1, such as on the last Wednesday and Thursday. Review and refine all the material from the last workshop. Then pick another 10% or 15% of the use cases that are architecturally significant and of high business value, and analyze them in detail for one or two days. When finished, perhaps 25% of the use cases and non-functional requirements will be written in detail. They won't be perfect.

5. On Friday morning, hold another iteration planning meeting for the next iteration.

6. Do iteration-2; similar steps.

7. Repeat, for four iterations and five requirements workshops, so that at the end of iteration-4, perhaps 80% or 90% of the requirements have been written in detail, but only 10% of the system has been implemented.

   ○ Note that this large, detailed set of requirements is based on feedback and evolution, and is thus of much higher quality than purely speculative waterfall specifications.

8. We are perhaps only 20% into the duration of the overall project. In UP terms, this is the end of the **elaboration phase**. At this point, estimate in

detail the effort and time for the refined, high-quality requirements. Because of the significant realistic investigation, feedback, and early programming and testing, the estimates of what can be done and how long it will take are much more reliable.

9. After this point, requirements workshops are unlikely; the requirements are stabilized—though never completely frozen. Continue in a series of three-week iterations, choosing the next step of work adaptively in each iteration planning meeting on the final Friday, re-asking the question each iteration, "Given what we know today, what are the most critical technical and business features we should do in the next three weeks?"

Figure 2.5 illustrates the approach for a 20-iteration project.

In this way, after a few iterations of early exploratory development, there comes a point when the team can more reliably answer "what, how much, when."

2.5   What is Risk-Driven and Client-Driven Iterative Planning?

The UP (and most new methods) encourage a combination of **risk-driven** and **client-driven** iterative planning. This means that the goals of the early iterations are chosen to 1) identify and drive down the highest risks, and 2) build visible features that the client cares most about.

Risk-driven iterative development includes more specifically the practice of **architecture-centric** iterative development, meaning that early iterations focus on building, testing, and stabilizing the core architecture. Why? Because not having a solid architecture is a common high risk.

Book Iterations vs. Real Project Iterations

Iteration-1 of the case studies in this book is driven by learning goals rather than true project goals. Therefore, iteration-1 is not architecture-centric or risk-driven. On a real project, we would tackle difficult and risky things first. But in the context of a book helping people learn fundamental OOA/D and UML, that's impractical—we need to start with problems illustrating basic principles, not the most difficult topics and problems.

2.6   What are Agile Methods and Attitudes?

Agile development methods usually apply timeboxed iterative and evolutionary development, employ adaptive planning, promote incremental delivery, and include other values and practices that encourage *agility*—rapid and flexible response to change.

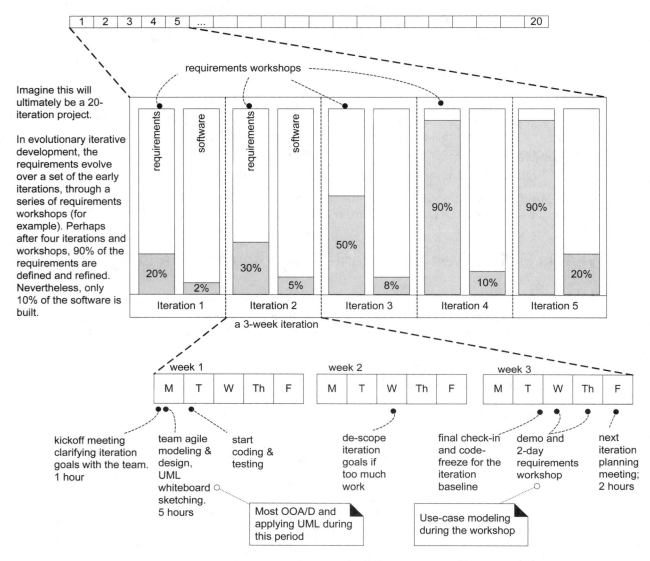

Figure 2.4 Evolutionary analysis and design—the majority in early iterations.

It is not possible to exactly define **agile methods**, as specific practices vary widely. However, short timeboxed iterations with evolutionary refinement of plans, requirements, and design is a basic practice the methods share. In addition, they promote practices and principles that reflect an agile sensibility of simplicity, lightness, communication, self-organizing teams, and more.

Example practices from the Scrum agile method include a *common project work-room* and *self-organizing teams* that coordinate through a daily stand-up meeting with four special questions each member answers. Example practices from the Extreme Programming (XP) method include *programming in pairs* and **test-driven development**.

TDD p. 385

Any iterative method, including the UP, can be applied in an agile spirit. And the UP itself is flexible, encouraging a "whatever works" attitude to include practices from Scrum, XP, and other methods.

The Agile Manifesto and Principles

The Agile Manifesto

Individuals and interactions	*over processes and tools*
Working software	*over comprehensive documentation*
Customer collaboration	*over contract negotiation*
Responding to change	*over following a plan*

The Agile Principles

1. Our highest priority is to satisfy the customer through early and continuous delivery of valuable software.

2. Welcome changing requirements, even late in development. Agile processes harness change for the customer's competitive advantage.

3. Deliver working software frequently, from a couple of weeks to a couple of months, with a preference to the shorter time scale.

4. Business people and developers must work together daily throughout the project.

5. Build projects around motivated individuals. Give them the environment and support they need, and trust them to get the job done.

6. The most efficient and effective method of conveying information to and within a development team is face-to-face conversation.

7. Working software is the primary measure of progress.

8. Agile processes promote sustainable development.

9. The sponsors, developers, and users should be able to maintain a constant pace indefinitely.

10. Continuous attention to technical excellence and good design enhances agility.

11. Simplicity—the art of maximizing the amount of work not done—is essential.

12. The best architectures, requirements, and designs emerge from self-organizing teams.

13. At regular intervals, the team reflects on how to become more effective, then tunes and adjusts its behavior accordingly.

In 2001 a group interested in iterative and agile methods (coining the term) met to find common ground. Out of this came the Agile Alliance (www.agilealliance.com) with a manifesto and statement of principles to capture the spirit of agile methods.

2.7   What is Agile Modeling?

more on agile modeling p. 214

Experienced analysts and modelers know the *secret of modeling*:

> The purpose of modeling (sketching UML, ...) is primarily to *understand*, not to document.

That is, the very act of modeling can and should provide a way to better understand the problem or solution space. From this viewpoint, the purpose of "doing UML" (which should really mean "doing OOA/D") is *not* for a designer to create many detailed UML diagrams that are handed off to a programmer (which is a very un-agile and waterfall-oriented mindset), but rather to quickly explore (more quickly than with code) alternatives and the path to a good OO design.

This view, consistent with agile methods, has been called **agile modeling** in the book (amazingly called) *Agile Modeling* [Ambler02]. It implies a number of practices and values, including:

- Adopting an agile method does not mean avoiding any modeling; that's a misunderstanding. Many agile methods, such as Feature-Driven Development, DSDM, and Scrum, normally include significant modeling sessions. Even the XP founders, from perhaps the most well-known agile method with the least emphasis on modeling, endorsed agile modeling as described by Ambler—and practiced by many modelers over the years.

- The purpose of modeling and models is primarily to support understanding and communication, not documentation.

- Don't model or apply the UML to all or most of the software design. Defer simple or straightforward design problems until programming—solve them while programming and testing. Model and apply the UML for the smaller percentage of unusual, difficult, tricky parts of the design space.

- Use the simplest tool possible. Prefer "low energy" creativity-enhancing simple tools that support rapid input and change. Also, choose tools that support large visual spaces. For example, prefer sketching UML on whiteboards, and capturing the diagrams with a digital camera.[2]

  - This doesn't mean UML CASE tools or word processors can't be used or have no value, but especially for the creative work of discovery, sketching on whiteboards supports quick creative flow and change. The key rule is ease and agility, whatever the technology.

---

2. Two whiteboard sketching tips: **One**: If you don't have enough whiteboards (and you should have many large ones), an alternative is "whiteboard" plastic cling sheets which cling to walls (with a static charge) to create whiteboards. The main product in North America is Avery Write-On Cling Sheets; the main product in Europe is LegaMaster Magic-Chart. **Two**: Digital photos of whiteboard images are often poor (due to reflection). Don't use a flash, but use a software "whiteboard image clean up" application to improve the images, if you need to clean them (as I did for this book).

- Don't model alone, model in pairs (or triads) at the whiteboard, in the awareness that the purpose of modeling is to discover, understand, and share that understanding. Rotate the pen sketching across the members so that all participate.

- Create models in parallel. For example, on one whiteboard start sketching a dynamic-view UML interaction diagram, and on another whiteboard, start sketching the complementary static-view UML class diagram. Develop the two models (two views) together, switching back and forth.

- Use "good enough" simple notation while sketching with a pen on whiteboards. Exact UML details aren't important, as long as the modelers understand each other. Stick to simple, frequently used UML elements.

- Know that all models will be inaccurate, and the final code or design different—sometimes dramatically different—than the model. Only tested code demonstrates the true design; all prior diagrams are incomplete hints, best treated lightly as throw-away explorations.

- Developers themselves should do the OO design modeling, for themselves, not to create diagrams that are given to other programmers to implement—an example of un-agile waterfall-oriented practices.

Agile Modeling in this Book: Why the Snapshots of UML Sketches?

UML-sketch modeling on whiteboards is a practice I—and many developers—have enthusiastically coached and practiced for years. Yet most of the UML diagrams in this book give the impression I don't work that way, because they've been drawn neatly with a tool, for readability. To balance that impression the book occasionally includes digital snapshot pictures of whiteboard UML sketches. It sacrifices legibility but reminds that agile modeling is useful and is the actual practice behind the case studies.

For example, Figure 2.5 is an unedited UML sketch created on a project I was coaching. It took about 20 minutes to draw, with four developers standing around. We needed to understand the inter-system collaboration. The act of drawing it together provided a context to contribute unique insights and reach shared understanding. This captures the feel of how agile modelers apply the UML.

2.8 What is an Agile UP?

The UP was not meant by its creators to be heavy or un-agile, although its large *optional* set of activities and artifacts have understandably led some to that impression. Rather, it was meant to be adopted and applied in the spirit of adaptability and lightness—an **agile UP**. Some examples of how this applies:

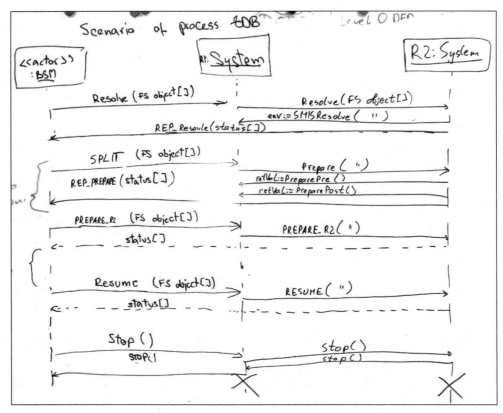

Figure 2.5 A UML sketch of a sequence diagram from a project.

customizing UP p. 37 ■ Prefer a *small* set of UP activities and artifacts. Some projects will benefit more than others, but, in general, keep it simple. Remember that all UP artifacts are optional, and avoid creating them unless they add value. Focus on early programming, not early documenting.

evolutionary A&D p. 25 ■ Since the UP is iterative and evolutionary, requirements and designs are not completed before implementation. They adaptively emerge through a series of iterations, based on feedback.

agile models p. 30 ■ Apply the UML with agile modeling practices.

agile PM p. 673 ■ There isn't a *detailed* plan for the entire project. There is a high-level plan (called the **Phase Plan**) that estimates the project end date and other major milestones, but it does not detail the fine-grained steps to those milestones. A detailed plan (called the **Iteration Plan**) only plans with greater detail one iteration in advance. Detailed planning is done adaptively from iteration to iteration.

The case studies emphasize a relatively small number of artifacts, and iterative development, in the spirit of an agile UP.

2.9 Are There Other Critical UP Practices?

The central idea to appreciate and practice in the UP is short timeboxed iterative, evolutionary, and adaptive development. Some additional best practices and key concepts in the UP:

- tackle high-risk and high-value issues in early iterations
- continuously engage users for evaluation, feedback, and requirements
- build a cohesive, core architecture in early iterations
- continuously verify quality; test early, often, and realistically
- apply use cases where appropriate
- do some visual modeling (with the UML)
- carefully manage requirements
- practice change request and configuration management

2.10 What are the UP Phases?

A UP project organizes the work and iterations across four major phases:

1. **Inception**—approximate vision, business case, scope, vague estimates.

2. **Elaboration**—refined vision, iterative implementation of the core architecture, resolution of high risks, identification of most requirements and scope, more realistic estimates.

3. **Construction**—iterative implementation of the remaining lower risk and easier elements, and preparation for deployment.

4. **Transition**—beta tests, deployment.

These phases are more fully defined in subsequent chapters.

This is *not* the old "waterfall" or sequential lifecycle of first defining all the requirements, and then doing all or most of the design.

Inception is not a requirements phase; rather, it is a feasibility phase, where just enough investigation is done to support a decision to continue or stop.

Similarly, elaboration is not the requirements or design phase; rather, it is a phase where the core architecture is iteratively implemented, and high-risk issues are mitigated.

Figure 2.6 illustrates common schedule-oriented terms in the UP. Notice that one development cycle (which ends in the release of a system into production) is composed of many iterations.

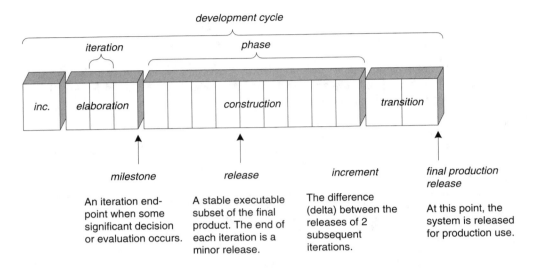

Figure 2.6 Schedule-oriented terms in the UP.

2.11   What are the UP Disciplines?

The UP describes work activities, such as writing a use case, within **disciplines**—a set of activities (and related artifacts) in one subject area, such as the activities within requirements analysis. In the UP, an **artifact** is the general term for any work product: code, Web graphics, database schema, text documents, diagrams, models, and so on.

There are several disciplines in the UP; this book focuses on some artifacts in the following three:

- **Business Modeling**—The Domain Model artifact, to visualize noteworthy concepts in the application domain.

- **Requirements**—The Use-Case Model and Supplementary Specification artifacts to capture functional and non-functional requirements.

- **Design**—The Design Model artifact, to design the software objects.

A longer list of UP disciplines is shown in Figure 2.7.

In the UP, **Implementation** means programming and building the system, not deploying it. The **Environment** discipline refers to establishing the tools and customizing the process for the project—that is, setting up the tool and process environment.

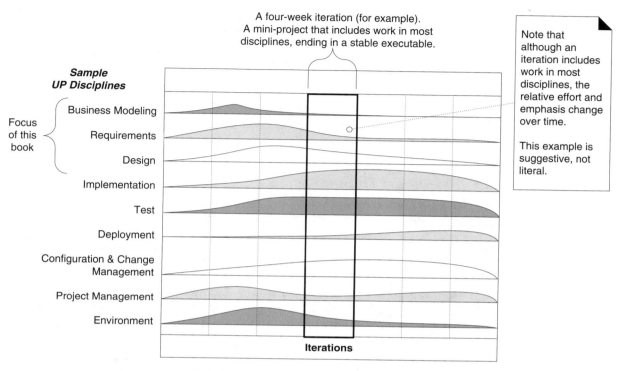

Figure 2.7 UP disciplines.

What is the Relationship Between the Disciplines and Phases?

As illustrated in Figure 2.7, during one iteration work goes on in most or all disciplines. However, the relative effort across these disciplines changes over time. Early iterations naturally tend to apply greater relative emphasis to requirements and design, and later ones less so, as the requirements and core design stabilize through a process of feedback and adaptation.

Relating this to the UP phases (inception, elaboration, ...), Figure 2.8 illustrates the changing relative effort with respect to the phases; please note these are suggestive, not literal. In elaboration, for example, the iterations tend to have a relatively high level of requirements and design work, although definitely some implementation as well. During construction, the emphasis is heavier on implementation and lighter on requirements analysis.

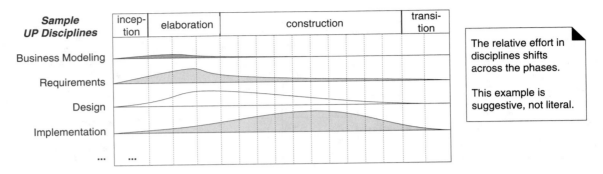

Figure 2.8 Disciplines and phases.

How is the Book Structure Influenced by UP Phases and Disciplines?

With respect to the phases and disciplines, what is the focus of the case studies?

The case studies emphasize the inception and elaboration phase. They focus on some artifacts in the Business Modeling, Requirements, and Design disciplines, as this is where requirements analysis, OOA/D, patterns, and the UML are primarily applied.

The earlier chapters introduce activities in inception; later chapters explore several iterations in elaboration. The following list and Figure 2.9 describe the organization with respect to the UP phases.

1. The inception phase chapters introduce the basics of requirements analysis.

2. Iteration 1 introduces fundamental OOA/D and assignment of responsibilities to objects.

3. Iteration 2 focuses on object design, especially on introducing some high-use "design patterns."

4. Iteration 3 introduces a variety of subjects, such as architectural analysis and framework design.

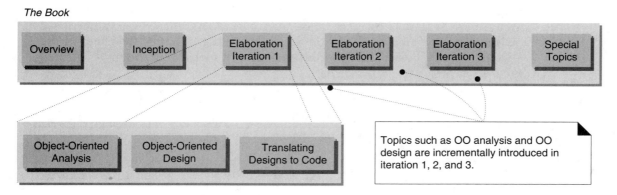

Figure 2.9 Book organization is related to the UP phases and iterations.

2.12 How to Customize the Process? The UP Development Case

Are There Optional Artifacts or Practices in the UP?

Yes! Almost everything is optional. That said, some UP practices and principles are invariant, such as iterative and risk-driven development, and continuous verification of quality.

However, a key insight into the UP is that all activities and artifacts (models, diagrams, documents, …) are *optional*—well, maybe not the code!

Analogy

The set of possible artifacts described in the UP should be viewed like a set of medicines in a pharmacy. Just as one does not indiscriminately take many medicines, but matches the choice to the ailment, likewise on a UP project, a team should select a small subset of artifacts that address its particular problems and needs. In general, focus on a *small* set of artifacts that demonstrate high practical value.

Definition: What is the Development Case?

The choice of practices and UP artifacts for a project may be written up in a short document called the **Development Case** (an artifact in the Environment discipline). For example, Table 2.1 could be the Development Case for the "NextGen Project" case study explored in this book.

Subsequent chapters describe the creation of some of these artifacts, including the Domain Model, Use-Case Model, and Design Model.

The example practices and artifacts presented in this case study are by no means sufficient for, or suitable for, all projects. For example, a machine control system may benefit from many state diagrams. A Web-based e-commerce system may require a focus on user interface prototypes. A "green-field" new development project has very different design artifact needs than a systems integration project.

Discipline	Practice	Artifact Iteration→	Incep. I1	Elab. E1..En	Const. C1..Cn	Trans. T1..T2
Business Modeling	agile modeling req. workshop	Domain Model		s		
Requirements	req. workshop vision box exercise dot voting	Use-Case Model	s	r		
		Vision	s	r		
		Supplementary Specification	s	r		
		Glossary	s	r		
Design	agile modeling test-driven dev.	Design Model		s	r	
		SW Architecture Document		s		
		Data Model		s	r	
Implementa-tion	test-driven dev. pair programming continuous integration coding standards	...				
Project Management	agile PM daily Scrum meeting	...				
...						

Table 2.1 Sample Development Case. s - start; r - refine

2.13 You Know You Didn't Understand Iterative Development or the UP When...

Here are some signs that you have not understood what it means to adopt iterative development and the UP in a healthy agile spirit.

- You try to define most of the requirements before starting design or implementation. Similarly, you try to define most of the design before starting implementation; you try to fully define and commit to an architecture before iterative programming and testing.

- You spend days or weeks in UML modeling before programming, or you think UML diagramming and design activities are a time to fully and accurately define designs and models in great detail. And you regard programming as a simple mechanical translation of these into code.

- You think that inception = requirements, elaboration = design, and construction = implementation (that is, superimposing the waterfall on the UP).

- You think that the purpose of elaboration is to fully and carefully define models, which are translated into code during construction.

- You believe that a suitable iteration length is three months long, rather than three weeks long.

- You think that adopting the UP means to do many of the possible activities and create many documents, and you think of or experience the UP as a formal, fussy process with many steps to be followed.

- You try to plan a project in detail from start to finish; you try to speculatively predict all the iterations, and what should happen in each one.

2.14   History

For the full story and citations, see "Iterative and Incremental Development: A Brief History" (*IEEE Computer*, June 2003, Larman and Basili), and also [Larman03]. Iterative methods go back farther than many realize. In the late 1950s, evolutionary, iterative, and incremental development (IID), rather than the waterfall, was applied on the Mercury space project, and in the early 1960s, on the Trident submarine project, in addition to many other large systems. The first published paper promoting iterative rather than waterfall development was published in 1968 at the IBM T.J. Watson Research Center.

IID was used on many large defense and aerospace projects in the 1970s, including the USA Space Shuttle flight control software (built in 17 iterations averaging about four weeks each). A dominant software engineering thought-leader of the 1970s, Harlan Mills, wrote at that time about the failure of the waterfall for software projects, and the need for IID. Tom Gilb, a private consultant, created and published the IID Evo method in the 1970s, arguably the first fully-formed iterative method. The USA Department of Defense had adopted a waterfall standard in the late 1970s and early 1980s (DoD-2167); by the late 1980s they were experiencing significant failure (estimates of at least 50% of software projects cancelled or unusable), and so it was dropped, and eventually (starting in 1987) replaced by IID method standards—although the legacy of waterfall influence still confuses some DoD projects.

Also in the 1980s, Dr. Frederick Brooks (of *Mythical Man-Month* fame), a major software engineering thoughtleader of that decade, wrote and spoke about the shortcomings of the waterfall and the need to instead use IID methods. Another 1980s milestone was the publication of the spiral model risk-driven IID method by Dr. Barry Boehm, citing the high risk of failure when the waterfall was applied.

By the early 1990s, IID was widely recognized as the successor to the waterfall, and there was a flowering of iterative and evolutionary methods: UP, DSDM, Scrum, XP, and many more.

2.15   Recommended Resources

A readable introduction to the UP and its refinement in the RUP is *The Rational Unified Process—An Introduction* by Philippe Kruchten. Also excellent is *The Rational Unified Process Made Easy*, by Kruchten and Kroll.

Agile and Iterative Development: A Manager's Guide [Larman03] discusses iterative and agile practices, four iterative methods (XP, UP, Scrum, and Evo), the evidence and history behind them, and the evidence of failure for the waterfall.

For other iterative and agile methods, the **Extreme Programming** (XP) series of books [Beck00, BF00, JAH00] are recommended, such as *Extreme Programming Explained*. Some XP practices are encouraged in later chapters of this book. Most XP practices (such as test-driven programming, continuous integration, and iterative development) are compatible with—or identical to—UP practices, and I encourage their adoption on a UP project.

The **Scrum** method is another popular iterative approach that applies 30-day timeboxed iterations, with a daily stand-up meeting with three special questions answered by each team member. *Agile Software Development with Scrum* is recommended reading.

Agile Modeling is described in *Agile Modeling*, by Scott Ambler.

IBM sells the online Web-based RUP documentation product, which provides comprehensive reading on RUP artifacts and activities, and templates for most artifacts. An organization can run a UP project just using mentors and books as learning resources, but some find the RUP product a useful learning and process aid.

For Web resources:

- **www.agilealliance.com**—Collects many articles specifically related to iterative and agile methods, plus links.

- **www.agilemodeling.com**—Articles on agile modeling.

- **www.cetus-links.org**—The Cetus Links site has specialized for years in object technology (OT). Under "OO Project Management—OOA/D Methods" it has many links to iterative and agile methods, even though they are not directly related to OT.

- **www.bradapp.net**—Brad Appleton maintains a large collection of links on software engineering, including iterative methods.

- **www.iturls.com**—The Chinese front page links to an English version, with a search engine referencing iterative and agile articles.

CASE STUDIES

Few things are harder to put up with than a good example.

—*Mark Twain*

Introduction

These case study problems (starting on p. 43) were chosen because they're familiar to many people, yet rich with complexity and interesting design problems. That allows us to concentrate on learning fundamental OOA/D, requirements analysis, UML and patterns, rather than explaining the problems.

What's Next? Having introduced iterative development, this chapter summarizes the case studies and our focus on the application logic layer. The next chapter introduces the inception phase of the case studies, emphasizing that inception is *not* the waterfall phase of "full" early requirements analysis.

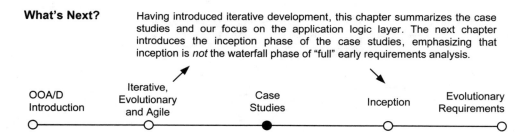

3.1   What is and isn't Covered in the Case Studies?

Generally, applications include UI elements, core application logic, database access, and collaboration with external software or hardware components.

> Although OO technology can be applied at all levels,
> this introduction to OOA/D focuses on the *core application logic layer*, with some secondary discussion of the other layers.

Exploring design of the other layers (such as the UI layer) will just focus on the design of their interface to the application logic layer.

definition of these layers p. 199

Why focus on OOA/D in the core application logic layer?

- Other layers are usually very technology/platform dependent. For example, to explore the OO design of a Web UI or rich client UI layer in Java, we would need to learn in detail about a framework such as Struts or Swing. But for .NET or Python, the choice and details are very different.

- In contrast, the OO design of the core logic layer is similar across technologies.

- The essential OO design skills learned in the context of the application logic layer are applicable to all other layers or components.

- The design approach/patterns for the other layers tends to change quickly as new frameworks or technologies emerge. For example, in the mid-1990s developers would probably build their own home-grown object-relational database access layer. Some years later, they were more likely to use a free, open-source solution such as Hibernate (if Java technology).

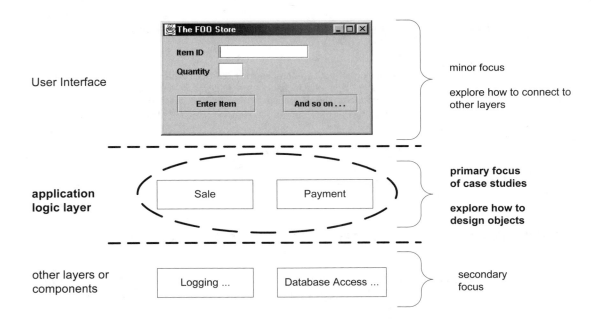

Figure 3.1 Sample layers and objects in an object-oriented system, and the case study focus.

3.2 Case Study Strategy: Iterative Development + Iterative Learning

This book is organized to show an iterative development strategy. OOA/D is applied to the case studies in multiple iterations; the first iteration is for some core functions. Later iterations expand the functionality (see Figure 3.2).

In conjunction with iterative development, the *presentation* of analysis and design topics, UML notation, and patterns is introduced iteratively and incrementally. In the first iteration, a core set of analysis and design topics and notation is presented. The second iteration expands into new ideas, UML notation, and patterns. And likewise in the third iteration.

Figure 3.2 Learning path follows iterations.

3.3 Case One: The NextGen POS System

The first case study is the NextGen point-of-sale (POS) system. In this apparently straightforward problem domain, we shall see that there are interesting requirement and design problems to solve. In addition, it's a real problem—groups really do develop POS systems with object technologies.

A POS system is a computerized application used (in part) to record sales and handle payments; it is typically used in a retail store. It includes hardware components such as a computer and bar code scanner, and software to run the system. It interfaces to various service applications, such as a third-party tax calculator and inventory control. These systems must be relatively fault-tolerant; that is, even if remote services are temporarily unavailable (such as the inventory system), they must still be capable of capturing sales and handling at least cash payments (so that the business is not crippled).

A POS system increasingly must support multiple and varied client-side terminals and interfaces. These include a thin-client Web browser terminal, a regular personal computer with something like a Java Swing graphical user interface, touch screen input, wireless PDAs, and so forth.

Furthermore, we are creating a commercial POS system that we will sell to different clients with disparate needs in terms of business rule processing. Each client will desire a unique set of logic to execute at certain predictable points in scenarios of using the system, such as when a new sale is initiated or when a new line item is added. Therefore, we will need a mechanism to provide this flexibility and customization.

Using an iterative development strategy, we are going to proceed through requirements, object-oriented analysis, design, and implementation.

3.4   Case Two: The Monopoly Game System

To show that the same practices of OOA/D can apply to *very* different problems, I've chosen a software version of the game of Monopoly® as another case study. Although the domain and requirements are not at all like a business system such as the NextGen POS, we will see that domain modeling, object design with patterns, and applying the UML are still relevant and useful. As with a POS, software versions of Monopoly are truly developed and sold, with both rich client and Web UIs.

I won't repeat the rules for Monopoly; it seems almost every person, in every country, has played this game as a child or teenager. If you have questions, the rules are available online at many websites.

The software version of the game will run as a simulation. One person will start the game and indicate the number of simulated players, and then watch while the game runs to completion, presenting a trace of the activity during the simulated player turns.

PART 2 INCEPTION

INCEPTION IS NOT THE REQUIREMENTS PHASE

Le mieux est l'ennemi du bien (The best is the enemy of the good).

—Voltaire

Objectives

- Define the inception step.
- Motivate the following chapters in this section.

Introduction

Inception is the initial short step to establish a common vision and basic scope for the project. It will include analysis of perhaps 10% of the use cases, analysis of the critical non-functional requirement, creation of a business case, and preparation of the development environment so that programming can start in the following elaboration phase.

What's Next?

Having introduced the case studies, this chapter explores the inception phase—which is not the waterfall requirements phase. The next chapter examines this point further: evolutionary vs. waterfall requirements.

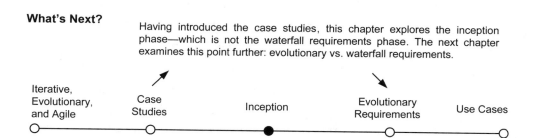

4.1 What is Inception?

Most projects require a short initial step in which the following kinds of questions are explored:

- What is the vision and business case for this project?
- Feasible?
- Buy and/or build?
- *Rough* unreliable range of cost: Is it $10K–100K or in the millions?
- Should we proceed or stop?

Defining the vision and obtaining an order-of-magnitude (unreliable) estimate requires doing *some* requirements exploration. However, ***the purpose of the inception phase is not to define all the requirements***, or generate a believable estimate or project plan.

Definition

This is a critical point, and repeatedly misunderstood on UP projects when people superimpose old "waterfall" thinking. The UP is not the waterfall, and the first phase, inception, is not the time do all requirements or create believable estimates or plans. That happens during elaboration.

At the risk of over-simplification, the idea is to do just enough investigation to form a rational, justifiable opinion of the overall purpose and feasibility of the potential new system, and decide if it is worthwhile to invest in deeper exploration (the purpose of the elaboration phase).

Most requirements analysis occurs during the elaboration phase, in parallel with early production-quality programming and testing.

Thus, the inception phase should be relatively short for most projects, such as one or a few weeks long. Indeed, on many projects, if it is more than a week long, then the point of inception has been missed: It is to decide if the project is worth a serious investigation (during elaboration), not to do that investigation.

Inception in one sentence:

Envision the product scope, vision, and business case.

The main problem solved in one sentence:

*Do the stakeholders have basic agreement on the vision
of the project, and is it worth investing in serious investigation?*

Does this Analogy Help?

In the oil business, when a new field is being considered, some of the steps include:

1. Decide if there is enough evidence or a business case to even justify exploratory drilling.

2. If so, do measurements and exploratory drilling.

3. Provide scope and estimate information.

4. Further steps…

The inception phase is like step one in this analogy. In step one people do not predict how much oil there is, or how much cost or effort is needed to extract it. Although it would be nice to be able to answer "how much" and "when" questions without the cost and effort of the exploration, in the oil business it is understood to not be realistic.

In UP terms, the realistic exploration step is the elaboration phase. The preceding inception phase is akin to a feasibility study to decide if it is even worth investing in exploratory drilling. Only after serious exploration (elaboration) do we have the data and insight to make somewhat believable estimates and plans. Therefore, in iterative development and the UP, plans and estimates are not to be considered reliable in the inception phase. They merely provide an order-of-magnitude sense of the level of effort, to aid the decision to continue or not.

4.2 How Long is Inception?

The intent of inception is to establish some initial common vision for the objectives of the project, determine if it is feasible, and decide if it is worth some serious investigation in elaboration. If it has been decided beforehand that the project will definitely be done, and it is clearly feasible (perhaps because the team has done projects like this before), then the inception phase will be especially brief. It may include the first requirements workshop, planning for the first iteration, and then quickly moving forward to elaboration.

4.3 What Artifacts May Start in Inception?

Table 4.1 lists common inception (or early elaboration) artifacts and indicates the issues they address. Subsequent chapters will examine some of these in greater detail, especially the Use-Case Model. A key insight regarding iterative development is to appreciate that these are only partially completed in this phase, will be refined in later iterations, and should not even be created unless it is deemed likely they will add real practical value. And since it is inception, the investigation and artifact content should be light.

For example, the Use-Case Model may list the *names* of most of the expected use cases and actors, but perhaps only describe 10% of the use cases in detail—done in the service of developing a rough high-level vision of the system scope, purpose, and risks.

Note that some programming work may occur in inception in order to create "proof of concept" prototypes, to clarify a few requirements via (typically) UI-oriented prototypes, and to do programming experiments for key "show stopper" technical questions.

Artifact†	Comment
Vision and Business Case	Describes the high-level goals and constraints, the business case, and provides an executive summary.
Use-Case Model	Describes the functional requirements. During inception, the names of most use cases will be identified, and perhaps 10% of the use cases will be analyzed in detail.
Supplementary Specification	Describes other requirements, mostly non-functional. During inception, it is useful to have some idea of the key non-functional requirements that have will have a major impact on the architecture.
Glossary	Key domain terminology, and data dictionary.
Risk List & Risk Management Plan	Describes the risks (business, technical, resource, schedule) and ideas for their mitigation or response.
Prototypes and proof-of-concepts	To clarify the vision, and validate technical ideas.
Iteration Plan	Describes what to do in the first elaboration iteration.
Phase Plan & Software Development Plan	Low-precision guess for elaboration phase duration and effort. Tools, people, education, and other resources.
Development Case	A description of the customized UP steps and artifacts for this project. In the UP, one always customizes it for the project.

†-These artifacts are only partially completed in this phase. They will be iteratively refined in subsequent iterations. Name capitalization implies an officially named UP artifact.

Table 4.1 Sample inception artifacts.

Isn't That a Lot of Documentation?

Recall that artifacts should be considered optional. Choose to create only those that really add value for the project, and drop them if their worth is not proved.

And since this is evolutionary development, the point is not to create complete specifications during this phase, but initial, rough documents, that are refined during the elaboration iterations, in response to the invaluable feedback from early programming and testing.

Also, often the point of creating artifacts or models is not the document or diagram itself, but the thinking, analysis, and proactive readiness. That's an Agile Modeling perspective: that the greatest value of modeling is to improve understanding, rather than to document reliable specifications. As General Eisenhower said, "In preparing for battle I have always found that plans are useless, but planning indispensable" [Nixon90, BF00].

Note also that artifacts from previous projects can be partially reused on later ones. It is common for there to be many similarities in risk, project management, testing, and environment artifacts across projects. All UP projects should organize artifacts the same way, with the same names (Risk List, Development Case, and so on). This simplifies finding reusable artifacts from prior projects on new engagements.

4.4   You Know You Didn't Understand Inception When...

- It is more than "a few" weeks long for most projects.

- There is an attempt to define most of the requirements.

- Estimates or plans are expected to be reliable.

- You define the architecture (this should be done iteratively in elaboration).

- You believe that the proper sequence of work should be: 1) define the requirements; 2) design the architecture; 3) implement.

- There is no Business Case or Vision artifact.

- All the use cases were written in detail.

- None of the use cases were written in detail; rather, 10–20% should be written in detail to obtain some realistic insight into the scope of the problem.

4.5   How Much UML During Inception?

The purpose of inception is to collect just enough information to establish a common vision, decide if moving forward is feasible, and if the project is worth serious investigation in the elaboration phase. As such, perhaps beyond simple UML use case diagrams, not much diagramming is warranted. There is more focus in inception on understanding the basic scope and 10% of the requirements, expressed mostly in text forms. In practice, and thus in this presentation, most UML diagramming will occur in the next phase—elaboration.

EVOLUTIONARY REQUIREMENTS

Ours is a world where people don't know what they
want and are willing to go through hell to get it.

—Don Marquis

Objectives

- Motivate doing evolutionary requirements.
- Define the FURPS+ model.
- Define the UP requirements artifacts.

Introduction

other UP practices p. 33

This chapter briefly introduces iterative and evolutionary requirements, and describes specific UP requirement artifacts, to provide context for the coming requirements-oriented chapters.

In also explores some evidence illustrating the futility and unskillfulness of waterfall-oriented requirements analysis approaches, in which there is an attempt to define so-called "complete" specifications before starting development.

What's Next? Having introduced inception, this chapter introduces requirements and their evolutionary refinement. The next covers use cases, the prime requirements practice in the UP and many modern methods.

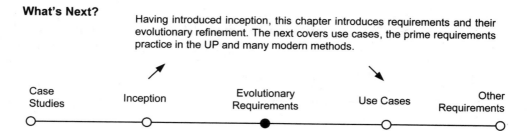

5.1 Definition: Requirements

Requirements are capabilities and conditions to which the system—and more broadly, the project—must conform [JBR99].

The UP promotes a set of best practices, one of which is *manage requirements*. This does not mean the waterfall attitude of attempting to fully define and stabilize the requirements in the first phase of a project before programming, but rather—in the context of inevitably changing and unclear stakeholder's wishes, this means—"a systematic approach to finding, documenting, organizing, and tracking the *changing* requirements of a system" [RUP].

In short, doing it iteratively and skillfully, and not being sloppy.

A prime challenge of requirements analysis is to find, communicate, and remember (that usually means write down) what is really needed, in a form that clearly speaks to the client and development team members.

5.2 Evolutionary vs. Waterfall Requirements

Notice the word *changing* in the definition of what it means to manage requirements. The UP embraces change in requirements as a fundamental driver on projects. That's incredibly important and at the heart of waterfall versus iterative and evolutionary thinking.

In the UP and other evolutionary methods (Scrum, XP, FDD, and so on), we start production-quality programming and testing long before most of the requirements have been analyzed or specified—perhaps when only 10% or 20% of the most architecturally significant, risky, and high-business-value requirements have been specified.

What are the process details? How to do partial, evolutionary requirements analysis combined with early design and programming, in iterations? See "How to do Iterative and Evolutionary Analysis and Design?" on page 25. It provides a brief description and a picture to help explain the process. See "Process: How to Work With Use Cases in Iterative Methods?" on page 95. It has more detailed discussion.

Caution!

If you find yourself on a so-called UP or iterative project that attempts to specify most or all of the requirements (use cases, and so forth) before starting to program and test, there is a profound misunderstanding—it is not a healthy UP or iterative project.

In the 1960s and 1970s (when I started work as a developer) there was still a common speculative belief in the efficacy of full, early requirements analysis for software projects (i.e., the waterfall). Starting in the 1980s, there arose evidence this was unskillful and led to many failures; the old belief was rooted in the wrong paradigm of viewing a software project as similar to predictable mass manufacturing, with low change rates. But software is in the domain of new product development, with high change ranges and high degrees of novelty and discovery.

change research p. 24

Recall the key statistic that, on average, 25% of the requirements change on software projects. Any method that therefore attempts to freeze or fully define requirements at the start is fundamentally flawed, based on a false assumption, and fighting or denying the inevitable change.

Underlining this point, for example, was a study of failure factors on 1,027 software projects [Thomas01]. The findings? Attempting waterfall practices (including detailed up-front requirements) was the single largest contributing factor for failure, being cited in 82% of the projects as the number one problem. To quote the conclusion:

> *... the approach of full requirements definition followed by a long gap before those requirements are delivered is no longer appropriate.*
>
> *The high ranking of changing business requirements suggests that any assumption that there will be little significant change to requirements once they have been documented is fundamentally flawed, and that spending significant time and effort defining them to the maximum level is inappropriate.*

Another relevant research result answers this question: When waterfall requirements analysis is attempted, how many of the prematurely early specified features are actually useful in the final software product? In a study [Johnson02] of thousands of projects, the results are quite revealing—45% of such features were never used, and an additional 19% were "rarely" used. See Figure 5.1. Almost 65% of the waterfall-specified features were of little or no value!

These results don't imply that the solution is to start pounding away at the code near Day One of the project, and forget about requirements analysis or recording requirements. There is a middle way: iterative and evolutionary requirements analysis combined with early timeboxed iterative development and frequent stakeholder participation, evaluation, and feedback on partial results.

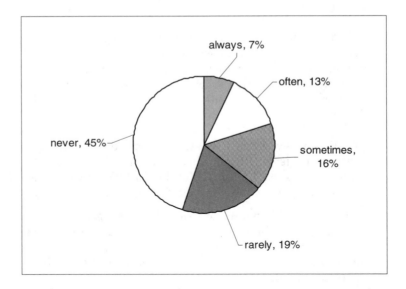

Figure 5.1 Actual use of waterfall-specified features.

5.3   What are Skillful Means to Find Requirements?

To review the UP best practice *manage requirements*:

> *...a systematic approach to finding, documenting, organizing, and tracking the changing requirements of a system. [RUP]*

Besides *changing*, the word *finding* is important; that is, the UP encourages skillful elicitation via techniques such as writing use cases with customers, requirements workshops that include both developers and customers, focus groups with proxy customers, and a demo of the results of each iteration to the customers, to solicit feedback.

The UP welcomes any requirements elicitation method that can add value and that increases user participation. Even the simple XP "story card" practice is acceptable on a UP project, if it can be made to work effectively (it requires the presence of a full-time customer-expert in the project room—an excellent practice but often difficult to achieve).

5.4   What are the Types and Categories of Requirements?

In the UP, requirements are categorized according to the FURPS+ model

[Grady92], a useful mnemonic with the following meaning:[1]

- **Functional**—features, capabilities, security.

- **Usability**—human factors, help, documentation.

- **Reliability**—frequency of failure, recoverability, predictability.

- **Performance**—response times, throughput, accuracy, availability, resource usage.

- **Supportability**—adaptability, maintainability, internationalization, configurability.

The "+" in FURPS+ indicates ancillary and sub-factors, such as:

- **Implementation**—resource limitations, languages and tools, hardware, ...

- **Interface**—constraints imposed by interfacing with external systems.

- **Operations**—system management in its operational setting.

- **Packaging**—for example, a physical box.

- **Legal**—licensing and so forth.

It is helpful to use FURPS+ categories (or some categorization scheme) as a checklist for requirements coverage, to reduce the risk of not considering some important facet of the system.

Some of these requirements are collectively called the **quality attributes**, **quality requirements**, or the "-ilities" of a system. These include usability, reliability, performance, and supportability. In common usage, requirements are categorized as **functional** (behavioral) or **non-functional** (everything else); some dislike this broad generalization [BCK98], but it is very widely used.

architectural analysis p. 541   As we shall see when exploring architectural analysis, the quality attributes have a strong influence on the architecture of a system. For example, a high-performance, high-reliability requirement will influence the choice of software and hardware components, and their configuration.

---

1. There are several systems of requirements categorization and quality attributes published in books and by standards organizations, such as ISO 9126 (which is similar to the FURPS+ list), and several from the Software Engineering Institute (SEI); any can be used on a UP project.

5.5   How are Requirements Organized in UP Artifacts?

The UP offers several requirements artifacts. As with all UP artifacts, they are optional. Key ones include:

- **Use-Case Model**—A set of typical scenarios of using a system. There are primarily for functional (behavioral) requirements.

- **Supplementary Specification**—Basically, everything not in the use cases. This artifact is primarily for all non-functional requirements, such as performance or licensing. It is also the place to record functional **features** not expressed (or expressible) as use cases; for example, a report generation.

- **Glossary**—In its simplest form, the Glossary defines noteworthy terms. It also encompasses the concept of the **data dictionary**, which records requirements related to data, such as validation rules, acceptable values, and so forth. The Glossary can detail any element: an attribute of an object, a parameter of an operation call, a report layout, and so forth.

- **Vision**—Summarizes high-level requirements that are elaborated in the Use-Case Model and Supplementary Specification, and summarizes the business case for the project. A short executive overview document for quickly learning the project's big ideas.

- **Business Rules**—Business rules (also called Domain Rules) typically describe requirements or policies that transcend one software project—they are required in the domain or business, and many applications may need to conform to them. An excellent example is government tax laws. Domain rule details *may* be recorded in the Supplementary Specification, but because they are usually more enduring and applicable than for one software project, placing them in a central Business Rules artifact (shared by all analysts of the company) makes for better reuse of the analysis effort.

What is the Correct Format for these Artifacts?

In the UP, all artifacts are information abstractions; they could be stored on Web pages (such as in a Wiki Web), wall posters, or any variation imaginable. The online RUP documentation product contains templates for the artifacts, but these are an optional aid, and can be ignored.

5.6   Does the Book Contain Examples of These Artifacts?

Yes! This book is primarily an introduction to OOA/D in an iterative process rather than requirements analysis, but exploring OOA/D without some example or context of the requirements gives an incomplete picture—it ignores the influence of requirements on OOA/D. And it's simply useful to have a larger example of key UP requirements artifacts. Where to find the examples:

Requirement Artifact	Where?	Comment
Use-Case Model	Introduction p. 61 Intermediate p. 493	Use cases are common in the UP and an input to OOA/D, and thus described in detail in an early chapter.
Supplementary Specification, Glossary, Vision, Business Rules	Case study examples p. 101	These are provided for consistency, but can be skipped—not an OOA/D topic.

5.7 Recommended Resources

References related to requirements with use cases are covered in a subsequent chapter. Use-case-oriented requirements texts, such as *Writing Effective Use Cases* [Cockburn01] are the recommended starting point in requirements study, rather than more general (and usually, traditional) requirements texts.

There is a broad effort to discuss requirements—and a wide variety of software engineering topics—under the umbrella of the Software Engineering Body of Knowledge (**SWEBOK**), available at www.swebok.org.

The SEI (www.sei.cmu.edu) has several proposals related to quality requirements. The ISO 9126, IEEE Std 830, and IEEE Std 1061 are standards related to requirements and quality attributes, and available on the Web at various sites.

A caution regarding general requirements books, even those that claim to cover use cases, iterative development, or indeed even requirements in the UP:

> Most are written with a waterfall bias of significant or "thorough" up-front requirements definition before moving on to design and implementation. Those books that also mention iterative development may do so superficially, perhaps with "iterative" material recently added to appeal to modern trends. They may have good requirements elicitation and organization tips, but don't represent an accurate view of iterative and evolutionary analysis.

Any variant of advice that suggests "try to define most of the requirements, and then move forward to design and implementation" is inconsistent with iterative evolutionary development and the UP.

USE CASES

The indispensable first step to getting the things
you want out of life: decide what you want.

—Ben Stein

Objectives

- Identify and write use cases.
- Use the brief, casual, and fully dressed formats, in an essential style.
- Apply tests to identify suitable use cases.
- Relate use case analysis to iterative development.

Introduction

intermediate use case topics p. 493

Use cases are text stories, widely used to discover and record requirements. They influence many aspects of a project—including OOA/D—and will be input to many subsequent artifacts in the case studies. This chapter explores basic concepts, including how to write use cases and draw a UML use case diagram. This chapter also shows the value of analysis skill over knowing UML notation; the UML use case diagram is trivial to learn, but the many guidelines to identify and write good use cases take weeks—or longer—to fully digest.

What's Next?

Having introduced requirements, this chapter explores use cases for functional requirements. The next covers other requirements in the UP, including the Supplementary Specification for non-functional requirements.

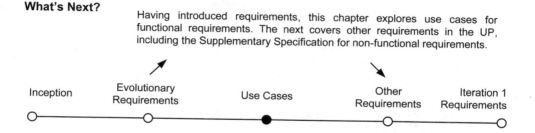

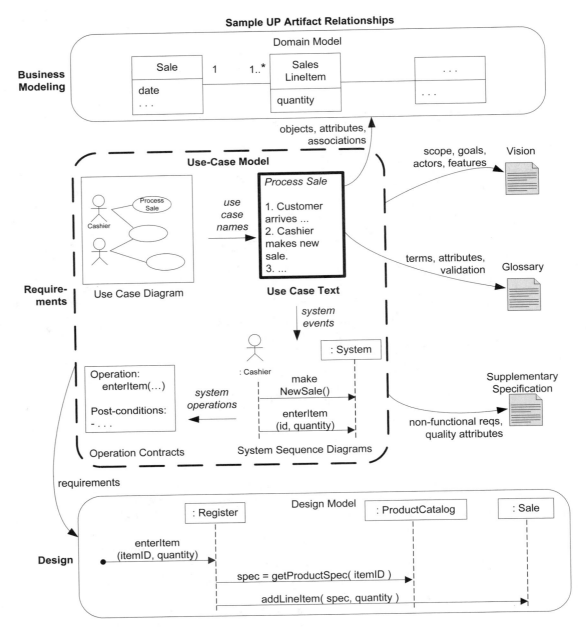

Figure 6.1 Sample UP artifact influence.

The influence of UP artifacts, with an emphasis on text use cases, is shown in Figure 6.1. High-level goals and use case diagrams are input to the creation of the use case text. The use cases can in turn influence many other analysis, design, implementation, project management, and test artifacts.

6.1 Example

Informally, use cases are *text stories* of some actor using a system to meet goals. Here is an example *brief format* use case:

> **Process Sale**: A customer arrives at a checkout with items to purchase. The cashier uses the POS system to record each purchased item. The system presents a running total and line-item details. The customer enters payment information, which the system validates and records. The system updates inventory. The customer receives a receipt from the system and then leaves with the items.

UML use case diagrams p. 89

Notice that **use cases are not diagrams, they are text**. Focusing on secondary-value UML use case diagrams rather than the important use case text is a common mistake for use case novices.

Use cases often need to be more detailed or structured than this example, but the essence is discovering and recording functional requirements by writing stories of using a system to fulfill user goals; that is, *cases of use*.[1] It isn't supposed to be a difficult idea, although it's often difficult to discover what's needed and write it well.

6.2 Definition: What are Actors, Scenarios, and Use Cases?

First, some informal definitions: an **actor** is something with behavior, such as a person (identified by role), computer system, or organization; for example, a cashier.

A **scenario** is a specific sequence of actions and interactions between actors and the system; it is also called a **use case instance**. It is one particular story of using a system, or one path through the use case; for example, the scenario of successfully purchasing items with cash, or the scenario of failing to purchase items because of a credit payment denial.

Informally then, a **use case** is a collection of related success and failure scenarios that describe an actor using a system to support a goal. For example, here is a *casual format* use case with alternate scenarios:

> **Handle Returns**
>
> *Main Success Scenario*: A customer arrives at a checkout with items to return. The cashier uses the POS system to record each returned item …
>
> *Alternate Scenarios*:

---

1. The original term in Swedish literally translates as "usage case."

If the customer paid by credit, and the reimbursement transaction to their credit account is rejected, inform the customer and pay them with cash.

If the item identifier is not found in the system, notify the Cashier and suggest manual entry of the identifier code (perhaps it is corrupted).

If the system detects failure to communicate with the external accounting system, ...

Now that scenarios (use case instances) are defined, an alternate, but similar definition of a use case provided by the RUP will make better sense:

A set of use-case instances, where each instance is a sequence of actions a system performs that yields an observable result of value to a particular actor [RUP].

6.3 Use Cases and the Use-Case Model

The UP defines the **Use-Case Model** within the Requirements discipline. Primarily, this is the set of all written use cases; it is a model of the system's functionality and environment.

> **Use cases are text documents,
> not diagrams, and use-case modeling is
> primarily an act of writing text, not drawing diagrams.**

other UP requirements p. 101

The Use-Case Model is not the only requirement artifact in the UP. There are also the Supplementary Specification, Glossary, Vision, and Business Rules. These are all useful for requirements analysis, but secondary at this point.

UML use case diagram p. 89

The Use-Case Model may optionally include a UML use case diagram to show the names of use cases and actors, and their relationships. This gives a nice **context diagram** of a system and its environment. It also provides a quick way to list the use cases by name.

There is nothing object-oriented about use cases; we're not doing OO analysis when writing them. That's not a problem—use cases are broadly applicable, which increases their usefulness. That said, use cases are a key requirements input to classic OOA/D.

6.4 Motivation: Why Use Cases?

We have goals and want computers to help meet them, ranging from recording sales to playing games to estimating the flow of oil from future wells. Clever analysts have invented *many* ways to capture goals, but the best are simple and familiar. Why? This makes it easier—especially for customers—to contribute to their definition and review. That lowers the risk of missing the mark. This may seem like an off-hand comment, but it's important. Researchers have concocted complex analysis methods that they understand, but that send your average business person into a coma! Lack of user involvement in software projects is near the top of the list of reasons for project failure [Larman03], so anything that can help keep them involved is truly desirable.

more motivation p. 92

Use cases are a good way to help keep it simple, and make it possible for domain experts or requirement donors to themselves write (or participate in writing) use cases.

Another value of use cases is that *they emphasize the user goals and perspective*; we ask the question "Who is using the system, what are their typical scenarios of use, and what are their goals?" This is a more user-centric emphasis compared to simply asking for a list of system features.

Much has been written about use cases, and though worthwhile, creative people often obscure a simple idea with layers of sophistication or over-complication. It is usually possible to spot a novice use-case modeler (or a serious Type-A analyst!) by an over-concern with secondary issues such as use case diagrams, use case relationships, use case packages, and so forth, rather than a focus on the hard work of simply *writing* the text stories.

That said, a strength of use cases is the ability to scale both up and down in terms of sophistication and formality.

6.5 Definition: Are Use Cases Functional Requirements?

FURPS+ p. 56

Use cases *are* requirements, primarily functional or behavioral requirements that indicate what the system will do. In terms of the FURPS+ requirements types, they emphasize the "F" (functional or behavioral), but can also be used for other types, especially when those other types strongly relate to a use case. In the UP—and many modern methods—use cases are the central mechanism that is recommended for their discovery and definition.

A related viewpoint is that a use case defines a *contract* of how a system will behave [Cockburn01].

To be clear: Use cases are indeed requirements (although not all requirements). Some think of requirements only as "the system shall do…" function or feature lists. Not so, and a key idea of use cases is to (usually) reduce the importance or use of detailed old-style feature lists and rather write use cases for the functional requirements. More on this point in a later section.

6.6   Definition: What are Three Kinds of Actors?

An **actor** is anything with behavior, including the system under discussion (SuD) itself when it calls upon the services of other systems.[2] Primary and supporting actors will appear in the action steps of the use case text. Actors are roles played not only by people, but by organizations, software, and machines. There are three kinds of external actors in relation to the SuD:

- **Primary actor**—has user goals fulfilled through using services of the SuD. For example, the cashier.
  - ○   Why identify? To find user goals, which drive the use cases.

- **Supporting actor**—provides a service (for example, information) to the SuD. The automated payment authorization service is an example. Often a computer system, but could be an organization or person.
  - ○   Why identify? To clarify external interfaces and protocols.

- **Offstage actor**—has an interest in the behavior of the use case, but is not primary or supporting; for example, a government tax agency.
  - ○   Why identify? To ensure that *all* necessary interests are identified and satisfied. Offstage actor interests are sometimes subtle or easy to miss unless these actors are explicitly named.

6.7   Notation: What are Three Common Use Case Formats?

Use cases can be written in different formats and levels of formality:

example p. 63
- **brief**—Terse one-paragraph summary, usually of the main success scenario. The prior *Process Sale* example was brief.
  - ○   When? During early requirements analysis, to get a quick sense of subject and scope. May take only a few minutes to create.

example p. 63
- **casual**—Informal paragraph format. Multiple paragraphs that cover various scenarios. The prior *Handle Returns* example was casual.
  - ○   When? As above.

---

2. This was a refinement and improvement to alternate definitions of actors, including those in early versions of the UML and UP [Cockburn97]. Older definitions inconsistently excluded the SuD as an actor, even when it called upon services of other systems. All entities may play multiple *roles*, including the SuD.

example p. 68

- **fully dressed**—All steps and variations are written in detail, and there are supporting sections, such as preconditions and success guarantees.

more on timing of
writing use cases
p. 95

  - ○ When? After many use cases have been identified and written in a brief format, then during the first requirements workshop a few (such as 10%) of the architecturally significant and high-value use cases are written in detail.

The following example is a fully dressed case for our NextGen case study.

6.8   Example: Process Sale, Fully Dressed Style

Fully dressed use cases show more detail and are structured; they dig deeper.

In iterative and evolutionary UP requirements analysis, 10% of the critical use cases would be written this way during the first requirements workshop. Then design and programming starts on the most architecturally significant use cases or scenarios from that 10% set.

Various format templates are available for detailed use cases. Probably the most widely used and shared format, since the early 1990s, is the template available on the Web at *alistair.cockburn.us*, created by Alistair Cockburn, the author of the most popular book and approach to use-case modeling. The following example illustrates this style.

First, here's the template:

Main Success Scenario and Extensions are the two major sections

Use Case Section	Comment
Use Case Name	Start with a verb.
Scope	The system under design.
Level	"user-goal" or "subfunction"
Primary Actor	Calls on the system to deliver its services.
Stakeholders and Interests	Who cares about this use case, and what do they want?
Preconditions	What must be true on start, *and* worth telling the reader?
Success Guarantee	What must be true on successful completion, *and* worth telling the reader.
Main Success Scenario	A typical, unconditional happy path scenario of success.
Extensions	Alternate scenarios of success or failure.
Special Requirements	Related non-functional requirements.

Use Case Section	Comment
Technology and Data Variations List	Varying I/O methods and data formats.
Frequency of Occurrence	Influences investigation, testing, and timing of implementation.
Miscellaneous	Such as open issues.

Here's an example, based on the template.

Please note that this is the book's primary case study example of a detailed use case; it shows many common elements and issues.

It probably shows much more than you ever wanted to know about a POS system! But, it's for a real POS, and shows the ability of use cases to capture complex real-world requirements, and deeply branching scenarios.

Use Case UC1: Process Sale

Scope: NextGen POS application
Level: user goal
Primary Actor: Cashier
Stakeholders and Interests:
— Cashier: Wants accurate, fast entry, and no payment errors, as cash drawer shortages are deducted from his/her salary.
— Salesperson: Wants sales commissions updated.
— Customer: Wants purchase and fast service with minimal effort. Wants easily visible display of entered items and prices. Wants proof of purchase to support returns.
— Company: Wants to accurately record transactions and satisfy customer interests. Wants to ensure that Payment Authorization Service payment receivables are recorded. Wants some fault tolerance to allow sales capture even if server components (e.g., remote credit validation) are unavailable. Wants automatic and fast update of accounting and inventory.
— Manager: Wants to be able to quickly perform override operations, and easily debug Cashier problems.
— Government Tax Agencies: Want to collect tax from every sale. May be multiple agencies, such as national, state, and county.
— Payment Authorization Service: Wants to receive digital authorization requests in the correct format and protocol. Wants to accurately account for their payables to the store.
Preconditions: Cashier is identified and authenticated.
Success Guarantee (or Postconditions): Sale is saved. Tax is correctly calculated. Accounting and Inventory are updated. Commissions recorded. Receipt is generated. Payment authorization approvals are recorded.

Main Success Scenario (or Basic Flow):
1. Customer arrives at POS checkout with goods and/or services to purchase.
2. Cashier starts a new sale.
3. Cashier enters item identifier.
4. System records sale line item and presents item description, price, and running total.
   Price calculated from a set of price rules.

Cashier repeats steps 3-4 until indicates done.
5. System presents total with taxes calculated.
6. Cashier tells Customer the total, and asks for payment.
7. Customer pays and System handles payment.
8. System logs completed sale and sends sale and payment information to the external Accounting system (for accounting and commissions) and Inventory system (to update inventory).
9. System presents receipt.
10. Customer leaves with receipt and goods (if any).

Extensions (or Alternative Flows):
*a. At any time, Manager requests an override operation:
    1. System enters Manager-authorized mode.
    2. Manager or Cashier performs one Manager-mode operation. e.g., cash balance change, resume a suspended sale on another register, void a sale, etc.
    3. System reverts to Cashier-authorized mode.
*b. At any time, System fails:

    To support recovery and correct accounting, ensure all transaction sensitive state and events can be recovered from any step of the scenario.
    1. Cashier restarts System, logs in, and requests recovery of prior state.
    2. System reconstructs prior state.
      2a. System detects anomalies preventing recovery:
        1. System signals error to the Cashier, records the error, and enters a clean state.
        2. Cashier starts a new sale.
1a. Customer or Manager indicate to resume a suspended sale.
    1. Cashier performs resume operation, and enters the ID to retrieve the sale.
    2. System displays the state of the resumed sale, with subtotal.
      2a. Sale not found.
        1. System signals error to the Cashier.
        2. Cashier probably starts new sale and re-enters all items.
    3. Cashier continues with sale (probably entering more items or handling payment).
2-4a. Customer tells Cashier they have a tax-exempt status (e.g., seniors, native peoples)
    1. Cashier verifies, and then enters tax-exempt status code.
    2. System records status (which it will use during tax calculations)
3a. Invalid item ID (not found in system):
    1. System signals error and rejects entry.
    2. Cashier responds to the error:
      2a. There is a human-readable item ID (e.g., a numeric UPC):
        1. Cashier manually enters the item ID.
        2. System displays description and price.
          2a. Invalid item ID: System signals error. Cashier tries alternate method.
      2b. There is no item ID, but there is a price on the tag:
        1. Cashier asks Manager to perform an override operation.

        2. Managers performs override.

        3. Cashier indicates manual price entry, enters price, and requests standard taxation for this amount (because there is no product information, the tax engine can't otherwise deduce how to tax it)

    2c. Cashier performs <u>Find Product Help</u> to obtain true item ID and price.

    2d. Otherwise, Cashier asks an employee for the true item ID or price, and does either manual ID or manual price entry (see above).

3b. There are multiple of same item category and tracking unique item identity not important (e.g., 5 packages of veggie-burgers):

    1. Cashier can enter item category identifier and the quantity.

3c. Item requires manual category and price entry (such as flowers or cards with a price on them):

    1. Cashier enters special manual category code, plus the price.

3-6a: Customer asks Cashier to remove (i.e., void) an item from the purchase:

This is only legal if the item value is less than the void limit for Cashiers, otherwise a Manager override is needed.

    1. Cashier enters item identifier for removal from sale.

    2. System removes item and displays updated running total.

        2a. Item price exceeds void limit for Cashiers:

            1. System signals error, and suggests Manager override.

            2. Cashier requests Manager override, gets it, and repeats operation.

3-6b. Customer tells Cashier to cancel sale:

    1. Cashier cancels sale on System.

3-6c. Cashier suspends the sale:

    1. System records sale so that it is available for retrieval on any POS register.

    2. System presents a "suspend receipt" that includes the line items, and a sale ID used to retrieve and resume the sale.

4a. The system supplied item price is not wanted (e.g., Customer complained about something and is offered a lower price):

    1. Cashier requests approval from Manager.

    2. Manager performs override operation.

    3. Cashier enters manual override price.

    4. System presents new price.

5a. System detects failure to communicate with external tax calculation system service:

    1. System restarts the service on the POS node, and continues.

        1a. System detects that the service does not restart.

            1. System signals error.

            2. Cashier may manually calculate and enter the tax, or cancel the sale.

5b. Customer says they are eligible for a discount (e.g., employee, preferred customer):

    1. Cashier signals discount request.

    2. Cashier enters Customer identification.

    3. System presents discount total, based on discount rules.

5c. Customer says they have credit in their account, to apply to the sale:

    1. Cashier signals credit request.

    2. Cashier enters Customer identification.

    3. Systems applies credit up to price=0, and reduces remaining credit.

6a. Customer says they intended to pay by cash but don't have enough cash:

    1. Cashier asks for alternate payment method.

        1a. Customer tells Cashier to cancel sale. Cashier cancels sale on System.

7a. Paying by cash:
    1. Cashier enters the cash amount tendered.
    2. System presents the balance due, and releases the cash drawer.
    3. Cashier deposits cash tendered and returns balance in cash to Customer.
    4. System records the cash payment.
7b. Paying by credit:
    1. Customer enters their credit account information.
    2. System displays their payment for verification.
    3. Cashier confirms.
        3a. Cashier cancels payment step:
            1. System reverts to "item entry" mode.
    4. System sends payment authorization request to an external Payment Authorization Service System, and requests payment approval.
        4a. System detects failure to collaborate with external system:
            1. System signals error to Cashier.
            2. Cashier asks Customer for alternate payment.
    5. System receives payment approval, signals approval to Cashier, and releases cash drawer (to insert signed credit payment receipt).
        5a. System receives payment denial:
            1. System signals denial to Cashier.
            2. Cashier asks Customer for alternate payment.
        5b. Timeout waiting for response.
            1. System signals timeout to Cashier.
            2. Cashier may try again, or ask Customer for alternate payment.
    6. System records the credit payment, which includes the payment approval.
    7. System presents credit payment signature input mechanism.
    8. Cashier asks Customer for a credit payment signature. Customer enters signature.
    9. If signature on paper receipt, Cashier places receipt in cash drawer and closes it.
7c. Paying by check…
7d. Paying by debit…
7e. Cashier cancels payment step:
    1. System reverts to "item entry" mode.
7f. Customer presents coupons:
    1. Before handling payment, Cashier records each coupon and System reduces price as appropriate. System records the used coupons for accounting reasons.
        1a. Coupon entered is not for any purchased item:
            1. System signals error to Cashier.
9a. There are product rebates:
    1. System presents the rebate forms and rebate receipts for each item with a rebate.
9b. Customer requests gift receipt (no prices visible):
    1. Cashier requests gift receipt and System presents it.
9c. Printer out of paper.
    1. If System can detect the fault, will signal the problem.
    2. Cashier replaces paper.
    3. Cashier requests another receipt.

Special Requirements:
- Touch screen UI on a large flat panel monitor. Text must be visible from 1 meter.
- Credit authorization response within 30 seconds 90% of the time.
- Somehow, we want robust recovery when access to remote services such the inventory system is failing.
- Language internationalization on the text displayed.
- Pluggable business rules to be insertable at steps 3 and 7.
- . . .

Technology and Data Variations List:
*a. Manager override entered by swiping an override card through a card reader, or entering an authorization code via the keyboard.
3a. Item identifier entered by bar code laser scanner (if bar code is present) or keyboard.
3b. Item identifier may be any UPC, EAN, JAN, or SKU coding scheme.
7a. Credit account information entered by card reader or keyboard.
7b. Credit payment signature captured on paper receipt. But within two years, we predict many customers will want digital signature capture.

Frequency of Occurrence: Could be nearly continuous.

Open Issues:
- What are the tax law variations?
- Explore the remote service recovery issue.
- What customization is needed for different businesses?
- Must a cashier take their cash drawer when they log out?
- Can the customer directly use the card reader, or does the cashier have to do it?

This use case is illustrative rather than exhaustive (although it is based on a real POS system's requirements—developed with an OO design in Java). Nevertheless, there is enough detail and complexity here to offer a realistic sense that a fully dressed use case can record many requirement details. This example will serve well as a model for many use case problems.

6.9   What do the Sections Mean?

Preface Elements

Scope

The scope bounds the system (or systems) under design. Typically, a use case describes use of one software (or hardware plus software) system; in this case it is known as a **system use case**. At a broader scope, use cases can also describe how a business is used by its customers and partners. Such an enterprise-level process description is called a **business use case** and is a good example of the wide applicability of use cases, but they aren't covered in this introductory book.

Level

EBP p. 88

see the use case "include" relationship for more on subfunction use cases p. 494

In Cockburn's system, use cases are classified as at the user-goal level or the subfunction level, among others. A **user-goal level** use case is the common kind that describe the scenarios to fulfill the goals of a primary actor to get work done; it roughly corresponds to an **elementary business process** (EBP) in business process engineering. A **subfunction-level** use case describes substeps required to support a user goal, and is usually created to factor out duplicate substeps shared by several regular use cases (to avoid duplicating common text); an example is the subfunction use case *Pay by Credit*, which could be shared by many regular use cases.

Primary Actor

The principal actor that calls upon system services to fulfill a goal.

Stakeholders and Interests List—Important!

This list is more important and practical than may appear at first glance. It suggests and bounds what the system must do. To quote:

> The [system] operates a contract between stakeholders, with the use cases detailing the behavioral parts of that contract...The use case, as the contract for behavior, captures *all and only* the behaviors related to satisfying the stakeholders' interests [Cockburn01].

This answers the question: What should be in the use case? The answer is: That which satisfies all the stakeholders' interests. In addition, by starting with the stakeholders and their interests before writing the remainder of the use case, we have a method to remind us what the more detailed responsibilities of the system should be. For example, would I have identified a responsibility for salesperson commission handling if I had not first listed the salesperson stakeholder and their interests? Hopefully eventually, but perhaps I would have missed it during the first analysis session. The stakeholder interest viewpoint provides a thorough and methodical procedure for discovering and recording all the required behaviors.

Stakeholders and Interests:
- Cashier: Wants accurate, fast entry and no payment errors, as cash drawer shortages are deducted from his/her salary.
- Salesperson: Wants sales commissions updated.
- …

Preconditions and Success Guarantees (Postconditions)

First, don't bother with a precondition or success guarantee unless you are stating something non-obvious and noteworthy, to help the reader gain insight. Don't add useless noise to requirements documents.

Preconditions state what *must always* be true before a scenario is begun in the use case. Preconditions are *not* tested within the use case; rather, they are conditions that are assumed to be true. Typically, a precondition implies a scenario of another use case, such as logging in, that has successfully completed. Note that there are conditions that must be true, but are not worth writing, such as "the system has power." Preconditions communicate noteworthy assumptions that the writer thinks readers should be alerted to.

Success guarantees (or **postconditions**) state what must be true on successful completion of the use case—either the main success scenario or some alternate path. The guarantee should meet the needs of all stakeholders.

> **Preconditions**: Cashier is identified and authenticated.
> **Success Guarantee (Postconditions)**: Sale is saved. Tax is correctly calculated. Accounting and Inventory are updated. Commissions recorded. Receipt is generated.

Main Success Scenario and Steps (or Basic Flow)

This has also been called the "happy path" scenario, or the more prosaic "Basic Flow" or "Typical Flow." It describes a typical success path that satisfies the interests of the stakeholders. Note that it often does *not* include any conditions or branching. Although not wrong or illegal, it is arguably more comprehensible and extendible to be very consistent and defer all conditional handling to the Extensions section.

Guideline

Defer all conditional and branching statements to the Extensions section.

The scenario records the steps, of which there are three kinds:

1. An interaction between actors.[3]

2. A validation (usually by the system).

3. A state change by the system (for example, recording or modifying something).

---

3. Note that the system under discussion itself should be considered an actor when it plays an actor role collaborating with other systems.

Step one of a use case does not always fall into this classification, but indicates the trigger event that starts the scenario.

It is a common idiom to always capitalize the actors' names for ease of identification. Observe also the idiom that is used to indicate repetition.

Main Success Scenario:
1. Customer arrives at a POS checkout with items to purchase.
2. Cashier starts a new sale.
3. Cashier enters item identifier.
4. ...
Cashier repeats steps 3-4 until indicates done.
5. ...

Extensions (or Alternate Flows)

Extensions are important and normally comprise the majority of the text. They indicate all the other scenarios or branches, both success and failure. Observe in the fully dressed example that the Extensions section was considerably longer and more complex than the Main Success Scenario section; this is common.

In thorough use case writing, the combination of the happy path and extension scenarios should satisfy "nearly" all the interests of the stakeholders. This point is qualified, because some interests may best be captured as non-functional requirements expressed in the Supplementary Specification rather than the use cases. For example, the customer's interest for a visible display of descriptions and prices is a usability requirement.

Extension scenarios are branches from the main success scenario, and so can be notated with respect to its steps 1...N. For example, at Step 3 of the main success scenario there may be an invalid item identifier, either because it was incorrectly entered or unknown to the system. An extension is labeled "3a"; it first identifies the condition and then the response. Alternate extensions at Step 3 are labeled "3b" and so forth.

Extensions:
3a. Invalid identifier:
    1. System signals error and rejects entry.
3b. There are multiple of same item category and tracking unique item identity not important (e.g., 5 packages of veggie-burgers):
    1. Cashier can enter item category identifier and the quantity.

An extension has two parts: the condition and the handling.

Guideline: When possible, write the condition as something that can be *detected* by the system or an actor. To contrast:

5a. System detects failure to communicate with external tax calculation system service:
5a. External tax calculation system not working:

The former style is preferred because this is something the system can detect; the latter is an inference.

Extension handling can be summarized in one step, or include a sequence, as in this example, which also illustrates notation to indicate that a condition can arise within a range of steps:

3-6a: Customer asks Cashier to remove an item from the purchase:
  1. Cashier enters the item identifier for removal from the sale.
  2. System displays updated running total.

At the end of extension handling, by default the scenario merges back with the main success scenario, unless the extension indicates otherwise (such as by halting the system).

Sometimes, a particular extension point is quite complex, as in the "paying by credit" extension. This can be a motivation to express the extension as a separate use case.

This extension example also demonstrates the notation to express failures within extensions.

7b. Paying by credit:
  1. Customer enters their credit account information.
  2. System sends payment authorization request to an external Payment Authorization Service System, and requests payment approval.
    2a. System detects failure to collaborate with external system:
      1. System signals error to Cashier.
      2. Cashier asks Customer for alternate payment.

If it is desirable to describe an extension condition as possible during any (or at least most) steps, the labels *a, *b, …, can be used.

---

*a. At any time, System crashes:
  In order to support recovery and correct accounting, ensure all transaction sensitive state and events can be recovered at any step in the scenario.
  1. Cashier restarts the System, logs in, and requests recovery of prior state.
  2. System reconstructs prior state.

Performing Another Use Case Scenario

Sometimes, a use case branches to perform another use case scenario. For example, the story *Find Product Help* (to show product details, such as description, price, a picture or video, and so on) is a distinct use case that is sometimes performed while within *Process Sale* (usually when the item ID can't be found). In

Cockburn notation, performing this second use case is shown with underlining, as this example shows:

> 3a. Invalid item ID (not found in system):
>   1. System signals error and rejects entry.
>   2. Cashier responds to the error:
>   2a. ...
>   2c. Cashier performs <u>Find Product Help</u> to obtain true item ID and price.

Assuming, as usual, that the use cases are written with a hyperlinking tool, then clicking on this underlined use case name will display its text.

Special Requirements

If a non-functional requirement, quality attribute, or constraint relates specifically to a use case, record it with the use case. These include qualities such as performance, reliability, and usability, and design constraints (often in I/O devices) that have been mandated or considered likely.

> **Special Requirements:**
> – Touch screen UI on a large flat panel monitor. Text must be visible from 1 meter.
> – Credit authorization response within 30 seconds 90% of the time.
> – Language internationalization on the text displayed.
> – Pluggable business rules to be insertable at steps 2 and 6.

Recording these with the use case is classic UP advice, and a reasonable location when *first* writing the use case. However, many practitioners find it useful to ultimately move and consolidate all non-functional requirements in the Supplementary Specification, for content management, comprehension, and readability, because these requirements usually have to be considered as a whole during architectural analysis.

Technology and Data Variations List

Often there are technical variations in *how* something must be done, but not what, and it is noteworthy to record this in the use case. A common example is a technical constraint imposed by a stakeholder regarding input or output technologies. For example, a stakeholder might say, "The POS system must support credit account input using a card reader and the keyboard." Note that these are examples of early design decisions or constraints; in general, it is skillful to avoid premature design decisions, but sometimes they are obvious or unavoidable, especially concerning input/output technologies.

It is also necessary to understand variations in data schemes, such as using UPCs or EANs for item identifiers, encoded in bar code symbology.

Congratulations: Use Cases are Written and Wrong (!)

The NextGen POS team is writing a few use cases in multiple short requirements workshops, in parallel with a series of short timeboxed development iterations that involve production-quality programming and testing. The team is incrementally adding to the use case set, and refining and adapting based on feedback from early programming, tests, and demos. Subject matter experts, cashiers, and developers actively participate in requirements analysis.

That's a good evolutionary analysis process—rather than the waterfall—but a dose of "requirements realism" is still needed. Written specifications and other models give the *illusion* of correctness, but models lie (unintentionally). Only code and tests reveals the truth of what's really wanted and works.

The use cases, UML diagrams, and so forth won't be perfect—guaranteed. They will lack critical information and contain wrong statements. The solution is not the waterfall attitude of trying to record specifications near-perfect and complete at the start—although of course we do the best we can in the time available, and should learn and apply great requirements practices. But it will never be enough.

This isn't a call to rush to coding without any analysis or modeling. There is a middle way, between the waterfall and ad hoc programming: iterative and evolutionary development. In this approach the use cases and other models are incrementally refined, verified, and clarified through early programming and testing.

You know you're on the wrong path if the team tries to write in detail all or most of the use cases before beginning the first development iteration—or the opposite.

This list is the place to record such variations. It is also useful to record variations in the data that may be captured at a particular step.

Technology and Data Variations List:
3a. Item identifier entered by laser scanner or keyboard.
3b. Item identifier may be any UPC, EAN, JAN, or SKU coding scheme.
7a. Credit account information entered by card reader or keyboard.
7b. Credit payment signature captured on paper receipt. But within two years, we predict many customers will want digital signature capture.

6.10 Notation: Are There Other Formats? A Two-Column Variation

Some prefer the two-column or conversational format, which emphasizes the interaction between the actors and the system. It was first proposed by Rebecca Wirfs-Brock in [Wirfs-Brock93], and is also promoted by Constantine and Lockwood to aid usability analysis and engineering [CL99]. Here is the same content using the two-column format:

Use Case UC1: Process Sale

Primary Actor: …
… as before …

Main Success Scenario:

Actor Action (or Intention)	System Responsibility
1. Customer arrives at a POS checkout with goods and/or services to purchase.	
2. Cashier starts a new sale.	
3. Cashier enters item identifier.	4. Records each sale line item and presents item description and running total.
Cashier repeats steps 3-4 until indicates done.	5. Presents total with taxes calculated.
6. Cashier tells Customer the total, and asks for payment.	
7. Customer pays.	8. Handles payment.
	9. Logs the completed sale and sends information to the external accounting (for all accounting and commissions) and inventory systems (to update inventory). System presents receipt.
…	…

The Best Format?

There isn't one best format; some prefer the one-column style, some the two-column. Sections may be added and removed; heading names may change. None of this is particularly important; the key thing is to write the details of the main success scenario and its extensions, in some form. [Cockburn01] summarizes many usable formats.

Personal Practice

This is my practice, not a recommendation. For some years, I used the two-column format because of its clear visual separation in the conversation. However, I have reverted to a one-column style as it is more compact and easier to format, and the slight value of the visually separated conversation does not for me outweigh these benefits. I find it still simple to visually identify the different parties in the conversation (Customer, System, …) if each party and the System responses are usually allocated to their own steps.

6.11   Guideline: Write in an Essential UI-Free Style

New and Improved! The Case for Fingerprinting

During a requirements workshop, the cashier may say one of his goals is to "log in." The cashier was probably thinking of a GUI, dialog box, user ID, and password. This is a mechanism to achieve a goal, rather than the goal itself. By investigating up the goal hierarchy ("What is the goal of that goal?"), the system analyst arrives at a mechanism-independent goal: "identify myself and get authenticated," or an even higher goal: "prevent theft ...".

This *root-goal* discovery process can open up the vision to new and improved solutions. For example, keyboards and mice with biometric readers, usually for a fingerprint, are now common and inexpensive. If the goal is "identification and authentication" why not make it easy and fast using a biometric reader on the keyboard? But properly answering that question involves some usability analysis work as well. Are their fingers covered in grease? Do they have fingers?

Essential Style Writing

This idea has been summarized in various use case guidelines as "keep the user interface out; focus on intent" [Cockburn01]. Its motivation and notation has been more fully explored by Larry Constantine in the context of creating better user interfaces (UIs) and doing usability engineering [Constantine94, CL99]. Constantine calls the writing style **essential** when it avoids UI details and focuses on the real user intent.[4]

In an essential writing style, the narrative is expressed at the level of the user's *intentions* and system's *responsibilities* rather than their concrete actions. They remain free of technology and mechanism details, especially those related to the UI.

Guideline

Write use cases in an essential style; keep the user interface out and focus on actor intent.

All of the previous example use cases in this chapter, such as *Process Sale*, were written aiming towards an essential style.

---

4. The term comes from "essential models" in *Essential Systems Analysis* [MP84].

Contrasting Examples

Essential Style

Assume that the *Manage Users* use case requires identification and authentication:

> . . .
> 1. Administrator identifies self.
> 2. System authenticates identity.
> 3. . . .

The design solution to these intentions and responsibilities is wide open: biometric readers, graphical user interfaces (GUIs), and so forth.

Concrete Style—Avoid During Early Requirements Work

In contrast, there is a **concrete use case** style. In this style, user interface decisions are embedded in the use case text. The text may even show window screen shots, discuss window navigation, GUI widget manipulation and so forth. For example:

> . . .
> 1. Adminstrator enters ID and password in dialog box (see Picture 3).
> 2. System authenticates Administrator.
> 3. System displays the "edit users" window (see Picture 4).
> 4. . . .

These concrete use cases may be useful as an aid to concrete or detailed GUI design work during a later step, but they are not suitable during the early requirements analysis work. During early requirements work, "keep the user interface out—focus on intent."

6.12   Guideline: Write Terse Use Cases

Do you like to read lots of requirements? I didn't think so. So, write terse use cases. Delete "noise" words. Even small changes add up, such as "System authenticates..." rather than "*The* System authenticates..."

6.13   Guideline: Write Black-Box Use Cases

Black-box use cases are the most common and recommended kind; they do not describe the internal workings of the system, its components, or design. Rather, the system is described as having *responsibilities*, which is a common unifying metaphorical theme in object-oriented thinking—software elements have responsibilities and collaborate with other elements that have responsibilities.

By defining system responsibilities with black-box use cases, one can specify *what* the system must do (the behavior or functional requirements) without deciding *how* it will do it (the design). Indeed, the definition of "analysis" versus "design" is sometimes summarized as "what" versus "how." This is an important theme in good software development: During requirements analysis avoid making "how" decisions, and specify the external behavior for the system, as a black box. Later, during design, create a solution that meets the specification.

Black-box style	Not
The system records the sale.	The system writes the sale to a database. ...or (even worse): The system generates a SQL INSERT statement for the sale...

6.14   Guideline: Take an Actor and Actor-Goal Perspective

Here's the RUP use case definition, from the use case founder Ivar Jacobson:

> A set of use-case instances, where each instance is a sequence of actions a system performs that yields an observable result of value *to a particular actor.*

The phrase *"an observable result of value to a particular actor"* is a subtle but important concept that Jacobson considers critical, because it stresses two attitudes during requirements analysis:

- Write requirements focusing on the users or actors of a system, asking about their goals and typical situations.

- Focus on understanding what the actor considers a valuable result.

function lists p. 92

Perhaps it seems obvious to stress providing observable user value and focusing on users' typical goals, but the software industry is littered with failed projects that did not deliver what people really needed. The old feature and function list approach to capturing requirements can contribute to that negative outcome because it did not encourage asking who is using the product, and what provides value.

6.15   Guideline: How to Find Use Cases

Use cases are defined to satisfy the goals of the primary actors. Hence, the basic procedure is:

1. Choose the system boundary. Is it just a software application, the hardware and application as a unit, that plus a person using it, or an entire organization?

2. Identify the primary actors—those that have goals fulfilled through using services of the system.

3. Identify the goals for each primary actor.

4. Define use cases that satisfy user goals; name them according to their goal. Usually, user-goal level use cases will be one-to-one with user goals, but there is at least one exception, as will be examined.

Of course, in iterative and evolutionary development, not all goals or use cases will be fully or correctly identified near the start. It's an evolving discovery.

Step 1: Choose the System Boundary

For this case study, the POS system itself is the system under design; everything outside of it is outside the system boundary, including the cashier, payment authorization service, and so on.

If the definition of the boundary of the system under design is not clear, it can be clarified by further definition of what is outside—the external primary and supporting actors. Once the external actors are identified, the boundary becomes clearer. For example, is the complete responsibility for payment authorization within the system boundary? No, there is an external payment authorization service actor.

Steps 2 and 3: Find Primary Actors and Goals

It is artificial to strictly linearize the identification of primary actors before user goals; in a requirements workshop, people brainstorm and generate a mixture of both. Sometimes, goals reveal the actors, or vice versa.

Guideline: Brainstorm the primary actors first, as this sets up the framework for further investigation.

Are There Questions to Help Find Actors and Goals?

In addition to obvious primary actors and goals, the following questions help identify others that may be missed:

Who starts and stops the system?	Who does system administration?
Who does user and security management?	Is "time" an actor because the system does something in response to a time event?

Is there a monitoring process that restarts the system if it fails?

Who evaluates system activity or performance?

How are software updates handled? Push or pull update?

Who evaluates logs? Are they remotely retrieved?

In addition to *human* primary actors, are there any external software or robotic systems that call upon services of the system?

Who gets notified when there are errors or failures?

How to Organize the Actors and Goals?

There are at least two approaches:

use case diagrams p. 89

1. As you discover the results, draw them in a use case diagram, naming the goals as use cases.

2. Write an actor-goal list first, review and refine it, and then draw the use case diagram.

If you create an actor-goal list, then in terms of UP artifacts it may be a section in the Vision artifact.

For example:

Actor	Goal		Actor	Goal
Cashier	process sales process rentals handle returns cash in cash out . . .		System Administrator	add users modify users delete users manage security manage system tables . . .
Manager	start up shut down . . .		Sales Activity System	analyze sales and performance data
. . .	. . .		. . .	. . .

The Sales Activity System is a remote application that will frequently request sales data from each POS node in the network.

Why Ask About Actor Goals Rather Than Use Cases?

Actors have goals and use applications to help satisfy them. The viewpoint of use case modeling is to find these actors and their goals, and create solutions that produce a result of value. This is slight shift in emphasis for the use case modeler. Rather than asking "What are the tasks?", one starts by asking: "Who uses the system and what are their goals?" In fact, the name of a use case for a user goal should reflect its name, to emphasize this viewpoint—Goal: capture or process a sale; use case: *Process Sale*.

Thus, here is a key idea regarding investigating requirements and use cases:

> Imagine we are together in a requirements workshop. We could ask either:
>
> ■ "What do you do?" (roughly a task-oriented question) or,
>
> ■ "What are your goals whose results have measurable value?"
>
> Prefer the second question.

Answers to the first question are more likely to reflect current solutions and procedures, and the complications associated with them.

Answers to the second question, especially combined with an investigation to move higher up the goal hierarchy ("what is the root goal?") open up the vision for new and improved solutions, focus on adding business value, and get to the heart of what the stakeholders want from the system.

Is the Cashier or Customer the Primary Actor?

Why is the cashier, and not the customer, a primary actor in the use case *Process Sale*?

The answer depends on the system boundary of the system under design, and who we are primarily designing the system for, as illustrated in Figure 6.2. If the enterprise or checkout service is viewed as an aggregate system, the customer *is* a primary actor, with the goal of getting goods or services and leaving. However, from the viewpoint of just the POS system (which is the choice of system boundary for this case study), the system services the goal of a trained cashier (and the store) to process the customer's sale. This assumes a traditional checkout environment with a cashier, although there are an increasing number of self-checkout POS systems in operation for direct use by customers.

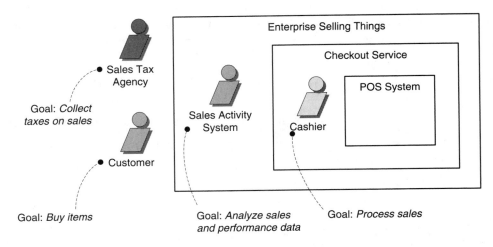

Figure 6.2 Primary actors and goals at different system boundaries.

The customer *is* an actor, but in the context of the NextGen POS, not a primary actor; rather, the cashier is the primary actor because the system is being designed to primarily serve the trained cashier's "power user" goals (to quickly process a sale, look up prices, etc.). The system does not have a UI and functionality that could equally be used by the customer or cashier. Rather, it is optimized to meet the needs and training of a cashier. A customer in front of the POS terminal wouldn't know how to use it effectively. In other words, it was designed for the cashier, not the customer, and so the cashier is not just a proxy for the customer.

On the other hand, consider a ticket-buying website that is identical for a customer to use directly or a phone agent to use, when a customer calls in. In this case, the agent is simply a proxy for the customer—the system is not designed to especially meet the unique goals of the agent. Then, showing the customer rather than the phone agent as the primary actor is correct.

Other Ways to Find Actors and Goals? Event Analysis

Another approach to aid in finding actors, goals, and use cases is to identify external events. What are they, where from, and why? Often, a group of events belong to the same use case. For example:

External Event	From Actor	Goal/Use Case
enter sale line item	Cashier	process a sale

External Event	From Actor	Goal/Use Case
enter payment	Cashier or Customer	process a sale
. . .		

Step 4: Define Use Cases

In general, define one use case for each user goal. Name the use case similar to the user goal—for example, Goal: process a sale; Use Case: *Process Sale*.

Start the name of use cases with a verb.

A common exception to one use case per goal is to collapse CRUD (create, retrieve, update, delete) separate goals into one CRUD use case, idiomatically called *Manage <X>*. For example, the goals "edit user," "delete user," and so forth are all satisfied by the *Manage Users* use case.

6.16　Guideline: What Tests Can Help Find Useful Use Cases?

Which of these is a valid use case?

- Negotiate a Supplier Contract
- Handle Returns
- Log In
- Move Piece on Game Board

An argument can be made that all of these are use cases *at different levels*, depending on the system boundary, actors, and goals.

But rather than asking in general, "What is a valid use case?", a more practical question is: "What is a useful level to express use cases for application requirements analysis?" There are several rules of thumb, including:

- The Boss Test
- The EBP Test
- The Size Test

The Boss Test

Your boss asks, "What have you been doing all day?" You reply: "Logging in!" Is your boss happy?

If not, the use case fails the Boss Test, which implies it is not strongly related to achieving results of measurable value. It may be a use case at some low goal level, but not the desirable level of focus for requirements analysis.

That doesn't mean to always ignore boss-test-failing use cases. User authentication may fail the boss test, but may be important and difficult.

The EBP Test

An **Elementary Business Process** (**EBP**) is a term from the business process engineering field,[5] defined as:

> A task performed by one person in one place at one time, in response to a business event, which adds measurable business value and leaves the data in a consistent state, e.g., Approve Credit or Price Order [original source lost].

Focus on use cases that reflect EBPs.

The EBP Test is similar to the Boss Test, especially in terms of the measurable business value qualification.

The definition can be taken too literally: Does a use case fail as an EBP if two people are required, or if a person has to walk around? Probably not, but the feel of the definition is about right. It's not a single small step like "delete a line item" or "print the document." Rather, the main success scenario is probably five or ten steps. It doesn't take days and multiple sessions, like "negotiate a supplier contract"; it is a task done during a single session. It is probably between a few minutes and an hour in length. As with the UP's definition, it emphasizes adding observable or measurable business value, and it comes to a resolution in which the system and data are in a stable and consistent state.

The Size Test

A use case is very seldom a single action or step; rather, a use case typically contains many steps, and in the fully dressed format will often require 3–10 pages of text. A common mistake in use case modeling is to define just a single step within a series of related steps as a use case by itself, such as defining a use case called *Enter an Item ID*. You can see a hint of the error by its small size—the use case name will wrongly suggest just one step within a larger series of steps, and if you imagine the length of its fully dressed text, it would be extremely short.

---

5. EBP is similar to the term **user task** in usability engineering, although the meaning is less strict in that domain.

Example: Applying the Tests

- Negotiate a Supplier Contract

  - Much broader and longer than an EBP. Could be modeled as a *business* use case, rather than a system use case.

- Handle Returns

  - OK with the boss. Seems like an EBP. Size is good.

- Log In

  - Boss not happy if this is all you do all day!

- Move Piece on Game Board

  - Single step—fails the size test.

Reasonable Violations of the Tests

Although the majority of use cases identified and analyzed for an application should satisfy the tests, exceptions are common.

see the use case "include" relationship for more on linking subfunction use cases p. 494

It is sometimes useful to write separate subfunction-level use cases representing subtasks or steps within a regular EBP-level use case. For example, a subtask or extension such as "paying by credit" may be repeated in several base use cases. If so, it is desirable to separate this into its own use case, even though it does not really satisfy the EBP and size tests, and link it to several base use cases, to avoid duplication of the text.

Authenticate User may not pass the Boss test, but be complex enough to warrant careful analysis, such as for a "single sign-on" feature.

6.17   Applying UML: Use Case Diagrams

The UML provides use case diagram notation to illustrate the names of use cases and actors, and the relationships between them (see Figure 6.3).[6]

> Use case diagrams and use case relationships are secondary in use case work. Use cases are text documents. Doing use case work means to write text.

A common sign of a novice (or academic) use case modeler is a preoccupation with use case diagrams and use case relationships, rather than writing text.

---

6. "Cash In" is the act of a cashier arriving with a drawer insert with cash, logging in, and recording the cash amount in the drawer insert.

World-class use case experts such as Fowler and Cockburn, among others, downplay use case diagrams and use case relationships, and instead focus on writing. With that as a caveat, a simple use case diagram provides a succinct visual context diagram for the system, illustrating the external actors and how they use the system.

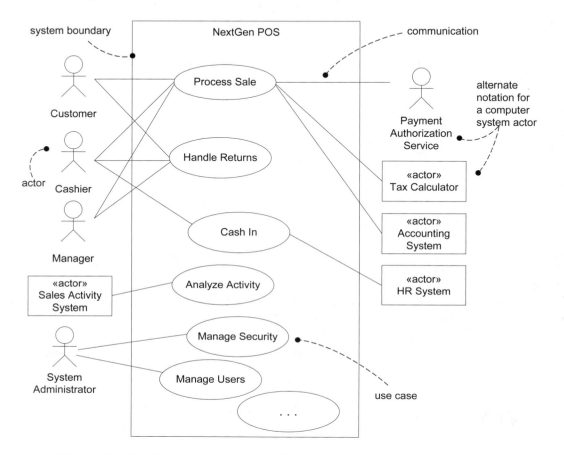

Figure 6.3 Partial use case context diagram.

Guideline

Draw a simple use case diagram in conjunction with an actor-goal list.

A use case diagram is an excellent picture of the system context; it makes a good **context diagram**, that is, showing the boundary of a system, what lies outside of it, and how it gets used. It serves as a communication tool that summarizes the behavior of a system and its actors. A sample *partial* use case context diagram for the NextGen system is shown in Figure 6.3.

Guideline: Diagramming

Figure 6.4 offers diagram advice. Notice the actor box with the symbol «actor». This style is used for UML **keywords** and **stereotypes**, and includes guillemet symbols—special *single*-character brackets («actor», not <<actor>>) most widely known by their use in French typography to indicate a quote.

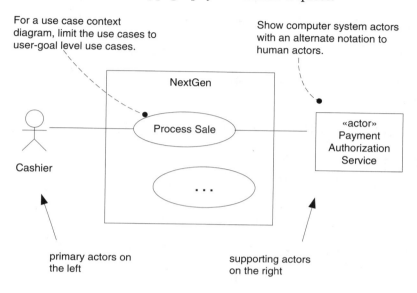

Figure 6.4 Notation suggestions.

To clarify, some prefer to highlight external computer system actors with an alternate notation, as illustrated in Figure 6.5.

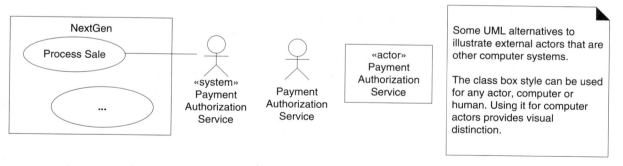

Figure 6.5 Alternate actor notation.

Guideline: Downplay Diagramming, Keep it Short and Simple

To reiterate, the important use case work is to write text, not diagram or focus on use case relationships. If an organization is spending many hours (or worse, days) working on a use case diagram and discussing use case relationships, rather than focusing on writing text, effort has been misplaced.

6.18   Applying UML: Activity Diagrams

UML activity diagrams p. 477

The UML includes a diagram useful to visualize workflows and business processes: activity diagrams. Because use cases involve process and workflow analysis, these can be a useful alternative or adjunct to writing the use case text, especially for *business* use cases that describe complex workflows involving many parties and concurrent actions.

6.19   Motivation: Other Benefits of Use Cases? Requirements in Context

motivation p. 64

A motivation for use cases is focusing on who the key actors are, their goals, and common tasks. Plus, in essence, use cases are a simple, widely-understood form (a story or scenario form).

Another motivation is to replace detailed, low-level function lists (which were common in 1970s traditional requirements methods) with use cases. These lists tended to look as follows:

ID	Feature
FEAT1.9	The system shall accept entry of item identifiers.
. . .	. . .
FEAT2.4	The system shall log credit payments to the accounts receivable system.

As implied by the title of the book *Uses Cases: Requirements in Context* [GK00], use cases organize a set of requirements *in the context of* the typical scenarios of using a system. That's a good thing—it improves cohesion and comprehension to consider and group requirements by the common thread of user-oriented scenarios (i.e., use cases). In a recent air traffic control system project: the requirements were originally written in the old-fashioned function list format, filling volumes of incomprehensible, unrelated specifications. A new leadership team analyzed and reorganized the massive requirements primarily by use cases. This provided a unifying and understandable way to pull the requirements together—into stories of requirements in context of use.

Supplementary Specification p. 104

To reiterate, however, use cases are not the only necessary requirements artifact. Non-functional requirements, report layouts, domain rules, and other hard-to-place elements are better captured in the UP Supplementary Specification.

High-Level System Feature Lists Are Acceptable

Vision p. 109

Although detailed function lists are undesirable, a terse, high-level feature list, called *system features,* added to a Vision document can usefully summarize system functionality. In contrast to 50 pages of low-level features, a system features list includes only a few dozen items. It provides a succinct summary of functionality, independent of the use case view. For example:

Summary of System Features

- sales capture
- payment authorization (credit, debit, check)
- system administration for users, security, code and constants tables, and so on
- …

When Are Detailed Feature Lists Appropriate Rather than Use Cases?

Sometimes use cases do not really fit; some applications cry out for a feature-driven viewpoint. For example, application servers, database products, and other middleware or back-end systems need to be primarily considered and evolved in terms of *features* ("We need Web Services support in the next release"). Use cases are not a natural fit for these applications or the way they need to evolve in terms of market forces.

6.20 Example: Monopoly Game

The only significant use case in the Monopoly software system is *Play Monopoly Game*—even if it doesn't pass the Boss Test! Since the game is run as a computer simulation simply watched by one person, we might say that person is an observer, not a player.

Supplementary Specification p. 104

This case study will show that use cases aren't always best for behavioral requirements. Trying to capture all the game rules in the use case format is awkward and unnatural. Where do the game rules belong? First, more generally, they are **domain rules** (sometimes called business rules). In the UP, domain rules can be part of the Supplementary Specification (SS). In the SS "domain rules" section there would probably be a reference to either the official paper booklet of rules, or to a website describing them. In addition, there may be a pointer to these rules from the use case text, as shown below.

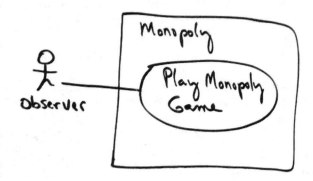

Figure 6.6 Use case diagram ("context diagram") for Monopoly system.

The text for this use case is very different than the NextGen POS problem, as it is a simple simulation, and the many possible (simulated) player actions are captured in the domain rules, rather than the Extensions section.

Use Case UC1: Play Monopoly Game

Scope: Monopoly application
Level: user goal
Primary Actor: Observer
Stakeholders and Interests:
– Observer: Wants to easily observe the output of the game simulation.

Main Success Scenario:
1. Observer requests new game initialization, enters number of players.
2. Observer starts play.

3. System displays game trace for next player move (see domain rules, and "game trace" in glossary for trace details).
Repeat step 3 until a winner or Observer cancels.

Extensions:
*a. At any time, System fails:
  (To support recovery, System logs after each completed move)
    1. Observer restarts System.
    2. System detects prior failure, reconstructs state, and prompts to continue.
    3. Observer chooses to continue (from last completed player turn).

Special Requirements:
– Provide both graphical and text trace modes.

6.21   Process: How to Work With Use Cases in Iterative Methods?

Use cases are central to the UP and many other iterative methods. The UP encourages **use-case driven development**. This implies:

- Functional requirements are primarily recorded in use cases (the Use-Case Model); other requirements techniques (such as functions lists) are secondary, if used at all.

- Use cases are an important part of iterative planning. The work of an iteration is—in part—defined by choosing some use case scenarios, or entire use cases. And use cases are a key input to estimation.

- **Use-case realizations** drive the design. That is, the team designs collaborating objects and subsystems in order to perform or realize the use cases.

- Use cases often influence the organization of user manuals.

- Functional or system testing corresponds to the scenarios of use cases.

- UI "wizards" or shortcuts may be created for the most common scenarios of important use cases to ease common tasks.

How to Evolve Use Cases and Other Specifications Across the Iterations?

This section reiterates a key idea in evolutionary iterative development: The timing and level of effort of specifications across the iterations. Table 6.1 presents a sample (not a recipe) that communicates the UP strategy of how requirements are developed.

Note that a technical team starts building the production core of the system when only perhaps 10% of the requirements are detailed, and in fact, the team deliberately delays in continuing with deep requirements work until near the end of the first elaboration iteration.

This is a key difference between iterative development and a waterfall process: Production-quality development of the core of a system starts quickly, long before all the requirements are known.

Observe that near the end of the first iteration of elaboration, there is a second requirements workshop, during which perhaps 30% of the use cases are written in detail. This staggered requirements analysis benefits from the feedback of having built a little of the core software. The feedback includes user evaluation, testing, and improved "knowing what we don't know." The act of building software rapidly surfaces assumptions and questions that need clarification.

In the UP, use case writing is encouraged in a requirements workshop. Figure 6.7 offers suggestions on the time and space for doing this work.

Discipline	Artifact	Comments and Level of Requirements Effort				
		Incep 1 week	Elab 1 4 weeks	Elab 2 4 weeks	Elab 3 3 weeks	Elab 4 3 weeks
Requirements	Use-Case Model	2-day requirements workshop. Most use cases identified by name, and summarized in a short paragraph. Pick 10% from the high-level list to analyze and write in detail. This 10% will be the most architecturally important, risky, and high-business value.	Near the end of this iteration, host a 2-day requirements workshop. Obtain insight and feedback from the implementation work, then complete 30% of the use cases in detail.	Near the end of this iteration, host a 2-day requirements workshop. Obtain insight and feedback from the implementation work, then complete 50% of the use cases in detail.	Repeat, complete 70% of all use cases in detail.	Repeat with the goal of 80–90% of the use cases clarified and written in detail. Only a small portion of these have been built in elaboration; the remainder are done in construction.
Design	Design Model	none	Design for a small set of high-risk architecturally significant requirements.	repeat	repeat	Repeat. The high risk and architecturally significant aspects should now be stabilized.
Implementation	Implementation Model (code, etc.)	none	Implement these.	Repeat. 5% of the final system is built.	Repeat. 10% of the final system is built.	Repeat. 15% of the final system is built.
Project Management	SW Development Plan	Very vague estimate of total effort.	Estimate starts to take shape.	a little better…	a little better…	Overall project duration, major milestones, effort, and cost estimates can now be rationally committed to.

Table 6.1 Sample requirements effort across the early iterations; this is not a recipe.

When Should Various UP Artifact (Including Use Cases) be Created?

Table 6.2 illustrates some UP artifacts, and an example of their start and refinement schedule. The Use-Case Model is started in inception, with perhaps only 10% of the architecturally significant use cases written in any detail. The majority are incrementally written over the iterations of the elaboration phase, so that by the end of elaboration, a large body of detailed use cases and other requirements (in the Supplementary Specification) are written, providing a realistic basis for estimation through to the end of the project.

Discipline	Artifact Iteration→	Incep. I1	Elab. E1..En	Const. C1..Cn	Trans. T1..T2
Business Modeling	Domain Model		s		
Requirements	*Use-Case Model*	s	r		
	Vision	s	r		
	Supplementary Specification	s	r		
	Glossary	s	r		
Design	Design Model		s	r	
	SW Architecture Document		s		

Table 6.2 Sample UP artifacts and timing. s - start; r - refine

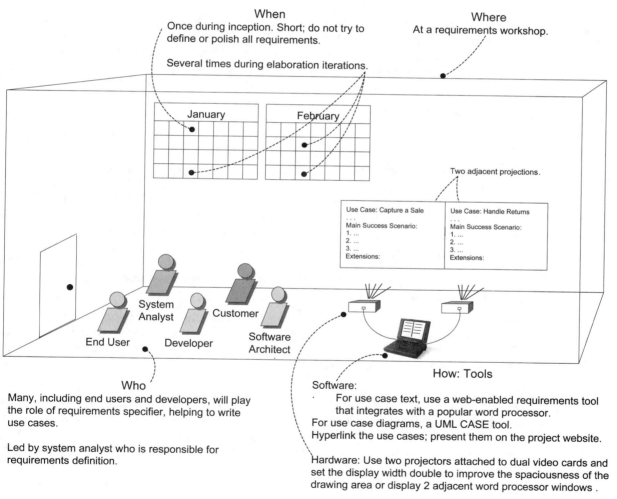

Figure 6.7 Process and setting context for writing use cases.

How to Write Use Cases in Inception?

The following discussion expands on the information in Table 6.1.

Not all use cases are written in their fully dressed format during the inception phase. Rather, suppose there is a two-day requirements workshop during the early NextGen investigation. The earlier part of the day is spent identifying goals and stakeholders, and speculating what is in and out of scope of the project. An actor-goal-use case table is written and displayed with the computer projector. A use case context diagram is started. After a few hours, perhaps 20 use cases are identified *by name*, including *Process Sale*, *Handle Returns*, and so on. Most of the interesting, complex, or risky use cases are written in brief format, each averaging around two minutes to write. The team starts to form a high-level picture of the system's functionality.

After this, 10% to 20% of the use cases that represent core complex functions, require building the core architecture, or that are especially risky in some dimension are rewritten in a fully dressed format; the team investigates a little deeper to better comprehend the magnitude, complexities, and hidden demons of the project through deep investigation of a small sample of influential use cases. Perhaps this means two use cases: *Process Sale* and *Handle Returns*.

How to Write Use Cases in Elaboration?

The following discussion expands on the information in Table 6.1.

This is a phase of multiple timeboxed iterations (for example, four iterations) in which risky, high-value, or architecturally significant parts of the system are incrementally built, and the "majority" of requirements identified and clarified. The feedback from the concrete steps of programming influences and informs the team's understanding of the requirements, which are iteratively and adaptively refined. Perhaps there is a two-day requirements workshop in each iteration—four workshops. However, not all use cases are investigated in each workshop. They are prioritized; early workshops focus on a subset of the most important use cases.

Each subsequent short workshop is a time to adapt and refine the vision of the core requirements, which will be unstable in early iterations, and stabilizing in later ones. Thus, there is an iterative interplay between requirements discovery, and building parts of the software.

During each requirements workshop, the user goals and use case list are refined. More of the use cases are written, and rewritten, in their fully dressed format. By the end of elaboration, "80–90%" of the use cases are written in detail. For the POS system with 20 user-goal level use cases, 15 or more of the most complex and risky should be investigated, written, and rewritten in a fully dressed format.

Note that elaboration involves programming parts of the system. At the end of this step, the NextGen team should not only have a better definition of the use cases, but some quality executable software.

How to Write Use Cases in Construction?

The construction phase is composed of timeboxed iterations (for example, 20 iterations of two weeks each) that focus on completing the system, once the risky and core unstable issues have settled down in elaboration. There may still be some minor use case writing and perhaps requirements workshops, but much less so than in elaboration.

Case Study: Use Cases in the NextGen Inception Phase

As described in the previous sections, not all use cases are written in their fully dressed form during inception. The Use-Case Model at this phase of the case study could be detailed as follows:

Fully Dressed	Casual	Brief
Process Sale Handle Returns	Process Rental Analyze Sales Activity Manage Security ...	Cash In Cash Out Manage Users Start Up Shut Down Manage System Tables ...

6.22 History

The idea of use cases to describe functional requirements was introduced in 1986 by Ivar Jacobson [Jacobson92], a main contributor to the UML and UP. Jacobson's use case idea was seminal and widely appreciated. Although many have made contributions to the subject, arguably the most influential and coherent next step in defining what use cases are and how to write them came from Alistair Cockburn (who was trained by Jacobson), based on his earlier work and writings stemming from 1992 onwards [e.g., Cockburn01].

6.23 Recommended Resources

The most popular use-case guide, translated into several languages, is *Writing Effective Use Cases* [Cockburn01].[7] This has emerged with good reason as the most widely read and followed use-case book and is therefore recommended as a primary reference. This introductory chapter is consequently based on and consistent with its content.

---

7. Note that Cockburn rhymes with *slow burn*.

Patterns for Effective Use Cases by Adolph and Bramble in some ways picks up where *Writing* leaves off, covering many useful tips—in pattern format—related to the process of creating excellent use cases (team organization, methodology, editing), and how to better structure and write them (patterns for judging and improving their content and organization).

Use cases are usually best written with a partner during a requirements workshop. An excellent guide to the art of running a workshop is *Requirements by Collaboration: Workshops for Defining Needs* by Ellen Gottesdiener.

Use Case Modeling by Bittner and Spence is another quality resource by two experienced modelers who also understand iterative and evolutionary development and the RUP, and present use case analysis in that context.

"Structuring Use Cases with Goals" [Cockburn97] is the most widely cited paper on use cases, available online at *alistair.cockburn.us*.

Use Cases: Requirements in Context by Kulak and Guiney is also worthwhile. It emphasizes the important viewpoint—as the title states—that use cases are not just another requirements artifact, but are the central vehicle that drives requirements work.

OTHER REQUIREMENTS

Fast, Cheap, Good: Choose any two.

—anonymous

Objectives

- Show Supplementary Specification, Glossary, Vision & Business Rules.
- Compare and contrast system features with use cases.
- Define quality attributes.

Introduction

There are a few other important UP requirement artifacts in addition to use cases; this chapter introduces them. If you want to skip this chapter—which deals with the secondary topic of requirements rather than OOA/D—no problem. Jump to the classic OOA subject of domain modeling on p. 131, after first reading the summary of iteration-1 requirements starting on p. 124.

So why include this chapter if it isn't central to learning OOA/D? Because it gives cohesion to the case studies and offers a more complete requirements example.

What's Next?

Having looked at use cases, this chapter explores other requirement artifacts in the UP. The next defines the scope of work for iteration-1.

Other Requirement Artifacts

Use cases aren't the whole story.

The **Supplementary Specification** captures and identifies other kinds of requirements, such as reports, documentation, packaging, supportability, licensing, and so forth.

The **Glossary** captures terms and definitions; it can also play the role of a data dictionary.

The **Vision** summarizes the "vision" of the project—an executive summary. It serves to tersely communicate the big ideas.

The **Business Rules** (or Domain Rules) capture long-living and spanning rules or policies, such as tax laws, that transcend one particular application.

7.1   How Complete are these Examples?

The book's prime goal is basic OOA/D, not the secondary POS requirement details discussed in this chapter. So rather than show exhaustive requirements examples,[1] the chapter presents partial examples.

Some sections are briefly shown to make connections between prior and future work, highlight noteworthy issues, provide a feel for the contents, and move forward quickly.

7.2   Guideline: Should We Analyze These Thoroughly During Inception?

No. The UP is an iterative and evolutionary method, which means that production-quality programming and testing should happen very early, long before most requirements have been fully analyzed or recorded. *Feedback* from early programming and tests evolve the requirements.

However, research shows that is useful to have a high-level "top ten" list of coarse-grained requirements near the start. It is also useful to spend non-trivial early time understanding the non-functional requirements (such as performance or reliability), as these have a significant impact on architectural choices.

---

1. Scope creep is not only a problem in requirements, but in *writing* about requirements!

Reliable Specifications: An Oxymoron?

The following written requirement examples could promote the illusion that the real requirements are understood and well-defined, and can (early on) be used to reliably estimate and plan the project. This illusion is more strong for non-software developers; programmers know from painful experience how unreliable it is. As mentioned, case studies (for example, [Thomas01] and [Larman03]) now show it is a misunderstanding to believe that early detailed requirements are useful or reliable on software projects. In fact, quite the opposite, as almost 50% of early waterfall-specified features are never used in a system.

What really matters is quickly building software that passes the acceptance tests defined by the users, and that meets their true goals—which are often not discovered until users are evaluating or working with the software.

Writing a Vision and Supplementary Specification is worthwhile as an exercise in clarifying a *first approximation* of what is wanted, the motivation for the product, and as a repository for the big ideas. But they are not—nor is any requirements artifact—a reliable specification. Only writing code, testing it, getting feedback, ongoing close collaboration with users and customers, and adapting, truly hit the mark.

This is not a call to abandon analysis and thinking, and just rush to code, but a suggestion to treat written requirements lightly, start programming early, and continually—ideally, daily—engage users and tests for feedback.

7.3 Guideline: Should These Artifacts be at the Project Website?

Definitely. Since this is a book, these examples and the use cases have a static and perhaps paper-oriented feel. Nevertheless, these should usually be digital artifacts recorded only online at the project website. And instead of being plain static documents, they may be hyperlinked, or recorded in tools other than a word processor or spreadsheet. For example, many of these could be stored in a Wiki Web.[2]

---

2. For an introduction to Wikis, see http://en.wikipedia.org/wiki/WikiWiki.

7.4   NextGen Example: (Partial) Supplementary Specification

Supplementary Specification

Revision History

Version	Date	Description	Author
Inception draft	Jan 10, 2031	First draft. To be refined primarily during elaboration.	Craig Larman

Introduction

This document is the repository of all NextGen POS requirements not captured in the use cases.

Functionality

(Functionality common across many use cases)

Logging and Error Handling

Log all errors to persistent storage.

Pluggable Rules

At various scenario points of several use cases (to be defined) support the ability to customize the functionality of the system with a set of arbitrary rules that execute at that point or event.

Security

All usage requires user authentication.

Usability

Human Factors

The customer will be able to see a large-monitor display of the POS. Therefore:

- Text should be easily visible from 1 meter.
- Avoid colors associated with common forms of color blindness.

Speed, ease, and error-free processing are paramount in sales processing, as the buyer wishes to leave quickly, or they perceive the purchasing experience (and seller) as less positive.

The cashier is often looking at the customer or items, not the computer display. Therefore, signals and warnings should be conveyed with sound rather than only via graphics.

Reliability

Recoverability

If there is failure to use external services (payment authorizer, accounting system, ...) try to solve with a local solution (e.g., store and forward) in order to still complete a sale. Much more analysis is needed here...

Performance

As mentioned under human factors, buyers want to complete sales processing *very* quickly. One bottleneck is external payment authorization. Our goal: authorization in less than1 minute, 90% of the time.

Supportability

Adaptability

Different customers of the NextGen POS have unique business rule and processing needs while processing a sale. Therefore, at several defined points in the scenario (for example, when a new sale is initiated, when a new line item is added) pluggable business rule will be enabled.

Configurability

Different customers desire varying network configurations for their POS systems, such as thick versus thin clients, two-tier versus N-tier physical layers, and so forth. In addition, they desire the ability to modify these configurations, to reflect their changing business and performance needs. Therefore, the system will be somewhat configurable to reflect these needs. Much more analysis is needed in this area to discover the areas and degree of flexibility, and the effort to achieve it.

Implementation Constraints

NextGen leadership insists on a Java technologies solution, predicting this will improve long-term porting and supportability, in addition to ease of development.

Purchased Components

- Tax calculator. Must support pluggable calculators for different countries.

Free Open Source Components

In general, we recommend maximizing the use of free Java technology open source components on this project.

Although it is premature to definitively design and choose components, we suggest the following as likely candidates:

- JLog logging framework
- ...

Interfaces

Noteworthy Hardware and Interfaces

- Touch screen monitor (this is perceived by operating systems as a regular monitor, and the touch gestures as mouse events)
- Barcode laser scanner (these normally attach to a special keyboard, and the scanned input is perceived in software as keystrokes)
- Receipt printer
- Credit/debit card reader
- Signature reader (but not in release 1)

Software Interfaces

For most external collaborating systems (tax calculator, accounting, inventory, ...) we need to be able to plug in varying systems and thus varying interfaces.

Application-Specific Domain (Business) Rules

(See the separate Business Rules document for general rules.)

ID	Rule	Changeability	Source
RULE1	Purchaser discount rules. Examples: Employee—20% off. Preferred Customer—10% off. Senior—15% off.	High. Each retailer uses different rules.	Retailer policy.
RULE2	Sale (transaction-level) discount rules. Applies to pre-tax total. Examples: 10% off if total greater than $100 USD. 5% off each Monday. 10% off all sales from 10am to 3pm today. Tofu 50% off from 9am-10am today.	High. Each retailer uses different rules, and they may change daily or hourly.	Retailer policy.
RULE3	Product (line item level) discount rules. Examples: 10% off tractors this week. Buy 2 veggieburgers, get 1 free.	High. Each retailer uses different rules, and they may change daily or hourly.	Retailer policy.

Legal Issues

We recommend some open source components if their licensing restrictions can be resolved to allow resale of products that include open source software.

All tax rules must, by law, be applied during sales. Note that these can change frequently.

Information in Domains of Interest

Pricing

In addition to the pricing rules described in the domain rules section, note that products have an *original price*, and optionally a *permanent markdown price*. A product's price (before further discounts) is the permanent markdown price, if present. Organizations maintain the original price even if there is a permanent markdown price, for accounting and tax reasons.

Credit and Debit Payment Handling

When an electronic credit or debit payment is approved by a payment authorization service, they are responsible for paying the seller, not the buyer. Consequently, for each payment, the seller needs to record monies owing in their accounts receivable, from the authorization service. Usually on a nightly basis, the authorization service will perform an electronic funds transfer to the seller's account for the daily total owing, less a (small) per transaction fee that the service charges.

Sales Tax

Sales tax calculations can be very complex, and regularly change in response to legislation at all levels of government. Therefore, delegating tax calculations to third-party calculator software (of which there are several available) is advisable. Tax may be owing to city, region, state, and national bodies. Some items may be tax exempt without qualification, or exempt depending on the buyer or target recipient (for example, a farmer or a child).

Item Identifiers: UPCs, EANs, SKUs, Bar Codes, and Bar Code Readers

The NextGen POS needs to support various item identifier schemes. UPCs (Universal Product Codes), EANs (European Article Numbering) and SKUs (Stock Keeping Units) are three common identifier systems for products that are sold. Japanese Article Numbers (JANs) are a kind of EAN version.

SKUs are completely arbitrary identifiers defined by the retailer.

However, UPCs and EANs have a standards and regulatory component. See www.adams1.com/pub/rus-sadam/upccode.html for a good overview. Also see www.uc-council.org and www.ean-int.org.

7.5 Commentary: Supplementary Specification

The **Supplementary Specification** captures other requirements, information, and constraints not easily captured in the use cases or Glossary, including system-wide "URPS+" (**u**sability, **r**eliability, **p**erformance, **s**upportability, and more) quality attributes or requirements.

Note that non-functional requirements specific to a use case can (and probably should) be first briefly written within the use case, in the *Special Requirements* section while you are thinking through the use case. But, after that informal step, these should then be moved to the Supplementary Specification, to keep all non-functional requirements in one place, and not duplicated.

Elements of the Supplementary Specification include:

- FURPS+ requirements—functionality, usability, reliability, performance, and supportability

- reports

- hardware and software constraints (operating and networking systems, ...)

- development constraints (for example, process or development tools)

- other design and implementation constraints

- internationalization concerns (units, languages)

- documentation (user, installation, administration) and help

- licensing and other legal concerns

- packaging

- standards (technical, safety, quality)

- physical environment concerns (for example, heat or vibration)

- operational concerns (for example, how do errors get handled, or how often should backups be done?)

- application-specific domain rules

- information in domains of interest (for example, what is the entire cycle of credit payment handling?)

Quality Attributes

Some requirements are called **quality attributes** [BCK98] (or "-ilities") of a system. These include usability, reliability, and so forth. Note that these are qualities of the system, not of the attributes themselves, which are not necessarily of high quality. For example, the quality of supportability might deliberately be chosen to be low if the product is not intended to serve a long-term purpose.

When we put on our "architect hat," the system-wide quality attributes (and thus the Supplementary Specification where one records them) are especially interesting because—as will be introduced in Chapter 33—*architectural analysis and design are largely concerned with the identification and resolution of the quality attributes in the context of the functional requirements.*

For example, suppose one of the quality attributes is that the NextGen system must be quite fault-tolerant when remote services fail. From an architectural viewpoint, that will have an overarching influence on large-scale design decisions.

Functionality in the Supplementary Spec? Shouldn't that be in the Use Cases?

Some functions or features don't fit in a use case format. In the 1990s I worked at a company that built a Java middleware and agent-based platform. For the next release (as with most middleware or server products) we didn't think of its functionality in terms of use cases—didn't make sense. But we did think of the functionality in terms of **features**, such as "add EJB Entity Bean 1.0 support."

The UP certainly allows this feature-oriented approach to requirements, in which case the feature list goes in the Supplementary Specification.

The UP encourages but does not require use cases for functionality; use cases are a great way to think about and pull together a related set of features in terms of typical scenarios of using a product. They don't always fit.

Application-Specific Domain (Business) Rules

General, broad domain rules such as tax laws belong in the UP Business Rules artifact, as a central shared repository. However, more narrow application-specific rules, such as how to calculate a line-item discount, can be recorded in the Supplementary Specification.

Information in Domains of Interest

It is often valuable for a subject matter expert to write (or provide URIs to) some explanation of domains related to the new software system (sales and accounting, the geophysics of underground oil/water/gas flows, ...), to provide context and deeper insight for the development team. That document may contain pointers to important literature or experts, formulas, laws, or other references. For example, the arcana of UPC and EAN coding schemes, and bar code symbology, must be understood to some degree by the NextGen team.

7.6   NextGen Example: (Partial) Vision

Vision

Revision History

Version	Date	Description	Author
inception draft	Jan 10, 2031	First draft. To be refined primarily during elaboration.	Craig Larman

Introduction

The analysis in this example is illustrative, but fictitious.

We envision a next generation fault-tolerant point-of-sale (POS) application, NextGen POS, with the flexibility to support varying customer business rules, multiple terminal and user interface mechanisms, and integration with multiple third-party supporting systems.

Positioning

Business Opportunity

Existing POS products are not adaptable to the customer's business, in terms of varying business rules and varying network designs (for example, thin client or not; 2, 3, or 4-tier architectures). In addition, they do not scale well as terminals and business increase. And, none can work in either on-line or off-line mode, dynamically adapting depending on failures. None easily integrate with many third-party systems. None allow for new terminal technologies such as mobile PDAs. There is marketplace dissatisfaction with this inflexible state of affairs, and demand for a POS that rectifies this.

Problem Statement

Traditional POS systems are inflexible, fault intolerant, and difficult to integrate with third-party systems. This leads to problems in timely sales processing, instituting improved processes that don't match the software, and accurate and timely accounting and inventory data to support measurement and planning, among other concerns. This affects cashiers, store managers, system administrators, and corporate management.

Product Position Statement

—*Terse summary of who the system is for, its outstanding features, and what differentiates it from the competition.*

Alternatives and Competition...

Understand who the players are, and their problems.

Stakeholder Descriptions

Market Demographics...

Stakeholder (Non-User) Summary...

User Summary...

Key High-Level Goals and Problems of the Stakeholders

Consolidate input from the Actor and Goals List, and the Stakeholder Interests section of the use cases.

A one-day requirements workshop with subject matter experts and other stakeholders, and surveys at several retail outlets led to identification of the following key goals and problems:

High-Level Goal	Priority	Problems and Concerns	Current Solutions
Fast, robust, integrated sales processing	high	Reduced speed as load increases. Loss of sales processing capability if components fail. Lack of up-to-date and accurate information from accounting and other systems due to non-integration with existing accounting, inventory, and HR systems. Leads to difficulties in measuring and planning. Inability to customize business rules to unique business requirements. Difficulty in adding new terminal or user interface types (for example, mobile PDAs).	Existing POS products provide basic sales processing, but do not address these problems.
. . .	. . .	. . .	. . .

User-Level Goals

This may be the Actor-Goal List created during use-case modeling, or a more terse summary.

The users (and external systems) need a system to fulfill these goals:

- *Cashier*: process sales, handle returns, cash in, cash out
- *System administrator*: manage users, manage security, manage system tables
- *Manager*: start up, shut down
- *Sales activity system*: analyze sales data
- ...

User Environment...

Product Overview

Product Perspective

The NextGen POS will usually reside in stores; if mobile terminals are used, they will be in close proximity to the store network, either inside or close outside. It will provide services to users, and collaborate with other systems, as indicated in Figure Vision-1.

Summarized from the use case diagram.

Context diagrams come in different formats with varying detail, but all show the major external actors related to a system.

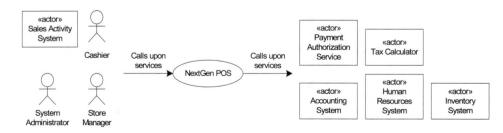

Figure Vision-1. NextGen POS system context diagram

Summary of Benefits

Similar to the Actor-Goal list, this table relates goals, benefits, and solutions, but at a higher level not solely related to use cases.

It summarizes the value and differentiating qualities of the product.

Supporting Feature	Stakeholder Benefit
Functionally, the system will provide all the common services a sales organization requires, including sales capture, payment authorization, return handling, and so forth.	Automated, fast point-of-sale services.
Automatic detection of failures, switching to local offline processing for unavailable services.	Continued sales processing when external components fail.
Pluggable business rules at various scenario points during sales processing.	Flexible business logic configuration.
Real-time transactions with third-party systems, using industry standard protocols.	Timely, accurate sales, accounting, and inventory information, to support measuring and planning.
...	...

Assumptions and Dependencies...

Cost and Pricing...

Licensing and Installation...

As discussed below, system features are a terse format to summarize functionality.

Summary of System Features

- sales capture

- payment authorization (credit, debit, check)

- system administration for users, security, code and constants tables, and so forth.

- automatic offline sales processing when external components fail

- real-time transactions, based on industry standards, with third-party systems, including inventory, accounting, human resources, tax calculators, and payment authorization services

- definition and execution of customized "pluggable" business rules at fixed, common points in the processing scenarios

- ...

Other Requirements and Constraints

Including design constraints, usability, reliability, performance, supportability, design constraints, documentation, packaging, and so forth: See the Supplementary Specification and use cases.

7.7   Commentary: Vision

When someone joins the project, it is useful to be able to say, "Welcome! Please go read the 7-page Vision at the project website." It is also useful to have an executive summary that briefly describes the project, as a context for the major players to establish a common vision of the project.

The Vision should not be long, nor should it attempt to describe firm requirements in detail. And it should summarize some of the information in the Use-Case Model and Supplementary Specification.

The Key High-Level Goals and Problems of the Stakeholders

This section summarizes the goals and problems at a high level—often higher than specific use cases—and reveals important non-functional and quality goals that may belong to one use case or span many, such as:

- *We need fault-tolerant sales processing.*
- *We need the ability to customize the business rules.*

Guideline: What are Some Facilitation Methods?

It is especially during activities such as high-level problem definition and goal identification that creative, investigative group work occurs. Here are some useful group facilitation techniques to discover root problems and goals, and support idea generation and prioritization: mind mapping, product vision box creation, fishbone diagrams, pareto diagrams, brainstorming, multi-voting, dot voting, nominal group process, brainwriting, and affinity grouping. Check them out on the Web. I prefer to apply several of these during the same workshop, to discover common problems and requirements from different angles.

Summary of System Features

Simply listing the use case names is not sufficient in the Vision to grasp the major features. Why?

- Too detailed or low-level. People want a short summary of the big ideas. There could be 30 or 50 use cases.

- The use case name can hide interesting major features stakeholders really want to know about. For example, suppose that the description of automated payment authorization functionality is embedded in the *Process Sale* use case. A reader of a list of use case names can't tell if the system will do payment authorization.

- Some noteworthy features span or are orthogonal to the use cases. For example, during the first NextGen requirements workshop, someone might say "The system should be able to interact with existing third-party accounting, inventory, and tax calculation systems."

Therefore, an alternative, complementary way to express system functions is with **features**, or more specifically in this context, **system features**, which are high-level, terse statements summarizing system functions. More formally, in the UP, a **system feature** is "an externally observable service provided by the system which directly fulfills a stakeholder need" [Kruchten00].

> *Definition*
>
> Features are behavioral functions a system can *do*. They should pass this linguistic test:
>
> > *The system does <feature X>.*

For example:

> *The system does payment authorization.*

Functional system features are to be contrasted with various kinds of non-functional requirements and constraints, such as: *"The system must run on Linux, must have 24/7 availability, and must have a touch-screen interface."* Note that these fail the linguistic test; for example, *the system does Linux.*

Guideline: How to Write the Feature List?

Terse is good in the Vision—indeed, in any document.

Here is a features example at a high level, for a large multi-system project of which the POS is just one element:

The major features include:

- *POS services*
- *Inventory management*
- *Web-based shopping*
- *...*

It is common to organize a two-level hierarchy of system features. But in the Vision document more than two levels leads to excessive detail; the point of system features in the Vision is to summarize the functionality, not decompose it into a long list of fine-grained elements. A reasonable example in terms of detail:

The major features include:

- *POS services:*
  - *sales capture*
  - *payment authorization*
  - *...*
- *Inventory management:*
  - *automatic reordering*
  - *...*

How many system features should the Vision contain?

> *Guideline*
>
> A Vision with less than 10 features is desirable—more can't be quickly grasped. If more, consider grouping and abstracting the features.

Guideline: Should We Duplicate Other Requirements in the Vision?

In the Vision, system features briefly summarize functional requirements often detailed in the use cases. Likewise, the Vision *can* summarize other requirements (for example, reliability and usability) that are detailed in the Supplementary Specification. But be careful to avoid going down the path of repeating yourself.

> *Guideline*
>
> For other requirements, avoid their duplication or near-duplication in both the Vision and Supplementary Specification (SS). Rather, record them only in the SS. In the Vision, direct the reader to the SS for the other requirements.

Guideline: Should You Write the Vision or Use Cases First?

It isn't useful to be rigid about the order. While developers are collaborating to create different requirements artifacts, a synergy emerges in which working on one artifact influences and helps clarify another. Nevertheless, a suggested sequence is:

1. Write a brief first draft of the Vision.

2. Identify user goals and the supporting use cases by name.

3. Write some use cases in detail, and start the Supplementary Specification.

4. Refine the Vision, summarizing information from these.

7.8 NextGen Example: A (Partial) Glossary

Glossary

Revision History

Version	Date	Description	Author
Inception draft	Jan 10, 2031	First draft. To be refined primarily during elaboration.	Craig Larman

Definitions

Term	Definition and Information	Format	Validation Rules	Aliases
item	A product or service for sale			
payment authorization	Validation by an external payment authorization service that they will make or guarantee the payment to the seller.			
payment authorization request	A composite of elements electronically sent to an authorization service, usually as a char array. Elements include: store ID, customer account number, amount, and timestamp.			
UPC	Numeric code that identifies a product. Usually symbolized with a bar code placed on products. See www.uc-council.org for details of format and validation.	12-digit code of several subparts.	Digit 12 is a check digit.	Universal Product Code
...	...			

7.9 Commentary: Glossary (Data Dictionary)

In its simplest form, the **Glossary** is a list of noteworthy terms and their definitions. It is surprisingly common that a term, often technical or particular to the domain, will be used in slightly different ways by different stakeholders; this needs to be resolved to reduce problems in communication and ambiguous requirements.

Guideline

Start the Glossary early. It will quickly become a useful repository of detailed information related to fine-grained elements.

Glossary as Data Dictionary

In the UP, the Glossary also plays the role of a **data dictionary**, a document that records data about the data—that is, **metadata**. During inception the glossary should be a simple document of terms and descriptions. During elaboration, it may expand into a data dictionary.

Term attributes could include:

- aliases
- description
- format (type, length, unit)
- relationships to other elements
- range of values
- validation rules

> Note that the range of values and validation rules in the Glossary constitute requirements with implications on the behavior of the system.

Guideline: Can We use the Glossary to Record Composite Terms?

The Glossary is not only for atomic terms such as "product price." It can and should include composite elements such as "sale" (which includes other elements, such as date and location) and nicknames used to describe a collection of data transmitted between actors in the use cases. For example, in the *Process Sale* use case, consider the following statement:

> System sends <u>payment authorization request</u> to an external Payment Authorization Service, and requests payment approval.

"Payment authorization request" is a nickname for an aggregate of data, which needs to be explained in the Glossary.

7.10   NextGen Example: Business Rules (Domain Rules)

Domain Rules

Revision History

Version	Date	Description	Author
inception draft	Jan 10, 2031	First draft. To be refined primarily during elaboration.	Craig Larman

Rule List

(See also the separate Application-specific Rules in the Supplementary Specification.)

ID	Rule	Changeability	Source
RULE1	Signature required for credit payments.	Buyer "signature" will continue to be required, but within 2 years most of our customers want signature capture on a digital capture device, and within 5 years we expect there to be demand for support of the new unique digital code "signature" now supported by USA law.	The policy of virtually all credit authorization companies.
RULE2	Tax rules. Sales require added taxes. See government statutes for current details.	High. Tax laws change annually, at all government levels.	law
RULE3	Credit payment reversals may only be paid as a credit to the buyer's credit account, not as cash.	Low	credit authorization company policy

7.11 Commentary: Domain Rules

Domain rules [Ross97, GK00] dictate how a domain or business may operate. They are not requirements of any one application, although an application's requirements are often influenced by domain rules. Company policies, physical laws (such as how oil flows underground), and government laws are common domain rules.

They are commonly called **business rules**, which is the most common type, but that term is poor, as many software applications are for non-business problems, such as weather simulation or military logistics. A weather simulation has "domain rules," related to physical laws and relationships, that influence the application requirements.

It's useful to identify and record domain rules in a separate application-independent artifact—what the UP calls the Business Rules artifact—so that this analysis can be shared and reused across the organization and across projects, rather than buried within a project-specific document.

The rules can help clarify ambiguities in the use cases, which emphasize the flow of the story rather than the details. For example, in the NextGen POS, if someone asks if the *Process Sale* use case should be written with an alternative to allow credit payments without signature capture, there is a business rule (RULE1) that clarifies whether this will not be allowed by any credit authorization company.

7.12   Process: Evolutionary Requirements in Iterative Methods

evolutionary requirements p. 25

As repeatedly stressed (as it's critical, yet too often ignored) in iterative methods, including the UP, these requirements are not fully analyzed and written near the start of the project. Rather, they evolve over a series of requirements workshops (for example), interspersed with early production-quality programming and testing. Feedback from early development refines the specifications.

As in the use case chapter, Table 7.1 summarizes a sample of artifacts and their possible timing in the UP. Usually, most requirements artifacts are started in inception and primarily developed during elaboration.

Discipline	Artifact	Incep.	Elab.	Const.	Trans.
	Iteration→	I1	E1..En	C1..Cn	T1..T2
Business Modeling	Domain Model		s		
Requirements	Use-Case Model	s	r		
	Vision	s	r		
	Supplementary Specification	s	r		
	Glossary	s	r		
	Business Rules	s	r		
Design	Design Model		s	r	
	SW Architecture Document		s		
	Data Model		s	r	

Table 7.1 Sample UP artifacts and timing. s - start; r - refine

Inception

Stakeholders need to decide if the project is worth serious investigation; that real investigation occurs during elaboration, not inception. During inception, the Vision summarizes the project idea in a form to help decision makers determine if it is worth continuing, and where to start.

Since most requirements analysis occurs during elaboration, the Supplementary Specification should be only lightly developed during inception, highlighting noteworthy quality attributes that expose major risks and challenges (for example, the NextGen POS must have recoverability when external services fail).

Input into these artifacts could be generated during an inception phase requirements workshop.

Elaboration

Through the elaboration iterations, the "vision" and the Vision are refined, based upon feedback from incrementally building parts of the system, adapting, and multiple requirements workshops held over several development iterations.

Through ongoing requirements investigation and iterative development, the other requirements will become more clear and can be recorded in the Supplementary Specification.

By the end of elaboration, it is feasible to have use cases, a Supplementary Specification, and a Vision that reasonably reflects the stabilized major features and other requirements to be completed for delivery. Nevertheless, the Supplementary Specification and Vision are not something to freeze and "sign off" on as a fixed specification; adaptation—not rigidity—is a core value of iterative development and the UP.

To clarify this "frozen sign off" comment: It is perfectly sensible—at the end of elaboration—to form an agreement with stakeholders about what will be done in the remainder of the project, and to make commitments (perhaps contractual) regarding requirements and schedule. At some point (the end of elaboration, in the UP), we need a reliable idea of "what, how much, and when." In that sense, a formal agreement on the requirements is normal and expected. It is also necessary to have a change control process (one of the explicit best practices in the UP) for formally considered and approved requirements changes, rather than chaotic and uncontrolled change.

But several points are implied by the "frozen sign off" comment:

- In iterative development and the UP it is understood that no matter how much due diligence is given to requirements specification, some change is inevitable, and should be acceptable. This change could be a late-breaking opportunistic improvement in the system that gives its owners a competitive advantage, or change due to improved insight.

- In iterative development, it is a core value to have continual engagement by the stakeholders to evaluate, provide feedback, and steer the project as they really want it. It does not benefit stakeholders to "wash their hands" of attentive engagement by signing off on a frozen set of requirements and waiting for the finished product, because they will seldom get what they really needed.

Construction

By construction, the major requirements—both functional and otherwise—should be stabilized—not finalized, but settled down to minor perturbation. Therefore, the Supplementary Specification and Vision are unlikely to experience much change in this phase.

7.13 Recommended Resources

Most books on software architecture include discussion of requirements analysis for quality attributes of the application, since these quality requirements tend to strongly influence architectural design. One example is *Software Architecture in Practice* [BCK98].

Business rules get an exhaustive treatment in *The Business Rule Book* [Ross97]. The book presents a broad, deep, and thoroughly-considered theory of business rules, but the method is not well-connected to other modern requirements techniques such as use cases, or to iterative development.

In the UP, Vision and Supplementary Specification work is a requirements discipline activity that could be initiated during a requirements workshop, along with use case analysis. A good guide for running a workshop is *Requirements by Collaboration: Workshops for Defining Needs* by Ellen Gottesdiener.

The RUP online product contains templates for the artifacts discussed in this chapter.

On the Web, templates for specifications are available from many sources, such as the ReadySET templates at *readyset.tigris.org*.

Part 3 Elaboration Iteration 1 — Basics

ITERATION 1—BASICS

The hard and stiff breaks. The supple prevails.

—Tao Te Ching

Objectives

- Define the first iteration in the elaboration phase.
- Motivate the following chapters in this section.
- Describe key inception and elaboration phase concepts.

Introduction

This chapter summarizes the iteration-1 requirements of the case studies, and then briefly discusses the process ideas of the inception and elaboration phases. Reading the chosen requirements is important to understand what's being tackled in the following chapters for this iteration; reading the remainder depends on your need or interest in iterative process issues.

What's Next?

Having looked at other requirements besides use cases, this chapter defines the scope of iteration-1. The next explores creating an OO domain model that illustrates the noteworthy concepts in the domain.

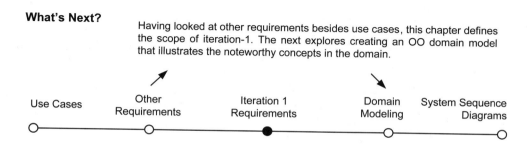

| Use Cases | Other Requirements | Iteration 1 Requirements | Domain Modeling | System Sequence Diagrams |

8.1   Iteration 1 Requirements and Emphasis: Core OOA/D Skills

In these case studies, iteration-1 of the elaboration phase emphasizes a range of fundamental and common OOA/D skills used in building object systems. Many other skills and steps—such as database design, usability engineering, and UI design—are of course needed to build software, but they are out of scope in this introduction focusing on OOA/D and applying the UML.

Book Iterations vs. Real Project Iterations

Iteration-1 of the case studies in this book is driven by learning goals rather than true project goals. Therefore, iteration-1 is not architecture-centric or risk-driven. On a UP project, we would tackle difficult, risky things first. But in the context of a book helping people learn fundamental OOA/D and UML, we want to start with easier topics.

NextGen POS

The requirements for the first iteration of the NextGen POS application follow:

- Implement a basic, key scenario of the *Process Sale* use case: entering items and receiving a cash payment.

- Implement a *Start Up* use case as necessary to support the initialization needs of the iteration.

- Nothing fancy or complex is handled, just a simple happy path scenario, and the design and implementation to support it.

- There is no collaboration with external services, such as a tax calculator or product database.

- No complex pricing rules are applied.

The design and implementation of the supporting UI, database, and so forth, would also be done, but is not covered in any detail.

Monopoly

The requirements for the first iteration of the Monopoly application follow:

- Implement a basic, key scenario of the *Play Monopoly Game* use case: players moving around the squares of the board.

- Implement a *Start Up* use case as necessary to support the initialization needs of the iteration.

- Two to eight players can play.

- A game is played as a series of rounds. During a round, each player takes one turn. In each turn, a player advances his piece clockwise around the board a number of squares equal to the sum of the number rolled on two six-sided dice.

- Play the game for only 20 rounds.

- After the dice are rolled, the name of the player and the roll are displayed. When the player moves and lands on a square, the name of the player and the name of the square that the player landed on are displayed.

- In iteration-1 there is no money, no winner or loser, no properties to buy or rent to pay, and no special squares of any kind.

- Each square has a name. Every player begins the game with their piece located on the square named "Go." The square names will be Go, Square 1, Square 2, ... Square 39

- Run the game as a simulation requiring no user input, other than the number of players.

Subsequent iterations will grow on these foundations.

In Iterative Development We Don't Implement All the Requirements at Once

Note that these requirements for iteration-1 are *subsets* of the complete requirements or use cases. For example, the NextGen POS iteration-1 requirements are a simplified version of the complete *Process Sale* use case; they describe one simple cash-only scenario.

Note also that we haven't done all the requirements analysis for the NextGen POS system, we've only analyzed the *Process Sale* use case in detail; many others are not yet analyzed.

This is a key understanding in iterative lifecycle methods (such as the UP, XP, Scrum, and so forth): We start production-quality programming and testing for a subset of the requirements, and we start that development *before* all the requirements analysis is complete—in contrast to a waterfall process.

Incremental Development for the Same Use Case Across Iterations

Notice that not all requirements in the *Process Sale* use case are being implemented in iteration-1. It is common to work on varying scenarios of the same use case over several iterations and gradually extend the system to ultimately handle all the functionality required (see Figure 8.1). On the other hand, short, simple use cases may be completed within one iteration.

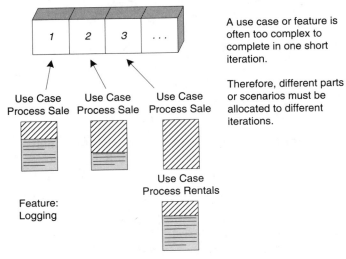

Figure 8.1 Use case implementation may be spread across iterations.

8.2   Process: Inception and Elaboration

In UP terms and our case studies, imagine we have finished the inception phase and are entering the elaboration phase.

What Happened in Inception?

The **inception** phase of the case studies may last only one week. Because this is *not* the requirements phase of the project, the artifacts created should be brief and incomplete, the phase quick, and the investigation light.

Inception is a short step to elaboration. It determines basic feasibility, risk, and scope, to decide if the project is worth more serious investigation. Not all activities that could reasonably occur in inception have been covered; this exploration emphasizes requirements-oriented artifacts. Some likely activities and artifacts in inception include:

- a short requirements workshop

- most actors, goals, and use cases named

- most use cases written in brief format; 10–20% of the use cases are written in fully dressed detail to improve understanding of the scope and complexity

- most influential and risky quality requirements identified

- version one of the Vision and Supplementary Specification written

- risk list

    ○ For example, leadership really wants a demo at the POSWorld trade show in Hamburg, in 18 months. But the effort for a demo cannot yet be even roughly estimated until deeper investigation.

- technical proof-of-concept prototypes and other investigations to explore the technical feasibility of special requirements ("Does Java Swing work properly on touch-screen displays?")

- user interface-oriented prototypes to clarify the vision of functional requirements

- recommendations on what components to buy/build/reuse, to be refined in elaboration

    ○ For example, a recommendation to buy a tax calculation package.

- high-level *candidate* architecture and components proposed

    ○ This is not a detailed architectural description, and it is not meant to be final or correct. Rather, it is brief speculation to use as a starting point of investigation in elaboration. For example, "A Java client-side application, no application server, Oracle for the database, ..." In elaboration, it may be proven worthy, or discovered to be a poor idea and rejected.

- plan for the first iteration

- candidate tools list

On to Elaboration

Elaboration is the initial series of iterations during which, on a normal project:

- the core, risky software architecture is programmed and tested

- the majority of requirements are discovered and stabilized

- the major risks are mitigated or retired

Elaboration is the initial series of iterations during which the team does serious investigation, implements (programs and tests) the core architecture, clarifies most requirements, and tackles the high-risk issues. In the UP, "risk" includes business value. Therefore, early work may include implementing scenarios that are deemed important, but are not especially technically risky.

Elaboration often consists of two or more iterations; each iteration is recommended to be between two and six weeks; prefer the shorter versions unless the team size is massive. Each iteration is timeboxed, meaning its end date is fixed.

Elaboration is not a design phase or a phase when the models are fully developed in preparation for implementation in the construction step—that would be an example of superimposing waterfall ideas on iterative development and the UP.

During this phase, one is not creating throw-away prototypes; rather, the code and design are production-quality portions of the final system. In some UP descriptions, the potentially misunderstood term "**architectural prototype**" is used to describe the partial system. This is not meant to be a prototype in the sense of a discardable experiment; in the UP, it means a production subset of the final system. More commonly it is called the **executable architecture** or **architectural baseline**.

> Elaboration in one sentence:
>
> *Build the core architecture, resolve the high-risk elements, define most requirements, and estimate the overall schedule and resources.*

Some key ideas and best practices will manifest in elaboration:

- do short timeboxed risk-driven iterations
- start programming early
- adaptively design, implement, and test the core and risky parts of the architecture
- test early, often, realistically
- adapt based on feedback from tests, users, developers
- write most of the use cases and other requirements in detail, through a series of workshops, once per elaboration iteration

What Artifacts May Start in Elaboration?

Table 8.1 lists *sample* artifacts that may be *started* in elaboration, and indicates the issues they address. Subsequent chapters will examine some of these in greater detail, especially the Domain Model and Design Model. For brevity, the table excludes artifacts that may have begun in inception; it introduces artifacts that are more likely to start in elaboration. Note these will not be completed in one iteration; rather, they will be refined over a series of iterations.

Artifact	Comment
Domain Model	This is a visualization of the domain concepts; it is similar to a static information model of the domain entities.
Design Model	This is the set of diagrams that describes the logical design. This includes software class diagrams, object interaction diagrams, package diagrams, and so forth.
Software Architecture Document	A learning aid that summarizes the key architectural issues and their resolution in the design. It is a summary of the outstanding design ideas and their motivation in the system.
Data Model	This includes the database schemas, and the mapping strategies between object and non-object representations.
Use-Case Storyboards, UI Prototypes	A description of the user interface, paths of navigation, usability models, and so forth.

Table 8.1 Sample elaboration artifacts, excluding those started in inception.

You Know You Didn't Understand Elaboration When...

- It is more than "a few" months long for most projects.

- It only has one iteration (with rare exceptions for well-understood problems).

- Most requirements were defined before elaboration.

- The risky elements and core architecture are not being tackled.

- It does not result in an *executable* architecture; there is no production-code programming.

- It is considered primarily a requirements or design phase, preceding an implementation phase in construction.

- There is an attempt to do a full and careful design before programming.

- There is minimal feedback and adaptation; users are not continually engaged in evaluation and feedback.

- There is no early and realistic testing.

- The architecture is speculatively finalized before programming.

- It is considered a step to do the proof-of-concept programming, rather than programming the production core executable architecture.

If a project exhibits these symptoms, the elaboration phase was not understood, and waterfall-thinking has been superimposed on the UP.

8.3   Process: Planning the Next Iteration

Planning and project management are important but large topics. A few ideas are briefly presented here, and there are some more tips starting on p. 673.

Organize requirements and iterations by risk, coverage, and criticality.

- **Risk** includes both technical complexity and other factors, such as uncertainty of effort or usability.

- **Coverage** implies that all major parts of the system are at least touched on in early iterations—perhaps a "wide and shallow" implementation across many components.

- **Criticality** refers to functions the client considers of high business value.

These criteria are used to rank work across iterations. Use cases or use case scenarios are ranked for implementation—early iterations implement high ranking scenarios. In addition, some requirements are expressed as high-level features unrelated to a particular use case, such as a logging service. These are also ranked.

The ranking is done before iteration-1, but then again before iteration-2, and so forth, as new requirements and new insights influence the order. That is, the plan of iterations is *adaptive*, rather than speculatively frozen at the beginning of the project. Usually based on some collaborative ranking technique, a grouping of requirements will emerge. For example:

Rank	Requirement (Use Case or Feature)	Comment
High	Process Sale Logging …	Scores high on all rankings. Pervasive. Hard to add late. …
Medium	Maintain Users …	Affects security subdomain. …
Low	…	…

Based on this ranking, we see that some key architecturally significant scenarios of the *Process Sale* use case should be tackled in early iterations. This list is not exhaustive; other requirements will also be tackled. In addition, an implicit or explicit *Start Up* use case will be worked on in each iteration, to meet its initialization needs.

DOMAIN MODELS

It's all very well in practice, but it will never work in theory.

—anonymous management maxim

Objectives

- Identify conceptual classes related to the current iteration.
- Create an initial domain model.
- Model appropriate attributes and associations.

Introduction

*more advanced
domain modeling
p. 501*

A domain model is the most important—and classic—model in OO *analysis*.[1] It illustrates noteworthy concepts in a domain. It can act as a source of inspiration for designing some software objects and will be an input to several artifacts explored in the case studies. This chapter also shows the value of OOA/D knowledge over UML notation; the basic notation is trivial, but there are subtle modeling guidelines for a useful model—expertise can take weeks or months. This chapter explores basic skills in creating domain models.

What's Next?

Having scoped the work for iteration-1, this chapter explores a partial domain model. The next examines the specific operations upon the system that are implied in the use case scenarios under design for this iteration.

| Other Requirements | Iteration 1 Requirements | Domain Modeling | System Sequence Diagrams | Operation Contracts |

---

1. Use cases are an important requirements analysis artifact, but are not *object*-oriented. They emphasize an activity view.

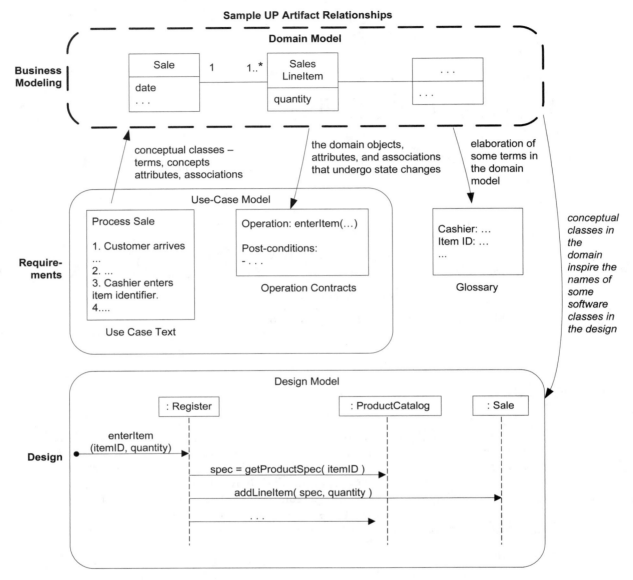

Figure 9.1 Sample UP artifact influence.

As with all things in an agile modeling and UP spirit, a domain model is optional. UP artifact influence emphasizing a domain model is shown in Figure 9.1. *Bounded by* the use case scenarios under development for the current iteration, the domain model can be evolved to show related noteworthy concepts. The related use case concepts and insight of experts will be input to its creation. The model can in turn influence operation contracts, a glossary, and the Design Model, especially the software objects in the **domain layer** of the Design Model.

domain layer
p. 136

9.1   Example

Figure 9.2 shows a partial domain model drawn with UML **class diagram** notation. It illustrates that the **conceptual classes** of *Payment* and *Sale* are significant in this domain, that a *Payment* is related to a *Sale* in a way that is meaningful to note, and that a *Sale* has a date and time, information attributes we care about.

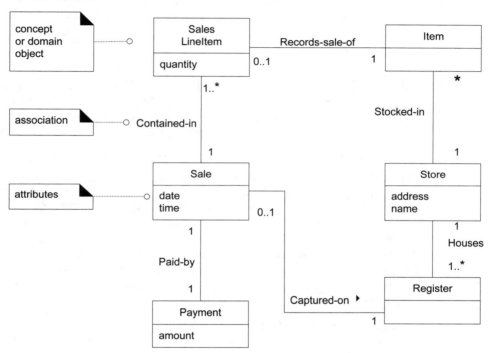

Figure 9.2 Partial domain model—a visual dictionary.

*conceptual
perspective p. 12*
Applying the UML class diagram notation for a domain model yields a *conceptual perspective* model.

Identifying a rich set of conceptual classes is at the heart of OO analysis. If it is done with skill and *short* time investment (say, no more than a few hours in each early iteration), it usually pays off during design, when it supports better understanding and communication.

Guideline

Avoid a waterfall-mindset big-modeling effort to make a thorough or "correct" domain model—it won't ever be either, and such over-modeling efforts lead to *analysis paralysis*, with little or no return on the investment.

9.2   What is a Domain Model?

The quintessential *object*-oriented analysis step is the decomposition of a domain into noteworthy concepts or objects.

A **domain model** is a *visual* representation of conceptual classes or real-situation objects in a domain [MO95, Fowler96]. Domain models have also been called **conceptual models** (the term used in the first edition of this book), **domain object models**, and **analysis object models**.[2]

Definition

In the UP, the term "Domain Model" means a representation of real-situation conceptual classes, not of software objects. The term does *not* mean a set of diagrams describing software classes, the domain layer of a software architecture, or software objects with responsibilities.

The UP defines the Domain Model[3] as one of the artifacts that may be created in the Business Modeling discipline. More precisely, the UP Domain Model is a specialization of the UP **Business Object Model** (BOM) "focusing on explaining 'things' and products important to a business domain" [RUP]. That is, a Domain Model focuses on one domain, such as POS related things. The more broad BOM, not covered in this introductory text and not something I encourage creating (because it can lead to too much up-front modeling), is an expanded, often very large and difficult to create, multi-domain model that covers the *entire* business and all its sub-domains.

Applying UML notation, a domain model is illustrated with a set of **class diagrams** in which no operations (method signatures) are defined. It provides a *conceptual perspective*. It may show:

- domain objects or conceptual classes

- associations between conceptual classes

- attributes of conceptual classes

Definition: Why Call a Domain Model a "Visual Dictionary"?

Please reflect on Figure 9.2 for a moment. See how it visualizes and relates words or concepts in the domain. It also shows an *abstraction* of the conceptual

---

2. They are also related to conceptual entity relationship models, which are capable of showing purely conceptual views of domains, but that have been widely re-interpreted as data models for database design. Domain models are not data models.

3. Capitalization of "Domain Model" or terms is used to emphasize it as an official model name defined in the UP, versus the general well-known concept of "domain models."

classes, because there are many other things one could communicate about registers, sales, and so forth.

The information it illustrates (using UML notation) could alternatively have been expressed in plain text (in the UP Glossary). But it's easy to understand the terms and especially their relationships in a visual language, since our brains are good at understanding visual elements and line connections.

Therefore, the domain model is a *visual dictionary* of the noteworthy abstractions, domain vocabulary, and information content of the domain.

Definition: Is a Domain Model a Picture of Software Business Objects?

A UP Domain Model, as shown in Figure 9.3, is a visualization of things in a real-situation domain of interest, *not* of software objects such as Java or C# classes, or software objects with responsibilities (see Figure 9.4). Therefore, the following elements are not suitable in a domain model:

- Software artifacts, such as a window or a database, unless the domain being modeled is of software concepts, such as a model of graphical user interfaces.

- Responsibilities or methods.[4]

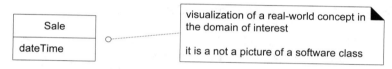

Figure 9.3 A domain model shows real-situation conceptual classes, not software classes.

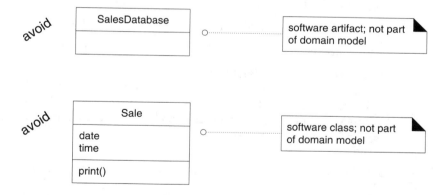

Figure 9.4 A domain model does not show software artifacts or classes.

---

4. In object modeling, we usually speak of responsibilities related to software objects. And methods are purely a software concept. But, the domain model describes real-situation concepts, not software objects. Considering object responsibilities during *design* work is very important; it is just not part of this model.

Definition: What are Two Traditional Meanings of "Domain Model"?

In the UP and thus this chapter, "Domain Model" is a conceptual perspective of objects in a real situation of the world, not a software perspective. But the term is overloaded; it also has been used (especially in the Smalltalk community where I did most of my early OO development work in the 1980s) to mean "the domain layer of software objects." That is, the layer of software objects below the presentation or UI layer that is composed of **domain objects**—software objects that represent things in the problem domain space with related "business logic" or "domain logic" methods. For example, a *Board* software class with a *getSquare* method.

Which definition is correct? Well, all of them! The term has long established uses in different communities to mean different things.

I've seen lots of confusion generated by people using the term in different ways, without explaining which meaning they intend, and without recognizing that others may be using it differently.

In this book, I'll usually write **domain layer** to indicate the second software-oriented meaning of domain model, as that's quite common.

Definition: What are Conceptual Classes?

The domain model illustrates conceptual classes or vocabulary in the domain. Informally, a **conceptual class** is an idea, thing, or object. More formally, a conceptual class may be considered in terms of its symbol, intension, and extension [MO95] (see Figure 9.5).

- **Symbol**—words or images representing a conceptual class.
- **Intension**—the definition of a conceptual class.
- **Extension**—the set of examples to which the conceptual class applies.

For example, consider the conceptual class for the event of a purchase transaction. I may choose to name it by the (English) symbol *Sale*. The intension of a *Sale* may state that it "represents the event of a purchase transaction, and has a date and time." The extension of *Sale* is all the examples of sales; in other words, the set of all sale instances in the universe.

Definition: Are Domain and Data Models the Same Thing?

A domain model is not a **data model** (which by definition shows persistent data to be stored somewhere), so do not exclude a class simply because the requirements don't indicate any obvious need to remember information about it (a criterion common in data modeling for relational database design, but not relevant to domain modeling) or because the conceptual class has no attributes. For example, it's valid to have attributeless conceptual classes, or conceptual classes that have a purely behavioral role in the domain instead of an information role.

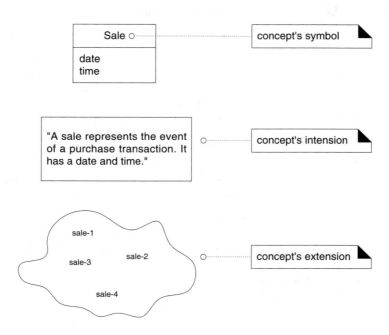

Figure 9.5 A conceptual class has a symbol, intension, and extension.

9.3 Motivation: Why Create a Domain Model?

I'll share a story that I've experienced many times in OO consulting and coaching. In the early 1990s I was working with a group developing a funeral services business system in Smalltalk, in Vancouver (you should see the domain model!). Now, I knew almost nothing about this business, so one reason to create a domain model was so that I could start to understand their key concepts and vocabulary.

domain layer
p. 206

We also wanted to create a **domain layer** of Smalltalk objects representing business objects and logic. So, we spent perhaps one hour sketching a UML-ish (actually OMT-ish, whose notation inspired UML) domain model, not worrying about software, but simply identifying the key terms. Then, those terms we sketched in the domain model, such as *Service* (like flowers in the funeral room, or playing "You Can't Always Get What You Want"), were also used as the names of key software classes in our domain layer implemented in Smalltalk.

This similarity of naming between the domain model and the domain layer (a real "service" and a Smalltalk *Service*) supported a lower gap between the software representation and our mental model of the domain.

Motivation: Lower Representational Gap with OO Modeling

This is a key idea in OO: Use software class names in the domain layer inspired from names in the domain model, with objects having domain-familiar information and responsibilities. Figure 9.6 illustrates the idea. This supports a **low representational gap** between our mental and software models. And that's not just a philosophical nicety—it has a practical time-and-money impact. For example, here's a source-code payroll program written in 1953:

1000010101000111101010101010001010101010101111010101 …

As computer science people, we know it runs, but the gap between this software representation and our mental model of the payroll domain is huge; that profoundly affects comprehension (and modification) of the software. OO modeling can lower that gap.

Of course, object technology is also of value because it can support the design of elegant, loosely coupled systems that scale and extend easily, as will be explored in the remainder of the book. A lowered representational gap is useful, but arguably secondary to the advantage objects have in supporting ease of change and extension, and managing and hiding complexity.

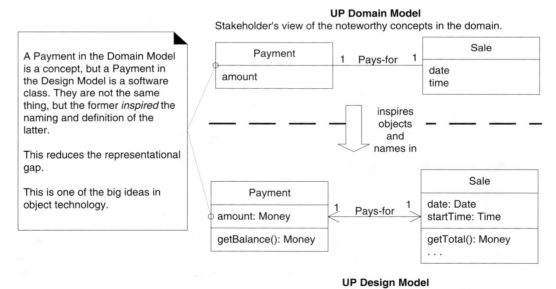

Figure 9.6 Lower representational gap with OO modeling.

9.4 Guideline: How to Create a Domain Model?

Bounded by the current iteration requirements under design:

1. Find the conceptual classes (see a following guideline).
2. Draw them as classes in a UML class diagram.
3. Add associations and attributes. See p. 149 and p. 158.

9.5 Guideline: How to Find Conceptual Classes?

Since a domain model shows conceptual classes, a central question is: How do I find them?

What are Three Strategies to Find Conceptual Classes?

1. Reuse or modify existing models. This is the first, best, and usually easiest approach, and where I will start if I can. There are published, well-crafted domain models and data models (which can be modified into domain models) for many common domains, such as inventory, finance, health, and so forth. Example books that I'll turn to include *Analysis Patterns* by Martin Fowler, *Data Model Patterns* by David Hay, and the *Data Model Resource Book* (volumes 1 and 2) by Len Silverston.
2. Use a category list.
3. Identify noun phrases.

Reusing existing models is excellent, but outside our scope. The second method, using a category list, is also useful.

Method 2: Use a Category List

We can kick-start the creation of a domain model by making a list of candidate conceptual classes. Table 9.1 contains many common categories that are usually worth considering, with an emphasis on business information system needs. The guidelines also suggest some priorities in the analysis. Examples are drawn from the 1) POS, 2) Monopoly, and 3) airline reservation domains.

Conceptual Class Category	Examples
business transactions *Guideline*: These are critical (they involve money), so start with transactions.	*Sale, Payment* *Reservation*
transaction line items *Guideline*: Transactions often come with related line items, so consider these next.	*SalesLineItem*
product or service related to a transaction or transaction line item *Guideline*: Transactions are *for* something (a product or service). Consider these next.	*Item* *Flight, Seat, Meal*
where is the transaction recorded? *Guideline*: Important.	*Register, Ledger* *FlightManifest*
roles of people or organizations related to the transaction; actors in the use case *Guideline*: We usually need to know about the parties involved in a transaction.	*Cashier, Customer, Store MonopolyPlayer Passenger, Airline*
place of transaction; place of service	*Store* *Airport, Plane, Seat*
noteworthy events, often with a time or place we need to remember	*Sale, Payment MonopolyGame Flight*
physical objects *Guideline*: This is especially relevant when creating device-control software, or simulations.	*Item, Register Board, Piece, Die Airplane*
descriptions of things *Guideline*: See p. 147 for discussion.	*ProductDescription* *FlightDescription*

Conceptual Class Category	Examples
catalogs *Guideline*: Descriptions are often in a catalog.	*ProductCatalog* *FlightCatalog*
containers of things (physical or information)	*Store, Bin* *Board* *Airplane*
things in a container	*Item* *Square (in a Board)* *Passenger*
other collaborating systems	*CreditAuthorizationSystem* *AirTrafficControl*
records of finance, work, contracts, legal matters	*Receipt, Ledger* *MaintenanceLog*
financial instruments	*Cash, Check, LineOfCredit* *TicketCredit*
schedules, manuals, documents that are regularly referred to in order to perform work	*DailyPriceChangeList* *RepairSchedule*

Table 9.1 Conceptual Class Category List.

Method 3: Finding Conceptual Classes with Noun Phrase Identification

Another useful technique (because of its simplicity) suggested in [Abbot83] is **linguistic analysis**: Identify the nouns and noun phrases in textual descriptions of a domain, and consider them as candidate conceptual classes or attributes.[5]

Guideline

Care must be applied with this method; a mechanical noun-to-class mapping isn't possible, and words in natural languages are ambiguous.

---

5. Linguistic analysis has become more sophisticated; it also goes by the name **natural language modeling**. See [Moreno97] for example.

Nevertheless, linguistic analysis is another source of inspiration. The fully dressed use cases are an excellent description to draw from for this analysis. For example, the current scenario of the *Process Sale* use case can be used.

Main Success Scenario (or Basic Flow):
1. **Customer** arrives at a **POS checkout** with **goods** and/or **services** to purchase.
2. **Cashier** starts a new **sale**.
3. **Cashier** enters **item identifier**.
4. System records **sale line item** and presents **item description**, **price**, and running **total**. Price calculated from a set of price rules.
Cashier repeats steps 2-3 until indicates done.
5. System presents total with **taxes** calculated.
6. Cashier tells Customer the total, and asks for **payment**.
7. Customer pays and System handles payment.
8. System logs the completed **sale** and sends sale and payment information to the external **Accounting** (for accounting and **commissions**) and **Inventory** systems (to update inventory).
9. System presents **receipt**.
10. Customer leaves with receipt and goods (if any).

Extensions (or Alternative Flows):

. . .

7a. Paying by cash:
    1. Cashier enters the cash **amount tendered**.
    2. System presents the **balance due**, and releases the **cash drawer**.
    3. Cashier deposits cash tendered and returns balance in cash to Customer.
    4. System records the cash payment.

The domain model is a visualization of noteworthy domain concepts and vocabulary. Where are those terms found? Some are in the use cases. Others are in other documents, or the minds of experts. In any event, use cases are one rich source to mine for noun phrase identification.

Some of these noun phrases are candidate conceptual classes, some may refer to conceptual classes that are ignored in this iteration (for example, "Accounting" and "commissions"), and some may be simply attributes of conceptual classes. See p. 160 for advice on distinguishing between the two.

A weakness of this approach is the imprecision of natural language; different noun phrases may represent the same conceptual class or attribute, among other ambiguities. Nevertheless, it is recommended in combination with the *Conceptual Class Category List* technique.

9.6   Example: Find and Draw Conceptual Classes

Case Study: POS Domain

iteration-1 requirements p. 124

From the category list and noun phrase analysis, a list is generated of candidate conceptual classes for the domain. Since this is a business information system, I'll focus first on the category list guidelines that emphasize business transactions and their relationship with other things. The list is constrained to the requirements and simplifications currently under consideration for iteration-1, the basic cash-only scenario of *Process Sale*.

Sale	*Cashier*
CashPayment	*Customer*
SalesLineItem	*Store*
Item	*ProductDescription*
Register	*ProductCatalog*
Ledger	

There is no such thing as a "correct" list. It is a somewhat arbitrary collection of abstractions and domain vocabulary that the modelers consider noteworthy. Nevertheless, by following the identification strategies, different modelers will produce similar lists.

In practice, I don't create a text list first, but immediately draw a UML class diagram of the conceptual classes as we uncover them. See Figure 9.7.

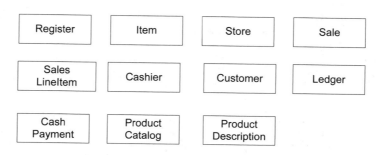

Figure 9.7 Initial POS domain model.

Adding the associations and attributes is covered in later sections.

Case Study: Monopoly Domain

iteration-1 requirements p. 124

From the Category List and noun phrase analysis, I generate a list of candidate conceptual classes for the iteration-1 simplified scenario of *Play a Monopoly Game* (see Figure 9.8). Since this is a simulation, I emphasize the noteworthy tangible, physical objects in the domain.

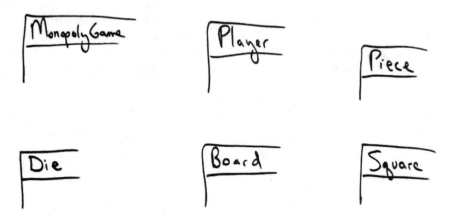

Figure 9.8 Initial Monopoly domain model.

9.7   Guideline: Agile Modeling—Sketching a Class Diagram

Notice the sketching style in the UML class diagram of Figure 9.8—keeping the bottom and right sides of the class boxes open. This makes it easier to grow the classes as we discover new elements. And although I've grouped the class boxes for compactness in this book diagram, on a whiteboard I'll spread them out.

9.8   Guideline: Agile Modeling—Maintain the Model in a Tool?

It's normal to miss significant conceptual classes during early domain modeling, and to discover them later during design sketching or programming. If you are taking an agile modeling approach, the purpose of creating a domain model is to quickly understand and communicate a rough approximation of the key concepts. Perfection is not the goal, and agile models are usually discarded shortly after creation (although if you've used a whiteboard, I recommend taking a digital snapshot). From this viewpoint, there is no motivation to maintain or update the model. But that doesn't mean it's wrong to update the model.

If someone wants the model maintained and updated with new discoveries, that's a good reason to redraw the whiteboard sketch within a UML CASE tool, or to originally do the drawing with a tool and a computer projector (for others to see the diagram easily). But, ask yourself: Who is going to use the updated model, and why? If there isn't a practical reason, don't bother. Often, the evolving *domain layer* of the software hints at most of the noteworthy terms, and a long-life OO analysis domain model doesn't add value.

9.9 Guideline: Report Objects—Include 'Receipt' in the Model?

Receipt is a noteworthy term in the POS domain. But perhaps it's only a *report* of a sale and payment, and thus duplicate information. Should it be in the domain model?

Here are some factors to consider:

- In general, showing a report of other information in a domain model is not useful since all its information is derived or duplicated from other sources. This is a reason to exclude it.

- On the other hand, it has a special role in terms of the business rules: It usually confers the right to the bearer of the (paper) receipt to return bought items. This is a reason to show it in the model.

Since item returns are not being considered in this iteration, *Receipt* will be excluded. During the iteration that tackles the *Handle Returns* use case, we would be justified to include it.

9.10 Guideline: Think Like a Mapmaker; Use Domain Terms

The mapmaker strategy applies to both maps and domain models.

> *Guideline*
>
> Make a domain model in the spirit of how a cartographer or mapmaker works:
>
> - Use the existing names in the territory. For example, if developing a model for a library, name the customer a "Borrower" or "Patron"—the terms used by the library staff.
>
> - Exclude irrelevant or out-of-scope features. For example, in the Monopoly domain model for iteration-1, cards (such as the "Get out of Jail Free" card) are not used, so don't show a *Card* in the model this iteration.
>
> - Do not add things that are not there.

The principle is similar to the *Use the Domain Vocabulary* strategy [Coad95].

9.11 Guideline: How to Model the *Unreal* World?

Some software systems are for domains that find very little analogy in natural or business domains; software for telecommunications is an example. Yet it is still possible to create a domain model in these domains. It requires a high degree of abstraction, stepping back from familiar non-OO designs, and listening carefully to the core vocabulary and concepts that domain experts use.

For example, here are candidate conceptual classes related to the domain of a telecommunication switch: *Message, Connection, Port, Dialog, Route, Protocol*.

9.12 Guideline: A Common Mistake with Attributes vs. Classes

Perhaps the most common mistake when creating a domain model is to represent something as an attribute when it should have been a conceptual class. A rule of thumb to help prevent this mistake is:

> *Guideline*
>
> If we do not think of some conceptual class X as a number or text in the real world, X is probably a conceptual class, not an attribute.

As an example, should *store* be an attribute of *Sale*, or a separate conceptual class *Store*?

Sale
store

or... ?

Sale

Store
phoneNumber

In the real world, a store is not considered a number or text—the term suggests a legal entity, an organization, and something that occupies space. Therefore, *Store* should be a conceptual class.

As another example, consider the domain of airline reservations. Should *destination* be an attribute of *Flight*, or a separate conceptual class *Airport*?

Flight
destination

or... ?

Flight

Airport
name

In the real world, a destination airport is not considered a number or text—it is a massive thing that occupies space. Therefore, *Airport* should be a concept.

9.13 Guideline: When to Model with 'Description' Classes?

A **description class** contains information that describes something else. For example, a *ProductDescription* that records the price, picture, and text description of an *Item*. This was first named the *Item-Descriptor* pattern in [Coad92].

Motivation: Why Use 'Description' Classes?

The following discussion may at first seem related to a rare, highly specialized issue. However, it turns out that the need for description classes is common in many domain models.

Assume the following:

- An *Item* instance represents a physical item in a store; as such, it may even have a serial number.

- An *Item* has a description, price, and itemID, which are not recorded anywhere else.

- Everyone working in the store has amnesia.

- Every time a real physical item is sold, a corresponding software instance of *Item* is deleted from "software land."

With these assumptions, what happens in the following scenario?

There is strong demand for the popular new vegetarian burger—ObjectBurger. The store sells out, implying that all *Item* instances of ObjectBurgers are deleted from computer memory.

Now, here is one problem: If someone asks, "How much do ObjectBurgers cost?", no one can answer, because the memory of their price was attached to inventoried instances, which were deleted as they were sold.

Here are some related problems: The model, if implemented in software similar to the domain model, has duplicate data, is space-inefficient, and error-prone (due to replicated information) because the description, price, and itemID are duplicated for every *Item* instance of the same product.

The preceding problem illustrates the need for objects that are *descriptions* (sometimes called *specifications*) of other things. To solve the *Item* problem, what is needed is a *ProductDescription* class that records information about items. A *ProductDescription* does not represent an *Item*, it represents a description of information *about* items. See Figure 9.9.

A particular *Item* may have a serial number; it represents a physical instance. A *ProductDescription* wouldn't have a serial number.

Switching from a conceptual to a software perspective, note that even if all inventoried items are sold and their corresponding *Item* software instances are deleted, the *ProductDescription* still remains.

The need for description classes is common in sales, product, and service domains. It is also common in manufacturing, which requires a *description* of a manufactured thing that is distinct from the thing itself.

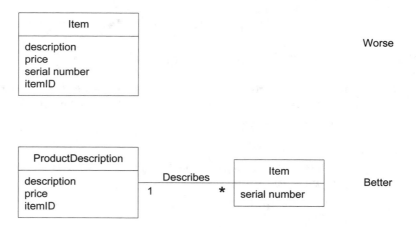

Figure 9.9 Descriptions about other things. The * means a multiplicity of "many." It indicates that one *ProductDescription* may describe many (*) *Items*.

Guideline: When Are Description Classes Useful?

Guideline

Add a description class (for example, *ProductDescription*) when:

- There needs to be a description about an item or service, independent of the current existence of any examples of those items or services.

- Deleting instances of things they describe (for example, *Item*) results in a loss of information that needs to be maintained, but was incorrectly associated with the deleted thing.

- It reduces redundant or duplicated information.

Example: Descriptions in the Airline Domain

As another example, consider an airline company that suffers a fatal crash of one of its planes. Assume that all the flights are cancelled for six months pending completion of an investigation. Also assume that when flights are cancelled, their corresponding *Flight* software objects are deleted from computer memory. Therefore, after the crash, all *Flight* software objects are deleted.

If the only record of what airport a flight goes to is in the *Flight* software instances, which represent specific flights for a particular date and time, then there is no longer a record of what flight routes the airline has.

The problem can be solved, both from a purely conceptual perspective in a domain model and from a software perspective in the software designs, with a *FlightDescription* that describes a flight and its route, even when a particular flight is not scheduled (see Figure 9.10).

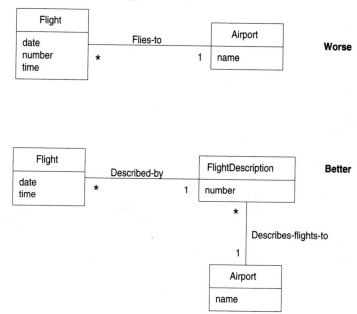

Figure 9.10 Descriptions about other things.

Note that the prior example is about a service (a flight) rather than a good (such as a veggieburger). Descriptions of services or service plans are commonly needed.

As another example, a mobile phone company sells packages such as "bronze," "gold," and so forth. It is necessary to have the concept of a description of the package (a kind of service plan describing rates per minute, wireless Internet content, the cost, and so forth) separate from the concept of an actual sold package (such as "gold package sold to Craig Larman on Jan. 1, 2047 at $55 per month"). Marketing needs to define and record this service plan or *MobileCommunicationsPackageDescription* before any are sold.

9.14   Associations

It's useful to find and show associations that are needed to satisfy the information requirements of the current scenarios under development, and which aid in understanding the domain.

An **association** is a relationship between classes (more precisely, instances of those classes) that indicates some meaningful and interesting connection (see Figure 9.11).

In the UML, associations are defined as "the semantic relationship between two or more classifiers that involve connections among their instances."

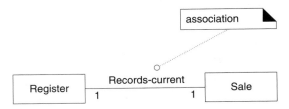

Figure 9.11 Associations.

Guideline: When to Show an Association?

Associations worth noting usually imply knowledge of a relationship that needs to be preserved for some duration—it could be milliseconds or years, depending on context. *In other words, between what objects do we need some **memory** of a relationship?*

For example, do we need to *remember* what *SalesLineItem* instances are associated with a *Sale* instance? Definitely, otherwise it would not be possible to reconstruct a sale, print a receipt, or calculate a sale total.

And we need to remember completed *Sales* in a *Ledger*, for accounting and legal purposes.

Because the domain model is a conceptual perspective, these statements about the need to remember refer to a need in a real situation of the world, not a software need, although during implementation many of the same needs will arise.

In the monopoly domain, we need to remember what *Square* a *Piece* (or *Player*) is on—the game doesn't work if that isn't remembered. Likewise, we need to remember what *Piece* is owned by a particular *Player*. We need to remember what *Squares* are part of a particular *Board*.

But on the other hand, there is no need to remember that the *Die* (or the plural, "dice") total indicates the *Square* to move to. It's true, but we don't need to have an ongoing memory of that fact, after the move has been made. Likewise, a *Cashier* may look up *ProductDescriptions*, but there is no need to remember the fact of a particular *Cashier* looking up particular *ProductDescriptions*.

> *Guideline*
>
> Consider including the following associations in a domain model:
>
> - Associations for which knowledge of the relationship needs to be preserved for some duration ("need-to-remember" associations).
>
> - Associations derived from the Common Associations List.

Guideline: Why Should We Avoid Adding Many Associations?

We need to avoid adding too many associations to a domain model. Digging back into our discrete mathematics studies, you may recall that in a graph with n nodes, there can be (n·(n-1))/2 associations to other nodes—a potentially very large number. A domain model with 20 classes could have 190 associations lines! Many lines on the diagram will obscure it with "visual noise." Therefore, be parsimonious about adding association lines. Use the criterion guidelines suggested in this chapter, and focus on "need-to-remember" associations.

Perspectives: Will the Associations Be Implemented In Software?

During domain modeling, an association is *not* a statement about data flows, database foreign key relationships, instance variables, or object connections in a software solution; it is a statement that a relationship is meaningful in a purely conceptual perspective—in the real domain.

That said, many of these relationships *will* be implemented in software as paths of navigation and visibility (both in the Design Model and Data Model). But the domain model is not a data model; associations are added to highlight our rough understanding of noteworthy relationships, not to document object or data structures.

Applying UML: Association Notation

An association is represented as a line between classes with a capitalized association name. See Figure 9.12.

The ends of an association may contain a multiplicity expression indicating the numerical relationship between instances of the classes.

The association is inherently bidirectional, meaning that from instances of either class, logical traversal to the other is possible. This traversal is purely abstract; it is *not* a statement about connections between software entities.

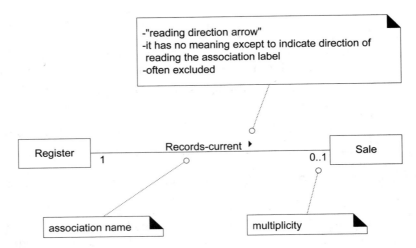

Figure 9.12 The UML notation for associations.

An optional "reading direction arrow" indicates the direction to read the association name; it does not indicate direction of visibility or navigation. If the arrow is not present, the convention is to read the association from left to right or top to bottom, although the UML does not make this a rule (see Figure 9.12).

Caution

The reading direction arrow has no meaning in terms of the model; it is only an aid to the reader of the diagram.

Guideline: How to Name an Association in UML?

Guideline

Name an association based on a *ClassName-VerbPhrase-ClassName* format where the verb phrase creates a sequence that is readable and meaningful.

Simple association names such as "Has" or "Uses" are usually poor, as they seldom enhance our understanding of the domain.

For example,

■ *Sale Paid-by CashPayment*

    ○ bad example (doesn't enhance meaning): *Sale Uses CashPayment*

■ *Player Is-on Square*

    ○ bad example (doesn't enhance meaning): *Player Has Square*

Association names should start with a capital letter, since an association represents a classifier of links between instances; in the UML, classifiers should start with a capital letter. Two common and equally legal formats for a compound association name are:

- *Records-current*

- *RecordsCurrent*

Applying UML: Roles

Each end of an association is called a **role**. Roles may optionally have:

- multiplicity expression

- name

- navigability

Multiplicity is examined next.

Applying UML: Multiplicity

Multiplicity defines how many instances of a class *A* can be associated with one instance of a class *B* (see Figure 9.13).

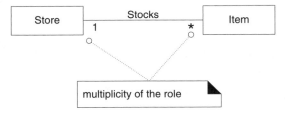

Figure 9.13 Multiplicity on an association.

For example, a single instance of a *Store* can be associated with "many" (zero or more, indicated by the *) *Item* instances.

Some examples of multiplicity expressions are shown in Figure 9.14.

The multiplicity value communicates how many instances can be validly associated with another, at a particular moment, rather than over a span of time. For example, it is possible that a used car could be repeatedly sold back to used car dealers over time. But at any particular moment, the car is only *Stocked-by* <u>one</u> dealer. The car is not *Stocked-by* <u>many</u> dealers at any particular moment. Similarly, in countries with monogamy laws, a person can be *Married-to* only <u>one</u> other person at any particular moment, even though over a span of time, that same person may be married to <u>many</u> persons.

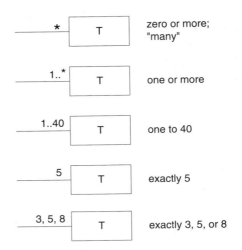

Figure 9.14 Multiplicity values.

The multiplicity value is dependent on our interest as a modeler and software developer, because it communicates a domain constraint that will be (or could be) reflected in software. See Figure 9.15 for an example and explanation.

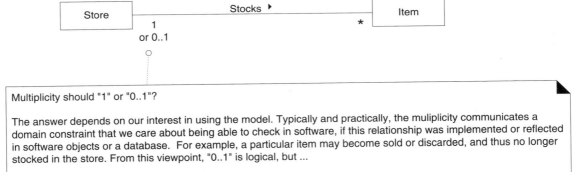

Figure 9.15 Multiplicity is context dependent.

Rumbaugh gives another example of *Person* and *Company* in the *Works-for* association [Rumbaugh91]. Indicating if a *Person* instance works for one or many *Company* instances is dependent on the context of the model; the tax department is interested in *many*; a union probably only *one*. The choice usually depends on why we are building the software.

Applying UML: Multiple Associations Between Two Classes

Two classes may have multiple associations between them in a UML class diagram; this is not uncommon. There is no outstanding example in the POS or Monopoly case study, but an example from the domain of the airline is the relationships between a *Flight* (or perhaps more precisely, a *FlightLeg*) and an *Airport* (see Figure 9.16); the flying-to and flying-from associations are distinctly different relationships, which should be shown separately.

Figure 9.16 Multiple associations.

Guideline: How to Find Associations with a Common Associations List

Start the addition of associations by using the list in Table 9.2. It contains common categories that are worth considering, especially for business information systems. Examples are drawn from the 1) POS, 2) Monopoly, and 3) airline reservation domains.

Category	Examples
A is a transaction related to another transaction B	*CashPayment—Sale* *Cancellation—Reservation*
A is a line item of a transaction B	*SalesLineItem—Sale*
A is a product or service for a transaction (or line item) B	*Item—SalesLineItem (or Sale)* *Flight—Reservation*
A is a role related to a transaction B	*Customer—Payment* *Passenger—Ticket*
A is a physical or logical part of B	*Drawer—Register* *Square—Board* *Seat—Airplane*

Category	Examples
A is physically or logically contained in/on B	*Register—Store, Item—Shelf* *Square—Board* *Passenger—Airplane*
A is a description for B	*ProductDescription—Item* *FlightDescription—Flight*
A is known/logged/recorded/reported/ captured in B	*Sale—Register* *Piece—Square* *Reservation—FlightManifest*
A is a member of B	*Cashier—Store* *Player—MonopolyGame* *Pilot—Airline*
A is an organizational subunit of B	*Department—Store* *Maintenance—Airline*
A uses or manages or owns B	*Cashier—Register* *Player—Piece* *Pilot—Airplane*
A is next to B	*SalesLineItem—SalesLineItem* *Square—Square* *City—City*

Table 9.2 Common Associations List.

9.15 Example: Associations in the Domain Models

Case Study: NextGen POS

The domain model in Figure 9.17 shows a set of conceptual classes and associations that are candidates for our POS domain model. The associations are primarily derived from the "need-to-remember" criteria of this iteration requirements, and the Common Association List. Reading the list and mapping the examples to the diagram should explain the choices. For example:

- **Transactions related to another transaction**—*Sale Paid-by CashPayment.*

- **Line items of a transaction**—*Sale Contains SalesLineItem.*

- **Product for a transaction (or line item)**—*SalesLineItem Records-sale-of Item*.

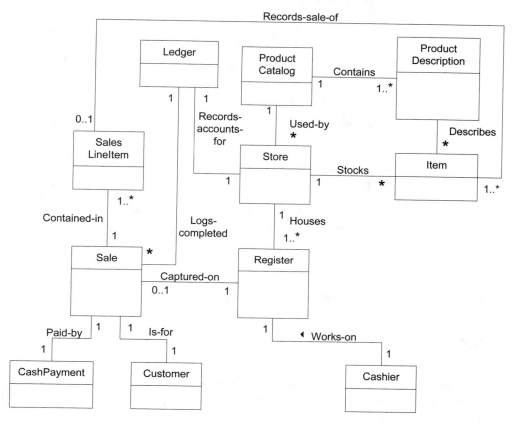

Figure 9.17 NextGen POS partial domain model.

Case Study: Monopoly

See Figure 9.18. Again, the associations are primarily derived from the "need-to-remember" criteria of this iteration requirements, and the Common Association List. For example:

- **A is contained in or on B**—*Board Contains Square*.
- **A owns B**—*Players Owns Piece*.
- **A is known in/on B**—*Piece Is-on Square*.
- **A is member of B**—*Player Member-of (or Plays) MonopolyGame*.

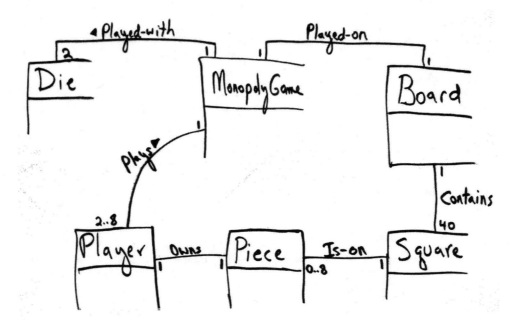

Figure 9.18 Monopoly partial domain model.

9.16   Attributes

It is useful to identify those attributes of conceptual classes that are needed to satisfy the information requirements of the current scenarios under development. An **attribute** is a logical data value of an object.

Guideline: When to Show Attributes?

Include attributes that the requirements (for example, use cases) suggest or imply a need to remember information.

For example, a receipt (which reports the information of a sale) in the *Process Sale* use case normally includes a date and time, the store name and address, and the cashier ID, among many other things.

Therefore,

■ *Sale* needs a *dateTime* attribute.

■ *Store* needs a *name* and *address*.

■ *Cashier* needs an *ID*.

Applying UML: Attribute Notation

Attributes are shown in the second compartment of the class box (see Figure 9.19). Their type and other information may optionally be shown.

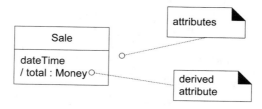

Figure 9.19 Class and attributes.

More Notation

detailed UML class diagram notation p. 249, and also on the back inside cover of the book

The full syntax for an attribute in the UML is:

visibility name : type multiplicity = default {property-string}

Some common examples are shown in Figure 9.20.

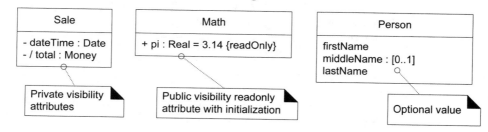

Figure 9.20 Attribute notation in UML.

As a convention, most modelers will assume attributes have private visibility (-) unless shown otherwise, so I don't usually draw an explicit visibility symbol.

{readOnly} is probably the most common property string for attributes.

Multiplicity can be used to indicate the optional presence of a value, or the number of objects that can fill a (collection) attribute. For example, many domains require that a first and last name be known for a person, but that a middle name is optional. The expression *middleName : [0..1]* indicates an optional value—0 or 1 values are present.

Guideline: Where to Record Attribute Requirements?

Notice that, subtly, *middleName : [0..1]* is a requirement or domain rule, embedded in the domain model. Although this is just a conceptual-perspective domain model, it probably implies that the software perspective should allow a missing value for *middleName* in the UI, the objects, and the database. Some modellers accept leaving such specifications only in the domain model, but I find this error-prone and scattered, as people tend to not look at the domain model in detail, or for requirements guidance. Nor do they usually maintain the domain model.

Instead, I suggest placing all such attribute requirements in the UP Glossary, which serves as a data dictionary. Perhaps I've spent an hour sketching a domain model with a domain expert; afterwards, I can spend 15 minutes looking through it and transferring implied attribute requirements into the Glossary.

Another alternative is to use a tool that integrates UML models with a data dictionary; then all attributes will automatically show up as dictionary elements.

Derived Attributes

The *total* attribute in the *Sale* can be calculated or derived from the information in the *SalesLineItems*. When we want to communicate that 1) this is a noteworthy attribute, but 2) it is derivable, we use the UML convention: a / symbol before the attribute name.

As another example, a cashier can receive a group of like items (for example, six tofu packages), enter the *itemID* once, and then enter a quantity (for example, six). Consequently, an individual *SalesLineItem* can be associated with more than one instance of an item.

The quantity that is entered by the cashier may be recorded as an attribute of the *SalesLineItem* (Figure 9.21). However, the quantity can be calculated from the actual multiplicity value of the association, so it may be characterized as a derived attribute—one that may be derived from other information.

Guideline: What are Suitable Attribute Types?

Focus on Data Type Attributes in the Domain Model

Informally, most attribute types should be what are often thought of as "primitive" data types, such as numbers and booleans. The type of an attribute should *not* normally be a complex domain concept, such as a *Sale* or *Airport*.

For example, the *currentRegister* attribute in the *Cashier* class in Figure 9.22 is undesirable because its type is meant to be a *Register*, which is not a simple data type (such as *Number* or *String*). The most useful way to express that a *Cashier* uses a *Register* is with an association, not with an attribute.

> *Guideline*
>
> The attributes in a domain model should preferably be **data types**. Very common data types include: *Boolean, Date (or DateTime), Number, Character, String (Text), Time.*
>
> Other common types include: *Address, Color, Geometrics (Point, Rectangle), Phone Number, Social Security Number, Universal Product Code (UPC), SKU, ZIP or postal codes, enumerated types*

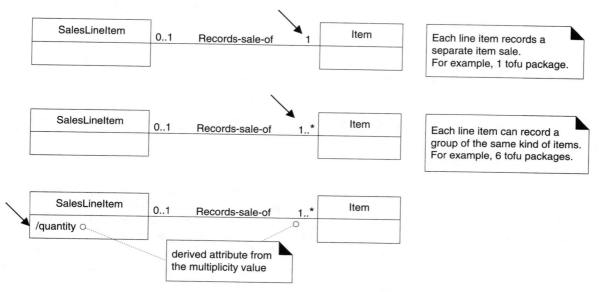

Figure 9.21 Recording the quantity of items sold in a line item.

To repeat an earlier example, a common confusion is modeling a complex domain concept as an attribute. To illustrate, a destination airport is not really a string; it is a complex thing that occupies many square kilometers of space. Therefore, *Flight* should be related to *Airport* via an association, not with an attribute, as shown in Figure 9.23.

> *Guideline*
>
> Relate conceptual classes with an association, not with an attribute.

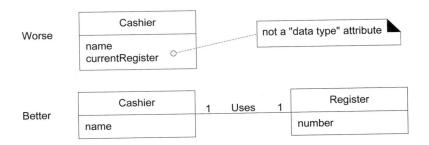

Figure 9.22 Relate with associations, not attributes.

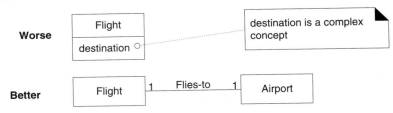

Figure 9.23 Don't show complex concepts as attributes; use associations.

Data Types

As said, attributes in the domain model should generally be **data types**; informally these are "primitive" types such as number, boolean, character, string, and enumerations (such as Size = {small, large}). More precisely, this is a UML term that implies a set of values for which unique identity is not meaningful (in the context of our model or system) [RJB99]. Said another way, equality tests are *not* based on identity, but instead on value.[6] For example, it is not (usually) meaningful to distinguish between:

■ Separate instances of the *Integer* 5.

■ Separate instances of the *String* 'cat'.

■ Separate instance of the *Date* "Nov. 13, 1990".

By contrast, it *is* meaningful to distinguish (by object identity) between two separate *Person* instances whose names are both "Jill Smith" because the two instances can represent separate individuals with the same name.

Also, data type values are usually immutable. For example, the instance '5' of *Integer* is immutable; the instance "Nov. 13, 1990" of *Date* is probably immutable. On the other hand, a *Person* instance may have its *lastName* changed for various reasons.

---

6. In Java, for example, a value test is done with the *equals* method, and an identity test with the == operator.

From a software perspective, there are few situations where one would compare the memory addresses (identity) of instances of *Integer* or *Date*; only value-based comparisons are relevant. On the other hand, the memory addresses of *Person* instances could conceivably be compared and distinguished, even if they had the same attribute values, because their unique identity is important.

Some OO and UML modeling books also speak of **value objects**, which are very similar to data types, but with minor variations. However, I found the distinctions rather fuzzy and subtle, and don't stress it.

Perspectives: What About Attributes in Code?

The recommendation that attributes in the domain model be mainly data types does *not* imply that C# or Java attributes must only be of simple, primitive data types. The domain model is a conceptual perspective, not a software one. In the Design Model, attributes may be of any type.

Guideline: When to Define New Data Type Classes?

In the NextGen POS system an *itemID* attribute is needed; it is probably an attribute of an *Item* or *ProductDescription*. Casually, it seems like just a number or perhaps a string. For example, *itemID : Integer* or *itemID : String*.

But it is more than that (item identifiers have subparts), and in fact it is useful to have a class named *ItemID* (or *ItemIdentifier*) in the domain model, and designate the type of the attribute as such. For example, *itemID : ItemIdentifier*.

Table 9.3 provides guidelines when it's useful to model with data types.

Applying these guidelines to the POS domain model attributes yields the following analysis:

- The item identifier is an abstraction of various common coding schemes, including UPC-A, UPC-E, and the family of EAN schemes. These numeric coding schemes have subparts identifying the manufacturer, product, country (for EAN), and a check-sum digit for validation. Therefore, there should be a data type *ItemID* class, because it satisfies many of the guidelines above.

- The *price* and *amount* attributes should be a data type *Money* class because they are quantities in a unit of currency.

- The *address* attribute should be a data type *Address* class because it has separate sections.

Guideline

Represent what may initially be considered a number or string as a new data type class in the domain model if:

- It is composed of separate sections.
    - phone number, name of person
- There are operations associated with it, such as parsing or validation.
    - social security number
- It has other attributes.
    - promotional price could have a start (effective) date and end date
- It is a quantity with a unit.
    - payment amount has a unit of currency
- It is an abstraction of one or more types with some of these qualities.
    - item identifier in the sales domain is a generalization of types such as Universal Product Code (UPC) and European Article Number (EAN)

Table 9.3 Guidelines for modeling data types.

Applying UML: Where to Illustrate These Data Type Classes?

Should the *ItemID* class be shown as a separate class in a domain model? It depends on what you want to emphasize in the diagram. Since *ItemID* is a **data type** (unique identity of instances is not used for equality testing), it may be shown only in the attribute compartment of the class box, as shown in Figure 9.24. On the other hand, if *ItemID* is a new type with its own attributes and associations, showing it as a conceptual class in its own box may be informative. There is no correct answer; resolution depends on how the domain model is being used as a tool of communication, and the significance of the concept in the domain.

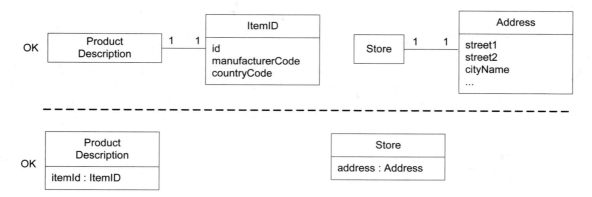

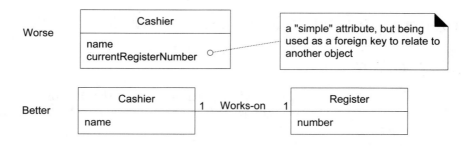

Figure 9.24 Two ways to indicate a data type property of an object.

Guideline: No Attributes Representing Foreign Keys

Attributes should *not* be used to relate conceptual classes in the domain model. The most common violation of this principle is to add a kind of **foreign key attribute**, as is typically done in relational database designs, in order to associate two types. For example, in Figure 9.25 the *currentRegisterNumber* attribute in the *Cashier* class is undesirable because its purpose is to relate the *Cashier* to a *Register* object. The better way to express that a *Cashier* uses a *Register* is with an association, not with a foreign key attribute. Once again, relate types with an association, not with an attribute.

There are many ways to relate objects—foreign keys being one—and we will defer how to implement the relation until design to avoid **design creep**.

Figure 9.25 Do not use attributes as foreign keys.

Guideline: Modeling Quantities and Units

Most numeric quantities should *not* be represented as plain numbers. Consider price or weight. Saying "the price was 13" or "the weight was 37" doesn't say much. Euros? Kilograms?

These are quantities with associated units, and it is common to require knowledge of the unit to support conversions. The NextGen POS software is for an international market and needs to support prices in multiple currencies. The domain model (and the software) should model quantities skillfully.

In the general case, the solution is to represent *Quantity* as a distinct class, with an associated *Unit* [Fowler96]. It is also common to show *Quantity* specializations. *Money* is a kind of quantity whose units are currencies. *Weight* is a quantity with units such as kilograms or pounds. See Figure 9.26.

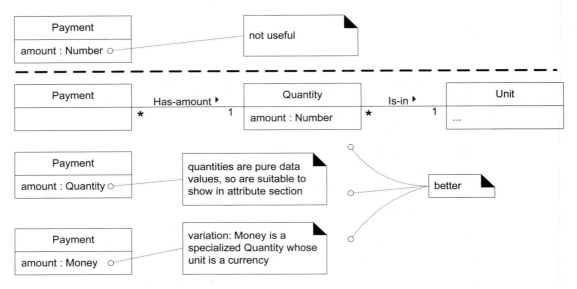

Figure 9.26 Modeling quantities.

9.17 Example: Attributes in the Domain Models

Case Study: NextGen POS

See Figure 9.27. The attributes chosen reflect the information requirements for this iteration—the *Process Sale* cash-only scenarios of this iteration. For example:

CashPayment	*amountTendered*—To determine if sufficient payment was provided, and to calculate change, an amount (also known as "amount tendered") must be captured.
Product-Description	*description*—To show the description on a display or receipt.
	itemId—To look up a *ProductDescription*.
	price—To calculate the sales total, and show the line item price.

Sale	*dateTime*—A receipt normally shows date and time of sale, and this is useful for sales analysis.
SalesLineItem	*quantity*—To record the quantity entered, when there is more than one item in a line item sale (for example, *five* packages of tofu).
Store	*address, name*—The receipt requires the name and address of the store.

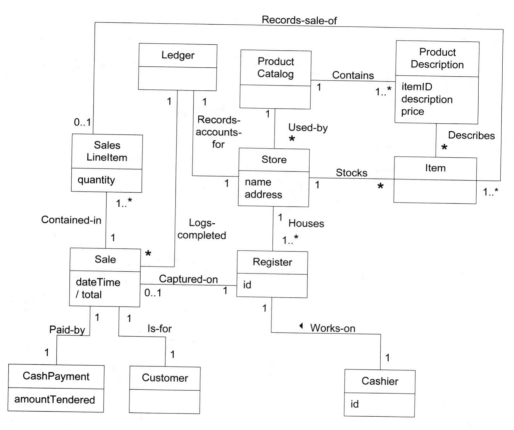

Figure 9.27 NextGen POS partial domain model.

Case Study: Monopoly

See Figure 9.28. The attributes chosen reflect the information requirements for this iteration—the simplified *Play Monopoly Game* scenario of this iteration. For example:

Die	*faceValue*—After rolling the dice, needed to calculate the distance of a move.
Square	*name*—To print the desired trace output.

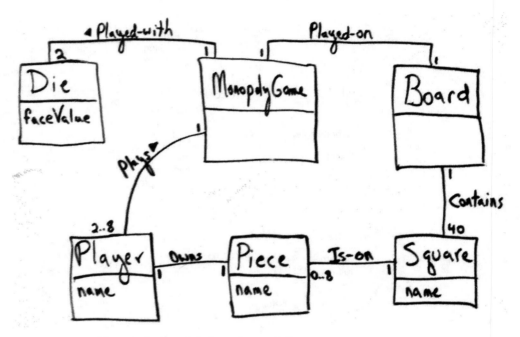

Figure 9.28 Monopoly partial domain model.

9.18   Conclusion: Is the Domain Model Correct?

There is no such thing as a single correct domain model. All models are approximations of the domain we are attempting to understand; the domain model is primarily a tool of understanding and communication among a particular group. A useful domain model captures the essential abstractions and information required to understand the domain in the context of the current requirements, and aids people in understanding the domain—its concepts, terminology, and relationships.

9.19 Process: Iterative and Evolutionary Domain Modeling

Although paradoxically a significant number of pages were devoted to explaining domain modeling, in experienced hands the development of a (partial, evolutionary) model in each iteration may take only 30 minutes. This is further shortened by the use of predefined analysis patterns.

In iterative development, we incrementally evolve a domain model over several iterations. In each, the domain model is limited to the prior and current scenarios under consideration, rather than expanding to a "big bang" waterfall-style model that early on attempts to capture all possible conceptual classes and relationships. For example, this POS iteration is limited to a simplified cash-only *Process Sale* scenario; therefore, a partial domain model will be created to reflect just that—not more.

And to reiterate advice from the start of this chapter:

Guideline

Avoid a waterfall-mindset big-modeling effort to make a thorough or "correct" domain model—it won't ever be either, and such over-modeling efforts lead to *analysis paralysis*, with little or no return on the investment.

Limit domain modeling to no more than a few hours per iteration.

Domain Models Within the UP

elaboration phase
p. 33

As suggested in the example of Table 9.4, the UP Domain Model is usually both started and completed in the elaboration phase.

Discipline	Artifact Iteration→	Incep. I1	Elab. E1..En	Const. C1..Cn	Trans. T1..T2
Business Modeling	***Domain Model***		s		
Requirements	Use-Case Model (SSDs)	s	r		
	Vision	s	r		
	Supplementary Specification	s	r		
	Glossary	s	r		
Design	Design Model		s	r	
	SW Architecture Document		s		
	Data Model		s	r	

Table 9.4 Sample UP artifacts and timing. s - start; r - refine

Inception

Domain models are not strongly motivated in inception, since inception's purpose is not to do a serious investigation, but rather to decide if the project is worth deeper investigation in an elaboration phase.

Elaboration

The Domain Model is primarily created during elaboration iterations, when the need is highest to understand the noteworthy concepts and map some to software classes during design work.

The UP Business Object Model vs. Domain Model

The UP Domain Model is an official variation of the less common UP Business Object Model (BOM). The UP BOM—not to be confused with the many other definitions of a BOM—is a kind of enterprise model that describes the entire business. It may be used when doing business process engineering or reengineering, independent of any one software application (such as the NextGen POS). To quote:

> [The UP BOM] serves as an abstraction of how business workers and business entities need to be related and how they need to collaborate in order to perform the business. [RUP]

The BOM is represented with several different diagrams (class, activity, and sequence) that illustrate how the entire enterprise runs (or should run). It is most useful if doing enterprise-wide business process engineering, but that is a less common activity than creating a single software application.

Consequently, the UP defines the Domain Model as the more commonly created subset artifact or specialization of the BOM. To quote:

> You can choose to develop an "incomplete" business object model, focusing on explaining "things" and products important to a domain. [...] This is often referred to as a domain model. [RUP]

9.20 Recommended Resources

Odell's *Object-Oriented Methods: A Foundation* provides a solid introduction to conceptual domain modeling. Cook and Daniel's *Designing Object Systems* is also useful.

Fowler's *Analysis Patterns* offers worthwhile patterns in domain models and is definitely recommended. Another good book that describes patterns in domain models is Hay's *Data Model Patterns: Conventions of Thought*. Advice from data modeling experts who understand the distinction between pure conceptual models and database schema models can be very useful for domain object modeling.

Java Modeling in Color with UML [CDL99] has much more relevant domain modeling advice than the title suggests. The authors identify common patterns in related types and their associations; the color aspect is really a visualization of the common categories of these types, such as *descriptions* (blue), *roles* (yellow), and *moment-intervals* (pink). Color is used to aid in seeing the patterns.

SYSTEM SEQUENCE DIAGRAMS

In theory, there is no difference between theory
and practice. But, in practice, there is.

—*Jan L.A. van de Snepscheut*

Objectives

- Identify system events.

- Create system sequence diagrams for use case scenarios.

Introduction

A system sequence diagram (SSD) is a fast and easily created artifact that illustrates input and output events related to the systems under discussion. They are input to operation contracts and—most importantly—object design.

The UML contains notation in the form of sequence diagrams to illustrate events from external actors to a system.

What's Next?   Having explored domain modeling, this chapter identifies system operations in an SSD. The next takes these operations and defines their effect on the domain model objects, using a pre- and post-condition operation contract notation.

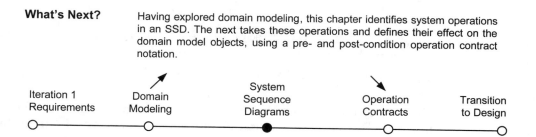

| Iteration 1 Requirements | Domain Modeling | System Sequence Diagrams | Operation Contracts | Transition to Design |

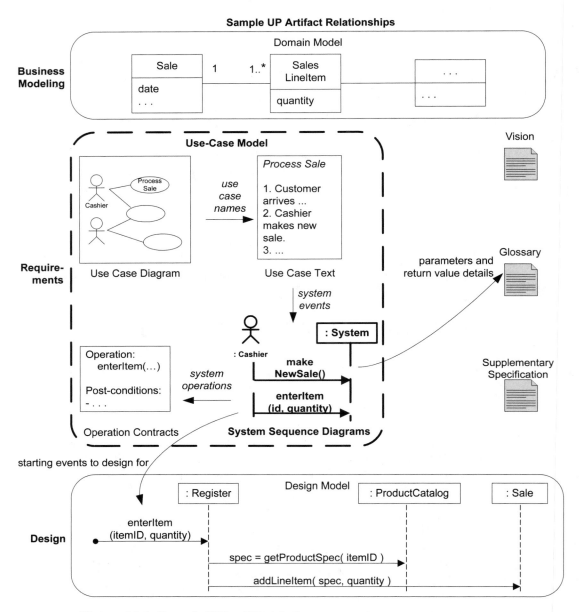

Figure 10.1 Sample UP artifact influence.

UP artifact influence emphasizing system sequence diagrams is shown in Figure 10.1. The use case text and its implied system events are input to SSD creation. The SSD operations (such as *enterItem*) can in turn be analyzed in the operation contracts, detailed in the Glossary, and—most important—serve as the starting point for designing collaborating objects.

10.1 Example: NextGen SSD

An SSD shows, for a particular course of events within a use case, the external actors that interact directly with the system, the system (as a black box), and the system events that the actors generate (see Figure 10.2). Time proceeds downward, and the ordering of events should follow their order in the scenario.

The Figure 10.2 example is for the main success scenario of a cash-only *Process Sale* scenario. It indicates that the cashier generates *makeNewSale, enterItem, endSale,* and *makePayment* system events. These events are implied or suggested by reading through the use case text.

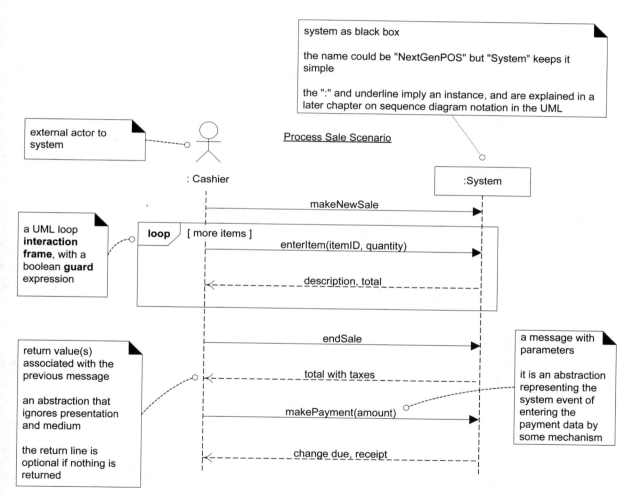

Figure 10.2 SSD for a *Process Sale* scenario.

10.2   What are System Sequence Diagrams?

Use cases describe how external actors interact with the software system we are interested in creating. During this interaction an actor generates **system events** to a system, usually requesting some **system operation** to handle the event. For example, when a cashier enters an item's ID, the cashier is requesting the POS system to record that item's sale (the *enterItem* event). That event initiates an operation upon the system. The use case text *implies* the *enterItem* event, and the SSD makes it concrete and explicit.

The UML includes **sequence diagrams** as a notation that can illustrate actor interactions and the operations initiated by them.

A **system sequence diagram** is a picture that shows, *for one particular scenario of a use case*, the events that external actors generate, their order, and inter-system events. All systems are treated as a black box; the emphasis of the diagram is events that cross the system boundary from actors to systems.

Guideline

Draw an SSD for a main success scenario of each use case, and frequent or complex alternative scenarios.

10.3   Motivation: Why Draw an SSD?

An interesting and useful question in software design is this: *What events are coming in to our system?* Why? Because we have to design the software to handle these events (from the mouse, keyboard, another system, ...) and execute a response. Basically, a software system reacts to three things: 1) external events from actors (humans or computers), 2) timer events, and 3) faults or exceptions (which are often from external sources).

Therefore, it is useful to know what, *precisely*, are the external input events—the **system events**. They are an important part of analyzing system behavior.

You may be familiar with the idea of identifying the messages that go into one software object. But this concept is useful at higher levels of components, including the entire system viewed (abstractly) as one thing or object.

Before proceeding to a detailed design of how a software application will work, it is useful to investigate and define its behavior as a "black box." **System behavior** is a description of *what* a system does, without explaining how it does it. One part of that description is a system sequence diagram. Other parts include the *contracts p. 181*   use cases and system operation contracts (to be discussed later).

10.4 Applying UML: Sequence Diagrams

UML sequence diagrams p. 227

The UML does not define something called a "system" sequence diagram but simply a "sequence diagram." The qualification is used to emphasize its application to systems as black boxes. Later, sequence diagrams will be used in another context—to illustrate the design of interacting software objects to fulfill work.

Loops in Sequence Diagrams

Notice in Figure 10.2 how **interaction frames** are used to show loops in sequence diagrams.

10.5 What is the Relationship Between SSDs and Use Cases?

An SSD shows system events *for one scenario of a use case*, therefore it is generated from inspection of a use case (see Figure 10.3).

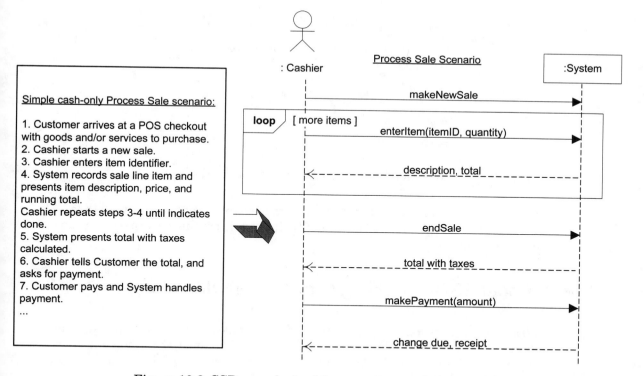

Figure 10.3 SSDs are derived from use cases; they show one scenario.

Applying UML: Should We Show Use Case Text in the SSD?

Not usually. If you name the SSD appropriately, you can indicate the use case; for example, *Process Sale Scenario*.

10.6 How to Name System Events and Operations?

Which is better, *scan(itemID)* or *enterItem(itemID)*?

System events should be expressed at the abstract level of intention rather than in terms of the physical input device.

Thus "enterItem" is better than "scan" (that is, laser scan) because it captures the *intent* of the operation while remaining abstract and noncommittal with respect to design choices about what interface is used to capture the system event. It could by via laser scanner, keyboard, voice input, or anything.

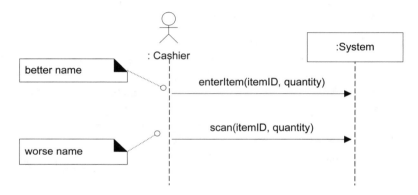

Figure 10.4 Choose event and operation names at an abstract level.

It also improves clarity to start the name of a system event with a verb (add..., enter..., end..., make...), as in Figure 10.4, since it emphasizes these are commands or requests.

10.7 How to Model SSDs Involving Other External Systems?

inter-system SSDs
p. 409

SSDs can also be used to illustrate collaborations between systems, such as between the NextGen POS and the external credit payment authorizer. However, this is deferred until a later iteration in the case study, since this iteration does not include remote systems collaboration.

10.8 What SSD Information to Place in the Glossary?

The elements shown in SSDs (operation name, parameters, return data) are terse. These may need proper explanation so that during design it is clear what is coming in and going out. The Glossary is a great place for these details.

For example, in Figure 10.2, there is a return line containing the description *"change due, receipt."* That's a vague description about the receipt—a complex report. So, the UP Glossary can have a *receipt* entry, that shows sample receipts (perhaps a digital picture), and detailed contents and layout.

Guideline

In general for many artifacts, show details in the Glossary.

10.9 Example: Monopoly SSD

use case text p. 93

The *Play Monopoly Game* use case is simple, as is the main scenario. The observing person initializes with the number of players, and then requests the simulation of play, watching a trace of the output until there is a winner. See Figure 10.5.

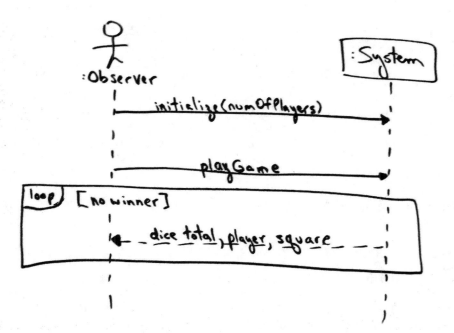

Figure 10.5 SSD for a *Play Monopoly Game* scenario.

10.10   Process: Iterative and Evolutionary SSDs

Don't create SSDs for all scenarios, unless you are using an estimation technique (such as function point counting) that requires identification of all system operations. Rather, draw them only for the scenarios chosen for the next iteration. And, they shouldn't take long to sketch—perhaps a few minutes or a half hour.

SSDs are also very useful when you want to understand the interface and collaborations of existing systems, or to document the architecture.

SSDs Within the UP

SSDs are part of the Use-Case Model—a visualization of the interactions implied in the scenarios of use cases. SSDs were not explicitly mentioned in the original UP description, although the UP creators are aware of and understand the usefulness of such diagrams. SSDs are an example of the many possible skillful and widely used analysis and design artifacts or activities that the UP or RUP documents do not mention. But the UP, being very flexible, encourages the inclusion of any and all artifacts and practices that add value.

UP Phases

Inception—SSDs are not usually motivated in inception, unless you are doing rough estimating (don't expect inception estimating to be reliable) involving a technique that is based on identifying system operations, such as **function points** or **COCOMO II** (see www.ifpug.org).

Elaboration—Most SSDs are created during elaboration, when it is useful to identify the details of the system events to clarify what major operations the system must be designed to handle, write system operation contracts, and possibly to support estimation (for example, macroestimation with unadjusted function points and COCOMO II).

10.11   History and Recommended Resources

Identifying a software system's public operations is a very old need, so variations of system interface diagrams that illustrate the I/O events for a system treated as a black box have been in widespread use for many decades. For example, in telecommunications they have been called call-flow diagrams. They were first popularized in OO methods in the Fusion method [Coleman+94], which provided a detailed example of the relationship of SSDs and system operations to other analysis and design artifacts.

OPERATION CONTRACTS

When ideas fail, words come in very handy.

—*Johann Wolfgang von Goethe*

Objectives

- Define system operations.
- Create contracts for system operations.

Introduction

Use cases or system features are the main ways in the UP to describe system behavior, and are usually sufficient. Sometimes a more detailed or precise description of system behavior has value. Operation contracts use a pre- and post-condition form to describe detailed changes to objects in a domain model, as the result of a system operation. A domain model is the most common OOA model, but operation contracts and state models (introduced on p. 485) can also be useful OOA-related artifacts.

Operation contracts may be considered part of the UP Use-Case Model because they provide more analysis detail on the effect of the system operations implied in the use cases.

What's Next? Having explored SSDs and system operations, this chapter takes the operations and defines their effect on the domain model objects. Then, having finished with analysis for this iteration, the next chapter summarizes the transition to design, a cycle that repeats each iteration.

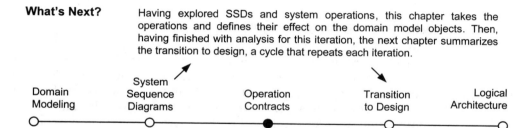

| Domain Modeling | System Sequence Diagrams | Operation Contracts | Transition to Design | Logical Architecture |

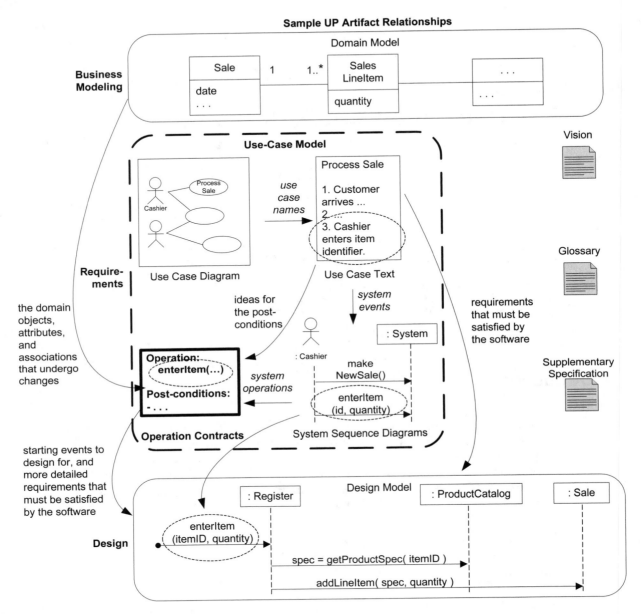

Figure 11.1 Sample UP artifact influence.

UP artifact influence emphasizing operation contracts is shown in Figure 11.1. The prime inputs to the contracts are the system operations identified in SSDs (such as *enterItem*), the domain model, and domain insight from experts. The contracts can in turn serve as input to the object design, as they describe changes that are likely required in the software objects or database.

11.1   Example

Here's an operation contract for the *enterItem* system operation. The critical element is the *postconditions*; the other parts are useful but less important.

Contract CO2: enterItem

Operation:	enterItem(itemID: ItemID, quantity: integer)
Cross References:	Use Cases: Process Sale
Preconditions:	There is a sale underway.
Postconditions:	– A SalesLineItem instance sli was created *(instance creation)*. – sli was associated with the current Sale *(association formed)*. – sli.quantity became quantity *(attribute modification)*. – sli was associated with a ProductDescription, based on itemID match *(association formed)*.

The categorizations such as "*(instance creation)*" are a learning aid, not properly part of the contract.

11.2   Definition: What are the Sections of a Contract?

A description of each section in a contract is shown in the following schema.

Operation:	Name of operation, and parameters
Cross References:	Use cases this operation can occur within
Preconditions:	Noteworthy assumptions about the state of the system or objects in the Domain Model before execution of the operation. These are non-trivial assumptions the reader should be told.
Postconditions:	This is the most important section. The state of objects in the Domain Model after completion of the operation. Discussed in detail in a following section.

11.3   Definition: What is a System Operation?

Operation contracts may be defined for **system operations**—operations that the system as a black box component offers in its public interface. System operations can be identified while sketching SSDs, as in Figure 11.2. To be more precise, the SSDs show **system events**—events or I/O messages relative to the system. Input system events imply the system has system operations to handle the events, just as an OO message (a kind of event or signal) is handled by an OO method (a kind of operation).

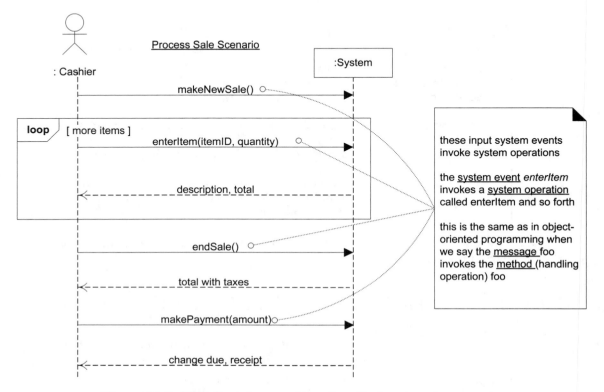

Figure 11.2 SSD. System operations handle input system events.

The entire set of system operations, across all use cases, defines the public **system interface**, viewing the system as a single component or class. In the UML, the system as a whole can be represented as one object of a class named (for example) *System*.

11.4   Definition: Postconditions

Notice that each of the postconditions in the *enterItem* example included a learning aid categorization such as *instance creation* or *association formed*. Here is a key point:

Definition

The **postconditions** describe changes in the state of objects in the domain model. Domain model state changes include instances created, associations formed or broken, and attributes changed.

Postconditions are not actions to be performed during the operation; rather, they are *observations* about the domain model objects that are true when the operation has finished—*after the smoke has cleared*.

To summarize, the postconditions fall into these categories:

- Instance creation and deletion.

- Attribute change of value.

- Associations (to be precise, UML *links*) formed and broken.

Breaking associations is rare. But as an example, consider an operation to allow the deletion of line items. The postcondition could read "The selected *SalesLineItem's* association with the *Sale* was broken." In other domains, when a loan is paid off or someone cancels their membership in something, associations are broken.

Instance deletion postconditions are most rare, because one does not usually care about explicitly enforcing the destruction of a thing in the real world. As an example: In many countries, after a person has declared bankruptcy and seven or ten years have passed, all records of their bankruptcy declaration must be destroyed, by law. Note that this is a conceptual perspective, not implementation. These are not statements about freeing up memory in a computer occupied by software objects.

How are Postconditions Related to the Domain Model?

These postconditions are expressed in the context of the Domain Model objects. What instances can be created?—those from the Domain Model; What associations can be formed?—those in the Domain Model; and so on.

Motivation: Why Postconditions?

First, they aren't always necessary. Most often, the effect of a system operation is relatively clear to the developers by virtue of reading the use case, talking with experts, or their own knowledge. But sometimes more detail and precision is useful. Contracts offer that.

Notice that the postconditions support fine-grained detail and precision in declaring what the outcome of the operation must be. It is also possible to express this level of detail in the use cases, but undesirable—they would be too verbose and low-level detailed.

A contract is an excellent tool of requirements analysis or OOA that describes in great detail the changes required by a system operation (in terms of the domain model objects) without having to describe *how* they are to be achieved.

In other words, the *design* can be deferred, and we can focus on the *analysis* of *what* must happen, rather than *how* it is to be accomplished.

Consider these postconditions:

Postconditions:	– A SalesLineItem instance sli was created (instance creation). – sli was associated with the current Sale (association formed). – sli.quantity became quantity (attribute modification). – sli was associated with a ProductDescription, based on itemID match (association formed).

No comment is made about how a *SalesLineItem* instance is created, or associated with a *Sale*. This could be a statement about writing on bits of paper and stapling them together, using Java technologies to create software objects and connect them, or inserting rows in a relational database.

Guideline: How to Write a Postcondition?

Express postconditions in the past tense to emphasize they are *observations* about state changes that arose from an operation, not an action to happen. That's why they are called **post**conditions! For example:

■ (better) A *SalesLineItem* **was** created.

rather than

■ (worse) Create a *SalesLineItem*, or, A *SalesLineItem* is created.

Analogy: The Spirit of Postconditions: The Stage and Curtain

Why write postconditions in the past tense? Think about them using the following image:

The system and its objects are presented on a theatre stage.

1. Before the operation, take a picture of the stage.

2. Close the curtains on the stage, and apply the system operation (*background noise of clanging, screams, and screeches...*).

3. Open the curtains and take a second picture.

4. Compare the before and after pictures, and express as postconditions the changes in the state of the stage (*A SalesLineItem was created...*).

Guideline: How Complete Should Postconditions Be? Agile vs. Heavy Analysis

Contracts may not be useful. This question is discussed in a subsequent section. But assuming some are useful, generating a complete and detailed set of post-conditions for all system operations is not likely—or necessary. In the spirit of Agile Modeling, treat their creation as an initial best guess, with the understanding they will not be complete and that "perfect" complete specifications are rarely possible or believable.

But understanding that light analysis is realistic and skillful doesn't mean to abandon a little investigation before programming—that's the other extreme of misunderstanding.

11.5   Example: *enterItem* Postconditions

The following section dissects the motivation for the postconditions of the *enterItem* system operation.

Instance Creation and Deletion

After the *itemID* and *quantity* of an item have been entered, what new object should have been created? A *SalesLineItem*. Thus:

- A *SalesLineItem* instance *sli* was created (instance creation).

Note the naming of the instance. This name will simplify references to the new instance in other post-condition statements.

Attribute Modification

After the itemID and quantity of an item have been entered by the cashier, what attributes of new or existing objects should have been modified? The *quantity* of the *SalesLineItem* should have become equal to the *quantity* parameter. Thus:

- *sli.quantity* became *quantity* (attribute modification).

Associations Formed and Broken

After the *itemID* and *quantity* of an item have been entered by the cashier, what associations between new or existing objects should have been formed or broken? The new *SalesLineItem* should have been related to its *Sale*, and related to its *ProductDescription*. Thus:

- *sli* was associated with the current *Sale* (association formed).

■ *sli* was associated with a *ProductDescription*, based on *itemID* match (association formed).

Note the informal indication that it forms a relationship with a *ProductDescription*—the one whose *itemID* matches the parameter. More fancy and formal language approaches are possible, such as using the Object Constraint Language (OCL). Recommendation: Keep it plain and simple.

11.6   Guideline: Should We Update the Domain Model?

It's common during the creation of the contracts to discover the need to record new conceptual classes, attributes, or associations in the domain model. Do not be limited to the prior definition of the domain model; enhance it as you make new discoveries while thinking through operation contracts.

> In iterative and evolutionary methods (and reflecting the reality of software projects), all analysis and design artifacts are considered partial and imperfect, and evolve in response to new discoveries.

11.7   Guideline: When Are Contracts Useful?

In the UP, the use cases are the main repository of requirements for the project. They may provide most or all of the detail necessary to know what to do in the design, in which case, contracts are not helpful. However, there are situations where the details and complexity of required state changes are awkward or too detailed to capture in use cases.

For example, consider an airline reservation system and the system operation *addNewReservation*. The complexity is very high regarding all the domain objects that must be changed, created, and associated. These fine-grained details *can* be written up in the use case, but it will make it extremely detailed (for example, noting each attribute in all the objects that must change).

Observe that the postcondition format offers and encourages a very precise, analytical language that supports detailed thoroughness.

If developers can comfortably understand what to do without them, then avoid writing contracts.

This case study shows more contracts than are necessary—for education. In practice, most of the details they record are obviously inferable from the use case text. On the other hand, "obvious" is a slippery concept!

11.8   Guideline: How to Create and Write Contracts

Apply the following advice to create contracts:

1. Identify system operations from the SSDs.

2. For system operations that are complex and perhaps subtle in their results, or which are not clear in the use case, construct a contract.

3. To describe the postconditions, use the following categories:

   ○ instance creation and deletion

   ○ attribute modification

   ○ associations formed and broken

Writing Contracts

- As mentioned, write the postconditions in a declarative, passive past tense form (*was ...*) to emphasize the *observation* of a change rather than a design of how it is going to be achieved. For example:

   ○ (better) A *SalesLineItem* **was** created.

   ○ (worse) Create a *SalesLineItem*.

- Remember to establish an association between existing objects or those newly created. For example, it is not enough that a new *SalesLineItem* instance is created when the *enterItem* operation occurs. After the operation is complete, it should also be true that the newly created instance was associated with *Sale*; thus:

   ○ The *SalesLineItem* was associated with the *Sale* (association formed).

What's the Most Common Mistake?

The most common problem is forgetting to include the *forming of associations*. Particularly when new instances are created, it is very likely that associations to several objects need be established. Don't forget!

11.9   Example: NextGen POS Contracts

System Operations of the Process Sale Use Case

Contract CO1: makeNewSale

Operation:	makeNewSale()
Cross References:	Use Cases: Process Sale
Preconditions:	none
Postconditions:	– A Sale instance s was created (instance creation).
	– s was associated with a Register (association formed).
	– Attributes of s were initialized.

Note the vague description in the last postcondition. If understandable, it's fine.

On a project, all these particular postconditions are so obvious from the use case that the *makeNewSale* contract should probably not be written.

Recall one of the guiding principles of healthy process and the UP: Keep it as light as possible, and avoid all artifacts unless they really add value.

Contract CO2: enterItem

Operation:	enterItem(itemID: ItemID, quantity: integer)
Cross References:	Use Cases: Process Sale
Preconditions:	There is a sale underway.
Postconditions:	– A SalesLineItem instance sli was created (instance creation).
	– sli was associated with the current Sale (association formed).
	– sli.quantity became quantity (attribute modification).
	– sli was associated with a ProductDescription, based on itemID match (association formed).

Contract CO3: endSale

Operation:	endSale()
Cross References:	Use Cases: Process Sale
Preconditions:	There is a sale underway.
Postconditions:	– Sale.isComplete became true (attribute modification).

Contract CO4: makePayment

Operation:	makePayment(amount: Money)
Cross References:	Use Cases: Process Sale
Preconditions:	There is a sale underway.
Postconditions:	– A Payment instance p was created (instance creation).
	– p.amountTendered became amount (attribute modification).
	– p was associated with the current Sale (association formed).
	– The current Sale was associated with the Store (association formed); (to add it to the historical log of completed sales)

Changes to the POS Domain Model

There is at least one point suggested by these contracts that is not yet represented in the domain model: completion of item entry to the sale. The *endSale* specification modifies it, and it is probably a good idea later during design work for the *makePayment* operation to test it, to disallow payments until a sale is complete (meaning, no more items to add).

One way to represent this information is with an *isComplete* attribute in the *Sale*:

Sale
isComplete: Boolean dateTime

There are alternatives, especially considered during design work. One technique is called the **State pattern**. Another is the use of "session" objects that track the state of a session and disallow out-of-order operations; this will be explored later.

11.10   Example: Monopoly Contracts

I'll use this case study to emphasize that many analysis artifacts aren't always needed, including contracts. The UP encourages *avoiding* creating an artifact unless it addresses a risk or solves a real problem. People who know the rules of the game from experience as a child or teenager (most people, it seems) can implement it without looking at many written details.

11.11   Applying UML: Operations, Contracts, and the OCL

What's the relationship between contracts in this chapter and the UML?

The UML formally defines **operations**. To quote:

> An operation is a specification of a transformation or query that an object may be called to execute. [RJB99]

For example, the elements of an interface are operations, in UML terms. An operation is an abstraction, not an implementation. By contrast, a **method** (in the UML) is an implementation of an operation. To quote:

> [A method is] the implementation of an operation. It specifies the algorithm or procedure associated with an operation. [OMG03a]

In the UML metamodel, an operation has a **signature** (name and parameters), and most importantly in this context, is associated with a set of UML **Constraint** objects classified as preconditions and postconditions that specify the semantics of the operation.

To summarize: The UML defines operation semantics via constraints, which are specifiable in the pre- and post-condition style. Note that, as emphasized in this chapter, a UML operation specification can *not* show an algorithm or solution, but only the state changes or effects of the operation.

In addition to using contracts to specify public operations of the entire *System* (that is, *system* operations), contracts can be applied to operations at any level of granularity: the public operations (or interface) of a subsystem, a component, an abstract class, and so forth. For example, operations can be defined for a single software class such as a *Stack*. The coarse-grained operations discussed in this chapter belong to a *System* class representing the overall system as a black box component, but in the UML operations can belong to any class or interface, all with pre- and post-conditions.

Operation Contracts Expressed with the OCL

The pre- and post-condition format in this chapter is informal natural language—perfectly acceptable in the UML, and desirable to be easily understood.

But also associated with the UML is a formal, rigorous language called the Object Constraint Language (**OCL**) [WK99], which can be used to express constraints of UML operations.

Guideline

Unless there is a compelling practical reason to require people to learn and use the OCL, keep things simple and use natural language. Although I'm sure there are real—and useful—applications, I've never seen a project that used OCL, even though I visit many clients and projects.

The OCL defines an official format for specifying pre- and postconditions for operations, as demonstrated in this fragment:

```
System::makeNewSale( )
   pre : <statements in OCL>
   post : …
```

Further OCL details are beyond the scope of this introduction.

11.12   Process: Operation Contracts Within the UP

A pre- and postcondition contract is a well-known style to specify an operation in the UML. In the UML, operations exists at many levels, from *System* down to fine-grained classes, such as *Sale*. Operation contracts for the *System* level are part of the Use-Case Model, although they were not formally highlighted in the original RUP or UP documentation; their inclusion in this model was verified with the RUP authors.[1]

Phases

Inception—Contracts are not motivated during inception—they are too detailed.

Elaboration—If used at all, most contracts will be written during elaboration, when most use cases are written. Only write contracts for the most complex and subtle system operations.

11.13   History

Operation contracts come out of the formal specifications area in computer science, originally from the prolific Tony Hoare. Hoare was working in industry in the mid-1960s to develop an ALGOL 60 compiler and read Bertrand Russell's *Introduction to Mathematical Philosophy*, which introduced him to the idea of axiomatic theory and assertions. He realized that computer programs could be expressed with assertions (pre- and post-conditions) relative to the results that were expected at the launch and termination of a program. In 1968 he joined academia, and his idea spread, along with other researchers' theories of formal specifications.

In 1974 at the IBM Lab in Vienna a PL/1 compiler was being developed, and the researchers desired an unambiguous formal specification of the language. Out of this need VDL—the Vienna Definition Language—was born by Peter Lucas. VDL borrowed the pre- and post-condition assertion form earlier explored by Hoare and Russel. VDL eventually evolved into the language used within the

---

1. Private communication.

Vienna Definition Method (**VDM**), a method that applied operation contract formal specifications and rigorous proof theory [BJ78].

In the 1980s, Bertrand Meyer—not surprisingly yet another compiler writer (the OO language Eiffel)—started to promote the use of pre- and post-condition assertions as first-class elements within his Eiffel language, to be applied to OOA/D. He contributed to a much wider awareness of formal specifications and operation contracts in his popular book *Object-Oriented Software Construction*, in which he also proposed the approach as a method called **Design by Contract** (DBC). In DBC, contracts are written for operations of fine-grained software class operations, not specifically the public operations of the overall "system." In addition, DBC promotes an *invariant* section, common in thorough contract specifications. Invariants define things that must not change state before and after the operation has executed. Invariants have not been used in this chapter for the sake of simplicity.

In the early 1990s, Grady Booch briefly discussed applying contracts to object operations in his **Booch Method**. Also, Derek Coleman and colleagues at HP Labs borrowed the operation contract idea and applied it to OOA and domain modeling, making it part of the influential OOA/D **Fusion method** [Coleman+94].

Programming Language Support for Contracts

Some languages, such as Eiffel, have first-class support for invariants and pre- and post-conditions. Using attributes, Javadoc tags, or pre-compilers, similar facilities can be provided in Java and C#, for example.

11.14   Recommended Resources

Many examples of OOA-oriented system operation contracts can be found in *Object-Oriented Development: The Fusion Method* by Coleman, et. al. *Object-Oriented Software Construction* by Meyer shows many program-level contract examples in Eiffel. Within the UML, operation contracts can also be specified more rigorously in the Object Constraint Language (OCL), for which Warmer and Kleppe's *The Object Constraint Language: Precise Modeling with UML* is recommended.

REQUIREMENTS TO DESIGN— ITERATIVELY

Hardware, n.: The parts of a computer system that can be kicked.

—*anonymous*

Objectives

- Quickly motivate the transition to design activities.
- Contrast the importance of object design skill versus UML notation knowledge.

Introduction

So far, the case studies have emphasized analysis of the requirements and objects. If following the UP guidelines, perhaps 10% of the requirements were investigated in inception, and a slightly deeper investigation was started in this first iteration of elaboration. The following chapters are a shift in emphasis toward designing a solution for this iteration in terms of collaborating software objects.

What's Next?   Having explored operation contracts, this chapter concludes the analysis work, and summarizes the transition to design, a cycle that repeats each iteration. The next chapter introduces a logical design architecture for the case studies, based on the Layers pattern.

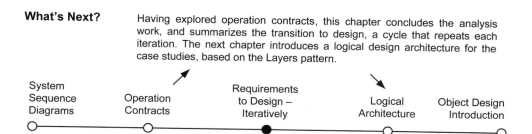

12.1   Iteratively Do the Right Thing, Do the Thing Right

The requirements and object-oriented analysis has focused on learning to *do the right thing*; that is, understanding some of the outstanding goals for the case studies, and related rules and constraints. By contrast, the following design work will stress *do the thing right*; that is, skillfully designing a solution to satisfy the requirements for this iteration.

In iterative development, a transition from primarily a requirements or analysis focus to primarily a design and implementation focus will occur in each iteration. Early iterations will spend relatively more time on analysis activities. As the vision and specifications start to stabilize based on early programming, test, and feedback, in later iterations it is common that analysis lessens; there's more focus on just building the solution.

12.2   Provoking Early Change

It is natural and healthy to discover and change some requirements during the design and implementation work, especially in the early iterations. Iterative and evolutionary methods "embrace change"—although we try to *provoke* that inevitable change in *early* iterations, so that we have a more stable goal (and estimate and schedule) for the later iterations. Early programming, tests, and demos help *provoke* the inevitable changes early on. Take note! This simple idea lies at the heart of why iterative development works.

The discovery of changing specifications will both clarify the purpose of the design work of this iteration and refine the requirements understanding for future iterations. Over the course of these early elaboration iterations, the requirements discovery should stabilize, so that by the end of elaboration, perhaps 80% of the requirements are reliably defined—defined and refined as a result of feedback, early programming and testing, rather than speculation, as occurs in a waterfall method.

12.3   Didn't All That Analysis and Modeling Take Weeks To Do?

After many chapters of detailed discussion, it must surely seem like the prior modeling would take weeks of effort. Not so!

When one is comfortable with the skills of use case writing, domain modeling, and so forth, the duration to do all the actual modeling that has been explored so far is realistically just *a few* hours or days.

However, that does not mean that only a few days have passed since the start of the project. Many other activities, such as proof-of-concept programming, finding resources (people, software, …), planning, setting up the environment, and so on, could consume a few weeks of preparation.

LOGICAL ARCHITECTURE AND UML PACKAGE DIAGRAMS

0x2B | ~0x2B

—Hamlet

Objectives

- Introduce a logical architecture using layers.
- Illustrate the logical architecture using UML package diagrams.

Introduction

First, to set the expectation level: This is a very short *introduction* to the topic of logical architecture, a fairly large topic. Learn more starting on p. 559.

Now that we have transitioned from analysis-oriented work to software design, let's start with the large-scale. At this level, the design of a typical OO system is based on several architectural layers, such as a UI layer, an application logic (or "domain") layer, and so forth. This chapter briefly explores a logical layered architecture and related UML notation.

What's Next? Having transitioned to design for this iteration, this chapter introduces a logical design architecture. The next chapter summarizes object design: static and dynamic modeling, and the relative importance of design skill over UML notation skill.

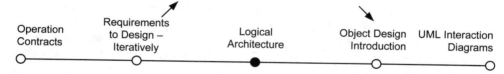

| Operation Contracts | Requirements to Design – Iteratively | Logical Architecture | Object Design Introduction | UML Interaction Diagrams |

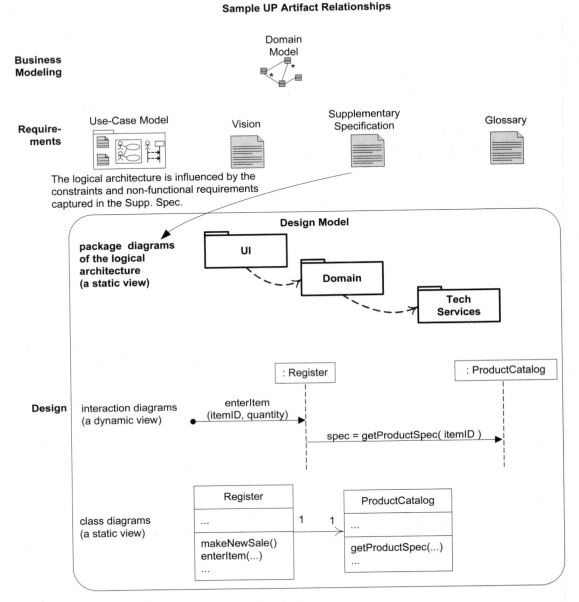

Figure 13.1 Sample UP artifact influence.

UP artifact influence, emphasizing the logical architecture (LA), is shown in Figure 13.1. UML package diagrams may illustrate the LA as part of the Design Model—and also be summarized as a view in the Software Architecture Document. The prime input is the architectural forces captured in the Supplementary Specification. The LA defines the packages within which software classes are defined.

13.1 Example

Figure 13.2 shows a partial layered, logical architecture drawn with UML **package diagram** notation.

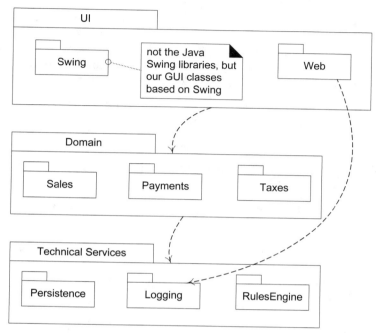

Figure 13.2 Layers shown with UML package diagram notation.

13.2 What is the Logical Architecture? And Layers?

The **logical architecture** is the large-scale organization of the software classes into packages (or namespaces), subsystems, and layers. It's called the *logical* architecture because there's no decision about how these elements are deployed across different operating system processes or across physical computers in a network (these latter decisions are part of the **deployment architecture**).

A **layer** is a very coarse-grained grouping of classes, packages, or subsystems that has cohesive responsibility for a major aspect of the system. Also, layers are organized such that "higher" layers (such as the UI layer) call upon services of "lower" layers, but not normally vice versa. Typically layers in an OO system include:

- **User Interface**.

- **Application Logic and Domain Objects**—software objects representing domain concepts (for example, a software class *Sale*) that fulfill application requirements, such as calculating a sale total.

- **Technical Services**—general purpose objects and subsystems that provide supporting technical services, such as interfacing with a database or error logging. These services are usually application-independent and reusable across several systems.

In a **strict layered architecture**, a layer only calls upon the services of the layer directly below it. This design is common in network protocol stacks, but not in information systems, which usually have a **relaxed layered architecture**, in which a higher layer calls upon several lower layers. For example, the UI layer may call upon its directly subordinate application logic layer, and also upon elements of a lower technical service layer, for logging and so forth.

A logical architecture doesn't have to be organized in layers. But it's *very* common, and hence, introduced at this time.

13.3   What Layers are the Focus in the Case Studies?

case studies p. 41   To reiterate a point made when the case studies were introduced:

> Although OO technology can be applied at all levels,
> this introduction to OOA/D focuses on the *core application logic*
> *(or "domain") layer*, with some secondary discussion of the other layers.

Exploring design of the other layers (such as the UI layer) will focus on the design of their interface to the application logic layer.

The discussion on p. 41 explains, but in brief, the other layers tend to be technology dependent (for example, very specific to Java or .NET), and in any case the OO design lessons learned in the context of the application logic (domain) layer are applicable to all other layers or components.

13.4   What is Software Architecture?

I touched on the logical and deployment architectures, so now is a good time to introduce a definition for **software architecture**. Here's one:

> An architecture is the set of significant decisions about the organization of a software system, the selection of the structural elements and their interfaces by which the system is composed, together with their behavior as specified in the collaborations among those elements, the composition of these structural and behavioral elements into progressively larger subsystems, and the architectural style that guides this organization—these elements and their interfaces, their collaborations, and their composition. [BRJ99]

Regardless of the definition (and there are many) the common theme in all software architecture definitions is that it has to do with the large scale—the Big Ideas in the motivations, constraints, organization, patterns, responsibilities, and connections of a system (or a system of systems).

13.5   Applying UML: Package Diagrams

UML package diagrams are often used to illustrate the logical architecture of a system—the layers, subsystems, packages (in the Java sense), etc. A layer can be modeled as a UML package; for example, the UI layer modeled as a package named UI.

A UML package diagram provides a way to group elements. A UML package can group anything: classes, other packages, use cases, and so on. Nesting packages is very common. A UML package is a more general concept than simply a Java package or .NET namespace, though a UML package can represent those—and more.

The package name may be placed on the tab if the package shows inner members, or on the main folder, if not.

It is common to want to show dependency (a coupling) between packages so that developers can see the large-scale coupling in the system. The UML **dependency line** is used for this, a dashed arrowed line with the arrow pointing towards the depended-on package.

A UML package represents a **namespace** so that, for example, a *Date* class may be defined in two packages. If you need to provide **fully-qualified names**, the UML notation is, for example, *java::util::Date* in the case that there was an outer package named "java" with a nested package named "util" with a *Date* class.

The UML provides alternate notations to illustrate outer and inner nested packages. Sometimes it is awkward to draw an outer package box around inner packages. Alternatives are shown in Figure 13.3.

UML Tools: Reverse-engineer Package Diagrams from Code

During early development, we may sketch a UML package diagram and then organize our code according to these package sketches. Over time, the code base grows and we spend more time programming and less on modeling or UML diagrams. At that point, a great use for a UML CASE tool is to reverse-engineer the source code and generate a package diagram automatically.

This practice is enhanced if we use the naming conventions on p. 204 suggested for code packages.

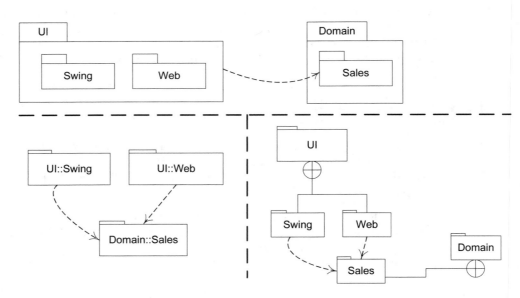

Figure 13.3 Alternate UML approaches to show package nesting, using embedded packages, UML fully-qualified names, and the circle-cross symbol.

13.6   Guideline: Design with Layers

The essential ideas of using layers [BMRSS96] are simple:

- Organize the large-scale logical structure of a system into discrete layers of distinct, related responsibilities, with a clean, cohesive separation of concerns such that the "lower" layers are low-level and general services, and the higher layers are more application specific.

- Collaboration and coupling is from higher to lower layers; lower-to-higher layer coupling is avoided.

Some more design issues are covered later, starting on p. 559. The idea is described as the **Layers pattern** in [BMRSS96] and produces a **layered architecture**. It has been applied and written about so often as a pattern that the *Pattern Almanac 2000* [Rising00] lists over 100 patterns that are variants of or related to the Layers pattern.

Using layers helps address several problems:

- Source code changes are rippling throughout the system—many parts of the systems are highly coupled.

- Application logic is intertwined with the user interface, so it cannot be reused with a different interface or distributed to another processing node.

- Potentially general technical services or business logic is intertwined with more application-specific logic, so it cannot be reused, distributed to another node, or easily replaced with a different implementation.

- There is high coupling across different areas of concern. It is thus difficult to divide the work along clear boundaries for different developers.

The purpose and number of layers varies across applications and application domains (information systems, operating systems, and so forth). Applied to information systems, typical layers are illustrated and explained in Figure 13.4.

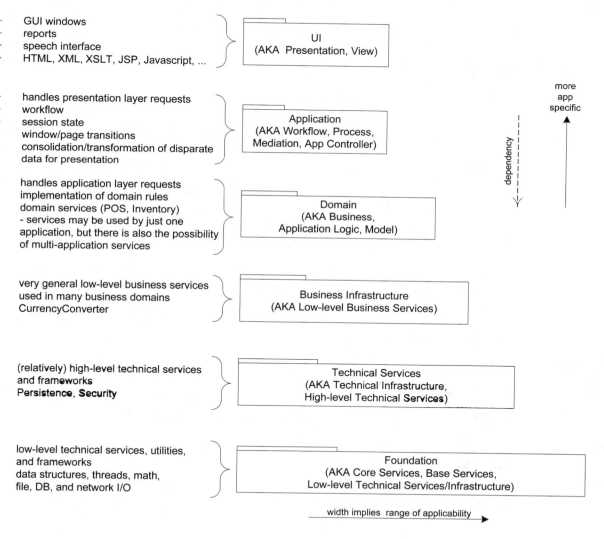

Figure 13.4 Common layers in an information system logical architecture.[1]

The *Application* layer in Figure 13.4 is discussed on p. 567.

Benefits of Using Layers

- In general, there is a separation of concerns, a separation of high from low-level services, and of application-specific from general services. This reduces coupling and dependencies, improves cohesion, increases reuse potential, and increases clarity.

- Related complexity is encapsulated and decomposable.

- Some layers can be replaced with new implementations. This is generally not possible for lower-level Technical Service or Foundation layers (e.g., *java.util*), but may be possible for UI, Application, and Domain layers.

- Lower layers contain reusable functions.

- Some layers (primarily the Domain and Technical Services) can be distributed.

- Development by teams is aided because of the logical segmentation.

Guideline: Cohesive Responsibilities; Maintain a Separation of Concerns

The responsibilities of the objects in a layer should be strongly related to each other and should not be mixed with responsibilities of other layers. For example, objects in the UI layer should focus on UI work, such as creating windows and widgets, capturing mouse and keyboard events, and so forth. Objects in the application logic or "domain" layer should focus on application logic, such as calculating a sales total or taxes, or moving a piece on a game board.

UI objects should not do application logic. For example, a Java Swing *JFrame* (window) object should not contain logic to calculate taxes or move a game piece. And on the other hand, application logic classes should not trap UI mouse or keyboard events. That would violate a clear **separation of concerns** and maintaining **high cohesion**—basic architectural principles.

high cohesion
p. 314

Model-View p. 209   Later chapters will explore these important principles, plus the **Model-View Separation Principle**, in greater detail.

Code: Mapping Code Organization to Layers and UML Packages

Most popular OO languages (Java, C#, C++, Python, ...) provide support for packages (called namespaces in C# and C++).

Here's an example, using Java, for mapping UML packages to code. The layers and packages illustrated in Figure 13.2 can map to Java package names as follows. Notice that the layer name is used as a section of the Java package name:

---

1. The width of the package is used to communicate range of applicability in this diagram, but this is not a general UML practice. AKA means Also known As.

```
// --- UI Layer

com.mycompany.nextgen.ui.swing
com.mycompany.nextgen.ui.web


// --- DOMAIN Layer

    // packages specific to the NextGen project
com.mycompany.nextgen.domain.sales
com.mycompany.nextgen.domain.payments


// --- TECHNICAL SERVICES Layer

    // our home-grown persistence (database) access layer
com.mycompany.service.persistence

    // third party
org.apache.log4j
org.apache.soap.rpc

// --- FOUNDATION Layer

    // foundation packages that our team creates
com.mycompany.util
```

Notice that, to support cross-project reuse, we avoided using a specific application qualifier ("nextgen") in the package names unless necessary. The UI packages are related to the NextGen POS application, so they are qualified with the application name *com.mycompany.nextgen.ui.**. But the utilities we write could be shared across many projects, hence the package name *com.mycompany.utils*, not *com.mycompany.nextgen.utils*.

UML Tools: Reverse-engineer Package Diagrams from Code

As mentioned earlier, a great use for a UML CASE tool is to reverse-engineer the source code and generate a package diagram automatically. This practice is enhanced if you use the recommended naming conventions in code. For example, if you include the partial name ".ui." in all packages for the UI layer, then the UML CASE tool will automatically group and nest sub-packages under a "ui" package, and you can see the layered architecture in both code and package diagram.

Definition: Domain Layer vs. Application Logic Layer; Domain Objects

> **This section describes a simple but key concept in OO design!**

A typical software system has UI logic and application logic, such as GUI widget creation and tax calculations. Now, here's a key question:

> How do we design the application logic with objects?

We could create one class called *XYZ* and put all the methods, for all the required logic, in that one class. It could technically work (though be a nightmare to understand and maintain), but it isn't the recommended approach in the spirit of OO thinking.

So, what is the recommended approach? Answer: To create software objects with names and information similar to the real-world domain, and assign application logic responsibilities to them. For example, in the real world of POS, there are sales and payments. So, in software, we create a *Sale* and *Payment* class, and give them application logic responsibilities. This kind of software object is called a **domain object**. It represents a thing in the problem domain space, and has related application or business logic, for example, a *Sale* object being able to calculate its total.

Designing objects this way leads to the application logic layer being more accurately called the **domain layer** of the architecture—the layer that contains domain objects to handle application logic work.

What's the Relationship Between the Domain Layer and Domain Model?

This is another key point: There's a relationship between the domain model and the domain layer. We look to the domain model (which is a visualization of noteworthy domain concepts) for inspiration for the names of classes in the domain layer. See Figure 13.5.

The domain layer is part of the software and the domain model is part of the conceptual-perspective analysis—they aren't the same thing. But by creating a domain layer with inspiration from the domain model, we achieve a **lower representational gap**, between the real-world domain, and our software design. For example, a *Sale* in the UP Domain Model helps inspire us to consider creating a software *Sale* class in the domain layer of the UP Design Model.

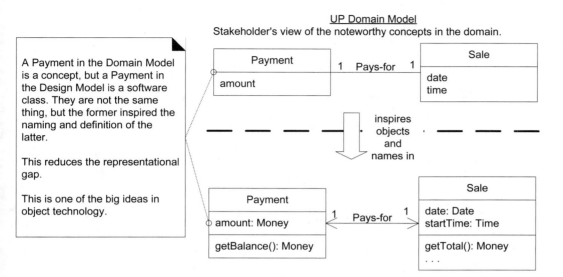

UP Domain Model
Stakeholder's view of the noteworthy concepts in the domain.

A Payment in the Domain Model is a concept, but a Payment in the Design Model is a software class. They are not the same thing, but the former inspired the naming and definition of the latter.

This reduces the representational gap.

This is one of the big ideas in object technology.

Domain layer of the architecture in the UP Design Model
The object-oriented developer has taken inspiration from the real world domain in creating software classes.

Therefore, the representational gap between how stakeholders conceive the domain, and its representation in software, has been lowered.

Figure 13.5 Domain layer and domain model relationship.

Definition: Tiers, Layers, and Partitions

The original notion of a **tier** in architecture was a logical layer, not a physical node, but the word has become widely used to mean a physical processing node (or cluster of nodes), such as the "client tier" (the client computer). This book will avoid the term for clarity, but bear this in mind when reading architecture literature.

The **layers** of an architecture are said to represent the vertical slices, while **partitions** represent a horizontal division of relatively parallel subsystems of a layer. For example, the *Technical Services* layer may be divided into partitions such as *Security* and *Reporting* (Figure 13.6).

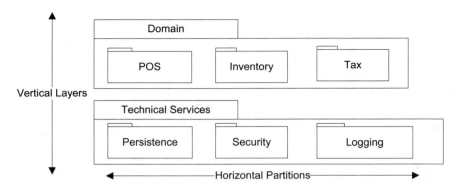

Figure 13.6 Layers and partitions.

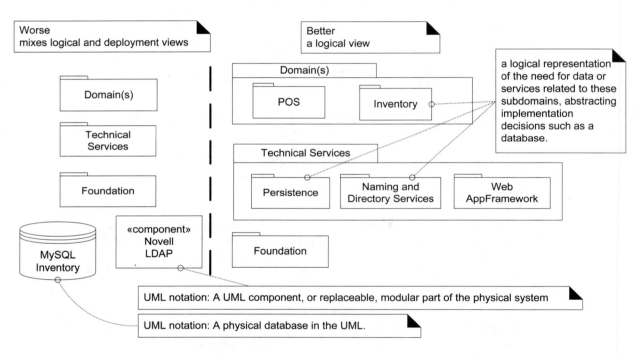

Figure 13.7 Mixing views of the architecture.

Guideline: Don't Show External Resources as the Bottom Layer

Most systems rely on external resources or services, such as a MySQL inventory database and a Novell LDAP naming and directory service. These are *physical* implementation components, not a layer in the *logical* architecture.

Showing external resources such as a particular database in a layer "below" the Foundation layer (for example) mixes up the logical view and the deployment views of the architecture.

Rather, in terms of the logical architecture and its layers, access to a particular set of persistent data (such as inventory data) can be viewed as a sub-domain of the *Domain* Layer—the *Inventory* sub-domain. And the general services that provide access to databases may be viewed as a Technical Service partition—the Persistence service. See Figure 13.7.

13.7   Guideline: The Model-View Separation Principle

What kind of visibility should other packages have to the UI layer? How should non-window classes communicate with windows?

Guideline: Model-View Separation Principle

This principle has at least two parts:

1. Do not connect or couple non-UI objects directly to UI objects. For example, don't let a *Sale* software object (a non-UI "domain" object) have a reference to a Java Swing *JFrame* window object. Why? Because the windows are related to a particular application, while (ideally) the non-windowing objects may be reused in new applications or attached to a new interface.

2. Do not put application logic (such as a tax calculation) in the UI object methods. UI objects should only initialize UI elements, receive UI events (such as a mouse click on a button), and delegate requests for application logic on to non-UI objects (such as domain objects).

---

*domain layer object
p. 206*

In this context, **model** is a synonym for the domain layer of objects (it's an old OO term from the late 1970s). **View** is a synonym for UI objects, such as windows, Web pages, applets, and reports.

The **Model-View Separation** principle[2] states that model (domain) objects should not have *direct* knowledge of view (UI) objects, at least as view objects. So, for example, a *Register* or *Sale* object should not directly send a message to a GUI window object *ProcessSaleFrame*, asking it to display something, change color, close, and so forth.

---

2. This is a key principle in the pattern *Model-View-Controller* (MVC). MVC was originally a small-scale Smalltalk-80 pattern, and related data objects (models), GUI widgets (views), and mouse and keyboard event handlers (controllers). More recently, the term "MVC" has been coopted by the distributed design community to also apply on a large-scale architectural level. The Model is the Domain Layer, the View is the UI Layer, and the Controllers are the workflow objects in the Application layer.

Observer p. 463

A legitimate relaxation of this principle is the Observer pattern, where the domain objects send messages to UI objects viewed only in terms of an interface such as *PropertyListener* (a common Java interface for this situation). Then, the domain object doesn't know that the UI object is a UI object—it doesn't know its concrete window class. It only knows the object as something that implements the *PropertyListener* interface.

A further part of this principle is that the domain classes encapsulate the information and behavior related to application logic. The window classes are relatively thin; they are responsible for input and output, and catching GUI events, but *do not* maintain application data or directly provide application logic. For example, a Java *JFrame* window should *not* have a method that does a tax calculation. A Web JSP page should *not* contain logic to calculate the tax. These UI elements should delegate to non-UI elements for such responsibilities.

The motivation for Model-View Separation includes:

- To support cohesive model definitions that focus on the domain processes, rather than on user interfaces.

- To allow separate development of the model and user interface layers.

- To minimize the impact of requirements changes in the interface upon the domain layer.

- To allow new views to be easily connected to an existing domain layer, without affecting the domain layer.

- To allow multiple simultaneous views on the same model object, such as both a tabular and business chart view of sales information.

- To allow execution of the model layer independent of the user interface layer, such as in a message-processing or batch-mode system.

- To allow easy porting of the model layer to another user interface framework.

13.8 What's the Connection Between SSDs, System Operations, and Layers?

During analysis work, we sketched some SSDs for use case scenarios. We identified input events from external actors into the system, calling upon system operations such as *makeNewSale* and *enterItem*.

The SSDs illustrate these system operations, but hide the specific UI objects. Nevertheless, normally it will be objects in the UI layer of the system that capture these system operation requests, usually with a rich client GUI or Web page.

In a well-designed layered architecture that supports high cohesion and a separation of concerns, the UI layer objects will then forward—or delegate—the request from the UI layer onto the domain layer for handling.

Now, here's the key point:

> The messages sent from the UI layer to the domain
> layer will be the messages illustrated on the SSDs, such as *enterItem*.

For example, in Java Swing, perhaps a GUI window class called *ProcessSaleFrame* in the UI layer will pick up the mouse and keyboard events requesting to enter an item, and then the *ProcessSaleFrame* object will send an *enterItem* message on to a software object in the domain layer, such as *Register*, to perform the application logic. See Figure 13.8.

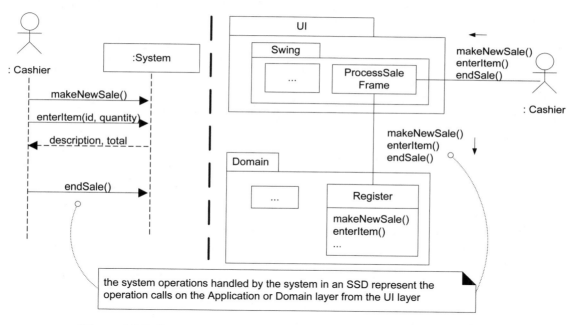

Figure 13.8 System operations in the SSDs and in terms of layers.

13.9 Example: NextGen Logical Architecture and Package Diagram

Figure 13.2 hints at the simple logical architecture for this iteration. Things get more interesting in later iterations; for example, see many examples of the NextGen logical architecture and package diagrams starting on p. 559.

13.10   Example: Monopoly Logical Architecture?

The Monopoly architecture is a simple layered design—UI, domain, and services. There is nothing novel to illustrate, so the NextGen case study is used for the architectural examples.

13.11   Recommended Resources

There's a wealth of literature on layered architectures, both in print and on the Web. A series of patterns in *Pattern Languages of Program Design*, volume 1, [CS95] first address the topic in pattern form, although layered architectures have been used and written about since at least the 1960s; volume 2 continues with further layers-related patterns. *Pattern-Oriented Software Architecture*, volume 1 [BMRSS96], provides a good treatment of the Layers pattern.

ON TO OBJECT DESIGN

*I do not like this word 'bomb.' It is not a bomb.
It is a device that is exploding.*

—*Ambassador Jacques le Blanc on nuclear 'weapons'*

Objectives

- Understand dynamic and static object design modeling.
- Try agile modeling, or a UML CASE tool for drawing.

Introduction

How do developers design objects? Here are three ways:

1. **Code**. Design-while-coding (Java, C#, ...), ideally with power tools such as **refactorings**. From mental model to code.

2. **Draw, then code.** Drawing some UML on a whiteboard or UML CASE tool, then switching to #1 with a text-strong IDE (e.g., Eclipse or Visual Studio).

3. **Only draw**. Somehow, the tool generates everything from diagrams. Many a dead tool vendor has washed onto the shores of this steep island. "Only draw" is a misnomer, as this still involves a text programming language attached to UML graphic elements.

What's Next?   Having structured the logical architecture in layers, this chapter introduces object design. The next chapter summarizes UML interaction diagram notation – a very useful tool when exploring detailed object design.

Requirements to Design – Iteratively	Logical Layered Architecture	On to Object Design	UML Interaction Diagrams	UML Class Diagrams

other design tech-niques p. 218

Of course, there are other ways to design, with other "languages."[1] If we use *Draw, then code* (the most popular approach with UML), the **drawing overhead** should be worth the effort. This chapter introduces object design and **lightweight drawing** before coding, suggesting ways to make it pay off.

14.1 Agile Modeling and Lightweight UML Drawing

agile modeling p. 30

Some aims of agile modeling [Ambler02] are to *reduce drawing overhead* and *model to understand and communicate*, rather than to document—though documenting is easy with digital photos. Try the simple agile modeling approach. Practices include using *lots* of whiteboards (ten in a room, not two) or special white plastic static cling sheets (that work like whiteboards) covering large wall

three ways to apply UML p. 11

areas, using markers, digital cameras, and printers to capture "UML as sketch"—one of the three ways to apply UML [Fowler03].

Agile modeling also includes

- **Modeling with others**.

- **Creating several models in parallel**. For example, five minutes on a wall of interaction diagrams, then five minutes on a wall of related class diagrams.

How big is the area you'd like to draw in? With your eyes and hands? Fifteen by two *meters* or 50 by 40 cm. (more monitor size)? Most people prefer big. But cheap virtual reality UML tools don't exist, yet. The simple alternative is lots of white static cling sheets (or whiteboards), reflecting the XP agile principle: *Do the simplest thing that could possibly work*.

More tips:

- It's easy to upload digital photos of wall drawings to an internal **wiki** (see www.twiki.org) that captures your project information.

- Popular brands of white plastic static cling sheets:

  ○ **North America** (and …): Avery Write-On Cling Sheets.

  ○ **Europe**: Legamaster Magic-Chart.[2]

---

1. What's a next-generation language? A 5GL? One view is that it's one that raises the level of the coding symbols, from bits to text to perhaps icons (or even gestures), packing more functionality into each symbol. Another view is that a 5GL is more declarative and goal-specifying rather than procedural, although 4GLs already exhibit this.

2. I like this roll style; it makes it easy to unroll a long sheet of cling-plastic.

14.2   UML CASE Tools

Please don't misinterpret my suggestion of wall-sketching and agile modeling as implying that UML CASE tools aren't also useful. Both can add value. These tools range from expensive to free and open source, and each year improve in usefulness. Each year's best choice changes, so I won't make a stale suggestion, but...

Guidelines

- Choose a UML CASE tool that integrates with popular text-strong IDEs, such as Eclipse or Visual Studio.

- Choose a UML tool that can reverse-engineer (generate diagrams from code) not only class diagrams (common), but also interaction diagrams (more rare, but very useful to learn call-flow structure of a program).

Many developers find it useful to code awhile in their favorite IDE, then press a button, reverse-engineer the code, and see a UML big-picture graphical view of their design.

Also, note:

**Agile modeling on the walls and using a
UML CASE tool integrated into a text-strong IDE can
be complementary. Try both during different phases of activity.**

14.3   How Much Time Spent Drawing UML Before Coding?

Guideline

For a three-week timeboxed iteration, ***spend a few hours or at most one day*** (with partners) near the start of the iteration "at the walls" (or with a UML CASE tool) drawing UML for the hard, creative parts of the detailed object design. Then stop—and if sketching—perhaps take digital photos, print the pictures, and transition to coding for the remainder of the iteration, using the UML drawings for inspiration as a starting point, but recognizing that the final design in code will diverge and improve. Shorter drawing/sketching sessions may occur throughout the iteration.

If agile modeling, then before each subsequent modeling session, reverse-engineer the growing code base into UML diagrams, print them out (perhaps on large plotter paper), and refer to them during the sketching session.

14.4   Designing Objects: What are Static and Dynamic Modeling?

There are two kinds of object models: dynamic and static. **Dynamic models**, such as UML interaction diagrams (**sequence diagrams** or **communication diagrams**), help design the logic, the behavior of the code or the method bodies. They tend to be the more interesting, difficult, important diagrams to create. **Static models**, such as UML class diagrams, help design the definition of packages, class names, attributes, and method signatures (but not method bodies). See Figure 14.1.

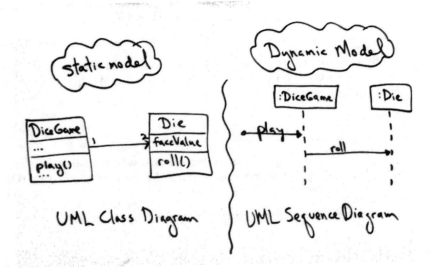

Figure 14.1 Static and dynamic UML diagrams for object modeling.

There's a relationship between static and dynamic modeling and the agile modeling practice of *create models in parallel:* Spend a short period of time on interaction diagrams (dynamics), then switch to a wall of related class diagrams (statics).

Dynamic Object Modeling

People new to UML tend to think that the important diagram is the static-view class diagram, but in fact, most of the challenging, interesting, useful design work happens while drawing the UML dynamic-view interaction diagrams. It's during dynamic object modeling (such as drawing sequence diagrams) that "the rubber hits the road" in terms of really thinking through the exact details of what objects need to exist and how they collaborate via messages and methods.

interaction dia-grams p. 221

Therefore, this book starts by introducing dynamic object modeling with interaction diagrams.

Guideline

Spend significant time doing *interaction* diagrams
(sequence or communication diagrams), not just class diagrams.

Ignoring this guideline is a very common worst-practice with UML.

RDD and GRASP p. 271

Note that it's especially during dynamic modeling that we apply **responsibility-driven design** and the **GRASP** principles. The subsequent chapters focus on these key topics of the book—and key skills in OO design.

There are other dynamic tools in the UML kit, including **state machine diagrams** (p. 485) and **activity diagrams** (p. 477).

Static Object Modeling

class diagrams p. 249

The most common static object modeling is with UML class diagrams. After first covering dynamic modeling with interaction diagrams, I introduce the details. Note, though, that if the developers are applying the agile modeling practice of *Create several models in parallel*, they will be drawing both interaction and class diagrams concurrently.

Other support in the UML for static modeling includes **package diagrams** (p. 197) and **deployment diagrams** (p. 651).

14.5 The Importance of Object Design Skill over UML Notation Skill

The following chapters explore detailed object design while applying UML diagrams. It's been said before, but is important to stress: What's important is knowing how to think and design in objects, and apply object design best-practice patterns, which is a very different and much more valuable skill than knowing UML notation.

While drawing a UML object diagram, we need to answer key questions: What are the responsibilities of the object? Who does it collaborate with? What design patterns should be applied? Far more important than knowing the difference between UML 1.4 and 2.0 notation! Therefore, the emphasis of the following chapters is on these principles and patterns in object design.

> *Object Design Skill vs. UML Notation Skill*
>
> Drawing UML is a reflection of making decisions about the design.
>
> The object design skills are what matter, not knowing how to draw UML. Fundamental object design requires knowledge of:
>
> ■ principles of responsibility assignment
>
> ■ design patterns

14.6 Other Object Design Techniques: CRC Cards

People prefer different design methods because of familiarity and, quite significantly, because of different *cognitive styles*. Don't assume that icons and pictures are better than text for everyone, or vice versa.

A popular text-oriented modeling technique is Class Responsibility Collaboration (**CRC**) cards, created by the agile, influential minds of Kent Beck and Ward Cunningham (also founders of the ideas of XP and design patterns).

CRC cards are paper index cards on which one writes the responsibilities and collaborators of classes. Each card represents one class. A CRC modeling session involves a group sitting around a table, discussing and writing on the cards as they play "what if" scenarios with the objects, considering what they must do and what other objects they must collaborate with. See Figure 14.2 and Figure 14.3.

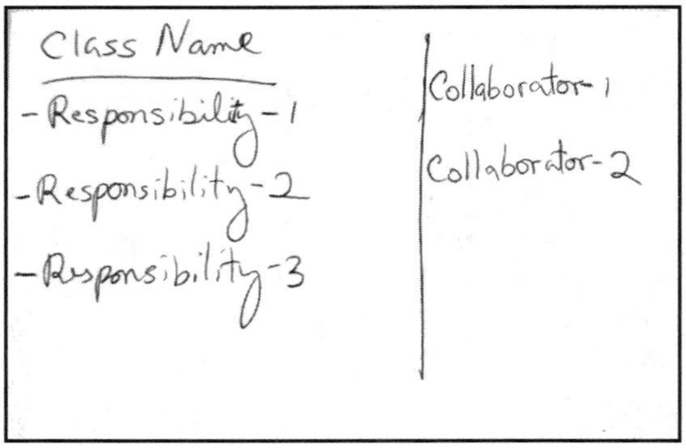

Figure 14.2 Template for a CRC card.

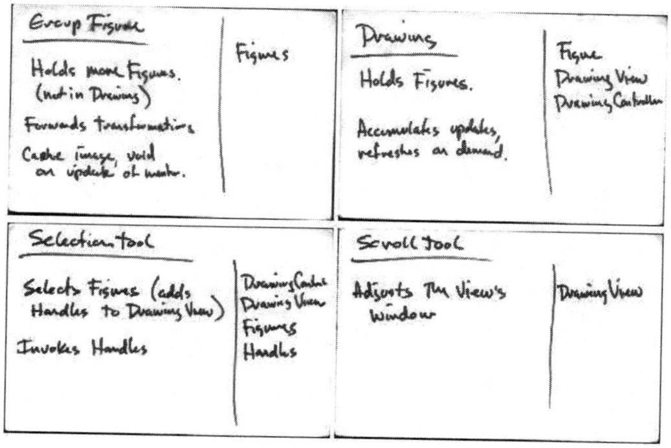

Figure 14.3 Four sample CRC cards. This minimized example is only meant to show the typical level of detail rather than the specific text.

UML INTERACTION DIAGRAMS

*Cats are smarter than dogs. You can't
get eight cats to pull a sled through snow.*

—*Jeff Valdez*

Objectives

- Provide a reference for frequently used UML interaction diagram notation—sequence and communication diagrams.

Introduction

The UML includes **interaction diagrams** to illustrate how objects interact via messages. They are used for **dynamic object modeling**. There are two common types: sequence and communication interaction diagrams. This chapter introduces the notation—view it as a *reference* to skim through—while subsequent chapters focus on a more important question: What are key principles in OO design?

In the following chapters, interaction diagrams are applied to help explain and demonstrate object design. Hence, it's useful to at least skim these examples before moving on.

What's Next?

Having introduced OO design (OOD), this chapter summarizes UML interaction diagrams for dynamic OO design. The next chapter summarizes UML class diagrams for static OO design.

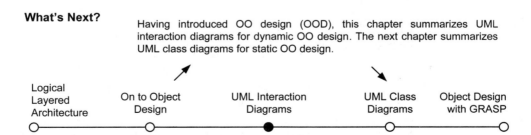

| Logical Layered Architecture | On to Object Design | UML Interaction Diagrams | UML Class Diagrams | Object Design with GRASP |

15.1   Sequence and Communication Diagrams

The term **interaction diagram** is a generalization of two more specialized UML diagram types:

- sequence diagrams

- communication diagrams

Both can express similar interactions.

A related diagram is the **interaction overview diagram**; it provides a big-picture overview of how a set of interaction diagrams are related in terms of logic and process-flow. However, it's new to UML 2, and so it's too early to tell if it will be practically useful.

Sequence diagrams are the more notationally rich of the two types, but communication diagrams have their use as well, especially for wall sketching. Throughout the book, both types will be used to emphasize the flexibility in choice.

Sequence diagrams illustrate interactions in a kind of fence format, in which each new object is added to the right, as shown in Figure 15.1.

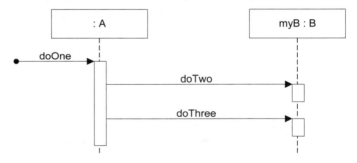

Figure 15.1 Sequence diagram.

What might this represent in code?[1] Probably, that class *A* has a method named *doOne* and an attribute of type *B*. Also, that class *B* has methods named *doTwo* and *doThree*. Perhaps the partial definition of class *A* is:

```
public class A
{
private B myB = new B();

public void doOne()
{
    myB.doTwo();
    myB.doThree();
}
// ...
}
```

---

1. Code mapping or generation rules will vary depending on the OO language.

Communication diagrams illustrate object interactions in a graph or network format, in which objects can be placed anywhere on the diagram (the essence of their wall sketching advantage), as shown in Figure 15.2.

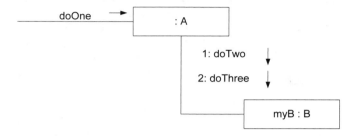

Figure 15.2 Communication diagram.

What are the Strengths and Weaknesses of Sequence vs. Communication Diagrams?

Each diagram type has advantages, and modelers have idiosyncratic preference—there isn't an absolutely "correct" choice. However, UML tools usually emphasize sequence diagrams, because of their greater notational power.

Sequence diagrams have some advantages over communication diagrams. Perhaps first and foremost, the UML specification is more sequence diagram centric—more thought and effort has been put into the notation and semantics. Thus, tool support is better and more notation options are available. Also, it is easier to see the call-flow sequence with sequence diagrams—simply read top to bottom. With communication diagrams we must read the sequence numbers, such as "1:" and "2:". Hence, sequence diagrams are excellent for documentation or to easily read a reverse-engineered call-flow sequence, generated from source code with a UML tool.

hree ways to use
JML p. 11

But on the other hand, communication diagrams have advantages when applying "UML as sketch" to draw on walls (an Agile Modeling practice) because they are *much* more space-efficient. This is because the boxes can be easily placed or erased anywhere—horizontal or vertical. Consequently as well, *modifying* wall sketches is easier with communication diagrams—it is simple (during creative high-change OO design work) to erase a box at one location, draw a new one elsewhere, and sketch a line to it. In contrast, new objects in a sequence diagrams must always be added to the right edge, which is limiting as it quickly consumes and exhausts right-edge space on a page (or wall); free space in the vertical dimension is not efficiently used. Developers doing sequence diagrams on walls rapidly feel the drawing pain when contrasted with communication diagrams.

Likewise, when drawing diagrams that are to be published on narrow pages (like this book), communication diagrams have the advantage over sequence diagrams of allowing *vertical* expansion for new objects—much more can be packed into a small visual space.

Type	Strengths	Weaknesses
sequence	clearly shows sequence or time ordering of messages large set of detailed notation options	forced to extend to the right when adding new objects; consumes horizontal space
communication	space economical—flexibility to add new objects in two dimensions	more difficult to see sequence of messages fewer notation options

Example Sequence Diagram: makePayment

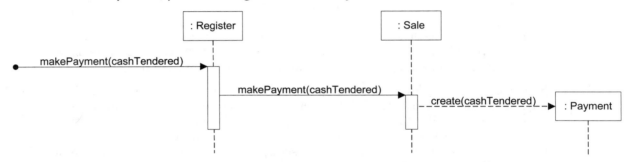

Figure 15.3 Sequence diagram.

The sequence diagram shown in Figure 15.3 is read as follows:

1. The message *makePayment* is sent to an instance of a *Register*. The sender is not identified.

2. The *Register* instance sends the *makePayment* message to a *Sale* instance.

3. The *Sale* instance creates an instance of a *Payment*.

From reading Figure 15.3, what might be some related code for the *Sale* class and its *makePayment* method?

```
public class Sale
{
private Payment payment;

public void makePayment( Money cashTendered )
{
    payment = new Payment( cashTendered );
    //…
}
// …
}
```

Example Communication Diagram: makePayment

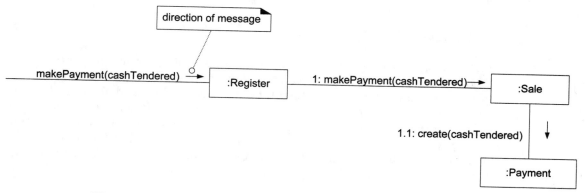

Figure 15.4 Communication diagram.

The communication diagram shown in Figure 15.3 has the same intent as the prior sequence diagram.

15.2 Novice UML Modelers Don't Pay Enough Attention to Interaction Diagrams!

Most UML novices are aware of class diagrams and usually think they are the only important diagram in OO design. Not true!

Although the static-view class diagrams are indeed useful, the dynamic-view interaction diagrams—or more precisely, *acts* of dynamic interaction modeling—are incredibly valuable.

Guideline
Spend time doing *dynamic* object modeling with interaction diagrams, not just static object modeling with class diagrams.

Why? Because it's when we have to think through the concrete details of what messages to send, and to whom, and in what order, that the "rubber hits the road" in terms of thinking through the true OO design details.

15.3 Common UML Interaction Diagram Notation

Illustrating Participants with Lifeline Boxes

In the UML, the boxes you've seen in the prior sample interaction diagrams are called **lifeline** boxes. Their precise UML definition is subtle, but informally they represent the **participants** in the interaction—related parts defined in the context of some structure diagram, such as a class diagram. It is not precisely accurate to say that a lifeline box equals an instance of a class, but informally and practically, the participants will often be interpreted as such. Therefore, in this text I'll often write something like "the lifeline representing a *Sale* instance," as a convenient shorthand. See Figure 15.5 for common cases of notation.

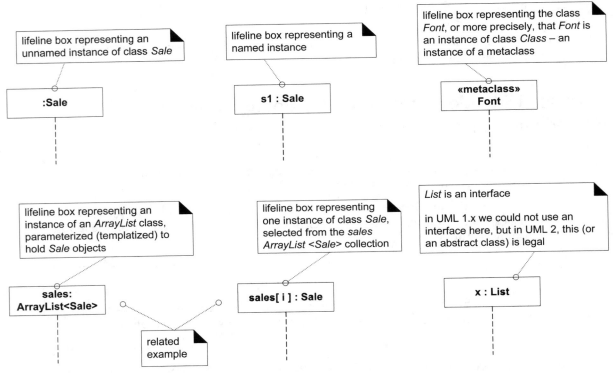

Figure 15.5 Lifeline boxes to show participants in interactions.

Basic Message Expression Syntax

Interaction diagrams show messages between objects; the UML has a standard syntax for these message expressions:[2]

---

2. An alternate syntax, such as C# or Java, is acceptable—and supported by UML tools.

```
return = message(parameter : parameterType) : returnType
```

Parentheses are usually excluded if there are no parameters, though still legal.

Type information may be excluded if obvious or unimportant.

For example:

```
initialize(code)
initialize
d = getProductDescription(id)
d = getProductDescription(id:ItemID)
d = getProductDescription(id:ItemID) : ProductDescription
```

Singleton Objects

Singleton p. 442

In the world of OO design patterns, there is one that is especially common, called the **Singleton** pattern. It is explained later, but an implication of the pattern is that there is only *one* instance of a class instantiated—never two. In other words, it is a "singleton" instance. In a UML interaction diagram (sequence or communication), such an object is marked with a '1' in the upper right corner of the lifeline box. It implies that the Singleton pattern is used to gain visibility to the object—the meaning of that won't be clear at this time, but will be upon reading its description on p. 442. See Figure 15.6.

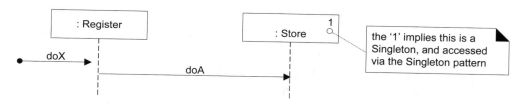

Figure 15.6 Singletons in interaction diagrams.

15.4   Basic Sequence Diagram Notation

Lifeline Boxes and Lifelines

feline boxes 226

In contrast to communication diagrams, in sequence diagrams the lifeline boxes include a vertical line extending below them—these are the actual lifelines. Although virtually all UML examples show the lifeline as dashed (because of UML 1 influence), in fact the UML 2 specification says it may be solid *or* dashed.

Messages

Each (typical synchronous) message between objects is represented with a message expression on a *filled-arrowed*[3] solid line between the vertical lifelines (see Figure 15.7). The time ordering is organized from top to bottom of lifelines.

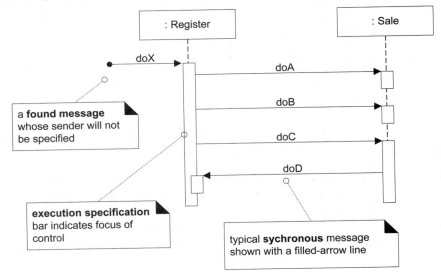

Figure 15.7 Messages and focus of control with execution specification bar.

In the example of Figure 15.7 the starting message is called a **found message** in the UML, shown with an opening solid ball; it implies the sender will not be specified, is not known, or that the message is coming from a random source. However, by convention a team or tool may ignore showing this, and instead use a regular message line without the ball, intending by convention it is a found message.[4]

Focus of Control and Execution Specification Bars

As illustrated in Figure 15.7, sequence diagrams may also show the focus of control (informally, in a regular blocking call, the operation is on the call stack) using an **execution specification** bar (previously called an **activation bar** or simply an **activation** in UML 1). The bar is optional.

Guideline: Drawing the bar is more common (and often automatic) when using a UML CASE tool, and less common when wall sketching.

---

3. An open message arrow means an asynchronous message in an interaction diagram.

4. Therefore, many of the book examples won't bother with the found message notation.

Illustrating Reply or Returns

There are two ways to show the return result from a message:

1. Using the message syntax *returnVar = message(parameter)*.

2. Using a reply (or return) message line at the end of an activation bar.

Both are common in practice. I prefer the first approach when sketching, as it's less effort. If the reply line is used, the line is normally labelled with an arbitrary description of the returning value. See Figure 15.8.

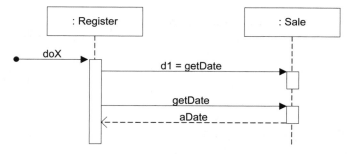

Figure 15.8 Two ways to show a return result from a message.

Messages to "self" or "this"

You can show a message being sent from an object to itself by using a nested activation bar (see Figure 15.9).

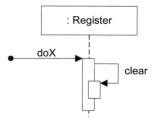

Figure 15.9 Messages to "this."

Creation of Instances

Object creation notation is shown in Figure 15.10. Note the UML-mandated *dashed* line.[5] The arrow is filled if it's a regular synchronous message (such as implying invoking a Java constructor), or open (stick arrow) if an asynchronous

---

5. I see no value in requiring a *dashed* line, but it's in the spec... Many author examples use a solid line, as early draft versions of the spec did as well.

call. The message name *create* is not required—anything is legal—but it's a UML idiom.

The typical interpretation (in languages such as Java or C#) of a *create* message on a dashed line with a filled arrow is "invoke the *new* operator and call the constructor".

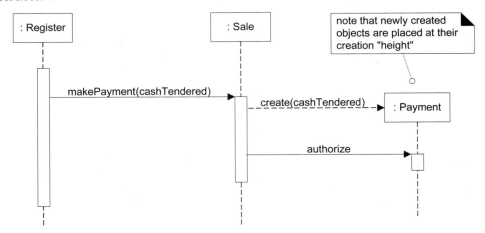

Figure 15.10 Instance creation and object lifelines.

Object Lifelines and Object Destruction

In some circumstances it is desirable to show explicit destruction of an object. For example, when using C++ which does not have automatic garbage collection, or when you want to especially indicate an object is no longer usable (such as a closed database connection). The UML lifeline notation provides a way to express this destruction (see Figure 15.11).

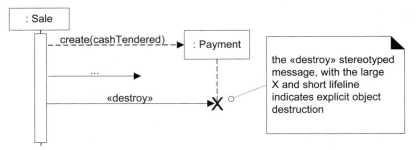

Figure 15.11 Object destruction.

Diagram Frames in UML Sequence Diagrams

To support conditional and looping constructs (among many other things), the UML uses **frames**.[6] Frames are regions or fragments of the diagrams; they have an operator or label (such as *loop*) and a guard[7] (conditional clause). See Figure 15.12.

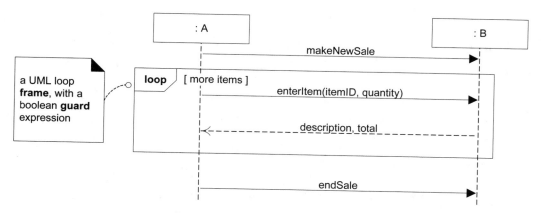

Figure 15.12 Example UML frame.

The following table summarizes some common frame operators:

Frame Operator	Meaning
alt	Alternative fragment for mutual exclusion conditional logic expressed in the guards.
loop	Loop fragment while guard is true. Can also write *loop(n)* to indicate looping n times. There is discussion that the specification will be enhanced to define a *FOR* loop, such as *loop(i, 1, 10)*
opt	Optional fragment that executes if guard is true.
par	Parallel fragments that execute in parallel.
region	Critical region within which only one thread can run.

Looping

The LOOP frame notation to show looping is shown in Figure 15.12.

Conditional Messages

An OPT frame is placed around one or more messages. Notice that the guard is

---

6. Also called **diagram frames** or **interaction frames**.

7. The *[boolean test]* guard should be placed *over* the lifeline to which it belongs.

placed *over* the related lifeline. See Figure 15.13.

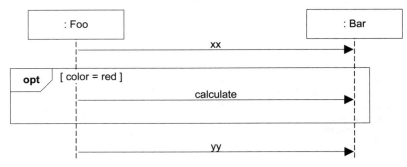

Figure 15.13 A conditional message.

Conditional Messages in UML 1.x Style—Still Useful?

The UML 2.x notation to show a single conditional message is heavyweight, requiring an entire OPT frame box around one message (see Figure 15.13). The older UML 1.x notation for *single* conditional messages in sequence diagrams is not legal in UML 2, but so simple that especially when sketching it will probably be popular for years to come. See Figure 15.14.

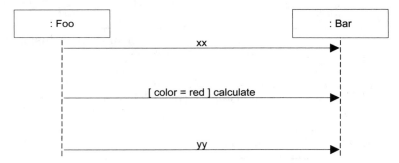

Figure 15.14 A conditional message in UML 1.x notation—a simple style.

Guideline: Use UML 1 style only for simple single messages when sketching.

Mutually Exclusive Conditional Messages

An ALT frame is placed around the mutually exclusive alternatives. See Figure 15.15.

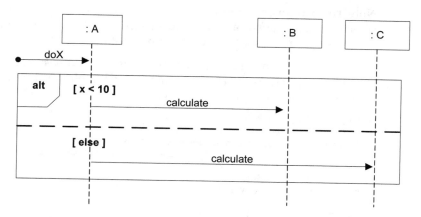

Figure 15.15 Mutually exclusive conditional messages.

Iteration Over a Collection

A common algorithm is to iterate over all members of a collection (such as a list or map), sending the same message to each. Often, some kind of iterator object is ultimately used, such as an implementation of *java.util.Iterator* or a C++ standard library iterator, although in the sequence diagram that low-level "mechanism" need not be shown in the interest of brevity or abstraction.

At the time of this writing, the UML specification did not (and may never) have an official idiom for this case. Two alternatives are shown—reviewed with the leader of the UML 2 interaction specification—in Figure 15.16 and Figure 15.17.

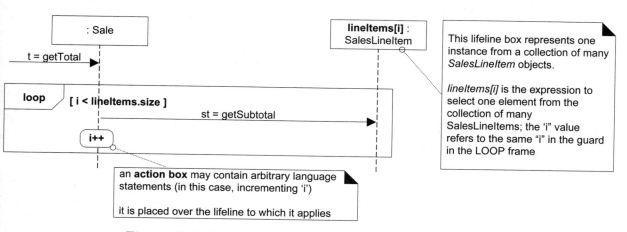

Figure 15.16 Iteration over a collection using relatively explicit notation.

Note the **selector** expression *lineItems[i]* in the lifeline of Figure 15.16. The selector expression is used to select one object from a group. Lifeline participants should represent one object, not a collection.

In Java, for example, the following code listing is a possible implementation that maps the explicit use of the incrementing variable *i* in Figure 15.16 to an idiomatic solution in Java, using its enhanced *for* statement (C# has the same).

```java
public class Sale
{
private List<SalesLineItem> lineItems =
                            new ArrayList<SalesLineItem>();


public Money getTotal()
{
    Money total = new Money();
    Money subtotal = null;

    for ( SalesLineItem lineItem : lineItems )
    {
        subtotal = lineItem.getSubtotal();
        total.add( subtotal );
    }
    return total;
}
// …
}
```

Another variation is shown in Figure 15.17; the intent is the same, but details are excluded. A team or tool could agree on this simple style by convention to imply iteration over all the collection elements.[8]

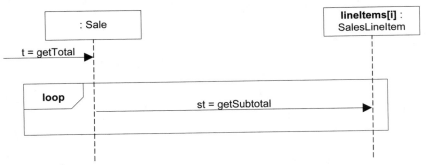

Figure 15.17 Iteration over a collection leaving things more implicit.

8. I use this style later in the book.

Nesting of Frames

Frames can be nested. See Figure 15.18.

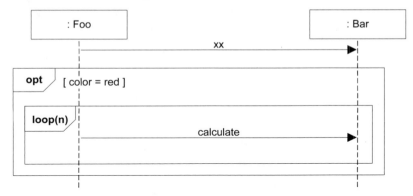

Figure 15.18 Nesting of frames.

How to Relate Interaction Diagrams?

Figure 15.19 illustrates probably better than words. An **interaction occurrence** (also called an **interaction use**) is a reference to an interaction within another interaction. It is useful, for example, when you want to simplify a diagram and factor out a portion into another diagram, or there is a reusable interaction occurrence. UML tools take advantage of them, because of their usefulness in relating and linking diagrams.

They are created with two related frames:

■ a frame around an entire sequence diagram[9], labeled with the tag **sd** and a name, such as *AuthenticateUser*

■ a frame tagged **ref**, called a **reference**, that refers to another named sequence diagram; it is the actual interaction occurrence

Interaction overview diagrams also contain a set of reference frames (interaction occurrences). These diagrams organized references into a larger structure of logic and process flow.

---

9. Interaction occurrences and *ref* frames can also be used for *communication* diagrams.

Guideline: Any sequence diagram can be surrounded with an *sd* frame, to name it. Frame and name one when you want to refer to it using a *ref* frame.

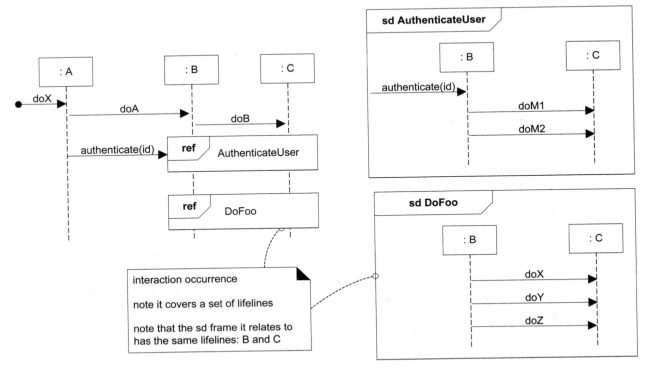

Figure 15.19 Example interaction occurrence, *sd* and *ref* frames.

Messages to Classes to Invoke Static (or Class) Methods

You can show class or static method calls by using a lifeline box label that indicates the receiving object is a class, or more precisely, an *instance* of a **metaclass** (see Figure 15.20).

What do I mean? For example, in Java and Smalltalk, all classes are conceptually or literally *instances* of class *Class*; in .NET classes are instances of class *Type*. The classes *Class* and *Type* are **metaclasses**, which means their instances are themselves classes. A specific class, such as class *Calendar*, is itself an instance of class *Class*. Thus, class *Calendar* is an instance of a metaclass! It may help to drink some beer before trying to understand this.

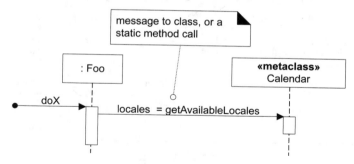

Figure 15.20 Invoking class or static methods; showing a class object as an instance of a metaclass.

In code, a likely implementation is:

```
public class Foo
{
public void doX()
{
    // static method call on class Calendar
    Locale[] locales = Calendar.getAvailableLocales();
    // ...
}
// ...
}
```

Polymorphic Messages and Cases

Polymorphism is fundamental to OO design. How to show it in a sequence diagram? That's a common UML question. One approach is to use multiple sequence diagrams—one that shows the polymorphic message to the abstract superclass or interface object, and then separate sequence diagrams detailing each polymorphic case, each starting with a *found* polymorphic message. Figure 15.21 illustrates.

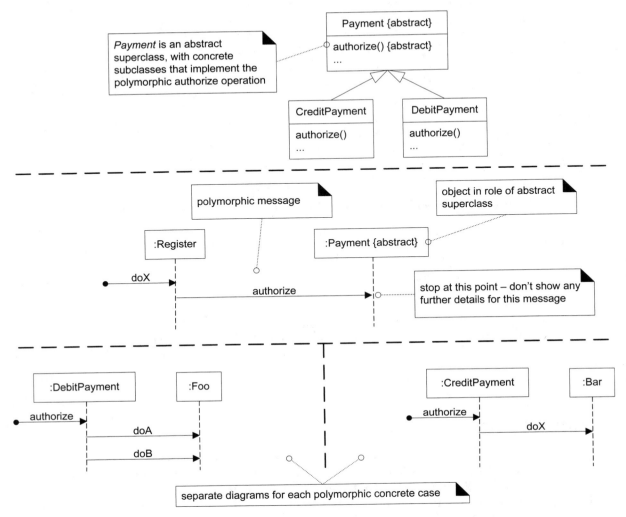

Figure 15.21 An approach to modeling polymorphic cases in sequence diagrams.

Asynchronous and Synchronous Calls

An **asynchronous message** call does not wait for a response; it doesn't *block*. They are used in multi-threaded environments such as .NET and Java so that new **threads** of execution can be created and initiated. In Java, for example, you may think of the *Thread.start* or *Runnable.run* (called by *Thread.start*) message as the asynchronous starting point to initiate execution on a new thread.

The UML notation for asynchronous calls is a stick arrow message; regular synchronous (blocking) calls are shown with a filled arrow (see Figure 15.22).

Guideline

This arrow difference is subtle. And when wall sketching UML, it is common to use a stick arrow to mean a synchronous call because it's easier to draw. Therefore, when reading a UML interaction diagram don't assume the shape of the arrow is correct!

An object such as the *Clock* in Figure 15.22 is also known as an **active object**— each instance runs on and controls its own thread of execution. In the UML, it may be shown with double vertical lines on the left and right sides of the lifeline box. The same notation is used for an **active class** whose instances are active objects.

active class p. 269

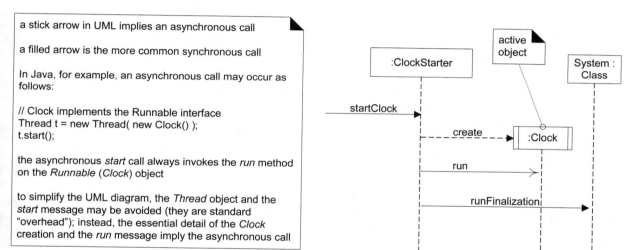

a stick arrow in UML implies an asynchronous call

a filled arrow is the more common synchronous call

In Java, for example, an asynchronous call may occur as follows:

// Clock implements the Runnable interface
Thread t = new Thread(new Clock());
t.start();

the asynchronous *start* call always invokes the *run* method on the *Runnable* (*Clock*) object

to simplify the UML diagram, the *Thread* object and the *start* message may be avoided (they are standard "overhead"); instead, the essential detail of the *Clock* creation and the *run* message imply the asynchronous call

Figure 15.22 Asynchronous calls and active objects.

In Java, a likely implementation for Figure 15.22 follows. Notice that the *Thread* object in the code is excluded from the UML diagram, because it is simply a consistent "overhead" mechanism to realize an asynchronous call in Java.

```
public class ClockStarter
{
public void startClock()
{
    Thread t = new Thread( new Clock() );
    t.start(); // asynchronous call to the 'run' method on the Clock
    System.runFinalization(); // example follow-on message
}
// ...
}
```

```
// objects should implement the Runnable interface
// in Java to be used on new threads

public class Clock implements Runnable
{
public void run()
{
    while ( true ) // loop forever on own thread
    {
        // …
    }
}
// …
}
```

15.5   Basic Communication Diagram Notation

Links

A **link** is a connection path between two objects; it indicates some form of navigation and visibility between the objects is possible (see Figure 15.23). More formally, a link is an instance of an association. For example, there is a link—or path of navigation—from a *Register* to a *Sale*, along which messages may flow, such as the *makePayment* message.

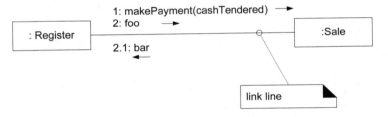

Figure 15.23 Link lines.

Note

Note that multiple messages, and messages *both* ways, flow along the same single link. There isn't one link line per message; all messages flow on the same line, which is like a road allowing two-way message traffic.

Messages

Each message between objects is represented with a message expression and small arrow indicating the direction of the message. Many messages may flow along this link (Figure 15.24). A sequence number is added to show the sequential order of messages in the current thread of control.

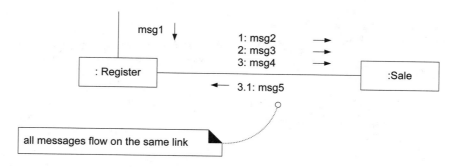

Figure 15.24 Messages.

Guideline

Don't number the starting message. It's legal to
do so, but simplifies the overall numbering if you don't.

Messages to "self" or "this"

A message can be sent from an object to itself (Figure 15.25). This is illustrated by a link to itself, with messages flowing along the link.

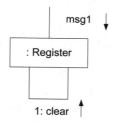

Figure 15.25 Messages to "this."

Creation of Instances

Any message can be used to create an instance, but the convention in the UML is to use a message named *create* for this purpose (some use *new*). See Figure 15.26. If another (less obvious) message name is used, the message may be annotated with a **UML stereotype**, like so: «*create*». The *create* message may include parameters, indicating the passing of initial values. This indicates, for example, a constructor call with parameters in Java. Furthermore, the **UML tagged value** *{new}* may optionally be added to the lifeline box to highlight the creation. Tagged values are a flexible extension mechanism in the UML to add semantically meaningful information to a UML element.

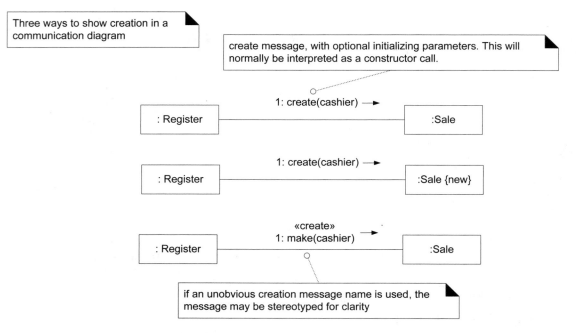

Figure 15.26 Instance creation.

Message Number Sequencing

The order of messages is illustrated with **sequence numbers**, as shown in Figure 15.27. The numbering scheme is:

1. The first message is not numbered. Thus, *msg1* is unnumbered.[10]

2. The order and nesting of subsequent messages is shown with a legal numbering scheme in which nested messages have a number appended to them. You denote nesting by prepending the incoming message number to the outgoing message number.

---

10. Actually, a starting number is legal, but it makes all subsequent numbering more awkward, creating another level of number-nesting deeper than otherwise necessary.

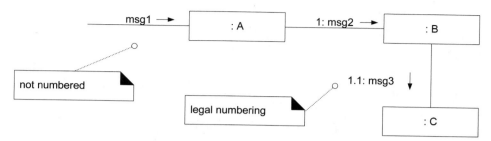

Figure 15.27 Sequence numbering.

Figure 15.28 shows a more complex case.

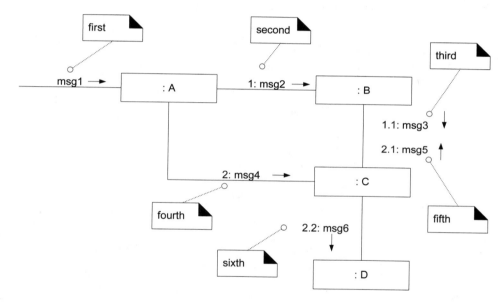

Figure 15.28 Complex sequence numbering.

Conditional Messages

You show a conditional message (Figure 15.29) by following a sequence number with a conditional clause in square brackets, similar to an iteration clause. The message is only sent if the clause evaluates to *true*.

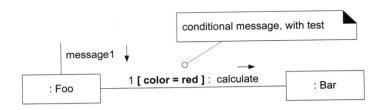

Figure 15.29 Conditional message.

Mutually Exclusive Conditional Paths

The example in Figure 15.30 illustrates the sequence numbers with mutually exclusive conditional paths.

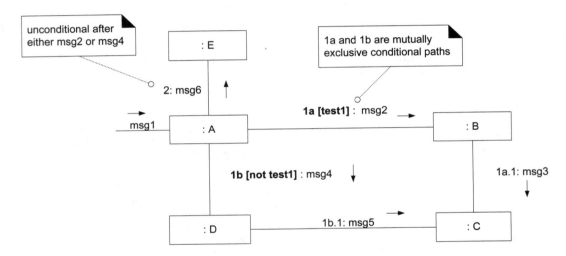

Figure 15.30 Mutually exclusive messages.

In this case we must modify the sequence expressions with a conditional path letter. The first letter used is **a** by convention. Figure 15.30 states that either *1a* or *1b* could execute after *msg1*. Both are sequence number 1 since either could be the first internal message.

Note that subsequent nested messages are still consistently prepended with their outer message sequence. Thus *1b.1* is nested message within *1b*.

Iteration or Looping

Iteration notation is shown in Figure 15.31. If the details of the iteration clause are not important to the modeler, a simple * can be used.

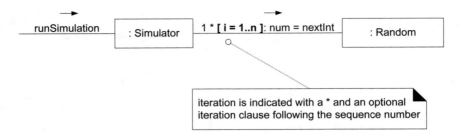

Figure 15.31 Iteration.

Iteration Over a Collection

A common algorithm is to iterate over all members of a collection (such as a list or map), sending the same message to each. In communication diagrams, this could be summarized as shown in Figure 15.32, although there is no official UML convention.

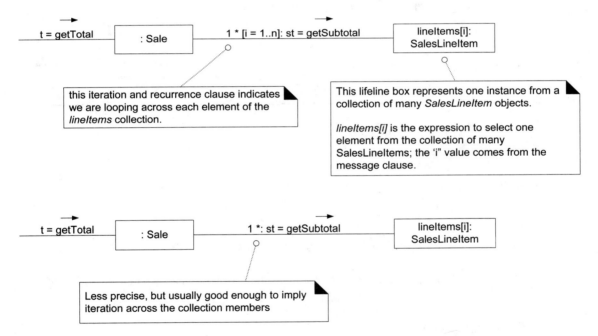

Figure 15.32 Iteration over a collection.

Messages to a Classes to Invoke Static (Class) Methods

See the discussion of metaclasses in the sequence diagram case on p. 236, to understand the purpose of the example in Figure 15.33.

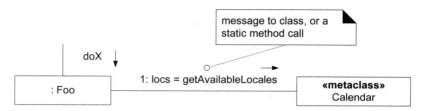

Figure 15.33 Messages to a class object (static method invocation).

Polymorphic Messages and Cases

Refer to Figure 15.21 for the related context, class hierarchy, and example for sequence diagrams. As in the sequence diagram case, multiple communication diagrams can be used to show each concrete polymorphic case (Figure 15.34).

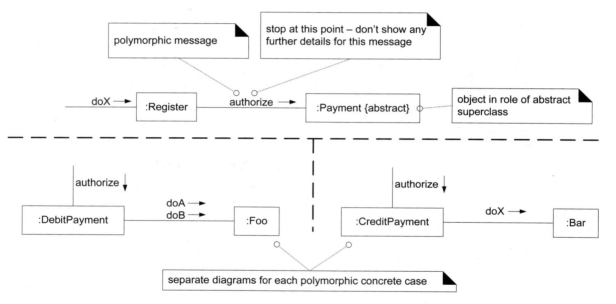

Figure 15.34 An approach to modeling polymorphic cases in communication diagrams.

Asynchronous and Synchronous Calls

As in sequence diagrams, asynchronous calls are shown with a stick arrow; synchronous calls with a filled arrow (see Figure 15.35).

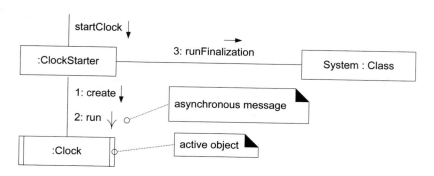

Figure 15.35 Asynchronous call in a communication diagram.

UML Class Diagrams

To iterate is human, to recurse, divine.

—anonymous

Objectives

- Provide a reference for frequently used UML class diagram notation.

Introduction

The UML includes **class diagrams** to illustrate classes, interfaces, and their associations. They are used for **static object modeling**. We've already introduced and used this UML diagram while domain modeling, applying class diagrams in a *conceptual perspective*. This chapter summarizes more of the notation, irrespective of the perspective (conceptual or software). As with the prior interaction diagram chapter, this is a *reference*.

Subsequent chapters focus on a more important question: What are key principles in OO design? Those chapters apply UML interaction and class diagrams to help explain and demonstrate object design. Hence, it's useful to first skim this chapter, but there's no need to memorize all these low-level details!

What's Next?   Having introduced interaction diagrams for dynamic OO design, this chapter does the same for class diagrams and static OO design. The next chapter is more important – it introduces key principles in OOD, with case study examples that apply the principles and UML modeling.

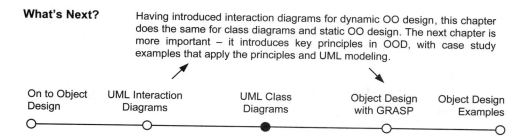

16.1 Applying UML: Common Class Diagram Notation

Much of the high-frequency class diagram notation can be summarized (and understood) in one figure:

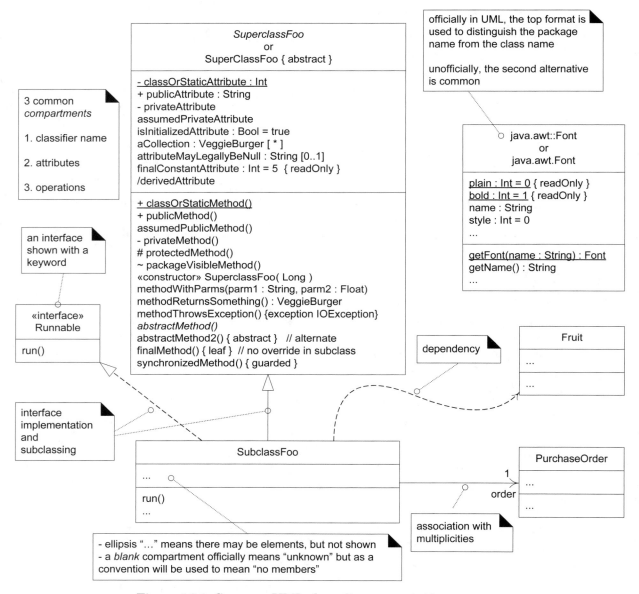

Figure 16.1 Common UML class diagram notation.

Most elements in Figure 16.1 are optional (e.g., +/- **visibility**, parameters, **compartments**). Modelers draw, show or hide them depending on context and the needs of the reader or UML tool.

Note

The OOA/D implications and modeling tips associated with the various UML class diagram elements shown here are distributed throughout the case study chapters. You will find cross-references to the OOA/D concepts are provided here and in the index.

---

applying associa-
tion classes p. 516

For example, this chapter summarizes UML **association class** notation, but doesn't explain the OOA/D modeling context. Likewise with many of the notation elements.

16.2   Definition: Design Class Diagram

As we've explored, the same UML diagram can be used in multiple perspectives (Figure 16.2). In a conceptual perspective the class diagram can be used to visualize a domain model. For discussion, we also need a unique term to clarify when the class diagram is used in a software or design perspective. A common modeling term for this purpose is **design class diagram** (**DCD**), which I'll use regularly in later chapters. In the UP, the set of all DCDs form part of the Design Model. Other parts of the Design Model include UML interaction and package diagrams.

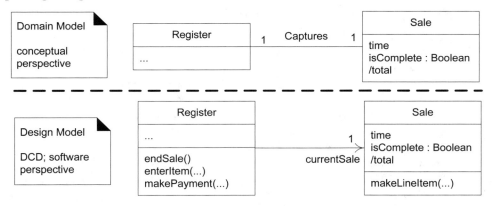

Figure 16.2 UML class diagrams in two perspectives.

16.3   Definition: Classifier

A UML **classifier** is "a model element that describes behavioral and structure features" [OMG03b]. Classifiers can also be specialized. They are a generalization of many of the elements of the UML, including classes, interfaces, use cases, and actors. In class diagrams, the two most common classifiers are regular classes and interfaces.

16.4 Ways to Show UML Attributes: Attribute Text and Association Lines

Attributes of a classifier (also called **structural properties** in the UML[1]) are shown several ways:

- **attribute text** notation, such as *currentSale : Sale*.

- **association line** notation

- **both** together

Figure 16.3 shows these notations being used to indicate that a *Register* object has an attribute (a reference to) one *Sale* object.

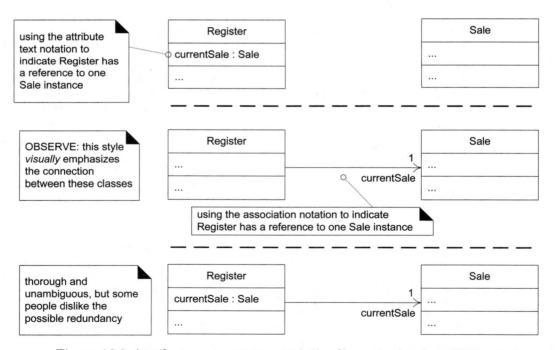

Figure 16.3 Attribute text versus association line notation for a UML attribute.

---

1. Often shortened to "property" — with the disadvantage of causing ambiguity versus the more general definition of a UML property (p. 260).

The full format of the attribute text notation is:

visibility name : type multiplicity = default {property-string}

Also, the UML allows any other programming language syntax to be used for the attribute declaration, as long as the reader or tool are notified.

As indicated in Figure 16.1, **visibility** marks include + (public), - (private), and so forth.

Guideline: Attributes are usually assumed private if no visibility is given.

Notice in Figure 16.3 that this attribute-as-association line has the following style:

- a **navigability arrow** pointing from the source (*Register*) to target (*Sale*) object, indicating a *Register* object has an attribute of one *Sale*
- a multiplicity at the target end, but not the source end
    - use the multiplicity notation described on p. 153
- a **rolename** (*currentSale*) only at the target end to show the attribute name
- no association name

Guideline: When showing attributes-as-associations, follow this style in DCDs, which is suggested by the UML specification. It is true that the UML metamodel also allows multiplicity and rolenames at the *source* end (e.g., the *Register* end in Figure 16.3), and also an association name, but they are not usually useful in the context of a DCD.

Guideline: On the other hand, when using class diagrams for a *domain model* do show association names but avoid navigation arrows, as a domain model is not a software perspective. See Figure 16.4.

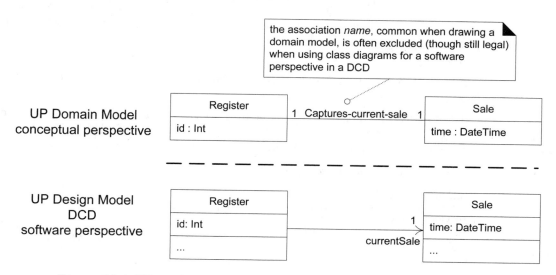

Figure 16.4 Idioms in association notation usage in different perspectives.

Note that this is not a new kind of association notation. It's the same UML notation for associations explored while applying class diagrams to domain modeling, on p. 149. This is an elaboration of the notation for use in the context of a software perspective DCD.

Guideline: When to Use Attribute Text versus Association Lines for Attributes?

This question was first explored in the context of domain modeling on p. 164. To review, a **data type** refers to objects for which unique identity is not important. Common data types are primitive-oriented types such as:

- Boolean, Date (or DateTime), Number, Character, String (Text), Time, Address, Color, Geometrics (Point, Rectangle), Phone Number, Social Security Number, Universal Product Code (UPC), SKU, ZIP or postal codes, enumerated types

Guideline: Use the attribute text notation for data type objects and the association line notation for others. Both are semantically equal, but showing an association line to another class box in the diagram (as in Figure 16.3) gives *visual emphasis*—it catches the eye, emphasizing the connection between the class of objects on the diagram. See Figure 16.5 for contrasting examples.

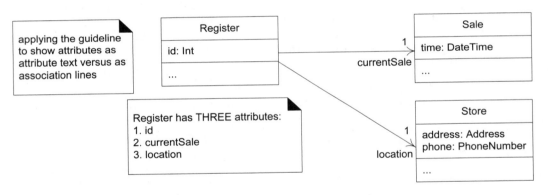

Figure 16.5 Applying the guidelines to show attributes in two notations.

Again, these different styles exist only in the UML surface notation; in code, they boil down to the same thing—the *Register* class of Figure 16.5 has three attributes. For example, in Java:

```java
public class Register
{
private int id;
private Sale currentSale;
private Store location;
// ...
}
```

The UML Notation for an Association End

As discussed, the end of an association can have a navigability arrow. It can also include an *optional* **rolename** (officially, an **association end name**) to indicate the attribute name. And of course, the association end may also show a **multiplicity** value, as explored earlier on p. 153, such as '*' or '0..1'. Notice in Figure 16.3 that the rolename *currentSale* is used to indicate the attribute name.

And as shown in Figure 16.6, a **property string** such as *{ordered}* or *{ordered, List}* is possible. *{ordered}* is a UML-defined **keyword** that implies the elements of the collection are (the suspense builds…) ordered. Another related keyword is *{unique}*, implying a *set* of unique elements.

The keyword *{List}* illustrates that the UML also supports user-defined keywords. I define *{List}* to mean the collection attribute *lineItems* will be implemented with an object implementing the *List* interface.

How to Show Collection Attributes with Attribute Text and Association Lines?

Suppose that a *Sale* software object holds a *List* (an interface for a kind of collection) of many *SalesLineItem* objects. For example, in Java:

```
public class Sale
{
private List<SalesLineItem> lineItems =
                        new ArrayList<SalesLineItem>();
// …
}
```

Figure 16.6 shows two ways to illustrate a collection attribute in class diagrams.

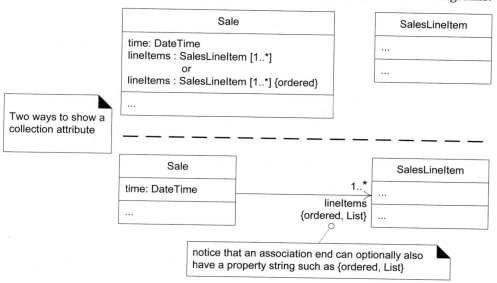

Figure 16.6 Two ways to show a collection attribute in the UML.

Notice also the optional use of property strings such as *{ordered}*.

16.5 Note Symbols: Notes, Comments, Constraints, and Method Bodies

Note symbols can be used on any UML diagram, but are especially common on class diagrams. A UML **note symbol** is displayed as a dog-eared rectangle with a dashed line to the annotated element; they've already been used throughout the book (for example, Figure 16.6). A note symbol may represent several things, such as:

- a UML **note** or **comment**, which by definition have no semantic impact
- a UML **constraint**, in which case it must be encased in braces '{...}' (see Figure 16.14)
- a **method** body—the implementation of a UML operation (see Figure 16.7)

16.6 Operations and Methods

Operations

One of the compartments of the UML class box shows the signatures of operations (see Figure 16.1 for many examples). At the time of this writing, the full, official format of the operation syntax is:

visibility name (parameter-list) {property-string}

Notice there is no *return type* element, an obvious problem, but purposefully injected into the UML 2 specification for inscrutable reasons. There is a chance that the specification will revert to a UML1-ish syntax, which in any event many authors show and UML tools will continue to support:

visibility name (parameter-list) : return-type {property-string}

Guideline: Assume the version that includes a return type.

Guideline: Operations are usually assumed public if no visibility is shown.

The property string contains arbitrary additional information, such as exceptions that may be raised, if the operation is abstract, and so forth.

In addition to the official UML operation syntax, the UML allows the operation signature to be written in any programming language, such as Java, assuming the reader or tool is notified. For example, both expressions are possible:

```
+ getPlayer( name : String ) : Player {exception IOException}

public Player getPlayer( String name ) throws IOException
```

An operation is *not* a method. A UML **operation** is a *declaration*, with a name, parameters, return type, exceptions list, and possibly a set of *constraints* of pre- and post-conditions. But, it isn't an implementation—rather, methods are implementations. When we explored operation contracts (p. 181), in UML terms we were exploring the definition of constraints for UML operations, as was discussed on p. 191.

How to Show Methods in Class Diagrams?

A UML **method** is the implementation of an operation; if constraints are defined, the method must satisfy them. A method may be illustrated several ways, including:

- in interaction diagrams, by the details and sequence of messages

- in class diagrams, with a UML note symbol stereotyped with «method»

Both styles will be used in subsequent chapters.

Figure 16.7 applies a UML note symbol to define the method body.

Notice, subtly, that when we use a UML note to show a method, we are *mixing static and dynamic views* in the same diagram. The method body (which defines dynamic behavior) adds a dynamic element to the static class diagram.

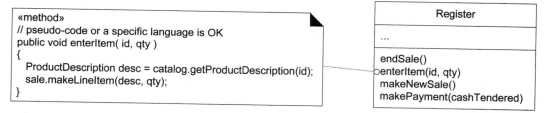

Figure 16.7 How to show a method body in a class diagram.

Note that this style is good for book or document diagrams and tool-generated output, but perhaps too fussy or stylized for sketching or tool input. Tools may provide a popup window to simply enter the code for a method.

Operation Issues in DCDs

The create Operation

The *create* message in an interaction diagram is normally interpreted as the invocation of the *new* operator and a constructor call in languages such as Java and C#. In a DCD this *create* message will usually be mapped to a constructor definition, using the rules of the language—such as the constructor name equal to the class name (Java, C#, C++, …). Figure 16.1 shows an example, with the *SuperclassFoo* constructor stereotyped «constructor» so that its category is clear.

Operations to Access Attributes

Accessing operations retrieve or set attributes, such as *getPrice* and *setPrice*. These operations are often excluded (or filtered) from the class diagram because of the high noise-to-value ratio they generate; for n attributes, there may be 2n uninteresting *getter* and *setter* operations. Most UML tools support filtering their display, and it's especially common to ignore them while wall sketching.

16.7   Keywords

A UML **keyword** is a textual adornment to categorize a model element. For example, the keyword to categorize that a classifier box is an interface is (shocking surprise!) «interface». Figure 16.1 illustrates the «interface» keyword. The «actor» keyword was used on p. 91 to replace the human stick-figure actor icon with a class box to model computer-system or robotic actors.

Guideline: When sketching UML—when we want speed, ease, and creative flow—modelers often simplify keywords to something like '<interface>' or '<I>'.

constraints p. 265   Most keywords are shown in guillemet (« »)[2] but some are shown in curly braces, such as *{abstract}*, which is a *constraint* containing the *abstract* keyword. In general, when a UML element says it can have a "property string"—such as a UML operation and UML association end have—some of the property string terms will be keywords (and some may be user defined terms) used in the curly brace format.

Figure 16.1 illustrates both the «interface» and *{abstract}* keywords.

A few sample predefined UML keywords include:[3]

Keyword	Meaning	Example Usage
«actor»	classifier is an actor	in class diagram, above classifier name
«interface»	classifier is an interface	in class diagram, above classifier name

---

2. Note that in UML 1, guillemet (« ») were only used for **stereotypes**. In UML 2, guillemets are used for both keywords and stereotypes.
3. There are many keywords. Refer to the UML specification for details.

Keyword	Meaning	Example Usage
{abstract}	abstract element; can't be instantiated	in class diagrams, after classifier name or operation name
{ordered}	a set of objects have some imposed order	in class diagrams, at an association end

16.8   Stereotypes, Profiles, and Tags

As with keywords, stereotypes are shown with guillemets symbols[4], such as «authorship». But, they are not keywords, which can be confusing. A **stereotype** represents a refinement of an existing modeling concept and is defined within a UML **profile**—informally, a collection of related stereotypes, tags, and constraints to specialize the use of the UML for a specific domain or platform, such as a UML profile for project management or for data modeling.

The UML predefines many stereotypes[5], such as «destroy» (used on sequence diagrams), and also allows user-defined ones. Thus, stereotypes provide an *extension mechanism* in the UML.

For example, Figure 16.8 shows a stereotype declaration, and its use. The stereotype declares a set of **tags**, using the attribute syntax. When an element (such as the *Square* class) is marked with a stereotype, all the tags apply to the element, and can be assigned values.

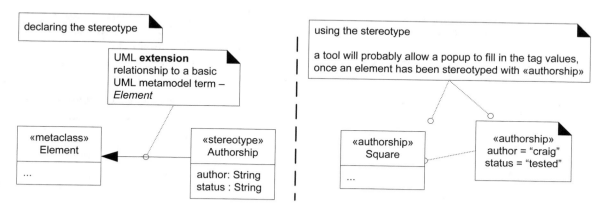

Figure 16.8 Stereotype declaration and use.

---

4. Guillemets are special *single*-character brackets most widely known by their use in French typography to indicate a quote. Typographically challenged tool vendors often substitute two angle brackets ('<< >>') for the more elegant '« »'.

5. See the UML specification.

16.9   UML Properties and Property Strings

In the UML, a **property** is "a named value denoting a characteristic of an element. A property has semantic impact." [OMG03b]. Some properties are predefined in the UML, such as *visibility*—a property of an operation. Others can be user-defined.

Properties of elements may be presented in many ways, but a textual approach is to use the UML **property string** *{name1=value1, name2=value2}* format, such as *{abstract, visibility=public}*. Some properties are shown without a value, such as *{abstract}*; this usually implies a boolean property, shorthand for *{abstract=true}*. Note that *{abstract}* is both an example of a *constraint* and a property string.

constraint p. 265

16.10   Generalization, Abstract Classes, Abstract Operations

Generalization in the UML is shown with a solid line and fat triangular arrow from the subclass to superclass (see Figure 16.1). What does it mean? In the UML, to quote:

> *Generalization—A taxonomic relationship between a more general classifier and a more specific classifier. Each instance of the specific classifier is also an indirect instance of the general classifier. Thus, the specific classifier indirectly has features of the more general classifier. [OMG03b]*

Is this the same as OO programming language (OOPL) **inheritance**? It depends. In a domain model conceptual-perspective class diagram, the answer is *no*. Rather, it implies the superclass is a superset and the subclass is a subset. On the other hand, in a DCD software-perspective class diagram, it implies OOPL inheritance from the superclass to subclass.

As shown in Figure 16.1, **abstract classes** and operations can be shown either with an *{abstract}* tag (useful when sketching UML) or by italicizing the name (easy to support in a UML tool).

The opposite case, **final classes** and operations that can't be overridden in subclasses, are shown with the *{leaf}* tag.

16.11   Dependency

Dependency lines may be used on any diagram, but are especially common on class and package diagrams. The UML includes a general **dependency relationship** that indicates that a **client** element (of any kind, including classes, packages, use cases, and so on) has knowledge of another **supplier** element and that a change in the supplier could affect the client. That's a broad relationship!

Dependency is illustrated with a dashed arrow line from the client to supplier.

Dependency can be viewed as another version of **coupling**, a traditional term in software development when an element is coupled to or depends on another.

There are many kinds of dependency; here are some common types in terms of objects and class diagrams:

- having an attribute of the supplier type
- sending a message to a supplier; the visibility to the supplier could be:
  - an attribute, a parameter variable, a local variable, a global variable, or class visibility (invoking static or class methods)
- receiving a parameter of the supplier type
- the supplier is a superclass or interface

All of these could be shown with a dependency line in the UML, but some of these types already have special lines that suggest the dependency. For example, there's a special UML line to show the superclass, one to show implementation of an interface, and one for attributes (the attribute-as-association line).

So, for those cases, it is not useful to use the dependency line. For example, in Figure 16.6 a *Sale* has some kind of dependency on *SalesLineItems* by virtue of the association line. Since there's already an association line between these two elements, adding a second dashed arrow dependency line is redundant.

Therefore, when to show a dependency?

Guideline: In class diagrams use the dependency line to depict global, parameter variable, local variable, and static-method (when a call is made to a static method of another class) dependency between objects.

For example, the following Java code shows an *updatePriceFor* method in the *Sale* class:

```
public class Sale
{
public void updatePriceFor( ProductDescription description )
{
    Money basePrice = description.getPrice();
    //…
}
// …
}
```

The *updatePriceFor* method receives a *ProductDescription* parameter object and then sends it a *getPrice* message. Therefore, the *Sale* object has parameter visibility to the *ProductDescription*, and message-sending coupling, and thus a dependency on the *ProductDescription*. If the latter class changed, the *Sale* class could be affected. This dependency can be shown in a class diagram (Figure 16.9).

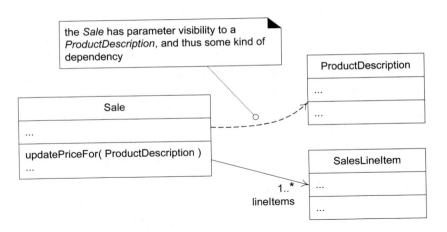

Figure 16.9 Showing dependency.

Another example: The following Java code shows a *doX* method in the *Foo* class:

```java
public class Foo
{
public void doX()
{
    System.runFinalization();
    //…
}
// …
}
```

The *doX* method invokes a static method on the *System* class. Therefore, the *Foo* object has a static-method dependency on the *System* class. This dependency can be shown in a class diagram (Figure 16.10).

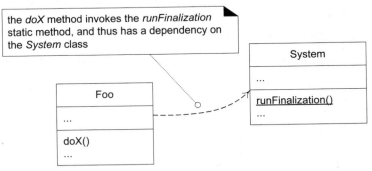

Figure 16.10 Showing dependency.

Dependency Labels

To show the type of dependency, or to help a tool with code generation, the dependency line can be labeled with keywords or stereotypes.[6] See Figure 16.11.

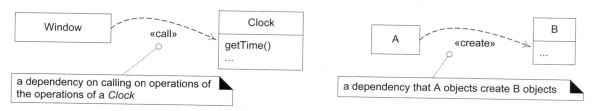

Figure 16.11 Optional dependency labels in the UML.

16.12 Interfaces

The UML provides several ways to show **interface** implementation, providing an interface to clients, and interface dependency (a **required interface**). In the UML, interface implementation is formally called **interface realization**. See Figure 16.12.

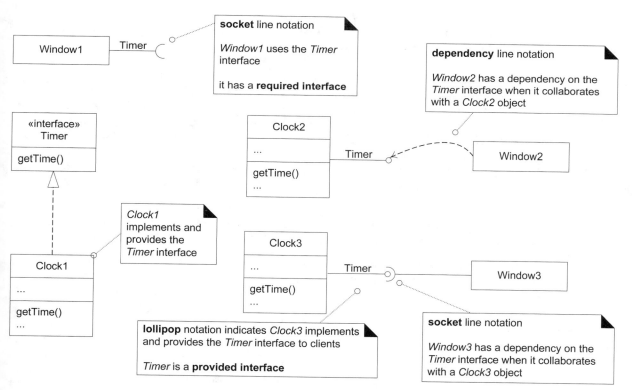

Figure 16.12 Different notations to show interfaces in UML.

---

6. See the UML specification for many predefined dependency labels.

The **socket notation** is new to UML 2. It's useful to indicate "Class X requires (uses) interface Y" without drawing a line pointing to interface Y.

16.13 Composition Over Aggregation

Aggregation is a vague kind of association in the UML that loosely suggests whole-part relationships (as do many ordinary associations). It has no meaningful distinct semantics in the UML versus a plain association, but the term is defined in the UML. Why? To quote Rumbaugh (one of the original and key UML creators):

In spite of the few semantics attached to aggregation, everybody thinks it is necessary (for different reasons). Think of it as a modeling placebo. [RJB04]

Guideline: Therefore, following the advice of UML creators, don't bother to use aggregation in the UML; rather, use *composition* when appropriate.

Composition, also known as **composite aggregation**, is a strong kind of whole-part aggregation and *is* useful to show in some models. A composition relationship implies that 1) an instance of the part (such as a *Square*) belongs to only *one* composite instance (such as one *Board*) at a time, 2) the part must *always belong* to a composite (no free-floating *Fingers)*, and 3) the composite is responsible for the creation and deletion of its parts—either by itself creating/deleting the parts, or by collaborating with other objects. Related to this constraint is that if the composite is destroyed, its parts must either be destroyed, or attached to another composite—no free-floating *Fingers* allowed! For example, if a physical paper Monopoly game board is destroyed, we think of the squares as being destroyed as well (a conceptual perspective). Likewise, if a software *Board* object is destroyed, its software *Square* objects are destroyed, in a DCD software perspective.

The UML notation for composition is a filled diamond on an association line, at the composite end of the line (see Figure 16.13).

Guideline: The association name in composition is always implicitly some variation of "Has-part," therefore don't bother to explicitly name the association.

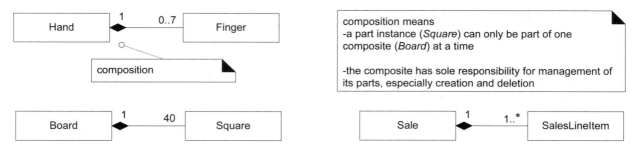

Figure 16.13 Composition in the UML.

16.14   Constraints

Constraints may be used on most UML diagrams, but are especially common on class diagrams. A UML **constraint** is a restriction or condition on a UML element. It is visualized in text between braces; for example: *{ size >= 0 }*. The text may be natural language or anything else, such as UML's formal specification language, the **Object Constraint Language** (OCL) [WK99]. See Figure 16.14.

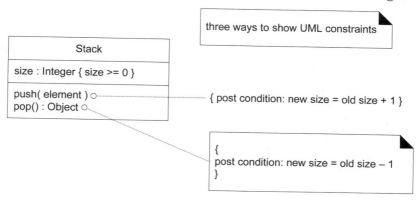

Figure 16.14 Constraints

16.15   Qualified Association

A **qualified association** has a **qualifier** that is used to select an object (or objects) from a larger set of related objects, based upon the qualifier key. Informally, in a software perspective, it suggests looking things up by a key, such as objects in a *HashMap*. For example, if a *ProductCatalog* contains many *ProductDescriptions*, and each one can be selected by an *itemID*, then the UML notation in Figure 16.15 can be used to depict this.

There's one subtle point about qualified associations: the change in multiplicity. For example, as contrasted in Figure 16.15 (a) vs. (b), qualification reduces the multiplicity at the target end of the association, usually down from many to one, because it implies the selection of usually one instance from a larger set.

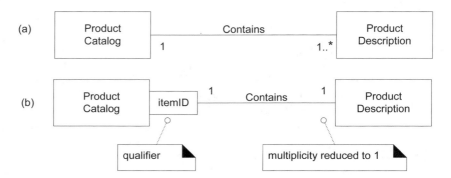

Figure 16.15 Qualified associations in the UML.

16.16   Association Class

An **association class** allows you treat an association itself as a class, and model it with attributes, operations, and other features. For example, if a *Company* employs many *Persons,* modeled with an *Employs* association, you can model the association itself as the *Employment* class, with attributes such as *startDate*.

In the UML, it is illustrated with a dashed line from the association to the association class. See Figure 16.16.

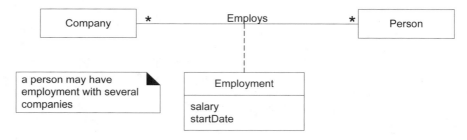

Figure 16.16 Association classes in the UML.

16.17   Singleton Classes

Singleton p. 442

In the world of OO design patterns, there is one that is especially common, called the **Singleton** pattern. It is explained later, but an implication of the pattern is that there is only *one* instance of a class instantiated—never two. In other words, it is a "singleton" instance. In a UML diagram, such a class can be marked with a '1' in the upper right corner of the name compartment. See Figure 16.17.

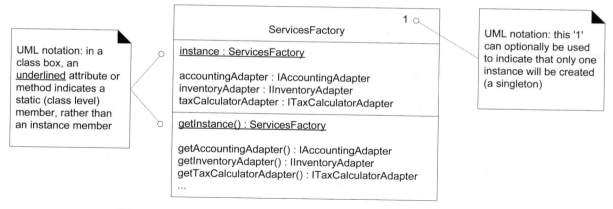

Figure 16.17 Showing a singleton.

16.18   Template Classes and Interfaces

Many languages (Java, C++, ...) support **templatized types**, also known (with shades of variant meanings) as **templates**, **parameterized types**, and **generics**.[7] They are most commonly used for the element type of collection classes, such as the elements of lists and maps. For example, in Java, suppose that a *Board* software object holds a *List* (an interface for a kind of collection) of many *Squares*. And, the concrete class that implements the *List* interface is an *ArrayList*:

```
public class Board
{
private List<Square> squares = new ArrayList<Square>();
// ...
}
```

Notice that the *List* interface and the *ArrayList* class (that implements the *List* interface) are parameterized with the element type *Square*. How to show template classes and interfaces in the UML? Figure 16.18 illustrates.

---

7. Motivations for template classes include increased type safety and performance.

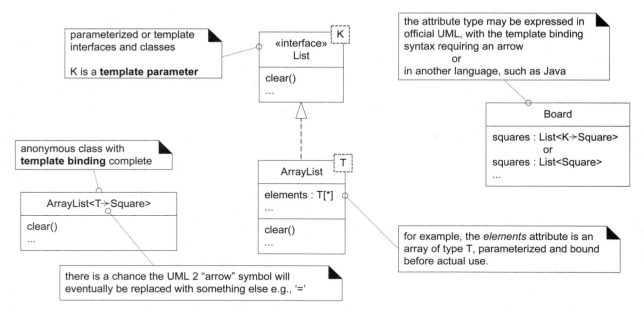

Figure 16.18 Templates in the UML.

16.19 User-Defined Compartments

In addition to common predefined **compartments** class compartments such as name, attributes, and operations, user-defined compartments can be added to a class box. Figure 16.19 shows an example.

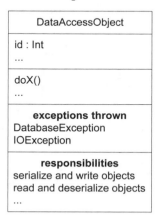

Figure 16.19 Compartments.

16.20   Active Class

active object p. 238   An **active object** runs on and controls its own thread of execution. Not surprisingly, the class of an active object is an **active class**. In the UML, it may be shown with double vertical lines on the left and right sides of the class box (Figure 16.20).

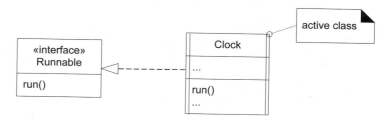

Figure 16.20 Active classes in the UML.

16.21   What's the Relationship Between Interaction and Class Diagrams?

When we draw interaction diagrams, a set of classes and their methods emerge from the creative design process of dynamic object modeling. For example, if we started with the (trivial for explanation) *makePayment* sequence diagram in Figure 16.21, we see that a *Register* and *Sale* class definition in a class diagram can be obviously derived.

Thus, from interaction diagrams the definitions of class diagrams can be generated. This suggests a linear ordering of drawing interaction diagrams *before* class diagrams, but in practice, especially when following the agile modeling practice of *models in parallel*, these complementary dynamic and static views are drawn concurrently. For example, 10 minutes on one, then 10 on the other.

Guideline: A good UML tool should automatically support changes in one diagram being reflected in the other. If wall sketching, use one wall for interaction diagrams, and an adjacent wall for class diagrams.

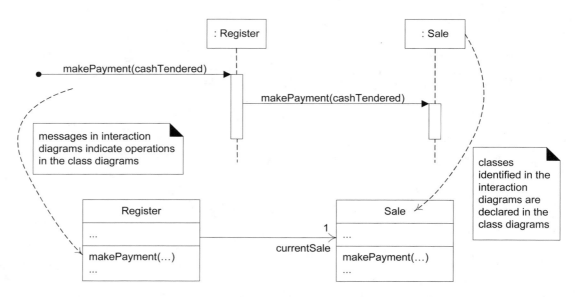

Figure 16.21 The influence of interaction diagrams on class diagrams.

GRASP: Designing Objects with Responsibilities

Understanding responsibilities is key to good object-oriented design.

—*Martin Fowler*

Objectives

- Learn to apply five of the GRASP principles or patterns for OOD.

This chapter and the next contribute significantly to an understanding of core OO design (OOD). OOD is sometimes taught as some variation of the following:

> After identifying your requirements and creating a domain model, then add methods to the appropriate classes, and define the messaging between the objects to fulfill the requirements.

Ouch! Such vague advice doesn't help us, because deep principles and issues are involved. Deciding what methods belong where and how objects should interact carries consequences and should be undertaken seriously. Mastering OOD—and this is its intricate charm—involves a large set of soft principles, with many degrees of freedom. It isn't magic—the patterns can be *named* (important!), explained, and applied. Examples help. Practice helps. And this small step helps: After studying these case studies, try recreating (from memory) the Monopoly solution on walls with partners, and apply the principles, such as Information Expert.

What's Next?   Having introduced basic dynamic and static UML notation to support OO design, this chapter introduces design principles. The next provides more detailed case study examples applying these principles and UML modeling.

UML Interaction Diagrams	UML Class Diagrams	Object Design with GRASP	Object Design Examples	Designing for Visibility

17.1   UML versus Design Principles

UML and silver bullet thinking p. 12

Since the UML is simply a standard visual modeling language, knowing its details doesn't teach you how to think in objects—that's a theme of this book. The UML is sometimes described as a "design tool" but that's not quite right…

The critical design tool for software development is a mind well educated in design principles. It is not the UML or any other technology.

17.2   Object Design: Example Inputs, Activities, and Outputs

This section summarizes a big-picture example of design in an iterative method:

- What's been done? — Prior activities (e.g., workshop) and artifacts.
- How do things relate? — Influence of prior artifacts (e.g., use cases) on OO design.
- How much design modeling to do, and how?
- What's the output?

Especially, I'd like you to understand how the analysis artifacts relate to object design.

What Are Inputs to Object Design?

Let's start with "process" inputs. Assume we are developers working on the POS NextGen project, and the following scenario is true:

The first **two-day requirements workshop** is finished.	The chief architect and business agree to implement and test some **scenarios of Process Sale in the first three-week** timeboxed iteration.
Three of the twenty use cases—those that are the most architecturally significant and of high business value—have been analyzed in detail, including, of course, the *Process Sale* use case. (The UP recommends, as typical with iterative methods, analyzing only **10%–20% of the requirements** in detail before starting to program.)	**Other artifacts** have been started: Supplementary Specification, Glossary, and Domain Model.
Programming experiments have resolved the show-stopper technical questions, such as whether a Java Swing UI will work on a touch screen.	The chief architect has drawn some ideas for the **large-scale logical architecture**, using UML package diagrams. This is part of the UP Design Model.

What are the *artifact* inputs and their relationship to object design?[1] They are summarized in Figure 17.1 and in the following table.

The **use case text** defines the visible behavior that the software objects must ultimately support—objects are designed to "realize" (implement) the use cases. In the UP, this OO design is called, not surprisingly, the **use case realization**.	The **Supplementary Specification** defines the non-functional goals, such as internalization, our objects must satisfy.
The **system sequence diagrams** identify the system operation messages, which are the starting messages on our interaction diagrams of collaborating objects.	The **Glossary** clarifies details of parameters or data coming in from the UI layer, data being passed to the database, and detailed item-specific logic or validation requirements, such as the legal formats and validation for product UPCs (universal product codes).
The **operation contracts** may complement the use case text to clarify what the software objects must achieve in a system operation. The post-conditions define detailed achievements.	The **Domain Model** suggests some names and attributes of software domain objects in the domain layer of the software architecture.

Not all of these artifacts are necessary. Recall that in the UP all elements are optional, possibly created to reduce some risk.

What Are Activities of Object Design?

We're ready to take off our analyst hats and put on our designer-modeler hats.

test first p. 386

Given one or more of these inputs, developers 1) start immediately coding (ideally with **test-first development**), 2) start some UML modeling for the object design, or 3) start with another modeling technique, such as CRC cards.[2]

In the UML case, the real point is not the UML, but visual modeling—using a language that allows us to explore more visually than we can with just raw text. In this case, for example, we draw both interaction diagrams and complementary class diagrams (dynamic and static modeling) during one **modeling day**. And most importantly, during the drawing (and coding) activity we apply various OO design principles, such as **GRASP** and the **Gang-of-Four (GoF) design patterns**. The overall approach to doing the OO design modeling will be based on the *metaphor* of **responsibility-driven design** (RDD), thinking about how to assign responsibilities to collaborating objects.

GRASP p. 277

GoF p. 435

RDD p. 276

> This and subsequent chapters explore what it means
> to apply RDD, GRASP, and some of the GoF design patterns.

---

1. Other artifact inputs could include design documents for an existing system being modified. It's also useful to reverse-engineer existing code into UML package diagrams to see the large-scale logical structure and some class and sequence diagrams.
2. All of these approaches are skillful depending on context and person.

On the modeling day, perhaps the team works in small groups for 2–6 hours either at the walls or with software modeling tools, doing different kinds of modeling for the difficult, creative parts of the design. This could include UI, OO, and database modeling with UML drawings, prototyping tools, sketches, and so forth.

During UML drawing, we adopt the realistic attitude (also promoted in agile modeling) that we are drawing the models primarily to *understand and communicate*, not to document. Of course, we expect some of the UML diagrams to be useful input to the definition (or automated code generation with a UML tool) of the code.

On Tuesday—still early in the three-week timeboxed iteration—the team stops modeling and puts on programmer hats to avoid a waterfall mentality of over-modeling before programming.

What Are the Outputs?

Figure 17.1 illustrates some inputs and their relationship to the output of a UML interaction and class diagram. Notice that we may refer to these analysis inputs during design; for example, re-reading the use case text or operation contracts, scanning the domain model, and reviewing the Supplementary Specification.

What's been created during the modeling day (for example)?

- specifically for object design, UML interaction, class, and package diagrams for the difficult parts of the design that we wished to explore before coding
- UI sketches and prototypes
- database models (with UML data modeling profile notation p. 625)
- report sketches and prototypes

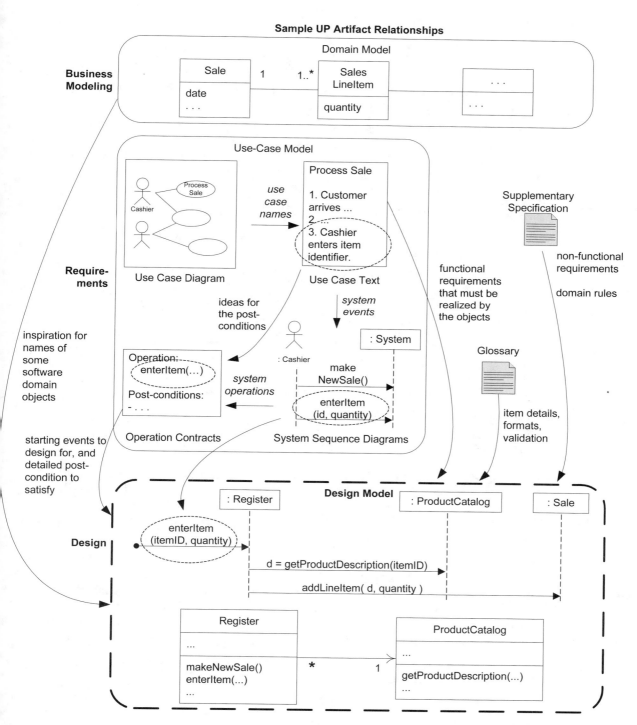

Figure 17.1 Artifact relationships emphasizing influence on OO design.

17.3   Responsibilities and Responsibility-Driven Design

A popular way of thinking about the design of software objects and also larger-scale components[3] is in terms of **responsibilities**, **roles**, and **collaborations**. This is part of a larger approach called **responsibility-driven design** or **RDD** [WM02].

In RDD, we think of software objects as having responsibilities—an abstraction of what they do. The UML defines a **responsibility** as "a contract or obligation of a classifier" [OMG03b]. Responsibilities are related to the obligations or behavior of an object in terms of its role. Basically, these responsibilities are of the following two types: *doing* and *knowing*.

Doing responsibilities of an object include:

- ❍   doing something itself, such as creating an object or doing a calculation

- ❍   initiating action in other objects

- ❍   controlling and coordinating activities in other objects

Knowing responsibilities of an object include:

- ❍   knowing about private encapsulated data

- ❍   knowing about related objects

- ❍   knowing about things it can derive or calculate

Responsibilities are assigned to classes of objects during object design. For example, I may declare that "a *Sale* is responsible for creating *SalesLineItems*" (a doing), or "a *Sale* is responsible for knowing its total" (a knowing).

low representational gap p. 138

Guideline: For software domain objects, the domain model, because of the attributes and associations it illustrates, often inspires the relevant responsibilities related to "knowing." For example, if the domain model *Sale* class has a *time* attribute, it's natural by the goal of **low representational gap** that a software *Sale* class knows its time.

The translation of responsibilities into classes and methods is influenced by the *granularity* of the responsibility. Big responsibilities take hundreds of classes and methods. Little responsibilities might take one method. For example, the responsibility to "provide access to relational databases" may involve two hundred classes and thousands of methods, packaged in a subsystem. By contrast, the responsibility to "create a *Sale*" may involve only one method in one class.

A responsibility is not the same thing as a method—it's an abstraction—but methods fulfill responsibilities.

---

3.   Thinking in terms of responsibilities can apply at any scale of software—from a small object to a system of systems.

RDD also includes the idea of **collaboration**. Responsibilities are implemented by means of methods that either act alone or collaborate with other methods and objects. For example, the *Sale* class might define one or more methods to know its total; say, a method named *getTotal*. To fulfill that responsibility, the *Sale* may collaborate with other objects, such as sending a *getSubtotal* message to each *SalesLineItem* object asking for its subtotal.

RDD is a Metaphor

RDD is a general metaphor for thinking about OO software design. Think of software objects as similar to people with responsibilities who collaborate with other people to get work done. RDD leads to viewing an OO design as a *community of collaborating responsible objects*.

Key point: GRASP names and describes some basic principles to assign responsibilities, so it's useful to know—to support RDD.

17.4 GRASP: A Methodical Approach to Basic OO Design

GRASP: A Learning Aid for OO Design with Responsibilities

It *is* possible to name and explain the detailed principles and reasoning required to grasp basic object design, assigning responsibilities to objects. The **GRASP** principles or patterns are a learning aid to help you understand essential object design and apply design reasoning in a methodical, rational, explainable way. This approach to understanding and using design principles is based on *patterns of assigning responsibilities*.

This chapter—and several others—uses GRASP as a tool to help master the basics of OOD and understanding responsibility assignment in object design.

Understanding how to apply GRASP
for object design is a key goal of the book.

So, GRASP is relevant, but on the other hand, it's just a learning aid to structure and name the principles—once you "grasp" the fundamentals, the specific GRASP terms (Information Expert, Creator, ...) aren't important.

17.5 What's the Connection Between Responsibilities, GRASP, and UML Diagrams?

You can think about assigning responsibilities to objects while coding or while modeling. Within the UML, drawing interaction diagrams becomes the occasion for considering these responsibilities (realized as methods).

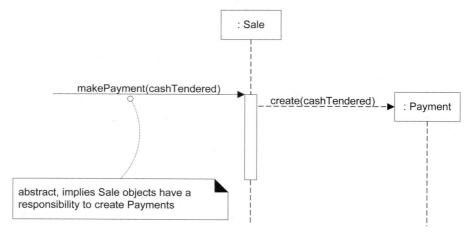

Figure 17.2 Responsibilities and methods are related.

Figure 17.2 indicates that *Sale* objects have been given a responsibility to create *Payments*, which is concretely invoked with a *makePayment* message and handled with a corresponding *makePayment* method. Furthermore, the fulfillment of this responsibility requires collaboration to create the *Payment* object and invoke its constructor.

Therefore, when we draw a UML interaction diagram, we are deciding on responsibility assignments. This chapter emphasizes fundamental principles— expressed in GRASP—to guide choices about assigning responsibilities. Thus, you can apply the GRASP principles while drawing UML interaction diagrams, and also while coding.

17.6   What are Patterns?

Experienced OO developers (and other software developers) build up a repertoire of both general principles and idiomatic solutions that guide them in the creation of software. These principles and idioms, if codified in a structured format describing the problem and solution and named, may be called **patterns**. For example, here is a sample pattern:

Pattern Name:	**Information Expert**
Problem:	What is a basic principle by which to assign responsibilities to objects?
Solution:	Assign a responsibility to the class that has the information needed to fulfill it.

In OO design, a **pattern** is a named description of a problem and solution that can be applied to new contexts; ideally, a pattern advises us on how to apply its solution in varying circumstances and considers the forces and trade-offs. Many patterns, given a specific category of problem, guide the assignment of responsibilities to objects.

> Most simply, a good **pattern** is a *named* and *well-known* problem/solution pair that can be applied in new contexts, with advice on how to apply it in novel situations and discussion of its trade-offs, implementations, variations, and so forth.

Patterns Have Names—Important!

Software development is a young field. Young fields lack well-established names for their principles—and that makes communication and education difficult. Patterns have names, such as *Information Expert* and *Abstract Factory*. Naming a pattern, design idea, or principle has the following advantages:

- It supports chunking and incorporating that concept into our understanding and memory.

- It facilitates communication.

When a pattern is named and widely published—and we all agree to use the name—we can discuss a complex design idea in shorter sentences (or shorter diagrams), a virtue of abstraction. Consider the following discussion between two software developers, using a vocabulary of pattern names:

Jill: "Hey Jack, for the persistence subsystem, let's expose the services with a *Facade*. We'll use an *Abstract Factory* for *Mappers*, and *Proxies* for lazy materialization."

Jack: "What the hell did you just say?!?"

Jill: "Here, read this…"

'New Pattern' is an Oxymoron

New pattern should be considered an oxymoron if it describes a new idea. The very term "pattern" suggests a long-repeating thing. The point of design patterns is *not* to express new design ideas. Quite the opposite—great patterns attempt to codify *existing* tried-and-true knowledge, idioms, and principles; the more honed, old, and widely used, the better.

Consequently, the GRASP patterns don't state new ideas; they name and codify widely used basic principles. To an OO design expert, the GRASP patterns—by idea if not by name—will appear fundamental and familiar. That's the point!

The Gang-of-Four Design Patterns Book

The idea of named patterns in software comes from Kent Beck (also of **Extreme Programming** fame) in the mid 1980s.[4] However, 1994 was a major milestone in the history of patterns, OO design, and software design books: The massive-selling and hugely influential book *Design Patterns* [GHJV95][5] was published, authored by Gamma, Helm, Johnson, and Vlissides. The book, considered the "Bible" of design pattern books, describes 23 patterns for OO design, with names such as *Strategy* and *Adapter*. These 23 patterns, authored by four people, are therefore called the **Gang of Four**[6] (or **GoF**) design patterns.

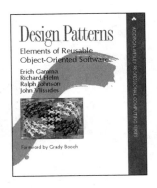

However, *Design Patterns* isn't an introductory book; it assumes significant prior OO design and programming knowledge, and most code examples are in C++.

Later—intermediate—chapters of *this* book, especially Chapter 26 (p. 435), Chapter 36 (p. 587), and Chapter 37 (p. 621) introduce many of the most frequently used GoF design patterns and apply them to our case studies. Also: See "Contents by Major Topics" on page ix.

It is a key goal of this text to *learn both GRASP and essential GoF patterns*.

Is GRASP a Set of Patterns or Principles?

GRASP defines nine basic OO design principles or basic building blocks in design. Some have asked, "Doesn't GRASP describe principles rather than patterns?" One answer is in the words of the Gang of Four authors, from the preface of their influential *Design Patterns* book:

One person's pattern is another person's primitive building block.

Rather than focusing on labels, this text focuses on the pragmatic value of using the pattern style as an excellent *learning aid* for naming, presenting, and remembering basic, classic design ideas.

---

4. The notion of patterns originated with the (building) architectural patterns of Christopher Alexander [AIS77]. Patterns for software originated in the 1980s with Kent Beck, who became aware of Alexander's pattern work in architecture, and then were developed by Beck with Ward Cunningham [BC87, Beck94] at Tektronix.
5. Publishers list the publication date as 1995, but it was released October 1994.
6. Also a subtle joke related to mid-1970s Chinese politics following Mao's death.

17.7　Where are We Now?

So far, this chapter has summarized the background for OO design:

1. The iterative **process background**—Prior artifacts? How do they relate to OO design models? How much time should we spend design modeling?

2. **RDD** as a metaphor for object design—a community of collaborating responsible objects.

3. **Patterns** as a way to name and explain OO design ideas—**GRASP** for basic patterns of assigning responsibilities, and **GoF** for more advanced design ideas. Patterns can be applied during modeling and during coding.

4. **UML** for OO design **visual modeling**, during which time both GRASP and GoF patterns can be applied.

With that understood, it's time to focus on some details of object design.

17.8　A Short Example of Object Design with GRASP

All the GRASP patterns are summarized on the inside front cover of this book.

Following sections explore GRASP in more detail, but let's start with a shorter example to see the big ideas, applied to the Monopoly case study. There are nine GRASP patterns; this example applies the following subset:

- Creator
- Information Expert
- Low Coupling
- Controller
- High Cohesion

Creator

Problem: Who creates the *Square* object?

One of the first problems you have to consider in OO design is: Who creates object X? This is a *doing* responsibility. For example, in the Monopoly case study, who creates a *Square* software object? Now, *any* object can create a *Square*, but what would many OO developers choose? And why?

How about having a *Dog* object (i.e., some arbitrary class) be the creator? No! We can feel it in our bones. Why? Because—and this is the critical point—it doesn't appeal to our mental model of the domain. *Dog* doesn't support **low representational gap** (**LRG**) between how we think of the domain and a straightforward correspondence with software objects. I've done this problem with literally thousands of developers, and virtually every one, from India to the USA, will say, "Make the *Board* object create the *Squares*." Interesting! It reflects an "intuition" that OO software developers often (exceptions are explored later) want "containers" to create the things "contained," such as *Boards* creating *Squares*.

By the way, why we are defining software classes with the names *Square* and *Board*, rather than the names *AB324* and *ZC17*? Answer: By LRG. This connects the UP Domain Model to the UP Design Model, or our mental model of the domain to its realization in the *domain layer* of the software architecture.

With that as background, here's the definition of the **Creator** pattern[7]:

Name:	**Creator**
Problem:	Who creates an A?
Solution: (this can be viewed as advice)	Assign class B the responsibility to create an instance of class A if one of these is true (the more the better):
	■ B "contains" or compositely aggregates A.
	■ B records A.
	■ B closely uses A.
	■ B has the initializing data for A.

Notice this has to do with responsibility assignment. Let's see how to apply Creator.

First, a subtle but important point in applying Creator and other GRASP patterns: *B* and *A* refer to *software* objects, not domain model objects. We first try to apply Creator by looking for existing *software* objects that satisfy the role of *B*. But what if we are just starting the OO design, and we have not yet defined any software classes? In this case, by LRG, *look to the domain model* for inspiration.

Thus, for the *Square* creation problem, since no software classes are yet defined, we look at the domain model in Figure 17.3 and see that a *Board contains Squares*. That's a conceptual perspective, not a software one, but of course we can mirror it in the Design Model so that a software *Board* object contains software *Square* objects. And then consistent with LRG and the Creator advice, the *Board* will create *Squares*. Also, *Squares* will always be a part of one *Board*, and *Board* manages their creation and destruction; thus, they are in a *composite aggregation* association with the *Board*.

Recall that an agile modeling practice is to create parallel complementary dynamic and static object models. Therefore, I've drawn *both* a partial sequence diagram and class diagram to reflect this design decision in which I've applied a GRASP pattern while drawing UML diagrams. See Figure 17.4 and Figure 17.5. Notice in Figure 17.4 that when the *Board* is created, it creates a *Square*. For brevity in this example, I'll ignore the side issue of drawing the loop to create all 40 squares.

---

7. Alternate creation patterns, such as *Concrete Factory* and *Abstract Factory*, are discussed later.

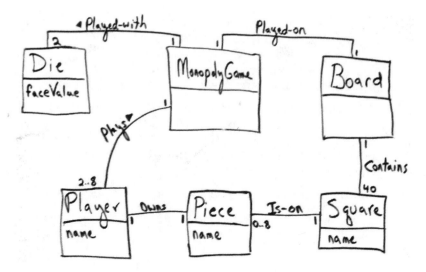

Figure 17.3 Monopoly iteration-1 domain model.

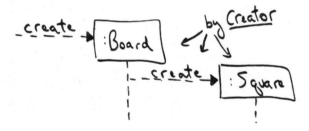

Figure 17.4 Applying the Creator pattern in a dynamic model.

Figure 17.5 In a DCD of the Design Model, *Board* has a composite aggregation association with *Squares*. We are applying Creator in a static model.

Information Expert

Problem: Who knows about a *Square* object, given a key?

The pattern Information Expert (often abbreviated to Expert) is one of the most basic responsibility assignment principles in object design.

Suppose objects need to be able to reference a particular *Square*, given its
name. Who should be responsible for
knowing a *Square*, given a key? Of
course, this is a *knowing* responsibility,
but Expert also applies to *doing*.

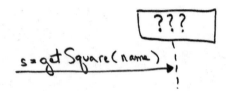

As with Creator, *any* object can be responsible, but what would many OO developers choose? And why? As with the Creator problem, most OO developers
choose the *Board* object. It seems sort of trivially obvious to assign this responsibility to a *Board*, but it is instructive to deconstruct why, and to learn to apply
this principle in more subtle cases. Later examples will get more subtle.

Information Expert explains why the *Board* is chosen:

Name:	**Information Expert**
Problem:	What is a basic principle by which to assign responsibilities to objects?
Solution: (advice)	Assign a responsibility to the class that has the information needed to fulfill it.

A responsibility needs information for its fulfillment—information about other
objects, an object's own state, the world around an object, information the object
can derive, and so forth. In this case, to be able to retrieve and present any one
Square—given its name—some object must know (have the information) about
all the *Squares*. We previously decided, as shown in Figure 17.5, that a software
Board will aggregate all the *Square* objects. Therefore, *Board* has the information necessary to fulfill this responsibility. Figure 17.6 illustrates applying
Expert in the context of drawing.

Figure 17.6 Applying Expert.

The next GRASP principle, Low Coupling, explains why Expert is a useful, core
principle of OO design.

Low Coupling

Question: Why *Board* over *Dog*?

Expert guides us to assign the responsibility to know a particular *Square*, given
a unique name, to the *Board* object because the *Board* knows about all the

Squares (it has the information—it is the Information Expert). But why does Expert give this advice?

The answer is found in the principle of Low Coupling. Briefly and informally, **coupling** is a measure of how strongly one element is connected to, has knowledge of, or depends on other elements. If there is coupling or dependency, then when the depended-upon element changes, the dependant may be affected. For example, a subclass is strongly coupled to a superclass. An object *A* that calls on the operations of object *B* has coupling to *B's* services.

The Low Coupling principle applies to many dimensions of software development; it's really one of the cardinal goals in building software. In terms of object design and responsibilities, we can describe the advice as follows:

Name:	**Low Coupling**
Problem:	How to reduce the impact of change?
Solution: (advice)	Assign responsibilities so that (unnecessary) coupling remains low. Use this principle to evaluate alternatives.

We use Low Coupling to *evaluate* existing designs or to evaluate the choice between new alternatives—all other things being equal, we should prefer a design whose coupling is lower than the alternatives.

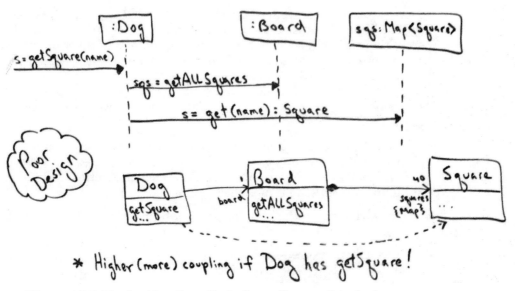

Figure 17.7 Evaluating the effect of coupling on this design.

For example, as we've decided in Figure 17.5, a *Board* object contains many *Squares*. Why not assign *getSquare* to *Dog* (i.e., some arbitrary other class)? Consider the impact in terms of low coupling. If a *Dog* has *getSquare*, as shown in the UML sketch in Figure 17.7, it must collaborate with the *Board* to get the collection of all the *Squares* in the *Board*. They are probably stored in a *Map* collection object, which allows retrieval by a key. Then, the *Dog* can access and return one particular *Square* by the key *name*.

But let's evaluate the total coupling with this poor *Dog* design versus our original design where *Board* does *getSquare*. In the *Dog* case, the *Dog* and the *Board* must both know about *Square* objects (two objects have coupling to *Square*); in the *Board* case, only *Board* must know about *Square* objects (one object has coupling to *Square*). Thus, the overall coupling is lower with the *Board* design, and all other things being equal, it is better than the *Dog* design, in terms of supporting the goal of Low Coupling.

At a higher-goal level, why is Low Coupling desirable? In other words, why would we want to reduce the impact of change? *Because Low Coupling tends to reduce the time, effort, and defects in modifying software.* That's a short answer, but one with big implications in building and maintaining software!

Key Point: Expert Supports Low Coupling

To return to the motivation for Information Expert: it guides us to a choice that supports Low Coupling. Expert asks us to find the object that has most of the information required for the responsibility (e.g., *Board*) and assign responsibility there.

If we put the responsibility anywhere else (e.g., *Dog*), the overall coupling will be higher because more information or objects must be shared away from their original source or home, as the squares in the *Map* collection had to be shared with the *Dog*, away from their home in the *Board*.

Applying UML: Please note a few UML elements in the sequence diagram in Figure 17.7:

- The return value variable *sqs* from the *getAllSquares* message is also used to name the lifeline object in *sqs : Map<Square>* (e.g., a collection of type *Map* that holds *Square* objects). Referencing a return value variable in a lifeline box (to send it messages) is common.

- The variable *s* in the starting *getSquare* message and the variable *s* in the later *get* message refer to the same object.

- The message expression *s = get(name) : Square* indicates that the type of *s* is a reference to a *Square* instance.

Controller

A simple layered architecture has a UI layer and a domain layer, among others. Actors, such as the human observer in the Monopoly game, generate UI events, such as clicking on a button with a mouse to play the game. The UI software objects (in Java for example, a *JFrame* window and a *JButton* button) must then react to the mouse click event and ultimately cause the game to play.

Model-View Separation p. 209

From the Model-View Separation Principle, we know the UI objects should *not* contain application or "business" logic such as calculating a player's move. Therefore, once the UI objects pick up the mouse event, they need to **delegate** (forward the task to another object) the request to *domain objects* in the *domain layer*.

The Controller pattern answers this simple question: What *first* object after or beyond the UI layer should receive the message from the UI layer?

To tie this back to system sequence diagrams, as a review of Figure 17.8 shows, the key system operation is *playGame*. Somehow the human observer generates a *playGame* request (probably by clicking on a GUI button labeled "Play Game") and the system responds.

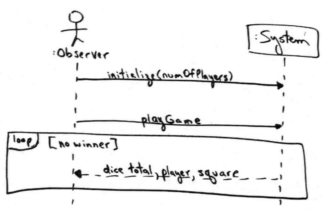

Figure 17.8 SSD for the Monopoly game. Note the *playGame* operation.

Figure 17.9 illustrates a finer-grained look at what's going on, assuming a Java Swing GUI *JFrame* window and *JButton* button.[8] Clicking on a *JButton* sends an *actionPerformed* message to some object, often to the *JFrame* window itself, as we see in Figure 17.9. Then—and this is the **key point**—the *JFrame* window must adapt that *actionPerformed* message into something more semantically meaningful, such as a *playGame* message (to correspond to the SSD analysis), and delegate the *playGame* message to a domain object in the domain layer.

> Do you see the connection between the SSD system operations and the detailed object design from the UI to domain layer? This is important.

Thus, Controller deals with a basic question in OO design: How to connect the UI layer to the application logic layer? Should the *Board* be the first object to receive the *playGame* message from the UI layer? Or something else?

---

8. Similar objects, messages, and collaboration patterns apply to .NET, Python, etc.

In some OOA/D methods, the name *controller* was given to the application logic object that received and "controlled" (coordinated) handling the request.

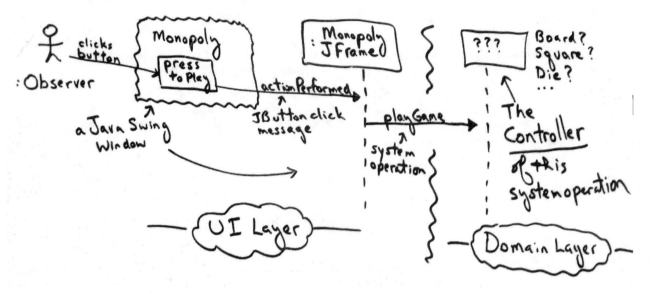

Figure 17.9 Who is the Controller for the *playGame* system operation?

The Controller pattern offers the following advice:

Name:	**Controller**
Problem:	What first object beyond the UI layer receives and coordinates ("controls") a system operation?
Solution: (advice)	Assign the responsibility to an object representing one of these choices:

- Represents the overall "system," a "root object," a device that the software is running within, or a major subsystem (these are all variations of a *facade controller*).

- Represents a use case scenario within which the system operation occurs (a use case or *session controller*)

Let's consider these options:

Option 1: Represents the overall "system," or a "root object"—such as an object called *MonopolyGame*.

Option 1: Represents a device that the software is running within—this option appertains to specialized hardware devices such as a phone or a bank cash machine (e.g., software class *Phone* or *BankCashMachine*); it doesn't apply in this case.

Option 2: Represents the use case or session. The use case that the *playGame* system operation occurs within is called *Play Monopoly Game*. Thus, a software class such as *PlayMonopolyGameHandler* (appending "*...Handler*" or "*...Session*" is an idiom in OO design when this version is used).

Option #1, class *MonopolyGame*, is reasonable if there are only a few system operations (more on the trade-offs when we discuss High Cohesion). Therefore, Figure 17.10 illustrates the design decision based on Controller.

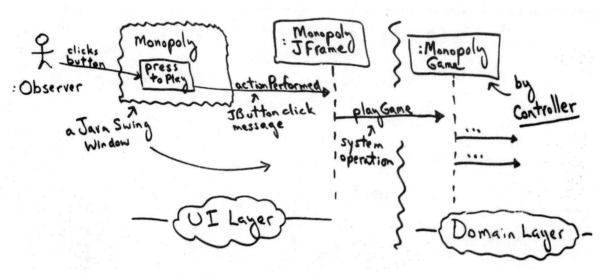

Figure 17.10 Applying the Controller pattern—using *MonopolyGame*. Connecting the UI layer to the domain layer of software objects.

High Cohesion

Based on the Controller decision, we are now at the design point shown in the sequence diagram to the right. The detailed design discussion of what comes next—consistently and methodically applying GRASP—is explored in a following chapter, but right now we have two contrasting design approaches worth considering, illustrated in Figure 17.11.

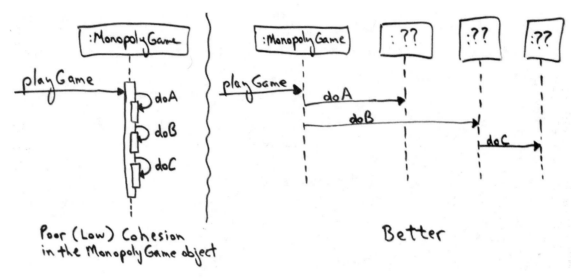

Figure 17.11 Contrasting the level of cohesion in different designs.

Notice in the left-hand version that the *MonopolyGame* object itself does all the work, and in the right-hand version it *delegates* and coordinates the work for the *playGame* request. In software design a basic quality known as **cohesion** informally measures how functionally related the operations of a software element are, and also measures how much work a software element is doing. As a simple contrasting example, an object *Big* with 100 methods and 2,000 source lines of code (SLOC) is doing a lot more than an object *Small* with 10 methods and 200 source lines. And if the 100 methods of *Big* are covering many different areas of responsibility (such as database access *and* random number generation), then *Big* has less focus or functional cohesion than *Small*. In summary, both the amount of code and the relatedness of the code are an indicator of an object's cohesion.

To be clear, bad cohesion (low cohesion) doesn't just imply an object does work only by itself; indeed, a low cohesion object with 2,000 SLOC probably collaborates with many other objects. Now, here's a *key point*: All that interaction tends to *also* create bad (high) coupling. Bad cohesion and bad coupling often go hand-in-hand.

In terms of the contrasting designs in Figure 17.11, the left-hand version of *MonopolyGame* has worse cohesion than the right-hand version, since the left-hand version is making the *MonopolyGame* object itself do all the work, rather than delegating and distributing work among objects. This leads to the principle of High Cohesion, which is used to evaluate different design choices. All other things being equal, prefer a design with higher cohesion.

Name:	**High Cohesion**
Problem:	How to keep objects focused, understandable, and manageable, and as a side effect, support Low Coupling?
Solution: (advice)	Assign responsibilities so that cohesion remains high. Use this to evaluate alternatives.

We can say that the right-hand design better supports High Cohesion than the left-hand version.

17.9 Applying GRASP to Object Design

All nine GRASP patterns are summarized on the inside front cover of this book.

GRASP stands for **G**eneral **R**esponsibility **A**ssignment **S**oftware **P**atterns.[9] The name was chosen to suggest the importance of *grasping* these principles to successfully design object-oriented software.

Understanding and being able to apply the ideas behind GRASP—while coding or while drawing interaction and class diagrams—enables developers new to object technology needs to master these basic principles as quickly as possible; they form a foundation for designing OO systems.

There are nine GRASP patterns:

Creator	Controller	Pure Fabrication
Information Expert	High Cohesion	Indirection
Low Coupling	Polymorphism	Protected Variations

The remainder of this chapter reexamines the first five in more detail; the remaining four are introduced in Chapter 25 starting on p. 413.

17.10 Creator

Problem Who should be responsible for creating a new instance of some class?

The creation of objects is one of the most common activities in an object-oriented system. Consequently, it is useful to have a general principle for the assignment of creation responsibilities. Assigned well, the design can support low coupling, increased clarity, encapsulation, and reusability.

---

9. Technically, one should write "GRAS Patterns" rather than "GRASP Patterns," but the latter sounds better.

Solution Assign class B the responsibility to create an instance of class A if one of these is true (the more the better):[10]

- B "contains" or compositely aggregates A.

- B records A.

- B closely uses A.

- B has the initializing data for A that will be passed to A when it is created. Thus B is an Expert with respect to creating A.

B is a *creator* of A objects.

If more than one option applies, usually prefer a class B which *aggregates* or *contains* class A.

Example In the NextGen POS application, who should be responsible for creating a *Sales-LineItem* instance? By Creator, we should look for a class that aggregates, contains, and so on, *SalesLineItem* instances. Consider the partial domain model in Figure 17.12.

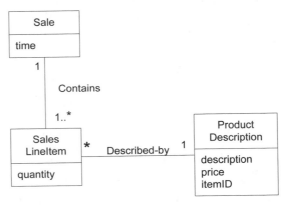

Figure 17.12 Partial domain model.

Since a *Sale* contains (in fact, aggregates) many *SalesLineItem* objects, the Creator pattern suggests that *Sale* is a good candidate to have the responsibility of creating *SalesLineItem* instances. This leads to the design of object interactions shown in Figure 17.13.

This assignment of responsibilities requires that a *makeLineItem* method be defined in *Sale*. Once again, the context in which we considered and decided on these responsibilities was while drawing an interaction diagram. The method section of a class diagram can then summarize the responsibility assignment results, concretely realized as methods.

---

10. Other creation patterns, such as *Concrete Factory* and *Abstract Factory*, are explored later.

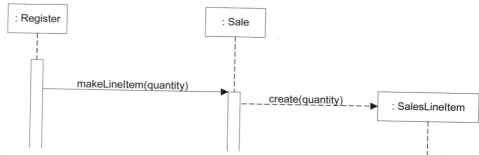

Figure 17.13 Creating a SalesLineItem.

Discussion Creator guides the assigning of responsibilities related to the creation of objects, a very common task. The basic intent of the Creator pattern is to find a creator that needs to be connected to the created object in any event. Choosing it as the creator supports low coupling.

Composite *aggregates* Part, Container *contains* Content, and Recorder *records*. Recorded are all very common relationships between classes in a class diagram. Creator suggests that the enclosing container or recorder class is a good candidate for the responsibility of creating the thing contained or recorded. Of course, this is only a guideline.

composite *aggregation p. 264* Note that we turned to the concept of **composition** in considering the Creator pattern. A composite object is an excellent candidate to make its parts.

Sometimes you identify a creator by looking for the class that has the initializing data that will be passed in during creation. This is actually an example of the Expert pattern. Initializing data is passed in during creation via some kind of initialization method, such as a Java constructor that has parameters. For example, assume that a *Payment* instance, when created, needs to be initialized with the *Sale* total. Since *Sale* knows the total, *Sale* is a candidate creator of the *Payment*.

Contraindications Often, creation requires significant complexity, such as using recycled instances for performance, conditionally creating an instance from one of a family of similar classes based upon some external property value, and so forth. In these cases, it is advisable to delegate creation to a helper class called a *Concrete Factory* or an *Abstract Factory* [GHJV95] rather than use the class suggested by *Creator*. Factories are discussed starting on p. 440.

Benefits ■ Low coupling is supported, which implies lower maintenance dependencies and higher opportunities for reuse. Coupling is probably not increased because the *created* class is likely already visible to the *creator* class, due to the existing associations that motivated its choice as creator.

Related Patterns
or Principles
- Low Coupling
- Concrete Factory and Abstract Factory
- Whole-Part [BMRSS96] describes a pattern to define aggregate objects that support encapsulation of components.

17.11 Information Expert (or Expert)

Problem What is a general principle of assigning responsibilities to objects?

A Design Model may define hundreds or thousands of software classes, and an application may require hundreds or thousands of responsibilities to be fulfilled. During object design, when the interactions between objects are defined, we make choices about the assignment of responsibilities to software classes. If we've chosen well, systems tend to be easier to understand, maintain, and extend, and our choices afford more opportunity to reuse components in future applications.

Solution Assign a responsibility to the information expert—the class that has the *information* necessary to fulfill the responsibility.

Example In the NextGEN POS application, some class needs to know the grand total of a sale.

> Start assigning responsibilities by clearly stating the responsibility.

By this advice, the statement is:

Who should be responsible for knowing the grand total of a sale?

By *Information Expert*, we should look for that class of objects that has the information needed to determine the total.

Now we come to a key question: Do we look in the Domain Model or the Design Model to analyze the classes that have the information needed? The Domain Model illustrates conceptual classes of the real-world domain; the Design Model illustrates software classes.

Answer:

1. If there are relevant classes in the Design Model, look there first.

2. Otherwise, look in the Domain Model, and attempt to use (or expand) its representations to inspire the creation of corresponding design classes.

For example, assume we are just starting design work and there is no, or a minimal, Design Model. Therefore, we look to the Domain Model for information experts; perhaps the real-world *Sale* is one. Then, we add a software class to the Design Model similarly called *Sale*, and give it the responsibility of knowing its total, expressed with the method named *getTotal*. This approach supports *low representational gap* in which the software design of objects appeals to our concepts of how the real domain is organized.

To examine this case in detail, consider the partial Domain Model in Figure 17.14.

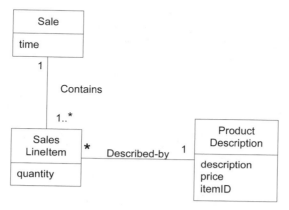

Figure 17.14 Associations of Sale.

What information do we need to determine the grand total? We need to know about all the *SalesLineItem* instances of a sale and the sum of their subtotals. A *Sale* instance contains these; therefore, by the guideline of Information Expert, *Sale* is a suitable class of object for this responsibility; it is an *information expert* for the work.

As mentioned, it is in the context of the creation of interaction diagrams that these questions of responsibility often arise. Imagine we are starting to work through the drawing of diagrams in order to assign responsibilities to objects. A partial interaction diagram and class diagram in Figure 17.15 illustrate some decisions.

Figure 17.15 Partial interaction and class diagrams.

We are not done yet. What information do we need to determine the line item subtotal? *SalesLineItem.quantity* and *ProductDescription.price*. The *Sales-LineItem* knows its quantity and its associated *ProductDescription*; therefore, by Expert, *SalesLineItem* should determine the subtotal; it is the *information expert*.

In terms of an interaction diagram, this means that the *Sale* should send *get-Subtotal* messages to each of the *SalesLineItems* and sum the results; this design is shown in Figure 17.16.

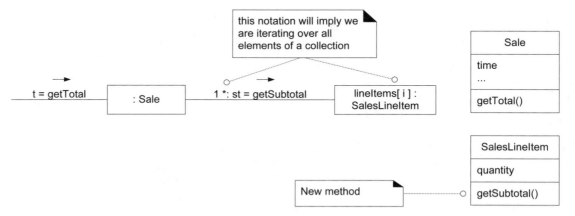

Figure 17.16 Calculating the Sale total.

To fulfill the responsibility of knowing and answering its subtotal, a *Sales-LineItem* has to know the product price.

The *ProductDescription* is an information expert on answering its price; therefore, *SalesLineItem* sends it a message asking for the product price.

The design is shown in Figure 17.17.

In conclusion, to fulfill the responsibility of knowing and answering the sale's total, we assigned three responsibilities to three design classes of objects as follows.

Design Class	Responsibility
Sale	knows sale total
SalesLineItem	knows line item subtotal
ProductDescription	knows product price

We considered and decided on these responsibilities in the context of drawing an interaction diagram. We could then summarize the methods in the method section of a class diagram.

The principle by which we assigned each responsibility was Information Expert—placing it with the object that had the information needed to fulfill it.

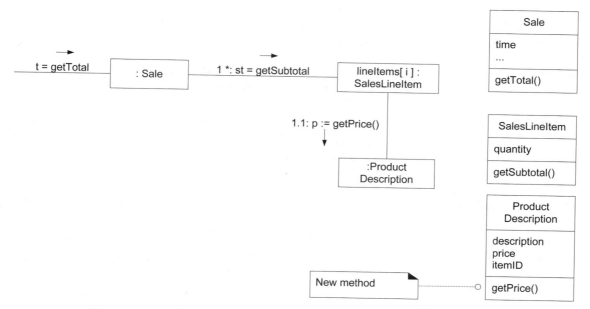

Figure 17.17 Calculating the *Sale* total.

Discussion Information Expert is frequently used in the assignment of responsibilities; it is a basic guiding principle used continuously in object design. Expert is not meant to be an obscure or fancy idea; it expresses the common "intuition" that objects do things related to the information they have.

Notice that the fulfillment of a responsibility often requires information that is spread across different classes of objects. This implies that many "partial" information experts will collaborate in the task. For example, the sales total problem ultimately required the collaboration of three classes of objects. Whenever information is spread across different objects, they will need to interact via messages to share the work.

Expert usually leads to designs where a software object does those operations that are normally done to the inanimate real-world thing it represents; Peter Coad calls this the "Do It Myself" strategy [Coad95]. For example, in the real world, without the use of electro-mechanical aids, a sale does not tell you its total; it is an inanimate thing. Someone calculates the total of the sale. But in object-oriented software land, all software objects are "alive" or "animated," and they can take on responsibilities and do things. Fundamentally, they do things related to the information they know. I call this the "animation" principle in object design; it is like being in a cartoon where everything is alive.

The Information Expert pattern—like many things in object technology—has a real-world analogy. We commonly give responsibility to individuals who have the information necessary to fulfill a task. For example, in a business, who should be responsible for creating a profit-and-loss statement? The person who has access to all the information necessary to create it—perhaps the chief financial officer. And just as software objects collaborate because the information is spread around, so it is with people. The company's chief financial officer may ask accountants to generate reports on credits and debits.

Contraindications   In some situations, a solution suggested by Expert is undesirable, usually because of problems in coupling and cohesion (these principles are discussed later in this chapter).

For example, who should be responsible for saving a *Sale* in a database? Certainly, much of the information to be saved is in the *Sale* object, and thus Expert could argue that the responsibility lies in the *Sale* class. And, by logical extension of this decision, each class would have its own services to save itself in a database. But acting on that reasoning leads to problems in cohesion, coupling, and duplication. For example, the *Sale* class must now contain logic related to database handling, such as that related to SQL and JDBC (Java Database Connectivity). The class no longer focuses on just the pure application logic of "being a sale." Now other kinds of responsibilities lower its cohesion. The class must be coupled to the technical database services of another subsystem, such as JDBC services, rather than just being coupled to other objects in the domain layer of software objects, so its coupling increases. And it is likely that similar database logic would be duplicated in many persistent classes.

All these problems indicate violation of a basic architectural principle: design for a separation of major system concerns. Keep application logic in one place (such as the domain software objects), keep database logic in another place (such as a separate persistence services subsystem), and so forth, rather than intermingling different system concerns in the same component.[11]

Supporting a separation of major concerns improves coupling and cohesion in a design. Thus, even though by Expert we could find some justification for putting the responsibility for database services in the *Sale* class, for other reasons (usually cohesion and coupling), we'd end up with a poor design.

Benefits   ■   Information encapsulation is maintained since objects use their own information to fulfill tasks. This usually supports low coupling, which leads to more robust and maintainable systems. Low Coupling is also a GRASP pattern that is discussed in a following section.

■   Behavior is distributed across the classes that have the required information, thus encouraging more cohesive "lightweight" class definitions that are easier to understand and maintain. High cohesion is usually supported (another pattern discussed later).

---

11. See Chapter 33 for a discussion of separation of concerns.

<table>
<tr><td>**Related Patterns or Principles**</td><td>■   Low Coupling

■   High Cohesion</td></tr>
<tr><td>**Also Known As; Similar To**</td><td>"Place responsibilities with data," "That which knows, does," "Do It Myself," "Put Services with the Attributes They Work On."</td></tr>
</table>

17.12   Low Coupling

Problem   How to support low dependency, low change impact, and increased reuse?

Coupling is a measure of how strongly one element is connected to, has knowledge of, or relies on other elements. An element with low (or weak) coupling is not dependent on too many other elements; "too many" is context dependent, but we examine it anyway. These elements include classes, subsystems, systems, and so on.

A class with high (or strong) coupling relies on many other classes. Such classes may be undesirable; some suffer from the following problems:

■   Forced local changes because of changes in related classes.

■   Harder to understand in isolation.

■   Harder to reuse because its use requires the additional presence of the classes on which it is dependent.

Solution   Assign a responsibility so that coupling remains low. Use this principle to evaluate alternatives.

Example   Consider the following partial class diagram from a NextGen case study:

Payment	Register	Sale

Assume we need to create a *Payment* instance and associate it with the *Sale*. What class should be responsible for this? Since a *Register* "records" a *Payment* in the real-world domain, the Creator pattern suggests *Register* as a candidate for creating the *Payment*. The *Register* instance could then send an *addPayment* message to the *Sale*, passing along the new *Payment* as a parameter. A possible partial interaction diagram reflecting this is shown in Figure 17.18.

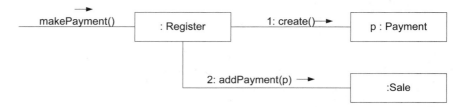

Figure 17.18 Register creates Payment.

This assignment of responsibilities couples the *Register* class to knowledge of the *Payment* class.

Applying UML: Note that the *Payment* instance is explicitly named *p* so that in message 2 it can be referenced as a parameter.

Figure 17.19 shows an alternative solution to creating the *Payment* and associating it with the *Sale*.

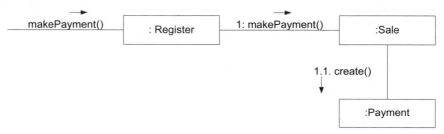

Figure 17.19 Sale creates Payment.

Which design, based on assignment of responsibilities, supports Low Coupling? In both cases we assume the *Sale* must eventually be coupled to knowledge of a *Payment*. Design 1, in which the *Register* creates the *Payment,* adds coupling of *Register* to *Payment*; Design 2, in which the *Sale* does the creation of a *Payment,* does not increase the coupling. Purely from the point of view of coupling, prefer Design 2 because it maintains overall lower coupling. This example illustrates how two patterns—Low Coupling and Creator—may suggest different solutions.

> In practice, the level of coupling alone can't be considered in isolation from other principles such as Expert and High Cohesion. Nevertheless, it is one factor to consider in improving a design.

Discussion Low Coupling is a principle to keep in mind during all design decisions; it is an underlying goal to continually consider. It is an **evaluative principle** that you apply while evaluating all design decisions.

In object-oriented languages such as C++, Java, and C#, common forms of coupling from *TypeX* to *TypeY* include the following:

- *TypeX* has an attribute (data member or instance variable) that refers to a *TypeY* instance, or *TypeY* itself.

- A *TypeX* object calls on services of a *TypeY* object.

- *TypeX* has a method that references an instance of *TypeY*, or *TypeY* itself, by any means. These typically include a parameter or local variable of type *TypeY*, or the object returned from a message being an instance of *TypeY*.

- *TypeX* is a direct or indirect subclass of *TypeY*.

- *TypeY* is an interface, and *TypeX* implements that interface.

Low Coupling encourages you to assign a responsibility so that its placement does not increase the coupling to a level that leads to the negative results that high coupling can produce.

Low Coupling supports the design of classes that are more independent, which reduces the impact of change. It can't be considered in isolation from other patterns such as Expert and High Cohesion, but rather needs to be included as one of several design principles that influence a choice in assigning a responsibility.

A subclass is strongly coupled to its superclass. Consider carefully any decision to derive from a superclass since it is such a strong form of coupling. For example, suppose that objects must be stored persistently in a relational or object database. In this case, you could follow the relatively common design practice of creating an abstract superclass called *PersistentObject* from which other classes derive. The disadvantage of this subclassing is that it highly couples domain objects to a particular technical service and mixes different architectural concerns, whereas the advantage is automatic inheritance of persistence behavior.

You cannot obtain an absolute measure of when coupling is too high. What is important is that you can gauge the current degree of coupling and assess whether increasing it will lead to problems. In general, classes that are inherently generic in nature and with a high probability for reuse should have especially low coupling.

The extreme case of Low Coupling is no coupling between classes. This case offends against a central metaphor of object technology: a system of connected objects that communicate via messages. Low Coupling taken to excess yields a poor design—one with a few incohesive, bloated, and complex active objects that do all the work, and with many passive zero-coupled objects that act as simple data repositories. Some moderate degree of coupling between classes is normal and necessary for creating an object-oriented system in which tasks are fulfilled by a collaboration between connected objects.

Contraindications   High coupling to stable elements and to pervasive elements is seldom a problem. For example, a J2EE application can safely couple itself to the Java libraries (*java.util,* and so on), because they are stable and widespread.

Pick Your Battles

It is not high coupling per se that is the problem; it is high coupling to elements that are *unstable* in some dimension, such as their interface, implementation, or mere presence.

This is an important point: As designers, we can add flexibility, encapsulate details and implementations, and in general design for lower coupling in many areas of the system. But, if we put effort into "future proofing" or lowering the coupling when we have no realistic motivation, this is not time well spent.

You must pick your battles in lowering coupling and encapsulating things. Focus on the points of realistic high instability or evolution. For example, in the Next-Gen project, we know that different third-party tax calculators (with unique interfaces) need to be connected to the system. Therefore, designing for low coupling at this variation point is practical.

Benefits ■ not affected by changes in other components

■ simple to understand in isolation

■ convenient to reuse

Background Coupling and cohesion are truly fundamental principles in design, and should be appreciated and applied as such by all software developers. Larry Constantine, also a founder of structured design in the 1970s and a current advocate of more attention to usability engineering [CL99], was primarily responsible in the 1960s for identifying and communicating coupling and cohesion as critical principles [Constantine68, CMS74].

Related Patterns ■ Protected Variation

17.13 Controller

Problem What first object beyond the UI layer receives and coordinates ("controls") a system operation?

System operations were first explored during the analysis of SSD. These are the major input events upon our system. For example, when a cashier using a POS terminal presses the "End Sale" button, he is generating a system event indicating "the sale has ended." Similarly, when a writer using a word processor presses the "spell check" button, he is generating a system event indicating "perform a spell check."

A **controller** is the first object beyond the UI layer that is responsible for receiving or handling a system operation message.

Solution Assign the responsibility to a class representing one of the following choices:

- Represents the overall "system," a "root object," a device that the software is running within, or a major subsystem—these are all variations of a *facade controller*.

- Represents a use case scenario within which the system event occurs, often named <UseCaseName>Handler, <UseCaseName>Coordinator, or <Use-CaseName>Session (*use case or session controller*).

  ○ Use the same controller class for all system events in the same use case scenario.

  ○ Informally, a session is an instance of a conversation with an actor. Sessions can be of any length but are often organized in terms of use cases (use case sessions).

Corollary: Note that "window," "view," and "document" classes are not on this list. Such classes should *not* fulfill the tasks associated with system events; they typically receive these events and delegate them to a controller.

Example Some get a better sense of applying this pattern with code examples. Look ahead in the Implementation section on p. 309 for Java examples of both rich client and Web UIs.

The NextGen application contains several system operations, as illustrated in Figure 17.20. This model shows the system itself as a class (which is legal and sometimes useful when modeling).

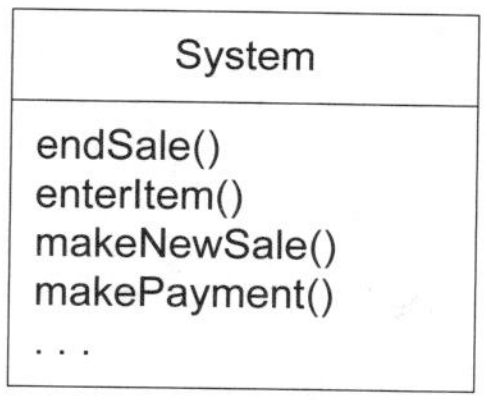

System
endSale() enterItem() makeNewSale() makePayment() . . .

Figure 17.20 Some system operations of the NextGen POS application.

During analysis, system operations may be assigned to the class *System* in some analysis model, to indicate they are system operations. However, this does *not* mean that a software class named *System* fulfills them during design. Rather, during design, a controller class is assigned the responsibility for system operations (see Figure 17.21).

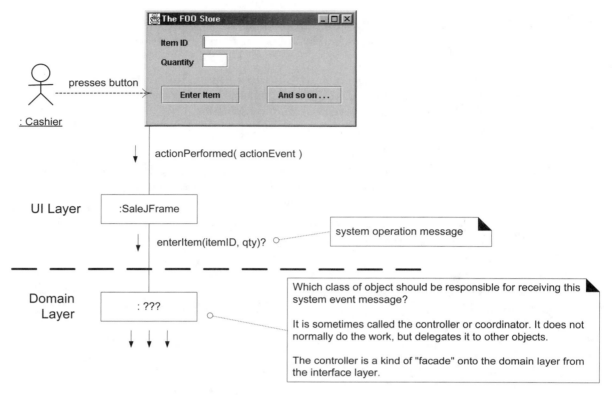

Figure 17.21 What object should be the Controller for enterItem?

Who should be the controller for system events such as *enterItem* and *endSale*?

By the Controller pattern, here are some choices:

> Represents the overall "system," "root object," device, or subsystem.   *Register, POSSystem*

> Represents a receiver or handler of all system events of a use case scenario.   *ProcessSaleHandler, ProcessSaleSession*

Note that in the domain of POS, a *Register* (called a *POS Terminal*) is a specialized device with software running in it.

In terms of interaction diagrams, one of the examples in Figure 17.22 could be useful.

The choice of which of these classes is the most appropriate controller is influenced by other factors, which the following section explores.

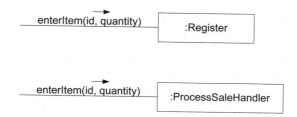

Figure 17.22 Controller choices.

During design, the system operations identified during system behavior analysis are assigned to one or more controller classes, such as *Register*, as shown in Figure 17.23.

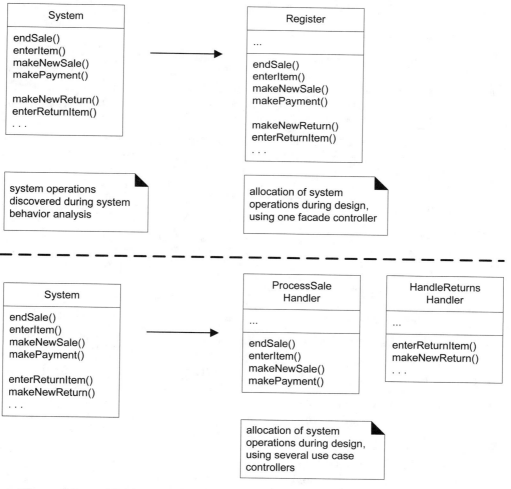

Figure 17.23 Allocation of system operations.

Discussion   Some get a better sense of applying this pattern with code examples. Look ahead in the Implementation section on p. 309 for examples in Java for both rich client and Web UIs.

Simply, this is a delegation pattern. In accordance with the understanding that the UI layer shouldn't contain application logic, UI layer objects must delegate work requests to another layer. When the "other layer" is the domain layer, the Controller pattern summarizes common choices that you, as an OO developer, make for the domain object delegate that receives the work requests.

Systems receive external input events, typically involving a GUI operated by a person. Other mediums of input include external messages, such as in a call-processing telecommunications switch or signals from sensors such as in process control systems.

In all cases, you must choose a handler for these events. Turn to the Controller pattern for guidance toward generally accepted, suitable choices. As illustrated in Figure 17.21, the controller is a kind of facade into the domain layer from the UI layer.

You will often want to use the same controller class for all the system events of one use case so that the controller can maintain information about the state of the use case. Such information is useful, for example, to identify out-of-sequence system events (for example, a *makePayment* operation before an *endSale* operation). Different controllers may be used for different use cases.

A common defect in the design of controllers results from over-assignment of responsibility. A controller then suffers from bad (low) cohesion, violating the principle of High Cohesion.

Guideline

Normally, a controller should *delegate* to other objects the work that needs to be done; it coordinates or controls the activity. It does not do much work itself.

Please see the "Issues and Solutions" section for elaboration.

The first category of controller is a facade controller representing the overall system, device, or a subsystem. The idea is to choose some class name that suggests a cover, or facade, over the other layers of the application and that provides the main point of service calls from the UI layer down to other layers. The facade could be an abstraction of the overall physical unit, such as a *Register*[12], *TelecommSwitch, Phone,* or *Robot*; a class representing the entire software sys-

---

12. Various terms are used for a physical POS unit, including register, point-of-sale terminal (POST), and so forth. Over time, "register" has come to embody the notion of both a physical unit and the logical abstraction of the thing that registers sales and payments.

tem, such as *POSSystem*; or any other concept which the designer chooses to represent the overall system or a subsystem, even, for example, *ChessGame* if it was game software.

Facade controllers are suitable when there are not "too many" system events, or when the user interface (UI) cannot redirect system event messages to alternating controllers, such as in a message-processing system.

If you choose a use case controller, then you will have a different controller for each use case. Note that this kind of controller is not a domain object; it is an artificial construct to support the system (a *Pure Fabrication* in terms of the GRASP patterns). For example, if the NextGen application contains use cases such as *Process Sale* and *Handle Returns*, then there may be a *ProcessSaleHandler* class and so forth.

When should you choose a use case controller? Consider it an alternative when placing the responsibilities in a facade controller leads to designs with low cohesion or high coupling, typically when the facade controller is becoming "bloated" with excessive responsibilities. A use case controller is a good choice when there are many system events across different processes; it factors their handling into manageable separate classes and also provides a basis for knowing and reasoning about the state of the current scenario in progress.

In the UP and Jacobson's older Objectory method [Jacobson92], there are the (optional) concepts of boundary, control, and entity classes. **Boundary objects** are abstractions of the interfaces, **entity objects** are the application-independent (and typically persistent) domain software objects, and **control objects** are use case handlers as described in this Controller pattern.

A important corollary of the Controller pattern is that UI objects (for example, window or button objects) and the UI layer should not have responsibility for fulfilling system events. In other words, system operations should be handled in the application logic or domain layers of objects rather than in the UI layer of a system. See the "Issues and Solutions" section for an example.

Web UIs and Server-Side Application of Controller

Please see p. 310 for a server-side example using Java Struts—a popular framework.

A similar delegation approach can be used in ASP.NET and WebForms: The "code behind" file that contains event handlers for Web browser button clicks will obtain a reference to a domain controller object (e.g., a *Register* object in the POS case study), and then delegate the request for work. This is in contrast to the common, fragile style of ASP.NET programming in which developers insert application logic handling in the "code behind" file, thus mixing application logic into the UI layer.

Server-side Web UI frameworks (such as Struts) embody the concept of the Web-MVC (Model-View-Controller) pattern. The "controller" in Web-MVC differs from this GRASP controller. The former is part of the UI layer and controls the

UI interaction and page flow. The GRASP controller is part of the domain layer and controls or coordinates the handling of the work request, essentially unaware of what UI technology is being used (e.g., a Web UI, a Swing UI, ...).

Also common with server-side designs when Java technologies are used is delegation from the Web UI layer (e.g., from a Struts *Action* class) to an Enterprise JavaBeans (**EJB**) *Session* object. Variant #2 of the Controller pattern—an object representing a user session or use case scenario—covers this case. In this case, the EJB *Session* object may itself delegate farther on to the domain layer of objects, and again, you can apply the Controller pattern to choose a suitable receiver in the pure domain layer.

All that said, the appropriate handling of server-side systems operations is strongly influenced by the chosen server technical frameworks and continues to be a moving target. But the underlying principle of Model-View Separation can and does still apply.

Even with a rich-client UI (e.g., a Swing UI) that interacts with a server, the Controller pattern still applies. The client-side UI forwards the request to the local client-side controller, and the controller forwards all or part of the request handling to remote services. This design lowers the coupling of the UI to remote services and makes it easier, for example, to provide the services either locally or remotely, through the *indirection* of the client-side controller.

Benefits
- *Increased potential for reuse* and *pluggable interfaces*—These benefits ensure that application logic is *not* handled in the interface layer. The responsibilities of a controller could technically be handled in an interface object, but such a design implies that program code and the fulfillment of application logic would be embedded in interface or window objects. An interface-as-controller design reduces the opportunity to reuse logic in future applications, since logic that is bound to a particular interface (for example, window-like objects) is seldom applicable in other applications. By contrast, delegating a system operation responsibility to a controller supports the reuse of the logic in future applications. And since the application logic is not bound to the interface layer, it can be replaced with a different interface.

- *Opportunity to reason about the state of the use case*—Sometimes we must ensure that system operations occur in a legal sequence, or we want to be able to reason about the current state of activity and operations within the use case that is underway. For example, we may have to guarantee that the *makePayment* operation cannot occur until the *endSale* operation has occurred. If so, we need to capture this state information somewhere; the controller is one reasonable choice, especially if we use the same controller throughout the use case (as recommended).

Implementation
The following examples use Java technologies for two common cases, a rich client in Java Swing and a Web UI with Struts on the server (a Servlet engine).

Please note that you should apply a similar approach in .NET **WinForms** and ASP.NET **WebForms**. A good practice in well-designed .NET (often ignored by MS programmers who violate the Model-View Separation Principle) is to *not* insert application logic code in the event handlers or in the "code behind" files (those are both part of the UI layer). Rather, in the .NET event handlers or "code behind" files, simply obtain a reference to a domain object (e.g., a *Register* object), and delegate to it.

Implementation with Java Swing: Rich Client UI

This section assumes you are familiar with basic Swing. The code contains comments to explain the key points. A few comments: Notice at ❶ that the *Process-SaleJFrame* window has a reference to the domain controller object, the *Register*. At ❷ I define the handler for the button click. At ❸ I show the key message—sending the *enterItem* message to the controller in the domain layer.

```
package com.craiglarman.nextgen.ui.swing;

    // imports…


    // in Java, a JFrame is a typical window
public class ProcessSaleJFrame extends JFrame
{

    // the window has a reference to the 'controller' domain object

❶   private Register register;


    // the window is passed the register, on creation
public ProcessSaleJFrame(Register _register)
{
    register = _register;
}

    // this button is clicked to perform the
    // system operation "enterItem"
private JButton BTN_ENTER_ITEM;


    // this is the important method!
    // here i show the message from the UI layer to domain layer
private JButton getBTN_ENTER_ITEM()
{
        // does the button exist?
    if (BTN_ENTER_ITEM != null)
        return BTN_ENTER_ITEM;


        // ELSE button needs to be initialized...
    BTN_ENTER_ITEM = new JButton();
    BTN_ENTER_ITEM.setText("Enter Item");


        // THIS IS THE KEY SECTION!
        // in Java, this is how you define
        // a click handler for a button
```

❷
```
      BTN_ENTER_ITEM.addActionListener(new ActionListener()
         {
         public void actionPerformed(ActionEvent e)
         {
               // Transformer is a utility class to
               // transform Strings to other data types
               // because the JTextField GUI widgets have Strings
            ItemID id = Transformer.toItemID(getTXT_ID().getText());
            int qty = Transformer.toInt(getTXT_QTY().getText());


               // here we cross the boundary from the
               // UI layer to the domain layer
               // delegate to the 'controller'
               // > > > THIS IS THE KEY STATEMENT < < <

❸          register.enterItem(id, qty);
         }
         } ); // end of the addActionListener call

      return BTN_ENTER_ITEM;
      } // end of method

   // …
   } // end of class
```

Implementation with Java Struts: Client Browser and WebUI

This section assumes you are familiar with basic Struts. Notice at ❶ that to obtain a reference to the *Register* domain object on the server side, the *Action* object must dig into the Servlet context. At ❷ I show the key message—sending the *enterItem* message to the domain controller object in the domain layer.

```
package com.craiglarman.nextgen.ui.web;

// … imports


   // in Struts, an Action object is associated with a
   // web browser button click, and invoked (on the server)
   // when the button is clicked.
public class EnterItemAction extends Action {


   // this is the method invoked on the server
   // when the button is clicked on the client browser
public ActionForward execute( ActionMapping mapping,
                              ActionForm form,
                              HttpServletRequest request,
                              HttpServletResponse response )
                              throws Exception
   {

      // the server has a Repository object that
      // holds references to several things, including
      // the POS "register" object
   Repository repository = (Repository)getServlet().
      getServletContext().getAttribute(Constants.REPOSITORY_KEY);
```

❶
```
      Register register = repository.getRegister();


        // extract the itemID and qty from the web form
      String txtId = ((SaleForm)form).getItemID();
      String txtQty = ((SaleForm)form).getQuantity();

        // Transformer is a utility class to
        // transform Strings to other data types
      ItemID id = Transformer.toItemID(txtId);
      int qty = Transformer.toInt(txtQty);


        // here we cross the boundary from the
        // UI layer to the domain layer
        // delegate to the 'domain controller'
        // > > > THIS IS THE KEY STATEMENT < < <
```

❷
```
      register.enterItem(id, qty);

      // …
    } // end of method
    } // end of class
```

Issues and Solutions

Bloated Controllers

Poorly designed, a controller class will have low cohesion—unfocused and handling too many areas of responsibility; this is called a **bloated controller**. Signs of bloating are:

- There is only a *single* controller class receiving *all* system events in the system, and there are many of them. This sometimes happens if a facade controller is chosen.

- The controller itself performs many of the tasks necessary to fulfill the system event, without delegating the work. This usually involves a violation of Information Expert and High Cohesion.

- A controller has many attributes, and it maintains significant information about the system or domain, which should have been distributed to other objects, or it duplicates information found elsewhere.

Among the cures for a bloated controller are these two:

1. Add more controllers—a system does not have to need only one. Instead of facade controllers, employ use case controllers. For example, consider an application with many system events, such as an airline reservation system.

It may contain the following controllers:

Use case controllers
MakeReservationHandler
ManageSchedulesHandler
ManageFaresHandler

2. Design the controller so that it primarily delegates the fulfillment of each system operation responsibility to other objects.

UI Layer Does Not Handle System Events

To reiterate: An important corollary of the Controller pattern is that UI objects (for example, window objects) and the UI layer should not have responsibility for handling system events. As an example, consider a design in Java that uses a *JFrame* to display the information.

Assume the NextGen application has a window that displays sale information and captures cashier operations. Using the Controller pattern, Figure 17.24 illustrates an acceptable relationship between the *JFrame* and the controller and other objects in a portion of the POS system (with simplifications).

Notice that the *SaleJFrame* class—part of the UI layer—delegates the *enterItem* request to the *Register* object. It did not get involved in processing the operation or deciding how to handle it; the window only delegated it to another layer.

Assigning the responsibility for system operations to objects in the application or domain layer by using the Controller pattern rather than the UI layer can increase reuse potential. If a UI layer object (like the *SaleJFrame*) handles a system operation that represents part of a business process, then business process logic would be contained in an interface (for example, window-like) object; the opportunity for reuse of the business logic then diminishes because of its coupling to a particular interface and application. Consequently, the design in Figure 17.25 is undesirable.

Placing system operation responsibility in a domain object controller makes it easier to reuse the program logic supporting the associated business process in future applications. It also makes it easier to unplug the UI layer and use a different UI framework or technology, or to run the system in an offline "batch" mode.

Message Handling Systems and the Command Pattern

Some applications are message-handling systems or servers that receive requests from other processes. A telecommunications switch is a common example. In such systems, the design of the interface and controller is somewhat different. The details are explored in a later chapter, but in essence, a common solution is to use the Command pattern [GHJV95] and Command Processor pattern [BMRSS96], introduced in Chapter 37.

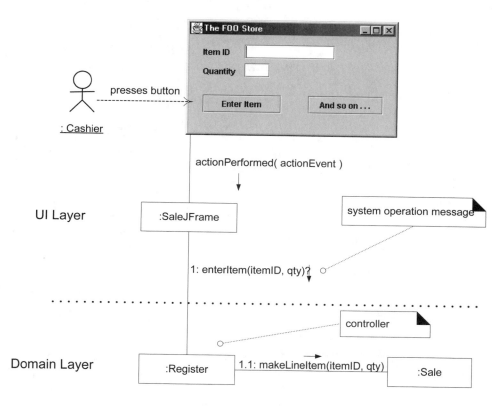

Figure 17.24 Desirable coupling of UI layer to domain layer.

Related Patterns

- **Command**—In a message-handling system, each message may be represented and handled by a separate Command object [GHJV95].

- **Facade**—A facade controller is a kind of Facade [GHJV95].

- **Layers**—This is a POSA pattern [BMRSS96]. Placing domain logic in the domain layer rather than the presentation layer is part of the Layers pattern.

- **Pure Fabrication**—This GRASP pattern is an arbitrary creation of the designer, not a software class whose name is inspired by the Domain Model. A use case controller is a kind of Pure Fabrication.

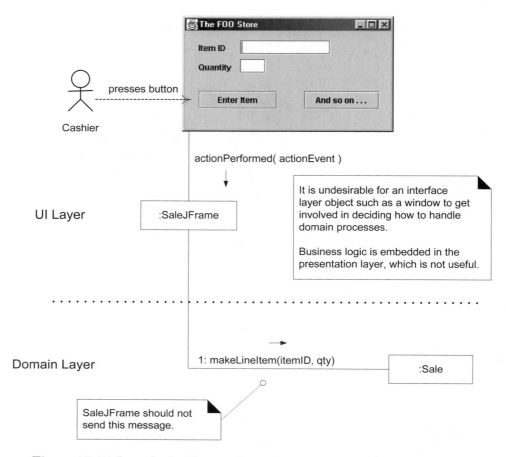

Figure 17.25 Less desirable coupling of interface layer to domain layer.

17.14   High Cohesion

Problem   How to keep objects focused, understandable, and manageable, and as a side effect, support Low Coupling?

In terms of object design, **cohesion** (or more specifically, functional cohesion) is a measure of how strongly related and focused the responsibilities of an element are. An element with highly related responsibilities that does not do a tremendous amount of work has high cohesion. These elements include classes, subsystems, and so on.

Solution   Assign a responsibility so that cohesion remains high. Use this to evaluate alternatives.

A class with low cohesion does many unrelated things or does too much work. Such classes are undesirable; they suffer from the following problems:

- hard to comprehend

- hard to reuse

- hard to maintain

- delicate; constantly affected by change

Low cohesion classes often represent a very "large grain" of abstraction or have taken on responsibilities that should have been delegated to other objects.

Example   Let's take another look at the example problem used in the Low Coupling pattern and analyze it for High Cohesion.

Assume we have a need to create a (cash) *Payment* instance and associate it with the *Sale*. What class should be responsible for this? Since *Register* records a *Payment* in the real-world domain, the Creator pattern suggests *Register* as a candidate for creating the *Payment*. The *Register* instance could then send an *addPayment* message to the *Sale*, passing along the new *Payment* as a parameter, as shown in Figure 17.26.

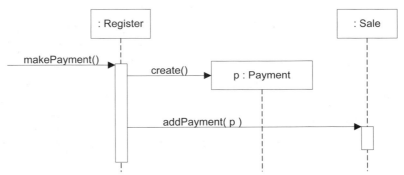

Figure 17.26 Register creates Payment.

This assignment of responsibilities places the responsibility for making a payment in the *Register*. The *Register* is taking on part of the responsibility for fulfilling the *makePayment* system operation.

In this isolated example, this is acceptable; but if we continue to make the *Register* class responsible for doing some or most of the work related to more and more system operations, it will become increasingly burdened with tasks and become incohesive.

Imagine fifty system operations, all received by *Register*. If *Register* did the work related to each, it would become a "bloated" incohesive object. The point is not that this single *Payment* creation task in itself makes the *Register* incohesive, but as part of a larger picture of overall responsibility assignment, it may suggest a trend toward low cohesion.

And most important in terms of developing skills as object designers, regardless of the final design choice, is the valuable achievement that at least we know to consider the impact on cohesion.

By contrast, as shown in Figure 17.27, the second design delegates the payment creation responsibility to the *Sale* supports higher cohesion in the *Register*.

Since the second design supports both high cohesion and low coupling, it is desirable.

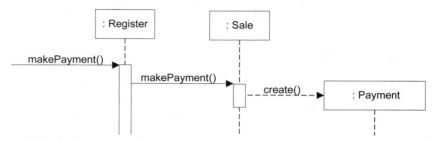

Figure 17.27 Sale creates Payment.

> In practice, the level of cohesion alone can't be considered in isolation from other responsibilities and other principles such as Expert and Low Coupling.

Discussion Like Low Coupling, High Cohesion is a principle to keep in mind during all design decisions; it is an underlying goal to continually consider. It is an evaluative principle that a designer applies while evaluating all design decisions.

Grady Booch describes high functional cohesion as existing when the elements of a component (such as a class) "all work together to provide some well-bounded behavior" [Booch94].

Here are some scenarios that illustrate varying degrees of functional cohesion:

1. *Very low cohesion*—A class is solely responsible for many things in very different functional areas.

   ○ Assume the existence of a class called *RDB-RPC-Interface* which is completely responsible for interacting with relational databases and for handling remote procedure calls. These are two vastly different functional areas, and each requires lots of supporting code. The responsibilities should be split into a family of classes related to RDB access and a family related to RPC support.

2. *Low cohesion*—A class has sole responsibility for a complex task in one functional area.

   ○ Assume the existence of a class called *RDBInterface* which is completely responsible for interacting with relational databases. The methods of the class are all related, but there are lots of them, and a tremendous amount of supporting code; there may be hundreds or thousands of methods. The class should split into a family of lightweight classes sharing the work to provide RDB access.

3. *High cohesion*—A class has moderate responsibilities in one functional area and collaborates with other classes to fulfill tasks.

○ Assume the existence of a class called *RDBInterface* that is only partially responsible for interacting with relational databases. It interacts with a dozen other classes related to RDB access in order to retrieve and save objects.

4. *Moderate cohesion*—A class has lightweight and sole responsibilities in a few different areas that are logically related to the class concept but not to each other.

○ Assume the existence of a class called *Company* that is completely responsible for (a) knowing its employees and (b) knowing its financial information. These two areas are not strongly related to each other, although both are logically related to the concept of a company. In addition, the total number of public methods is small, as is the amount of supporting code.

As a rule of thumb, a class with high cohesion has a relatively small number of methods, with highly related functionality, and does not do too much work. It collaborates with other objects to share the effort if the task is large.

A class with high cohesion is advantageous because it is relatively easy to maintain, understand, and reuse. The high degree of related functionality, combined with a small number of operations, also simplifies maintenance and enhancements. The fine grain of highly related functionality also supports increased reuse potential.

The High Cohesion pattern—like many things in object technology—has a real-world analogy. It is a common observation that if a person takes on too many unrelated responsibilities—especially ones that should properly be delegated to others—then the person is not effective. This is observed in some managers who have not learned how to delegate. These people suffer from low cohesion; they are ready to become "unglued."

Another Classic Principle: Modular Design

Coupling and cohesion are old principles in software design; designing with objects does not imply ignoring well-established fundamentals. Another of these—which is strongly related to coupling and cohesion—is to promote **modular design**. To quote:

> Modularity is the property of a system that has been decomposed into a set of cohesive and loosely coupled modules [Booch94].

We promote a modular design by creating methods and classes with high cohesion. At the basic object level, we achieve modularity by designing each method with a clear, single purpose and by grouping a related set of concerns into a class.

Cohesion and Coupling; Yin and Yang

Bad cohesion usually begets bad coupling, and vice versa. I call cohesion and coupling the *yin and yang of software engineering* because of their interdependent influence. For example, consider a GUI widget class that represents and paints a widget, saves data to a database, and invokes remote object services. Not only is it profoundly incohesive, but it is coupled to many (and disparate) elements.

Contraindications   In a few cases, accepting lower cohesion is justified.

One case is the grouping of responsibilities or code into one class or component to simplify maintenance by one person—although be warned that such grouping may also worsen maintenance. But suppose an application contains embedded SQL statements that by other good design principles should be distributed across ten classes, such as ten "database mapper" classes. Now, commonly only one or two SQL experts know how to best define and maintain this SQL. Even if dozens of object-oriented (OO) programmers work on the project, few OO programmers may have strong SQL skills. Suppose the SQL expert is not even a comfortable OO programmer. The software architect may decide to group all the SQL statements into one class, *RDBOperations*, so that it is easy for the SQL expert to work on the SQL in one location.

Another case for components with lower cohesion is with distributed server objects. Because of overhead and performance implications associated with remote objects and remote communication, it is sometimes desirable to create fewer and larger, less cohesive server objects that provide an interface for many operations. This approach is also related to the pattern called **Coarse-Grained Remote Interface**. In that pattern the remote operations are made more coarse-grained so that they can to do or request more work in remote operation calls to alleviate the performance penalty of remote calls over a network. As a simple example, instead of a remote object with three fine-grained operations *setName*, *setSalary*, and *setHireDate*, there is one remote operation, *setData*, which receives a set of data. This results in fewer remote calls and better performance.

Benefits   ■ Clarity and ease of comprehension of the design is increased.

■ Maintenance and enhancements are simplified.

■ Low coupling is often supported.

■ Reuse of fine-grained, highly related functionality is increased because a cohesive class can be used for a very specific purpose.

17.15   Recommended Resources

The metaphor of RDD especially emerged from the influential object work in Smalltalk at Tektronix in Portland, from Kent Beck, Ward Cunningham, Rebecca Wirfs-Brock, and others. *Designing Object-Oriented Software* [WWW90] is the landmark text, and is as relevant today as when it was written. Wirfs-Brock has more recently released another RDD text, *Object Design: Roles, Responsibilities, and Collaborations* [WM02].

Two other recommended texts emphasizing fundamental object design principles are *Object-Oriented Design Heuristics* by Riel and *Object Models* by Coad.

OBJECT DESIGN EXAMPLES WITH GRASP

To invent, you need a good imagination and a pile of junk.

—*Thomas Edison*

Objectives

- Design use case realizations.
- Apply GRASP to assign responsibilities to classes.
- Apply UML to illustrate and think through the design of objects.

Introduction

This chapter applies OO design principles and the UML to the case studies, to show larger examples of reasonably designed objects with responsibilities and collaborations. Please note that the GRASP patterns by name are not important; they're just a learning aid that helps us think methodically about basic OO design.

What's Next?
Having introduced basic OO design principles with GRASP, this chapter applies them to the case studies. The next clarifies the small but necessary issue of designing for visibility between objects.

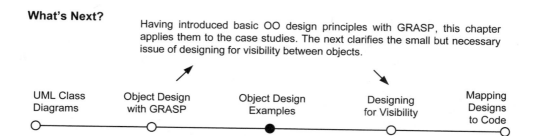

| UML Class Diagrams | Object Design with GRASP | Object Design Examples | Designing for Visibility | Mapping Designs to Code |

Key Point

The assignment of responsibilities and design of collaborations are very important and creative steps during design, both while diagraming and while coding.

The No-Magic Zone

This chapter invites you to learn through detailed explanations how an OO developer might reason while designing by principles. In fact, over a short time of practice, these principles become ingrained, and some of the decision-making happens almost at a subconscious level.

But *first,* I wish to exhaustively illustrate that no "magic" is needed in object design, no unjustifiable decisions are necessary—assignment of responsibilities and the choice of collaborations can be rationally explained and learned. OO software design really can be more science than art, though there is plenty of room for creativity and elegant design.

18.1   What is a Use Case Realization?

The last chapter on basic OO design principles looked at little fragments of design problems. In contrast, this chapter demonstrates the larger picture of designing the domain objects[1] for an entire use case scenario. You will see larger-scale collaborations and more complex UML diagrams.

To quote, "A **use-case realization** describes how a particular use case is realized within the Design Model, in terms of collaborating objects" [RUP]. More precisely, a designer can describe the design of one or more *scenarios* of a use case; each of these is called a use case realization (though non-standard, perhaps better called a **scenario realization**). *Use case realization* is a UP term used to remind us of the connection between the requirements expressed as use cases and the object design that satisfies the requirements.

UML diagrams are a common language to illustrate use case realizations. And as we explored in the prior chapter, we can apply principles and patterns of object design, such as Information Expert and Low Coupling, during this use case realization design work.

To review, Figure 18.1 illustrates the relationship between some UP artifacts, emphasizing the Use Case Model and the Design Model—use case realizations.

---

1. Recall, as explained on p. 200, that the case studies focus on the domain layer, not the UI or service layers, which are nevertheless important.

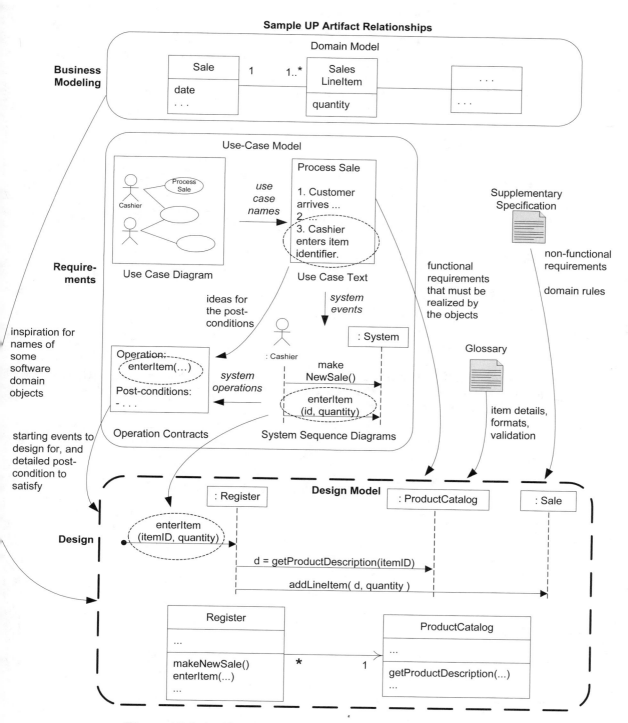

Figure 18.1 Artifact relationships, emphasizing use case realization.

Some relevant artifact-influence points include the following:

- The use case suggests the system operations that are shown in SSDs.

- The system operations become the starting messages entering the Controllers for domain layer interaction diagrams. See Figure 18.2.

  ○ This is a **key point** often missed by those new to OOA/D modeling.

- Domain layer interaction diagrams illustrate how objects interact to fulfill the required tasks—the use case realization.

18.2 Artifact Comments

SSDs, System Operations, Interaction Diagrams, and Use Case Realizations

In the current NextGen POS iteration we are considering scenarios and system operations identified on the SSDs of the *Process Sale* use case:

- *makeNewSale*
- *enterItem*
- *endSale*
- *makePayment*

If we use communication diagrams to illustrate the use case realizations, we will draw a different communication diagram to show the handling of each system operation message. Of course, the same is true for sequence diagrams. For example, see Figure 18.2 and Figure 18.3.

Key Point

The system operations in the SSDs are used as the
starting messages into the domain layer controller objects.

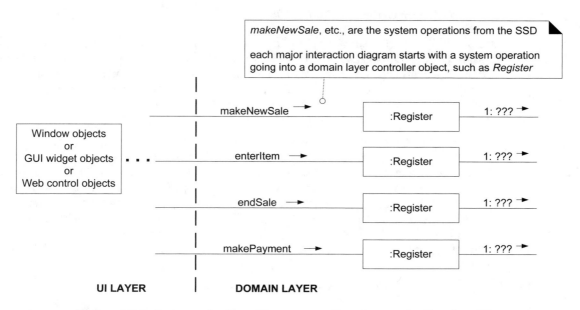

Figure 18.2 Communication diagrams and system operation handling.

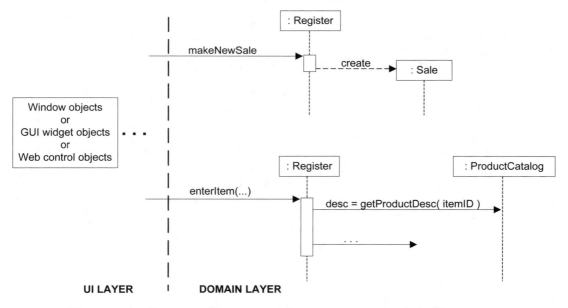

Figure 18.3 Sequence diagrams and system operation handling.

Use Cases and Use Case Realizations

Naturally, use cases are a prime input to use case realizations. The use case text and related requirements expressed in the Supplementary Specifications, Glossary, UI prototypes, report prototypes, and so forth, all inform developers what needs to be built. But bear in mind that written requirements are imperfect—often very imperfect.

Involve the Customer Frequently

The above section gives the impression that documents are the critical requirements input to doing software design and development. Truly, though, it is hard to beat the ongoing participation of customers in evaluating demos, discussing requirements and tests, prioritizing, and so forth. One of the principles of agile methods is "Business people and developers must work together daily throughout the project"—a very worthy goal.

Operation Contracts and Use Case Realizations

As discussed, use case realizations could be designed directly from the use case text or from one's domain knowledge. For some complex system operations, contracts may have been written that add more analysis detail. For example:

Contract CO2: enterItem

Operation:	enterItem(itemID : ItemID, quantity : integer)
Cross References:	Use Cases: Process Sale
Preconditions:	There is a sale underway.
Postconditions:	– A SalesLineItem instance sli was created (instance creation).
	– ...

In conjunction with contemplating the use case text, for each contract, we work through the postcondition state changes and design message interactions to satisfy the requirements. For example, given this partial *enterItem* system operation, we diagram a partial interaction that satisfies the state change of *SalesLineItem* instance creation, as shown in Figure 18.4.

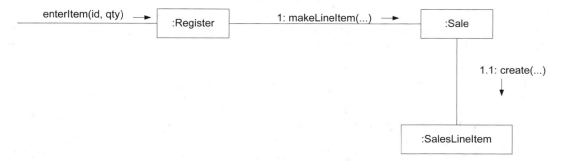

Figure 18.4 Partial interaction diagram satisfies a contract postcondition.

The Domain Model and Use Case Realizations

In the interaction diagrams, the Domain Model inspires some of the software objects, such as a *Sale* conceptual class and *Sale* software class. The existing Domain Model—as with all analysis artifacts—won't be perfect; you should expect errors and omissions. You will discover new concepts that were previously missed, ignore concepts that were previously identified, and do likewise with associations and attributes.

Must you limit the design classes in the Design Model to classes with names inspired from the Domain Model? Not at all. It's normal to discover new conceptual classes during design work that were missed during earlier domain analysis and to make up software classes whose names and purpose are completely unrelated to the Domain Model.

18.3   What's Next?

The remainder of this chapter is organized as follows:

1. A relatively detailed discussion of the design of the NextGen POS.

2. Likewise, for the Monopoly case study, starting on p. 349.

Applying UML and patterns to these case studies, let's get into the details...

18.4   Use Case Realizations for the NextGen Iteration

The following sections explore the choices and decisions made during the design of a use case realization with objects based on the GRASP patterns. I intentionally detail explanations, to show that there's no magic in OO design—it's based on justifiable principles.

Initialization and the 'Start Up' Use Case

The *Start Up* use case realization is the design context in which to consider creating most of the 'root' or long-lived objects. See p. 347 for some of the design details.

Guideline

When coding, program at least some *Start Up* initialization first. But during OO design modeling, consider the *Start Up* initialization design *last*, after you have discovered what really needs to be created and initialized. Then, design the initialization to support the needs of other use case realizations.

Based on this guideline, we will explore the *Process Sale* use case realization before the supporting *Start Up* design.

How to Design makeNewSale?

The *makeNewSale* system operation occurs when a cashier initiates a request to start a new sale, after a customer has arrived with things to buy. The use case may have been sufficient to decide what was necessary, but for this case study we wrote contracts for all the system operations, to demonstrate the approach.

Contract CO1: makeNewSale

Operation:	makeNewSale()
Cross References:	Use Cases: Process Sale
Preconditions:	none
Postconditions:	– A Sale instance s was created (instance creation).
	– s was associated with the Register (association formed).
	– Attributes of s were initialized.

Choosing the Controller Class

Our first design choice involves choosing the controller for the system operation message *enterItem*. By the Controller pattern, here are some choices:

Represents the overall "system," "root object," a specialized device, or a major subsystem.	*Store*—a kind of root object because we think of most of the other domain objects as "within" the *Store*.
	Register—a specialized device that the software runs on; also called a *POSTerminal*.
	POSSystem—a name suggesting the overall system
Represents a receiver or handler of all system events of a use case scenario.	*ProcessSaleHandler*—constructed from the pattern <use-case-name> "Handler" or "Session"
	ProcessSaleSession

Choosing a device-object facade controller like *Register* is satisfactory if there are only a few system operations and if the facade controller is not taking on too many responsibilities (in other words, if it is not becoming incohesive). Choosing a use case controller is suitable when we have many system operations and we wish to distribute responsibilities in order to keep each controller class light-weight and focused (in other words, cohesive). In this case, *Register* suffices since there are only a few system operations.

> Remember, this *Register* is a software object in the Design Model. It isn't a physical register.

Thus, based on the Controller pattern, the interaction diagram shown in Figure 18.5 begins by sending the system operation *makeNewSale* message to a *Register* software object.

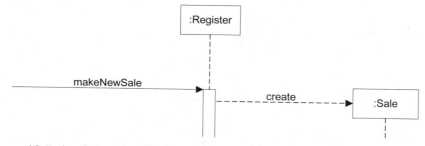

Figure 18.5 Applying the GRASP Controller pattern.

Creating a New Sale

We must create a software *Sale* object, and the GRASP Creator pattern suggests assigning the responsibility for creation to a class that aggregates, contains, or records the object to be created.

Analyzing the Domain Model reveals that a *Register* may be thought of as recording a *Sale*; indeed, the word "register" in business has for hundreds of years meant the thing that recorded (or registered) account transactions, such as sales.

Thus, *Register* is a reasonable candidate for creating a *Sale*. Note how this supports a low representational gap (LRG). And by having the *Register* create the *Sale*, we can easily associate the *Register* with it over time so that during future operations within the session, the *Register* will have a reference to the current *Sale* instance.

In addition to the above, when the *Sale* is created, it must create an empty collection (such as a Java *List*) to record all the future *SalesLineItem* instances that will be added. This collection will be contained within and maintained by the *Sale* instance, which implies by Creator that the *Sale* is a good candidate for creating the collection.

Therefore, the *Register* creates the *Sale*, and the *Sale* creates an empty collection, represented by a multiobject in the interaction diagram.

Hence, the interaction diagram in Figure 18.6 illustrates the design.

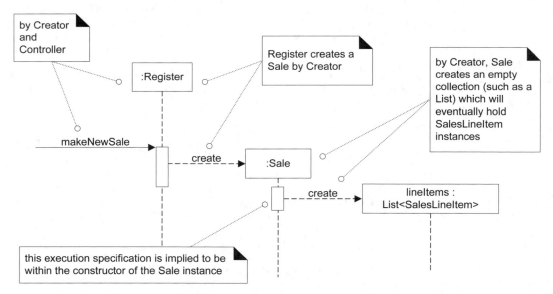

Figure 18.6 Sale and the collection creation.

Conclusion

The design was not difficult, but the point of its careful explanation in terms of Controller and Creator was to illustrate that the details of a design can be rationally and methodically decided and explained in terms of principles and patterns, such as GRASP.

How to Design enterItem?

The *enterItem* system operation occurs when a cashier enters the *itemID* and (optionally) the quantity of something to be purchased. Here is the complete contract:

Contract CO2: enterItem

Operation:	enterItem(itemID : ItemID, quantity : integer)
Cross References:	Use Cases: Process Sale
Preconditions:	There is an underway sale.
Postconditions:	— A SalesLineItem instance sli was created (instance creation).
	— sli was associated with the current Sale (association formed).
	— sli.quantity became quantity (attribute modification).
	— sli was associated with a ProductDescription, based on itemID match (association formed).

We now construct an interaction diagram to satisfy the postconditions of *enterItem*, using the GRASP patterns to help with the design decisions.

Choosing the Controller Class

Our first choice involves handling the responsibility for the system operation message *enterItem*. Based on the Controller pattern, as for *makeNewSale*, we will continue to use *Register* as a controller.

Display Item Description and Price?

Because of a principle of Model-View Separation, it is not the responsibility of non-GUI objects (such as a *Register* or *Sale*) to get involved in output tasks. Therefore, although the use case states that the description and price are displayed after this operation, we ignore the design at this time.

All that is required with respect to responsibilities for the display of information is that the information is known, which it is in this case.

Creating a New SalesLineItem

The *enterItem* contract postconditions indicate the creation, initialization, and association of a *SalesLineItem*. Analysis of the Domain Model reveals that a *Sale* contains *SalesLineItem* objects. Taking inspiration from the domain, we determine that a software *Sale* may similarly contain software *SalesLineItem*. Hence, by Creator, a software *Sale* is an appropriate candidate to create a *SalesLineItem*.

We can associate the *Sale* with the newly created *SalesLineItem* by storing the new instance in its collection of line items. The postconditions indicate that the new *SalesLineItem* needs a quantity when created; therefore, the *Register* must pass it along to the *Sale*, which must pass it along as a parameter in the *create* message. In Java, that would be implemented as a constructor call with a parameter.

Therefore, by Creator, a *makeLineItem* message is sent to a *Sale* for it to create a *SalesLineItem*. The *Sale* creates a *SalesLineItem*, and then stores the new instance in its permanent collection.

The parameters to the *makeLineItem* message include the *quantity*, so that the *SalesLineItem* can record it, and the *ProductDescription* that matches the *itemID*.

Finding a ProductDescription

The *SalesLineItem* needs to be associated with the *ProductDescription* that matches the incoming *itemID*. This implies that we must retrieve a *ProductDescription,* based on an *itemID* match.

Before considering *how* to achieve the lookup, we want to consider *who* should be responsible for it. Thus, a first step is:

Start assigning responsibilities by clearly stating the responsibility.

To restate the problem:

> Who should be responsible for knowing a *ProductDescription*, based on an *itemID* match?

This is neither a creation problem nor one of choosing a controller for a system event. Now we see our first application of Information Expert in the design.

In many cases, the Expert pattern is the principal one to apply. Information Expert suggests that the object that has the information required to fulfill the responsibility should do it. Who knows about all the *ProductDescription* objects?

Analyzing the Domain Model reveals that the *ProductCatalog* logically contains all the *ProductDescriptions*. Once again, taking inspiration from the domain, we design software classes with similar organization: a software *ProductCatalog* will contain software *ProductDescriptions*.

With that decided, then by Information Expert *ProductCatalog* is a good candidate for this lookup responsibility since it knows all the *ProductDescription* objects.

The lookup can be implemented, for example, with a method called *getProductDescription* (abbreviated as *getProductDesc* in some of the diagrams).[2]

Visibility to a ProductCatalog

Who should send the *getProductDescription* message to the *ProductCatalog* to ask for a *ProductDescription*?

It is reasonable to assume that a long-life *Register* and a *ProductCatalog* instance were created during the initial *Start Up* use case and that the *Register* object is permanently connected to the *ProductCatalog* object. With that assumption (which we might record on a task list of things to ensure in the design when we get to designing the initialization), we know that the *Register* can send the *getProductDescription* message to the *ProductCatalog*.

This implies another concept in object design: visibility. **Visibility** is the ability of one object to "see" or have a reference to another object.

> For an object to send a message to another object, it must have visibility to it.

Since we assume that the *Register* has a permanent connection—or reference—to the *ProductCatalog*, it has visibility to it, and hence can send it messages such as *getProductDescription*. A following chapter explores the question of visibility more closely.

The Final Design

Given the above discussion, the interaction diagram in Figure 18.7 and the DCD in Figure 18.8 (dynamic and static views) reflects the decisions regarding the assignment of responsibilities and how objects should interact. Mark the considerable reflection on the GRASP patterns, that brought us to this design; the design of object interactions and responsibility assignment requires some deliberation.

---

2. The name of access methods is idiomatic to each language. Java always uses the *object.getFoo()* form; C++ tends to use *object.foo()*; and C# uses *object.Foo,* which hides (like Eiffel and Ada) whether access is by a method call or is direct access of a public attribute.

Yet, once these principles are deeply "grasped" the decisions often come quickly, almost subconsciously.

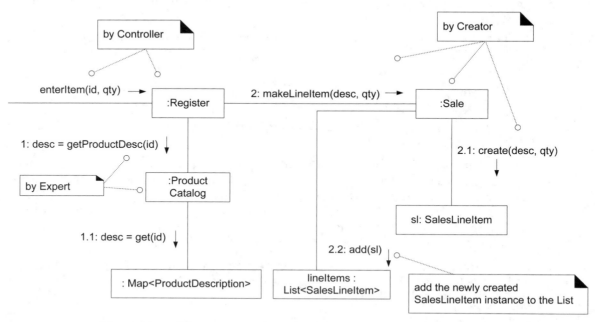

Figure 18.7 The *enterItem* interaction diagram. Dynamic view.

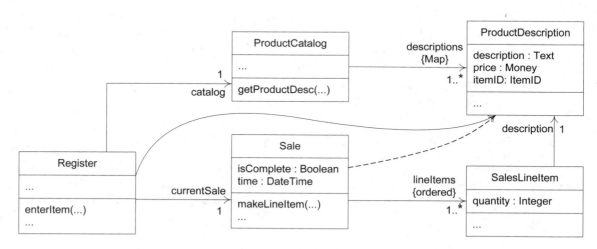

Figure 18.8 Partial DCD related to the *enterItem* design. Static view.

Retrieving ProductDescriptions from a Database

In the final version of the NextGen POS application, it is unlikely that *all* the *ProductDescriptions* will be in memory. They will most likely be stored in a relational database and retrieved on demand; some may be locally cached for performance or fault-tolerance reasons. However, in the interest of simplicity, we defer for now the issues surrounding retrieval from a database and assume that all the *ProductDescriptions* are in memory.

Chapter 37 explores the topic of database access of persistent objects, which is a larger topic influenced by the choice of technologies, such as Java or .NET.

How to Design endSale?

The *endSale* system operation occurs when a cashier presses a button indicating the end of entering line items into a sale (another name could have been *endItemEntry*). Here is the contract:

Contract CO3: endSale

Operation:	endSale()
Cross References:	Use Cases: Process Sale
Preconditions:	There is an underway sale.
Postconditions:	Sale.isComplete became true (attribute modification).

Choosing the Controller Class

Our first choice involves handling the responsibility for the system operation message *endSale*. Based on the Controller GRASP pattern, as for *enterItem*, we will continue to use *Register* as a controller.

Setting the Sale.isComplete Attribute

The contract postconditions state:

- *Sale.isComplete* became *true* (attribute modification).

As always, Expert should be the first pattern considered unless the problem is a controller or creation problem (which it is not).

Who should be responsible for setting the *isComplete* attribute of the *Sale* to true?

By Expert, it should be the *Sale* itself, since it owns and maintains the *isComplete* attribute. Thus, the *Register* will send a *becomeComplete* message to the *Sale* to set it to *true* (see Figure 18.9).[3]

---

3. That style is especially a Smalltalk idiom. Probably in Java, *setComplete(true)*.

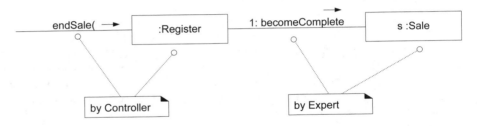

Figure 18.9 Completion of item entry.

Calculating the Sale Total

Consider this fragment of the *Process Sale* use case:

Main Success Scenario:
3. Customer arrives ...
4. Cashier tells System to create a new sale.
5. Cashier enters item identifier.
6. System records sale line item and ...
Cashier repeats steps 3-4 until indicates done.
7. System presents total with taxes calculated.

In step 5, a total is presented (or displayed). Because of the Model-View Separation principle, we should not concern ourselves with the design of how the sale total will be displayed, but we must ensure that the total is known. Note that no design class currently knows the sale total, so we need to create a design of object interactions that satisfies this requirement.

As always, Information Expert should be a pattern to consider unless the problem is a controller or creation problem (which it is not).

You have probably figured out by Expert that the *Sale* itself should be responsible for knowing its total. But to make *crystal clear* the reasoning process to find an Expert, follow the analysis of this simple example.

1. State the responsibility:

    o   Who should be responsible for knowing the sale total?

2. Summarize the information required:

    o   The sale total is the sum of the subtotals of all the sales line-items.

    o   sales line-item subtotal := line-item quantity * product description price

3. List the information required to fulfill this responsibility and the classes that know this information.

Information Required for Sale Total	Information Expert
ProductDescription.price	*ProductDescription*
SalesLineItem.quantity	*SalesLineItem*
all the *SalesLineItems* in the current Sale	*Sale*

Next we analyze the reasoning process in more detail:

- Who should be responsible for calculating the *Sale* total? By Expert, it should be the *Sale* itself, since it knows about all the *SalesLineItem* instances whose subtotals must be summed to calculate the sale total. Therefore, *Sale* will have the responsibility of knowing its total, implemented as a *getTotal* method.

- For a *Sale* to calculate its total, it needs the subtotal for each *SalesLineItem*. Who should be responsible for calculating the *SalesLineItem* subtotal? By Expert, it should be the *SalesLineItem* itself, since it knows the quantity and the *ProductDescription* it is associated with. Therefore, *SalesLineItem* will have the responsibility of knowing its subtotal, implemented as a *getSubtotal* method.

- For the *SalesLineItem* to calculate its subtotal, it needs the price of the *ProductDescription*. Who should be responsible for providing the *ProductDescription* price? By Expert, it should be the *ProductDescription* itself, since it encapsulates the price as an attribute. Therefore, *ProductDescription* will have the responsibility of knowing its price, implemented as a *getPrice* operation.

My goodness, that was detailed!

Although the above analysis is trivial in this case and the degree of excruciating elaboration presented is uncalled for in actual design practice, the same reasoning strategy to find an Expert can and should be applied in more difficult situations. If you follow the above logic, you can see how to apply Expert to almost any problem.

The Sale.getTotal Design

Given the above discussion, let us construct an interaction diagram that illustrates what happens when a *Sale* is sent a *getTotal* message. The first message in this diagram is *getTotal*, but observe that the *getTotal* message is not a system operation message (such as *enterItem* or *makeNewSale*).

This leads to the following observation:

> Not all interaction diagrams start with a system operation message; they can start with any message for which the designer wishes to show interactions.

The interaction diagram is shown in Figure 18.10. First, the *getTotal* message is sent to a *Sale* instance. The *Sale* then sends a *getSubtotal* message to each related *SalesLineItem* instance. The *SalesLineItem* in turn sends a *getPrice* message to its associated *ProductDescriptions*.

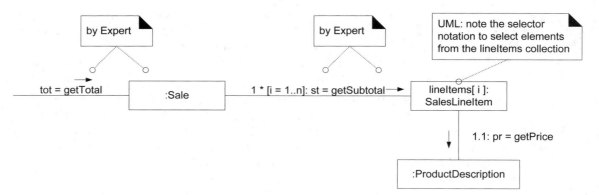

Figure 18.10 Sale.getTotal interaction diagram.

Since arithmetic is not (usually) illustrated via messages, we can illustrate the details of the calculations by attaching algorithms or constraints to the diagram that defines the calculations.

Who will send the *getTotal* message to the *Sale*? Most likely, it will be an object in the UI layer, such as a Java *JFrame*.

Observe in Figure 18.12 the use of the "method" note symbol style in UML 2.

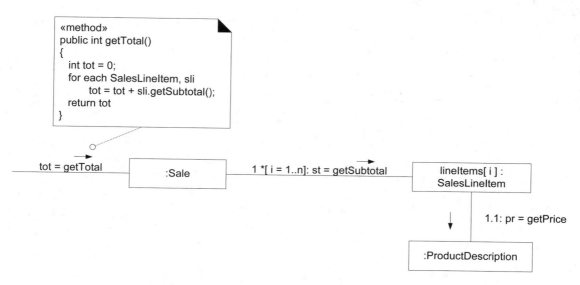

Figure 18.11 Showing a method in a note symbol.

How to Design makePayment?

The *makePayment* system operation occurs when a cashier enters the amount of cash tendered for payment. Here is the complete contract:

Contract CO4: makePayment

Operation:	makePayment(amount: Money)
Cross References:	Use Cases: Process Sale
Preconditions:	There is an underway sale.
Postconditions:	– A Payment instance p was created (instance creation).
	– p.amountTendered became amount (attribute modification).
	– p was associated with the current Sale (association formed).
	– The current Sale was associated with the Store (association formed); (to add it to the historical log of completed sales).

We construct a design to satisfy the postconditions of *makePayment*.

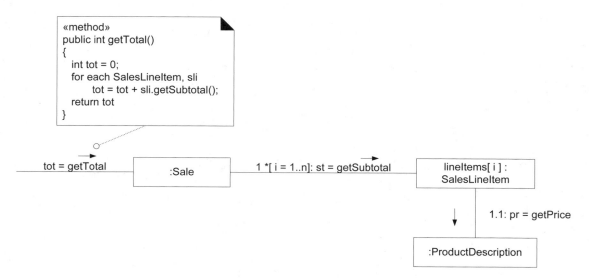

«method»
public int getTotal()
{
    int tot = 0;
    for each SalesLineItem, sli
        tot = tot + sli.getSubtotal();
    return tot
}

tot = getTotal   :Sale   1 *[i = 1..n]: st = getSubtotal   lineItems[i] : SalesLineItem

1.1: pr = getPrice

:ProductDescription

Figure 18.12 Showing a method in a note symbol.

Creating the Payment

One of the contract postconditions states:

- A *Payment* instance p was created (instance creation).

This is a creation responsibility, so we consider the Creator GRASP pattern.

Who records, aggregates, most closely uses, or contains a *Payment*? There is some appeal in stating that a *Register* logically records a *Payment* because in the real domain a "register" records account information; this motivates *Register*'s candidacy by the goal of reducing the representational gap in the software design. Additionally, we can reasonably expect that *Sale* software will closely use a *Payment*; thus, it, too, may be a candidate.

Another way to find a creator is to use the Expert pattern in terms of who the Information Expert is with respect to initializing data—the amount tendered in this case. The *Register* is the controller that receives the system operation *make-Payment* message, so it will initially have the amount tendered. Consequently the *Register* is again a candidate.

In summary, there are two candidates:

- *Register*
- *Sale*

Now, this leads to a key design idea:

Guideline

When there are alternative design choices, take a closer look at the **cohesion** and **coupling** implications of the alternatives, and possibly at the future evolution pressures on the alternatives. Choose an alternative with good cohesion, coupling, and stability in the presence of likely future changes.

Consider some of the implications of these choices in terms of the High Cohesion and Low Coupling GRASP patterns. If we choose the *Sale* to create the *Payment*, the work (or responsibilities) of the *Register* is lighter—leading to a simpler *Register* definition. Also, the *Register* does not need to know about the existence of a *Payment* instance because it can be recorded indirectly via the *Sale*—leading to lower coupling in the *Register*. This leads to the design shown in Figure 18.13.

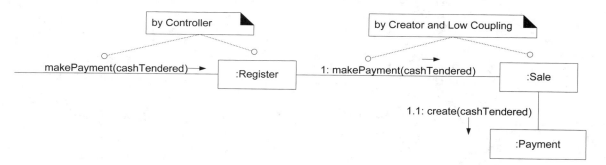

Figure 18.13 Register.makePayment interaction diagram.

This interaction diagram satisfies the postconditions of the contract: the *Payment* has been created, associated with the *Sale*, and its *amountTendered* has been set.

Logging a Sale

Once complete, the requirements state that the sale should be placed in an historical log. As always, Information Expert should be an early pattern considered unless the problem is a controller or creation problem (which it is not), and the responsibility should be stated:

> Who is responsible for knowing all the logged sales and doing the logging?

By the goal of low representational gap in the software design (in relation to our concepts of the domain), we can reasonably expect a *Store* to know all the logged sales since they are strongly related to its finances. Other alternatives include classic accounting concepts, such as a *SalesLedger*. Using a *SalesLedger* object makes sense as the design grows and the *Store* becomes incohesive (see Figure 18.14).

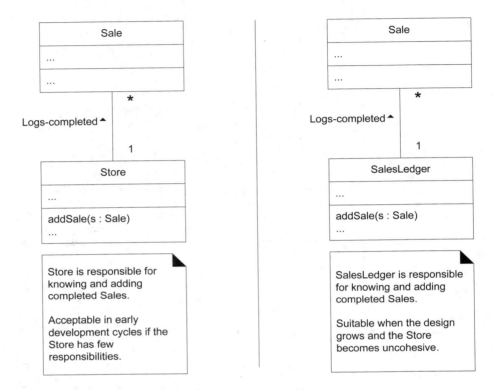

Figure 18.14 Who should be responsible for knowing the completed sales?

Note also that the postconditions of the contract indicate relating the *Sale* to the *Store*. This is an example of postconditions not being what we want to actually achieve in the design. Perhaps we didn't think of a *SalesLedger* earlier, but now that we have, we choose to use it instead of a *Store*. If this were the case, we would (ideally) add *SalesLedger* to the Domain Model as well since a sales ledger is a concept in the real-world domain. This kind of discovery and change during design work is to be expected.

In this case, we stick with the original plan of using the *Store* (see Figure 18.15).

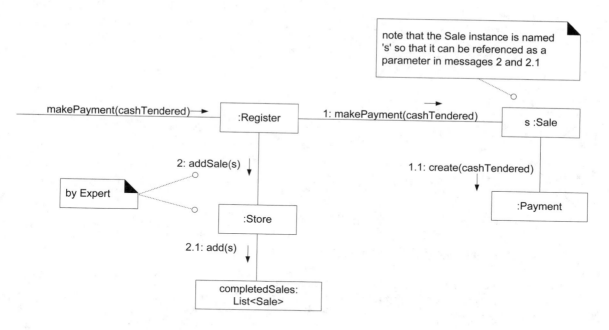

Figure 18.15 Logging a completed sale.

Calculating the Balance

The *Process Sale* use case implies that the balance due from a payment be printed on a receipt and displayed somehow.

Because of the Model-View Separation principle, we should not concern ourselves with how the balance will be displayed or printed, but we must ensure that it is known. Note that no class currently knows the balance, so we need to create a design of object interactions that satisfies this requirement.

As always, Information Expert should be considered unless the problem is a controller or creation problem (which it is not), and the responsibility should be stated:

Who is responsible for knowing the balance?

To calculate the balance, we need the sale total and payment cash tendered. Therefore, *Sale* and *Payment* are partial Experts on solving this problem.

If the *Payment* is primarily responsible for knowing the balance, it needs visibility to the *Sale*, to ask the *Sale* for its total. Since it does not currently know about the *Sale*, this approach would increase the overall coupling in the design—it would not support the Low Coupling pattern.

In contrast, if the *Sale* is primarily responsible for knowing the balance, it needs visibility to the *Payment*, to ask it for its cash tendered. Since the *Sale* already has visibility to the *Payment*—as its creator—this approach does not increase the overall coupling and is therefore a preferable design.

Consequently, the interaction diagram in Figure 18.16 provides a solution for knowing the balance.

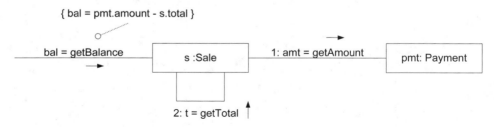

Figure 18.16 Sale.getBalance interaction diagram.

The Final NextGen DCD for Iteration-1

In accordance with the design decisions in this chapter, Figure 18.17 illustrates a static-view DCD of the emerging design for the *domain layer*, reflecting the use case realizations for the chosen scenarios of *Process Sale* in iteration-1.

Of course, we still have more OO design work—either while coding or while modeling—to do in other layers, include the UI layer and services layers.

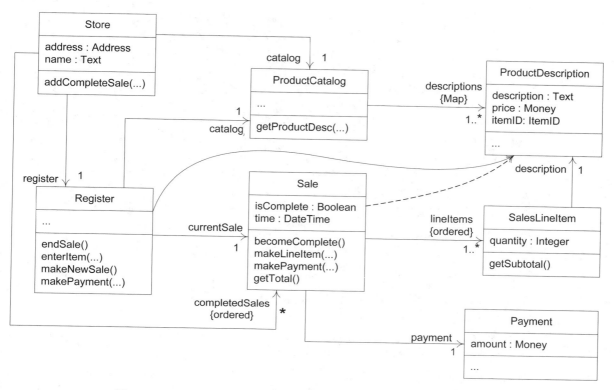

Figure 18.17 A more complete DCD reflecting most design decisions.

How to Connect the UI Layer to the Domain Layer?

Common designs by which objects in the UI layer obtain visibility to objects in the domain layer include the following:

- An initializer object (for example, a *Factory* object) called from the application starting method (e.g., the Java *main* method) creates both a UI and a domain object and passes the domain object to the UI.

- A UI object retrieves the domain object from a well-known source, such as a factory object that is responsible for creating domain objects.

Once the UI object has a connection to the *Register* instance (the facade controller in this design), it can forward system event messages, such as the *enterItem* and *endSale* message, to it (see Figure 18.18).

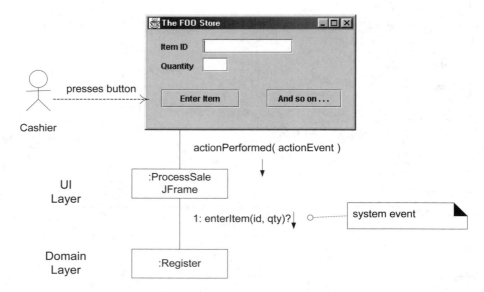

Figure 18.18 Connecting the UI and domain layers.

In the case of the *enterItem* message, we want the window to show the running total after each entry. Design solutions are:

- Add a *getTotal* method to the *Register*. The UI sends the *getTotal* message to the *Register*, which delegates to the *Sale*. This has the possible advantage of maintaining lower coupling from the UI to the domain layer—the UI only knows of the *Register* object. But it starts to expand the interface of the *Register* object, making it less cohesive.

- A UI asks for a reference to the current *Sale* object, and then when it requires the total (or any other information related to the sale), it directly sends messages to the *Sale*. This design increases the coupling from the UI to the domain layer. However, as we explored in the Low Coupling GRASP pattern discussion, higher coupling in and of itself is not a problem; rather, coupling to *unstable* things is a real problem. Assume we decide the *Sale* is a stable object that will be an integral part of the design—which is reasonable. Then, coupling to the *Sale* is not a major problem.

As illustrated in Figure 18.19, this design follows the second approach.

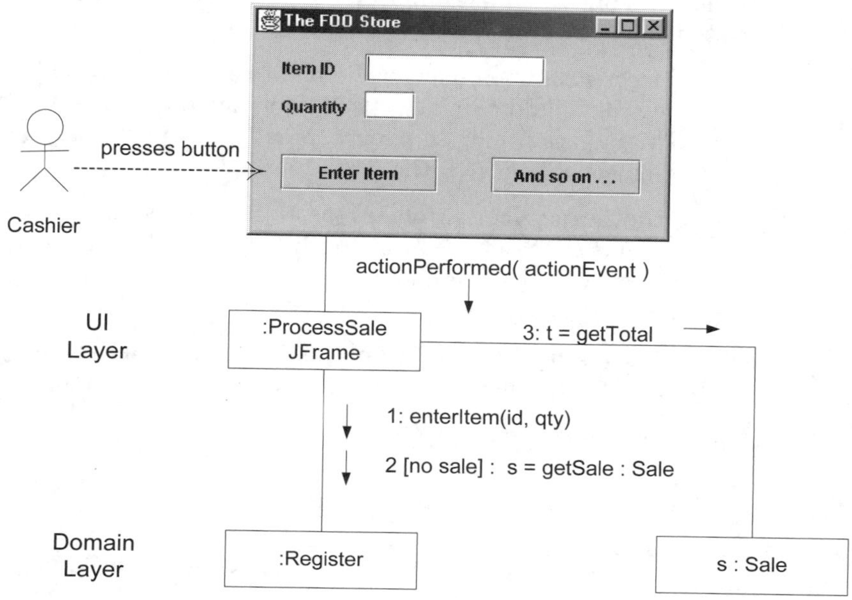

Figure 18.19 Connecting the UI and domain layers.

Initialization and the 'Start Up' Use Case

When to Create the Initialization Design?

Most, if not all, systems have either an implicit or explicit *Start Up* use case and some initial system operation related to the starting up of the application. Although abstractly, a *startUp* system operation is the earliest one to execute, delay the development of an interaction diagram for it until after all other system operations have been considered. This practice ensures that information has been discovered concerning the initialization activities required to support the later system operation interaction diagrams.

Guideline

Do the initialization design last.

How do Applications Start Up?

The *startUp* or *initialize* system operation of a *Start Up* use case abstractly represents the initialization phase of execution when an application is launched. To understand how to design an interaction diagram for this operation, you must first understand the contexts in which initialization can occur. How an application starts and initializes depends on the programming language and operating system.

In all cases, a common design idiom is to create an **initial domain object** or a set of peer initial domain objects that are the first software "domain" objects created. This creation may happen explicitly in the starting *main* method or in a *Factory* object called from the *main* method.

Often, the initial domain object (assuming the singular case), once created, is responsible for the creation of its direct child domain objects. For example, a *Store* chosen as the initial domain object may be responsible for the creation of a *Register* object.

In a Java application, for example, the *main* method may create the initial domain object or delegate the work to a *Factory* object that creates it.

```
public class Main
{

public static void main( String[] args )
{
    // Store is the initial domain object.
    // The Store creates some other domain objects.

    Store store = new Store();

    Register register = store.getRegister();

    ProcessSaleJFrame frame = new ProcessSaleJFrame( register );
    ...
}

}
```

Choosing the Initial Domain Object

What should the class of the initial domain object be?

Guideline

Choose as an initial domain object a class at or near the root of the containment or aggregation hierarchy of domain objects. This may be a facade controller, such as *Register*, or some other object considered to contain all or most other objects, such as a *Store*.

High Cohesion and Low Coupling considerations influence the choice between these alternatives. In this application, we chose the *Store* as the initial object.

Store.create Design

The tasks of creation and initialization derive from the needs of the prior design work, such as the design for handling *enterItem* and so on. By reflecting on the prior interaction designs, we identify the following initialization work:

- Create a *Store, Register, ProductCatalog,* and *ProductDescription*s.
- Associate the *ProductCatalog* with *ProductDescriptions.*
- Associate *Store* with *ProductCatalog.*
- Associate *Store* with *Register.*
- Associate *Register* with *ProductCatalog.*

Figure 18.20 shows the design. We chose the *Store* to create the *ProductCatalog* and *Register* by the Creator pattern. Likewise, we chose *ProductCatalog* to create the *ProductDescription*s. Recall that this approach to creating the specifications is temporary. In the final design, we will materialize them from a database, as needed.

Applying UML: Observe that the creation of all the *ProductDescription* instances and their addition to a container happens in a repeating section, indicated by the * following the sequence numbers.

An interesting deviation between modeling the real-world domain and the design is illustrated in the fact that the software *Store* object only creates *one Register* object. A real store may house *many* real registers or POS terminals. However, we are considering a software design, not real life. In our current requirements, our software *Store* only needs to create a single instance of a software *Register.*

> Multiplicity between classes of objects in the
> Domain Model and Design Model may not be the same.

18.5 Use Case Realizations for the Monopoly Iteration

First, an education point: Please don't dismiss this case study because it isn't a business application. The logic, especially in later iterations, becomes quite complex, with rich OO design problems to solve. The core object design principles that it illustrates—applying Information Expert, evaluating the coupling and cohesion of alternatives—are relevant to object design in all domains.

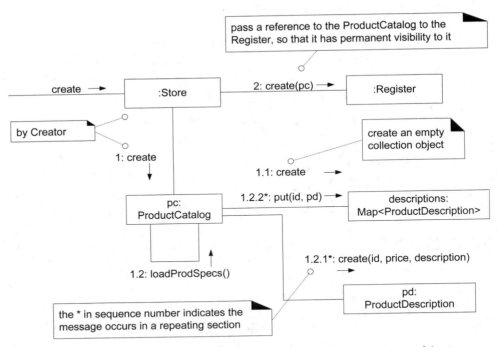

pass a reference to the ProductCatalog to the Register, so that it has permanent visibility to it

create →

:Store

2: create(pc) →

:Register

by Creator

1: create

create an empty collection object

1.1: create →

pc:
ProductCatalog

1.2.2*: put(id, pd) →

descriptions:
Map<ProductDescription>

1.2: loadProdSpecs()

1.2.1*: create(id, price, description) →

pd:
ProductDescription

the * in sequence number indicates the message occurs in a repeating section

Figure 18.20 Creation of the initial domain object and subsequent objects.

iteration-1 requirements p. 44

We are designing a simplified version of Monopoly in iteration-1 for a scenario of the use case *Play Monopoly Game*. It has two system operations: *initialize* (or *startUp*) and *playGame*. Following our guideline, we will ignore initialization design until the last step and focus first on the main system operations—only *playGame* in this case.

Also, to support the goal of low representational gap (LRG), we look again at Figure 18.21, which shows the Domain Model. We turn to it for inspiration as we design the domain layer of the Design Model.

How to Design playGame?

The *playGame* system operation occurs when the human game observer performs some UI gesture (such as clicking a "play game" button) to request the game to play as a simulation while the observer watches the output.

We didn't write a detailed use case or an operation contract for this case study, as most people know the rules; our focus is the design issues, not the requirements.

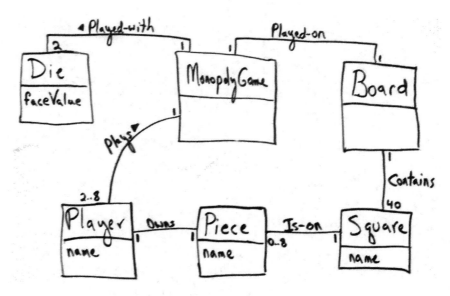

Figure 18.21 Iteration-1 Domain Model for Monopoly.

Choosing the Controller Class

Our first design choice involves selecting the controller for the system operation message *playGame* that comes from the UI layer into the domain layer. By the Controller pattern, here are some choices:

Represents the overall "system," "root object," a specialized device, or a major subsystem.	*MonopolyGame*—a kind of root object: We think of most of the other domain objects as "contained within" the *MonopolyGame*. Abbreviated *MGame* in most of the UML sketches.
	MonopolyGameSystem—a name suggesting the overall system
Represents a receiver or handler of all system events of a use case scenario.	*PlayMonopolyGameHandler*— constructed from the pattern <use-case-name> "Handler"
	PlayMonopolyGameSession

Choosing a root-object facade controller like *MonopolyGame* (*MGame* in Figure 18.22) is satisfactory if there are only a few system operations (there are only two in this use case) and if the facade controller is not taking on too many responsibilities (in other words, if it is not becoming incohesive).

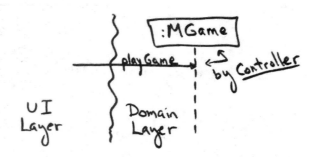

Figure 18.22 Applying Controller to the *playGame* system operation.

The Game-Loop Algorithm

Before discussing OO design choices, we prepare by considering the basic algorithm of the simulation. First, some terminology:

- *turn*—a player rolling the dice and moving the piece
- *round*—all the players taking one turn

Now the game loop:

```
for N rounds
    for each Player p
        p takes a turn
```

Recall that the iteration-1 version does not have a winner, so the simulation simply runs for *N* rounds.

Who is Responsible for Controlling the Game Loop?

Reviewing the algorithm: The first responsibility is game loop control—looping for *N* rounds and having a turn played for each player. This is a *doing* responsibility and is not a creation or controller problem, so naturally, Expert should be considered. Applying Expert means asking, "What information is needed for the responsibility?" Here's the analysis:

Information Needed	Who Has the Information?
the current round count	No object has it yet, but by LRG, assigning this to the *MonopolyGame* object is justifiable.
all the players (so that each can be used in taking a turn)	Taking inspiration from the domain model, *MonopolyGame* is a good candidate.

Therefore, by Expert, *MonopolyGame* is a justifiable choice to control the game loop and coordinate the playing of each round. Figure 18.23 illustrates in UML. Notice the use of a private (internal) *playRound* helper method; it accomplishes at least two goals:

1. It factors the play-single-round logic into a helper method; it is good to organize cohesive chunks of behavior into small separate methods.

   ○ Good OO method design encourages small methods with a single purpose. This supports High Cohesion at the method level.

2. The name *playRound* is inspired by domain vocabulary—that's desirable, it improves comprehension.

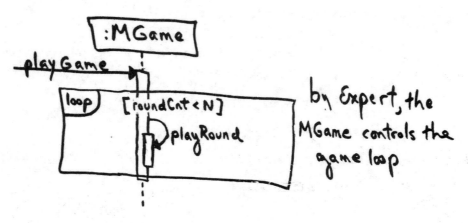

Figure 18.23 Game loop.

Who Takes a Turn?

Taking a turn involves rolling the dice and moving a piece to the square indicated by the total of the dice face values.

What object should be responsible for taking the turn of a player? This is a *doing* responsibility. Again, Expert applies.

Now, a naive reaction might be to say "a *Player* object should take the turn" because in the real world a human player takes a turn. However—and this is a **key point**—OO designs are not one-to-one simulations of how a real domain works, especially with respect to how *people* behave. If you applied the (wrong) guideline "put responsibilities in software objects as they are assigned to people" then, for example in the POS domain, a *Cashier* software object would do almost everything! A violation of High Cohesion and Low Coupling. Big fat objects.

Rather, object designs distribute responsibilities among many objects by the principle of Information Expert (among many others).

Therefore, we should not choose a *Player* object just because a human player takes a turn.

Yet, as we shall see, *Player* turns out to be a good choice for taking a turn. But the justification will be by Expert, not inspiration from how humans behave. Applying Expert means asking, "What information is needed for the responsibility?" Here's the analysis:

Information Needed	Who Has the Information?
current location of the player (to know the starting point of a move)	Taking inspiration from the domain model, a *Piece* knows its *Square* and a *Player* knows its *Piece*. Therefore, a *Player* software object could know its location by LRG.
the two *Die* objects (to roll them and calculate their total)	Taking inspiration from the domain model, *MonopolyGame* is a candidate since we think of the dice as being part of the game.
all the squares—the square organization (to be able to move to the correct new square)	By LRG, *Board* is a good candidate.

Now, this is an interesting problem! There are three *partial* information experts for the "take a turn" responsibility: *Player*, *MonopolyGame*, and *Board*.

What's interesting about this problem is how to resolve it—the evaluations and trade-offs an OO developer may consider. Here's the first guideline to solve the problem:

Guideline: When there are multiple *partial* information experts to choose from, place the responsibility in the *dominant* information expert—the object with the majority of the information. This tends to best support Low Coupling.

Unfortunately, in this case, are all rather equal, each with about one-third of the information—no dominant expert.

So, here's another guideline to try:

Guideline: When there are alternative design choices, consider the coupling and cohesion impact of each, and choose the best.

OK, that can be applied. *MonopolyGame* is already doing some work, so giving it more work impacts its cohesion, especially when contrasted with a *Player* and *Board* object, which are not doing anything yet. But we still have a two-way tie with these objects.

So, here's another guideline:

Guideline: When there is no clear winner from the alternatives other guidelines, consider probable *future evolution* of the software objects and the impact in terms of Information Expert, cohesion, and coupling.

For example, in iteration-1, taking a turn doesn't involve much information. However, consider the complete set of game rules in a later iteration. Then, taking a turn can involve buying a property that the player lands on, if the player has enough money or if its color fits in with the player's "color strategy." What object would be expected to know a player's cash total? Answer: a *Player* (by LRG). What object would be expected to know a player's color strategy? Answer: a *Player* (by LRG, as it involves a player's current holdings of properties).

Thus, in the end, by these guidelines *Player* turns out to be a good candidate, justified by Expert when we consider the full game rules.

My goodness, that was detailed!

Surely this discussion was more detailed than you normally want to read! Yet, if you can now follow its reasoning and apply it in new situations, it will serve you very well for the remainder of your career as an OO developer, and thus have been worth the effort.

Based on the above, Figure 18.24 illustrates the emerging dynamic design and static design.

Applying UML: Notice the approach to indicating that the *takeTurn* message is sent to each player in a collection named *players*.

Taking a Turn

Taking a turn means:

1. calculating a random number total between 2 and 12 (the range of two dice)

2. calculating the new square location

3. moving the player's piece from an old location to a new square location

First, the random number problem: By LRG, we'll create a *Die* object with a *faceValue* attribute. Calculating a new random *faceValue* involves changing information in the *Die*, so by Expert *Die* should be able to "roll" itself (generate a new random value, using domain vocabulary), and answer its *faceValue*.

Second, the new square location problem: By LRG, it's reasonable that a *Board* knows all its *Squares*. Then by Expert a *Board* will be responsible for knowing a new square location, given an old square location, and some offset (the dice total).

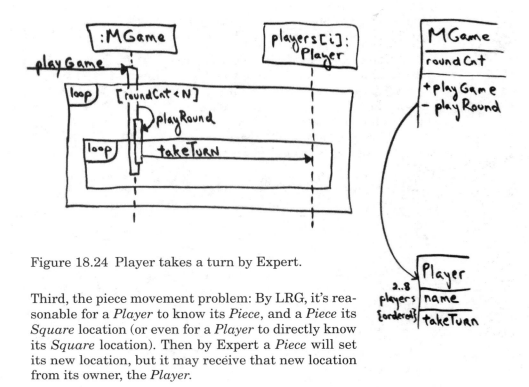

Figure 18.24 Player takes a turn by Expert.

Third, the piece movement problem: By LRG, it's reasonable for a *Player* to know its *Piece*, and a *Piece* its *Square* location (or even for a *Player* to directly know its *Square* location). Then by Expert a *Piece* will set its new location, but it may receive that new location from its owner, the *Player*.

Who Coordinates All This?

The above three steps need to be coordinated by some object. Since the *Player* is responsible for taking a turn, the *Player* should coordinate.

The Problem of Visibility

However, that the *Player* coordinates these steps implies its collaboration with the *Die*, *Board*, and *Piece* objects. And this implies a **visibility** need—the *Player* must have an object reference to those objects.

Since the *Player* will need visibility to the *Die*, *Board*, and *Piece* objects each and every turn, we can usefully initialize the *Player* during startup with permanent references to those objects.

The Final Design of playGame

Based on the above design decisions, the emerging dynamic design is as shown in Figure 18.25 and the static design as in Figure 18.26. Notice that each message, each allocation of responsibility, was methodically and rationally motivated by the GRASP principles. As you come to master these principles, you will be able to reason through a design and evaluate existing ones in terms of coupling, cohesion, Expert, and so forth.

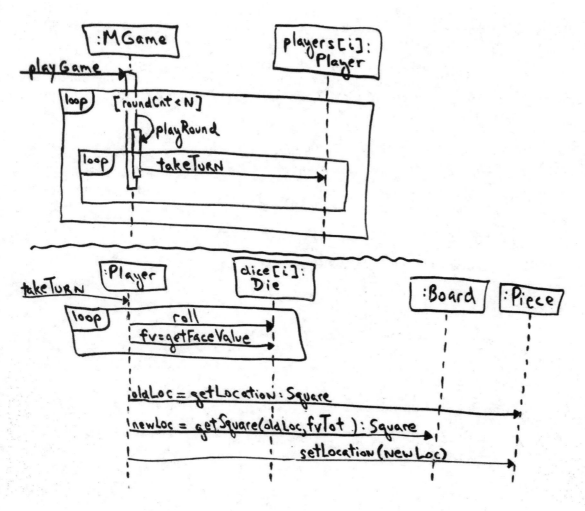

Figure 18.25 Dynamic design for *playGame*.

Applying UML:

- Notice in Figure 18.25 that I show two sequence diagrams. In the top, the *takeTurn* message to a *Player* is not expanded. Then, in the bottom diagram, I expand the *takeTurn* message. This is a common sketching style, so that each wall diagram is not too large. The two diagrams are related informally. More formally, I could use UML *sd* and *ref* frames (see p. 235), which would be easy and appropriate in a UML tool; but for wall sketching, informality suffices.

- Notice again, with the *roll* and *getFaceValue* messages to a *Die* object, the convention of drawing a loop frame around messages to a collection selection object, to indicate collection over each element in a collection.

- Notice the parameter *fvTot* in the *getSquare* message. I am informally suggesting this is the total of all the *Die faceValues*. This kind of informality is appropriate when we apply "UML as sketch," assuming the audience understands the context.

The Command-Query Separation Principle

Notice in Figure 18.25 that the message to *roll* the *Die* is followed by a second *getFaceValue* to retrieve its new *faceValue*. In particular, the *roll* method is *void*—it has no return value. For example:

```
// style #1; used in the official solution
public void roll()
{
    faceValue = // random num generation
}


public int getFaceValue()
{
    return faceValue;
}
```

Why not make *roll* non-void and combine these two functions so that the *roll* method returns the new *faceValue*, as follows?

```
// style #2; why is this poor?
public int roll()
{
    faceValue = // random num generation
    return faceValue;
}
```

You can find *many* examples of code that follow style #2, but it is considered undesirable because it violates the **Command-Query Separation Principle**, (CQS) a classic OO design principle for methods [Meyer88]. This principle states that every method should either be:

- a command method that performs an action (updating, coordinating, …), often has side effects such as changing the state of objects, and is *void* (no return value); or

- a query that returns data to the caller and has no side effects—it should not permanently change the state of any objects

But—and this is the key point—a method should *not be both*.

The *roll* method is a command—it has the side effect of changing the state of the *Die's faceValue*. Therefore, it should not also return the new *faceValue*, as then the method also becomes a kind of query and violates the "must be void" rule.

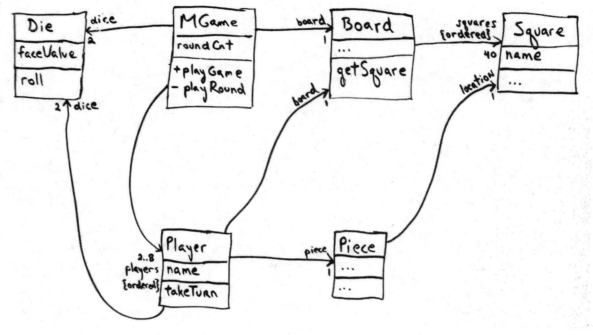

Figure 18.26 Static design for *playGame*.

Motivation: Why Bother?

CQS is widely considered desirable in computer science theory because with it, you can more easily reason about a program's state without simultaneously modifying that state. And it makes designs simpler to understand and anticipate. For example, if an application consistently follows CQS, you know that a query or *getter* method isn't going to modify anything and a command isn't going to return anything. Simple pattern. This often turns out to be nice to rely on, as the alternative can be a nasty surprise—violating the **Principle of Least Surprise** in software development.

Consider this contrived but explosive counter-example in which a query method violates CQS:

```
Missile m = new Missile();
    // looks harmless to me!
String name = m.getName();

...
```

```
public class Missile
{
// ...
public String getName()
{
    launch(); // launch missile!
    return name;
}
} // end of class
```

Initialization and the 'Start Up' Use Case

The *initialize* system operation occurs, at least abstractly, in a *Start Up* use case. For this design, we must first choose a suitable *root object* that will be the creator of some other objects. For example, *MonopolyGame* is itself a good candidate root object. By Creator, the *MonopolyGame* can justifiably create the *Board* and *Players*, for example—and the *Board* can justifiably create the *Squares*, for example. We could show the details of the dynamic design with UML interaction diagrams, but I'll use this case as an opportunity to show a UML dependency line stereotyped with «create», in a class diagram. Figure 18.27 illustrates a static view diagram that suggests the creation logic. I ignore the fine details of the interactions. In fact, that's probably suitable, because from this UML sketch we (the developers who drew this) can pretty easily figure out the creation details while coding.

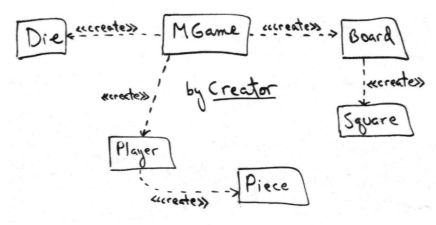

Figure 18.27 Creation dependencies.

18.6   Process: Iterative and Evolutionary Object Design

I've made many suggestions about iterative and evolutionary object design for use case realizations over the last few chapters, including

- "On to Object Design" on page 213
- "Object Design: Example Inputs, Activities, and Outputs" on page 272

The essential point: Keep it light and short, move quickly to code and test, and don't try to detail everything in UML models. Model the creative, difficult parts of the design.

Figure 18.28 offers suggestions on the time and space for doing this work.

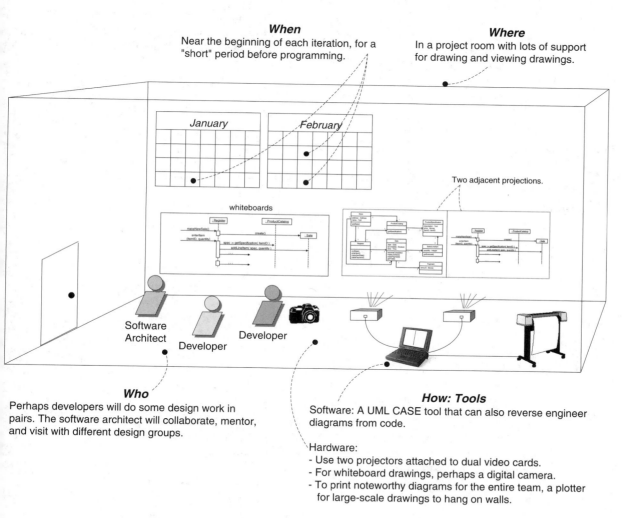

Figure 18.28 Sample process and setting context.

Object Design Within the UP

To again consider the UP as the example iterative method: use case realizations are part of the UP Design Model.

Inception—The Design Model and use case realizations will not usually be started until elaboration because they involve detailed design decisions, which are premature during inception.

Elaboration—During this phase, use case realizations may be created for the most architecturally significant or risky scenarios of the design. However, UML diagramming will not be done for every scenario, and not necessarily in complete and fine-grained detail. The idea is to do interaction diagrams for the key use case realizations that benefit from some forethought and exploration of alternatives, focusing on the major design decisions.

Construction—Use case realizations are created for remaining design problems.

Table 18.1 summarizes.

Discipline	Artifact	Incep.	Elab.	Const.	Trans.
	Iteration➜	I1	E1..En	C1..Cn	T1..T2
Business Modeling	Domain Model		s		
Requirements	Use Case Model (SSDs)	s	r		
	Supplementary Specification	s	r		
	Glossary	s	r		
Design	*Design Model*		s	r	
	SW Architecture Document		s		
	Data Model		s	r	

Table 18.1 Sample UP artifacts and timing. s - start; r - refine

18.7   Summary

Designing object interactions and assigning responsibilities is at the heart of object design. These choices can have a profound impact on the extensibility, clarity, and maintainability of an object software system, plus on the degree and quality of reusable components. There are principles by which the choices of responsibility assignment can be made; the GRASP patterns summarize some of the most general and common ones used by object-oriented designers.

DESIGNING FOR VISIBILITY

A mathematician is a device for turning coffee into theorems.

—*Paul Erdös*

Objectives

- Identify four kinds of visibility.
- Design to establish visibility.

Introduction

Visibility is the ability of one object to see or have reference to another. This chapter explores this basic but necessary design issue; those new to object design sometimes don't think about and design to achieve necessary visibility.

What's Next? Having dived into the case studies, this chapter clarifies the small but necessary issue of designing for visibility between objects. The next introduces mapping our design to code in an OO language.

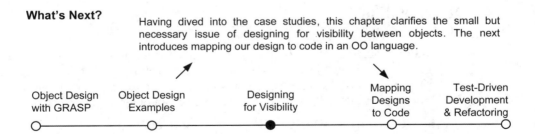

| Object Design with GRASP | Object Design Examples | Designing for Visibility | Mapping Designs to Code | Test-Driven Development & Refactoring |

9.1 Visibility Between Objects

The designs created for the system operations (*enterItem*, and so on) illustrate messages between objects. For a sender object to send a message to a receiver object, the sender must be *visible* to the receiver—the sender must have some kind of reference or pointer to the receiver object.

For example, the *getProductDescription* message sent from a *Register* to a *ProductCatalog* implies that the *ProductCatalog* instance is visible to the *Register* instance, as shown in Figure 19.1.

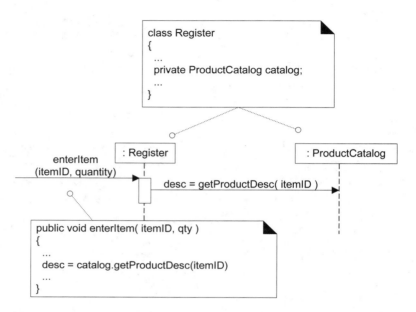

Figure 19.1 Visibility from the Register to ProductCatalog is required.[1]

When creating a design of interacting objects, it is necessary to ensure that the necessary visibility is present to support message interaction.

19.2   What is Visibility?

In common usage, **visibility** is the ability of an object to "see" or have a reference to another object. More generally, it is related to the issue of scope: Is one resource (such as an instance) within the scope of another? There are four common ways that visibility can be achieved from object *A* to object *B*:

- **Attribute visibility**—B is an attribute of A.

- **Parameter visibility**—B is a parameter of a method of A.

- **Local visibility**—B is a (non-parameter) local object in a method of A.

---

1. In this and subsequent code examples, language simplifications may be made for the sake of brevity and clarity.

- **Global visibility**—B is in some way globally visible.

The motivation to consider visibility is this:

> For an object A to send a message to an object B, B must be visible to A.

For example, to create an interaction diagram in which a message is sent from a *Register* instance to a *ProductCatalog* instance, the *Register* must have visibility to the *ProductCatalog*. A typical visibility solution is that a reference to the *ProductCatalog* instance is maintained as an attribute of the *Register*.

Attribute Visibility

Attribute visibility from A to B exists when B is an attribute of A. It is a relatively permanent visibility because it persists as long as A and B exist. This is a very common form of visibility in object-oriented systems.

To illustrate, in a Java class definition for *Register*, a *Register* instance may have attribute visibility to a *ProductCatalog*, since it is an attribute (Java instance variable) of the *Register*.

```
public class Register
{
...
private ProductCatalog catalog;
...
}
```

This visibility is required because in the *enterItem* diagram shown in Figure 19.2, a *Register* needs to send the *getProductDescription* message to a *Product-Catalog*:

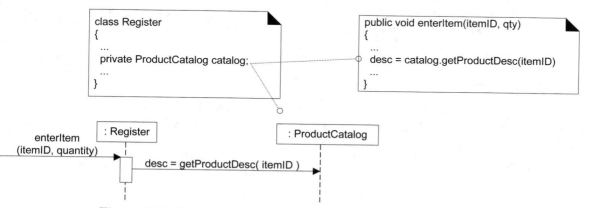

Figure 19.2 Attribute visibility.

Parameter Visibility

Parameter visibility from A to B exists when B is passed as a parameter to a method of A. It is a relatively temporary visibility because it persists only within the scope of the method. After attribute visibility, it is the second most common form of visibility in object-oriented systems.

To illustrate, when the *makeLineItem* message is sent to a *Sale* instance, a *ProductDescription* instance is passed as a parameter. Within the scope of the *makeLineItem* method, the *Sale* has parameter visibility to a *ProductDescription* (see Figure 19.3).

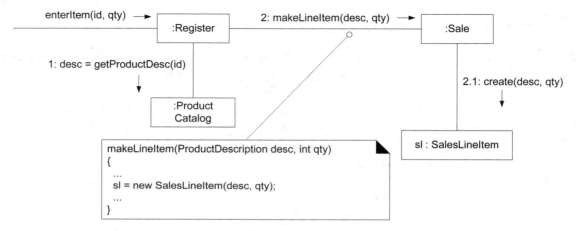

Figure 19.3 Parameter visibility.

It is common to transform parameter visibility into attribute visibility. When the *Sale* creates a new *SalesLineItem*, it passes the *ProductDescription* in to its initializing method (in C++ or Java, this would be its **constructor**). Within the initializing method, the parameter is assigned to an attribute, thus establishing attribute visibility (Figure 19.4).

Local Visibility

Local visibility from A to B exists when B is declared as a local object within a method of A. It is a relatively temporary visibility because it persists only within the scope of the method. After parameter visibility, it is the third most common form of visibility in object-oriented systems.

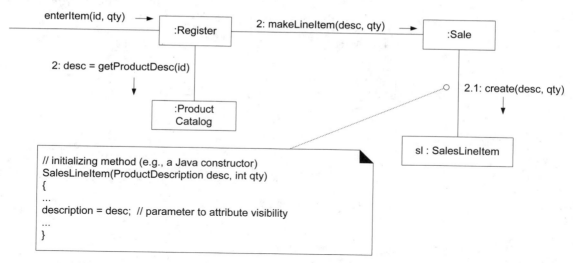

Figure 19.4 Parameter to attribute visibility.

Two common means by which local visibility is achieved are:

- Create a new local instance and assign it to a local variable.
- Assign the returning object from a method invocation to a local variable.

As with parameter visibility, it is common to transform locally declared visibility into attribute visibility.

An example of the second variation (assigning the returning object to a local variable) can be found in the *enterItem* method of class *Register* (Figure 19.5).

A subtle version on the second variation is when the method does not explicitly declare a variable, but one implicitly exists as the result of a returning object from a method invocation. For example:

```
// there is implicit local visibility to the foo object
// returned via the getFoo call

anObject.getFoo().doBar();
```

Global Visibility

Global visibility from A to B exists when B is global to A. It is a relatively permanent visibility because it persists as long as A and B exist. It is the least common form of visibility in object-oriented systems.

One way to achieve global visibility is to assign an instance to a global variable, which is possible in some languages, such as C++, but not others, such as Java.

The preferred method to achieve global visibility is to use the **Singleton** pattern [GHJV95], which is discussed in a later chapter.

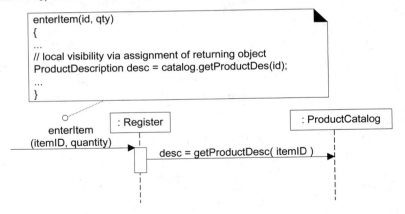

Figure 19.5 Local visibility.

MAPPING DESIGNS TO CODE

Beware of bugs in the above code;
I have only proved it correct, not tried it.

—Donald Knuth

Objectives

- Map design artifacts to code in an object-oriented language.

Introduction

With the completion of interaction diagrams and DCDs for the current iteration of the case studies, there's more than enough thought and detail to cut some code for the domain layer of objects.

The UML artifacts created during the design work—the interaction diagrams and DCDs—will be used as input to the code generation process.

In UP terms, there exists an **Implementation Model**. This is all the implementation artifacts, such as the source code, database definitions, JSP/XML/HTML pages, and so forth. Thus, the code being created in this chapter can be considered part of the UP Implementation Model.

What's Next?   Having wrapped up design issues with visibility, this chapter introduces mapping our design to code in an OO language. The next is related, introducing important OO programming practices: TDD and refactoring.

Object Design Examples	Designing for Visibility	Mapping Designs to Code	Test-Driven Development & Refactoring	UML Tools & UML as Blueprint

Java is used for the examples because of its widespread use and familiarity. However, this is not meant to imply a special endorsement of Java; C#, Visual Basic, C++, Smalltalk, Python, and many more languages are amenable to the object design principles and mapping to code presented in this case study.

20.1 Programming and Iterative, Evolutionary Development

The prior design modeling should not be taken to imply that there is no prototyping or design-while-programming; modern development tools provide an excellent environment to quickly explore and refactor alternate approaches, and some (often lots) design-while-programming is worthwhile.

The creation of code in an OO language—such as Java or C#—is not part of OOA/D—it's an end goal. The artifacts created in the Design Model provide some of the information necessary to generate the code.

A strength of use cases plus OOA/D plus OO programming is that they provide an end-to-end roadmap from requirements through to code. The various artifacts feed into later artifacts in a traceable and useful manner, ultimately culminating in a running application. This is not to suggest that the road will be smooth, or can simply be mechanically followed—there are many variables. But having a roadmap provides a starting point for experimentation and discussion.

Creativity and Change During Implementation

Some decision-making and creative work was accomplished during design work. It will be seen during the following discussion that the generation of the code in these examples a relatively mechanical translation process.

However, in general, the programming work is not a trivial code generation step—quite the opposite! Realistically, the results generated during design modeling are an incomplete first step; during programming and testing, myriad changes will be made and detailed problems will be uncovered and resolved.

Done well, the *ideas* and *understanding* (not the diagrams or documents!) generated during OO design modeling will provide a great base that scales up with elegance and robustness to meet the new problems encountered during programming. But, expect and plan for lots of change and deviation from the design during programming. That's a key—and pragmatic—attitude in iterative and evolutionary methods.

20.2   Mapping Designs to Code

Implementation in an object-oriented language requires writing source code for:

- class and interface definitions
- method definitions

The following sections discuss their generation in Java (as a typical case). The discussion is more-or-less independent of using a UML tool for code generation or working from some wall sketches.

20.3   Creating Class Definitions from DCDs

At the very least, DCDs depict the class or interface name, superclasses, operation signatures, and attributes of a class. This is sufficient to create a basic class definition in an OO language. If the DCD was drawn in a UML tool, it can generate the basic class definition from the diagrams.

Defining a Class with Method Signatures and Attributes

From the DCD, a mapping to the attribute definitions (Java *fields*) and method signatures for the Java definition of *SalesLineItem* is straightforward, as shown in Figure 20.1.

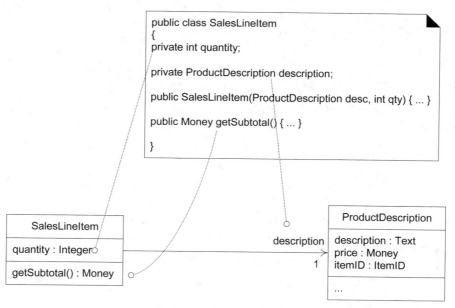

Figure 20.1 SalesLineItem in Java.

Note the addition in the source code of the Java constructor *SalesLineItem(...)*. It is derived from the *create(desc, qty)* message sent to a *SalesLineItem* in the *enterItem* interaction diagram. This indicates, in Java, that a constructor supporting these parameters is required. The *create* method is often excluded from the class diagram because of its commonality and multiple interpretations, depending on the target language.

20.4   Creating Methods from Interaction Diagrams

The sequence of the messages in an interaction diagram translates to a series of statements in the method definitions. The *enterItem* interaction diagram in Figure 20.2 illustrates the Java definition of the *enterItem* method. For this example, we will explore the implementation of the *Register* and its *enterItem* method. A Java definition of the *Register* class is shown in Figure 20.3.

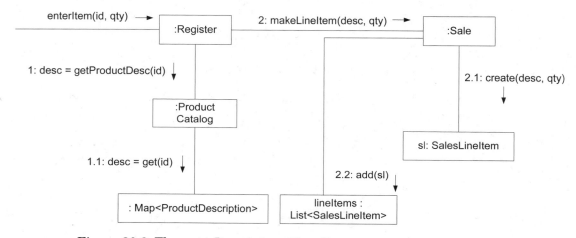

Figure 20.2 The enterItem interaction diagram.

The *enterItem* message is sent to a *Register* instance; therefore, the *enterItem* method is defined in class *Register*.

```
public void enterItem(ItemID itemID, int qty)
```

Message 1: A *getProductDescription* message is sent to the *ProductCatalog* to retrieve a *ProductDescription*.

```
ProductDescription desc = catalog.getProductDescription(itemID);
```

Message 2: The *makeLineItem* message is sent to the *Sale*.

```
currentSale.makeLineItem(desc, qty);
```

In summary, each sequenced message within a method, as shown on the interaction diagram, is mapped to a statement in the Java method.

The complete *enterItem* method and its relationship to the interaction diagram is shown in Figure 20.4.

The Register.enterItem Method

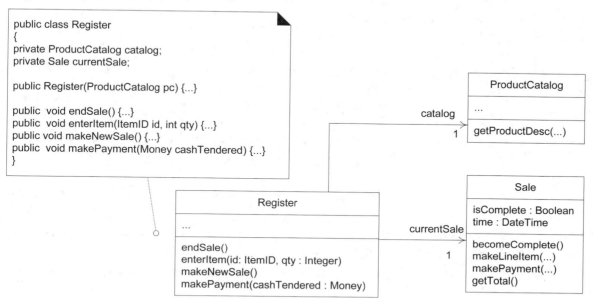

Figure 20.3 The Register class.

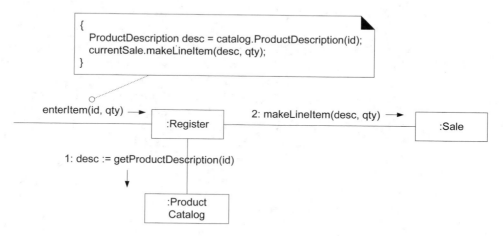

Figure 20.4 The enterItem method.

20.5   Collection Classes in Code

One-to-many relationships are common. For example, a *Sale* must maintain visibility to a group of many *SalesLineItem* instances, as shown in Figure 20.5. In OO programming languages, these relationships are usually implemented with the introduction of a **collection** object, such as a *List* or *Map*, or even a simple array.

For example, the Java libraries contain collection classes such as *ArrayList* and *HashMap*, which implement the *List* and *Map* interfaces, respectively. Using *ArrayList*, the *Sale* class can define an attribute that maintains an ordered list of *SalesLineItem* instances.

The choice of collection class is of course influenced by the requirements; key-based lookup requires the use of a *Map*, a growing ordered list requires a *List*, and so on.

As a small point, note that the *lineItems* attribute is declared in terms of its interface.

Guideline: If an object implements an interface, declare the variable in terms of the interface, not the concrete class.

For example, in Figure 20.5 the definition for the *lineItems* attribute demonstrates this guideline:

```
private List lineItems = new ArrayList();
```

20.6   Exceptions and Error Handling

Exception handling has been ignored so far in the development of a solution. This was intentional to focus on the basic questions of responsibility assignment and object design. However, in application development, it's wise to consider the large-scale exception handling strategies during design modeling (as they have a large-scale architectural impact), and certainly during implementation. Briefly, in terms of the UML, exceptions can be indicated in the property strings of messages and operation declarations (see p. 256, for example).

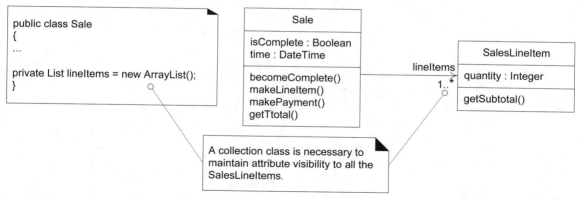

Figure 20.5 Adding a collection.

20.7 Defining the Sale.makeLineItem Method

As a final example, the *makeLineItem* method of class *Sale* can also be written by inspecting the *enterItem* collaboration diagram. An abridged version of the interaction diagram, with the accompanying Java method, is shown in Figure 20.6.

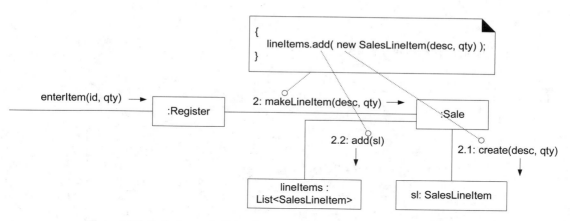

Figure 20.6 Sale.makeLineItem method.

20.8 Order of Implementation

Classes need to be implemented (and ideally, fully unit tested) from least-coupled to most-coupled (see Figure 20.7). For example, possible first classes to implement are either *Payment* or *ProductDescription*; next are classes only dependent on the prior implementations—*ProductCatalog* or *SalesLineItem*.

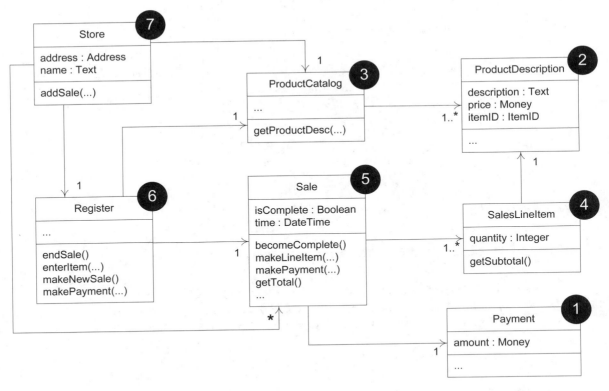

Figure 20.7 Possible order of class implementation and testing.

20.9 Test-Driven or Test-First Development

TDD p. 386

An excellent practice promoted by the Extreme Programming (XP) method [Beck00], and applicable to the UP and other iterative methods (as most XP practices are), is **test-driven development** (TDD) or **test-first development**. In this practice, unit testing code is written *before* the code to be tested, and the developer writes unit testing code for *all* production code. The basic rhythm is to write a little test code, then write a little production code, make it pass the test, then write some more test code, and so forth. This is explore in more detail in a following chapter.

20.10 Summary of Mapping Designs to Code

As demonstrated, there is a translation process from UML class diagrams to class definitions, and from interaction diagrams to method bodies. There is still lots of room for creativity, evolution, and exploration during programming work.

20.11 Introduction to the NextGen POS Program Solution

This section presents a sample domain layer of classes in Java for this iteration. The code generation is largely derived from the design class diagrams and interaction diagrams defined in the design work, based on the principles of mapping designs to code as previously explored.

> The main point of this listing is to show that there is a translation from design artifacts to a foundation of code. This code defines a simple case; it is not meant to illustrate a robust, fully developed Java program with synchronization, exception handling, and so on.

Comments excluded on purpose, in the interest of brevity, as the code is simple.

Class Payment

```java
// all classes are probably in a package named
// something like:
package com.foo.nextgen.domain;


public class Payment
{
    private Money amount;

    public Payment( Money cashTendered ){ amount = cashTendered; }
    public Money getAmount() { return amount; }
}
```

Class ProductCatalog

```java
public class ProductCatalog
{
    private Map<ItemID, ProductDescription>
        descriptions = new HashMap()<ItemID, ProductDescription>;

    public ProductCatalog()
    {
        // sample data
        ItemID id1 = new ItemID( 100 );
        ItemID id2 = new ItemID( 200 );
        Money price = new Money( 3 );

        ProductDescription desc;
        desc = new ProductDescription( id1, price, "product 1" );
        descriptions.put( id1, desc );
        desc = new ProductDescription( id2, price, "product 2" );
        descriptions.put( id2, desc );
    }

    public ProductDescription getProductDescription( ItemID id )
    {
```

```
        return descriptions.get( id );
    }
}
```

Class Register

```
public class Register
{
    private ProductCatalog catalog;
    private Sale currentSale;

    public Register( ProductCatalog catalog )
    {
        this.catalog = catalog;
    }

    public void endSale()
    {
        currentSale.becomeComplete();
    }

    public void enterItem( ItemID id, int quantity )
    {
        ProductDescription desc = catalog.getProductDescription( id );

        currentSale.makeLineItem( desc, quantity );
    }

    public void makeNewSale()
    {
        currentSale = new Sale();
    }

    public void makePayment( Money cashTendered )
    {
        currentSale.makePayment( cashTendered );
    }

}
```

Class ProductDescription

```
public class ProductDescription
{
    private ItemID id;
    private Money price;
    private String description;

    public ProductDescription
        ( ItemID id, Money price, String description )
    {
        this.id = id;
        this.price = price;
        this.description = description;
    }

    public ItemID getItemID() { return id;}

    public Money getPrice() { return price; }
```

```java
    public String getDescription() { return description; }
}
```

Class Sale

```java
public class Sale
{
    private List<SalesLineItem> lineItems =
                        new ArrayList()<SalesLineItem>;
    private Date date = new Date();
    private boolean isComplete = false;
    private Payment payment;

    public Money getBalance()
    {
        return payment.getAmount().minus( getTotal() );
    }

    public void becomeComplete() { isComplete = true; }

    public boolean isComplete() { return isComplete; }

    public void makeLineItem
        ( ProductDescription desc, int quantity )
    {
        lineItems.add( new SalesLineItem( desc, quantity ) );
    }

    public Money getTotal()
    {
        Money total = new Money();
        Money subtotal = null;

        for ( SalesLineItem lineItem : lineItems )
        {
            subtotal = lineItem.getSubtotal();
            total.add( subtotal );
        }
    return total;
    }

    public void makePayment( Money cashTendered )
    {
        payment = new Payment( cashTendered );
    }
}
```

Class SalesLineItem

```java
public class SalesLineItem
{
    private int quantity;
    private ProductDescription description;

    public SalesLineItem (ProductDescription desc, int quantity )
    {
        this.description = desc;
        this.quantity = quantity;
    }
```

```
    public Money getSubtotal()
    {
        return description.getPrice().times( quantity );
    }
}
```

Class Store

```
public class Store
{
    private ProductCatalog catalog = new ProductCatalog();
    private Register register = new Register( catalog );

    public Register getRegister() { return register; }
}
```

20.12   Introduction to the Monopoly Program Solution

This section presents a sample domain layer of classes in Java for this iteration.
Iteration-2 will lead to refinements and improvements in this code and design.
Comments excluded on purpose, in the interest of brevity, as the code is simple.

Class Square

```
// all classes are probably in a package named
// something like:
package com.foo.monopoly.domain;

public class Square
{
    private String name;
    private Square nextSquare;
    private int index;

    public Square( String name, int index )
    {
        this.name = name;
        this.index = index;
    }

    public void setNextSquare( Square s )
    {
        nextSquare = s;
    }

    public Square getNextSquare(  )
    {
        return nextSquare;
    }

    public String getName(  )
    {
        return name;
    }

  public int getIndex()
```

```
    {
       return index;
    }
  }
```

Class Piece

```
public class Piece
{

  private Square location;

  public Piece(Square location)
  {
    this.location = location;
  }

  public Square getLocation()
  {
    return location;
  }

  public void setLocation(Square location)
  {
    this.location = location;
  }
}
```

Class Die

```
public class Die
{
    public static final int MAX   = 6;
    private int             faceValue;

    public Die( )
    {
       roll( );
    }

    public void roll( )
    {
       faceValue = (int) ( ( Math.random( ) * MAX ) + 1 );
    }

    public int getFaceValue( )
    {
       return faceValue;
    }
}
```

Class Board

```
public class Board
{

  private static final int SIZE    = 40;
  private List             squares = new ArrayList(SIZE);
```

```
public Board()
{
  buildSquares();
  linkSquares();
}

public Square getSquare(Square start, int distance)
{
  int endIndex = (start.getIndex() + distance) % SIZE;
  return (Square) squares.get(endIndex);
}

public Square getStartSquare()
{
  return (Square) squares.get(0);
}

private void buildSquares()
{
  for (int i = 1; i <= SIZE; i++)
  {
    build(i);
  }
}

private void build(int i)
{
  Square s = new Square("Square " + i, i - 1);
  squares.add(s);
}

private void linkSquares()
{
  for (int i = 0; i < (SIZE - 1); i++)
  {
    link(i);
  }

  Square first = (Square) squares.get(0);
  Square last = (Square) squares.get(SIZE - 1);
  last.setNextSquare(first);
}

private void link(int i)
{
  Square current = (Square) squares.get(i);
  Square next = (Square) squares.get(i + 1);
  current.setNextSquare(next);
}
}
```

Class Player

```
public class Player
{
  private String name;
  private Piece  piece;
  private Board  board;
  private Die[]  dice;

  public Player(String name, Die[] dice, Board board)
```

```java
{
  this.name = name;
  this.dice = dice;
  this.board = board;
  piece = new Piece(board.getStartSquare());
}

public void takeTurn()
{
    // roll dice
  int rollTotal = 0;
  for (int i = 0; i < dice.length; i++)
  {
    dice[i].roll();
    rollTotal += dice[i].getFaceValue();
  }

  Square newLoc = board.getSquare(piece.getLocation(), rollTotal);
  piece.setLocation(newLoc);

}

public Square getLocation()
{
  return piece.getLocation();
}

public String getName()
{
  return name;
}

}
```

Class MonopolyGame

```java
public class MonopolyGame
{
    private static final int ROUNDS_TOTAL  = 20;
    private static final int PLAYERS_TOTAL = 2;
    private List players = new ArrayList( PLAYERS_TOTAL );
    private Board    board = new Board(  );
    private Die[]    dice  = { new Die(), new Die() };

    public MonopolyGame(  )
    {
        Player p;
        p = new Player( "Horse", dice, board );
        players.add( p );
        p = new Player( "Car", dice, board  );
        players.add( p );
    }

    public void playGame(  )
    {
        for ( int i = 0; i < ROUNDS_TOTAL; i++ )
        {
            playRound();
        }
    }

    public List getPlayers(  )
```

```
    {
        return players;
    }

    private void playRound(   )
    {
        for ( Iterator iter = players.iterator(   ); iter.hasNext(   ); )
        {
            Player player = (Player) iter.next();
            player.takeTurn();
        }
    }
}
```

TEST-DRIVEN DEVELOPMENT AND REFACTORING

Logic is the art of going wrong with confidence.

—*Joseph Wood Krutch*

Objectives

- Introduce these two important development practices in the context of the case studies.

Introduction

Extreme Programming (XP) promoted an important testing practice: writing the tests *first*. It also promoted continuously refactoring code to improve its quality—less duplication, increased clarity, and so forth. Modern tools support both practices, and many OO developers swear by their value.

What's Next?

Having explored mapping our design to code, this chapter explores two important development skills in OO programming. The next introduces the use of UML CASE tools—a rapidly moving target!

Designing for Visibility	Mapping Designs to Code	Test-Driven Development & Refactoring	UML Tools & UML as Blueprint	Iteration 2– Requirements

21.1   Test-Driven Development

An excellent practice promoted by the iterative and agile XP method [Beck00], and applicable to the UP (as most XP practices are), is **test-driven development** (TDD) [Beck00]. It is also known as **test-first development**. TDD covers more than just **unit testing** (testing individual components), but this introduction will focus on its application to unit testing individual classes.

In OO unit testing TDD-style, test code is written *before* the class to be tested, and the developer writes unit testing code for nearly *all* production code.

The basic rhythm is to write a little test code, then write a little production code, make it pass the test, then write some more test code, and so forth.

Key Point: The test is written *first*, imagining the code to be tested is written.

Advantages include:

- **The unit tests actually get written**—Human (or at least programmer) nature is such that avoidance of writing unit tests is very common, if left as an afterthought.

- **Programmer satisfaction leading to more consistent test writing**— This is more important than it sounds for sustainable, enjoyable testing work. If, following the traditional style, a developer first writes the production code, informally debugs it, and then as an afterthought is expected to add unit tests, it doesn't feel satisfying. This is *test-last development*, also known as *Just-this-one-time-I'll-skip-writing-the-test* development. It's human psychology. However, if the test is written first, we feel a worthwhile challenge and question in front of us: Can I write code to pass this test? And then, after the code is cut to pass the tests, there is some feeling of accomplishment—meeting a goal. And a very useful goal—an executable, repeatable test. The psychological aspects of development can't be ignored— programming is a human endeavor.

- **Clarification of detailed interface and behavior**—This sounds subtle, but it turns out in practice to be a major value of TDD. Consider your state of mind if you write the test for an object first: As you write the test code, you must *imagine* that the object code exists. For example, if in your test code you write *sale.makeLineItem(description, 3)* to test the *makeLineItem* method (which doesn't exist yet), you must think through the details of the public view of the method—its name, return value, parameters, and behavior. That reflection improves or clarifies the detailed design.

- **Provable, repeatable, automated verification**—Obviously, having hundreds or thousands of unit tests that build up over the weeks provides some meaningful verification of correctness. And because they can be run automatically, it's easy. Over time, as the test base builds from 10 tests to 50 tests to 500 tests, the early, more painful investment in writing tests starts to really feel like it's paying off as the size of the application grows.

■ **The confidence to change things**—In TDD, there will eventually be hundreds or thousands of unit tests, and a unit test class for each production class. When a developer needs to change existing code—written by themselves or others—there is a unit test suite that can be run[1], providing immediate feedback if the change caused an error.

The most popular unit testing framework is the **xUnit** family (for many languages), available at www.junit.org.[2] For Java, the popular version is **JUnit**. There's also an **NUnit** for .NET, and so forth. JUnit is integrated into most of the popular Java IDEs, such as **Eclipse** (www.eclipse.org).

Example

Suppose we are using JUnit and TDD to create the *Sale* class. *Before* programming the *Sale* class, we write a unit testing method in a *SaleTest* class that does the following:

1. Create a *Sale*—the thing to be tested (also known as the **fixture**).

2. Add some line items to it with the *makeLineItem* method (the *makeLineItem* method is the public method we wish to test).

3. Ask for the total, and verify that it is the expected value, using the *assertTrue* method. JUnit will indicate a failure if any *assertTrue* statement does not evaluate to *true*.

Each testing method follows this pattern:

1. Create the fixture.

2. Do something to it (some operation that you want to test).

3. Evaluate that the results are as expected.

A *key point* to note is that we do *not* write all the unit tests for *Sale* first; rather, we write only one test method, implement the solution in class *Sale* to make it pass, and then repeat.

To use JUnit, you must create a test class that extends the JUnit *TestCase* class; your test class inherits various unit testing behaviors.

In JUnit you create a separate testing method for *each* Sale method that you want to test. In general you will write unit testing methods (perhaps several) for each *public* method of the *Sale* class. Exceptions include trivial (and usually auto-generated) *get* and *set* methods.

To test method *doFoo*, it is an idiom to name the testing method *testDoFoo*.

---

1. A popular free open source tool to automatically re-build the application and run all unit tests is **CruiseControl**. Find it on the Web.

2. The xUnit family, and JUnit, was started by Kent Beck (creator of XP) and Eric Gamma (one of the Gang-of-Four design pattern authors, and the chief architect of the popular Eclipse IDE).

For example:

```
public class SaleTest extends TestCase
{
    // …

    // test the Sale.makeLineItem method
  public void testMakeLineItem()
    {
        // STEP 1: CREATE THE FIXTURE

        // -this is the object to test
        // -it is an idiom to name it 'fixture'
        // -it is often defined as an instance field rather than
        // a local variable
      Sale fixture = new Sale();

        // set up supporting objects for the test
      Money total = new Money( 7.5 );
      Money price = new Money( 2.5 );
      ItemID id = new ItemID( 1 );
      ProductDescription desc =
              new ProductDescription( id, price, "product 1" );


        // STEP 2: EXECUTE THE METHOD TO TEST

        // NOTE: We write this code **imagining** there
        // is a makeLineItem method. This act of imagination
        // as we write the test tends to improve or clarify
        // our understanding of the detailed interface to
        // to the object. Thus TDD has the side-benefit of
        // clarifying the detailed object design.

        // test makeLineItem
      sale.makeLineItem( desc, 1 );
      sale.makeLineItem( desc, 2 );


        // STEP 3: EVALUATE THE RESULTS

        // there could be many assertTrue statements
        // for a complex evaluation

        // verify the total is 7.5
      assertTrue( sale.getTotal().equals( total ));
    }
}
```

Only after this *testMakeLineItem* test method is written do we then write the *Sale.makeLineItem* method to pass this test. Hence, the term test-*driven* or test-*first* development.

IDE Support for TDD and xUnit

Most IDEs have built-in support for some xUnit tool. For example, Eclipse supports JUnit. JUnit includes a visual cue—if all the tests pass when executed, it displays a green bar. This gave rise to the TDD mantra: *Keep the bar green to keep the code clean.* Figure 21.1 illustrates.

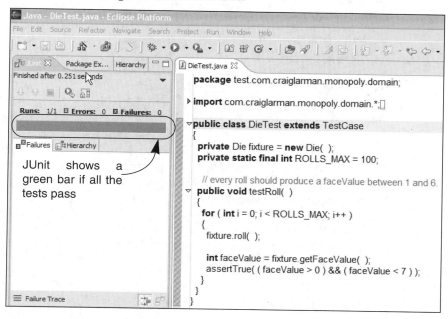

Figure 21.1 Support for TDD and JUnit in a popular IDE, Eclipse.

21.2 Refactoring

Refactoring [Fowler99] is a *structured, disciplined* method to rewrite or restructure existing code without changing its external behavior, applying small transformation steps combined with re-executing tests each step. Continuously refactoring code is another XP practice and applicable to all iterative methods (including the UP).[3]

The essence of refactoring is applying small *behavior preserving transformations* (each called a 'refactoring'), one at a time. After each transformation, the unit tests are re-executed to prove that the refactoring did not cause a regression (failure). Therefore, there's a relationship between refactoring and TDD—all those unit tests support the refactoring process.

Each refactoring is small, but a series of transformations—each followed by executing the unit tests again—can, of course, produce a major restructuring of the code and design (for the better), all the while ensuring the behavior remains the same.

---

3. Ralph Johnson (one of the Gang-of-Four design pattern authors) and Bill Opdyke first discussed refactoring in 1990. Kent Beck (XP creator), along with Martin Fowler, are two other refactoring pioneers.

What are the activities and goals refactoring? They are simply the activities and goals of good programming:

- remove duplicate code
- improve clarity
- make long methods shorter
- remove the use of hard-coded literal constants
- and more…

Code that's been well-refactored is short, tight, clear, and without duplication—it looks like the work of a master programmer. Code that doesn't have these qualities *smells bad* or has *code smells*. In other words, there is a poor design. **Code smells** is a metaphor in refactoring—they are *hints* that something *may* be wrong in the code. The name *code smell* was chosen to suggest that when we look into the smelly code, it might turn out to be alright and not need improvement. That's in contrast to **code stench**—truly putrid code crying out for clean up! Some code smells include:

- duplicated code
- big method
- class with many instance variables
- class with lots of code
- strikingly similar subclasses
- little or no use of interfaces in the design
- high coupling between many objects
- and so many other ways bad code is written…[4]

The remedy to smelly code are the refactorings. Like patterns, refactorings have names, such as *Extract Method*. There are about 100 named refactorings; here's a sample to get a sense of them:

Refactoring	Description
Extract Method	Transform a long method into a shorter one by factoring out a portion into a private helper method.
Extract Constant	Replace a literal constant with a constant variable.

---

4. See the original and major OO, patterns, XP, and refactoring Wiki *c2.com / cgi / wiki* for many Wiki pages on code smells and refactoring. Fascinating site…

Refactoring	Description
Introduce Explaining Variable (specialization of Extract Local Variable)	Put the result of the expression, or parts of the expression, in a temporary variable with a name that explains the purpose.
Replace Constructor Call with Factory Method	In Java, for example, replace using the *new* operator and constructor call with invoking a helper method that creates the object (hiding the details).

Example

This example demonstrates the common Extract Method refactoring. Notice in the Figure 21.2 listing that the *takeTurn* method in the *Player* class has an initial section of code that rolls the dice and calculates the total in a loop. This code is itself a distinct, cohesive unit of behavior; we can make the *takeTurn* method shorter, clearer, and better supporting High Cohesion by extracting that code into a private helper method called *rollDice*. Notice that the *rollTotal* value is required in *takeTurn*, so this helper method must return the *rollTotal*.[5]

```
public class Player
{
    private Piece   piece;
    private Board   board;
    private Die[]   dice;
    // …

public void takeTurn()
{
        // roll dice
    int rollTotal = 0;
    for (int i = 0; i < dice.length; i++)
    {
        dice[i].roll();
        rollTotal += dice[i].getFaceValue();
    }

    Square newLoc = board.getSquare(piece.getLocation(), rollTotal);
    piece.setLocation(newLoc);

}

} // end of class
```

Figure 21.2 The takeTurn method before refactoring.

---

5. That violates the Command-Query Separation Principle (p. 358), but the principle is more easily relaxed for *private* methods. It is a guideline, not a rule.

Now here's the code after applying the Extract Method refactoring:

```
public class Player
{
    private Piece   piece;
    private Board   board;
    private Die[]   dice;
    // …

public void takeTurn()
{
        // the refactored helper method
    int rollTotal = rollDice();

    Square newLoc = board.getSquare(piece.getLocation(), rollTotal);
    piece.setLocation(newLoc);
}

private int rollDice()
{
    int rollTotal = 0;
    for (int i = 0; i < dice.length; i++)
    {
        dice[i].roll();
        rollTotal += dice[i].getFaceValue();
    }
    return rollTotal;
}

} // end of class
```

Figure 21.3 The code after refactoring with Extract Method.

We will see in iteration-2 that this *rollDice* helper method is not a great solution—the Pure Fabrication pattern will suggest an alternative that also preserves the Command-Query Separation Principle—but it suffices to illustrate the refactoring operation.

As a second short example, one of my favorite simple refactorings is *Introduce Explaining Variable* because it clarifies, simplifies, and reduces the need for comments. The listings in Figure 21.4 and Figure 21.5 illustrate.

```
    // good method name, but the logic of the body is not clear
boolean isLeapYear( int year )
{
    return ( ( ( year % 400 ) == 0 ) ||
         ( ( ( year % 4 ) == 0 ) && ( ( year % 100 ) != 0 ) ) );
}
```

Figure 21.4 Before introducing an explaining variable.

```
    // that's better!
boolean isLeapYear( int year )
{
    boolean isFourthYear = ( ( year % 4 ) == 0 );
    boolean isHundrethYear = ( ( year % 100 ) == 0);
    boolean is4HundrethYear = ( ( year % 400 ) == 0);
    return (
        is4HundrethYear
        || ( isFourthYear && ! isHundrethYear ) );
}
```

Figure 21.5 After introducing an explaining variable.

IDE Support for Refactoring

Most of the dominant IDEs include automated refactoring support. See Figure 21.6 and Figure 21.7 for an example in the Eclipse IDE of applying the Extract Method refactoring. The *rollDice* method is automatically generated, as is the call to it from the *takeTurn* method. Notice that the tool is smart enough to see the need to return the *rollTotal* variable. Nice!

1.3   Recommended Resources

For TDD on the Web:

- www.junit.org
- www.testdriven.com

There are several useful texts, including *Test Driven Development: By Example* by Beck, *Test Driven Development* by Astels, and *JUnit Recipes* by Rainsberger.

For refactoring on the Web:

- www.refactoring.com
- c2.com/cgi/wiki?WhatIsRefactoring (a major Wiki on many subjects)

The classic code-level refactoring text is *Refactoring: Improving the Design of Existing Code* by Martin Fowler. Also excellent, at a higher design level, is *Refactoring to Patterns* by Joshua Kerievsky.

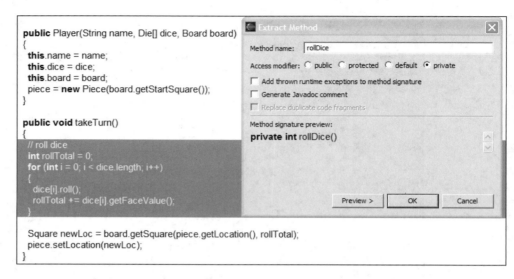

Figure 21.6 IDE before refactoring.

```
public void takeTurn()
{
  int rollTotal = rollDice();

  Square newLoc = board.getSquare(piece.getLocation(), rollTotal);
  piece.setLocation(newLoc);
}

private int rollDice()
{
  // roll dice
  int rollTotal = 0;
  for (int i = 0; i < dice.length; i++)
  {
    dice[i].roll();
    rollTotal += dice[i].getFaceValue();
  }
  return rollTotal;
}
```

Figure 21.7 IDE after refactoring.

UML Tools and UML as Blueprint

*Experience is that marvelous thing that enables you
to recognize a mistake when you make it again.*

—F. P. Jones

Objectives

- Define forward, reverse, and round-trip engineering.
- Suggestions for choosing a UML tool.
- Suggestions on how to integrate UML wall sketching and tools.

Introduction

It isn't useful to discuss specific UML tools in detail because this is a rapidly changing subject—information is quickly stale. However, this chapter points out some common features and the use of such tools for "UML as blueprint."

What's Next? Having introduced TDD and refactoring, this chapter briefly explores UML tools. This ends iteration-1. Next we introduce the new requirements for iteration-2.

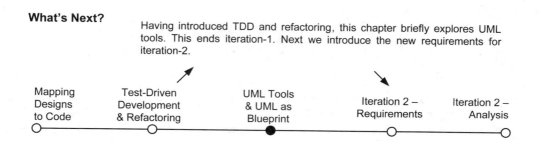

| Mapping Designs to Code | Test-Driven Development & Refactoring | UML Tools & UML as Blueprint | Iteration 2 – Requirements | Iteration 2 – Analysis |

As mentioned, three ways people wish to apply UML include:

- **UML as sketch**.

- **UML as blueprint**—This applies to both code and diagram generation. Relatively detailed diagrams guide some code generation (e.g., Java) with a tool. And diagrams are generated from the code to visualize the code base. After generating code, many fine details are usually filled in by developers while programming.

- **UML as programming language**—Complete executable specification of a software system in UML. Executable code will be automatically generated (or a virtual machine directly interprets UML), but is not normally seen or modified by developers; one works only in the UML "programming language."

The first and second ways are common. Most UML tools support the second approach, UML as blueprint, rather than UML as programming language.

22.1   Forward, Reverse, and Round-Trip Engineering

In the **CASE** (Computer Aided Software Engineering) tool world, **forward engineering** means the generation of code from diagrams; **reverse engineering** means generation of diagrams from code and **round-trip engineering** closes the loop—the tool supports generation in either direction and can synchronize between UML diagrams and code, ideally automatically and immediately as either is changed.

All UML tools claim to support these features, but many are half crippled. Why? Because many of the tools can only do the static models: They can generate class diagrams from code, but can't generate interaction diagrams. Or for forward engineering, they can generate the basic (e.g., Java) class definition from a class diagram, but not the method bodies from interaction diagrams.

Yet, code isn't just declarations of variables, it's dynamic behavior! For example, suppose you want to understand the basic call-flow structure of an existing application or framework. If your tool can generate a sequence diagram from the code, you can then much more easily follow the call-flow logic of the system to learn its basic collaborations.

22.2   What is a Common Report of Valuable Features?

Over the years, I've had the opportunity to visit or consult with many large clients who have tried UML tools. Rather consistently, the developers eventually report, after trying the tool for some time, that it seems to "get in the way" more than help (versus simply a text-powerful IDE). This is not always true—I'm reporting averages. And, the experience of value seems to improve with each new generation of tools. All that said, the most consistent long-term report of UML tool value that I hear clients claim is their value for reverse engineering, as a *visualization learning aid* to understand existing code. Generating UML package, class, and interaction diagrams from code and then viewing the diagrams on a monitor, or printing them on large plotter paper, seems to consistently be useful when developers want to "get their head around" a large code base. And I agree.

With time, as more UML tools become well-integrated with text-strong IDEs (such as Eclipse and Visual Studio), and their usability improves, I predict that there will be more consistent value reported in using the tools for both forward and round-trip engineering.

22.3   What to Look For in a Tool?

Given the above comments, here's a summary of some advice when choosing a UML tool, based on what clients—often in hindsight after spending too much money—have shared with me.

- First, try a free UML tool. There are several options. Only buy a tool after the free options have been exhausted.

- Once you've chosen a tentative tool, especially in the context of a company-standard tool or a large purchasing decision, try it on a real project with as many developers as possible, before making a decision. Decide based on the guidance of your developers who have really used it for a long period, not based on the opinion of architects or others who have only made a cursory investigation.

- Choose a UML tool that integrates into your favorite text-strong IDE.

- Choose a UML tool that supports reverse engineering sequence diagrams from code. Or, if an otherwise satisfactory free tool doesn't support this, use the free tool for most developers, and buy just a few copies of a commercial tool that does, for when you want to understand call-flow patterns.

- Choose a tool that supports printouts to a plotter, on large plotter paper, in large font and diagram sizes, so that large-scale visualization is possible.

22.4   If Sketching UML, How to Update the Diagrams After Coding?

If you are using a UML tool integrated with an IDE, working alone, and not doing wall sketching, then synchronizing the diagrams is a simple reverse-engineering operation in the IDE.

But what if you are working with a small team and want to spend a modeling day each iteration at the whiteboards, applying UML as sketch. Consider this scenario:

1. At the start of a three-week timeboxed iteration, there was a modeling day involving UML wall sketches.

2. This is followed by about three weeks of code and test.

3. Finally, it's time to start the next iteration's modeling day.

At this point, if you wanted to do some wall sketching again, based on the existing state of the code base, how to proceed? Here's a suggestion: Just before the modeling day, use a UML tool to reverse engineer the code into UML diagrams—package, class, and interaction diagrams. Then, for the most interesting ones, print them large on long plotter paper, on a plotter. Hang them relatively high in the modeling room on the walls, so that during the modeling day developers can refer to them, sketch on top of them, and sketch below them on whiteboards or static cling sheets.

22.5   Recommended Resources

Software tools are naturally a fast-changing subject. A relatively complete list of UML tools is maintained at:

www.objectsbydesign.com/tools/umltools_byCompany.html

PART 4 ELABORATION ITERATION 2 — MORE PATTERNS

ITERATION 2—MORE PATTERNS

Objectives

- Define the requirements for iteration-2.

Introduction

The inception phase chapters and those for iteration-1 in the elaboration phase emphasized a wide range of fundamental analysis and object design skills, in order to share information on a breadth of common steps in building object systems.

In this iteration, the case study just emphasizes:

- essential object design

- the use of patterns to create a solid design

- applying the UML to visualize the models

These are primary objectives of the book, and critical skills.

What's Next?   Having completed iteration-1, this chapter introduces the new requirements for iteration-2. The next very briefly examines some analysis changes, bearing in mind that this iteration focuses on OO design.

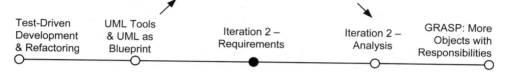

There is minimal discussion of requirements analysis or domain modeling, and the explanation of the design is more succinct, now that (in iteration-1) a detailed explanation of the basics of how to think in objects has been presented. Many other analysis, design, and implementation activities would of course occur in this iteration, but these are de-emphasized in favor of sharing information about how to do object design.

23.1 From Iteration 1 to 2

When iteration-1 ends, the following should be accomplished:

- All the software has been vigorously tested: unit, acceptance, load, usability, and so on. The idea in the UP is to do early, realistic, and continuous verification of quality and correctness, so that early feedback guides the developers to adapt and improve the system, finding its "true path."

- Customers have been regularly engaged in evaluating the partial system, to obtain feedback for adaptation and clarification of requirements. And the customers get to see early visible progress with the system.

- The system, across all subsystems, has been completely integrated and stabilized as a baselined internal release.

In the interest of brevity, many activities concluding iteration-1 and initiating iteration-2 are skipped, since the emphasis of this presentation is an introduction to OOA/D. Comments on a few of the myriad activities that are skipped include:

- An iteration planning meeting to decide what to work on in the next iteration, resolve questions, and identify major tasks.

- At the start of the new iteration, use a UML tool to reverse engineer diagrams from the source code of the last iteration (the results are part of the UP Design Model). These can be printed in large size on a plotter and posted on the walls of the project room, as a communication aid to illustrate the starting point of the logical design for the next iteration.

- Usability analysis and engineering for the UI is underway. This is an extraordinarily important skill and activity for the success of many systems. However, the subject is detailed and non-trivial, and outside the scope of this book.

- Database modeling and implementation is underway.

- Another two-day (for example) requirements workshop occurs, in which more use cases are written in their fully dressed format. During elaboration, while perhaps 10% of the most risky requirements are being designed and implemented, there is a *parallel* activity to deeply explore and define perhaps 80% of the use cases for the system, even though most of these requirements won't be implemented until later iterations.

  ○ Participants will include a few developers (including the software architect) from the first iteration, so that the investigation and questioning during this workshop is informed from the insights (and confusions) gained from actually quickly building some software. There's nothing like building software to discover what we really don't know about the requirements—this is a key idea in the UP and iterative, evolutionary methods.

Simplifications in the Case Study

In a skillful UP project, the requirements chosen for the early iterations are organized by risk and high business value, so that the high-risk issues are identified and resolved early. However, if this case study exactly followed that strategy, it would not be possible to help explain fundamental ideas and principles of OOA/D in the early iterations. Therefore, some license is taken with the prioritization of requirements, preferring those that support the educational goals, rather than project risk goals.

23.2 Iteration-2 Requirements and Emphasis: Object Design and Patterns

As mentioned, for these case studies iteration-2 largely ignores requirements analysis and domain analysis, and focuses on object design with responsibilities and GRASP, and applying some GoF design patterns.

NextGen POS

iteration-1 requirements p. 124

Iteration-2 of the NextGen POS application handles several interesting requirements:

1. Support for variations in third-party external services. For example, different tax calculators must be connectable to the system, and each has a unique interface. Likewise with different accounting systems and so forth. Each will offer a different API and protocol for a core of common functions.

2. Complex pricing rules.

3. A design to refresh a GUI window when the sale total changes.

These requirements will only be considered (for this iteration) in the context of scenarios of the *Process Sale* use case.

Please note that these are not newly discovered requirements; they were identified during inception. For example, the original *Process Sale* use case indicates the pricing problem:

Main Success Scenario:
1. Customer arrives at a POS checkout with goods and/or services to purchase.
2. Cashier tells System to create a new sale.
3. Cashier enters item identifier.

> 4. System records sale line item and presents item description, price, and running total.
> ***Price calculated from a set of price rules.***
>
> ...

Furthermore, sections in the Supplementary Specification record details of the domain rules for pricing, and indicate the need to support varying external systems:

Supplementary Specification

...

Interfaces

Software Interfaces

For most external collaborating systems (tax calculator, accounting, inventory, ...) we need to be able to plug in varying systems and thus varying interfaces.

...

Domain (Business) Rules

ID	Rule	Changeability	Source
RULE4	Purchaser discount rules. Examples: Employee—20% off. Preferred Customer—10% off. Senior—15% off.	High. Each retailer uses different rules.	Retailer policy.
...	...	...	...

Information in Domains of Interest

Pricing

In addition to the pricing rules described in the domain rules section, note that products have an *original price*, and optionally a *permanent markdown price*. A product's price (before further discounts) is the permanent markdown price, if present. Organizations maintain the original price even if there is a permanent markdown price, for accounting and tax reasons.

...

Incremental Development for a Use Case Across Iterations

Because of these requirements, we are revisiting the *Process Sale* use case in iteration-2, but implementing more *scenarios*, so that the system incrementally grows. It is common to work on varying scenarios or features of the same use case over several iterations and gradually extend the system to ultimately handle all the functionality required. On the other hand, short, simple use cases may be completely implemented within one iteration.

However, one scenario should not be split across iterations; an iteration should complete one or more end-to-end scenarios.

Iteration-1 made simplifications so that the problem and solution were not overly complex to explore. Once again—for the same reason—a relatively small amount of additional functionality is considered.

Monopoly

*iteration-1 require-
ments p. 405*

The additional requirements for the second iteration of the Monopoly application include:

- Again, implement a basic, key scenario of the *Play Monopoly Game* use case: players moving around the squares of the board. And as before, run the game as a simulation requiring no user input, other than the number of players. However, in iteration-2 some of the special square rules apply. These are described in the following points…

- Each player receives $1500 at the beginning of the game. Consider the game to have an unlimited amount of money.

- When a player lands on the Go square, the player receives $200.

- When a player lands on the Go-To-Jail square, they move to the Jail square.

   ○ However, unlike the complete rules, they get out easily. On their next turn, they simply roll and move as indicated by the roll total.

- When a player lands on the Income-Tax square, the player pays the minimum of $200 or 10% of their worth.

QUICK ANALYSIS UPDATE

Any sufficiently advanced bug is indistinguishable from a feature.

—*Rich Kulawiec*

Objectives

- Quickly highlight some analysis artifact changes, especially in the Monopoly domain model.

Introduction

This chapter briefly points out some changes in the requirements and domain analysis. The noteworthy modeling and UML tips of interest are related to the NextGen SSDs and the Monopoly domain model.

What's Next?   Having introduced the requirements, this chapter summarizes a few key analysis changes. The next explores the remaining GRASP principles and shows more examples of object design with responsibilities for the case studies.

UML Tools & UML as Blueprint	Iteration 2 – Requirements	Iteration 2 – Analysis	GRASP: More Objects with Responsibilities	Applying GoF Design Patterns

24.1   Case Study: NextGen POS

Use Cases

No refinement is needed for the use cases this iteration.

However, at a process level I recommend (as does the UP) a second short one- or two-day requirements workshop this iteration (near the end of iteration-1 and again near the end of iteration-2), within which more requirements will be investigated and written in detail. The previously fully analyzed use cases (for example, *Process Sale*) will be revisited and probably refined based on insights gained from iteration-1 programming and tests. In iterative methods, note the interplay of early programming and testing with parallel requirements analysis that is improved by feedback from early development.

SSDs

This iteration includes adding support for third-party external systems with varying interfaces, such as a tax calculator. The NextGen POS system will be remotely communicating with external systems. Consequently, the SSDs should be updated to reflect at least some of the inter-system collaborations, in order to clarify what the new system-level events are.

Figure 24.1 illustrates an SSD for one scenario of paying by credit, which requires collaboration with several external systems. Even though the design of paying by credit is not handled in this iteration, the modeler (me) has drawn an SSD based on it (and probably several others as well), to better understand the inter-system collaboration, and thus the required support for varying interfaces in the external systems.

Domain Model

After a little experience in domain modeling, a modeler can estimate if a set of new requirements will have a minor or major impact on the Domain Model in terms of many new concepts, associations, and attributes. In contrast to the prior iteration, the requirements being tackled this time do not involve many new domain concepts. A brief survey of the new requirements suggests something like *PriceRule* as a domain concept, but there are probably not dozens of new things.

In this situation, it is quite reasonable to skip refining the Domain Model, move quickly on to design work, and let the discovery of new domain concepts occur during object design in the Design Model, when the developers are thinking through a solution, or indeed even while coding.

A sign of process maturity with the UP is understanding when creating an artifact will add significant value, or is a kind of mechanical "make work" step and better skipped.

On the other hand, there can be not only too much modeling, but too little. Developers often avoid any analysis or modeling because it seems like a low-value and time-consuming affair. Yet, modeling can add value if one masters the basic guidelines of analysis and design, becomes comfortable with the "languages"—be they use cases or UML or UI prototypes on a wall—and applies these in the spirit of agile modeling.

System Operation Contracts

No new system operations are being considered in this iteration, and thus contracts are not required. In any event, contracts are only an option to consider when the detailed precision they offer is an improvement over the descriptions in the use cases.

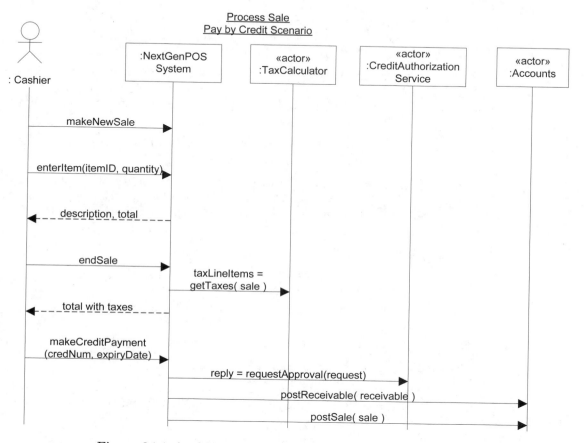

Figure 24.1 An SSD scenario that illustrates some external systems.

24.2   Case Study: Monopoly

Use Cases, etc.

Uses case were skipped, as most know the rules of the game. No update to the SSD is required, and no operations contracts were written.

Domain Model

The concepts *Square, GoSquare, IncomeTaxSquare,* and *GoToJailSquare* are all similar—they are variations on a square. In this situation, it is possible (and often useful) to organize them into a **generalization-specialization class hierarchy** (or simply **class hierarchy**) in which the **superclass** *Square* represents a more general concept and the **subclasses** more specialized ones.

In the UML, generalization-specialization relationships are shown with a large triangular arrow pointing from the specialization class to the more general class, as shown in Figure 24.2.

Generalization is the activity of identifying commonality among concepts and defining superclass (general concept) and subclass (specialized concept) relationships. It is a way to construct taxonomic classifications among concepts that are then illustrated in class hierarchies.

The subject of generalization and specialization is covered more thoroughly in a later chapter. See "Generalization" on page 503.

Identifying a superclass and subclasses is of value in a domain model because their presence allows us to understand concepts in more general, refined and abstract terms. It leads to economy of expression, improved comprehension and a reduction in repeated information.

When to show subclasses? The following are common motivations:

Guideline

Create a conceptual subclass of a superclass when:

1. The subclass has additional attributes of interest.

2. The subclass has additional associations of interest.

3. The subclass concept is operated on, handled, reacted to, or manipulated differently than the superclass or other subclasses, in noteworthy ways.

Criteria #3 applies to the case of the different kinds of squares. The *GoSquare* is treated differently than other kinds of squares according to the domain rules. It is a *noteworthy* distinct concept—and the domain model is especially useful as a place to identify noteworthy concepts.

Therefore, an updated domain model is shown in Figure 24.2. Note that each distinct square that is treated differently by the domain rules is shown as a separate class.

Guidelines: A few more domain modeling guidelines and points are illustrated in this model:

- The class *Square* is defined *{abstract}*.

  - ○ ***Guideline***: Declare superclasses abstract. Although this is a conceptual perspective unrelated to software, it is also a common OO guideline that all *software* superclasses be abstract.

- Each subclass name appends the superclass name—*IncomeTaxSquare* rather than *IncomeTax*. That's a good idiom, and also more accurate, as, for example, we really aren't modeling the concept of income tax, but modeling the concept of an income tax square in a monopoly game.

  - ○ ***Guideline***: Append the superclass name to the subclass.

- A *RegularSquare* that does nothing special is also a distinct concept.

- Now that money is involved, the Player has a *cash* attribute.

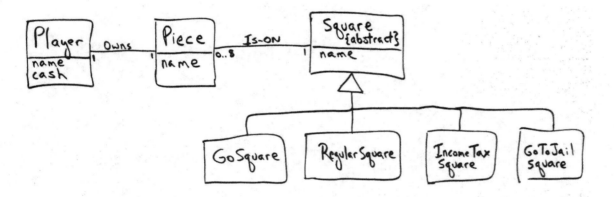

Figure 24.2 Monopoly domain model changes for iteration-2.

GRASP: More Objects with Responsibilities

Luck is the residue of design.

—*Branch Rickey*

Objectives

- Learn to apply the remaining GRASP patterns.

Introduction

Previously, we applied five GRASP patterns:

- Information Expert, Creator, High Cohesion, Low Coupling, and Controller

The final four GRASP patterns are covered in this chapter. They are:

- Polymorphism
- Indirection
- Pure Fabrication
- Protected Variations

What's Next?   Having highlighted some analysis changes, this chapter explores the remaining GRASP principles and applies them to the case studies. The next introduces the important subject of GoF design patterns, also applied to the case studies.

Iteration 2 – Requirements	Iteration 2 – Analysis	GRASP: More Objects with Responsibilities	Applying GoF Design Patterns	Iteration-3 Requirements

Once these have been explained, we will have a rich and shared vocabulary with which to discuss designs. And as some of the "Gang-of-Four" (GoF) design patterns (such as Strategy and Abstract Factory) are also introduced in subsequent chapters, that vocabulary will grow. A short sentence, such as "I suggest a Strategy generated from a Abstract Factory to support Protected Variations and low coupling with respect to <X>" communicates lots of information about the design, since pattern names tersely convey a complex design concept.

Subsequent chapters introduce other useful patterns and apply them to the development of the second iteration of the case studies.

25.1   Polymorphism

Problem   How handle alternatives based on type? How to create pluggable software components?

Alternatives based on type—Conditional variation is a fundamental theme in programs. If a program is designed using if-then-else or case statement conditional logic, then if a new variation arises, it requires modification of the case logic—often in many places. This approach makes it difficult to easily extend a program with new variations because changes tend to be required in several places—wherever the conditional logic exists.

Pluggable software components—Viewing components in client-server relationships, how can you replace one server component with another, without affecting the client?

Solution   When related alternatives or behaviors vary by type (class), assign responsibility for the behavior—using polymorphic operations—to the types for which the behavior varies.[1]

Corollary: Do not test for the type of an object and use conditional logic to perform varying alternatives based on type.

Examples   **NextGen Problem: How Support Third-Party Tax Calculators?**

In the NextGen POS application, there are multiple external third-party tax calculators that must be supported (such as Tax-Master and Good-As-Gold Tax-Pro); the system needs to be able to integrate with different ones. Each tax calculator has a different interface, so there is similar but varying behavior to adapt to each of these external fixed interfaces or APIs. One product may sup-

---

1. **Polymorphism** has several related meanings. In this context, it means "giving the same name to services in different objects" [Coad95] when the services are similar or related. The different object types usually implement a common interface or are related in an implementation hierarchy with a common superclass, but this is language-dependent; for example, dynamic binding languages such as Smalltalk do not require this.

port a raw TCP socket protocol, another may offer a SOAP interface, and a third may offer a Java RMI interface.

What objects should be responsible for handling these varying external tax calculator interfaces?

Since the behavior of calculator adaptation varies by the type of calculator, by Polymorphism we should assign the responsibility for adaptation to different calculator (or calculator adapter) objects themselves, implemented with a polymorphic *getTaxes* operation (see Figure 25.1).

These calculator adapter objects are not the external calculators, but rather, local software objects that represent the external calculators, or the adapter for the calculator. By sending a message to the local object, a call will ultimately be made on the external calculator in its native API.

Each *getTaxes* method takes the *Sale* object as a parameter, so that the calculator can analyze the sale. The implementation of each *getTaxes* method will be different: *TaxMasterAdapter* will adapt the request to the API of Tax-Master, and so on.

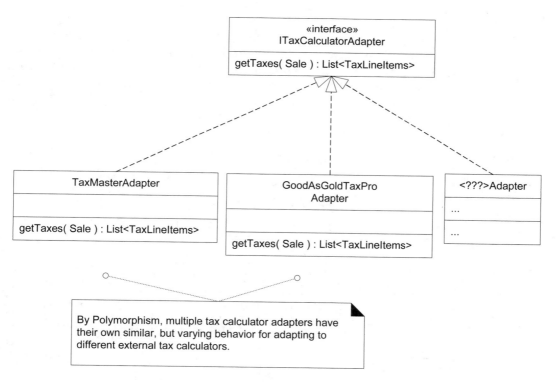

Figure 25.1 Polymorphism in adapting to different external tax calculators.

UML—Notice the interface and interface realization notation in Figure 25.1.

Monopoly Problem: How to Design for Different Square Actions?

To review, when a player lands on the Go square, they receive $200. There's a different action for landing on the Income Tax square, and so forth. Notice that there is a different rule for different types of squares. Let's review the Polymorphism design principle:

> When related alternatives or behaviors vary by type (class), assign responsibility for the behavior—using polymorphic operations—to the types for which the behavior varies. *Corollary*: Do not test for the type of an object and use conditional logic to perform varying alternatives based on type.

From the corollary, we know we should *not* design with case logic (a *switch* statement in Java or C#) as in the following pseudocode:

```
    // bad design
SWITCH ON square.type

CASE GoSquare: player receives $200
CASE IncomeTaxSquare: player pays tax
...
```

Rather, the principle advises us to create a polymorphic operation for each type for which the behavior varies. It varies for the types (classes) *RegularSquare*, *GoSquare*, and so on. What is the operation that varies? It's what happens when a player lands on a square. Thus, a good name for the polymorphic operation is *landedOn* or some variation. Therefore, by Polymorphism, we'll create a separate class for each kind of square that has a different *landedOn* responsibility, and implement a *landedOn* method in each. Figure 25.2 illustrates the static-view class design.

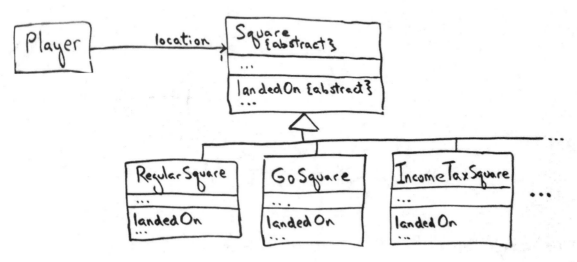

Figure 25.2 Applying Polymorphism to the Monopoly problem.

Applying UML: Notice in Figure 25.2 the use of the *{abstract}* keyword for the *landedOn* operation.

Guideline: Unless there is a default behavior in the superclass, declare a polymorphic operation in the superclass to be *{abstract}*.

The remaining interesting problem is the dynamic design: How should the interaction diagrams evolve? What object should send the *landedOn* message to the square that a player lands on? Since a *Player* software object already knows its location square (the one it landed on), then by the principles of Low Coupling and by Expert, class *Player* is a good choice to send the message, as a *Player* already has visibility to the correct square.

Naturally, this message should be sent at the end of the *takeTurn* method. Please review the iteration-1 *takeTurn* design on p. 355 to see our starting point. Figure 25.3 and Figure 25.4 illustrate the evolving dynamic design.

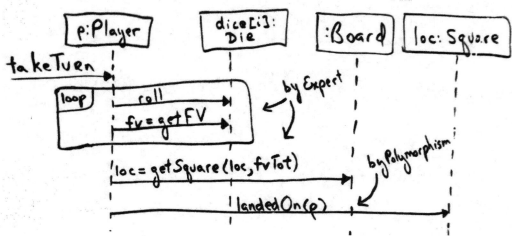

Figure 25.3 Applying Polymorphism.

Applying UML:

- Notice in Figure 25.3 and Figure 25.4 the informal approach to showing the
  UML frames p. 235
  polymorphic cases in separate diagrams when sketching UML. An alternative—especially when using a UML tool—is to use *sd* and *ref* frames.

- Notice in Figure 25.3 that the *Player* object is labeled 'p' so that in the *landedOn* message we can refer to that object in the parameter list. (You will see in Figure 25.4 that it is useful for the *Square* to have parameter visibility to the *Player*.)

- Notice in Figure 25.3 that the *Square* object is labeled *loc* (short for 'location') and this is the same label as the return value variable in the *getSquare* message. This implies they are the same object.

Let's consider each of the polymorphic cases in terms of GRASP and the design issues:

- *GoSquare*—See Figure 25.4. By low representational gap, the *Player* should know its cash. Therefore, by Expert, it should be sent an *addCash* message. Thus the square needs visibility to the *Player* so it can send the message; consequently, the *Player* is passed as a parameter 'p' in the *landedOn* message to achieve parameter visibility.

- *RegularSquare*—See Figure 25.5. In this case, *nothing* happens. I've informally labeled the diagram to indicate this, though a UML note box could be used as well. In code, the body of this method will be empty—sometimes called a **NO-OP** (no operation) method. Note that to make the magic of polymorphism work, we need to use this approach to avoid special case logic.

- *IncomeTaxSquare*—See Figure 25.6. We need to calculate 10% of the player's net worth. By low representational gap and by Expert, who should know this? The *Player*. Thus the square asks for the player's worth, and then deducts the appropriate amount.

- *GoToJailSquare*—See Figure 25.7. Simply, the Player's location must be changed. By Expert, it should receive a *setLocation* message. Probably, the *GoToJailSquare* will be initialized with an attribute referencing the *JailSquare*, so that it can pass this square as a parameter to the *Player*.

UML as Sketch: Notice in Figure 25.4 that the vertical lifeline is drawn as a solid line, rather than the traditional dashed line. This is more convenient when hand sketching. Furthermore, UML 2 allows either format—although in any event conformance to correct UML is not so important when sketching, only that the participants understand each other.

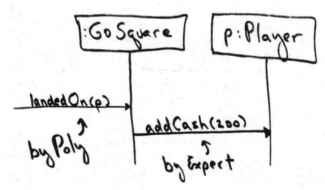

Figure 25.4 The *GoSquare* case.

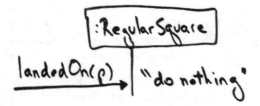

Figure 25.5 The *RegularSquare* case.

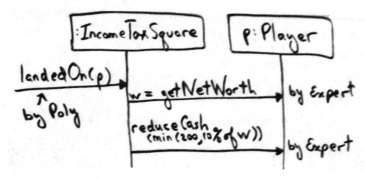

Figure 25.6 The *IncomeTaxSquare* case.

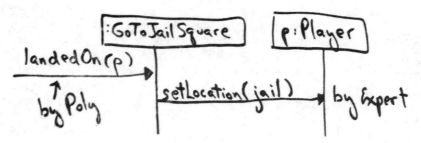

Figure 25.7 The *GoToJailSquare* case.

Improving the Coupling

As a small OO design refinement, notice in Figure 18.25 on p. 357 for iteration-1 that the *Piece* remembers the square location but the *Player* does not, and thus the *Player* must extract the location from the *Piece* (to send the *getSquare* message to the *Board*), and then re-assign the new location to the *Piece*. That's a weak design point, and in this iteration, when the *Player* must also send the *landedOn* message to its *Square*, it becomes even weaker. Why? What's wrong with it? Answer: Problems in *coupling*.

Clearly the *Player* needs to permanently know its own *Square* location object rather than the *Piece*, since the *Player* keeps collaborating with its *Square*. You should see this as a refactoring opportunity to improve coupling—when object A keeps needing the data in object B it implies either 1) object A should hold that data, or 2) object B should have the responsibility (by Expert) rather than object A.

Therefore, in iteration-2 I've refined the design so that the *Player* rather than the *Piece* knows its square; this is reflected in both the DCD of Figure 25.2 and the interaction diagram of Figure 25.3.

In fact, one can even question if the *Piece* is a useful object in the Design Model. In the real world, a little plastic piece sitting on the board is a useful proxy for a human, because we're big and go to the kitchen for cold beer! But in software, the *Player* object (being a tiny software blob) can fulfill the role of the *Piece*.

Discussion Polymorphism is a fundamental principle in designing how a system is organized to handle similar variations. A design based on assigning responsibilities by Polymorphism can be easily extended to handle new variations. For example, adding a new calculator adapter class with its own polymorphic *getTaxes* method will have minor impact on the existing design.

Guideline: When to Design with Interfaces?

Polymorphism implies the presence of abstract superclasses or interfaces in most OO languages. When should you consider using an interface? The general answer is to introduce one when you want to support polymorphism without being committed to a particular class hierarchy. If an abstract superclass AC is used without an interface, any new polymorphic solution must be a subclass of AC, which is very limiting in single-inheritance languages such as Java and C#. As a rule-of-thumb, if there is a class hierarchy with an abstract superclass C1, consider making an interface I1 that corresponds to the public method signatures of C1, and then declare C1 to implement the I1 interface. Then, even if there is no immediate motivation to *avoid* subclassing under C1 for a new polymorphic solution, there is a flexible evolution point for unknown future cases.

Contraindications Sometimes, developers design systems with interfaces and polymorphism for speculative "future-proofing" against an unknown possible variation. If the variation point is definitely motivated by an immediate or very probable variability, then the effort of adding the flexibility through polymorphism is of course rational. But critical evaluation is required, because it is not uncommon to see unnecessary effort being applied to future-proofing a design with polymorphism at variation points that in fact are improbable and will never actually arise. Be realistic about the true likelihood of variability before investing in increased flexibility.

Benefits
- Extensions required for new variations are easy to add.

- New implementations can be introduced without affecting clients.

Related Patterns
- Protected Variations

- A number of popular GoF design patterns [GHJV95], which will be discussed in this book, rely on polymorphism, including Adapter, Command, Composite, Proxy, State, and Strategy.

Also Known As; Similar To   Choosing Message, Don't Ask "What Kind?"

5.2   Pure Fabrication

Problem   What object should have the responsibility, when you do not want to violate High Cohesion and Low Coupling, or other goals, but solutions offered by Expert (for example) are not appropriate?

Object-oriented designs are sometimes characterized by implementing as software classes representations of concepts in the real-world problem domain to lower the representational gap; for example a *Sale* and *Customer* class. However, there are many situations in which assigning responsibilities only to domain layer software classes leads to problems in terms of poor cohesion or coupling, or low reuse potential.

Solution   Assign a highly cohesive set of responsibilities to an artificial or convenience class that does not represent a problem domain concept—something made up, to support high cohesion, low coupling, and reuse.

Such a class is a *fabrication* of the imagination. Ideally, the responsibilities assigned to this fabrication support high cohesion and low coupling, so that the design of the fabrication is very clean, or *pure*—hence a pure fabrication.

Finally, in English *pure fabrication* is an idiom that implies making something up, which we do when we're desperate!

Examples   **NextGen Problem: Saving a Sale Object in a Database**

For example, suppose that support is needed to save *Sale* instances in a relational database. By Information Expert, there is some justification to assign this responsibility to the *Sale* class itself, because the sale has the data that needs to be saved. But consider the following implications:

- The task requires a relatively large number of supporting database-oriented operations, none related to the concept of sale-ness, so the *Sale* class becomes incohesive.

- The *Sale* class has to be coupled to the relational database interface (such as JDBC in Java technologies), so its coupling goes up. And the coupling is not even to another domain object, but to a particular kind of database interface.

- Saving objects in a relational database is a very general task for which many classes need support. Placing these responsibilities in the *Sale* class suggests there is going to be poor reuse or lots of duplication in other classes that do the same thing.

Thus, even though *Sale* is a logical candidate by virtue of Information Expert to save itself in a database, it leads to a design with low cohesion, high coupling, and low reuse potential—exactly the kind of desperate situation that calls for making something up.

A reasonable solution is to create a new class that is solely responsible for saving objects in some kind of persistent storage medium, such as a relational database; call it the *PersistentStorage*.[2] This class is a Pure Fabrication—a figment of the imagination.

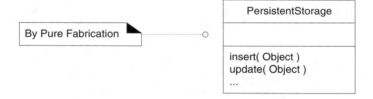

Notice the name: *PersistentStorage*. This is an understandable concept, yet the name or concept "persistent storage" is not something one would find in the Domain Model. And if a designer asked a business-person in a store, "Do you work with persistent storage objects?" they would not understand. They understand concepts such as "sale" and "payment." *PersistentStorage* is not a domain concept, but something made up or fabricated for the convenience of the software developer.

---

2. In a real persistence framework, more than a single pure fabrication class is ultimately necessary to create a reasonable design. This object will be a front-end facade on to a large number of back-end helper objects.

This Pure Fabrication solves the following design problems:

- The *Sale* remains well-designed, with high cohesion and low coupling.

- The *PersistentStorage* class is itself relatively cohesive, having the sole purpose of storing or inserting objects in a persistent storage medium.

- The *PersistentStorage* class is a very generic and reusable object.

Creating a pure fabrication in this example is exactly the situation in which their use is called for—eliminating a bad design based on Expert, with poor cohesion and coupling, with a good design in which there is greater potential for reuse.

Note that, as with all the GRASP patterns, the emphasis is on where responsibilities should be placed. In this example the responsibilities are shifted from the *Sale* class (motivated by Expert) to a Pure Fabrication.

Monopoly Problem: Handling the Dice

In the refactoring chapter, I used the example of dice rolling behavior (rolling and summing the dice totals) to apply Extract Method (p. 391) in the *Player.takeTurn* method. At the end of the example I also mentioned that the refactored solution itself was not ideal, and a better solution would be presented later.

In the current design, the *Player* rolls all the dice and sums the total. Dice are very general objects, usable in many games. By putting this rolling and summing responsibility in a Monopoly game *Player*, the summing service is not generalized for use in other games. Another weakness: It is not possible to simply ask for the current dice total without rolling the dice again.

But, choosing any other object inspired from the Monopoly game domain model leads to the same problems. And that leads us to Pure Fabrication—make something up to conveniently provide related services.

Although there is no cup for the dice in Monopoly, many games do use a dice cup in which one shakes all the dice and rolls them onto a table. Therefore, I propose a Pure Fabrication called *Cup* (notice that I'm still trying to use similar domain-relevant vocabulary) to hold all the dice, roll them, and know their total. The new design is shown in Figure 25.8 and Figure 25.9. The *Cup* holds a collection of many *Die* objects. When one sends a *roll* message to a *Cup*, it sends a *roll* message to all its dice.

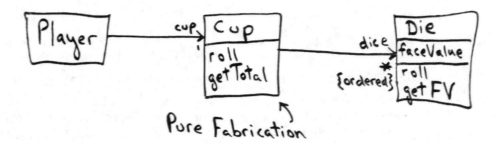

Figure 25.8 DCD for a *Cup*.

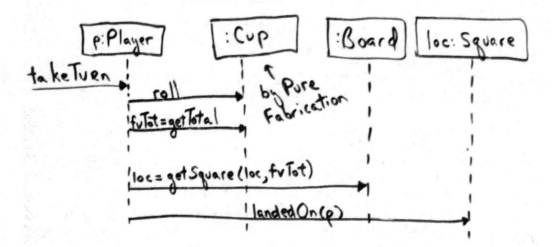

Figure 25.9 Using the *Cup* in the Monopoly game.

Discussion The design of objects can be broadly divided into two groups:

1. Those chosen by **representational decomposition**.

2. Those chosen by **behavioral decomposition**.

For example, the creation of a software class such as *Sale* is by representational decomposition; the software class is related to or represents a thing in a domain. Representational decomposition is a common strategy in object design and supports the goal of low representational gap. But sometimes, we desire to assign responsibilities by grouping behaviors or by algorithm, without any concern for creating a class with a name or purpose that is related to a real-world domain concept.

A good example is an "algorithm" object such as a *TableOfContentsGenerator,* whose purpose is (surprise!) to generate a table of contents and was created as a helper or convenience class by a developer, without any concern for choosing a name from the domain vocabulary of books and documents. It exists as a convenience class conceived by the developer to group together some related behavior or methods, and is thus motivated by *behavioral decomposition*.

To contrast, a software class named *TableOfContents* is inspired by *representational decomposition*, and should contain information consistent with our concept of the real domain (such as chapter names).

Identifying a class as a Pure Fabrication is not critical. It's an educational concept to communicate the general idea that some software classes are inspired by representations of the domain, and some are simply "made up" as a convenience for the object designer. These convenience classes are usually designed to group together some common behavior, and are thus inspired by behavioral rather than representational decomposition.

Said another way, a Pure Fabrication is usually partitioned based on related functionality, so it is a kind of function-centric or behavioral object.

Many existing object-oriented design patterns are examples of Pure Fabrications: Adapter, Strategy, Command, and so on [GHJV95].

As a final comment worth reiterating: Sometimes a solution offered by Information Expert is not desirable. Even though the object is a candidate for the responsibility by virtue of having much of the information related to the responsibility, in other ways, its choice leads to a poor design, usually due to problems in cohesion or coupling.

Benefits
- High Cohesion is supported because responsibilities are factored into a fine-grained class that only focuses on a very specific set of related tasks.

- Reuse potential may increase because of the presence of fine-grained Pure Fabrication classes whose responsibilities have applicability in other applications.

Contraindications
Behavioral decomposition into Pure Fabrication objects is sometimes overused by those new to object design and more familiar with decomposing or organizing software in terms of functions. To exaggerate, functions just become objects. There is nothing inherently wrong with creating "function" or "algorithm" objects, but it needs to be balanced with the ability to design with representational decomposition, such as the ability to apply Information Expert so that a representational class such as *Sale* also has responsibilities. Information Expert supports the goal of co-locating responsibilities with the objects that know the information needed for those responsibilities, which tends to support lower coupling. If overused, Pure Fabrication could lead to too many behavior objects that have responsibilities *not* co-located with the information required for their fulfillment, which can adversely affect coupling. The usual symptom is that most of the data inside the objects is being passed to other objects to reason with it.

Related Patterns and Principles

- Low Coupling.
- High Cohesion.
- A Pure Fabrication usually takes on responsibilities from the domain class that would be assigned those responsibilities based on the Expert pattern.
- All GoF design patterns [GHJV95], such as Adapter, Command, Strategy, and so on, are Pure Fabrications.
- Virtually all other design patterns are Pure Fabrications.

25.3 Indirection

Problem   Where to assign a responsibility, to avoid direct coupling between two (or more) things? How to de-couple objects so that low coupling is supported and reuse potential remains higher?

Solution   Assign the responsibility to an intermediate object to mediate between other components or services so that they are not directly coupled.

The intermediary creates an *indirection* between the other components.

Examples   **TaxCalculatorAdapter**

These objects act as intermediaries to the external tax calculators. Via polymorphism, they provide a consistent interface to the inner objects and hide the variations in the external APIs. By adding a level of indirection and adding polymorphism, the adapter objects protect the inner design against variations in the external interfaces (see Figure 25.10).

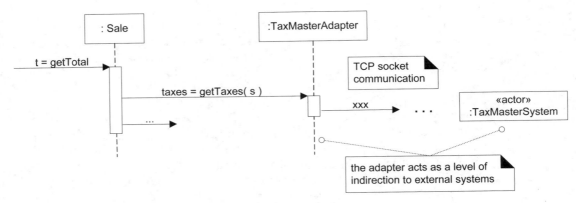

Figure 25.10 Indirection via the adapter.

Applying UML: Notice how the external TaxMaster remote service application is modeled in Figure 25.10: It's labeled with the «actor» keyword to indicate it's an external software component to our NextGen system.

PersistentStorage

The Pure Fabrication example of decoupling the *Sale* from the relational database services through the introduction of a *PersistentStorage* class is also an example of assigning responsibilities to support Indirection. The *PersistentStorage* acts as a intermediary between the *Sale* and the database.

Discussion "Most problems in computer science can be solved by another level of indirection" is an old adage with particular relevance to object-oriented designs. [3]

Just as many existing design patterns are specializations of Pure Fabrication, many are also specializations of Indirection. Adapter, Facade, and Observer are examples [GHJV95]. In addition, many Pure Fabrications are generated because of Indirection. The motivation for Indirection is usually Low Coupling; an intermediary is added to decouple other components or services.

Benefits ■ Lower coupling between components.

Related Patterns and Principles
■ Protected Variations

■ Low Coupling

■ Many GoF patterns, such as Adapter, Bridge, Facade, Observer, and Mediator [GHJV95].

■ Many Indirection intermediaries are Pure Fabrications.

25.4   Protected Variations

Problem How to design objects, subsystems, and systems so that the variations or instability in these elements does not have an undesirable impact on other elements?

Solution Identify points of predicted variation or instability; assign responsibilities to create a stable interface around them.

Note: The term "interface" is used in the broadest sense of an access view; it does not literally only mean something like a Java interface.

Example For example, the prior external tax calculator problem and its solution with Polymorphism illustrate Protected Variations (Figure 25.1). The point of insta-

---

3. By David Wheeler. Note there is also the counter-adage: "Most problems in performance can be solved by removing another layer of indirection!"

bility or variation is the different interfaces or APIs of external tax calculators. The POS system needs to be able to integrate with many existing tax calculator systems, and also with future third-party calculators not yet in existence.

By adding a level of indirection, an interface, and using polymorphism with various *ITaxCalculatorAdapter* implementations, protection within the system from variations in external APIs is achieved. Internal objects collaborate with a stable interface; the various adapter implementations hide the variations to the external systems.

Discussion This is a *very* important, fundamental principle of software design! Almost every software or architectural design trick in book—data encapsulation, polymorphism, data-driven designs, interfaces, virtual machines, configuration files, operating systems, and much more—is a specialization of Protected Variations.

Protected Variations (PV) was first published as a named pattern by Cockburn in [VCK96], although this very fundamental design principle has been around for decades under various terms, such as the term **information hiding** [Parnas72].

Mechanisms Motivated by Protected Variations

PV is a root principle motivating most of the mechanisms and patterns in programming and design to provide flexibility and protection from variations—variations in data, behavior, hardware, software components, operating systems, and more.

At one level, the maturation of a developer or architect can be seen in their growing knowledge of ever-wider mechanisms to achieve PV, to pick the appropriate PV battles worth fighting, and their ability to choose a suitable PV solution. In the early stages, one learns about data encapsulation, interfaces, and polymorphism—all core mechanisms to achieve PV. Later, one learns techniques such as rule-based languages, rule interpreters, reflective and metadata designs, virtual machines, and so forth—all of which can be applied to protect against some variation.

For example:

Core Protected Variations Mechanisms

Data encapsulation, interfaces, polymorphism, indirection, and standards are motivated by PV. Note that components such as virtual machines and operating systems are complex examples of indirection to achieve PV.

Data-Driven Designs

Data-driven designs cover a broad family of techniques including reading codes, values, class file paths, class names, and so forth, from an external source in order to change the behavior of, or "parameterize" a system in some way at runtime. Other variants include style sheets, metadata for object-relational mapping, property files, reading in window layouts, and much more. The system is protected from the impact of data, metadata, or declarative variations by externalizing the variant, reading it in, and reasoning with it.

Service Lookup

Service lookup includes techniques such as using naming services (for example, Java's JNDI) or traders to obtain a service (for example, Java's Jini, or UDDI for Web services). Clients are protected from variations in the location of services, using the stable interface of the lookup service. It is a special case of data-driven design.

Interpreter-Driven Designs

Interpreter-driven designs include rule interpreters that execute rules read from an external source, script or language interpreters that read and run programs, virtual machines, neural network engines that execute nets, constraint logic engines that read and reason with constraint sets, and so forth. This approach allows changing or parameterizing the behavior of a system via external logic expressions. The system is protected from the impact of logic variations by externalizing the logic, reading it in, and using an interpreter.

Reflective or Meta-Level Designs

An example of this approach is using the *java.beans.Introspector* to obtain a *BeanInfo* object, asking for the getter *Method* object for bean property X, and calling *Method.invoke*. The system is protected from the impact of logic or external code variations by reflective algorithms that use introspection and meta-language services. It may be considered a special case of data-driven designs.

Uniform Access

Some languages, such as Ada, Eiffel, and C#, support a syntactic construct so that both a method and field access are expressed the same way. For example, *aCircle.radius* may invoke a *radius():float* method or directly refer to a public field, depending on the definition of the class. We can change from public fields to access methods, without changing the client code.

Standard Languages

Official language standards such as SQL provide protection against a proliferation of varying languages.

The Liskov Substitution Principle (LSP)

LSP [Liskov88] formalizes the principle of protection against variations in different implementations of an interface, or subclass extensions of a superclass.

To quote:

> What is wanted here is something like the following substitution property: If for each object *o1* of type *S* there is an object *o2* of type *T* such that for all programs *P* defined in terms of *T*, the behavior of *P* is unchanged when o1 is substituted for o2 then S is a subtype of *T* [Liskov88].

Informally, software (methods, classes, …) that refers to a type T (some interface or abstract superclass) should work properly or as expected with any substituted implementation or subclass of T—call it S. For example:

```
public void addTaxes( ITaxCalculatorAdapter calculator, Sale sale )
{
    List taxLineItems = calculator.getTaxes( sale );
    // ...
}
```

For this method *addTaxes*, no matter what implementation of *ITaxCalculatorAdapter* is passed in as an actual parameter, the method should continue to work "as expected." LSP is a simple idea, intuitive to most object developers, that formalizes this intuition.

Structure-Hiding Designs

In the first edition of this book, an important, classic object design principle called **Don't Talk to Strangers** or the **Law of Demeter** [Lieberherr88] was expressed as one of the nine GRASP patterns. Briefly, it means to avoid creating designs that traverse long object structure paths and send messages (or talk) to distant, indirect (stranger) objects. Such designs are fragile with respect to changes in the object structures—a common point of instability. But in the second edition the more general PV replaced Don't Talk to Strangers, because the latter is a special case of the former. That is, a mechanism to achieve protection from structure changes is to apply the Don't Talk to Strangers rules.

Don't Talk to Strangers places constraints on what objects you should send messages to within a method. It states that within a method, messages should only be sent to the following objects:

1. The *this* object (or *self*).

2. A parameter of the method.

3. An attribute of *this*.

4. An element of a collection which is an attribute of *this*.

5. An object created within the method.

The intent is to avoid coupling a client to knowledge of indirect objects and the object connections between objects.

Direct objects are a client's "familiars," indirect objects are "strangers." A client should talk to familiars, and avoid talking to strangers.

Here is an example that (mildly) violates Don't Talk to Strangers. The comments explain the violation.

```
class Register
{
private Sale sale;

public void slightlyFragileMethod()
{
    // sale.getPayment() sends a message to a "familiar" (passes #3)
```

```
    // but in sale.getPayment().getTenderedAmount()
    // the getTenderedAmount() message is to a "stranger" Payment

    Money amount = sale.getPayment().getTenderedAmount();

    // ...
}
    // ...
}
```

This code traverses structural connections from a familiar object (the *Sale*) to a stranger object (the *Payment*), and then sends it a message. It is very slightly fragile, as it depends on the fact that *Sale* objects are connected to *Payment* objects. Realistically, this is unlikely to be a problem.

But, consider this next fragment, which traverses farther along the structural path:

```
public void moreFragileMethod()
{
    AccountHolder holder =
        sale.getPayment().getAccount().getAccountHolder();

    // ...
}
```

Or more generally:

```
public void doX()
{
    F someF =
        foo.getA().getB().getC().getD().getE().getF();

    // ...
}
```

The example is contrived, but you see the pattern: Traversing farther along a path of object connections in order to send a message to a distant, indirect object—talking to a distant stranger. The design is coupled to a particular structure of how objects are connected. *The farther along a path the program traverses, the more fragile it is*. Why? Because the object structure (the connections) may change. This is especially true in young applications or early iterations.

Karl Lieberherr and his colleagues have done research into good object design principles, under the umbrella of the Demeter project. This Law of Demeter (Don't Talk to Strangers) was identified because of the frequency with which they saw change and instability in object structure, and thus frequent breakage in code that was coupled to knowledge of object connections.

Yet, as will be examined in the following "Speculative PV and Picking your Battles" section, it is not always necessary to protect against this; it depends on the instability of the object structure. In standard libraries (such as the Java libraries) the structural connections between classes of objects are relatively stable. In mature systems, the structure is more stable. In new systems in early iteration, it isn't stable.

In general, the farther along a path one traverses, the more fragile it is, and thus it is more useful to conform to Don't Talk to Strangers.

Strictly obeying this law—protection against structural variations—requires adding new public operations to the "familiars" of an object; these operations provide the ultimately desired information, and hide how it was obtained. For example, to support Don't Talk to Strangers for the previous two cases:

```
// case 1
Money amount = sale.getTenderedAmountOfPayment();

// case 2
AccountHolder holder = sale.getAccountHolderOfPayment();
```

Contraindications *Caution: Speculative PV and Picking Your Battles*

First, two points of change are worth defining:

- **variation point**—Variations in the existing, current system or requirements, such as the multiple tax calculator interfaces that must be supported.

- **evolution point**—Speculative points of variation that may arise in the future, but which are not present in the existing requirements.[4]

PV is applied to both variation and evolution points.

A caution: Sometimes the cost of speculative "future-proofing" at evolution points outweighs the cost incurred by a simple, more "brittle" design that is reworked as necessary in response to the true change pressures. That is, the cost of engineering protection at evolution points can be higher than reworking a simple design.

For example, I recall a pager message-handling system where the architect added a scripting language and interpreter to support flexibility and protected variation at an evolution point. However, during rework in an incremental release, the complex (and inefficient) scripting was removed—it simply wasn't needed. And when I started OO programming (in the early 1980s) I suffered the disease of "generalize-itis" in which I tended to spend many hours creating superclasses of the classes I really needed to write. I would make everything very general and flexible (and protected against variations), for that future situation when it would really pay off—which never came. I was a poor judge of when it was worth the effort.

The point is not to advocate rework and brittle designs. If the need for flexibility and protection from change is realistic, then applying PV is motivated. But if it

---

4. In the UP, evolution points can be formally documented in **Change Cases**; each describes relevant aspects of an evolution point for the benefit of a future architect.

is for speculative future-proofing or speculative "reuse" with very uncertain probabilities, then restraint and critical thinking is called for.

Novice developers tend toward brittle designs, intermediate developers tend toward overly fancy and flexible, generalized ones (in ways that never get used). Expert designers choose with insight; perhaps a simple and brittle design whose cost of change is balanced against its likelihood.

Benefits

- Extensions required for new variations are easy to add.

- New implementations can be introduced without affecting clients.

- Coupling is lowered.

- The impact or cost of changes can be lowered.

Related Patterns and Principles

- Most design principles and patterns are mechanisms for protected variation, including polymorphism, interfaces, indirection, data encapsulation, most of the GoF design patterns, and so on.

- In [Pree95] variation and evolution points are called "hot spots."

Also Known As; Similar To

PV is essentially the same as the information hiding and open-closed principles, which are older terms. As an "official" pattern in the pattern community, it was named "Protected Variations" in 1996 by Cockburn in [VCK96].

Information Hiding

David Parnas's famous paper *On the Criteria To Be Used in Decomposing Systems Into Modules* [Parnas72] is an example of classics often cited but seldom read. In it, Parnas introduces the concept of **information hiding**. Perhaps because the term sounds like the idea of data encapsulation, it has been *misinterpreted* as data encapsulation, and some books erroneously define the concepts as synonyms. Rather, Parnas intended information hiding to mean *hide information about the design from other modules, at the points of difficulty or likely change*. To quote his discussion of information hiding as a guiding design principle:

> We propose instead that one begins with a list of difficult design decisions or design decisions which are likely to change. Each module is then designed to hide such a decision from the others.

That is, Parnas's information hiding is the same principle expressed in PV, and not simply data encapsulation—which is but one of many techniques to hide information about the design. However, the term has been so widely reinterpreted as a synonym for data encapsulation that it is no longer possible to use it in its original sense without misunderstanding.

Open-Closed Principle

The **Open-Closed Principle** (OCP), described by Bertrand Meyer in [Meyer88], is essentially equivalent to the PV pattern and to information hiding. A definition of OCP is:

> Modules should be both open (for extension; adaptable) and closed (the module is closed to modification in ways that affect clients).

OCP and PV are essentially two expressions of the same principle, with different emphasis: protection at variation and evolution points. In OCP, "module" includes all discrete software elements, including methods, classes, subsystems, applications, and so forth.

In the context of OCP, the phrase "closed with respect to X" means that clients are not affected if X changes. For example, "the class is closed with respect to instance field definitions" through the mechanism of data encapsulation with private fields and public accessing methods. At the same time, they are open to modifying the definitions of the private data, because outside clients are not directly coupled to the private data.

As another example, "the tax calculator adapters are closed with respect to their public interface" through implementing the stable *ITaxCalculatorAdapter* interface. However, the adapters are open to extension by being privately modified in response to changes in the APIs of the external tax calculators, in ways that do not break their clients.

APPLYING GOF DESIGN PATTERNS

*The shift of focus (to patterns) will have a profound and
enduring effect on the way we write programs.*

—*Ward Cunningham and Ralph Johnson*

Objectives

- Introduce and apply some GoF design patterns.
- Show GRASP principles as a generalization of other design patterns.

Introduction

This chapter explores OO design for use-case realizations for the NextGen case
study, providing support for external third-party services whose interfaces may
vary, more complex product pricing rules, and pluggable business rules. The
emphasis is to show how to apply the Gang-of-Four (GoF) and the more basic
GRASP patterns. It illustrates that object design and the assignment of responsibilities can be explained and learned based on the application of patterns—a
vocabulary of principles and idioms that can be combined to design objects.

What's Next? Having applied the remaining GRASP principles, this chapter introduces the
important subject of GoF design patterns. That concludes this iteration; the
next chapter presents iteration-3 requirements.

Iteration 2 – Analysis	GRASP: More Objects with Responsibilities	Applying GoF Design Patterns	Iteration-3 Requirements	UML Activity Diagrams

Some of the 23 GoF design patterns are introduced here, but more are also covered in later chapters, including:

- "More Object Design with GoF Patterns" on page 587
- "Designing a Persistence Framework with Patterns" on page 621

The Gang-of-Four Design Patterns

GoF design patterns, and their seminal influence, were first introduced on p. 280. As a brief review, these were first described in *Design Patterns* [GHJV95], a seminal and extremely popular work that presents 23 patterns useful during object design.

Not all of the 23 patterns are widely used; perhaps 15 are common and most useful.

A thorough study of the *Design Patterns* book is recommended to grow as an object designer, although that book assumes the reader is already an OO designer with significant experience—and has a background in C++ and Smalltalk. In contrast, this book offers an introduction.

26.1   Adapter (GoF)

The NextGen problem explored on p. 414 to motivate the Polymorphism pattern and its solution is more specifically an example of the GoF **Adapter** pattern.

Name:	**Adapter**
Problem:	How to resolve incompatible interfaces, or provide a stable interface to similar components with different interfaces?
Solution: (advice)	Convert the original interface of a component into another interface, through an intermediate adapter object.

To review: The NextGen POS system needs to support several kinds of external third-party services, including tax calculators, credit authorization services, inventory systems, and accounting systems, among others. Each has a different API, which can't be changed.

A solution is to add a level of indirection with objects that adapt the varying external interfaces to a consistent interface used within the application. The solution is illustrated in Figure 26.1.

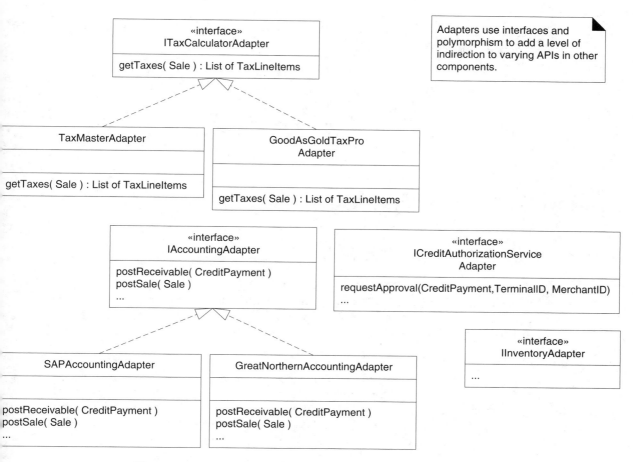

Figure 26.1 The Adapter pattern.

As illustrated in Figure 26.2, a particular adapter instance will be instantiated for the chosen external service[1], such as SAP for accounting, and will adapt the *postSale* request to the external interface, such as a SOAP XML interface over HTTPS for an intranet Web service offered by SAP.

---

1. In the J2EE Connector Architecture, these adapters to external services are more specifically called **resource adapters**.

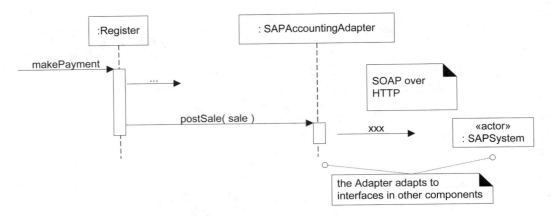

Figure 26.2 Using an Adapter.

Guideline: Include Pattern in Type Name

Notice that the type names include the pattern name "Adapter." This is a relatively common style and has the advantage of easily communicating to others reading the code or diagrams what design patterns are being used.

Related Patterns A resource adapter that hides an external system may also be considered a Facade object (another GoF pattern discussed in this chapter), as it wraps access to the subsystem or system with a single object (which is the essence of Facade). However, the motivation to call it a resource adapter especially exists when the wrapping object provides adaptation to varying external interfaces.

26.2   Some GRASP Principles as a Generalization of Other Patterns

The previous use of the Adapter pattern can be viewed as a specialization of some GRASP building blocks:

> Adapter supports *Protected Variations* with respect to changing external interfaces or third-party packages through the use of an *Indirection* object that applies interfaces and *Polymorphism*.

What's the Problem? Pattern Overload!

The *Pattern Almanac 2000* [Rising00] lists around 500 design patterns. And many hundreds more have been published since then. The curious developer has no time to actually program given this reading list!

A Solution: See the Underlying Principles

Yes, it's important for an experienced designer to know in detail and by memory 50+ of the most important design patterns, but few of us can learn or remember 1,000 patterns, or even start to organize that pattern plethora into a useful taxonomy.

But there's good news: Most design patterns can be seen as specializations of a few basic GRASP principles. Although it is indeed helpful to study detailed design patterns to accelerate learning, it is even more helpful to see their underlying basic themes (Protected Variations, Polymorphism, Indirection, …) to help us to cut through the myriad details and see the essential "alphabet" of design techniques being applied.

Example: Adapter and GRASP

Figure 26.1 illustrates my point that detailed design patterns can be analyzed in terms of the basic underlying "alphabet" of GRASP principles. UML generalization relationships are used to suggest the conceptual connections. At this point perhaps this idea seems academic or overly analytical. But it is truly the case that as you spend some years applying and reflecting on myriad design patterns, you will increasingly come to feel that it's the underlying themes that are important, and the fine details of Adapter or Strategy or whatever will become secondary.

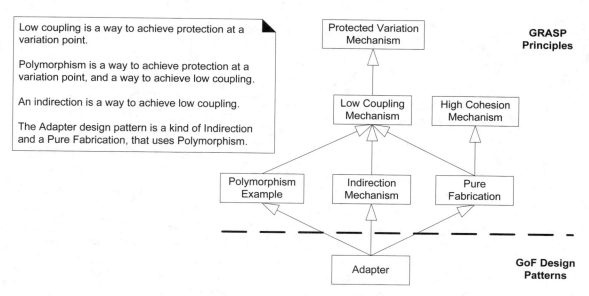

Figure 26.3 Relating Adapter to some core GRASP principles.

26.3 "Analysis" Discoveries During Design: Domain Model

Observe that in the Adapter design in Figure 26.1, the *getTaxes* operation returns a list of *TaxLineItems*. That is, on deeper reflection and investigation of how taxes are handled and tax calculators work, the modeler (me) realized that a list of tax line items are associated with a sale, such as state tax, federal tax, and so forth (there is always the chance governments will invent new taxes!).

In addition to being a newly created software class in the Design Model, this is a domain concept. It is normal and common to discover noteworthy domain concepts and refined understanding of the requirements during design or programming—iterative development supports this kind of incremental discovery.

Should this discovery be reflected in the Domain Model (or Glossary)? If the Domain Model will be used in the future as a source of inspiration for later design work, or as a visual learning aid to communicate the key domain concepts, then adding it could have value. Figure 26.4 illustrates an updated Domain Model.

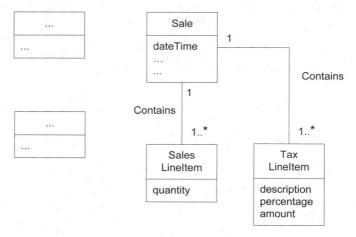

Figure 26.4 Updated partial Domain Model.

26.4 Factory

This is also called **Simple Factory** or **Concrete Factory**. This pattern is not a GoF design pattern, but extremely widespread. It is also a simplification of the GoF Abstract Factory pattern (p. 605), and often described as a variation of Abstract Factory, although that's not strictly accurate. Nevertheless, because of its prevalence and association with GoF, it is presented now.

The adapter raises a new problem in the design: In the prior Adapter pattern solution for external services with varying interfaces, who creates the adapters? And how to determine which class of adapter to create, such as *TaxMaster-*

Adapter or *GoodAsGoldTaxProAdapter?*

If some domain object creates them, the responsibilities of the domain object are going beyond pure application logic (such as sales total calculations) and into other concerns related to connectivity with external software components.

This point underscores another fundamental design principle (usually considered an architectural design principle): Design to maintain a **separation of concerns**. That is, modularize or separate distinct concerns into different areas, so that each has a cohesive purpose. Fundamentally, it is an application of the GRASP High Cohesion principle. For example, the domain layer of software objects emphasizes relatively pure application logic responsibilities, whereas a different group of objects is responsible for the concern of connectivity to external systems.

Therefore, choosing a domain object (such as a *Register*) to create the adapters does not support the goal of a separation of concerns, and lowers its cohesion.

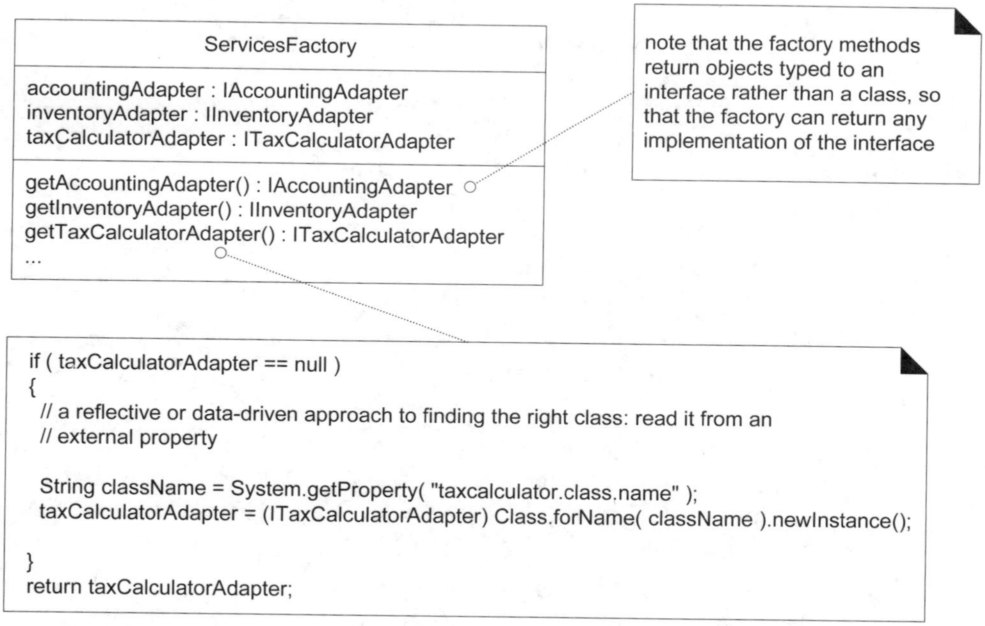

```
ServicesFactory
─────────────────────────────────────────
accountingAdapter : IAccountingAdapter
inventoryAdapter : IInventoryAdapter
taxCalculatorAdapter : ITaxCalculatorAdapter
─────────────────────────────────────────
getAccountingAdapter() : IAccountingAdapter
getInventoryAdapter() : IInventoryAdapter
getTaxCalculatorAdapter() : ITaxCalculatorAdapter
...
```

note that the factory methods return objects typed to an interface rather than a class, so that the factory can return any implementation of the interface

```
if ( taxCalculatorAdapter == null )
{
    // a reflective or data-driven approach to finding the right class: read it from an
    // external property

    String className = System.getProperty( "taxcalculator.class.name" );
    taxCalculatorAdapter = (ITaxCalculatorAdapter) Class.forName( className ).newInstance();

}
return taxCalculatorAdapter;
```

Figure 26.5 The Factory pattern.

A common alternative in this case is to apply the **Factory** pattern, in which a Pure Fabrication "factory" object is defined to create objects.

Factory objects have several advantages:

- Separate the responsibility of complex creation into cohesive helper objects.

- Hide potentially complex creation logic.

- Allow introduction of performance-enhancing memory management strategies, such as object caching or recycling.

441

Name:	**Factory**
Problem:	Who should be responsible for creating objects when there are special considerations, such as complex creation logic, a desire to separate the creation responsibilities for better cohesion, and so forth?
Solution: (advice)	Create a Pure Fabrication object called a Factory that handles the creation.

A Factory solution is illustrated in Figure 26.5.

Note that in the *ServicesFactory*, the logic to decide which class to create is resolved by reading in the class name from an external source (for example, via a system property if Java is used) and then dynamically loading the class. This is an example of a partial **data-driven design**. This design achieves Protected Variations with respect to changes in the implementation class of the adapter. Without changing the source code in this factory class, we can create instances of new adapter classes by changing the property value and ensuring that the new class is visible in the Java class path for loading.

Related Patterns   Factories are often accessed with the Singleton pattern.

26.5   Singleton (GoF)

The *ServicesFactory* raises another new problem in the design: Who creates the factory itself, and how is it accessed?

First, observe that only one instance of the factory is needed within the process. Second, quick reflection suggests that the methods of this factory may need to be called from various places in the code, as different places need access to the adapters for calling on the external services. Thus, there is a visibility problem: How to get visibility to this single *ServicesFactory* instance?

One solution is pass the *ServicesFactory* instance around as a parameter to wherever a visibility need is discovered for it, or to initialize the objects that need visibility to it, with a permanent reference. This is possible but inconvenient; an alternative is the **Singleton** pattern.

Occasionally, it is desirable to support global visibility or a single access point to a single instance of a class rather than some other form of visibility. This is true for the *ServicesFactory* instance.

Name: **Singleton**

Problem: Exactly one instance of a class is allowed—it is a "singleton." Objects need a global and single point of access.

Solution: Define a static method of the class that returns the singleton.
(advice)

For example, Figure 26.6 shows an implementation of the Singleton pattern.

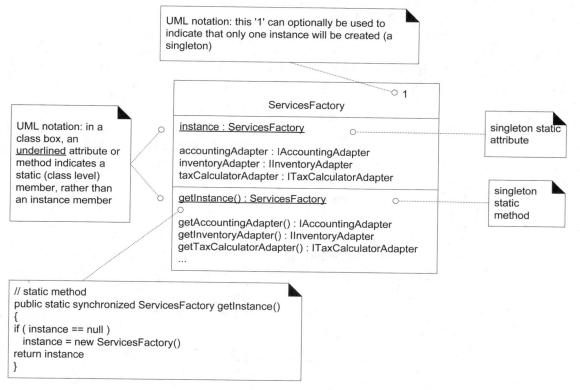

Figure 26.6 The Singleton pattern in the *ServicesFactory* class.

Applying UML: Notice how a singleton is illustrated, with a '1' in the top right corner of the name compartment.

Thus, the key idea is that class X defines a static method *getInstance* that itself provides a single instance of X.

With this approach, a developer has global visibility to this single instance, via the static *getInstance* method of the class, as in this example:

```
public class Register
{

public void initialize()
{
    … do some work …

    // accessing the singleton Factory via the getInstance call
    accountingAdapter =
        ServicesFactory.getInstance().getAccountingAdapter();

    … do some work …
}

// other methods…

} // end of class
```

Since visibility to public classes is global in scope (in most languages), at any point in the code, in any method of any class, one can write

SingletonClass.getInstance()

in order to obtain visibility to the singleton instance, and then send it a message, such as *SingletonClass.getInstance().doFoo()*. And it's hard to beat the feeling of being able to globally *doFoo*!

Implementation and Design Issues

A Singleton *getInstance* method is often frequently called. In multi-threaded applications, the creation step of the **lazy initialization** logic is a critical section requiring thread concurrency control. Thus, assuming the instance is lazy initialized, it is common to wrap the method with concurrency control. In Java, for example:

```
public static synchronized ServicesFactory getInstance()
{
    if ( instance == null )
    {
        // critical section if multithreaded application
        instance = new ServicesFactory();
    }
    return instance;
}
```

On the subject of lazy initialization, why not prefer **eager initialization**, as in this example?

```
public class ServicesFactory
{

// eager initialization
private static ServicesFactory instance =
    new ServicesFactory();
```

```
public static ServicesFactory getInstance()
{
    return instance;
}

// other methods...

}
```

The first approach of lazy initialization is usually preferred for at least these reasons:

- Creation work (and perhaps holding on to "expensive" resources) is avoided, if the instance is never actually accessed.

- The *getInstance* lazy initialization sometimes contains complex and conditional creation logic.

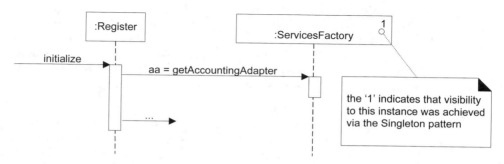

Figure 26.7 Implicit *getInstance* Singleton pattern message indicated in the UML because of the '1' mark.

Another common Singleton implementation question is: Why not make all the service methods *static* methods of the class itself, instead of using an instance object with instance-side methods? For example, what if we add a *static* method called *getAccountingAdapter* to *ServicesFactory*. But, an instance and instance-side methods are usually preferred for these reasons:

- Instance-side methods permit subclassing and refinement of the singleton class into subclasses; static methods are not polymorphic (virtual) and don't permit overriding in subclasses in most languages (Smalltalk excluded).

- Most object-oriented remote communication mechanisms (for example, Java's RMI) only support remote-enabling of instance methods, not static methods. A singleton instance could be remote-enabled, although that is admittedly rarely done.

- A class is not always a singleton in all application contexts. In application X, it may be a singleton, but it may be a "multi-ton" in application Y. It is also not uncommon to start off a design thinking the object will be a singleton, and then discovering a need for multiple instances in the same process. Thus, the instance-side solution offers flexibility.

Related Patterns The Singleton pattern is often used for Factory objects and Facade objects—another GoF pattern that will be discussed.

26.6 Conclusion of the External Services with Varying Interfaces Problem

A combination of Adapter, Factory, and Singleton patterns have been used to provide Protected Variations from the varying interfaces of external tax calculators, accounting systems, and so forth. Figure 26.8 illustrates a larger context of using these in the use-case realization.

This design may not be ideal, and there is always room for improvement. But one of the goals strived for in this case study is to illustrate that at least a design can be constructed from a set of principles or pattern "building blocks," and that there is a methodical approach to doing and explaining a design. It is my sincere hope that it is possible to see how the design in Figure 26.8 arose from reasoning based on Controller, Creator, Protected Variations, Low Coupling, High Cohesion, Indirection, Polymorphism, Adapter, Factory, and Singleton.

Note how succinct a designer can be in conversation or documentation when there is a shared understanding of patterns. I can say, "To handle the problem of varying interfaces for external services, let's use Adapters generated from a Singleton Factory." Object designers really do have conversations that sound like this; using patterns and pattern names supports raising the level of abstraction in design communication.

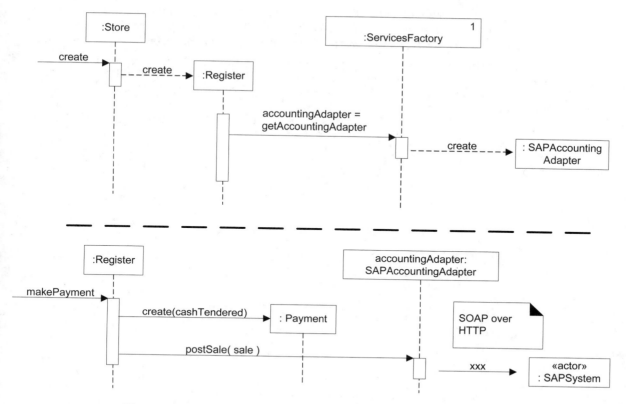

Figure 26.8 Adapter, Factory, and Singleton patterns applied to the design.

26.7   Strategy (GoF)

The next design problem to be resolved is to provide more complex pricing logic, such as a store-wide discount for the day, senior citizen discounts, and so forth.

The pricing strategy (which may also be called a rule, policy, or algorithm) for a sale can vary. During one period it may be 10% off all sales, later it may be $10 off if the sale total is greater than $200, and myriad other variations. How do we design for these varying pricing algorithms?

Name:	**Strategy**
Problem:	How to design for varying, but related, algorithms or policies? How to design for the ability to change these algorithms or policies?
Solution: (advice)	Define each algorithm/policy/strategy in a separate class, with a common interface.

Since the behavior of pricing varies by the strategy (or algorithm), we create multiple *SalePricingStrategy* classes, each with a polymorphic *getTotal* method (see Figure 26.9). Each *getTotal* method takes the *Sale* object as a parameter, so that the pricing strategy object can find the pre-discount price from the *Sale*, and then apply the discounting rule. The implementation of each *getTotal* method will be different: *PercentDiscountPricingStrategy* will discount by a percentage, and so on.

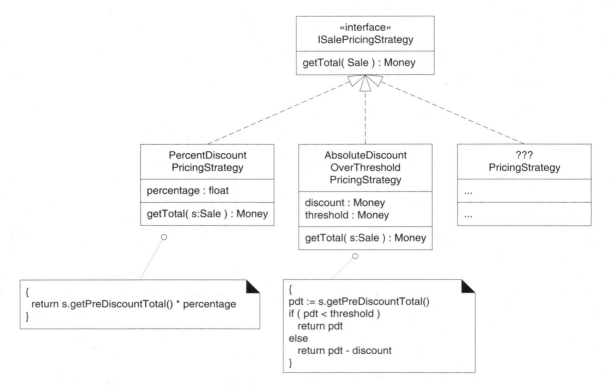

Figure 26.9 Pricing Strategy classes.

A strategy object is attached to a **context object**—the object to which it applies the algorithm. In this example, the context object is a *Sale*. When a *getTotal* message is sent to a *Sale*, it delegates some of the work to its strategy object, as illustrated in Figure 26.10. It is not required that the message to the context object and the strategy object have the same name, as in this example (for example, *getTotal* and *getTotal*), but it is common. However, it is common—indeed, usually required—that the context object pass a reference to itself (*this*) on to the strategy object, so that the strategy has parameter visibility to the context object, for further collaboration.

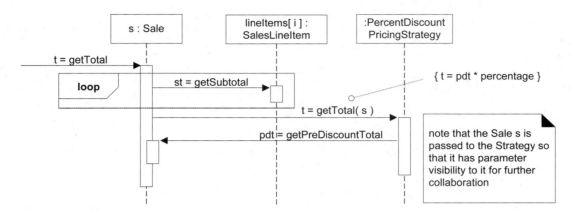

Figure 26.10 Strategy in collaboration.

Observe that the context object (*Sale*) needs attribute visibility to its strategy. This is reflected in the DCD in Figure 26.11.

Creating a Strategy with a Factory

There are different pricing algorithms or strategies, and they change over time. Who should create the strategy? A straightforward approach is to apply the Factory pattern again: A *PricingStrategyFactory* can be responsible for creating all strategies (all the pluggable or changing algorithms or policies) needed by the application. As with the *ServicesFactory*, it can read the name of the implementation class of the pricing strategy from a system property (or some external data source), and then make an instance of it. With this partial *data-driven design* (or reflective design) one can dynamically change at any time—while the NextGen POS application is running—the pricing policy, by specifying a different class of Strategy to create.

Observe that a new factory was used for the strategies; that is, different than the *ServicesFactory*. This supports the goal of High Cohesion—each factory is cohesively focused on creating a related family of objects.

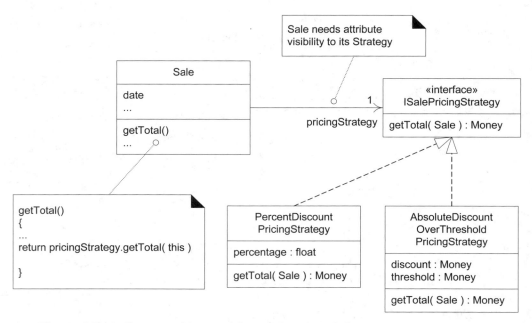

Figure 26.11 Context object needs attribute visibility to its strategy.

UML—Observe that in Figure 26.11 the reference via a directed association is to the interface *ISalePricingStrategy*, not to a concrete class. This indicates that the reference attribute in the *Sale* will be declared in terms of the interface, not a class, so that any implementation of the interface can be bound to the attribute.

Note that because of the frequently changing pricing policy (it could be every hour), it is *not* desirable to cache the created strategy instance in a field of the *PricingStrategyFactory*, but rather to re-create one each time, by reading the external property for its class name, and then instantiating the strategy.

And as with most factories, the *PricingStrategyFactory* will be a singleton (one instance) and accessed via the Singleton pattern (see Figure 26.12).

When a *Sale* instance is created, it can ask the factory for its pricing strategy, as shown in Figure 26.13.

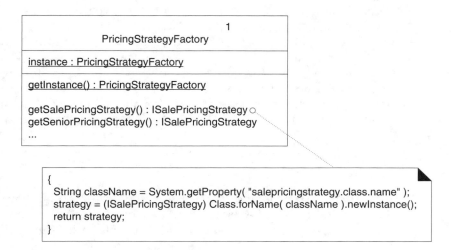

Figure 26.12 Factory for strategies.

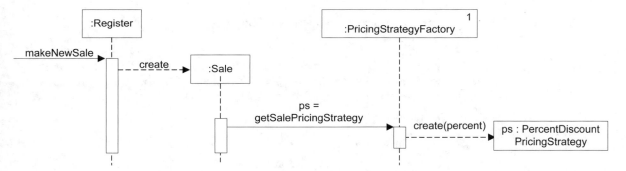

Figure 26.13 Creating a strategy.

Reading and Initializing the Percentage Value

Finally, a design problem that has been ignored until now is the issue of how to find the different numbers for the percentage or absolute discounts. For example, on Monday, the *PercentageDiscountPricingStrategy* may have a percentage value of 10%, but 20% on Tuesday.

Note also that a percentage discount may be related to the type of buyer, such as a senior citizen, rather than to a time period.

These numbers will be stored in some external data store, such as a relational database, so they can be easily changed. So, what object will read them and ensure they are assigned to the strategy? A reasonable choice is the *Strategy-Factory* itself, since it is creating the pricing strategy, and can know which percentage to read from a data store ("current store discount," "senior discount," and so forth).

Designs to read these numbers from external data stores vary from the simple to the complex, such as a plain JDBC SQL call (if Java technologies, as an example) or collaborating with objects that add levels of indirection in order to hide the particular location, data query language, or type of data store. Analyzing the variation and evolution points with respect to the data store will reveal if there is a need for protected variation. For example, we could ask, "Are we all comfortable with a long-term commitment to using a relational database that understands SQL?". If so, a simple JDBC call from within the *StrategyFactory* may suffice.

Summary

Protected Variations with respect to dynamically changing pricing policies has been achieved with the Strategy and Factory patterns. Strategy builds on Polymorphism and interfaces to allow pluggable algorithms in an object design.

Related Patterns   Strategy is based on Polymorphism, and provides Protected Variations with respect to changing algorithms. Strategies are often created by a Factory.

26.8   Composite (GoF) and Other Design Principles

To raise yet another interesting requirements and design problem: How do we handle the case of multiple, conflicting pricing policies? For example, suppose a store has the following policies in effect today (Monday):

- 20% senior discount policy

- preferred customer discount of 15% off sales over $400

- on Monday, there is $50 off purchases over $500

- buy 1 case of Darjeeling tea, get 15% discount off of everything

Suppose a senior who is also a preferred customer buys 1 case of Darjeeling tea, and $600 of veggieburgers (clearly an enthusiastic vegetarian who loves chai). What pricing policy should be applied?

To clarify: There are now pricing strategies that attach to the sale by virtue of three factors:

1. time period (Monday)

2. customer type (senior)

3. a particular line item product (Darjeeling tea)

Another point of clarification: Three of the four example policies are really just "percentage discount" strategies, which simplifies our view of the problem.

Part of the answer to this problem requires defining the store's **conflict resolution strategy**. Usually, a store applies the "best for the customer" (lowest price) conflict resolution strategy, but this is not required, and it could change. For example, during a difficult financial period, the store may have to use a "highest price" conflict resolution strategy.

The first point to note is that there can exist multiple co-existing strategies, that is, one sale may have several pricing strategies. Another point to note is that a pricing strategy can be related to the type of customer (for example, a senior). This has creation design implications: The customer type must be known by the *StrategyFactory* at the time of creation of a pricing strategy for the customer.

Similarly, a pricing strategy can be related to the type of product being bought (for example, Darjeeling tea). This likewise has creation design implications: The *ProductDescription* must be known by the *StrategyFactory* at the time of creation of a pricing strategy influenced by the product.

Is there a way to change the design so that the *Sale* object does not know if it is dealing with one or many pricing strategies, and also offer a design for the conflict resolution? Yes, with the Composite pattern.

Name:	**Composite**
Problem:	How to treat a group or composition structure of objects the same way (polymorphically) as a non-composite (atomic) object?
Solution: (advice)	Define classes for composite and atomic objects so that they implement the same interface.

For example, a new class called *CompositeBestForCustomerPricingStrategy* (well, at least it's descriptive) can implement the *ISalesPricingStrategy* and itself contain other *ISalesPricingStrategy* objects. Figure 26.14 explains the design idea in detail.

Observe that in this design, the composite classes such as *CompositeBestForCustomerPricingStrategy* inherit an attribute *pricingStrategies* that contains a list of more *ISalePricingStrategy* objects. This is a signature feature of a composite object: The outer composite object contains a list of inner objects, and both the outer and inner objects implement the same interface. That is, the composite class itself implements the *ISalePricingStrategy* interface.

Thus, we can attach either a composite *CompositeBestForCustomerPricingStrategy* object (which contains other strategies inside of it) or an atomic *PercentDiscountPricingStrategy* object to the *Sale* object, and the *Sale* does not know or care if its pricing strategy is an atomic or composite strategy—it looks the same to the *Sale* object. It is just another object that implements the *ISalePricingStrategy* interface and understands the *getTotal* message (Figure 26.15).

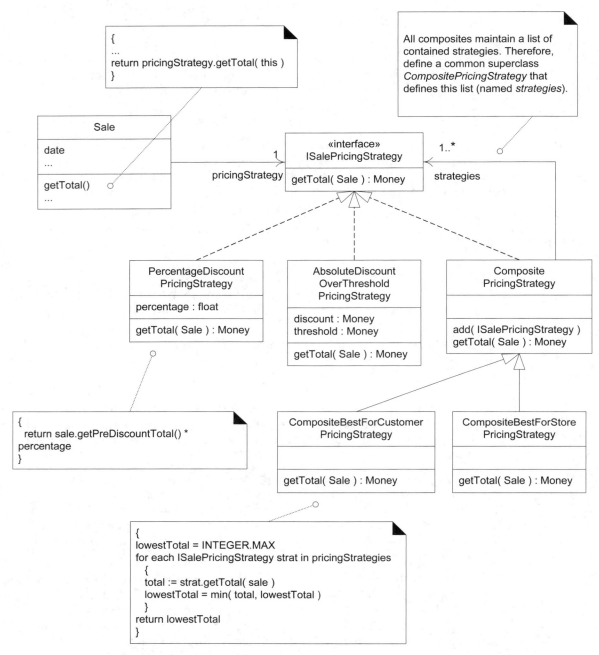

{
...
return pricingStrategy.getTotal(this)
}

All composites maintain a list of contained strategies. Therefore, define a common superclass *CompositePricingStrategy* that defines this list (named *strategies*).

Sale

date
...

getTotal()
...

pricingStrategy

1

«interface»
ISalePricingStrategy

getTotal(Sale) : Money

1..*

strategies

PercentageDiscount PricingStrategy

percentage : float

getTotal(Sale) : Money

AbsoluteDiscount OverThreshold PricingStrategy

discount : Money
threshold : Money

getTotal(Sale) : Money

Composite PricingStrategy

add(ISalePricingStrategy)
getTotal(Sale) : Money

{
 return sale.getPreDiscountTotal() *
percentage
}

CompositeBestForCustomer PricingStrategy

getTotal(Sale) : Money

CompositeBestForStore PricingStrategy

getTotal(Sale) : Money

{
lowestTotal = INTEGER.MAX
for each ISalePricingStrategy strat in pricingStrategies
  {
  total := strat.getTotal(sale)
  lowestTotal = min(total, lowestTotal)
  }
return lowestTotal
}

Figure 26.14 The Composite pattern.

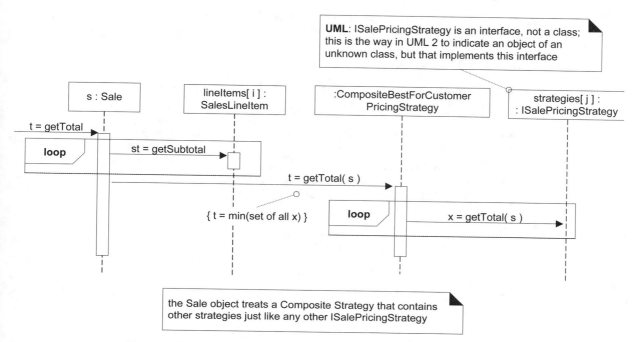

Figure 26.15 Collaboration with a Composite.

UML—In Figure 26.15, please note a way to indicate objects that implement an interface, when we don't care to specify the exact implementation class.

To clarify with some sample code in Java, the *CompositePricingStrategy* and one of its subclasses are defined as follows:

```
// superclass so all subclasses can inherit a List of strategies

public abstract class CompositePricingStrategy
    implements ISalePricingStrategy
{

protected List strategies = new ArrayList();

public add( ISalePricingStrategy s )
{
    strategies.add( s );
}

public abstract Money getTotal( Sale sale )

} // end of class




// a Composite Strategy that returns the low
// of its inner SalePricingStrategies
```

```
public class CompositeBestForCustomerPricingStrategy
    extends CompositePricingStrategy
{

public Money getTotal( Sale sale )
{
    Money lowestTotal = new Money( Integer.MAX_VALUE );

    // iterate over all the inner strategies

    for( Iterator i = strategies.iterator(); i.hasNext(); )
    {
        ISalePricingStrategy strategy =
            (ISalePricingStrategy)i.next();
        Money total = strategy.getTotal( sale );
        lowestTotal = total.min( lowestTotal );
    }
return lowestTotal;
}


} // end of class
```

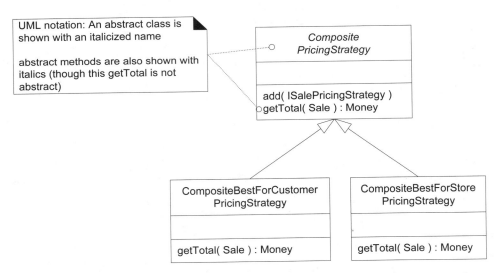

Figure 26.16 Abstract superclasses, abstract methods, and inheritance in the UML.

Creating Multiple SalePricingStrategies

With the Composite pattern, we have made a group of multiple (and conflicting) pricing strategies look to the *Sale* object like a single pricing strategy. The composite object that contains the group also implements the *ISalePricingStrategy* interface. The more challenging (and interesting) part of this design problem is: When do we create these strategies?

A desirable design will start by creating a Composite that contains the present moment's store discount policy (which could be set to 0% discount if none is active), such as some *PercentageDiscountPricingStrategy*. Then, if at a later step in the scenario, another pricing strategy is discovered to also apply (such as senior discount), it will be easy to add it to the composite, using the inherited *CompositePricingStrategy.add* method.

There are three points in the scenario where pricing strategies may be added to the composite:

1. Current store-defined discount, added when the sale is created.

2. Customer type discount, added when the customer type is communicated to the POS.

3. Product type discount (if bought Darjeeling tea, 15% off the overall sale), added when the product is entered to the sale.

The design of the first case is shown in Figure 26.17. As in the original design discussed earlier, the strategy class name to instantiate could be read as a system property, and a percentage value could be read from an external data store.

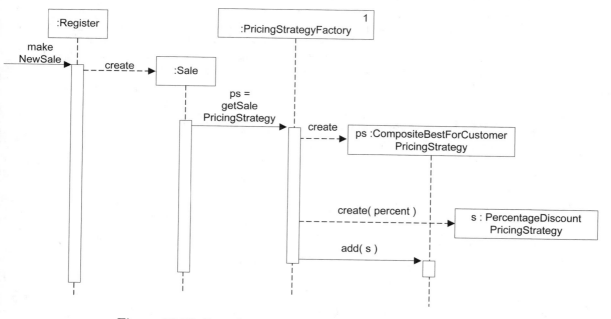

Figure 26.17 Creating a composite strategy.

For the second case of a customer type discount, first recall the use case extension which previously recognized this requirement:

Use Case UC1: Process Sale

...
Extensions (or Alternative Flows):
5b. Customer says they are eligible for a discount (e.g., employee, preferred customer)
    1. Cashier signals discount request.
    2. Cashier enters Customer identification.
    3. System presents discount total, based on discount rules.

This indicates a new system operation on the POS system, in addition to *make-NewSale*, *enterItem*, *endSale*, and *makePayment*. We will call this fifth system operation *enterCustomerForDiscount*; it may optionally occur after the *endSale* operation. It implies that some form of customer identification will have to come in through the user interface, the *customerID*. Perhaps it can be captured from a card reader, or via the keyboard.

The design of the second case is shown in Figure 26.18 and Figure 26.19. Not surprisingly, the factory object is responsible for the creation of the additional pricing strategy. It may make another *PercentageDiscountPricingStrategy* that represents, for example, a senior discount. But as with the original creation design, the choice of class will be read in as a system property, as will the specific percentage for the customer type, to provide Protected Variations with respect to changing the class or values. Note that by virtue of the Composite pattern, the *Sale* may have two or three conflicting pricing strategies attached to it, but it continues to look like a single strategy to the *Sale* object.

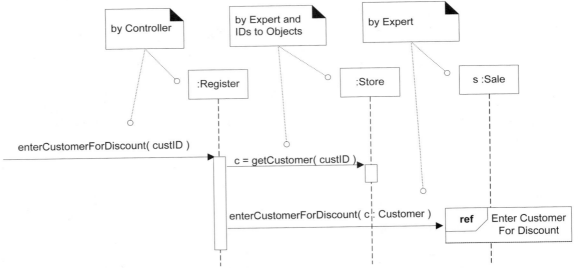

Figure 26.18 Creating the pricing strategy for a customer discount, part 1.

UML—Figure 26.18 and Figure 26.19 show an important UML 2 idea in interaction diagrams: Using the ref and sd frame to relate diagrams.

Considering GRASP and Other Principles in the Design

To review thinking in terms of some basic GRASP patterns: For this second case, why not have the *Register* send a message to the *PricingStrategyFactory*, to create this new pricing strategy and then pass it to the *Sale*? One reason is to support Low Coupling. The *Sale* is already coupled to the factory; by making the *Register* also collaborate with it, the coupling in the design would increase. Furthermore, the *Sale* is the Information Expert that knows its current pricing strategy (which is going to be modified); so by Expert, it is also justified to delegate to the *Sale*.

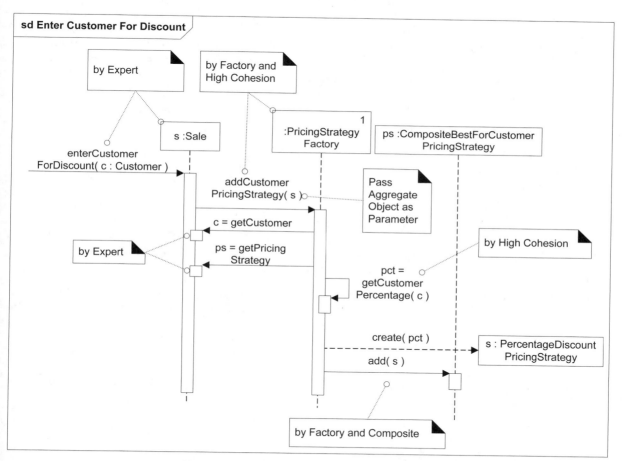

Figure 26.19 Creating the pricing strategy for a customer discount, part 2.

Observe in the design that *customerID* is transformed into a *Customer* object via the *Register* asking the *Store* for a *Customer*, given an ID. First, it is justifiable to give the *getCustomer* responsibility to the *Store*; by Information Expert and the goal of low representational gap, the *Store* can know all the *Customers*. And the *Register* asks the *Store*, because the *Register* already has attribute visibility to the *Store* (from earlier design work); if the *Sale* had to ask the *Store*, the *Sale* would need a reference to the *Store*, increasing the coupling beyond its current levels, and therefore not supporting Low Coupling.

IDs to Objects

Second, why transform the *customerID* (an "ID"—perhaps a number) into a *Customer* object? This is a common practice in object design—to transform keys and IDs for things into true objects. This transformation often takes place shortly after an ID or key enters the domain layer of the Design Model from the UI layer. It doesn't have a pattern name, but it could be a candidate for a pattern because it is such a common idiom among experienced object designers—perhaps *IDs to Objects*. Why bother? Having a true *Customer* object that encapsulates a set of information about the customer, and which can have behavior (related to Information Expert, for example), frequently becomes beneficial and flexible as the design grows, even if the designer does not originally perceive a need for a true object and thought instead that a plain number or ID would be sufficient. Note that in the earlier design, the transformation of the *itemID* into a *ProductDescription* object is another example of this *IDs to Objects* pattern.

Pass Aggregate Object as Parameter

Finally, note that in the *addCustomerPricingStrategy(s:Sale)* message we pass a *Sale* to the factory, and then the factory turns around and asks for the *Customer* and *PricingStrategy* from the *Sale*.

Why not just extract these two objects from the *Sale*, and instead pass in the *Customer* and *PricingStrategy* to the factory? The answer is another common object design idiom: Avoid extracting child objects out of parent or aggregate objects, and then passing around the child objects. Rather, pass around the aggregate object that contains child objects.

Following this principle increases flexibility, because then the factory can collaborate with the entire *Sale* in ways we may not have previously anticipated as necessary (which is very common), and as a corollary, it reduces the need to anticipate what the factory object needs; the designer just passes as a parameter the entire *Sale*, without knowing what more particular objects the factory may need. Although this idiom does not have a name, it is related to Low Coupling and Protected Variations. Perhaps it could be called the *Pass Aggregate Object as Parameter* pattern.

Summary

This design problem was squeezed for many tips in object design. A skilled object designer has many of these patterns committed to memory through studying their published explanations, and has internalized core principles, such as those described in the GRASP family.

Please note that although this application of Composite was to a Strategy family, the Composite pattern can be applied to other kinds of objects, not just strategies. For example, it is common to create "macro commands"—commands that contain other commands—through the use of Composite. The Command pattern is described in a subsequent chapter.

Related Patterns   Composite is often used with the Strategy and Command patterns. Composite is based on Polymorphism and provides Protected Variations to a client so that it is not impacted if its related objects are atomic or composite.

26.9   Facade (GoF)

Another requirement chosen for this iteration is *pluggable business rules*. That is, at predictable points in the scenarios, such as when *makeNewSale* or *enterItem* occurs in the *Process Sale* use case, or when a cashier starts cashing in, different customers who wish to purchase the NextGen POS would like to customize its behavior slightly.

To be more precise, assume that rules are desired that can invalidate an action. For example:

- Suppose when a new sale is created, it is possible to identify that it will be paid by a gift certificate (this is possible and common). Then, a store may have a rule to only allow one item to be purchased if a gift certificate is used. Consequently, subsequent *enterItem* operations, after the first, should be invalidated.

- If the sale is paid by a gift certificate, invalidate all payment types of change due back to the customer except for another gift certificate. For example, if the cashier requested change in the form of cash, or as a credit to the customer's store account, invalidate those requests.

- Suppose when a new sale is created, it is possible to identify that it is for a charitable donation (from the store to the charity). A store may also have a rule to only allow item entries less than $250 each, and also to only add items to the sale if the currently logged in "cashier" is a manager.

In terms of requirements analysis, the specific scenario points across all use cases (*enterItem*, *chooseCashChange*, ...) must be identified. For this exploration, only the *enterItem* point will be considered, but the same solution applies equally to all points.

Suppose that the software architect wants a design that has low impact on the existing software components. That is, she or he wants to design for a separation of concerns, and factor out this rule handling into a separate concern. Furthermore, suppose that the architect is unsure of the best implementation for this pluggable rule handling, and may want to experiment with different solutions for representing, loading, and evaluating the rules. For example, rules can be implemented with the Strategy pattern, or with free open-source rule interpreters that read and interpret a set of IF-THEN rules, or with commercial, purchased rule interpreters, among other solutions.

To solve this design problem, the Facade pattern can be used.

Name:	**Facade**
Problem:	A common, unified interface to a disparate set of implementations or interfaces—such as within a subsystem—is required. There may be undesirable coupling to many things in the subsystem, or the implementation of the subsystem may change. What to do?
Solution: (advice)	Define a single point of contact to the subsystem—a facade object that wraps the subsystem. This facade object presents a single unified interface and is responsible for collaborating with the subsystem components.

A Facade is a "front-end" object that is the single point of entry for the services of a subsystem[2]; the implementation and other components of the subsystem are private and can't be seen by external components. Facade provides Protected Variations from changes in the implementation of a subsystem.

For example, we will define a "rule engine" subsystem, whose specific implementation is not yet known.[3] It will be responsible for evaluating a set of rules against an operation (by some hidden implementation), and then indicating if any of the rules invalidated the operation.

The facade object to this subsystem will be called *POSRuleEngineFacade*. See Figure 26.20. The designer decides to place calls to this facade near the start of the methods that have been defined as the points for pluggable rules, as in this example:

```
public class Sale
{

public void makeLineItem( ProductDescription desc, int quantity )
{
    SalesLineItem sli = new SalesLineItem( desc, quantity );

    // call to the Facade
    if ( POSRuleEngineFacade.getInstance().isInvalid( sli, this ) )
        return;

    lineItems.add( sli );
}

// ...

} // end of class
```

---

2. "Subsystem" is here used in an informal sense to indicate a separate grouping of related components, not exactly as defined in the UML.

3. There are several free open source and commercial rule engines. For example, Jess, a free-for-academic-use rule engine available at http://herzberg.ca.sandia.gov/jess/.

Note the use of the Singleton pattern. Facades are often accessed via Singleton.

With this design, the complexity and implementation of how rules will be represented and evaluated are hidden in the "rules engine" subsystem, accessed via the *POSRuleEngineFacade* facade. Observe that the subsystem hidden by the facade object could contain dozens or hundreds of classes of objects, or even a non-object-oriented solution, yet as a client to the subsystem, we see only its one public access point.

And a separation of concerns has been achieved to some degree—all the rule-handling concerns have been delegated to another subsystem.

Summary

The Facade pattern is simple and widely used. It hides a subsystem behind an object.

Related Patterns Facades are usually accessed via the Singleton pattern. They provide Protected Variations from the implementation of a subsystem, by adding an Indirection object to help support Low Coupling. External objects are coupled to one point in a subsystem: the facade object.

As described in the Adapter pattern, an adapter object may be used to wrap access to external systems with varying interfaces. This is a kind of facade, but the emphasis is to provide adaptation to varying interfaces, and thus it is more specifically called an adapter.

26.10 Observer/Publish-Subscribe/Delegation Event Model (GoF)

Another requirement for the iteration is adding the ability for a GUI window to refresh its display of the sale total when the total changes (see Figure 26.21). The idea is to solve the problem for this one case, and then in later iterations, extend the solution to refreshing the GUI display for other changing data as well.

Why not do the following as a solution? When the *Sale* changes its total, the *Sale* object sends a message to a window, asking it to refresh its display.

To review, the Model-View Separation principle discourages such solutions. It states that "model" objects (non-UI objects such as a *Sale*) should not know about view or presentation objects such as a window. It promotes Low Coupling from other layers to the presentation (UI) layer of objects.

A consequence of supporting this low coupling is that it allows the replacement of the view or presentation layer by a new one, or of particular windows by new windows, without impacting the non-UI objects. If model objects do not know about Java Swing objects (for example), then it is possible to unplug a Swing interface, or unplug a particular window, and plug in something else.

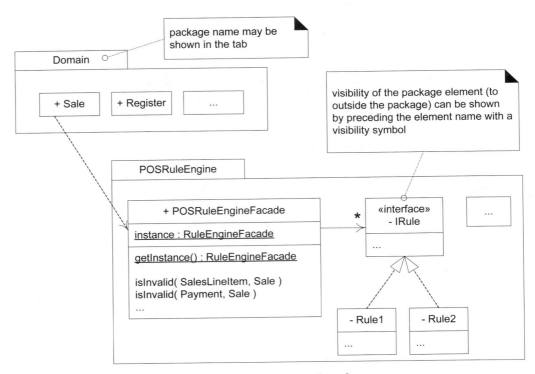

Figure 26.20 UML package diagram with a Facade.

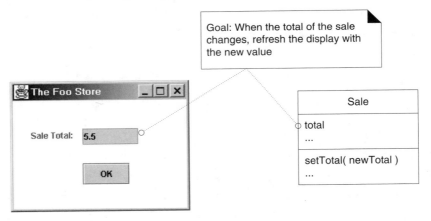

Figure 26.21 Updating the interface when the sale total changes.

Thus, Model-View Separation supports Protected Variations with respect to a changing user interface.

To solve this design problem, the Observer pattern can be used.

Name:	**Observer (Publish-Subscribe)**
Problem:	Different kinds of subscriber objects are interested in the state changes or events of a publisher object, and want to react in their own unique way when the publisher generates an event. Moreover, the publisher wants to maintain low coupling to the subscribers. What to do?
Solution: (advice)	Define a "subscriber" or "listener" interface. Subscribers implement this interface. The publisher can dynamically register subscribers who are interested in an event and notify them when an event occurs.

An example solution is described in detail in Figure 26.22.

The major ideas and steps in this example:

1. An interface is defined; in this case, *PropertyListener* with the operation *onPropertyEvent*.

2. Define the window to implement the interface.

    ○ *SaleFrame1* will implement the method *onPropertyEvent*.

3. When the *SaleFrame1* window is initialized, pass it the *Sale* instance from which it is displaying the total.

4. The *SaleFrame1* window registers or *subscribes* to the *Sale* instance for notification of "property events," via the *addPropertyListener* message. That is, when a property (such as total) changes, the window wants to be notified.

5. Note that the *Sale* does not know about *SaleFrame1* objects; rather, it only knows about objects that implement the *PropertyListener* interface. This lowers the coupling of the *Sale* to the window—the coupling is only to an interface, not to a GUI class.

6. The *Sale* instance is thus a *publisher* of "property events." When the total changes, it iterates across all subscribing *PropertyListeners*, notifying each.

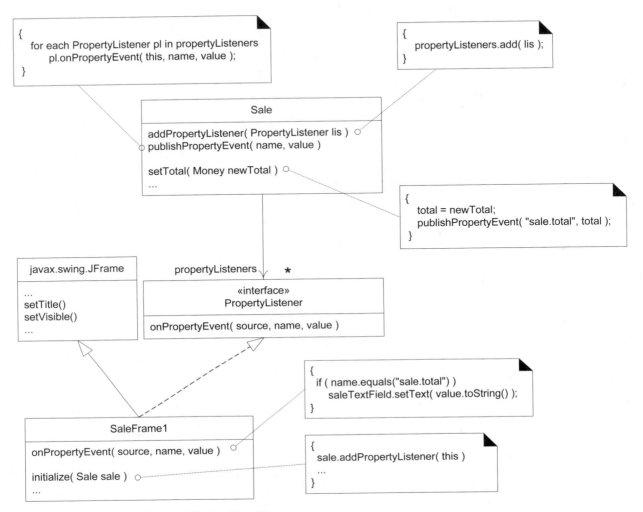

Figure 26.22 The Observer pattern.

The *SaleFrame1* object is the observer/subscriber/listener. In Figure 26.23, it *subscribes* to interest in property events of the *Sale*, which is a *publisher* of property events. The *Sale* adds the object to its list of *PropertyListener* subscribers. Note that the *Sale* does not know about the *SaleFrame1* as a *SaleFrame1* object, but only as a *PropertyListener* object; this lowers the coupling from the model up to the view layer.

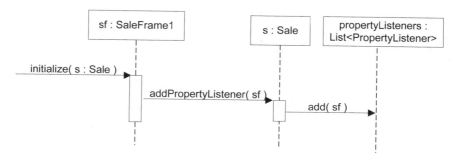

Figure 26.23 The observer *SaleFrame1* subscribes to the publisher *Sale*.

As illustrated in Figure 26.24, when the Sale total changes, it iterates across all its registered subscribers, and "publishes an event" by sending the *onPropertyEvent* message to each.

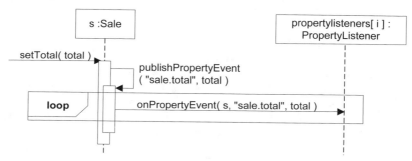

Figure 26.24 The Sale publishes a property event to all its subscribers.

Applying UML: Note the approach to handing polymorphic messages in an interaction diagram, in Figure 26.24. The *onPropertyEvent* message is polymorphic; the specific cases of polymorphic implementation will be shown in other diagrams, as in Figure 26.25.

SaleFrame1, which implements the *PropertyListener* interface, thus implements an *onPropertyEvent* method. When the *SaleFrame1* receives the message, it sends a message to its *JTextField* GUI widget object to refresh with the new sale total. See Figure 26.25.

In this pattern, there is still some coupling from the model object (the *Sale*) to the view object (the *SaleFrame1*). But it is a loose coupling to an interface independent of the presentation layer—the *PropertyListener* interface. And the design does not require any subscriber objects to actually be registered with the publisher (no objects have to be listening). That is, the list of registered *PropertyListeners* in the *Sale* can be empty. In summary, coupling to a generic interface of objects that do not need to be present, and which can be dynamically added (or removed), supports low coupling. Therefore, Protected Variations with respect to a changing user interface has been achieved through the use of an interface and polymorphism.

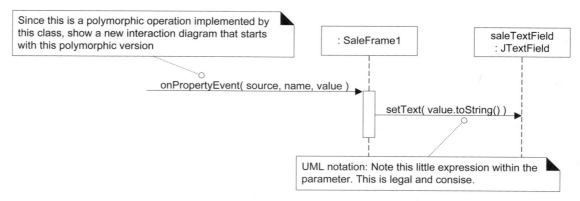

Figure 26.25 The subscriber SaleFrame1 receives notification of a published event.

Why Is It Called Observer, Publish-Subscribe, or Delegation Event Model?

Originally, this idiom was called publish-subscribe, and it is still widely known by that name. One object "publishes events," such as the *Sale* publishing the "property event" when the total changes. No object may be interested in this event, in which case, the *Sale* has no registered subscribers. But objects that are interested, "subscribe" or register to interest in an event by asking the publishing to notify them. This was done with the *Sale.addPropertyListener* message. When the event happens, the registered subscribers are notified by a message.

It has been called Observer because the listener or subscriber is observing the event; that term was popularized in Smalltalk in the early 1980s.

It has also been called the Delegation Event Model (in Java) because the publisher delegates handling of events to "listeners" (subscribers; see Figure 26.26).

Observer Is Not Only for Connecting UIs and Model Objects

The previous example illustrated connecting a non-UI object to a UI object with Observer. However, other uses are common.

The most prevalent use of this pattern is for GUI widget event handling, in both Java technologies (AWT and Swing) and in Microsoft's .NET. Each widget is a publisher of GUI-related events, and other objects can subscribe to interest in these. For example, a Swing *JButton* publishes an "action event" when it is pressed. Another object will register with the button so that when it is pressed, the object is sent a message and can take some action.

As another example, Figure 26.27 illustrates an *AlarmClock,* which is a publisher of alarm events and various subscribers. This example is illustrative in that it emphasizes that many classes can implement the *AlarmListener* interface, many objects can simultaneously be registered listeners, and all can react to the "alarm event" in their own unique way.

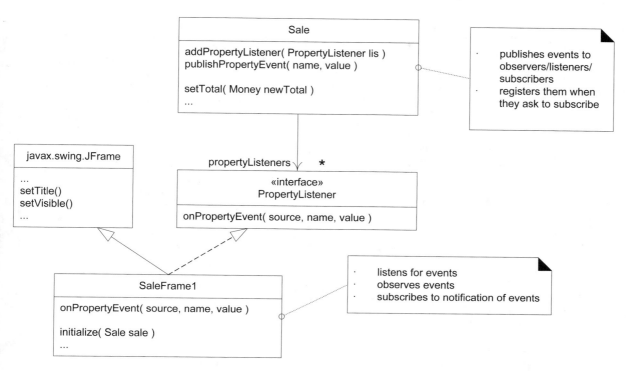

Figure 26.26 Who is the observer, listener, subscriber, and publisher?

One Publisher Can Have Many Subscribers for an Event

As suggested in Figure 26.27, one publisher instance could have from zero to many registered subscribers. For example, one instance of an *AlarmClock* could have three registered *AlarmWindows*, four *Beepers*, and one *ReliabilityWatch-Dog*. When an alarm event happens, all eight of these *AlarmListeners* are notified via an *onAlarmEvent*.

Implementation

Events

In both the Java and C# .NET implementations of Observer, an "event" is communicated via a regular message, such as *onPropertyEvent*. Moreover, in both cases, the event is more formally defined as a class, and filled with appropriate event data. The event is then passed as a parameter in the event message.

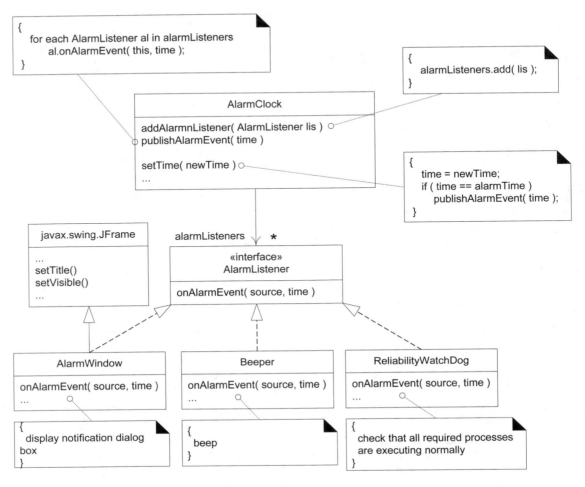

Figure 26.27 Observer applied to alarm events, with different subscribers.

For example:

```java
class PropertyEvent extends Event
{
    private Object sourceOfEvent;
    private String propertyName;
    private Object oldValue;
    private Object newValue;
    //...
}

//...

class Sale
{
    private void publishPropertyEvent(
        String name, Object old, Object new )
        {
```

```
    PropertyEvent evt =
     new PropertyEvent( this, "sale.total", old, new);

    for each AlarmListener al in alarmListeners
     al.onPropertyEvent( evt );
  }

  //...
}
```

Java

When the JDK 1.0 was released in January 1996, it contained a weak publish-subscribe implementation based on a class and interface called *Observable* and *Observer*, respectively. This was essentially copied without improvement from an early 1980s approach to publish-subscribe implemented in Smalltalk.

Therefore, in late 1996, as part of the JDK 1.1 effort, the Observable-Observer design was effectively replaced by the more robust Java Delegation Event Model (DEM) version of publish-subscribe, although the original design was kept for backward-compatibility (but in general to be avoided).

The designs that have been described in this chapter are consistent with the DEM, but slightly simplified to emphasize the core ideas.

Summary

Observer provides a way to loosely couple objects in terms of communication. Publishers know about subscribers only through an interface, and subscribers can register (or de-register) dynamically with the publisher.

Related Patterns   Observer is based on Polymorphism, and provides Protected Variations in terms of protecting the publisher from knowing the specific class of object, and number of objects, that it communicates with when the publisher generates an event.

26.11 Conclusion

The main lesson to draw from this exposition is that objects can be designed and responsibilities assigned with the support of patterns. These provide an explainable set of idioms by which well-designed object-oriented systems can be built.

26.12 Recommended Resources

Design Patterns by Gamma, Helm, Johnson, and Vlissides is the seminal patterns text, and essential reading for all object designers.

Each year there is a "Pattern Languages of Programs" (PLOP) conference, from which is published an annual compendium of patterns, in the series *Pattern Languages of Program Design*, volumes 1, 2, and so forth. The entire series is recommended.

Pattern-Oriented Software Architecture, volumes 1 and 2, furthered the discussion of patterns to larger-scale architectural concerns. Volume 1 presented a taxonomy of patterns.

There are hundreds of published patterns. *The Pattern Almanac* by Rising summarizes a respectable percentage of them.

PART 5   ELABORATION ITERATION 3 — INTERMEDIATE TOPICS

ITERATION 3—INTERMEDIATE TOPICS

Objectives

- Define the requirements for iteration-3.

Introduction

Inception and iteration-1 explored many basic OOA/D modeling basics. Iteration-2 narrowly emphasized object design. This third iteration takes a broader view again, exploring a variety of analysis and design topics, including:

- more GoF design pattern, and their application to the design of frameworks—in particular, a persistence framework

- architectural analysis; documenting architecture with the N+1 view model

- process modeling with UML activity diagrams

- generalization and specialization

- the design of packages

What's Next?

Having concluded iteration-2, this chapter presents iteration-3 requirements. The next briefly explores modeling processes with UML activity diagrams.

GRASP: More Objects with Responsibilities	Applying GoF Design Patterns	Iteration-3 Requirements	UML Activity Diagrams	UML State Machine Diagrams

27.1 NextGen POS

Requirements in iteration-3 include:

- Provide failover to local services when the remote services cannot be accessed. For example, if the remote product database can't be accessed, use a local version with cached data.

- Provide support for POS device handling, such as the cash drawer and coin dispenser.

- Handle credit payment authorization.

- Support for persistent objects.

27.2 Monopoly

Requirements in iteration-3 include:

- Again, implement a basic, key scenario of the *Play Monopoly Game* use case: players moving around the squares of the board. And as before, run the game as a simulation requiring no user input, other than the number of players. However, in iteration-3 more of the complete set of rules apply. These are described in the following points.

- There are now Lots, Railroads, and Utility squares. When a player lands on a Lot, Railroad or Utility square, the following logic applies…

- If the Lot, Railroad or Utility square is not owned, the player who landed on the square may buy it. If they buy it, the price of the Lot, Railroad or Utility square is deducted from the player's money and the player becomes its owner.

  - The price is set when the game starts, but is arbitrary—for example, the official Monopoly prices may be used.

- If the Lot, Railroad or Utility square is owned by the player that landed on it, nothing happens.

- If the Lot, Railroad or Utility square is owner by a player other than the player that landed on it, the player that landed on the square must pay its owner rent. The rent calculations are:

  - Lot rent is (index position) dollars; e.g., if position 5, then $5.

  - Railroad rent is 25 dollars times the number of Railroads owned by the owner; e.g., if own 3 Railroads, then $75.

  - Utilities rent is 4 times the number shown on the dice when the player lands on the square (do not roll again)

UML Activity Diagrams and Modeling

If it wasn't backed-up, then it wasn't important.

—The Sysadmin Motto

Objectives

- Introduce UML activity diagram notation, with examples, and various modeling applications.

Introduction

A UML activity diagram shows sequential and parallel activities in a process. They are useful for modeling business processes, workflows, data flows, and complex algorithms.

What's Next?

Having defined iteration-3 requirements, this chapter introduces process modeling with UML activity diagrams. The next summarizes state machine modeling.

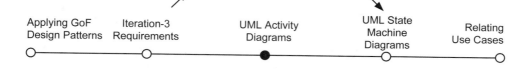

| Applying GoF Design Patterns | Iteration-3 Requirements | UML Activity Diagrams | UML State Machine Diagrams | Relating Use Cases |

28.1 Example

Basic UML **activity diagram** notation is shown in Figure 28.1, illustrating an **action**, **partition**, **fork**, **join**, and **object node**. In essence, this diagram shows a sequence of actions, some of which may be parallel. Most of the notation is self-explanatory; two subtle points:

- once an action is finished, there is an automatic outgoing transition
- the diagram can show both *control* flow and *data* flow

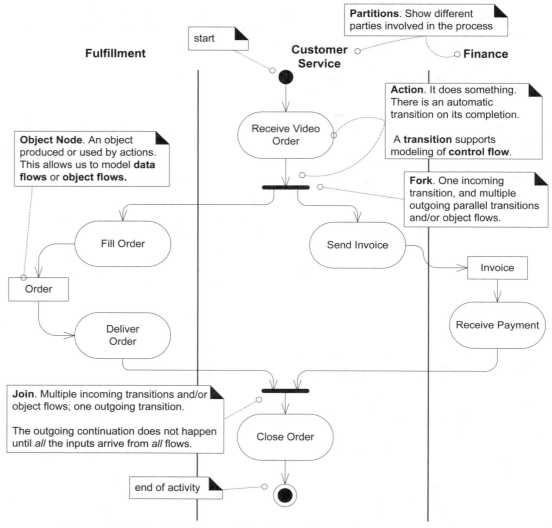

Figure 28.1 Basic UML activity diagram notation.

28.2   How to Apply Activity Diagrams?

A UML **activity diagram** offers rich notation to show a sequence of activities, including parallel activities. It may be applied to any perspective or purpose, but is popular for visualizing business workflows and processes, and use cases.

Business Process Modeling

One of my clients is in the express parcel shipping business. The process of shipping a parcel is *very* non-trivial; there are many parties involved (customer, driver, …) and many steps. Although this process can be captured in text (in use case text), in this case activity diagrams are a great example of pictures being worth a thousand words. My client uses activity diagrams to understand their current complex business processes by visualizing them. The partitions are useful to see the multiple parties and parallel actions involved in the shipping process, and the object nodes illustrate what's moving around. After modeling their current process they visually explore changes and optimizations. See Figure 28.1 for a simple example of applying UML activity diagrams to business process modeling. To show the process model for my shipping client would fill an entire wall!

Data Flow Modeling

Starting in the 1970s, **data flow diagrams** (DFD) became a popular way to visualize the major steps and data involved in software system processes. This is not the same as business process modeling; rather, DFDs were usually used to show data flows in a computer system, although they could in theory be applied to business process modeling. DFDs were useful to document the major data flows or to explore a new high-level design in terms of data flow. See Figure 28.2 for an example DFD in the classic Gane-Sarson notation. Observe that the process steps are numbered, to indicate order.

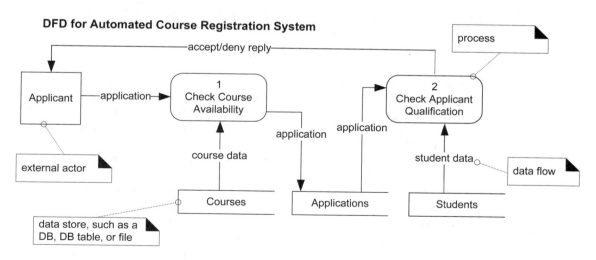

Figure 28.2 Classic DFD in Gane-Sarson notation.

The information modeled in a DFD is useful, both for documentation and discovery, but the UML does not include DFD notation. Fortunately, UML activity diagrams can satisfy the same goals—they can be used for data flow modeling, replacing traditional DFD notation. Figure 28.3 illustrates the same information as the DFD in Figure 28.2, but using a UML activity diagram. Notice that in addition to *object nodes* being useful to show data flow, the UML **datastore node** is applicable.

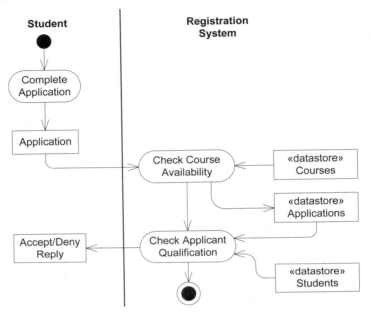

Figure 28.3 Applying activity diagram notation to show a data flow model.

Concurrent Programming and Parallel Algorithm Modeling

Although the details are beyond this introduction, parallel algorithms in concurrent programming problems involve multiple partitions, and fork and join behavior. For example, such algorithms are used in 3D simulations with finite element or finite difference modeling, and are applied to oil reservoir modeling, materials stress analysis, and weather modeling. The overall physical space is subdivided into large blocks, and many parallel threads (or processes) execute, one for each sub-block. In these cases the UML activity diagram partitions can be used to represent different operating system threads or processes. The object nodes can be used to model the shared objects and data. And of course, forking can be used to model the creation and parallel execution of multiple threads or processes, one per partition.

28.3 More UML Activity Diagram Notation

How to show that an activity is expanded in another activity diagram? Figure 28.4 and Figure 28.5 illustrate, using the **rake** symbol.

How to show conditional branches? See the **decision** symbol used in Figure 28.5. The related **merge** symbol shows how flows can come back together.

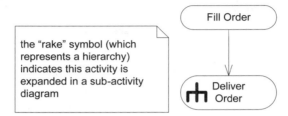

Figure 28.4 An activity will be expanded in another diagram.

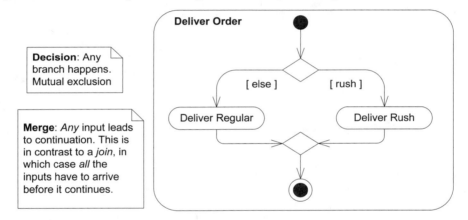

Figure 28.5 The expansion of an activity.

Signals are shown in Figure 28.6. They are useful, for example, when you need to model events such as time triggering an action, or a cancellation request.

There's a *lot* more UML activity notation available. This short introduction merely highlights some of the most common elements.

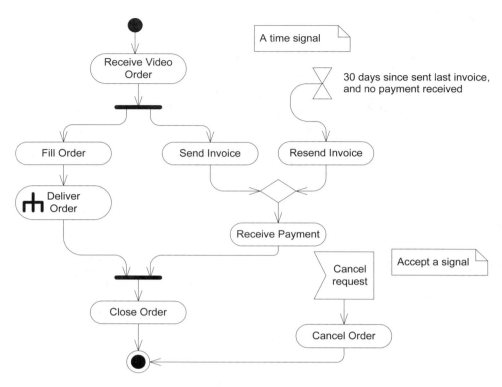

Figure 28.6 Signals.

28.4   Guidelines

A few guidelines have emerged in activity modeling; these include:

- This technique proves most valuable for very complex processes, usually involving many parties. Use-case text suffices for simple processes.

- If modeling a business process, take advantage of the "rake" notation and sub-activity diagrams. On the first overview "level 0" diagram, keep all the actions at a very high level of abstraction, so that the diagram is short and sweet. Expand the details in sub-diagrams at the "level 1" level, and perhaps even more at the "level 2" level, and so forth.

- Related to the above, strive to make the level of abstraction of action nodes roughly equal within a diagram. As a poor counter-example, suppose in a "level 0" diagram there is an action node labeled "Deliver Order." And, a second action node "Calculate Tax." Those are very different levels of abstraction.

28.5   Example: NextGen Activity Diagram

The partial model in Figure 28.7 illustrates applying the UML to the *Process Sale* use case process. I've shown this case-study example for completeness, but in reality would not bother to create this, as the use case text and relative simplicity of the process make it of marginal value.

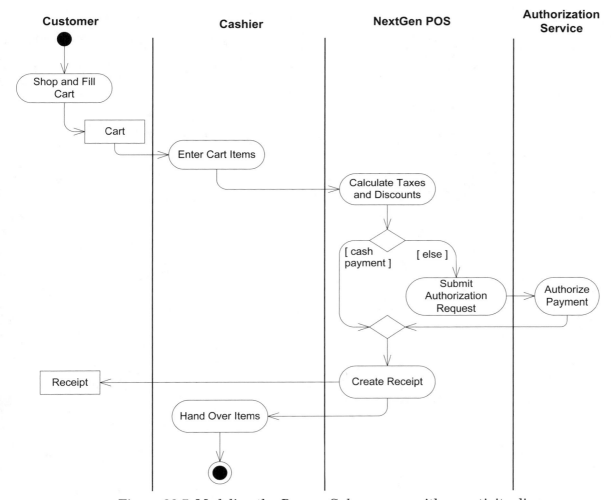

Figure 28.7 Modeling the *Process Sale* use case with an activity diagram.

28.6   Process: Activity Diagrams in the UP

One of the UP disciplines is **Business Modeling**; its purpose is to understand and communicate "the structure and the dynamics of the organization in which a system is to be deployed" [RUP]. A key artifact of the Business Modeling discipline is the **Business Object Model** (a superset of the UP Domain Model), which essentially visualizes how a business works, using UML class, sequence, and activity diagrams. Thus, activity diagrams are especially applicable within the Business Modeling discipline of the UP.

28.7 Background

A plethora of process modeling and data flow diagramming languages have been around since forever. Each year, UML activity diagrams become more popular as a common standard, though there is still significant variation.

The semantics of activity diagrams are loosely based on **Petri nets**, an important computational theory in computer science. The metaphor—or actualization—of Petri nets is that there are **tokens** flowing through the activity graph. For example, when a token arrives at an action node, it executes. When all the required input tokens arrive at a join, an output token is created.

UML State Machine Diagrams and Modeling

No, no, you're not thinking, you're just being logical.

—*Niels Bohr*

Objectives

- Introduce UML state machine diagram notation, with examples, and various modeling applications.

Introduction

As with activity diagrams, UML state diagrams show a dynamic view. The UML includes notation to illustrate the events and states of things—transactions, use cases, people, and so forth.

The most important notational features are shown, but there are many rare elements not covered in this introduction.

What's Next?   Having introduced activity diagrams, this chapter summarizes state machine modeling. The next explores how to relate use cases; for example, when one use case refers to another use case.

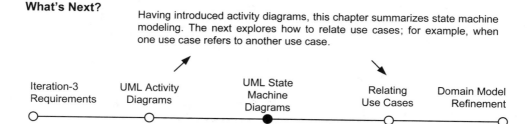

| Iteration-3 Requirements | UML Activity Diagrams | UML State Machine Diagrams | Relating Use Cases | Domain Model Refinement |

29.1   Example

A UML **state machine diagram**, as shown in Figure 29.1, illustrates the interesting events and states of an object, and the behavior of an object in reaction to an event. Transitions are shown as arrows, labeled with their event. States are shown in rounded rectangles. It is common to include an initial pseudo-state, which automatically transitions to another state when the instance is created.

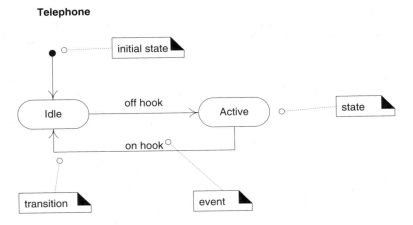

Figure 29.1 State machine diagram for a telephone.

A state machine diagram shows the lifecycle of an object: what events it experiences, its transitions, and the states it is in between these events. It need not illustrate every possible event; if an event arises that is not represented in the diagram, the event is ignored as far as the state machine diagram is concerned. Therefore, we can create a state machine diagram that describes the lifecycle of an object at arbitrarily simple or complex levels of detail, depending on our needs.

29.2   Definitions: Events, States, and Transitions

An **event** is a significant or noteworthy occurrence. For example:

■   A telephone receiver is taken off the hook.

A **state** is the condition of an object at a moment in time—the time between events. For example:

- A telephone is in the state of being "idle" after the receiver is placed on the hook and until it is taken off the hook.

A **transition** is a relationship between two states that indicates that when an event occurs, the object moves from the prior state to the subsequent state. For example:

- When the event "off hook" occurs, transition the telephone from the "idle" to "active" state.

29.3   How to Apply State Machine Diagrams?

State-Independent and State-Dependent Objects

If an object always responds the same way to an event, then it is considered **state-independent** (or modeless) with respect to that event. For example, if an object receives a message, and the responding method always does the same thing. The object is state-independent with respect to that message. If, for all events of interest, an object always reacts the same way, it is a **state-independent object**. By contrast, **state-dependent objects** react differently to events depending on their state or mode.

Guideline

Consider state machines for state-dependent objects with complex behavior, not for state-independent objects.

For example, a telephone is very state-dependent. The phone's reaction to pushing a particular button (generating an event) depends on the current mode of the phone—off hook, engaged, in a configuration subsystem, and so forth.

It's for these kind of complex state-dependent problems that a state machine diagram may add value to either understand or document something.

Guideline

In general, business information systems have few complex state-dependent classes. It is seldom helpful to apply state machine modeling.

By contrast, process control, device control, protocol handlers, and telecommunication domains often have many state-dependent objects. If you work in these domains, definitely know and consider state machine modeling.

Modeling State-dependent Objects

Broadly, state machines are applied in two ways:

1. To model the behavior of a complex reactive object in response to events.

2. To model legal sequences of operations—protocol or language specifications.

   ○ This approach may be considered a specialization of #1, if the "object" is a language, protocol, or process. A formal grammar for a context-free language is a kind of state machine.

The following is a list of common objects which are often state-dependent, and for which it may be useful to create a state machine diagram:

Complex Reactive Objects

- **Physical Devices** controlled by software

  ○ Phone, car, microwave oven: They have complex and rich reactions to events, and the reaction depends upon their current mode.

- **Transactions** and related **Business Objects**

  ○ How does a business object (a sale, order, payment) react to an event? For example, what should happen to an *Order* if a *cancel* event occurs? And understanding all the events and states that a *Package* can go through in the shipping business can help with design, validation, and process improvement.

- **Role Mutators**—These are objects that change their role.

  ○ A *Person* changing roles from being a civilian to a veteran. Each role is represented by a state.

Protocols and Legal Sequences

- **Communication Protocols**

  ○ TCP, and new protocols, can be easily and clearly understood with a state machine diagram. The diagram illustrates when operations are legal. For example, a TCP "close" request should be ignored if the protocol handler is already in the "closed" state.

- **UI Page/Window Flow or Navigation**—When doing UI modeling, it can be useful to understand the legal sequence between Web pages or windows; this is often complex. A state machine is a great tool to model UI navigation.

- **UI Flow Controllers or Sessions**—This is related to UI navigation modeling, but specifically focused on the server-side object that controls page flow. These are usually server-side objects representing an ongoing session or conversations with a client. For example, a Web application that remembers the state of the session with a Web client and controls the transitions to new Web pages, or the modified display of the current Web page, based upon the state of the session and the next operation that is received.

- **Use Case System Operations**
  - ○ Do you recall the system operations for *Process Sale*: *makeNewSale*, *enterItem*, and so forth? These should arrive in a legal order; for example, *endSale* should only come after one or more *enterItem* operations. Usually, the order is trivially obvious, but if complex, a state machine can model this, treating the use case itself as an object.

- **Individual UI Window Event Handling**
  - ○ Understanding the events and legal sequences for one window or form. For example, the Edit-Paste action is only valid if there is something in the "clipboard" to paste.

29.4   More UML State Machine Diagram Notation

Transition Actions and Guards

A transition can cause an action to fire. In a software implementation, this may represent the invocation of a method of the class of the state machine diagram.

A transition may also have a conditional guard—or boolean test. The transition only occurs if the test passes. See Figure 29.2.

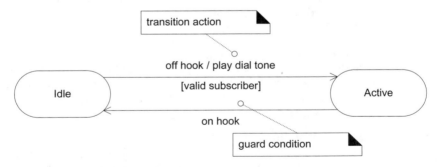

Figure 29.2 Transition action and guard notation.

Nested States

A state allows nesting to contain substates; a substate inherits the transitions of its superstate (the enclosing state). See Figure 29.3. This was a key contribution of the Harel statechart approach that the UML is based on, as it leads to succinct state machine diagrams. Substates may be graphically shown by nesting them in a superstate box.

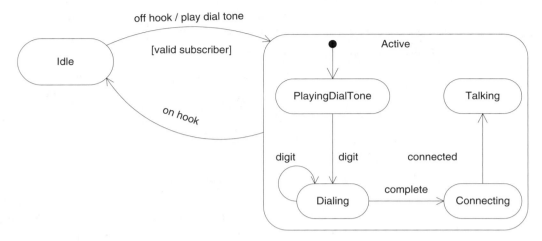

Figure 29.3 Nested states.

For example, when a transition to the *Active* state occurs, creation and transition into the *PlayingDialTone* substate occurs. No matter what substate the object is in, if the *on hook* event related to the *Active* superstate occurs, a transition to the *Idle* state occurs.

29.5 Example: UI Navigation Modeling with State Machines

Some UI applications, especially Web UI applications, have complex page flows. State machines are a great way to document that, for understanding, and a great way to model page flows, during creative design.

A common technique in UI agile modeling and UI prototyping is to model a UI with large paper sheets on walls. Each sheet represents a Web page. Post-it notes are place on the sheets to represent elements; perhaps yellow is information and pink is a control, such as a button. Each sheet is labeled, e.g., "Help Page," "Product Page," and so on.

In addition to modeling the page content with this "low tech, high touch" method, it is useful to model the flow between these pages. Therefore, on a whiteboard adjacent to the wall of Web pages, I'll sketch a UML state machine diagram. The states represent the pages and the events represent the events that cause transfer from one page to another, such as a button click. See Figure 29.4 for an example of this UI **navigation model**. Of course, this small example doesn't do justice to the usefulness of the practice; it's value becomes evident for large, complex page structures.

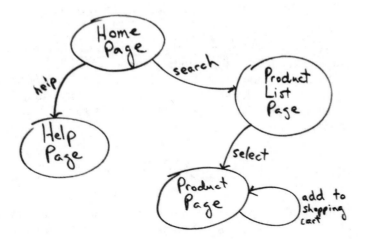

Figure 29.4 Applying a state machine to Web page navigation modeling.

9.6 Example: NextGen Use Case State Machine Diagram

There are no really interesting complex reactive objects in the case studies, so I'll illustrate a state machine diagram to show legal sequencing of use case operation. See Figure 29.5 for its application to the *Process Sale* use case.

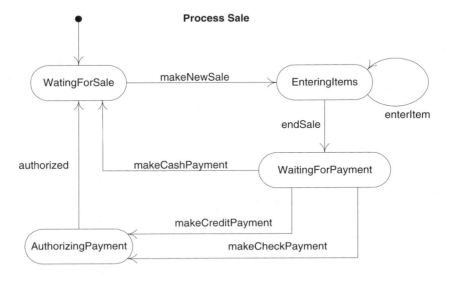

Figure 29.5 A sample state machine for legal sequence of use case operations.

29.7 Process: State Machine Diagrams in the UP

There is not one model in the UP called the "state model." Rather, any element in any model (Design Model, Domain Model, Business Object Model, and so forth) may have a state machine to better understand or communicate its dynamic behavior in response to events. For example, a state machine associated with the *Sale* design class of the Design Model is itself part of the Design Model.

29.8 Recommended Resources

The application of state models to OOA/D is well-covered in *Designing Object Systems* by Cook and Daniels. *Real Time UML* by Douglass also provides an excellent discussion of state modeling; the content emphasizes real-time systems, but is broadly applicable.

RELATING USE CASES

*Why do programmers get Halloween and
Christmas mixed up? Because OCT(31) = DEC(25)*

Objectives

- Relate use cases with *include* and *extend* associations, in both text and diagram formats.

Introduction

Use cases can be related to each other. For example, a subfunction use case such as *Handle Credit Payment* may be part of several regular use cases, such as *Process Sale* and *Process Rental*. Organizing use cases into relationships has no impact on the behavior or requirements of the system. Rather, it is simply an organization mechanism to (ideally) improve communication and comprehension of the use cases, reduce duplication of text, and improve management of the use case documents.

What's Next?   Having introduced state diagrams, this chapter examines use case relationships. The next goes more deeply into refining the domain model for iteration-3, applying new OOA modeling tips, such as association classes.

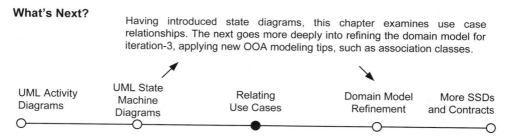

| UML Activity Diagrams | UML State Machine Diagrams | Relating Use Cases | Domain Model Refinement | More SSDs and Contracts |

Guideline: Avoid Agonizing Over Use Case Relationships

In some organizations working with use cases, way too much unproductive time is spent debating how to relate use cases in a use case diagram, rather than the important use case work: ***writing text***. It actually a reflects a deeper problem in analysis-oriented work on software projects: Too much time wasted on low-value analysis and modeling. It's part of the larger problem of waterfall thinking rather than iterative and evolutionary thinking; if you think you have to "get it right" at the start, everything becomes bogged down in analysis paralysis.

Consequently, although this chapter discusses relating use cases, the subject and its effort should be put in perspective: It has some value, but the important work is writing use case text. Specifying the requirements is done by writing text, not by organizing use cases—an optional step to possibly improve their comprehension or reduce duplication. If a team starts off use-case modeling by spending hours (or worse, days) discussing a use case diagram and use case relationships ("Should that be an *include* or an *extend* relationship? Should we *specialize* this use case?"), rather than quickly focusing on writing the key use case text, relative effort was misplaced.

Plus, in the UP and other iterative methods, the organization of use cases into relationships can iteratively evolve in small steps over the elaboration phase; it is not helpful to attempt a waterfall-like effort of fully defining and refining a complete use case diagram and set of relationships in one step near the start of a project.

30.1 The include Relationship

This is the most common and important relationship.

It is common to have some partial behavior that is common across several use cases. For example, the description of paying by credit occurs in several use cases, including *Process Sale, Process Rental, Contribute to Lay-away Plan*, and so forth. Rather than duplicate this text, it is desirable to separate it into its own subfunction use case, and indicate its inclusion. This is simply refactoring and linking text to avoid duplication.[1]

For example:

UC1: Process Sale

...
Main Success Scenario:
1. Customer arrives at a POS checkout with goods and/or services to purchase.
...
7. Customer pays and System handles payment.
...

Extensions:
7b. Paying by credit: Include _Handle Credit Payment_.
7c. Paying by check: Include _Handle Check Payment_.
...

---

1. It is helpful if the links are implemented with navigable hyperlinks as well.

UC7: Process Rental

> ...
> **Extensions:**
> 6b. Paying by credit: Include *Handle Credit Payment*.
> ...

UC12: Handle Credit Payment

> ...
> **Level:** Subfunction
> **Main Success Scenario:**
> 1. Customer enters their credit account information.
> 2. System sends payment authorization request to an external Payment Authorization Service System, and requests payment approval.
>
> 3. System receives payment approval and signals approval to Cashier.
> 4. ...
> **Extensions:**
> 2a. System detects failure to collaborate with external system:
>   1. System signals error to Cashier.
>   2. Cashier asks Customer for alternate payment.
> ...

This is the **include** relationship.

A slightly shorter (and thus perhaps preferred) notation to indicate an included use case is simply to underline it or highlight it in some fashion. For example:

UC1: Process Sale

> ...
> **Extensions:**
> 7b. Paying by credit: *Handle Credit Payment*.
> 7c. Paying by check: *Handle Check Payment*.
> ...

Notice that the *Handle Credit Payment* subfunction use case was originally in the *Extensions* section of the *Process Sale* use case, but was factored out to avoid duplication. Also note that the same *Main Success* and *Extensions* structures are used in the subfunction use case as in the regular elementary business process use cases such as *Process Sale*.

A simple, practical guideline of when to use the include relationship is offered by Fowler [Fowler03]:

> Use *include* when you are repeating yourself in two or more separate use cases and you want to avoid repetition.

Another motivation is simply to decompose an overwhelmingly long use case into subunits to improve comprehension.

Using include with Asynchronous Event Handling

Yet another use of the include relationship is to describe the handling of an asynchronous event, such as when a user is able to, at any time, select or branch to a particular window, function, or Web page, or within a range of steps.

In fact, the use case notation to support this asynchronous branching was already explored in the introduction to use cases in Chapter 6, but at that time the addition of calling out to an included sub-use case was not discussed.

The basic notation is to use the $a*$, $b*$, ... style labels in the Extensions section. Recall that these imply an extension or event that can happen at any time. A minor variation is a range label, such as *3-9*, to be used when the asynchronous event can occur within a relatively large range of the use case steps, but not all.

UC1: Process FooBars

> ...
> **Main Success Scenario:**
> 1. ...
> **Extensions:**
> a*. At any time, Customer selects to edit personal information: *Edit Personal Information*.
> b*. At any time, Customer selects printing help: *Present Printing Help*.
> 2-11. Customer cancels: *Cancel Transaction Confirmation*.
> ...

Summary

The include relationship can be used for most use case relationship problems. To summarize:

Factor out subfunction use cases and use the *include* relationship when:

- They are duplicated in other use cases.

- A use case is *very* complex and long, and separating it into subunits aids comprehension.

As will be explained, there are other relationships: extend and generalization. But Cockburn, an expert use-case modeler, advises to prefer the include relationship over extend or generalization:

> As a first rule of thumb, always use the *include* relationship between use cases. People who follow this rule report they and their readers have less confusion with their writing than people who mix *include* with *extend* and *generalizes* [Cockburn01].

30.2 Terminology: Concrete, Abstract, Base, and Addition Use Cases

A **concrete use case** is initiated by an actor and performs the entire behavior desired by the actor [RUP]. These are the elementary business process use cases. For example, *Process Sale* is a concrete use case. By contrast, an **abstract use case** is never instantiated by itself; it is a subfunction use case that is part of another use case. *Handle Credit Payment* is abstract; it doesn't stand on its own, but is always part of another story, such as *Process Sale*.

A use case that includes another use case, or that is extended or specialized by another use case is called a **base use case**. *Process Sale* is a base use case with respect to the included *Handle Credit Payment* subfunction use case. On the other hand, the use case that is an inclusion, extension, or specialization is called an **addition use case**. *Handle Credit Payment* is the addition use case in the include relationship to *Process Sale*. Addition use cases are usually abstract. Base use cases are usually concrete.

30.3 The extend Relationship

Suppose a use case's text should not be modified (at least not significantly) for some reason. Perhaps continually modifying the use case with myriad new extensions and conditional steps is a maintenance headache, or the use case has been baselined as a stable artifact, and can't be touched. How to append to the use case without modifying its original text?

The **extend** relationship provides an answer. The idea is to create an extending or addition use case, and within it, describe where and under what condition it extends the behavior of some base use case. For example:

UC1: Process Sale (the base use case)

> ...
> **Extension Points:** *VIP Customer*, step 1. *Payment*, step 7.
> **Main Success Scenario:**
> 1. Customer arrives at a POS checkout with goods and/or services to purchase.
> ...
> 7. Customer pays and System handles payment.
> ...

UC15: Handle Gift Certificate Payment (the extending use case)

> ...
> **Trigger:** Customer wants to pay with gift certificate.
> **Extension Points:** Payment in Process Sale.
> **Level:** Subfunction
> **Main Success Scenario:**
> 1. Customer gives gift certificate to Cashier.

> 2. Cashier enters gift certificate ID.
>
> ...

This is an example of an **extend** relationship. Note the use of an **extension point**, and that the extending use case is triggered by some condition. Extension points are labels in the base use case which the extending use case references as the point of extension, so that the step numbering of the base use case can change without affecting the extending use case—indirection yet again.

Sometimes, the extension point is simply "At any point in use case X." This is especially common in systems with many asynchronous events, such as a word processor ("do a spell check now," "do a thesaurus lookup now"), or reactive control systems. Note however, as described in the prior include relationship section, that include can also be used to describe asynchronous event handling. The extend alternative is an option when the base use case is closed to modification.

Note that a signature quality of the extend relationship is that the base use case (*Process Sale*) has no reference to the extending use case (*Handle Gift Certificate Payment*), and therefore, does not define or control the conditions under which the extensions trigger. *Process Sale* is complete and whole by itself, without knowing about the extending use case.

Observe that this *Handle Gift Certificate Payment* addition use case could alternatively have been referenced within *Process Sale* with an include relationship, as with *Handle Credit Payment*. That is often suitable. But this example was motivated by the constraint that the *Process Sale* use case was not to be modified, which is the situation in which to use extend rather than include.

Further, note that this gift certificate scenario could simply have been recorded by adding it as an extension in the *Extensions* section of *Process Sale*. This approach avoids both the include and extend relationships, and the creation of a separate subfunction use case.

> Indeed, just updating the *Extensions* section is usually the preferred solution, rather than creating complex use case relationships.

Some use case guidelines recommend using extending use cases and the extend relationship to model conditional or optional behavior inserted into the base use case. This is not inaccurate, but it misses the point that optional and conditional behavior can simply be recorded as text in the *Extensions* section of the base use case. The complication of using the extend relationship and more use cases is not motivated only by optional behavior.

What most practically motivates using the extend technique is when it is undesirable for some reason to modify the base use case.

30.4 The generalize Relationship

Discussion of the generalize relationship is outside the scope of this introduction. However, note that use case experts have been successfully doing use case work without this optional relationship, which adds another level of complexity to use cases, and there is not yet agreement by practitioners on the best-practice guidelines of how to get value from this idea. A common observation by use case consultants is that complications result and unproductive time is spent on the addition of many use case relationships.

30.5 Use Case Diagrams

Figure 30.1 illustrates the UML notation for the include relationship, which is the only one being used in the case study, following the advice of use-case experts to keep things simple and prefer the include relationship.

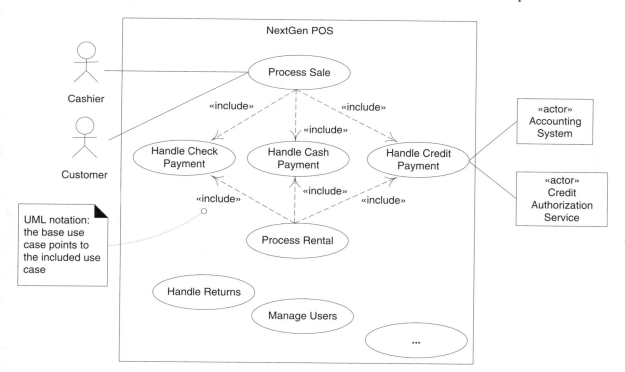

Figure 30.1 Use case include relationship in the Use-Case Model.

The extend relationship notation is illustrated in Figure 30.2.

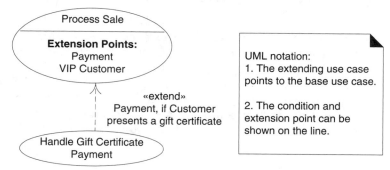

Figure 30.2 The extend relationship.

DOMAIN MODEL REFINEMENT

*Crude classifications and false generalizations
are the curse of the organized life.*

—A generalization by H.G. Wells

Objectives

- Refine the domain model with generalizations, specializations, association classes, time intervals, composition, and packages.

- Identify when showing a subclass is worthwhile.

Introduction

Generalization and specialization are fundamental concepts in domain modeling that support an economy of expression; further, conceptual class hierarchies are often the basis of inspiration for software class hierarchies that exploit inheritance and reduce duplication of code. Association classes capture information about an association itself. Time intervals capture the important concept that some business objects are valid for a limited time. And packages are a way to organize large domain models into smaller units. Most of these concepts are introduced in the context of the NextGen case study; a refined Monopoly domain model is shown starting on p. 532.

What's Next?

Having introduced state diagrams, this chapter examines use case relationships. The next goes more deeply into refining the domain model for iteration-3, applying new OOA modeling tips, such as association classes.

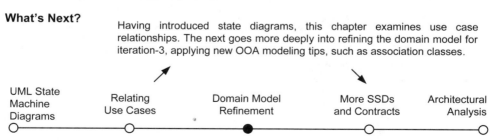

| UML State Machine Diagrams | Relating Use Cases | Domain Model Refinement | More SSDs and Contracts | Architectural Analysis |

31.1 New Concepts for the NextGen Domain Model

As in iteration-1, the Domain Model may be incrementally developed by considering the concepts in the requirements for this iteration. Techniques such as the *Concept Category List* and noun phrase identification will help. An effective approach to developing a robust and rich domain model is to study the work of other authors on this subject, such as [Fowler96].

Concepts Category List

Table 31.1 shows some noteworthy concepts being considered in this iteration.

Category	Examples
physical or tangible objects	*CreditCard, Check*
transactions	*CashPayment, CreditPayment, CheckPayment*
other computer or electro-mechanical systems external to our system	*CreditAuthorizationService, CheckAuthorizationService*
abstract noun concepts	
organizations	*CreditAuthorizationService, CheckAuthorizationService*
records of finance, work, contracts, legal matters	*AccountsReceivable*

Table 31.1 Category Concepts List

Noun Phrase Identification from the Use Cases

To reiterate, noun phrase identification cannot be mechanically applied to identify relevant concepts to include in the domain model. Judgement must be applied and suitable abstractions developed, since natural language is ambiguous and relevant concepts are not always explicit or clear in existing text. However, it is a practical technique in domain modeling since it is straightforward.

This iteration handles the scenarios of the *Process Sale* use case for credit and check payments. The following shows some noun phrase identification from these extensions:

Use Case UC1: Process Sale

...

Extensions:

7b. Paying by credit:
1. Customer enters their **credit account information**.
2. System sends **payment authorization request** to an external **Payment Authorization Service** System, and requests **payment approval**.
   2a. System detects failure to collaborate with external system:
      1. System signals error to Cashier.
      2. Cashier asks Customer for alternate payment.
3. System receives **payment approval** and signals approval to Cashier.
   3a. System receives **payment denial**:
      1. System signals denial to Cashier.
      2. Cashier asks Customer for alternate payment.
4. System records the **credit payment**, which includes the payment approval.
5. System presents credit payment signature input mechanism.
6. Cashier asks Customer for a credit payment signature. Customer enters signature.

7c. Paying by check:
1. The Customer writes a **check**, and gives it and their **driver's license** to the Cashier.
2. Cashier writes the driver's license number on the check, enters it, and requests **check payment authorization**.
3. Generates a **check payment request** and sends it to an external **Check Authorization Service**.
4. Receives a check payment approval and signals approval to Cashier.
5. System records the **check payment**, which includes the payment approval.

...

Authorization Service Transactions

The noun phrase identification reveals concepts such as *CreditPaymentRequest* and *CreditApprovalReply*. These may in fact be viewed as types of transactions with external services, and in general, it is useful to identify such transactions because activities and processes tend to revolve around them.

These transactions do not have to represent computer records or bits travelling over a line. They represent the abstraction of the transaction independent of its means of execution. For example, a credit payment request may be executed by people talking on the phone, by two computers sending records or messages to each other, and so on.

31.2   Generalization

The concepts *CashPayment*, *CreditPayment,* and *CheckPayment* are all very similar. In this situation, it is possible (and useful[1]) to organize them (as in Figure

---

1. Later in the chapter, we will investigate reasons to define class hierarchies.

31.1) into a **generalization-specialization class hierarchy** (or simply **class hierarchy**) in which the **superclass** *Payment* represents a more general concept, and the **subclasses** more specialized ones.

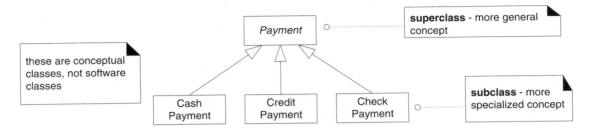

Figure 31.1 Generalization-specialization hierarchy.

Note that the discussion of classes in this chapter refers to *conceptual* classes, not software classes.

Generalization is the activity of identifying commonality among concepts and defining superclass (general concept) and subclass (specialized concept) relationships. It is a way to construct taxonomic classifications among concepts which are then illustrated in class hierarchies.

Identifying a superclass and subclasses is of value in a domain model because their presence allows us to understand concepts in more general, refined and abstract terms. It leads to economy of expression, improved comprehension and a reduction in repeated information. And although we are focusing now on the UP Domain Model and not the software Design Model, the later design and implementation of super- and subclass as software classes that use inheritance yields better software.

Thus:

Guideline

Identify domain superclasses and subclasses relevant to the current iteration, and illustrate them in the Domain Model.

UML—To review the generalization notation introduced in a prior chapter, in the UML the generalization relationship between elements is indicated with a large hollow triangle pointing to the more general element from the more specialized one (see Figure 31.2). Either a separate target or shared target arrow style may be used.

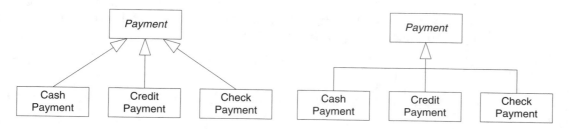

Figure 31.2 Class hierarchy with separate and shared arrow notations.

31.3 Defining Conceptual Superclasses and Subclasses

Since it is valuable to identify conceptual super- and subclasses, it is useful to clearly and precisely understand generalization, superclasses, and subclasses in terms of class definition and class sets.[2] This following sections explore these.

Generalization and Conceptual Class Definition

What is the relationship of a conceptual superclass to a subclass?

Definition

A conceptual superclass definition is more general or encompassing than a subclass definition.

For example, consider the superclass *Payment* and its subclasses (*CashPayment*, and so on). Assume the definition of *Payment* is that it represents the transaction of transferring money (not necessarily cash) for a purchase from one party to another, and that all payments have an amount of money transferred. The model corresponding to this is shown in Figure 31.3.

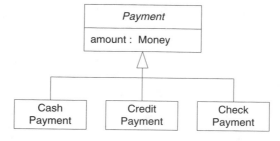

Figure 31.3 Payment class hierarchy.

---

2. That is, a class's intension and extension. This discussion was inspired by [MO95].

A *CreditPayment* is a transfer of money via a credit institution which needs to be authorized. My definition of *Payment* encompasses and is more general than my definition of *CreditPayment*.

Generalization and Class Sets

Conceptual subclasses and superclasses are related in terms of set membership.

Definition

All members of a conceptual subclass set are members of their superclass set.

For example, in terms of set membership, all instances of the set *CreditPayment* are also members of the set *Payment*. In a Venn diagram, this is shown as in Figure 31.4.

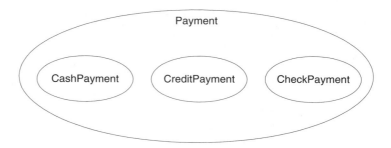

Figure 31.4 Venn diagram of set relationships.

Conceptual Subclass Definition Conformance

When a class hierarchy is created, statements about superclasses that apply to subclasses are made. For example, Figure 31.5 states that all *Payments* have an *amount* and are associated with a *Sale*.

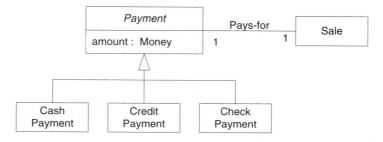

Figure 31.5 Subclass conformance.

All *Payment* subclasses must conform to having an amount and paying for a *Sale*. In general, this rule of conformance to a superclass definition is the *100% Rule*:

Guideline: 100% Rule

100% of the conceptual superclass's definition should be applicable to the subclass. The subclass must conform to 100% of the superclass's:

- attributes
- associations

Conceptual Subclass Set Conformance

A conceptual subclass should be a member of the set of the superclass. Thus, *CreditPayment* should be a member of the set of *Payments*.

Informally, this expresses the notion that the conceptual subclass *is a kind of* superclass. *CreditPayment is a kind of Payment*. More tersely, *is-a-kind-of* is called *is-a*.

This kind of conformance is the *Is-a Rule*:

Guideline: Is-a Rule

All the members of a subclass set must be members of their superclass set.

In natural language, this can usually be informally tested by forming the statement: *Subclass **is a** Superclass*.

For instance, the statement *CreditPayment is a Payment* makes sense, and conveys the notion of set membership conformance.

What Is a Correct Conceptual Subclass?

From the above discussion, apply the following tests[3] to define a correct subclass when constructing a domain model:

Guideline

A potential subclass should conform to the:

- 100% Rule (definition conformance)
- Is-a Rule (set membership conformance)

31.4   When to Define a Conceptual Subclass?

Rules to ensure that a subclass is correct have been examined (the Is-a and 100% rules). However, *when* should we even bother to define a subclass? First, a definition: A **conceptual class partition** is a division of a conceptual class into disjoint subclasses (or **types** in Odell's terminology) [MO95]. The question may be restated as: "When is it useful to show a conceptual class partition?"

For example, in the POS domain, *Customer* may be correctly partitioned (or subclassed) into *MaleCustomer* and *FemaleCustomer*. But is it relevant or useful to show this in our model (see Figure 31.6)? This partition is not useful for our domain; the next section explains why.

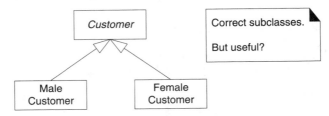

Figure 31.6 Legal conceptual class partition, but is it useful in our domain?

Motivations to Partition a Conceptual Class into Subclasses

The following are strong motivations to partition a class into subclasses:

Guideline

Create a conceptual subclass of a superclass when:

1. The subclass has additional attributes of interest.

2. The subclass has additional associations of interest.

3. The subclass concept is operated on, handled, reacted to, or manipulated differently than the superclass or other subclasses, in ways that are of interest.

4. The subclass concept represents an animate thing (for example, animal, robot) that behaves differently than the superclass or other subclasses, in ways that are of interest.

Based on the above criteria, it is not compelling to partition *Customer* into the subclasses *MaleCustomer* and *FemaleCustomer* because they have no additional

---

3. These rule names have been chosen for their mnemonic support rather than precision.

attributes or associations, are not operated on (treated) differently, and do not behave differently in ways that are of interest[4].

Table 31.2 shows some examples of class partitions from the domain of payments and other areas, using these criteria.

Conceptual Subclass Motivation	Examples
The subclass has additional attributes of interest.	Payments—not applicable. Library—*Book*, subclass of *LoanableResource,* has an *ISBN* attribute.
The subclass has additional associations of interest.	Payments—*CreditPayment*, subclass of *Payment,* is associated with a *CreditCard*. Library—*Video*, subclass of *LoanableResource,* is associated with *Director*.
The subclass concept is operated upon, handled, reacted to, or manipulated differently than the superclass or other subclasses, in ways that are of interest.	Payments—*CreditPayment*, subclass of *Payment,* is handled differently than other kinds of payments in how it is authorized. Library—*Software*, subclass of *LoanableResource*, requires a deposit before it may be loaned.
The subclass concept represents an animate thing (for example, animal, robot) that behaves differently than the superclass or other subclasses, in ways that are of interest.	Payments—not applicable. Library—not applicable. Market Research—*MaleHuman*, subclass of *Human*, behaves differently than *FemaleHuman* with respect to shopping habits.

Table 31.2 Example subclass partitions.

---

4. Men and women do exhibit different shopping habits. However, these are not relevant to our current use case requirements—the criterion that bounds our investigation.

31.5   When to Define a Conceptual Superclass?

Generalization into a common superclass is usually advised when commonality is identified among potential subclasses. The following are motivations to generalize and define a superclass:

Guideline

Create a superclass in a generalization relationship to subclasses when:

■   The potential conceptual subclasses represent variations of a similar concept.

■   The subclasses will conform to the 100% and Is-a rules.

■   All subclasses have the same attribute that can be factored out and expressed in the superclass.

■   All subclasses have the same association that can be factored out and related to the superclass.

The following sections illustrate these points.

31.6   NextGen POS Conceptual Class Hierarchies

Payment Classes

Based on the above criteria for partitioning the *Payment* class, it is useful to create a class hierarchy of various kinds of payments. The justification for the superclass and subclasses is shown in Figure 31.7.

Authorization Service Classes

Credit and check authorization services are variations on a similar concept, and have common attributes of interest. This leads to the class hierarchy in Figure 31.8.

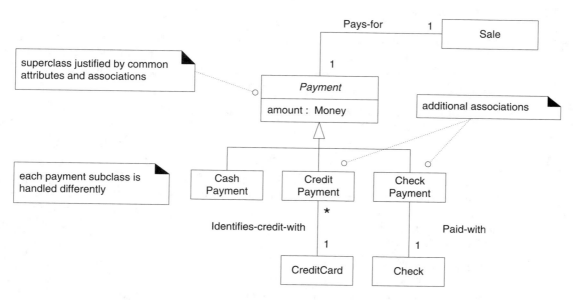

Figure 31.7 Justifying *Payment* subclasses.

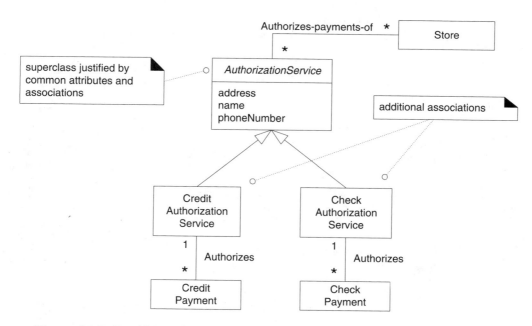

Figure 31.8 Justifying the AuthorizationService hierarchy.

Authorization Transaction Classes

Modeling the various kinds of authorization service transactions (requests and replies) presents an interesting case. In general, transactions with external services are useful to show in a domain model because activities and processes tend to revolve around them. They are important concepts.

Should the modeler illustrate *every* variation of an external service transaction? It depends. As mentioned, domain models are not necessarily correct or wrong, but rather more or less useful. They are useful, because each transaction class is related to different concepts, processes, and business rules.[5]

A second interesting question is the degree of generalization that is useful to show in the model. For argument's sake, let us assume that every transaction has a date and time. These common attributes, plus the desire to create an ultimate generalization for this family of related concepts, justifies the creation of *PaymentAuthorizationTransaction*.

But is it useful to generalize a reply into a *CreditPaymentAuthorizationReply* and *CheckPaymentAuthorizationReply,* as shown in Figure 31.9, or is it sufficient to show less generalization, as depicted in Figure 31.10?

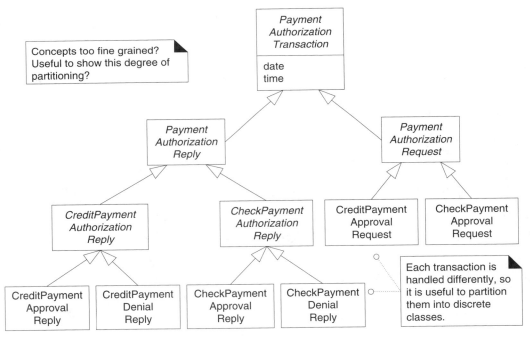

Figure 31.9 One possible class hierarchy for external service transactions.

---

5. In telecommunications domain models, it is similarly useful to identify each kind of exchange or switch message.

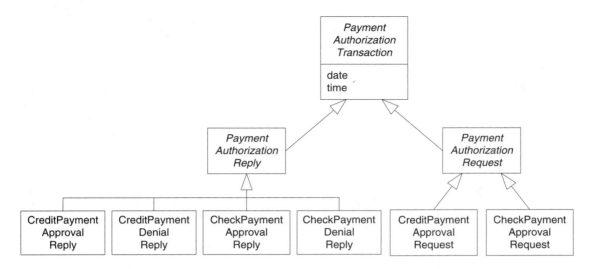

Figure 31.10 An alternate transaction class hierarchy.

The class hierarchy shown in Figure 31.10 is sufficiently useful in terms of generalization, because the additional generalizations do not add obvious value. The hierarchy of Figure 31.9 expresses a finer granularity of generalization that does not significantly enhance our understanding of the concepts and business rules, but it does make the model more complex—and added complexity is undesirable unless it confers other benefits.

31.7 Abstract Conceptual Classes

It is useful to identify abstract classes in the domain model because they constrain what classes it is possible to have concrete instances of, thus clarifying the rules of the problem domain.

Definition

If every member of a class C must also be a member of a subclass, then class C is called an **abstract conceptual class**.

For example, assume that every *Payment* instance must more specifically be an instance of the subclass *CreditPayment*, *CashPayment,* or *CheckPayment*. This is illustrated in the Venn diagram of Figure 31.11 (b). Since every *Payment* member is also a member of a subclass, *Payment* is an abstract conceptual class by definition.

By contrast, if there can be *Payment* instances that are not members of a subclass, it is not an abstract class, as illustrated in Figure 31.11 (a).

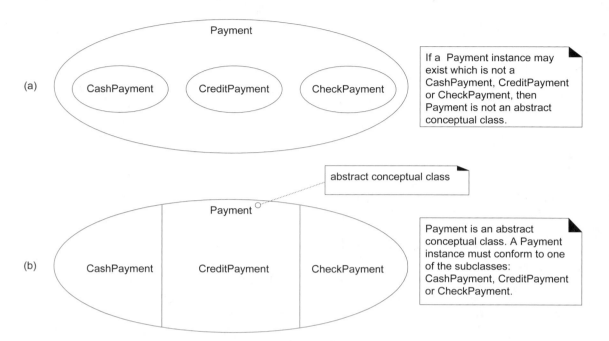

Figure 31.11 Abstract conceptual classes.

In the POS domain, every *Payment* is really a member of a subclass. Figure 31.11 (b) is the correct depiction of payments; therefore, *Payment* is an abstract conceptual class.

Abstract Class Notation in the UML

To review, the UML provides a notation to indicate abstract classes—the class name is italicized (see Figure 31.12).

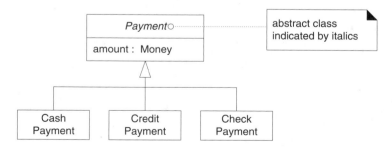

Figure 31.12 Abstract class notation.

31.8   Modeling Changing States

Assume that a payment can either be in an unauthorized or authorized state, and it is meaningful to show this in the domain model (it may not really be, but assume so for the discussion). As shown in Figure 31.13, one modeling approach is to define subclasses of *Payment*: *UnauthorizedPayment* and *AuthorizedPayment*. However, note that a payment does not stay in one of these states; it typically transitions from unauthorized to authorized. This leads to the following guideline:

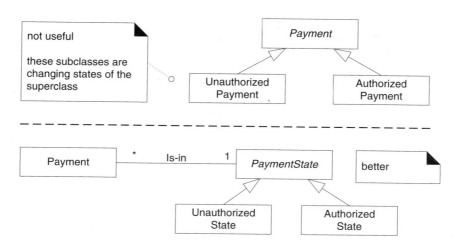

Figure 31.13 Modeling changing states.

31.9   Class Hierarchies and Inheritance in Software

This discussion of conceptual class hierarchies has not mentioned *inheritance*, because the discussion is focused on a domain model conceptual perspective, not software objects. In an object-oriented language, a software subclass **inherits** the attribute and operation definitions of its superclasses by the creation of **software class hierarchies**. **Inheritance** is a software mechanism to make superclass things applicable to subclasses. It supports refactoring code from subclasses and pushing it up class hierarchies. Therefore, inheritance has no real part to play in the discussion of the domain model, although it most definitely does when we transition to the design and implementation view.

The conceptual class hierarchies generated here may or may not be reflected in the Design Model. For example, the hierarchy of authorization service transaction classes may be collapsed or expanded into alternate software class hierarchies, depending on language features and other factors. For instance, C++ templatized classes can sometimes reduce the number of classes.

31.10   Association Classes

The following domain requirements set the stage for association classes:

■   Authorization services assign a merchant ID to each store for identification during communications.

■   A payment authorization request from the store to an authorization service needs the merchant ID that identifies the store to the service.

■   Furthermore, a store has a different merchant ID for each service.

Where in the UP Domain Model should the merchant ID attribute reside?

Placing *merchantID* in *Store* is incorrect because a *Store* can have more than one value for *merchantID*. The same is true with placing it in *Authorization-Service* (see Figure 31.14).

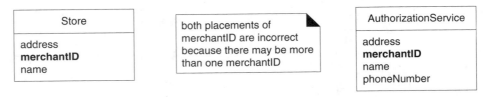

Figure 31.14 Inappropriate use of an attribute.

This leads to the following modeling principle:

Guideline

In a domain model, if a class C can simultaneously have many values for the same kind of attribute A, do not place attribute A in C. Place attribute A in another class that is associated with C.

For example:

■ A *Person* may have many phone numbers. Place phone number in another class, such as *PhoneNumber* or *ContactInformation*, and associate many of these to *Person*.

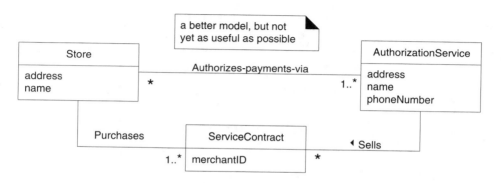

Figure 31.15 First attempt at modeling the merchantID problem.

The above principle suggests that something like the model in Figure 31.15 is more appropriate. In the business world, what concept formally records the information related to the services that a service provides to a customer?—A *Contract* or *Account*.

The fact that both *Store* and *AuthorizationService* are related to *ServiceContract* is a clue that it is dependent on the relationship between the two. The *merchantID* may be thought of as an attribute related to the association between *Store* and *AuthorizationService*.

This leads to the notion of an **association class**, in which we can add features to the association itself. *ServiceContract* may be modeled as an association class related to the association between *Store* and *AuthorizationService*.

In the UML, this is illustrated with a dashed line from the association to the association class. Figure 31.16 visually communicates the idea that a *Service-Contract* and its attributes are related to the association between a *Store* and *AuthorizationService*, and that the lifetime of the *ServiceContract* is dependent on the relationship.

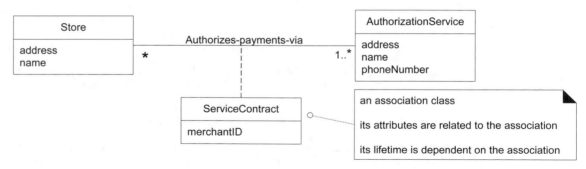

Figure 31.16 An association class.

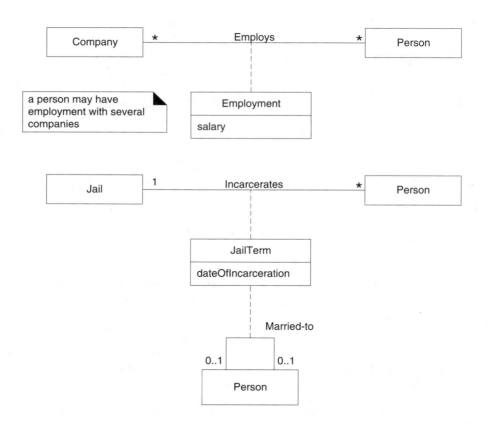

Figure 31.17 Association classes.

Guidelines for adding association classes include the following:

Guideline

Clues that an association class might be useful in a domain model:

- An attribute is related to an association.

- Instances of the association class have a lifetime dependency on the association.

- There is a many-to-many association between two concepts and information associated with the association itself.

The presence of a many-to-many association is a common clue that a useful association class is lurking in the background somewhere; when you see one, consider an association class.

Figure 31.17 illustrates some other examples of association classes.

31.11 Aggregation and Composition

These first few paragraphs repeat the introduction on p. 264. **Aggregation** is a vague kind of association in the UML that loosely suggests whole-part relationships (as do many ordinary associations). It has no meaningful distinct semantics in the UML versus a plain association, but the term is defined in the UML. Why? To quote Rumbaugh (one of the original and key UML creators):

> *In spite of the few semantics attached to aggregation, everybody thinks it is necessary (for different reasons). Think of it as a modeling placebo. [RJB04]*

Guideline: Therefore, following the advice of UML creators, don't bother to use aggregation in the UML; rather, use *composition* when appropriate.

Composition, also known as **composite aggregation**, is a strong kind of whole-part aggregation and *is* useful to show in some models. A composition relationship implies that 1) an instance of the part (such as a *Square*) belongs to only *one* composite instance (such as one *Board*) at a time, 2) the part must *always belong* to a composite (no free-floating *Fingers),* and 3) the composite is responsible for the creation and deletion of its parts—either by itself creating/deleting the parts, or by collaborating with other objects. Related to this constraint is that if the composite is destroyed, its parts must either be destroyed, or attached to another composite—no free-floating *Fingers* allowed! For example, if a physical paper Monopoly game board is destroyed, we think of the squares as being destroyed as well (a conceptual perspective). Likewise, if a software *Board* object is destroyed, its software *Square* objects are destroyed, in a DCD software perspective.

How to Identify Composition

In some cases, the presence of composition is obvious—usually in physical assemblies. But sometimes, it is not clear.

Guideline

On composition: If in doubt, leave it out.

Here are some guidelines that suggest when to show aggregation:

Guideline

Consider showing composition when:

- The lifetime of the part is bound within the lifetime of the composite— there is a create-delete dependency of the part on the whole.

- There is an obvious whole-part physical or logical assembly.

- Some properties of the composite propagate to the parts, such as the location.

- Operations applied to the composite propagate to the parts, such as destruction, movement, recording.

A Benefit of Showing Composition

Identifying and illustrating composition is *not* profoundly important; it is quite reasonable to exclude it from a domain model. Most—if not all—experienced domain modelers have seen unproductive time wasted debating the fine points of these associations.

Discover and show composition because it has the following benefits, most of which relate to the design rather than the analysis, which is why its exclusion from the domain model is not very significant.

- It clarifies the domain constraints regarding the eligible existence of the part independent of the whole. In composite aggregation, the part may not exist outside of the lifetime of the whole.

  - During design work, this has an impact on the create-delete dependencies between the whole and part software classes and database elements (in terms of referential integrity and cascading delete paths).

- It assists in the identification of a creator (the composite) using the GRASP Creator pattern.

- Operations—such as copy and delete—applied to the whole often propagate to the parts.

Composition in the NextGen Domain Model

In the POS domain, the *SalesLineItems* may be considered a part of a composite *Sale*; in general, transaction line items are viewed as parts of an aggregate transaction (see Figure 31.18). In addition to conformance to that pattern, there is a create-delete dependency of the line items on the *Sale*—their lifetime is bound within the lifetime of the *Sale*.

By similar justification, *ProductCatalog* is a composite of *ProductDescriptions*.

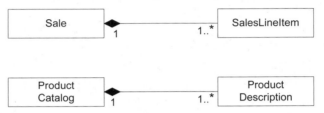

Figure 31.18 Aggregation in the point-of-sale application.

No other relationship is a compelling combination that suggests whole-part semantics, a create-delete dependency, and "If in doubt, leave it out."

1.12   Time Intervals and Product Prices—Fixing an Iteration 1 "Error"

In the first iteration, *SalesLineItems* were associated with *ProductDescriptions*, that recorded the price of an item. This was a reasonable simplification for early iterations, but needs to be amended. It raises the interesting—and widely applicable—issue of **time intervals** associated with information, contracts, and the like.

If a *SalesLineItem* always retrieved the current price recorded in a *ProductDescriptions*, then when the price was changed in the object, old sales would refer to new prices, which is incorrect. What is needed is a distinction between the historical price when the sale was made, and the current price.

Depending on the information requirements, there are at least two ways to model this. One is to simply copy the product price into the *SalesLineItem*, and maintain the current price in the *ProductDescriptions*.

The other approach, more robust, is to associate a collection of *ProductPrices* with a *ProductDescriptions*, each with an associated applicable time interval. Thus, the organization can record all past prices (to resolve the sale price problem, and for trend analysis) and also record future planned prices (see Figure 31.19). See [CLD99] for a broader discussion of time intervals, under the category of **Moment-Interval** archetypes.

It is common that a collection of time interval related information needs to be maintained, rather than a simple value. Physical, medical, and scientific measurements, and many accounting and legal artifacts have this requirement.

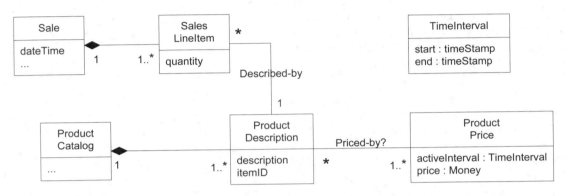

Figure 31.19 ProductPrices and time intervals.

31.13 Association Role Names

Each end of an association is a role, which has various properties, such as:

- name

- multiplicity

A role name identifies an end of an association and ideally describes the role played by objects in the association. Figure 31.20 shows role name examples.

An explicit role name is not required—it is useful when the role of the object is not clear. It usually starts with a lowercase letter. If not explicitly present, assume that the default role name is equal to the related class name, though starting with a lowercase letter.

As covered previously, roles used in DCDs may be interpreted as the basis for attribute names during code generation.

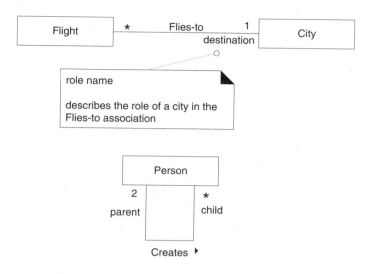

Figure 31.20 Role names.

31.14   Roles as Concepts versus Roles in Associations

In a domain model, a real-world role—especially a human role—may be modeled in a number of ways, such as a discrete concept, or expressed as a role in an association.[6] For example, the role of cashier and manager may be expressed in at least the two ways illustrated in Figure 31.21.

The first approach may be called "roles in associations"; the second, "roles as concepts." Both approaches have advantages.

Roles in associations are appealing because they are a relatively accurate way to express the notion that the same instance of a person takes on multiple (and dynamically changing) roles in various associations. I, a person, simultaneously or in sequence, may take on the role of writer, object designer, parent, and so on.

On the other hand, roles as concepts provides ease and flexibility in adding unique attributes, associations, and additional semantics. Furthermore, the implementation of roles as separate classes is easier because of limitations of current popular object-oriented programming languages—it is not convenient to dynamically mutate an instance of one class into another, or dynamically add behavior and attributes as the role of a person changes.

---

6. For simplicity, other excellent solutions such as those discussed in [Fowler96] are not covered.

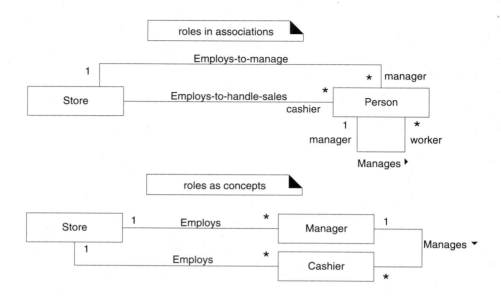

Figure 31.21 Two ways to model human roles.

31.15 Derived Elements

A derived element can be determined from others. Attributes and associations are the most common derived elements. When should derived elements be shown?

Guideline

Avoid showing derived elements in a diagram, since they add complexity without new information. However, add a derived element when it is prominent in the terminology, and excluding it impairs comprehension.

For example, a *Sale total* can be derived from *SalesLineItem* and *ProductDescriptions* information (see Figure 31.22). In the UML, it is shown with a "/" preceding the element name.

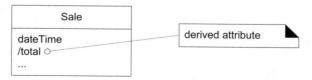

Figure 31.22 Derived attribute.

As another example, a *SalesLineItem quantity* is actually derivable from the number of instances of *Items* associated with the line item (see Figure 31.23).

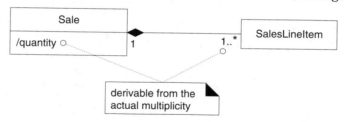

Figure 31.23 Derived attribute related to multiplicity.

31.16 Qualified Associations

A **qualifier** may be used in an association; it distinguishes the set of objects at the far end of the association based on the qualifier value. An association with a qualifier is a **qualified association**.

For example, *ProductDescriptions* may be distinguished in a *ProductCatalog* by their *itemID*, as illustrated in Figure 31.24 (b). As contrasted in Figure 31.24 (a) vs. (b), qualification reduces the multiplicity at the far end from the qualifier, usually down from many to one. Depicting a qualifier in a domain model communicates how, in the domain, things of one class are distinguished in relation to another class. They should not, in the domain model, be used to express design decisions about lookup keys, although that is suitable in other diagrams illustrating design decisions.

Qualifiers do not usually add compelling useful new information, and we can fall into the trap of "design-think." However, used judiciously, they can sharpen understanding about the domain. The qualified associations between *ProductCatalog* and *ProductDescriptions* provide a reasonable example of a value-added qualifier.

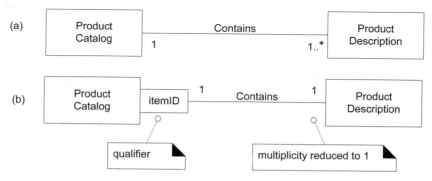

Figure 31.24 Qualified association.

31.17   Reflexive Associations

A concept may have an association to itself; this is known as a **reflexive association**[7] (see Figure 31.25).

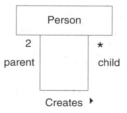

Figure 31.25 Reflexive association.

31.18   Using Packages to Organize the Domain Model

A domain model can easily grow large enough that it is desirable to factor it into packages of strongly related concepts, as an aid to comprehension and parallel analysis work in which different people do domain analysis within different subdomains. The following sections illustrate a package structure for the UP Domain Model.

To review, a UML package is shown as a tabbed folder (see Figure 31.26). Subordinate packages may be shown within it. The package name is within the tab if the package depicts its elements; otherwise, it is centered within the folder itself.

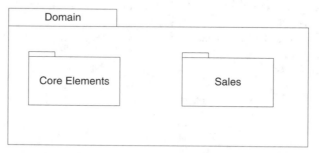

Figure 31.26 A UML package.

---

7. [MO95] constrains the definition of reflexive associations further.

Ownership and References

An element is *owned* by the package within which it is defined, but may be *referenced* in other packages. In that case, the element name is qualified by the package name using the pathname format *PackageName::ElementName* (see Figure 31.27). A class shown in a foreign package may be modified with new associations, but must otherwise remain unchanged.

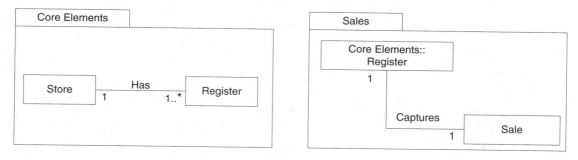

Figure 31.27 A referenced class in a package.

Package Dependencies

If a model element is in some way dependent on another, the dependency may be shown with a dependency relationship, depicted with an arrowed line. A package dependency indicates that elements of the dependent package in some way know about or are coupled to elements in the target package.

For example, if a package references an element owned by another, a dependency exists. Thus, the *Sales* package has a dependency on the *Core Elements* package (see Figure 31.28).

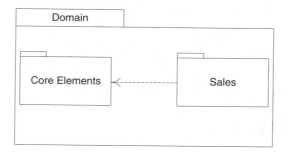

Figure 31.28 A package dependency.

How to Partition the Domain Model

How should the classes in a domain model be organized within packages? Apply the following general guidelines:

Guideline

To partition the domain model into packages, place elements together that:

- are in the same subject area—closely related by concept or purpose
- are in a class hierarchy together
- participate in the same use cases
- are strongly associated

It is useful if all elements related to the domain model are rooted in a package called *Domain*, and all widely shared, common, core concepts are defined in a packaged named something like *Core Elements* or *Common Concepts*, in the absence of any other meaningful package within which to place them.

POS Domain Model Packages

Based on the above criteria, the package organization for the POS Domain Model is shown in Figure 31.29.

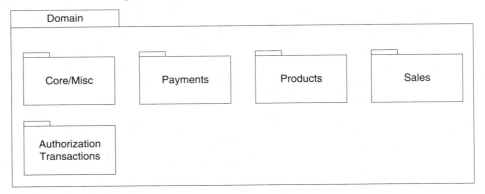

Figure 31.29 Domain concept packages.

Core/Misc Package

A Core/Misc package (see Figure 31.30) is useful to own widely shared concepts or those without an obvious home. In later references, the package name will be abbreviated to *Core*.

There are no new concepts or associations particular to this iteration in this package.

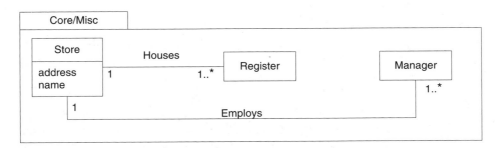

Figure 31.30 Core package.

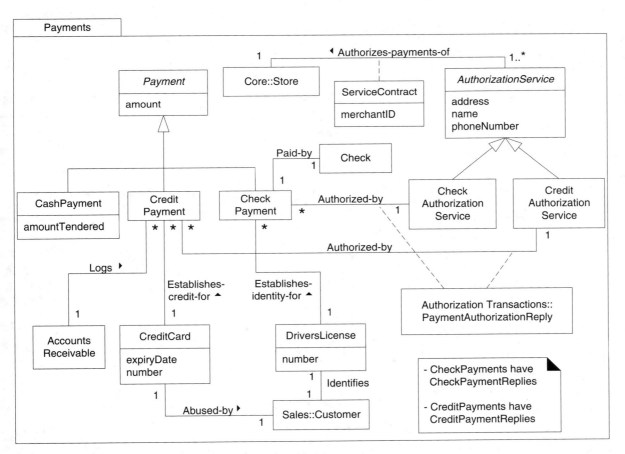

Figure 31.31 Payments package.

Payments

As in iteration 1, new associations are primarily motivated by a need-to-know criterion. For example, there is a need to remember the relationship between *CreditPayment* and *CreditCard*. In contrast, some associations are added more for comprehension, such as *DriversLicense Identifies Customer* (see Figure 31.31).

Note that *PaymentAuthorizationReply* is expressed as an association class. A reply arises out of association between a payment and its authorization service.

Products

With the exception of composite aggregation, there are no new concepts or associations particular to this iteration (see Figure 31.32).

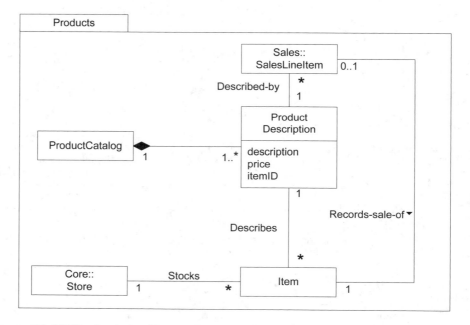

Figure 31.32 Products package.

Sales

With the exception of composite aggregation and derived attributes, there are no new concepts or associations particular to this iteration (see Figure 31.33).

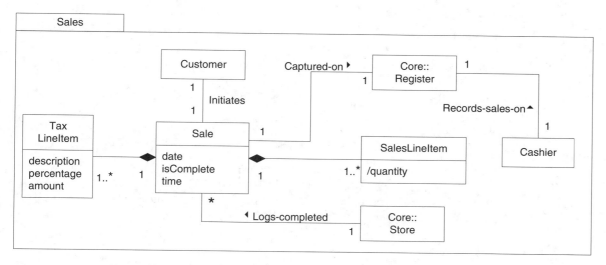

Figure 31.33 Sales package.

Authorization Transactions

Although providing meaningful names for associations is recommended, in some circumstances it may not be compelling, especially if the purpose of the association is considered obvious to the audience. A case in point is the associations between payments and their transactions. Their names have been left unspecified because we can assume the audience reading the class diagram in Figure 31.34 will understand that the transactions are for the payment; adding the names merely makes the diagram more busy.

Is this diagram too detailed, showing too many specializations? It depends. The real criteria is usefulness. Although it is not incorrect, does it add any value in improving understanding of the domain? The answer should influence how many specializations to illustrate in a domain model.

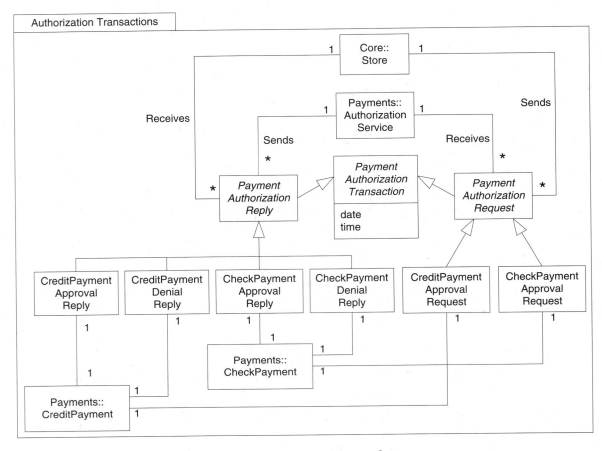

Figure 31.34 Authorization transaction package.

31.19 Example: Monopoly Domain Model Refinements

Figure 31.35 shows refinements to the Monopoly domain model. These include:

- Different kinds of property squares (*LotSquare*, ...). This reflects the guideline that if the domain rules treat a noteworthy concept in a different or distinct manner, then show it a separate specialization.

- An abstract superclass *PropertySquare*. This is justified because all the subclasses have a *price* attribute and an *Owns* association with a *Player*.

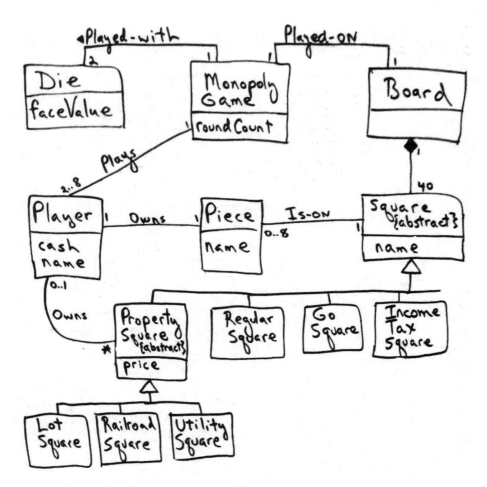

Figure 31.35 Iteration-3 Monopoly domain model.

MORE SSDS AND CONTRACTS

Virtue is insufficient temptation.

—George Bernard Shaw

Objectives

■ Define SSDs and operation contracts for the current iteration.

Introduction

The chapter quickly summarizes updates to SSDs and system operation contracts for this iteration of the NextGen case study. No changes are necessary for the Monopoly problem.

What's Next? Having refined the domain model, this chapter quickly summarizes SSD and contract changes. The next introduces how to analyze the architecturally significant forces for an application.

| Relating Use Cases | Domain Model Refinement | More SSDs and Contracts | Architectural Analysis | Logical Architecture Refinement |

32.1 NextGen POS

New System Sequence Diagrams

In the current iteration, the new payment handling requirements involve new collaborations with external systems. To review, SSDs use sequence diagram notation to illustrate inter-system collaborations, treating each system as a blackbox. It is useful to illustrate the new system events in SSDs in order to clarify:

- new system operations that the NextGen POS system will need to support

- calls to other systems, and the responses to expect from these calls

Common Beginning of Process Sale Scenario

The SSD for the beginning portion of a basic scenario includes *makeNewSale*, *enterItem*, and *endSale* system events; it is common regardless of the payment method (see Figure 32.1).

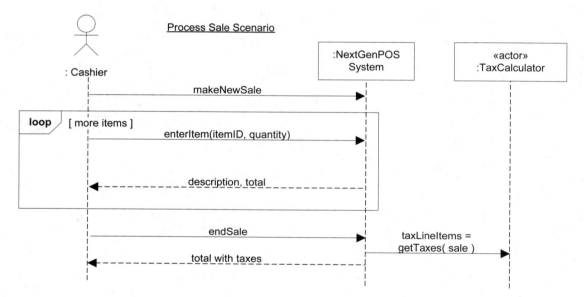

Figure 32.1 SSD common beginning.

Credit Payment

This credit payment scenario SSD starts after the common beginning (see Figure 32.2).

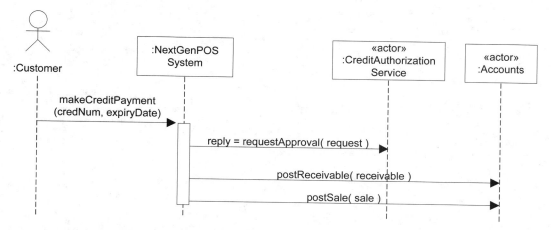

Figure 32.2 Credit payment SSD.

In both cases of credit and check payments, a simplifying assumption is made (for this iteration) that the payment is exactly equal to the sale total, and thus a different "tendered" amount does not have be an input parameter.

Note that the call to the external *CreditAuthorizationService* is modeled as a regular synchronous message with a return value. This is an abstraction; it could be implemented with a SOAP request over secure HTTPS, or any remote communication mechanism. The resource adapters defined in the prior iteration will hide the specific protocol.

The *makeCreditPayment* system operation—and the use case—assume that the credit information of the customer is coming from a credit card, and thus a credit account number and expiry date enter the system (probably via a card reader). Although it is recognized that in the future, alternative mechanisms for communicating credit information will arise, the assumption that credit cards will be supported is very stable.

Recall that when a credit authorization service approves a credit payment, it owes the store for the payment; thus, a receivables entry needs to be added to the accounts receivable system.

Check Payment

The SSD for the check payment scenario is shown in Figure 32.3.

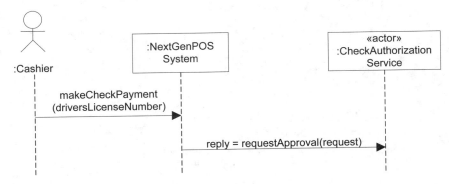

Figure 32.3 Check payment SSD.

According to the use case, the cashier must enter the driver's license number for validation.

New System Operations

In this iteration, the new system operations that our system must handle are:

- *makeCreditPayment*
- *makeCheckPayment*

In the first iteration, the system operation for the cash payment was simply *makePayment*. Now that the payments are of different types, it is renamed to *makeCashPayment*.

New System Operation Contracts

To review, system operation contracts are an optional requirements artifact (part of the Use-Case Model) that adds fine detail regarding the results of a system operation. Usually, the use case text is itself sufficient, and these contracts aren't useful. But on occasion they bring value by their precise and detailed approach to identifying what happens when a complex operation is invoked on the system, in terms of state changes to objects defined in the Domain Model.

Here are contracts for the new system operations:

Contract CO5: makeCreditPayment

Operation:	makeCreditPayment(creditAccountNumber, expiryDate)
Cross References:	Use Cases: Process Sale
Preconditions:	An underway sale exists and all items have been entered.

Postconditions:	– a CreditPayment pmt was created
	– pmt was associated with the current Sale sale
	– a CreditCard cc was created; cc.number = creditAccountNumber, cc.expiryDate = expiryDate
	– cc was associated with pmt
	– a CreditPaymentRequest cpr was created
	– pmt was associated with cpr
	– a ReceivableEntry re was created
	– re was associated with the external AccountsReceivable
	– sale was associated with the Store as a completed sale

Note the postcondition indicating the association of a new receivable entry in accounts receivable. Although this responsibility is outside the bounds of the NextGen system, the accounts receivable system is within the control of the business, so the statement has been added as a correctness check.

For example, during testing it is clear from this post-condition that the accounts receivable system should be tested for the presence of a new receivable entry.

Contract CO6: makeCheckPayment

Operation:	makeCheckPayment(driversLicenceNumber)
Cross References:	Use Cases: Process Sale
Preconditions:	An underway sale exists and all items have been entered.
Postconditions:	– a CheckPayment pmt was created
	– pmt was associated with the current Sale sale
	– a DriversLicense dl was created; dl.number = driversLicenseNumber
	– dl was associated with pmt
	– a CheckPaymentRequest cpr was created.
	– pmt was associated with cpr
	– sale was associated with the Store as a completed sale

ARCHITECTURAL ANALYSIS

Error, no keyboard — press F1 to continue.

—early PC BIOS message

Objectives

- Create architectural factor tables.
- Create technical memos that record architectural decisions.

Introduction

Architectural analysis can be viewed as a specialization of requirements analysis, with a focus on requirements that strongly influence the "architecture." For example, identifying the need for a highly-secure system.

The essence of architectural analysis is to identify factors that should influence the architecture, understand their variability and priority, and resolve them. The difficult part is knowing what questions to ask, weighing the trade-offs, and knowing the many ways to resolve an architecturally significant factor, ranging from benign neglect, to fancy designs, to third-party products.

A good architect earns her salary by having the experience to know what questions to ask and choosing skillful means to resolve the factors.

What's Next? Having summarized SSD and contract changes, this chapter introduces how to analyze the architecturally significant forces for an application. The next explores some intermediate topics in layered architectures.

Domain Model Refinement	More SSDs and Contracts	Architectural Analysis	Logical Architecture Refinement	Package Design

Why is architectural analysis important? It's useful to:

- reduce the risk of missing something centrally important in the design of the systems

- avoid applying excessive effort to low priority issues

- help align the product with business goals

This chapter is an introduction to basic steps and ideas in architectural analysis from a UP perspective; that is, to the method, rather than to tips and tricks of master architects. Thus, it is not a cookbook of architectural solutions—a very large and context-dependent subject that is beyond the scope of this introductory book. Nevertheless, the NextGen POS case study comments in the chapter do provide concrete examples of architectural solutions.

33.1   Process: When Do We Start Architectural Analysis?

In the UP, architectural analysis should start even before the first development iteration, as architectural issues need to be identified and resolved in early development work. Failure to do so is a high risk. For example, deferring an architecturally-significant factor such as "must be internationalized to support English, Chinese, and Hindi" or "must handle 500 concurrent transactions with on-average one-second response time" until late in development is a recipe for pain and suffering.

However, since the UP is iterative and evolutionary—not the waterfall—we start programming and testing in early iterations before all the architectural analysis is complete. Analysis and early development proceed hand-in-hand.

But this important topic was deferred until this point of the book so that fundamentals of OOA/D could be first presented.

33.2   Definition: Variation and Evolution Points

First, two points of change in a software system (first introduced in the Protected Variations pattern) are worth reiterating:

- **variation point**—Variations in the existing current system or requirements, such as the multiple tax calculator interfaces that must be supported.

- **evolution point**—Speculative points of variation that may arise in the future, but which are not present in the existing requirements.

As will be seen, variation and evolution points are recurring key elements in architectural analysis.

33.3 Architectural Analysis

Architectural analysis is concerned with the identification and resolution of the system's non-functional requirements (for example, security), in the context of the functional requirements (for example, processing sales). It includes identifying variation points and the most probable evolution points.

In the UP, the term encompasses both architectural investigation (identification) and architectural design (resolution). Here are some examples of the many issues to be identified and resolved at an architectural level:

- How do reliability and fault-tolerance requirements affect the design?

    ○ For example, in the NextGen POS, for what remote services (e.g., tax calculator) will fail-over to local services be allowed? Why? Do they provide exactly the same services locally as remotely, or are there differences?

- How do the licensing costs of purchased subcomponents affect profitability?

    ○ For example, the producer of the excellent database server, *Clueless,* wants 2% of each NextGen POS sale, if their product is used as a subcomponent. Using their product will speed development (and time to market) because it is robust and provides many services, and many developers know it, but at a price. Should the team instead use the less robust, open source *YourSQL* database server? At what risk? How does it restrict the ability to charge for the NextGen product?

- How do the adaptability and configurability requirements affect the design?

    ○ For example, most retailers have variations in business rules they want represented in their POS applications. What are the variations? What is the "best" way to design for them? What is the criteria for best? Can NextGen make more money by requiring customized programming for each customer (and how much effort will that be?), or with a solution that allows the customer to add the customization easily themselves? Should "more money" be the goal in the short-run?

- How does brand name and branding affect the architecture?

    ○ A little-known story is that Microsoft's Windows XP was not originally named "Windows XP." The name was a relatively last-minute change from the marketing department. You may appreciate that the operating system name is displayed in many places, both as raw text and as a graphic image. Because the Microsoft architects did not identify a name change as a likely *evolution point*, there was no Protected Variation solution for this point, such as the label existing in only one place in a configuration file. Therefore, at the last minute, a small team scoured the millions of lines of source code and image files, and made hundreds of changes.

  ○ Similarly, how should potential changes to the brand name of the NextGen product and related logos, icons, and so forth affect its architecture?

- How do the adaptability and configurability requirements affect the design?

  ○ For example, most retailers have variations in business rules they want represented in their POS applications. What are the variations? What is the "best" way to design for them? What is the criteria for best? Can NextGen make more money by requiring customized programming for each customer (and how much effort will that be?), or with a solution that allows the customer to add the customization easily themselves? Should "more money" be the goal in the short-run?

33.4 Common Steps in Architectural Analysis

There are several methods of architectural analysis. Common to most of these is some variation of the following steps:

1. Identify and analyze the non-functional requirements that have an impact on the architecture. Functional requirements are also relevant (especially in terms of variability or change), but the non-functional are given thorough attention. In general, all these may be called **architectural factors** (also known as the **architectural drivers**).

  ○ This step could be characterized as regular requirements analysis, but since it is done in the context of identifying architectural impact and deciding high-level architectural solutions, it is considered a part of architectural analysis in the UP.

  ○ In terms of the UP, some of these requirements will be roughly identified and recorded in the Supplementary Specification or use cases during inception. During architectural analysis, which occurs in early elaboration, the team investigates these requirements more closely.

2. For those requirements with a significant architectural impact, analyze alternatives and create solutions that resolve the impact. These are **architectural decisions**.

  ○ Decisions range from "remove the requirement," to a custom solution, to "stop the project," to "hire an expert."

This presentation introduces these basic steps in the context of the NextGen POS case study. For simplicity, it avoids architectural deployment issues such as the hardware and operating system configuration, which are very context and time sensitive.

33.5 The Science: Identification and Analysis of Architectural Factors

Architectural Factors

FURPS+ p. 56

Any and all of the FURPS+ requirements may have a significant influence on the architecture of a system, ranging from reliability, to schedule, to skills, and to cost constraints. For example, a case of tight schedule with limited skills and sufficient money probably favors buying or outsourcing to specialists, rather than building all components in-house.

However, the factors with the strongest architectural influence tend to be within the high-level FURPS+ categories of functionality, reliability, performance, supportability, implementation, and interface. Interestingly, it is usually the non-functional quality attributes (such as reliability or performance) that give a particular architecture its unique flavor, rather than its functional requirements. For example, the design in the NextGen system to support different third-party components with unique interfaces, and the design to support easily plugging in different sets of business rules.

In the UP, these factors with architectural implications are called **architecturally significant requirements**. "Factors" is used here for brevity.

Many technical and organizational factors can be characterized as *constraints* that restrict the solution in some way (such as, must run on Linux, or, the budget for purchasing third-party components is X).

Quality Scenarios

When defining quality requirements during architectural factor analysis, **quality scenarios**[1] are recommended, as they define measurable (or at least observable) responses, and thus can be verified. It is not much use to vaguely state "the system will be easy to modify" without some measure of what that means.[2]

Quantifying some things, such as performance goals and mean time between failure, are well known practices, but quality scenarios extend this idea and encourage recording all (or at least, most) factors as measurable statements.

---

1. A term used in various architectural methods promoted by the Software Engineering Institute (SEI); for example, in the *Architecture Based Design* method.
2. Tom Gilb, the creator of perhaps the first iterative and evolutionary method, Evo, is also a long-time proponent of the need to quantify and measure non-functional goals. His **PLanguage** structured requirements language emphasizes quantification.

Quality scenarios are short statements of the form <stimulus> <measurable response>; for example:

- When the completed sale is sent to the remote tax calculator to add the taxes, the result is returned within 2 seconds "most" of the time, measured in a production environment under "average" load conditions.

- When a bug report arrives from a NextGen beta test volunteer, reply with a phone call within 1 working day.

Note that "most" and "average" will need further investigation and definition by the NextGen architect; a quality scenario is not really valid until it is testable, which implies fully specified. Also, observe the qualification in the first quality scenario in terms of the environment to which it applies. It does little good to specify a quality scenario, verify that it passes in a lightly loaded development environment, but fail to evaluate it in a realistic production environment.

Pick Your Battles

A caution: Writing these quality scenarios can be a mirage of usefulness. It's easy to *write* these detailed specifications, but not to realize them. Will anyone ever really test them? How and by whom? A strong dose of realism is required when writing these; there's no point in listing many sophisticated goals if no one will ever really follow through on testing them.

pick your battles p. 432

There is a relationship here to the "pick your battles" discussion that was presented in an earlier chapter on the Protected Variations pattern. What are the really critical make-or-break quality scenarios? For example, in an airline reservation system, consistently fast transaction completion under very high load conditions is truly critical to the success of the system—it must definitely be tested. In the NextGen system, the application really must be fault-tolerant and fail over to local replicated services when the remote ones fail—it must definitely be properly tested and validated. Therefore, focus on writing quality scenarios for the important battles, and follow through with a plan for their evaluation.

Describing Factors

One important goal of architectural analysis is to understand the influence of the factors, their priorities, and their variability (immediate need for flexibility and future evolution). Therefore, most architectural methods (for example, see [HNS00]) advocate creating a table or tree with variations of the following information (the format varies depending on the method). The following style shown in Table 33.1 is called a **factor table**, which in the UP is part of the Supplementary Specification.

Factor	Measures and quality scenarios	Variability (current flexibility and future evolution)	Impact of factor (and its variability) on stakeholders, architecture and other factors	Priority for Success	Difficulty or Risk
Reliability—Recoverability					
Recovery from remote service failure	When a remote service fails, reestablish connectivity with it within 1 minute of its detected re-availability, under normal store load in a production environment.	current flexibility - our SME says local client-side simplified services are acceptable (and desirable) until reconnection is possible. evolution - within 2 years, some retailers may be willing to pay for full local replication of remote services (such as the tax calculator). Probability? High.	High impact on the large-scale design. Retailers really dislike it when remote services fail, as it prevents or restricts them from using a POS to make sales.	H	M
...	...	...	...		

Table 33.1 Sample factor table. Legend: H-high. M-medium. SME-subject matter expert.

Notice the categorization scheme: *Reliability—Recoverability* (from the FURPS+ categories). This isn't presented as the best or only scheme, but it is useful to group architectural factors into categories. For example, certain categories (such as reliability and performance) strongly relate to identifying and defining test plans, and thus it is useful to group them.

The basic priority and risk code values of H/M/L are simply suggestive of using some codes the team finds useful; there are a variety of coding schemes (numeric and qualitative) from different architectural methods and standards (such as ISO 9126). A caution: If the extra effort of using a more complex scheme does not lead to any practical action, it isn't worthwhile.

Factors and UP Artifacts

The central functional requirements repository in the UP are the use cases, and they, along with the Vision and Supplementary Specification, are an important source of inspiration when creating a factor table. In the use cases, the *Special Requirements*, *Technology Variations*, and *Open Issues* should be reviewed, and their implied or explicit architectural factors consolidated in the Supplementary Specification.

It is reasonable to at first record use-case related factors with the use case during its creation, because of the obvious relationship, but it is ultimately more convenient (in terms of content management, tracking, and readability) to consolidate all the architectural factors in one location—in the factor table in the Supplementary Specification.

Use Case UC1: Process Sale

Main Success Scenario:

1. ...

Special Requirements:
– Credit authorization response within 30 seconds 90% of the time.
– Somehow, we want robust recovery when access to remote services such the inventory system is failing.
– . . .

Technology and Data Variations List:
2a. Item identifier entered by bar code laser scanner (if bar code is present) or keyboard.

....

Open Issues:
– What are the tax law variations?
– Explore the remote service recovery issue.

33.6 Example: Partial NextGen POS Architectural Factor Table

The partial factor table in Table 33.2 shows some factors related to later discussion.

Factor	Measures and quality scenarios	Variability (current flexibility and future evolution)	Impact of factor (and its variability) on stakeholders, architecture and other factors	Priority for Success	Difficulty or Risk
Reliability—Recoverability					
Recovery from remote service failure	When a remote service fails, reestablish connectivity with it within 1 minute of its detected re-availability, under normal store load in a production environment.	current flexibility - our SME says local client-side simplified services are acceptable (and desirable) until reconnection is possible. evolution - within 2 years, some retailers may be willing to pay for full local replication of remote services (such as the tax calculator). Probability? High.	High impact on the large-scale design. Retailers really dislike it when remote services fail, as it prevents them from using a POS to make sales.	H	M
Recovery from remote product database failure	as above	current flexibility - our SME says local client-side use of cached "most common" product info is acceptable (and desirable) until reconnection is possible. evolution - within 3 years, client-side mass storage and replication solutions will be cheap and effective, allowing permanent complete replication and thus local usage. Probability? High.	as above	H	M
Supportability - Adaptability					

Factor	Measures and quality scenarios	Variability (current flexibility and future evolution)	Impact of factor (and its variability) on stakeholders, architecture and other factors	Priority for Success	Difficulty or Risk
Support many third-party services (tax calculator, inventory, HR, accounting). They will vary at each installation.	When a new third-party system must be integrated, it can be, and within 10 person days of effort.	current flexibility - as described by factor evolution - none	Required for product acceptance. Small impact on design.	H	L
Support wireless PDA terminals for the POS client?	When support is added, it does not require a change to the design of the non-UI layers of the architecture.	current flexibility - not required at present evolution - within 3 years, we think the probability is very high that wireless "PDA" POS clients will be desired by the market.	High design impact in terms of protected variation from many elements. For example, the operating systems and UIs are different on small devices.	L	H
Other - Legal					
Current tax rules must be applied.	When the auditor evaluates conformance, 100% conformance will be found. When tax rules change, they will be operational within the period allowed by government.	current flexibility - conformance is inflexible, but tax rules can change almost weekly because of the many rules and levels of government taxation (national, state, ...) evolution - none	Failure to comply is a criminal offense. Impacts tax calculation services. Difficult to write our own service--complex rules, constant change, need to track all levels of government. But, easy/low risk if buy a package.	H	L

Table 33.2 Partial factor table for the NextGen architectural analysis.

33.7 The Art: Resolution of Architectural Factors

One could say the *science* of architecture is the collection and organization of information about the architectural factors, as in the factor table. The *art* of architecture is making skillful choices to resolve these factors, in light of trade-offs, interdependencies, and priorities.

Adept architects have knowledge in a variety of areas (for example, architectural styles and patterns, technologies, products, pitfalls, and trends) and apply this to their decisions.

Recording Architectural Alternatives, Decisions, and Motivation

Ignoring for now principles of architectural decision-making, virtually all architectural methods recommend keeping a record of alternative solutions, decisions, influential factors, and motivations for the noteworthy issues and decisions.

Such records have been called **technical memos** [Cunningham96], **issue cards** [HNS00], and **architectural approach documents** (SEI architectural proposals), with varying degrees of formality and sophistication. In some methods, these memos are the basis for yet another step of review and refinement.

In the UP, the memos should be recorded in the SAD.

An important aspect of the technical memo is the *motivation* or rationale. When a future developer or architect needs to modify the system,[3] it is immensely helpful to understand the motivations behind the design, such as *why* a particular approach to recovery from remote service failure in the NextGen POS was chosen and others rejected, in order to make informed decisions about changing the system.

Explaining the rationale of rejecting the alternatives is important, as during future product evolution, an architect may reconsider these alternatives, or at least want to know what alternatives were considered, and why one was chosen.

A sample technical memo follows that records an architectural decision for the NextGen POS. The exact format is, of course, not important. Keep it simple and just record information that will help the future reader make an informed decision when changing the system.

Technical Memo
Issue: Reliability—Recovery from Remote Service Failure

Solution Summary: Location transparency using service lookup, failover from remote to local, and local service partial replication.

Factors

- Robust recovery from remote service failure (e.g., tax calculator, inventory)
- Robust recovery from remote product (e.g., descriptions and prices) database failure

Solution

Achieve protected variation with respect to location of services using an Adapter created in a Services-Factory. Where possible, offer local implementations of remote services, usually with simplified or constrained behavior. For example, the local tax calculator will use constant tax rates. The local product information database will be a small cache of the most common products. Inventory updates will be stored and forwarded at reconnection.

See also the *Adaptability—Third-Party Services* technical memo for the adaptability aspects of this solutions, because remote service implementations will vary at each installation.

To satisfy the quality scenarios of reconnection with the remote services ASAP, use smart Proxy objects for the services, that on each service call test for remote service reactivation, and redirect to them when possible.

---

3. Or when four weeks have passed and the original architect has forgotten their own rationale!

Motivation

Retailers really don't want to stop making sales! Therefore, if the NextGen POS offers this level of reliability and recovery, it will be a very attractive product, as none of our competitors provide this capability. The small product cache is motivated by very limited client-side resources. The real third-party tax calculator is not replicated on the client primarily because of the higher licensing costs, and configuration efforts (as each calculator installation requires almost weekly adjustments). This design also supports the evolution point of future customers willing and able to permanently replicate services such as the tax calculator to each client terminal.

Unresolved Issues

Alternatives Considered

A "gold level" quality of service agreement with remote credit authorization services to improve reliability. It was available, but much too expensive.

Note as illustrated in this example—and this is a key point—that an architectural decision described in one technical memo may resolve a group of factors, not only one.

Priorities

There is a hierarchy of goals that guides architectural decisions:

1. Inflexible constraints, including safety and legal compliance.
    - The NextGen POS must correctly apply tax policies.

2. Business goals.
    - Demo of noteworthy features ready for the POSWorld trade show in Hamburg in 18 months.

    - Has qualities and features attractive to department stores in Europe (for example, multi-currency support and customizable business rules).

3. All other goals
    - These can often be traced back to directly stated business goals, but are indirect. For example, "easily extendible: can add <some unit of functionality> in 10 person weeks" could trace to a business goal of "new release every six months."

In the UP, many of these goals are recorded in the Vision artifact. Mind that the *Priority for Success* scores in the factor table should reflect the priority of these goals.

There is a distinguishing aspect of decision-making at this level vs. small-scale object design: one has to simultaneously consider more (and often globally influential) goals and their trade-offs. Furthermore, the business goals become central to the technical decisions (or at least they should). For example:

Technical Memo

Issue: Legal—Tax Rule Compliance

Solution Summary: Purchase a tax calculator component.

Factors

■ Current tax rules must be applied, by law.

Solution

Purchase a tax calculator with a licensing agreement to receive ongoing tax rule updates. Note that different calculators may be used at different installations.

Motivation

Time-to-market, correctness, low maintenance requirements, and happy developers (see alternatives). These products are costly, which affects our cost-containment and product pricing business goals, but the alternative is considered unacceptable.

Unresolved Issues

What are the leading products and their qualities?

Alternatives Considered

Build one by the NextGen team? It is estimated to take too long, be error prone, and create an ongoing costly and uninteresting (to the company's developers) maintenance responsibility, which affects the goal of "happy developers" (surely, the most important goal of all).

Priorities and Evolution Points: Under- and Over-engineering

Another distinguishing feature of architectural decision-making is prioritization by probability of **evolution points**—points of variability or change that *may* arise in the future. For example, in NextGen, there is a chance that wireless handheld client terminals will become desirable. Designing for this has a significant impact because of differences in operating systems, user interface, hardware resources, and so forth.

The company could spend a huge amount of money (and increase a variety of risks) to achieve this "future proofing." If it turns out in the future that this was not relevant, doing it would be a very expensive exercise in over-engineering. Note also that future proofing is arguably rarely perfect, since it is speculation; even if the predicted change occurs, some change in the speculated design is likely.

On the other hand, future proofing against the Y2K date problem would have been money very well spent; instead, there was under-engineering with a wickedly expensive result.

> The art of the architect is knowing what battles are worth fighting—where it's worth investing in designs that provide protection against evolutionary change.

To decide if early "future-proofing" should be avoided, realistically consider the scenario of deferring the change to the future, when it is called for. How much of the design and code will actually have to change? What will be the effort? Perhaps a close look at the potential change will reveal that what was at first considered a gigantic issue to protect against, is estimated to consume only a few person-weeks of effort.

This is just a hard problem; "Prediction is very difficult, especially if it's about the future" (unverifiably attributed to Niels Bohr).

Basic Architectural Design Principles

The core design principles explored in much of this book that were applicable to small-scale object design are still dominant principles at the large-scale architectural level:

- low coupling

- high cohesion

- protected variation (interfaces, indirection, service lookup, and so forth)

However, the granularity of the components is larger—it is low coupling between applications, subsystems, or process rather than between small objects.

Furthermore, at this larger scale, there are more or different mechanisms to achieve qualities such as low coupling and protected variation. For example, consider this technical memo:

Technical Memo
Issue: Adaptability—Third-Party Services

Solution Summary: Protected Variation using interfaces and Adapters

Factors

- Support many, changeable third-party services (tax calculators, credit authorization, inventory, ...)

Solution

Achieve protected variation as follows: Analyze several commercial tax calculator products (and so forth for the other product categories) and construct common interfaces for the lowest common denominators of functionality. Then use Indirection via the Adapter pattern. That is, create a resource Adapter object that implements the interface and acts as connection and translator to a particular back-end tax calculator. See also the *Reliability—Recovery from Remote Service Failure* technical memo for the location transparency aspects of this solution.

Motivation

Simple. Cheaper, and faster communication than using a messaging service (see alternatives), and in any event a messaging service can't be used to directly connect to the external credit authorization service.

Unresolved Issues

Will the lowest common denominator interfaces create an unforeseen problem, such as too limited?

Alternatives Considered

Apply indirection by using a messaging or publish-subscribe service (e.g., a JMS implementation) between the client and tax calculator, with adapters. But not directly usable with a credit authorizer, costly (for reliable ones), and more reliability in message delivery than is practically needed.

The point is that at the architectural level, there are usually new mechanisms to achieve protected variation (and other goals), often in collaboration with third-party components, such as using a Java Messaging Service (JMS) or EBJ server.

Separation of Concerns and Localization of Impact

Another basic principle applied during architectural analysis is to achieve a **separation of concerns**. It is also applicable at the scale of small objects, but achieves prominence during architectural analysis.

Cross-cutting concerns are those with a wide application or influence in the system, such as data persistence or security. One *could* design persistence support in the NextGen application such that each object (that contained application logic code) itself also communicated with a database to save its data. This would weave the concern of persistence in with the concern of application logic, in the source code of the classes—so too with security. Cohesion drops and coupling rises.

In contrast, designing for a separation of concerns factors out persistence support and security support into separate "things" (there are very different mechanisms for this separation). An object with application logic just has application logic, not persistence or security logic. Similarly, a persistence subsystem focuses on the concern of persistence, not security. A security subsystem doesn't do persistence.

Separation of concerns is a large-scale way of thinking about low coupling and high cohesion at an architectural level. It also applies to small-scale objects, because its absence results in incohesive objects that have multiple areas of responsibility. But it is especially an architectural issue because the concerns are broad, and the solutions involve major, fundamental design choices.

There are several large-scale techniques to achieve a separation of concerns:

1. Modularize the concern into a separate component (for example, subsystem) and invoke its services.

   ○ This is the most common approach. For example, in the NextGen system, the persistence support could be factored into a subsystem called the *persistence service*. Via a facade, it can offer a public interface of services to other components. Layered architectures also illustrate this separation of concerns.

2. Use decorators.

   ○ This is the second most common approach; first popularized in the Microsoft Transaction Service, and afterwards with EJB servers. In this approach, the concern (such as security) is decorated onto other objects with a Decorator object that wraps the inner object and interposes the service. The Decorator is called a **container** in EJB terminology. For example, in the NextGen POS system, security control to remote services such as the HR system can be achieved with an EJB container that adds security checks in the outer Decorator, around the application logic of the inner object.

3. Use post-compilers and aspect-oriented technologies.

   ○ For example, with EJB entity beans one can add persistence support to classes such as *Sale*. One specifies in a property descriptor file the persistence characteristics of the *Sale* class. Then, a post-compiler (by which I mean another compiler that executes after the "regular" compiler) will add the necessary persistence support in a modified *Sale* class (modifying just the bytecode) or subclass. The developer continues to see the original class as a "clean" application-logic-only class. Another variation is **aspect-oriented** technologies such as AspectJ (www.aspectj.org), which similarly support post-compilation weaving in of cross-cutting concerns into the code, in a manner that is transparent to the developer. These approaches maintain the illusion of separation during development work, and weave in the concern before execution.

Promotion of Architectural Patterns

An exploration of architectural patterns and how they could apply (or misapply) to the NextGen case study is out of scope in this introductory text. However, a few pointers:

Probably the most common mechanism to achieve low coupling, protected variation, and a separation of concerns at the architectural level is the Layers pattern, which has been introduced a previous chapter. This is an example of the most common separation technique—modularizing concerns into separate components or layers.

There is a large and growing body of written architectural patterns. Studying these is the fastest way I know of to learn architectural solutions. Please see the recommended readings.

33.8 Summary of Themes in Architectural Analysis

The *first* theme to note is that "architectural" concerns are especially related to non-functional requirements, and include an awareness of the business or market context of the application. At the same time, the functional requirements (for example, processing sales) cannot be ignored; they provide the context within which these concerns must be resolved. Further, identification of their variability is architecturally significant.

A *second* theme is that architectural concerns involve system-level, large-scale, and broad problems whose resolution usually involves large-scale or fundamental design decisions; for example, the choice of—or even use of—an application server.

A *third* theme in architectural analysis is interdependencies and trade-offs. For example, improved security may affect performance or usability, and most choices affect cost.

A *fourth* theme in architecture analysis is the generation and evaluation of alternative solutions. A skilled architect can offer design solutions that involve building new software, and also suggest solutions (or partial solutions) using commercial or publicly available software and hardware. For example, recovery in a remote server of the NextGen POS can be achieved through designing and programming "watchdog" processes, or perhaps through clustering, replication, and fail-over services offered by some operating system and hardware components. Good architects know third-party hardware and software products.

The opening definition of architectural concerns provides the framework for how to think about the subject of architecture: identifying the issues with large-scale or system-level implications, and resolving them.

Definition

Architectural analysis is concerned with the identification and resolution of the system's non-functional requirements in the context of the functional requirements.

33.9 Process: Iterative Architecture in the UP

The UP is an architecture-centric iterative and evolutionary method. This does *not* mean a waterfall attempt to fully identify all architectural requirements before development, nor an attempt to fully design the "correct" architecture before program and test. Rather, it means that early iterations focus on programming and testing architecturally significant concerns (such as security) and using, proving, developing and stabilizing the key architectural elements (subsystems, interfaces, frameworks, and so on).

In the UP, the architecture evolves and stabilizes through early development and test with an architecture-focus, not through speculation on paper, or "PowerPoint Architecture."

documenting archi-
tecture and the
SAD p. 655

In the UP, the architectural factors—or requirements—are recorded in the Supplementary Specification, and the architectural decisions that resolve them are recorded in the **Software Architecture Document** (SAD). Because the UP is not the waterfall, the SAD is not fully created before programming, but rather, after programming—once the code has stabilized. Then, the SAD documents the actual system as a learning aid for others.

Architectural analysis starts early, during the inception phase, and is a focus of the elaboration phase; it is a high-priority and very influential activity in software development.

Architectural Information in the UP Artifacts

- The architectural factors (for example, in a factor table) are recorded in the Supplementary Specification.

- The architectural decisions are recorded in the SAD. This includes the technical memos and descriptions of the architectural views.

Phases

Inception—If it is unclear whether it is technically possible to satisfy the architecturally significant requirements, the team may implement an **architectural proof-of-concept** (POC) to determine feasibility. In the UP, its creation and assessment is called **Architectural Synthesis**. This is distinct from plain old small POC programming experiments for isolated technical questions. An architectural POC lightly covers *many* of the architecturally significant requirements to assess their *combined* feasibility.

Elaboration—A major goal of this phase is to implement the core risky architectural elements, thus most architectural analysis is completed during elaboration. It is normally expected that the majority of factor table, technical memo, and SAD content can be completed by the end of elaboration.

Transition—Although ideally the architecturally significant factors and decisions were resolved long before transition, the SAD will need a review and possible revision at the end of this phase to ensure it accurately describes the final deployed system.

Subsequent evolution cycles—Before the design of new versions, it is common to revisit architectural factors and decisions. For example, the decision in version 1.0 to create a single remote tax calculator service, rather than one duplicated on each POS node, could have been motivated by cost (to avoid multiple licenses). But perhaps in the future the cost of tax calculators is reduced, and thus, for fault tolerance or performance reasons, the architecture is changed to use multiple local tax calculators.

33.10 Recommended Resources

There is a growing body of architecture-related patterns, and general software architecture advice. Suggestions:

- *Beyond Software Architecture* [Hohman03]. This useful guide, from someone experienced as both architect and product manager, brings a business-oriented emphasis to architecture. Hohman shares his experience with important issues seldom covered, such as the impact of the business model, licensing, and upgrades on the software architecture.

- *Patterns of Enterprise Application Architecture* [Fowler02].

- *Software Architecture in Practice* [BCK98].

- *Pattern-Oriented Software Architecture*, both volumes.

- *Pattern Languages of Program Design*, all volumes. Each volume has a section on architecture-related patterns.

LOGICAL ARCHITECTURE REFINEMENT

Alcohol and calculus don't mix... Don't drink and derive.

—anonymous

Objectives

- Explore more issues in logical architecture and the Layers pattern, including inter-layer collaboration.
- Present the logical architecture for this iteration of the case studies.
- Apply the Facade, Observer, and Controller patterns in the context of architectural layers.

Introduction

Logical architecture and the Layers pattern was introduced starting on p. 197. This chapter dives a bit deeper—looking at some intermediate topics related to layered architectures.

What's Next?   Having introduced architectural analysis, this chapter explores more issues in the Layers pattern and logical architecture. The next introduces how to design packages—a design subject that doesn't receive enough attention.

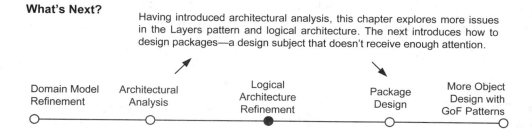

| Domain Model Refinement | Architectural Analysis | Logical Architecture Refinement | Package Design | More Object Design with GoF Patterns |

34.1   Example: NextGen Logical Architecture

example of common layers p. 202   Figure 34.1 illustrates a partial logical layered architecture for this iteration of NextGen application.

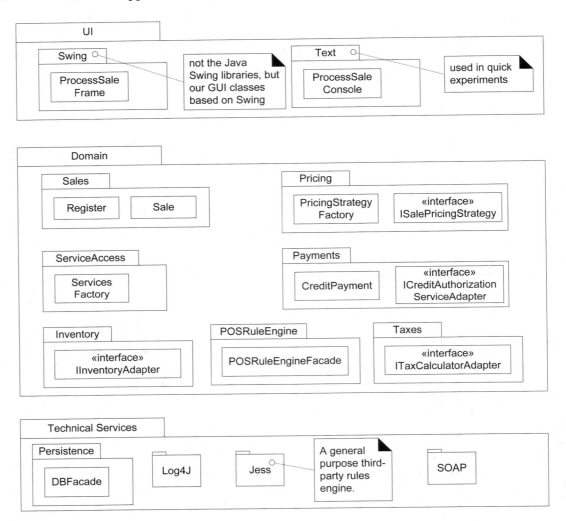

Figure 34.1 Partial logical view of layers in the NextGen application.

Note the absence of an Application layer for this iteration of the design; as discussed later, it is not always necessary.

Since this is iterative development, it is normal to create a design of layers that starts simple, and evolves over the iterations of the elaboration phase. One goal of this phase is to have the core architecture established (designed and implemented) by the end of the iterations in elaboration, but this does not mean doing a large up-front speculative architectural design before starting to program. Rather, a tentative logical architecture is designed in the early iterations, and it evolves incrementally through the elaboration phase.

Observe that just a few sample types are present in this package diagram; this is not only motivated by limited page space in formatting this book, but is a signature quality of an **architectural view** diagram—it only shows a few noteworthy elements in order to concisely convey the big ideas of the architecturally significant aspects. The idea in a UP architectural view document is to say to the reader, "I've chosen this small set of instructive elements to convey the big ideas."

Comments on Figure 34.1:

- There are other types in these packages; only a few are shown to indicate noteworthy aspects.

- The Foundation layer was not shown in this view; the architect (me) decided it did not add interesting information, even though the development team will certainly be adding some Foundation classes, such as more advanced *String* manipulation utilities.

- For now, a separate Application layer is not used. The responsibilities of control or session objects in the Application layer are handled by the *Register* object. The architect will add an Application layer in a later iteration as the behavior grows in complexity, and alternative client interfaces are introduced (such as a Web browser and wireless networked handheld PDA).

Inter-Layer and Inter-Package Coupling

To help someone understand the NextGen logical architecture, it's also informative to include a diagram in the logical view that illustrates noteworthy coupling between the layers and packages. A partial example is illustrated in Figure 34.2.

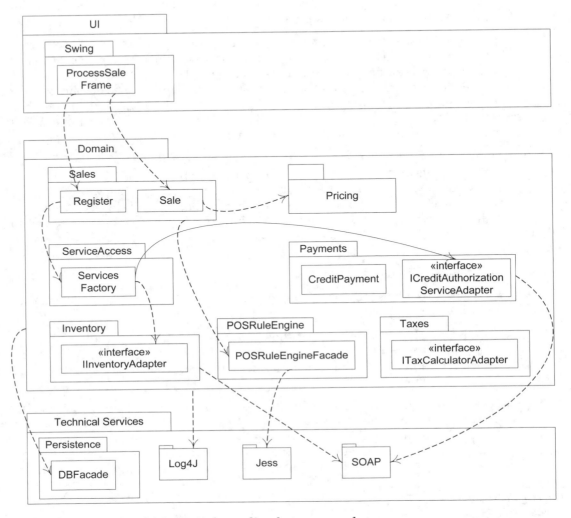

Figure 34.2 Partial coupling between packages.

Applying UML:

- Observe that dependency lines can be used to communicate coupling between packages or types in packages. Plain dependency lines are excellent when the communicator does not care to be more specific on the exact dependency (attribute visibility, subclassing, ...), but just wants to highlight general dependencies.

- Note also the use of a dependency line emitting from a package rather than a particular type, such as from the *Sales* package to *POSRuleEngineFacade* class, and the *Domain* package to the *Log4J* package. This is useful when either the specific dependent type is not interesting, or the communicator wants to suggest that many elements of the package may share that dependency.

Another common use of a package diagram is to hide the specific types, and focus on illustrating the package-package coupling, as in the partial diagram of Figure 34.3.

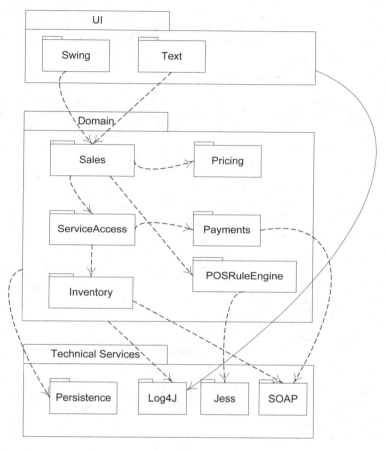

Figure 34.3 Partial package coupling.

In fact, Figure 34.3 illustrates probably the most common style of logical architecture diagram in the UML—a package diagram that shows between perhaps 5 to 20 major packages, and their dependencies.

Inter-Layer and Inter-Package Interaction Scenarios

Package diagrams show static information. To help someone understand the *dynamics* in the NextGen logical architecture, it's also useful to include a diagram of how objects across the layers connect and communicate. Thus, an interaction diagram is helpful. In the spirit of an "architectural view" which hides uninteresting details, and emphasizes what the architect wants to convey, an interaction diagram in the logical view of the architecture focuses on the collaborations as they cross layer and package boundaries. A set of interaction diagrams that illustrate **architecturally significant scenarios** (in the sense that they illustrate many aspects of the large-scale or big ideas in the design) is thus useful.

For example, Figure 34.4 illustrates part of a *Process Sale* scenario that emphasizes the connection points across the layers and packages.

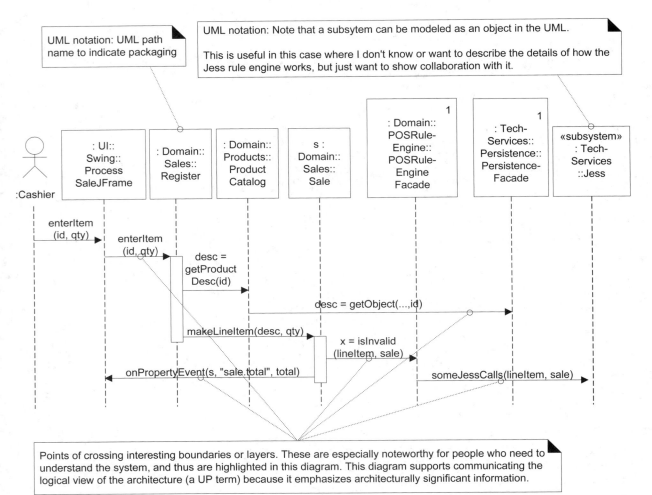

Figure 34.4 An architecturally significant interaction diagram that emphasizes cross-boundary connections.

Applying UML:

■ The package of a type can optionally be shown by qualifying the type with the UML **path name** expression *<PackageName>::<TypeName>*. For example, *Domain::Sales::Register*. This can be exploited to highlight to the reader the inter-package and inter-layer connections in the interaction diagram.

- Note also the use of the «subsystem» stereotype. In the UML, a subsystem is a discrete entity that has behavior and interfaces. A subsystem can be modeled as a special kind of package, or—as shown here—as an object, which is useful when one wants to show inter-subsystem (or system) collaborations. In the UML, the entire system is also a "subsystem" (the root one), and thus can also be shown as an object in interaction diagrams (such as an SSD).

- Note the use of the '1' in the top right corner to indicate a singleton, and suggest access using the GoF Singleton pattern.

Observe that the diagram ignores showing some messages, such as certain *Sale* collaborations, in order to highlight architecturally significant interactions.

34.2 Collaborations with the Layers Pattern

Two design decisions at an architectural level are:

1. What are the big parts?

2. How are they connected?

Whereas the architectural Layers pattern guides defining the big parts, micro-architectural design patterns such as Facade, Controller, and Observer are commonly used for the design of the connections between layers and packages. This section examines patterns in connection and communication between layers and packages.

Simple Packages versus Subsystems

Some packages or layers are not just conceptual groups of things, but are true subsystems with behavior and interfaces. To contrast:

- The *Pricing* package is not a subsystem; it simply groups the factory and strategies used in pricing. Likewise with Foundation packages such as *java.util*.

- On the other hand, the *Persistence, POSRuleEngine,* and *Jess* packages are subsystems. They are discrete engines with cohesive responsibilities that do work.

In the UML, a subsystem can be identified with a stereotype, as in Figure 34.5.

Facade

For packages that represent subsystems, the most common pattern of access is Facade, a GoF design pattern. That is, a public facade object defines the services for the subsystem, and clients collaborate with the facade, not internal subsystem components. This is true of the *POSRuleEngineFacade* and the *PersistenceFacade* for access to the rules engine and persistence subsystem.

The facade should not normally expose many low-level operations. Rather, it is desirable for the facade to expose a small number of high-level operations—the coarse-grained services. When a facade does expose many low-level operations, it tends to become incohesive. Furthermore, if the facade will be, or might become, a distributed or remote object (such as an EJB session bean, or RMI server object), fine-grained services lead to remote communication performance problems—lots of little remote calls are a performance bottleneck in distributed systems.

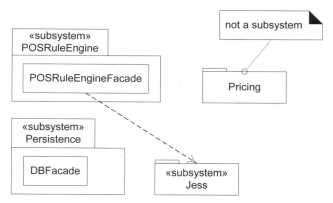

Figure 34.5 Subsystem stereotypes.

Also, a facade does not normally do its own work. Rather, it is consolidator or mediator to the underlying subsystem objects, which do the work.

For example, the *POSRuleEngineFacade* is the wrapper and single point of access into the rules engine for the POS application. Other packages do not see the implementation of this subsystem, as it is hidden behind the facade. Suppose (this is just one of many implementations) that the POS rules engine subsystem is implemented by collaborating with the Jess rules engine. Jess is a subsystem that exposes many fine-grained operations (this is common for very general, third-party subsystems). But the *POSRuleEngineFacade* does not expose the low-level Jess operations in its interface. Rather, it provides only a few high-level operation such as *isInvalid(lineItem, sale)*.

If the application has only a "small" number of system operations, then it is common for the Application or Domain layer to expose only one object to an upper layer. On the other hand, the Technical Services layer, which contains several subsystems, exposes at least one facade (or several public objects, if facades aren't used) for each subsystem to upper layers. See Figure 34.6.

Session Facades and the Application Layer

In contrast to Figure 34.6, when an application has many system operations and supports many use cases, it is common to have more than one object mediating between the UI and Domain layers.

In the current version of the NextGen system, there is a simple design of a single *Register* object acting as the facade onto the Domain layer (by virtue of the GRASP controller pattern).

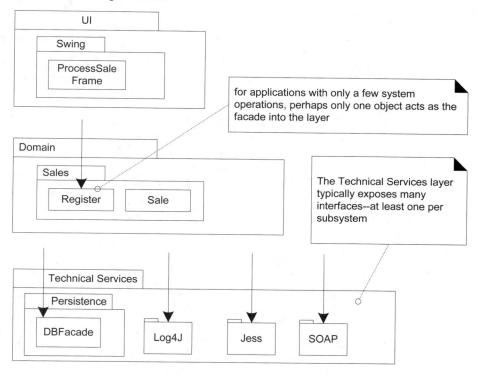

Figure 34.6 Number of interfaces exposed to upper layers.

However, as the system grows to handle many use cases and system operations, it is not uncommon to introduce an Application layer of objects that maintain session state for the operations of a use case, where each session instance represents a session with one client. These are called Session Facades, and their use is another recommendation of the GRASP Controller pattern, such as in the use-case session facade controller variant of the pattern. See Figure 34.7 for an example of how the NextGen architecture may evolve with an Application layer and session facades.

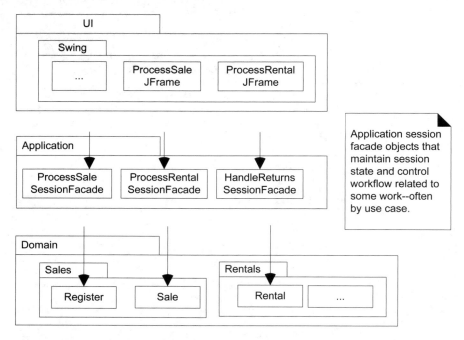

Application session facade objects that maintain session state and control workflow related to some work--often by use case.

Figure 34.7 Session facades and an Application Layer.

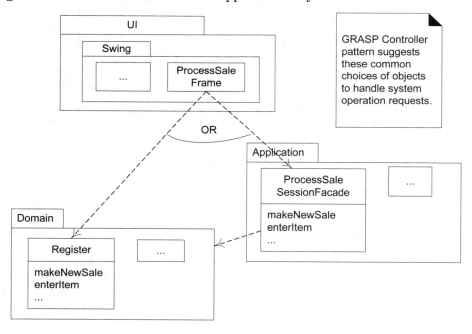

GRASP Controller pattern suggests these common choices of objects to handle system operation requests.

Figure 34.8 The Controller choices.

Controller

The GRASP Controller pattern describes common choices in client-side handlers (or controllers, as they've been called) for system operation requests emitting from the UI layer. Figure 34.8 illustrates.

System Operations and Layers

The SSDs illustrate the system operations, hiding UI objects from the diagram. The system operations being invoked on the system in Figure 34.9 are requests being generated by an actor via the UI layer, onto the Application or Domain layer.

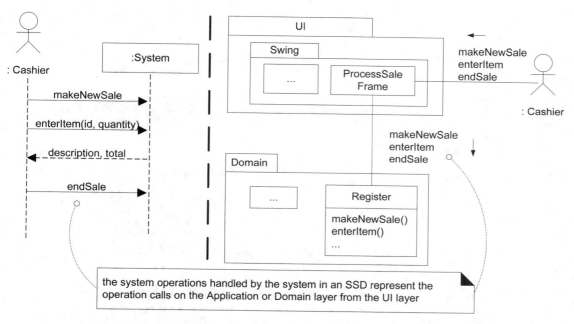

Figure 34.9 System operations in the SSDs and in terms of layers.

Upward Collaboration with Observer

The Facade pattern is commonly used for "downward" collaboration from a higher to a lower layer, or for access to services in another subsystem of the same layer. When the lower Application or Domain layer needs to communicate upward with the UI layer, it is usually via the Observer pattern. That is, UI objects in the higher UI layer implement an interface such as *PropertyListener* or *AlarmListener*, and are subscribers or listeners to events (such as property or alarm events) coming from objects in the lower layers. The lower layer objects are directly sending messages to the upper layer UI objects, but the coupling is only to the objects viewed as things that implement an interface, such as *PropertyListener*, not viewed as specific GUI windows.

This was examined when the Observer pattern was introduced. Figure 34.10 summarizes the idea in relation to layers.

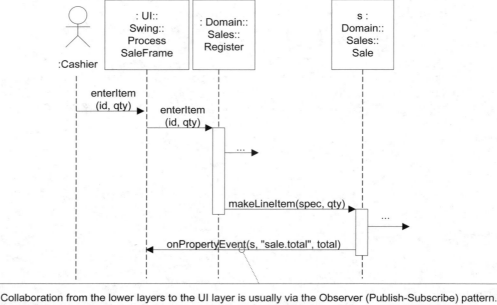

Figure 34.10 Observer for "upward" communication to the UI layer.

Relaxed Layered Coupling

The layers in most layered architectures are *not* coupled in the same limited sense as a network protocol based on the OSI 7-Layer Model. In the protocol model, there is strict restriction that elements of layer N only access the services of the immediate lower layer N-1.

This is rarely followed in information system architectures. Rather, the standard is a "relaxed layered" or "transparent layered" architecture [BMRSS96], in which elements of a layer collaborate with or are coupled to several other layers.

Comments on typical coupling between layers:

- All higher layers have dependencies on the Technical Services and Foundations layer.

    o For example, in Java all layers depend on *java.util* package elements.

- It is primarily the Domain layer that has dependency on the Business Infrastructure layer.

- The UI layer makes calls on the Application layer, which makes service calls on the Domain layer; the UI layer does not call on the Domain, unless there is no Application layer.

- If it is a single-process "desktop" application, software objects in the Domain layer are directly visible to, or passed between, UI, Application, and to a lesser extent, Technical Services.

  ○ For example, assuming the NextGen POS system is of this type, a *Sale* and a *Payment* object could be directly visible to the GUI UI Layer, and also passed into the Persistence subsystem in the Technical Services layer.

- On the other hand, if it is a distributed system, then serializable **replicates** (also known as **data holder** or **value objects**) of objects in the Domain layer are usually passed to a UI layer. In this case, the Domain layer is deployed on a server computer, and client nodes get copies of server data.

Isn't Coupling to Technical and Foundation Layers Dangerous?

As the GRASP Protected Variations and Low Coupling discussions explored, it is not coupling per se that is a problem, but unnecessary coupling to variation and evolution points that are unstable and expensive to fix. There is very little justification in spending time and money attempting to abstract or hide something that is unlikely to change, or if it did, the change impact cost would be negligible. For example, if building a Java technologies application, what value is there in hiding the application from access to the Java libraries? High coupling into many points of the libraries is an unlikely problem, as they are (relatively) stable and ubiquitous.

34.3   Other Layer Pattern Issues

In addition to the structural and collaboration issues discussed above for the Layers pattern, other issues include the following.

Logical versus Process and Deployment Views of the Architecture

The architectural layers are a logical view of the architecture, not a deployment view of elements to processes and processing nodes. Depending on the platform, *all* layers could be deployed within the same process on the same node, such as an application within a handheld PDA, or spread across many computers and processes for a large-scale Web application.

The UP Deployment Model that maps this logical architecture to processes and nodes is strongly influenced by the choice of software and hardware platform and associated application frameworks. For example, J2EE versus .NET influence the deployment architecture.

There are many ways to slice and dice these logical layers for deployment, and in general the subject of deployment architecture will only be lightly introduced, as it is non-trivial, largely outside the scope of the book, and dependent on detailed discussion of the chosen software platform, such as J2EE.

Is the Application Layer Optional?

If present, the Application layer contains objects responsible for knowing the session state of clients, mediating between the UI and Domain layers, and controlling the flow of work.

The flow may be organized by controlling the order of windows or web pages, for example.

In terms of the GRASP patterns, GRASP Controller objects such as a use case facade controller are part of this layer. In distributed systems, components such as EJB session beans (and stateful session objects in general) are part of this layer.

In some applications, this layer is not required. It is useful (this is not an exhaustive list) when one or more of the following is true:

- Multiple user interfaces (for example, web pages and a Swing GUI) will be used for the system. The Application layer objects can act as Adapters that collect and consolidate the data as needed for different UIs, and as Facades that wrap and hide access to the Domain layer.

- It is a distributed system and the Domain layer is on a different node than the UI layer, and shared by multiple clients. It is usually necessary to keep track of session state, and Application layer objects are a useful choice for this responsibility.

- The Domain Layer cannot or should not maintain session state.

- There is a defined workflow in terms of the controlled order of windows or Web pages that must be presented.

Fuzzy Set Membership in Different Layers

Some elements are strongly a member of one layer; a *Math* class is part of the Foundation layer. However, especially between the Technical Services and Foundation layers, and Domain and Business Infrastructure, some elements are harder to classify, because the differentiation between these layers is, roughly, "high" versus "low," or "specific" versus "general." which are fuzzy set terms. This is normal, and it is seldom necessary to decide upon a definitive categorization—the development team may consider an element roughly part of the Technical Services and/or Foundations layer considered as a group, broadly called the Infrastructure layer.[1]

For example:

- Suppose this is a Java technologies project, and the open source logging framework *Log4J* (part of the Jakarta project) has been chosen. Is logging part of the Technical Service or Foundation layer? Log4J is a low-level, small, general framework. It is moderately a member of both the Technical Services and the Foundations fuzzy sets.

- Suppose this is a Web application, and the Jakarta *Struts* framework for web applications has been chosen. Struts is a relatively high-level, large, specific technical framework. It is arguably strongly a member of the Technical Services set, and weakly a member of the Foundation set.

But, one person's High-level Technical Service is another's Foundation...

Finally, it is not the case that the libraries provided by a software platform only represent low-level Foundation services. For example, in both .NET and J2SE+J2EE, services include relatively high-level functions such as naming and directory services.

Contraindications and Liabilities for Layers

- In some contexts, adding layers introduces performance problems. For example, in a high-performance graphics-intensive game, adding layers of abstraction and indirection on top of direct access to graphics card components may introduce performance problems.

- The Layers pattern is one of several core architectural patterns; it is not applicable to every problem. For example, an alternate is Pipes and Filters [BMRSS96]. This is useful when the main theme of the application involves processing something through a series transformations, such as image transformations, and the ordering of the transformations is changeable. Yet even in the case when the highest level architectural pattern is Pipes and Filters, individual pipes or filters can be design, with Layers.

Known Uses

A vast number of modern object-oriented systems (from desktop applications to distributed J2EE Web systems) are developed with Layers; it might be harder to find one that is not, than is. Going farther back in history:

Virtual Machines and Operating Systems

Starting in the 1960s, operating system architects advocated the design of operating systems in terms of clearly defined layers, where the "lower" layers encapsulated access to the physical resources and provided process and I/O services,

---

1. Note that there are not well-established naming conventions for layers, and name overloading and contradiction in the architecture literature is common.

and higher layers called on these services. These included Multics [CV65] and the THE system [Dijkstra68].

Earlier still—in the 1950s—researchers suggested the idea of a virtual machine (VM) with a bytecode universal machine language (for example, UNCOL [Conway1958]), so that applications could be written at higher layers in the architecture (and executed without recompilation across different platforms), on top of the virtual machine layer, which in turn would sit on top of the operating system and machine resources. A VM layered architecture was applied by Alan Kay in his landmark Flex object-oriented personal computer system [Kay68] and later (1972) by Kay and Dan Ingalls in the influential Smalltalk virtual machine [GK76]—the progenitor of more recent VMs such as the Java Virtual Machine.

Information Systems: The Classic Three-Tier Architecture

An early influential description of a layered architecture for information systems that included a user interface and persistent storage of data was known as a **three-tier architecture** (Figure 34.11), described in the 1970s in [TK78]. The phrase did not achieve popularity until the mid 1990s, in part due to its promotion in [Gartner95] as a solution to problems associated with the widespread use of two-tier architectures.

The original term is now less common, but its motivation is still relevant.

A classic description of the vertical tiers in a three-tier architecture is:

1. **Interface**—windows, reports, and so on.

2. **Application Logic**—tasks and rules that govern the process.

3. **Storage**—persistent storage mechanism.

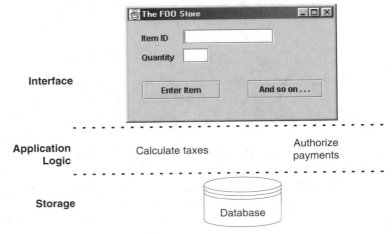

Figure 34.11 Classic view of a three-tier architecture.

The singular quality of a three-tier architecture is the separation of the application logic into a distinct logical middle tier of software. The interface tier is relatively free of application processing; windows or Web pages forward task requests to the middle tier. The middle tier communicates with the back-end storage layer.

There was some misunderstanding that the original description implied or required a physical deployment on three computers, but the intended description was purely logical; the allocation of the tiers to compute nodes could vary from one to three. See Figure 34.12.

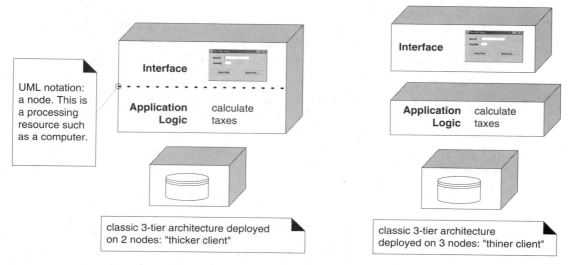

Figure 34.12 A three-tier logical division deployed in two physical architectures.

The three-tier architecture was contrasted by the Gartner Group with a **two-tier** design, in which, for example, application logic is placed within window definitions, which read and write directly to a database; there is no middle tier that separates out the application logic. Two-tier client-server architectures became especially popular with the rise of tools such as Visual Basic and PowerBuilder.

Two-tier designs have (in some cases) the advantage of initial quick development, but can suffer the complaints covered in the *Problems* section. Nevertheless, there are applications that are primarily simple CRUD (create, retrieve, update, delete) data intensive systems, for which this is a suitable choice.

Related Patterns

- Indirection—layers can add a level of indirection to lower-level services.

- Protected Variation—layers can protect against the impact of varying implementations.

- Low Coupling and High Cohesion—layers strongly support these goals.

■ Its application specifically to object-oriented information systems is described in [Fowler96].

Also Known As

The Layers pattern is also known as Layered Architecture [Shaw96, Gemstone00].

34.4   Model-View Separation and "Upward" Communication

How can windows obtain information to display? Usually, it is sufficient for them to send messages to domain objects, querying for information which they then display in widgets—a **polling** or **pull-from-above** model of display updates.

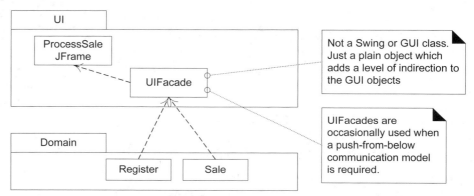

Figure 34.13 A UI layer UIFacade is occasionally used for push-from-below designs.

However, a polling model is sometimes insufficient. For example, polling every second across thousands of objects to discover only one or two changes, which are then used to refresh a GUI display, is not efficient. In this case it is more efficient for the few changing domain objects to communicate with windows to cause a display update as the state of domain objects changes. Typical situations of this case include:

■ Monitoring applications, such as telecommunications network management.

■ Simulation applications that require visualization, such as aerodynamics modeling.

In these situations, a **push-from-below** model of display update is required. Because of the restriction of the Model-View Separation pattern, this leads to the need for "indirect" communication from lower objects up to windows—pushing up notification to update from below.

There are two common solutions:

1. The Observer pattern, via making the GUI object simply appear as an object that implements an interface such as *PropertyListener*.

2. A UI facade object. That is, adding a facade within the UI layer that receives requests from below. This is an example of adding Indirection to provide Protected Variation if the GUI changes. For example, see Figure 34.13.

34.5 Recommended Resources

There's a wealth of literature on layered architectures, both in print and on the Web. A series of patterns in *Pattern Languages of Program Design*, volume 1, [CS95] first address the topic in pattern form, although layered architectures have been used and written about since at least the 1960s; volume 2 continues with further layers-related patterns. *Pattern-Oriented Software Architecture* volume 1 [BMRSS96] provides a good treatment of the Layers pattern.

PACKAGE DESIGN

*If you were plowing a field, which would you
rather use? Two strong oxen or 1024 chickens?*

—*Seymour Cray*

Objectives

- Organize packages to reduce the impact of changes.
- Know alternative UML package structure notation.

Introduction

If some package X is widely depended upon by the development team, it is undesirable for X to be very unstable (going through many new versions), since it increases the impact on the team in terms of constant version re-synchronization and fixing dependent software that breaks in response to changes in X (**version thrashing**).

This sounds—and is—obvious, but sometimes a team does not pay attention to identifying and stabilizing the most depended-upon packages, and ends up experiencing more version thrashing than necessary, unaware of the underlying cause.

What's Next?   Having explored more issues in the Layers pattern, this chapter introduces how to design packages—a design subject that doesn't receive enough attention. The next explores applying more GoF and GRASP patterns for the use-case realizations of the case studies.

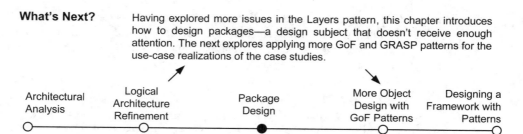

| Architectural Analysis | Logical Architecture Refinement | Package Design | More Object Design with GoF Patterns | Designing a Framework with Patterns |

This chapter builds on previous chapter's introduction to layers and packages, by suggesting more fine-grained heuristics for the organization of packages, to reduce these kinds of change impact. The goal is to create a robust physical package design.

One feels the pain of fragile dependency-sensitive package organization much more quickly in C++ than in Java because of the hyper-sensitive compile and link dependencies in C++; a change in one class can have a strong transitive dependency impact leading to recompilation of many classes, and re-linking.[1] Therefore, these suggestions are especially helpful for C++ projects and moderately so for Java or C# (as examples) projects.

The useful work of Robert Martin [Martin95], who has grappled with physical design and packaging of C++ applications, influenced some of the following guidelines.

Source Code Physical Design in the Implementation Model

This issue is an aspect of **physical design**—the UP Implementation Model for source code packaging.

While simply diagramming a package design on a whiteboard or CASE tool, we can arbitrarily place types in any functionally cohesive package without impact. But during source code physical design—the organization of types into physical units of release as Java or C++ "packages"—our choices will influence the degree of developer impact when changes in those packages occur, if there are many developers sharing a common code base.

35.1 Package Organization Guidelines

Guideline: Package Functionally Cohesive Vertical and Horizontal Slices

The basic "intuitive" principle is modularization based on functional cohesion—types (classes and interfaces) are grouped together that are strongly related in terms of their participation in a common purpose, service, collaborations, policy, and function. For example, all the types in the NextGen *Pricing* package are related to product pricing. The layers and packages in the NextGen design are organized by functional groups.

In addition to the usually sufficient informal guesswork on grouping by function ("I think class *SalesLineItem* belongs in *Sales*") another clue to functional grouping is a cluster of types with strong internal coupling and weaker extra-cluster

---

1. In C++ the packages may be realized as namespaces, but more likely it means the organization of the source code into separate physical directories—one for each "package."

coupling. For example, *Register* has a strong coupling to *Sale*, which has a strong coupling to *SalesLineItem*.

Internal package coupling, or **relational cohesion**, can be quantified, although such formal analysis is rarely of practical necessity. For the curious, one measure is:

$$RC = \frac{NumberOfInternalRelations}{NumberOfTypes}$$

Where *NumberOfInternalRelations* includes attribute and parameter relations, inheritance, and interface implementations between types in the package.

A package of 6 types with 12 internal relations has RC=2. A package of 6 types with 3 intra-type relations has RC=0.5. Higher numbers suggest more cohesion or relatedness for the package.

Note that this measure is less applicable to packages of mostly interfaces; it is most useful for packages that contain some implementation classes.

A very low RC value suggests either:

- The package contains unrelated things and is not factored well.

- The package contains unrelated things and the designer deliberately does not care. This is common with utility packages of disparate services (e.g., *java.util*), where high or low RC is not important.

- It contains one or more subset clusters with high RC, but overall does not.

Guideline: Package a Family of Interfaces

Place a family of functionally related *interfaces* in a separate package—separate from implementation classes. The Java technologies EJB package *javax.ejb* is an example: It is a package of at least twelve interfaces; implementations are in separate packages.

Guideline: Package by Work and by Clusters of Unstable Classes

The context for this discussion is that packages are usually the basic unit of development work and of release. It is less common to work on and release just one class. Unless a package is massive or very complex, a developer is often responsible for all the types within it.

Suppose 1) there is an existing large package P1 with thirty classes, and 2) there is a work trend that a particular subset of ten classes (C1 through C10) is regularly modified and re-released.

In this case, refactor P1 into P1-a and P1-b, where P1-b contains the ten frequently worked on classes.

Thus, the package has been refactored into more stable and less stable subsets, or more generally, into groups related to work. That is, if most types in a package are worked on together, then it is a useful grouping.

Ideally, fewer developers have a dependency on P1-b than on P1-a, and by factoring out this unstable part to a separate package, not as many developers are affected by new releases of P1-b as by re-releasing the larger original package P1.

Note that this refactoring is in reaction to an emerging work trend. It is difficult to speculatively identify a good package structure in very early iterations. It incrementally evolves over the elaboration iterations, and it should be a goal of the elaboration phase (because it is architecturally significant) to have the majority of the package structure stabilized by elaboration completion.

This guideline illustrates the basic strategy: **Reduce widespread dependency on unstable packages**.

Guideline: Most Responsible Are Most Stable

If the most responsible (depended-on) packages are unstable, there is a greater chance of widespread change dependency impact. As an extreme case, if a widely used utility package such as *com.foo.util* changed frequently, many things could break. Therefore, Figure 35.1 illustrates an appropriate dependency structure.

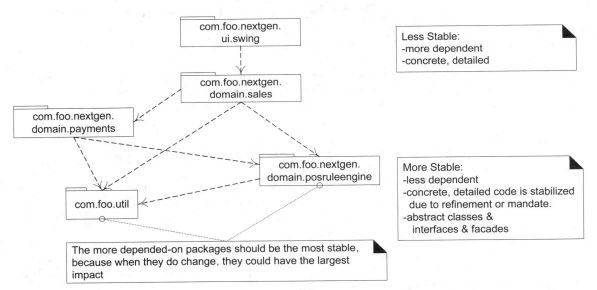

Figure 35.1 More responsible packages should be more stable.

Visually, the lower packages in this diagram should be the most stable.

There are different ways to increase stability in a package:

- It contains only or mostly interfaces and abstract classes.
    - For example, *java.sql* contains eight interfaces and six classes, and the classes are mostly simple, stable types such as *Time* and *Date*.
- It has no dependencies on other packages (it is independent), or it depends on other very stable packages, or it encapsulates its dependencies such that dependents are not affected.
    - For example, *com.foo.nextgen.domain.posruleengine* hides its rule engine implementation behind a single facade object. Even if the implementation changes, dependent packages are not affected.
- It contains relatively stable code because it was well-exercised and refined before release.
    - For example, *java.util*.
- It is mandated to have a slow change schedule.
    - For example, *java.lang*, the core package in the Java libraries, is simply not allowed to change frequently.

Guideline: Factor out Independent Types

Organize types that can be used independently or in different contexts into separate packages. Without careful consideration, grouping by common functionality may not provide the right level of granularity in the factoring of packages.

For example, suppose that a subsystem for persistence services has been defined in one package *com.foo.service.persistence*. In this package are two very general utility/helper classes *JDBCUtililities* and *SQLCommand*. If these are general utilities for working with JDBC (Java's services for relational database access), then they can be used independently of the persistence subsystem, for any occasion when the developer is using JDBC. Therefore, it is better to migrate these types into a separate package, such as *com.foo.util.jdbc*. Figure 35.2 illustrates.

Guideline: Use Factories to Reduce Dependency on Concrete Packages

One way to increase package stability is to reduce its dependency on concrete classes in other packages. Figure 35.3 illustrates the "before" situation.

Suppose that both *Register* and *PaymentMapper* (a class that maps payment objects to/from a relational database) create instances of *CreditPayment* from package *Payments*. One mechanism to increase the long-term stability of the *Sales* and *Persistence* packages is to stop explicitly creating concrete classes defined in other packages (*CreditPayment* in *Payments*).

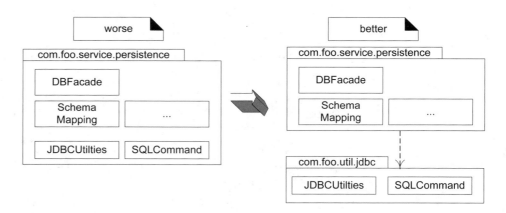

Figure 35.2 Factoring out independent types.

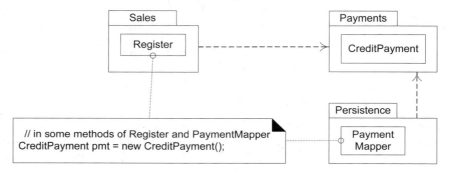

Figure 35.3 Direct coupling to concrete package due to creation.

We can reduce the coupling to this concrete package by using a factory object that creates the instances, but whose create methods return objects declared in terms of interfaces rather than classes. See Figure 35.4.

Domain Object Factory Pattern

The use of domain object factories with interfaces for the creation of *all* domain objects is a common design idiom. I have seen it mentioned informally in design literature as the Domain Object Factory pattern, but don't know of a published reference.

Guideline: No Cycles in Packages

If a group of packages have cyclic dependency, then they may need to be treated as one larger package in terms of a release unit. This is undesirable because releasing larger packages (or package aggregates) increases the likelihood of affecting something.

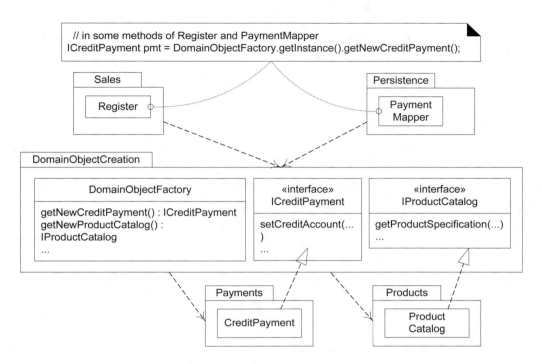

Figure 35.4 Reduced coupling to a concrete package by using a factory object.

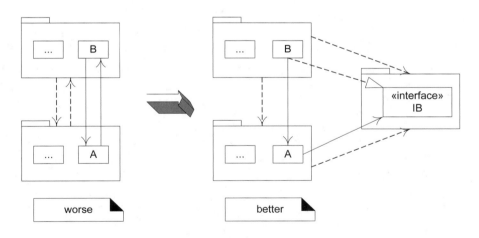

Figure 35.5 Breaking a cyclic dependency.

There are two solutions:

1. Factor out the types participating in the cycle into a new smaller package.
2. Break the cycle with an interface.

The steps to break the cycle with an interface are:

1. Redefine the depended-on classes in one of the packages to implement new interfaces.

2. Define the new interfaces in a new package.

3. Redefine the dependent types to depend on the interfaces in the new package, rather than the original classes.

Figure 35.5 illustrates this strategy.

35.2   Recommended Resources

Most of the detailed work—not surprisingly—on improving package design to reduce dependency impact comes from the C++ community, although the principles apply to other languages. Martin's *Designing Object-Oriented C++ Applications Using the Booch Method* [Martin95] provides good coverage, as does *Large-Scale C++ Software Design* [Lakos96]. The subject is also introduced in *Java 2 Performance and Idiom Guide* [GL99].

MORE OBJECT DESIGN WITH GoF PATTERNS

On two occasions I have been asked (by members of Parliament), "Pray, Mr. Babbage, if you put into the machine wrong figures, will the right answers come out?" I am not able rightly to apprehend the kind of confusion of ideas that could provoke such a question.

—Charles Babbage

Objectives

■ Apply GoF and GRASP in the design of the use-case realizations.

Introduction

This chapter explores more OO designs, applying GoF and GRASP patterns, to the current iteration of both case studies. For NextGen POS, we tackle requirements such as failover to local services, POS device handling, and payment authorization, while demonstrating applying GoF patterns. For the Monopoly problem, we tackle landing on property squares and buying or paying rent. Monopoly (starting on p. 615) demonstrates applying basic GRASP principles.

What's Next?

Having explored detailed package design, this chapter explores applying more GoF and GRASP patterns. And the next applies GoF patterns to the design of a framework—an important OO design skill.

| Logical Architecture Refinement | Package Design | More Object Design with GoF Patterns | Designing a Framework with Patterns | UML Deployment & Component Diagrams |

36.1   Example: NextGen POS

The following sections explore applying patterns and principles to various iteration-3 NextGen requirements, including:

- failover to a local service when a remote service fails

- local caching

- support for third-party POS devices, such as different scanners

- handling credit, debit, and check payments

36.2   Failover to Local Services; Performance with Local Caching

One of the NextGen requirements is some degree of recovery from remote service failure, such as a (temporarily) unavailable product database.

Access to product information is the first case used to explore the recovery and failover design strategy. Afterwards, access to the accounting service is explored, which has a slightly different solution.

To review part of the technical memo:

Technical Memo

Issue: Reliability—Recovery from Remote Service Failure

Solution Summary: Location transparency using service lookup, failover from remote to local, and local service partial replication.

Factors

- Robust recovery from remote service failure (e.g., tax calculator, inventory)
- Robust recovery from remote product (e.g., descriptions and prices) database failure

Solution

Achieve protected variation with respect to location of services using the Adapter served up from a ServicesFactory. Where possible, offer local implementations of remote services, usually with simplified or constrained behavior. For example, the local tax calculator will use constant tax rates. The local product information database will be a small cache of the most common products. Inventory updates will be stored and forwarded at reconnection.

See also the *Adaptability—Third-Party Services* technical memo for the adaptability aspects of this solutions, because remote service implementations will vary at each installation.

To satisfy the quality scenarios of reconnection with the remote services, use smart Proxy objects for the services, that on each service call test for remote service reactivation, and redirect to them when possible.

Motivation

Retailers really don't want to stop making sales! Therefore, if the NextGen POS offers this level of reliability and recovery, it will be a very attractive product, as none of our competitors provide this capability.

Before solving the failover and recovery aspects, note that for both performance reasons and to improve recoverability when access to the remote database fails, the architect (me) has recommended a local cache (reliably persisted on the local hard disk in a simple file) of *ProductDescription* objects. Therefore, the local cache should always be searched for a "cache hit" before attempting a remote access.

This can be neatly achieved with our existing adapter and factory design:

1. The *ServicesFactory* will always return an adapter to a local product information service.

2. The local products "adapter" is not really an adapter to another component. It will itself implement the responsibilities of the local service.

3. The local service is initialized to a reference to a second adapter to the true remote product service.

4. If the local service finds the data in its cache, it returns it; otherwise, it forwards the request to the adapter for the external service.

Note that there are two levels of client-side cache:

1. The in-memory *ProductCatalog* object will maintain an in-memory collection (such as a Java *HashMap*) of some (for example, 1,000) *ProductDescription* objects that have been retrieved from the product information service. The size of this collection can be adjusted depending on local memory availability.

2. The local products service will maintain a larger persistent (hard disk based) cache that maintains some quantity of product information (such as 1 or 100MB of file space). Again, it can be adjusted depending on the local configuration. This persistent cache is important for fault tolerance, so that even if the POS application crashes and the in-memory cache of the *ProductCatalog* object is lost, the persistent cache remains.

This design does not break existing code—the new local service object is inserted without affecting the design of the *ProductCatalog* object (which collaborates with the product service).

So far, no new patterns have been introduced; Adapter and Factory are used.

Figure 36.1 illustrates the types in the design, and Figure 36.2 illustrates the initialization..

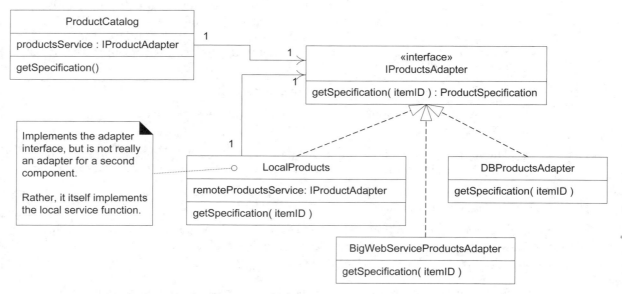

Figure 36.1 Adapters for product information.

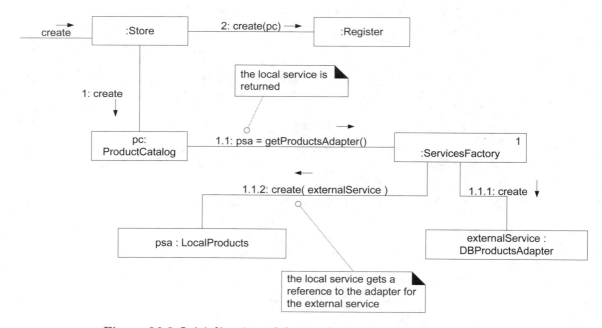

Figure 36.2 Initialization of the product information service.

Figure 36.3 shows the initial collaboration from the catalog to the products service.

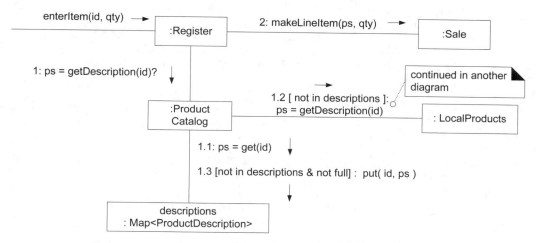

Figure 36.3 Starting the collaboration with the products service.

If the local product service does not have the product in its cache, it collaborates with the adapter to the external service, as shown in Figure 36.4. Note that the local product service caches the *ProductDescription* objects as true serialized objects.

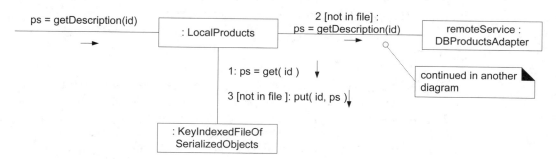

Figure 36.4 Continuing the collaboration for product information.

If the true external service was changed from a database to a new Web service, only the factory's configuration of the remote service needs to change. See Figure 36.5.

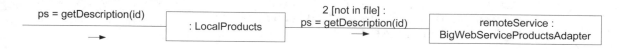

Figure 36.5 New external services do not affect the design.

To continue with the case of collaborating with the *DBProductsAdapter*, it will interact with an object-relational (O-R) mapping persistence subsystem (see Figure 36.6).

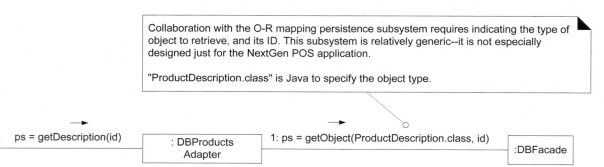

Figure 36.6 Collaboration with the persistence subsystem.

Caching Strategies

Consider the alternatives for loading the in-memory *ProductCatalog* cache and the *LocalProducts* file-based cache: One approach is lazy initialization, in which the caches fill slowly as external product information is retrieved; another approach is eager initialization, in which the caches are loaded during the *StartUp* use case. If the designer is unsure which approach to use and wants to experiment with alternatives, a family of different *CacheStrategy* objects based on the Strategy pattern can neatly solve the problem.

Stale Cache

Since product prices change quickly, and perhaps at the whim of the store manager, caching the product price creates a problem—the cache contains stale data; this is always a concern when data is replicated. One solution is to add a remote service operation that answers today's current changes; the *LocalProducts* object queries it every n minutes and updates its cache.

Threads in the UML

If the *LocalProducts* object is going to solve the stale cache problem with a query for updates every n minutes, one approach to the design is to make it an **active object** that owns a thread of control. The thread will sleep for n minutes, wake up, the object will get the data, and the thread will go back to sleep. The UML provides notation to illustrate threads and asynchronous calls, as shown in Figure 36.7 and Figure 36.8.

36.3   Handling Failure

The preceding design provides a solution for client-side caching of *ProductDescription* objects in a persistent file, to improve performance, and also to provide at least a partial fall-back solution if the external products service can't be accessed. Perhaps 10,000 products are cached in the local file, which may satisfy most requests for product information even when the external service fails.

What to do in the case where there isn't a local cache hit and access to the external products service fails? Suppose that the stakeholders asked us create a solution that signals the cashier to manually enter the price and description, or cancel the line item entry.

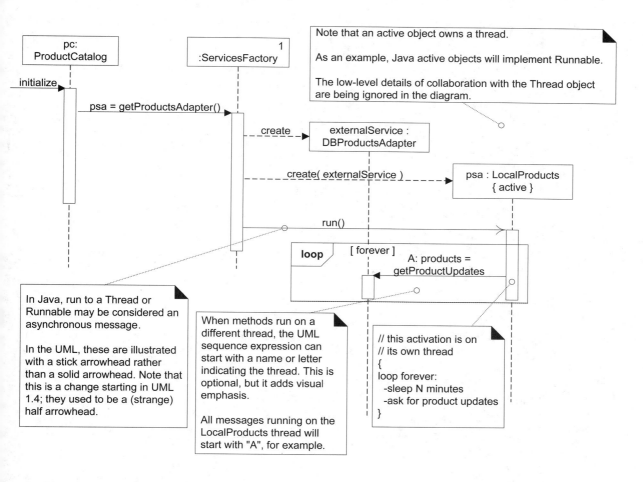

Figure 36.7 Threads and asynchronous messages in the UML.

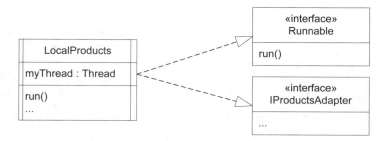

Figure 36.8 Active class notation.

This is an example of an error or failure condition, and it will be used as a context to describe some general patterns in dealing with failures and exception handling. Exception and error handling is a large topic, and this introduction will just focus on some patterns specific to the context of the case study. First, some terminology:

- **Fault**—the ultimate origin or cause of misbehavior.

    o Programmer misspelled the name of a database.

- **Error**—a manifestation of the fault in the running system. Errors are detected (or not).

    o When calling the naming service to obtain a reference to the database (with the misspelled name), it signals an error.

- **Failure**—a denial of service caused by an error.

    o The Products subsystem (and the NextGen POS) fails to provide a product information service.

Throwing Exceptions

A straightforward approach to signaling the failure under consideration is to throw an exception.

Guideline

Exceptions are especially appropriate when dealing with resource failures (disk, memory, network or database access, and other external services).

An exception will be thrown from within the persistence subsystem (actually, probably starting from within something like a Java JDBC implementation), where a failure to use the external products database is first detected. The exception will unwind the call stack back up to an appropriate point for its handling.[1]

Suppose that the original exception (using Java as an example) is a *java.sql.SQLException*. Should a *SQLException* per se be thrown all the way up to the presentation layer? No. It is at the wrong level of abstraction. This leads to a common exception handling pattern:

Pattern: Convert Exceptions [Brown01]

Within a subsystem, avoid emitting lower level exceptions coming from lower subsystems or services. Rather, convert the lower level exception into one that is meaningful at the level of the subsystem. The higher level exception usually wraps the lower-level exception, and adds information, to make the exception more contextually meaningful to the higher level.

This is a guideline, not an absolute rule.

"Exception" is used here in the vernacular sense of something that can be thrown; in Java, the equivalent is a *Throwable*.

Also known as Exception Abstraction [Renzel97].

For example, the persistence subsystem catches a particular *SQLException*, and (assuming it can't handle it[2]) throws a new *DBUnavailableException*, which contains the *SQLException*. Note that the *DBProductAdapter* is like a facade onto a logical subsystem for product information. Thus, the higher level *DBProductAdapter* (as the representative for a logical subsystem) catches the lower level *DBUnavailableException* and (assuming it can't handle it) throws a new *ProductInfoUnavailableException*, which wraps the *DBUnavailableException*.

Consider the names of these exceptions: Why *DBUnavailableException* rather than, say, *PersistenceSubsystemException*? There is a pattern for this:

Pattern: Name The Problem Not The Thrower [Grosso00]

What to call an exception? Assign a name that describes why the exception is being thrown, not the thrower. The benefit is that it makes it easier for the programmer to understand the problem, and it the highlights the essential similarity of many classes of exceptions (in a way that naming the thrower does not).

---

1. Checked vs. unchecked exception handling is not covered, as it is not supported in all popular OO languages—C++, C#, and Smalltalk, for example.
2. Resolving an exception near the level at which it was raised is a laudable but difficult goal, because the requirement for how to handle an error is often application-specific.

Exceptions in the UML

This is an appropriate time to introduce the UML notation for throwing[3] and catching exceptions.

Two common notation questions in the UML are:

1. In a class diagram, how to show what exceptions a class catches and throws?

2. In an interaction diagram, how to show throwing an exception?

For a class diagram, Figure 36.9 presents the notation:

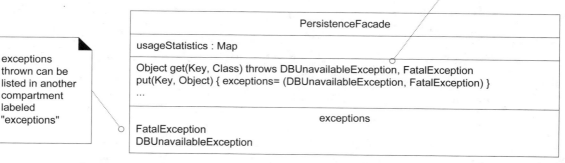

UML: One can specify exceptions several ways.

1. The UML allows the operation syntax to be any other language, such as Java. In addition, some UML CASE tools allow display of operations explicitly in Java syntax. Thus,

    Object get(Key, Class) throws DBUnavailableException, FatalException

2. The default UML syntax allows exceptions to be defined in a property string. Thus,

    put(Object, id) { exceptions= (DBUnavailableException, FatalException) }

3. Some UML tools allow one to specify (in a dialog box) the exceptions that an operation throws.

exceptions thrown can be listed in another compartment labeled "exceptions"

PersistenceFacade
usageStatistics : Map
Object get(Key, Class) throws DBUnavailableException, FatalException put(Key, Object) { exceptions= (DBUnavailableException, FatalException) } ...
exceptions FatalException DBUnavailableException

Figure 36.9 Exceptions caught and thrown by a class.

In the UML, an *Exception* is a specialization of a *Signal*, which is the specification of an asynchronous communication between objects. This means that in interaction diagrams, exceptions are illustrated as **asynchronous messages**.[4]

---

3. Officially in the UML, one *sends* an exception, but *throws* is a sufficient and more familiar usage.

4. Note that starting in UML 1.4, the notation for an asynchronous message changed from a half arrowhead to a stick arrowhead.

Figure 36.10 shows the notation, using the prior description of *SQLException* translated to *DBUnavailableException* as an example.

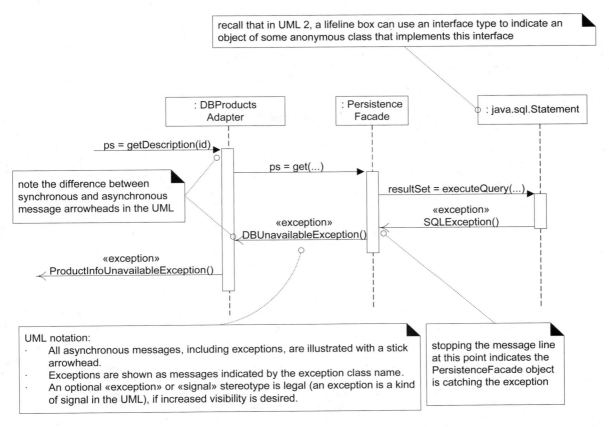

Figure 36.10 Exceptions in an interaction diagram.

In summary, UML notation exists to show exceptions. However, it is rarely used.

This is not a recommendation to avoid early consideration of exception handling. Quite the opposite: At an architectural level, the basic patterns, policies, and collaborations for exception handling need to be established early, because it is awkward to insert exception handling as an afterthought. However, the low-level design of handling particular exceptions is felt by many developers to be most appropriately decided during programming or via less detailed design descriptions, rather than via detailed UML diagrams.

Handling Errors

One side of the design has been considered: throwing exceptions, in terms of converting, naming, and illustrating them. The other side is the handling of an exception.

Two patterns to apply in this and most cases are:

Pattern: Centralized Error Logging [Renzel97]

Use a Singleton-accessed central error logging object and report all exceptions to it. If it is a distributed system, each local singleton will collaborate with a central error logger. Benefits:

- Consistency in reporting.

- Flexible definition of output streams and format.

Also known as Diagnostic Logger [Harrison98].

It is a simple pattern. The second is:

Pattern: Error Dialog [Renzel97]

Use a standard Singleton-accessed, application-independent, non-UI object to notify users of errors. It wraps one or more UI "dialog" objects (such as a GUI modal dialog, text console, sound beeper, or speech generator) and delegates the notification of the error to the UI objects. Thus, output could go to both a GUI dialog and to a speech generator. It will also report the exception to the centralized error logger. A Factory reading from system parameters will create the appropriate UI objects. Benefits:

- Protected Variations with respect to changes in the output mechanism.

- Consistent style of error reporting; for example, all GUI windows can call on this singleton to display the error dialog.

- Centralized control of the common strategy for error notification.

- Minor performance gain; if an "expensive" resource such as a GUI dialog is used, it is easy to hide and cache it for recycled use, rather than recreate a dialog for each error.

Should a UI object (for example, *ProcessSaleFrame*) handle an error by catching the exception and notifying the user? For applications with only a few windows, and simple, stable navigation paths between windows, this straightforward design is fine. This is currently true for the NextGen application.

Keep in mind, however, that this places some "application logic" related to error handling in the presentation (GUI) layer. The error handling relates to user notification, so this is logical, but it is a trend to watch. It is not inherently a problem for simple UIs with a low chance of UI replacement, but it is a point of fragility. For example, suppose a team wants to replace a Java Swing UI with the IBM Java MicroView GUI framework for handheld computers. There is now some application logic in the Swing version that has to be identified and replicated in the MicroView version. To some degree, this is inevitable with UI replacements; but it will be aggravated as more application logic migrates upwards. In general, as more non-UI application logic responsibilities migrate to the presentation layer, the probability of design or maintenance headaches increases.

For systems with many windows and complex (perhaps even changing) navigation paths, there are other solutions. For example, an application layer of one or more controllers can be inserted between the presentation and domain layers.

Furthermore, a "view manager mediator" object [GHJV95, BMRSS96] that is responsible for having a reference to all open windows, and knowing the transitions between windows, given some event E1 (such as an error), can be inserted.

This mediator is abstractly a state machine that encapsulates the states (displayed window) and transitions between states, based on events. It may read the state (window) transition model from an external file, so that the navigation paths can be data-driven (source code changes are not necessary). It can also close all the application windows, or tile or minimize them, since it has a reference to all windows.

In this design, an application layer controller may be designed with a reference to this view manager mediator (hence, the application controller is coupled "upwards" to the presentation layer). The application controller may catch the exception and collaborate with the view manager mediator to cause notification (based on the Error Dialog pattern). In this way, the application controller is involved with workflow for the application, and some error logic handling is kept out of the windows.

Detailed UI control and navigation design is outside the scope of this introduction, and the simple design of the window catching the exception will suffice. A design using an Error Dialog is shown in Figure 36.11.

36.4　Failover to Local Services with a Proxy (GoF)

Failover to a local service for the product information was achieved by inserting the local service in front of the external service; the local service is always tried first. However, this design is not appropriate for all services; sometimes the external service should be tried first, and a local version second. For example, consider the posting of sales to the accounting service. Business wants them posted as soon as possible, for real-time tracking of store and register activity.

In this case, another GoF pattern can solve the problem: Proxy. Proxy is a simple pattern, and widely used in its **Remote Proxy** variant. For example, in Java's RMI and in CORBA, a local client-side object (called a "stub") is called upon to access a remote object's services. The client-side stub is a local proxy, or a representative for a remote object.

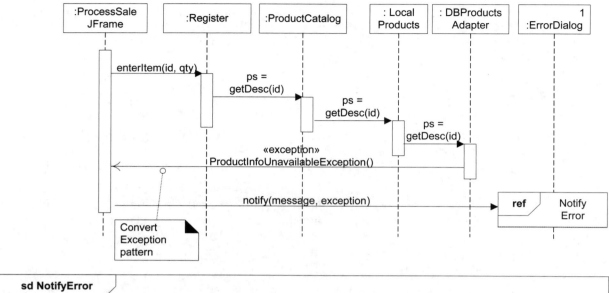

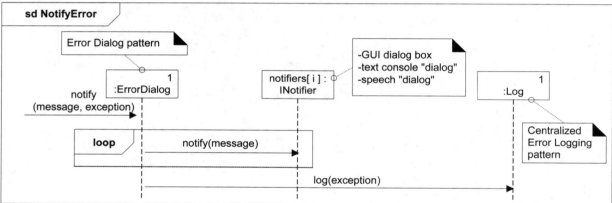

Figure 36.11 Handling the exception.

This NextGen example use of Proxy is not the Remote Proxy variant, but rather the **Redirection Proxy** (also known as a **Failover Proxy**) variant.

Regardless of the variant, the structure of Proxy is always the same; the variations are related to what the proxy does once called.

A proxy is simply an object that implements the same interface as the subject object, holds a reference to the real subject, and is used to control access to it. For the general structure, see Figure 36.12.

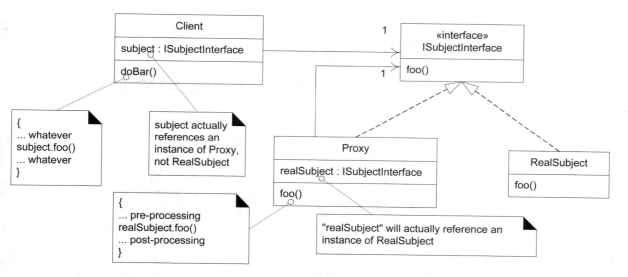

Figure 36.12 General structure of the Proxy pattern.

Applied to the NextGen case study for external accounting service access, a redirection proxy is used as follows:

1. Send a *postSale* message to the redirection proxy, treating it as though it was the actual external accounting service.

2. If the redirection proxy fails to make contact with the external service (via its adapter), then it redirects the *postSale* message to a local service, which locally stores the sales for forwarding to the accounting service, when it is active.

Figure 36.13 illustrates a class diagram of the interesting elements.

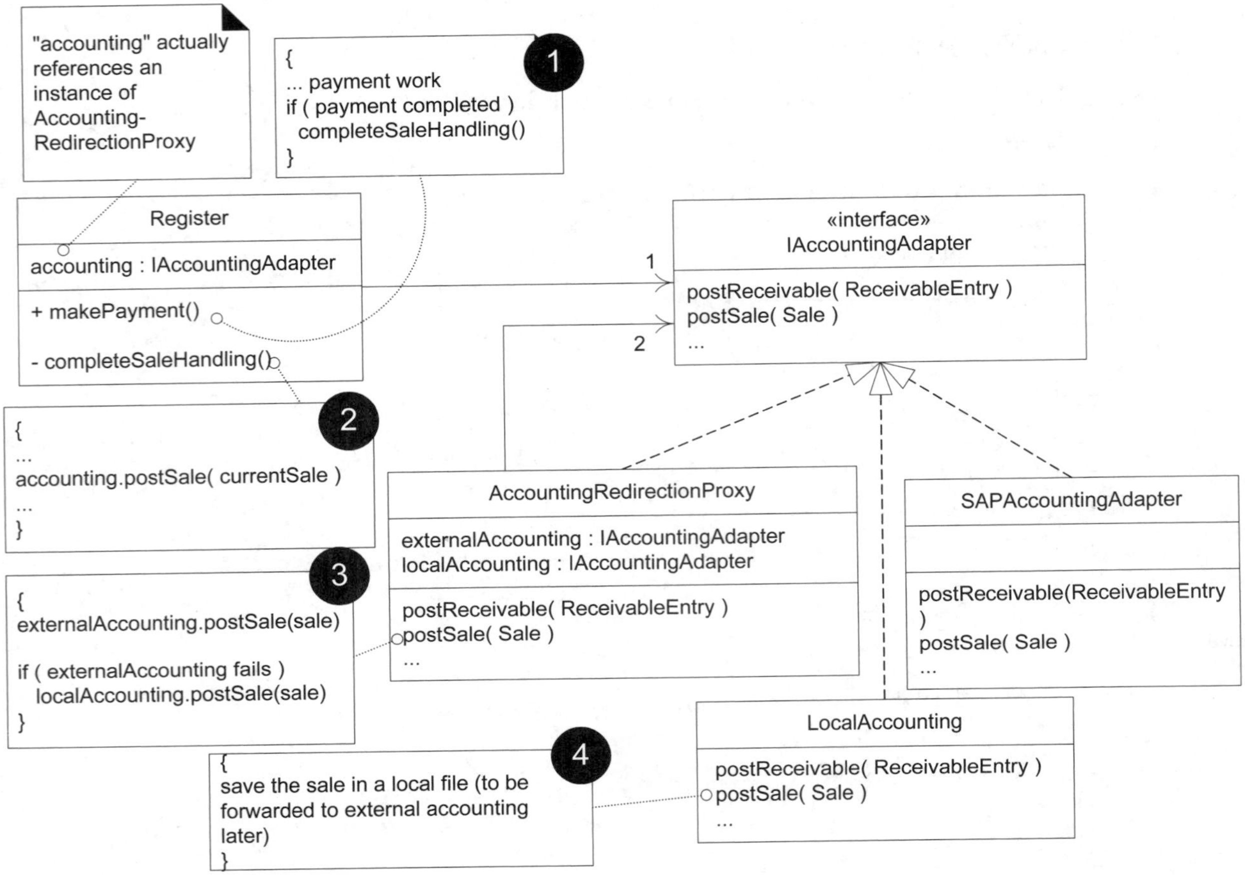

Figure 36.13 NextGen use of a redirection proxy.

Applying UML:

■ To avoid creating an interaction diagram to show the dynamic behavior, observe how this static diagram uses numbering to convey the sequence of interaction. An interaction diagram is usually preferred, but this style is presented to illustrate an alternative style.

■ Observe the public and private (+, -) visibility markers beside *Register* methods. If absent, they are unspecified, rather than defaulting to public or private. However, by common convention, unspecified visibility is interpreted by most readers (and code generating CASE tools) as meaning private attributes and public methods. However, in this diagram, I especially want to convey the fact that *makePayment* is public, and by contrast, *completeSaleHandling* is private. Visual noise and information overload are always concerns in communication, so it is desirable to exploit conventional interpretation to keep the diagrams simple.

To summarize, a proxy is an outer object that wraps an inner object, and both implement the same interface. A client object (such as a *Register*) does not know that it references a proxy—it is designed as though it is collaborating with the real subject (for example, the *SAPAccountingAdapter*). The Proxy intercepts calls in order to enhance access to the real subject, in this case by redirecting the operation to a local service (*LocalAccounting*) if the external service is not accessible.

36.5 Designing for Non-Functional or Quality Requirements

Before moving on to the next section, notice that the design work up to this point in the chapter did not relate to business logic, but to non-functional or quality requirements related to reliability and recovery.

Interestingly—and this a key point in software architecture—it is common that the large-scale themes, patterns, and structures of the software architecture are shaped by the designs to resolve the non-functional or quality requirements, rather than the basic business logic.

36.6 Accessing External Physical Devices with Adapters

Another requirement in this iteration is to interact with physical devices that comprise a POS terminal, such as opening a cash drawer, dispensing change from the coin dispenser, and capturing a signature from the digital signature device.

The NextGen POS must work with a variety of POS equipment, including that sold by IBM, Epson, NCR, Fujitsu, and so forth.

Fortunately, the software architect has done some investigation, and has discovered that there is now an industry standard, UnifiedPOS (www.nrf-arts.org), that defines standard object-oriented interfaces (in the UML sense) for all common POS devices. Furthermore, there is the JavaPOS (www.javapos.com)—a Java mapping of the UnifiedPOS.

Therefore, in the Software Architecture Document, the architect adds a technical memo to communicate this significant architectural choice:

Technical Memo
Issue: POS Hardware Device Control

Solution Summary: Use Java software from the device manufacturers that conforms to the JavaPOS standard interfaces.

Factors

- Correctly controls the devices
- Cost to buy vs. build and maintain

Solution

The UnifiedPOS (www.nrf-arts.org) defines an industry standard UML model of interfaces for POS devices. The JavaPOS (www.javapos.com) is an industry standard mapping of UnifiedPOS to Java. POS device manufactures (e.g., IBM, NCR) sell Java implementations of these interfaces that control their devices.

Buy these, rather than build them.

Use a Factory that reads from a system property to load IBM or NCR (etc.) set of classes, and return instances based on their interface.

Motivation

Based on an informal survey, we believe they work well, and the manufacturers have a regular update process for their improvement. It is difficult to get the expertise and other resources to write these ourselves.

Alternatives Considered

Writing them ourselves--difficult and risky.

Figure 36.14 shows some of the interfaces, which have been added as another package of the domain layer in our Design Model.

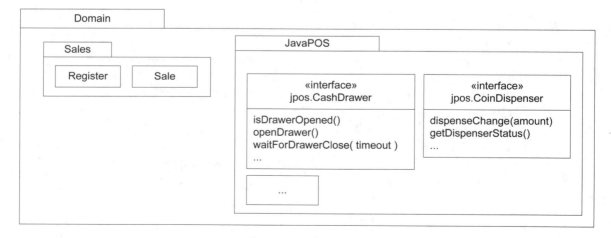

Figure 36.14 Standard JavaPOS interfaces.

Assume that the major manufacturers of POS equipment now provide JavaPOS implementations. For example, if we buy an IBM POS terminal with a cash drawer, coin dispenser, and so forth, we can also get Java classes from IBM that implement the JavaPOS interfaces, and that control the physical devices.

> Consequently, this part of the architecture is resolved by buying software components, rather than building them. Encouraging the use of existing components is one of the UP best practices.

How do they work? At a low level, a physical device has a device driver for the underlying operating system. A Java class (for example, one that implements *jpos.CashDrawer*) uses JNI (Java Native Interface) to make calls out to these device drivers.

> These Java classes adapt the low-level device driver to the JavaPOS interfaces, and thus can be characterized as Adapter objects in the GoF pattern sense. They can also be called Proxy objects—local proxies that control or enhance access to the physical devices.
>
> It is not uncommon to be able to classify a design in terms of multiple patterns.

36.7 Abstract Factory (GoF) for Families of Related Objects

The JavaPOS implementations will be purchased from manufacturers. For example[5]:

```
// IBM's drivers
com.ibm.pos.jpos.CashDrawer (implements jpos.CashDrawer)
com.ibm.pos.jpos.CoinDispenser (implements jpos.CoinDispenser)
...
// NCR's drivers
com.ncr.posdrivers.CashDrawer (implements jpos.CashDrawer)
com.ncr.posdrivers.CoinDispenser (implements jpos.CoinDispenser)
...
```

Now, how to design the NextGen POS application to use the IBM Java drivers if IBM hardware is used, NCR drivers if appropriate, and so forth?

Note that there are families of classes (*CashDrawer+CoinDispenser+...*) that need to be created, and each family implements the same interfaces.

---

5. These are fictitious package names.

For this situation, a commonly used GoF pattern exists: Abstract Factory.

Abstract Factory

Context / Problem

How to create families of related classes that implement a common interface?

Solution

Define a factory interface (the abstract factory). Define a concrete factory class for each family of things to create. Optionally, define a true abstract class that implements the factory interface and provides common services to the concrete factories that extend it.

Figure 36.15 illustrates the basic idea; it is improved upon in the next section.

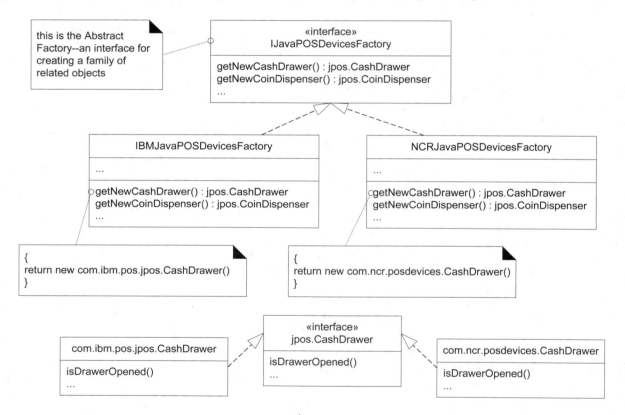

Figure 36.15 A basic abstract factory.

An Abstract Class Abstract Factory

A common variation on Abstract Factory is to create an abstract class factory that is accessed using the Singleton pattern, reads from a system property to decide which of its subclass factories to create, and then returns the appropriate subclass instance. This is used, for example, in the Java libraries with the *java.awt.Toolkit* class, which is an abstract class abstract factory for creating families of GUI widgets for different operating system and GUI subsystems.

The advantage of this approach is that it solves this problem: How does the application know which abstract factory to use? *IBMJavaPOSDevicesFactory*? *NCRJavaPOSDevicesFactory*?

The following refinement solves this problem. Figure 36.16 illustrates the solution.

With this abstract class factory and Singleton pattern *getInstance* method, objects can collaborate with the abstract superclass, and obtain a reference to one of its subclass instances. For example, consider the statement:

```
cashDrawer = JavaPOSDevicesFactory.getInstance().getNewCashDrawer();
```

The expression *JavaPOSDevicesFactory.getInstance()* will return an instance of *IBMJavaPOSDevicesFactory* or *NCRJavaPOSDevicesFactory,* depending on the system property that is read in. Notice that by changing the external system property *"jposfactory.classname"* (which is the class name as a String) in a properties file, the NextGen system will use a different family of JavaPOS drivers. Protected Variations with respect to a changing factory has been achieved with a data-driven (reading a properties file) and reflective programming design, using the *c.newInstance()* expression.

Interaction with the factory will occur in a *Register*. By the goal of low representational gap, it is reasonable for the software *Register* (whose name is suggestive of the overall POS terminal) to hold a reference to devices such as *CashDrawer*. For example:

```
class Register
{
private jpos.CashDrawer cashDrawer;
private jpos.CoinDispenser coinDispenser;

public Register()
{
    cashDrawer =
        JavaPOSDevicesFactory.getInstance().getNewCashDrawer();
    //...
}
//...
}
```

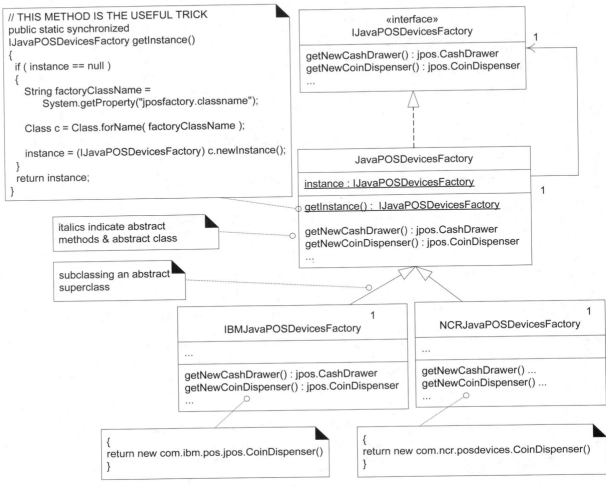

```
// THIS METHOD IS THE USEFUL TRICK
public static synchronized
IJavaPOSDevicesFactory getInstance()
{
  if ( instance == null )
  {
    String factoryClassName =
        System.getProperty("jposfactory.classname");

    Class c = Class.forName( factoryClassName );

    instance = (IJavaPOSDevicesFactory) c.newInstance();
  }
  return instance;
}
```

«interface»
IJavaPOSDevicesFactory

getNewCashDrawer() : jpos.CashDrawer
getNewCoinDispenser() : jpos.CoinDispenser
...

italics indicate abstract
methods & abstract class

subclassing an abstract
superclass

JavaPOSDevicesFactory

instance : IJavaPOSDevicesFactory

getInstance() : IJavaPOSDevicesFactory

getNewCashDrawer() : jpos.CashDrawer
getNewCoinDispenser() : jpos.CoinDispenser
...

IBMJavaPOSDevicesFactory

...

getNewCashDrawer() : jpos.CashDrawer
getNewCoinDispenser() : jpos.CoinDispenser
...

NCRJavaPOSDevicesFactory

...

getNewCashDrawer() ...
getNewCoinDispenser() ...
...

```
{
  return new com.ibm.pos.jpos.CoinDispenser()
}
```

```
{
  return new com.ncr.posdevices.CoinDispenser()
}
```

Figure 36.16 An abstract class abstract factory.

36.8   Handling Payments with Polymorphism and Do It Myself

One of the common ways to apply polymorphism (and Information Expert) is in the context of what Peter Coad calls the "Do It Myself" strategy or pattern [Coad95]. That is:

> *Do It Myself*
>
> "I (a software object) do those things that are normally done to the actual object that I'm an abstraction of." [Coad95]

This is the classic object-oriented design style: *Circle* objects draw themselves, *Square* objects draw themselves, *Text* objects spell-check themselves, and so forth.

Notice that a *Text* object spell-checking itself is an example of Information Expert: *The object that has the information related to the work does it* (a *Dictionary* is also a candidate, by Expert).

Do It Myself and Information Expert usually lead to the same choice.

Similarly, notice that *Circle* and *Square* objects drawing themselves are examples of Polymorphism: *When related alternatives vary by type, assign responsibility using polymorphic operations to the types for which the behavior varies.*

Do It Myself and Polymorphism usually lead to the same choice.

Yet, as was explored in the Pure Fabrication discussion, it is often contraindicated due to problems in coupling and cohesion, and instead, a designer uses pure fabrications such as strategies, factories, and the like.

Nevertheless, when appropriate, Do It Myself is attractive in part because of its support for low representational gap. The design for handling payments will be accomplished with Do It Myself and Polymorphism.

One of the requirements for this iteration is to handle multiple payment types, which essentially means to handle the authorization and accounting steps. Different kinds of payments are authorized in different ways:

- Credit and debit payments are authorized with an external authorization service. Both require recording a receivable entry in accounts receivable—money owing from the financial institution that does the authorization.

- Cash payments are authorized in some stores (it is a trend in some countries) using a special paper bill analyzer attached to the POS terminal that checks for counterfeit money. Other stores do not do this.

- Check payments are authorized in some stores using a computerized authorization service. Other stores do not do authorize checks.

CreditPayments are authorized in one way; *CheckPayments* are authorized in another. This is a classic case for Polymorphism.

Thus, as shown in Figure 36.17, each *Payment* subclass has its own *authorize* method.

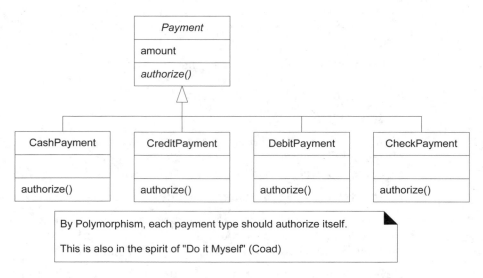

Figure 36.17 Classic polymorphism with multiple *authorize* methods.

For example, as illustrated in Figure 36.18 and Figure 36.19, a *Sale* instantiates a *CreditPayment* or *CheckPayment* and asks it to authorize itself. .

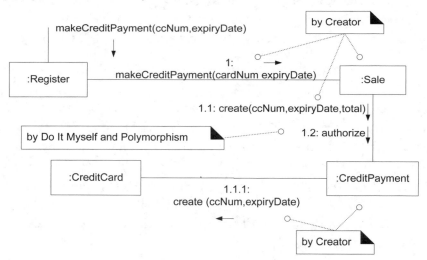

Figure 36.18 Creating a CreditPayment.

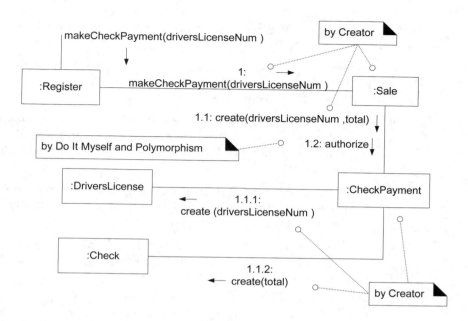

Figure 36.19 Creating a CheckPayment.

Fine-Grained Classes?

Consider the creation of the *CreditCard*, *DriversLicense,* and *Check* software objects. Our first impulse might be to record the data they hold simply in their related payment classes, and eliminate such fine-grained classes. However, it is usually a more profitable strategy to use them; they often end up providing useful behavior and being reusable. For example, the *CreditCard* is a natural Expert on telling you its credit company type (Visa, MasterCard, and so on). This behavior will turn out to be necessary for our application.

Credit Payment Authorization

The system must communicate with an external credit authorization service, and we have already created the basis of the design based on adapters to support this.

Relevant Credit Payment Domain Information

Some context for the upcoming design:

- POS systems are physically connected with external authorization services in several ways, including phone lines (which must be dialed) and always-on broadband Internet connections.

- Different application-level protocols and associated data formats are used, such as Secure Electronic Transaction (SET). New ones may become popular, such as XMLPay.

- Payment authorization can be viewed as a regular synchronous operation: a POS thread blocks, waiting for a reply from the remote service (within the limits of a time-out period).

- All payment authorization protocols involve sending identifiers uniquely identifying the store (with a "merchant ID"), and the POS terminal (with a "terminal ID"). A reply includes an approval or denial code, and a unique transaction ID.

- A store may use different external authorization services for different credit card types (one for Visa, one for MasterCard). For each service, the store has a different merchant ID.

- The credit company type can be deduced from the card number. For example, numbers starting with 5 are MasterCard; numbers starting with 4 are Visa.

- The adapter implementations will protect the upper layers of the system against all these variations in payment authorization. Each adapter is responsible for ensuring the authorization request transaction is in the appropriate format, and for collaborating with the external service. As discussed in a prior iteration, the *ServicesFactory* is responsible for delivering the appropriate *ICreditAuthorizationServiceAdapter* implementation.

A Design Scenario

Figure 36.20 starts the presentation of an annotated design that satisfies these details and requirements. Messages are annotated to illustrate the reasoning.

Once the correct *ICreditAuthorizationServiceAdapter* is found, it is given the responsibility for completing the authorization, as shown in Figure 36.21.

Once a reply is obtained by *CreditPayment* (which has been given the responsibility for handling its completion by Polymorphism and Do It Myself), assuming it is approved, it completes its tasks, as shown in Figure 36.22.

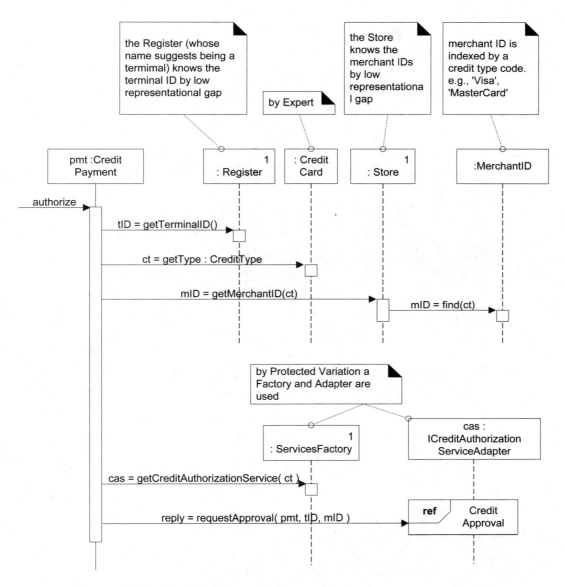

Figure 36.20 Handling a credit payment.

UML—Observe in this sequence diagram that some objects were stacked. This is legal, although few CASE tools support it. It is helpful in publishing, where width is constrained.

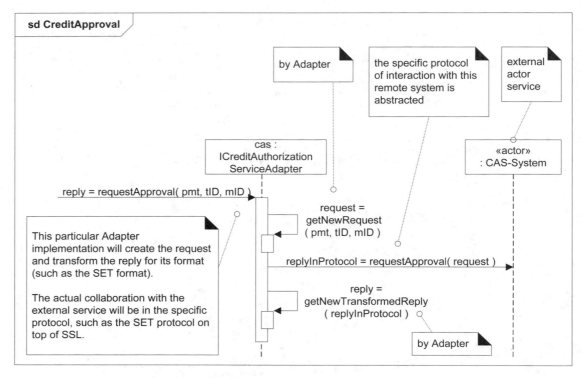

Figure 36.21 Completing the authorization.

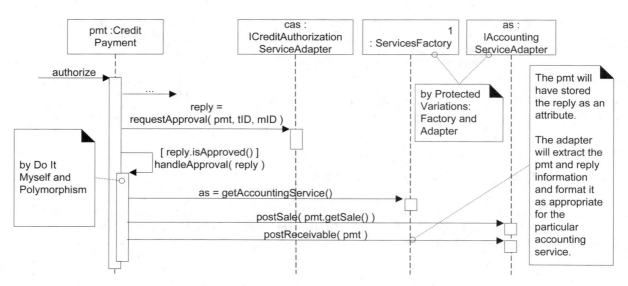

Figure 36.22 Completion of an approved credit payment.

36.9   Example: Monopoly

First, let's briefly review the new domain rules and requirements in iteration-3: If a player lands on a property square (a lot, railroad, or utility) then they buy it if they have enough cash and it's not owned. If it is owned by another player, they pay rent according to square-specific rules.

Let's also review the essential design, as shown in Figure 36.23 and Figure 36.24. Polymorphism is applied; for each kind of square that has a different landed-on behavior, there is a polymorphic *landedOn* method. When a *Player* software object lands on a *Square*, it sends it a *landedOn* message.

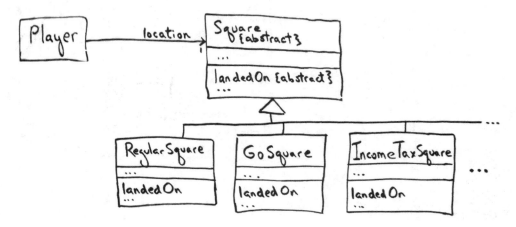

Figure 36.23 DCD for the polymorphic *landedOn* design strategy.

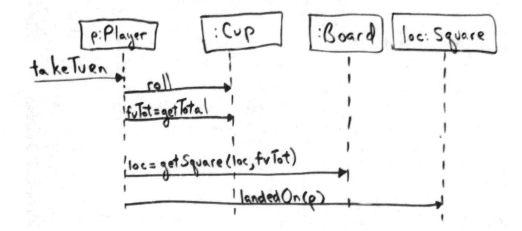

Figure 36.24 Dynamic collaborations for the *landedOn* design strategy.

The existing design shows off the beauty of polymorphism to handle new, similar cases. For this iteration, we will simply add new square types (*LotSquare*, *Rail-RoadSquare*, *UtilitySquare*) and add more polymorphic *landedOn* methods.

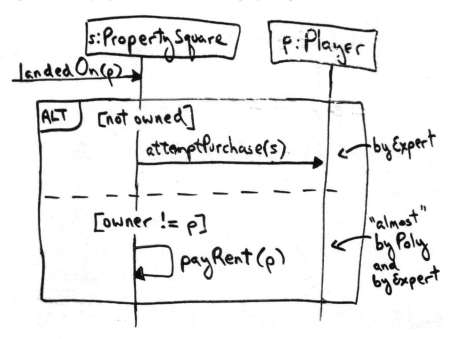

Figure 36.25 Landing on a PropertySquare.

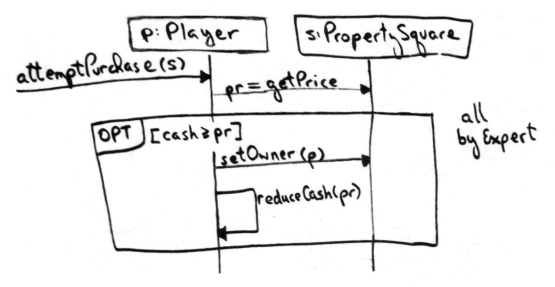

Figure 36.26 Attempting to purchase a property.

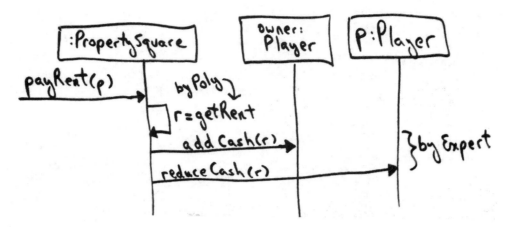

Figure 36.27 Paying rent.

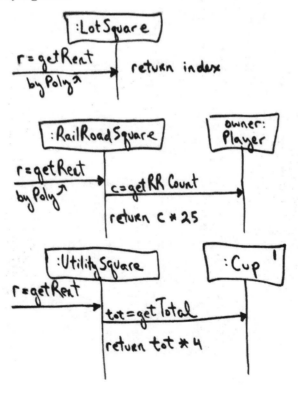

Figure 36.28 Polymorphic *getRent* methods.

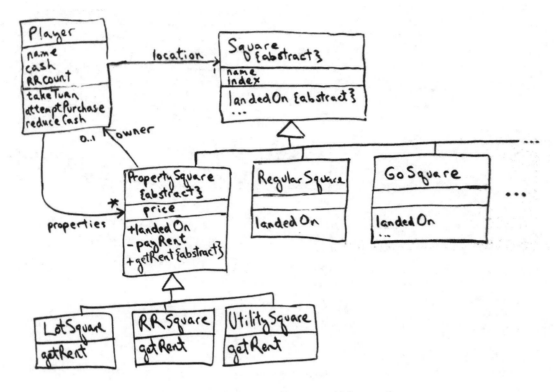

Figure 36.29 Partial DCD for iteration-3 of Monopoly.

Notice in Figure 36.25 that all the *PropertySquares* have identical *landedOn* behavior, so this method can be implemented once in the superclass and inherited by the subclasses of *PropertySquare*. The only behavior that is unique to each subclass is the calculation of the rent; thus by the Polymorphism principle, there is a *getRent* polymorphic operation in each subclass (see Figure 36.28).

36.10 Conclusion

The point of these case studies was not to show the correct solution—there isn't a single best solution, and I'm sure readers can improve on what I've suggested. My sincere hope has been to demonstrate that doing object design can be reasoned through by core principles such as low coupling and the application of patterns, rather than being a mysterious process.

Caution: Pattern-itis

This presentation has used GoF design patterns at many points. But there have been reports of designers excessively force-fitting patterns in a creative frenzy of *pattern-itis*. I think a conclusion to draw from this is that patterns require study in multiple examples to be well-digested. A popular learning vehicle is a lunch-time or after-work study group in which participants share ways they have seen or could see the application of patterns, and discuss a section of a patterns book.

DESIGNING A PERSISTENCE FRAMEWORK WITH PATTERNS

The most likely way for the world to be destroyed, most experts agree, is by accident. That's where we come in; we're computer professionals. We cause accidents.

—*Nathaniel Borenstein*

Objectives

- Design part of a framework with the Template Method, State, and Command patterns.
- Introduce issues in object-relational (O-R) mapping.
- Implement lazy materialization with Virtual Proxies.

Introduction

The point of this chapter is not actually the design of a persistence framework, but, more generally, to introduce key OO framework design principles and patterns, using persistence as an interesting case study.

What's Next?   Having explored more GoF and GRASP patterns, this chapter applies GoF patterns to the design of a framework—an important OO design skill. The next summarizes more UML notation, useful in documenting an architecture with UML.

| Package Design | More Object Design with GoF Patterns | Designing a Framework with Patterns | UML Deployment & Component Diagrams | Documenting Architecture: The N+1 View Model |

The NextGen application—like most—requires storing and retrieving information in a persistent storage mechanism, such as a relational database (RDB). This chapter explores the design of a framework for storing persistent objects.

Caution! Don't Try This at Home!

There are excellent free, robust, industrial-strength open source persistence frameworks, and thus seldom a need to create one yourself. For example, **Hibernate** is very widely used in the Java domain (www.hibernate.org). It solves most or all problems in object-relational mapping, performance, transaction support, and so forth.

This persistence framework is presented to introduce framework design applied to a common and problem-rich domain. It is not recommended for an industrial persistence service. At least for Java technologies, there is no need to create one yourself.

37.1   The Problem: Persistent Objects

Assume that in the NextGen application, *ProductDescription* data resides in a relational database. It must be brought into local memory during application use. **Persistent objects** are those that require persistent storage, such as *ProductDescription* instances.

Storage Mechanisms and Persistent Objects

Object databases—If an object database is used to store and retrieve objects, no additional custom or third-party persistence services are required. This is one of several attractions for its use. However, they are relatively rare.

Relational databases—Because of the prevalence of RDBs, their use is often required, rather than the more OO-natural object databases. If this is the case, a number of problems arise due to the mismatch between record-oriented and object-oriented representations of data; these problems are explored later. A special O-R mapping service is required.

Other—In addition to RDBs, it is sometimes desirable to store objects in other storage mechanisms or formats, such as flat files, XML structures, Palm OS PDB files, hierarchical databases, and so on. As with relational databases, a representation mismatch exists between objects and these non-object-oriented formats. And as with RDBs, special services are required to make them work with objects.

37.2   The Solution: A Persistence Service from a Persistence Framework

A **persistence framework** is a general-purpose, reusable, and extendable set of types that provides functionality to support persistent objects. A **persistence service** (or subsystem) actually provides the service, and will be created with a persistence framework. A persistence service is usually written to work with RDBs, in which case it is also called an **O-R mapping service**. Typically, a persistence service must translate objects into records (or some other form of structured data such as XML) and save them in a database, and translate records into objects when retrieving from a database.

In terms of the layered architecture of the NextGen application, a persistence service is a subsystem within the technical services layer.

37.3   Frameworks

At the risk of oversimplification, a framework is an *extendable* set of objects for related functions. The quintessential example is a GUI framework, such as Java's Swing framework.

The signature quality of a framework is that it provides an implementation for the core and unvarying functions, and includes a mechanism to allow a developer to plug in the varying functions, or to extend the functions.

For example, Java's Swing GUI framework provides many classes and interfaces for core GUI functions. Developers can add specialized widgets by subclassing from the Swing classes and overriding certain methods. Developers can also plug in varying event response behavior to predefined widget classes (such as *JButton*) by registering listeners or subscribers based on the Observer pattern. That's a framework.

In general, a **framework**:

- Is a cohesive set of interfaces and classes that collaborate to provide services for the core, unvarying part of a logical subsystem.

- Contains concrete (and especially) abstract classes that define interfaces to conform to, object interactions to participate in, and other invariants.

- Usually (but not necessarily) requires the framework user to define subclasses of existing framework classes to make use of, customize, and extend the framework services.

- Has abstract classes that may contain both abstract and concrete methods.

- Relies on the **Hollywood Principle**— *"Don't call us, we'll call you."* This means that the user-defined classes (for example, new subclasses) will receive messages from the predefined framework classes. These are usually handled by implementing superclass abstract methods.

The following persistence framework example will demonstrate these principles.

Frameworks Are Reusable

Frameworks offer a high degree of reuse—much more so than individual classes. Consequently, if an organization is interested (and who isn't?) in increasing its degree of software reuse, then it should emphasize the creation of frameworks.

37.4 Requirements for the Persistence Service and Framework

For the NextGen POS application, we need a persistence service to be built with a persistence framework (which could be used to also create other persistence services). Let's call the framework PFW (Persistence Framework). PFW is a simplified framework—a full-blown, industrial-strength persistence framework is outside the scope of this introduction.

The framework should provide functions such as:

- store and retrieve objects in a persistent storage mechanism
- *commit* and *rollback* transactions

The design should be extendable to support different storage mechanisms and formats, such as RDBs, records in flat files, or XML in files.

37.5 Key Ideas

The following key ideas will be explored in subsequent sections:

- **Mapping**—There must be some mapping between a class and its persistent store (for example, a table in a database), and between object attributes and the fields (columns) in a record. That is, there must be a **schema mapping** between the two schemas.

- **Object identity**—To easily relate records to objects, and to ensure there are no inappropriate duplicates, records and objects have a unique object identifier.

- **Database mapper**—A Pure Fabrication database mapper is responsible for materialization and dematerialization.

- **Materialization and dematerialization**—Materialization is the act of transforming a non-object representation of data (for example, records) from a persistent store into objects. Dematerialization is the opposite activity (also known as passivation).

- **Caches**—Persistence services cache materialized objects for performance.

- **Transaction state of object**—It is useful to know the state of objects in terms of their relationship to the current transaction. For example, it is useful to know which objects have been modified (are *dirty*) so that it is possible to determine if they need to be saved back to their persistent store.

- **Transaction operations**—Commit and rollback operations.

- **Lazy materialization**—Not all objects are materialized at once; a particular instance is only materialized on-demand, when needed.

- **Virtual proxies**—Lazy materialization can be implemented using a smart reference known as a virtual proxy.

37.6　Pattern: Representing Objects as Tables

How do you map an object to a record or relational database schema?

The **Representing Objects as Tables** pattern [BW96] proposes defining a table in an RDB for each persistent object class. Object attributes containing primitive data types (number, string, boolean, and so on) map to columns.

If an object has only attributes of primitive data types, the mapping is straightforward. But as we will see, matters are not that simple, since objects may have attributes that refer to other complex objects, while the relational model requires that values be atomic (that is, First Normal Form) (see Figure 37.1).

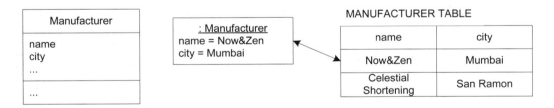

Figure 37.1　Mapping objects and tables.

37.7　UML Data Modeling Profile

While on the subject of RDBs, not surprisingly, the UML has become a popular notation for **data models**. Note that one of the official UP artifacts is the Data Model, which is part of the Design discipline. Figure 37.2 illustrates some notation in the UML for data modeling.

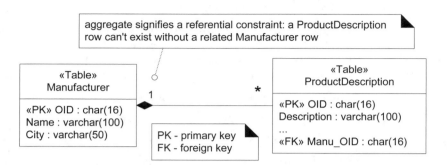

aggregate signifies a referential constraint: a ProductDescription row can't exist without a related Manufacturer row

«Table»
Manufacturer

«PK» OID : char(16)
Name : varchar(100)
City : varchar(50)

1

*

«Table»
ProductDescription

«PK» OID : char(16)
Description : varchar(100)
...
«FK» Manu_OID : char(16)

PK - primary key
FK - foreign key

Figure 37.2 UML Data Modeling Profile example.

These stereotypes are not part of the core UML—they are an extension. To generalize, the UML has the concept of a **UML profile**: a coherent set of UML stereotypes, tagged values, and constraints for a particular purpose. Figure 37.2 illustrates part of a proposed Data Modeling Profile.

37.8   Pattern: Object Identifier

It is desirable to have a consistent way to relate objects to records, and to be able to ensure that repeated materialization of a record does not result in duplicate objects.

The **Object Identifier** pattern [BW96] proposes assigning an **object identifier** (OID) to each record and object (or proxy of an object).

An OID is usually an alphanumeric value; each is unique to a specific object. There are various approaches to generating unique IDs for OIDs, ranging from unique to one database, to globally unique: database sequence generators, the High-Low key generation strategy [Ambler00], and others.

Within object land, an OID is represented by an OID interface or class that encapsulates the actual value and its representation. In an RDB, it is usually stored as a fixed length character value.

Every table will have an OID as primary key, and each object will (directly or indirectly) also have an OID. If every object is associated with an OID, and every table has an OID primary key, every object can be uniquely mapped to some row in some table (see Figure 37.3).

This is a simplified view of the design. In reality, the OID may not actually be placed in the persistent object—although that is possible. Instead, it may be placed in a Proxy object wrapping the persistent object. The design is influenced by the choice of language.

An OID also provides a consistent key type to use in the interface to the persistence service.

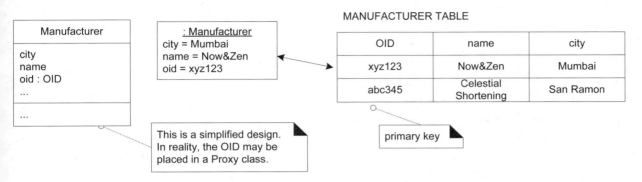

Figure 37.3 Object identifiers link objects and records.

37.9   Accessing a Persistence Service with a Facade

Step one in the design of this subsystem is to define a facade for its services; recall that Facade is a common pattern to provide a unified interface to a subsystem. To begin, an operation is needed to retrieve an object given an OID. But in addition to an OID, the subsystem needs to know what type of object to materialize; therefore, the class type will also be provided. Figure 37.4 illustrates some operations of the facade and its use in collaboration with one of the Next-Gen service adapters.

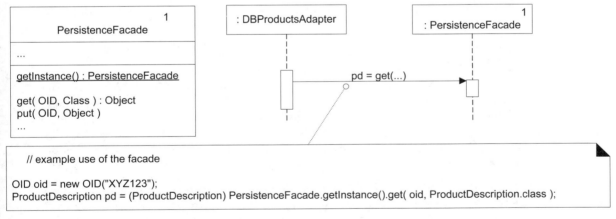

Figure 37.4 The PersistenceFacade.

37.10 Mapping Objects: Database Mapper or Database Broker Pattern

The *PersistenceFacade*—as true of all facades—does not do the work itself, but delegates requests to subsystem objects.

Who should be responsible for materialization and dematerialization of objects (for example, a *ProductDescription*) from a persistent store?

The Information Expert pattern suggests that the persistent object class itself (*ProductDescription*) is a candidate, because it has some of the data (the data to be saved) required by the responsibility.

If a persistent object class defines the code to save itself in a database, it is called a **direct mapping** design. Direct mapping is workable *if* the database related code is automatically generated and injected into the class by a post-processing compiler, and the developer never has to see or maintain this complex database code cluttering his or her class.

But if direct mapping is manually added and maintained, it has a number of defects and does not tend to scale well in terms of programming and maintenance. Problems include:

- Strong coupling of the persistent object class to persistent storage knowledge—violation of Low Coupling.

- Complex responsibilities in a new and unrelated area to what the object was previously responsible for—violation of High Cohesion and maintaining a separation of concerns. Technical service concerns are mixing with application logic concerns.

We will explore a classic **indirect mapping** approach, that uses other objects to do the mapping for persistent objects.

Part of this approach is to use the **Database Broker** pattern [BW95]. It proposes making a class that is responsible for materialization, dematerialization, and object caching. This has also been called the **Database Mapper** pattern in [Fowler01], which is a better name than Database Broker, as it describes its responsibility, and the term "broker" in distributed systems [BMRSS96] design has a long-standing and different meaning.[1]

A different mapper class is defined for each persistent object class. Figure 37.5 illustrates that each persistent object may have its own mapper class, and that there may be different kinds of mappers for different storage mechanisms. A snippet of code:

---

1. In distributed systems, a **broker** is a front-end server process that delegates tasks to back-end server processes.

```
class PersistenceFacade
{
//...
public Object get( OID oid, Class persistenceClass )
{
    // an IMapper is keyed by the Class of the persistent object
    IMapper mapper = (IMapper) mappers.get( persistenceClass );

    // delegate
    return mapper.get( oid );
}
//...
}
```

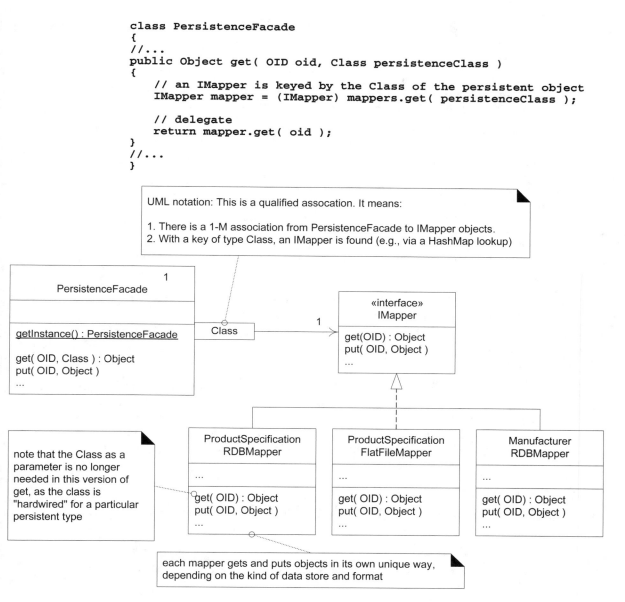

Figure 37.5 Database Mappers.

Although this diagram indicates two *ProductDescription* mappers, only one will be active within a running persistence service.

Metadata-Based Mappers

More flexible, but more involved, is a mapper design based on **metadata** (data about data). In contrast to hand-crafting individual mapper classes for different persistent types, metadata-based mappers dynamically generate the mapping from an object schema to another schema (such as relational) based on reading in metadata that describes the mapping, such as "TableX maps to Class Y; column Z maps to object property P" (it gets much more complex). This approach is feasible for languages with reflective programming capabilities, such as Java, C#, or Smalltalk, and awkward for those that don't, such as C++.

With metadata-based mappers, we can change the schema mapping in an external store and it will be realized in the running system, without changing source code—Protected Variations with respect to schema variations.

Nevertheless, a useful quality of the framework presented here is that hand-coded or metadata mappers can be used without affecting clients—encapsulation of the implementation.

37.11 Framework Design with the Template Method Pattern

The next section describes some of the essential design features of the Database Mappers, which are a central part of the PFW. These design features are based on the **Template Method** GoF design pattern [GHJV95].[2] This pattern is at the heart of framework design,[3] and is familiar to most OO programmers by practice if not by name.

The idea is to define a method (the Template Method) in a superclass that defines the skeleton of an algorithm, with its varying and unvarying parts. The Template Method invokes other methods, some of which are methods that may be overridden in a subclass. Thus, subclasses can override the varying methods in order to add their own unique behavior at points of variability (see Figure 37.6).

37.12 Materialization with the Template Method Pattern

If we were to program two or three mapper classes, some commonality in the code would become apparent. The basic repeating algorithm structure for materializing an object is:

```
if (object in cache)
    return it
else
    create the object from its representation in storage
    save object in cache
    return it
```

---

2. This pattern is unrelated to C++ templates. It describes the *template* of an algorithm.

3. More specifically, of **whitebox frameworks**. These are usually class hierarchy and subclassing-oriented frameworks that require the user to know something about their design and structure; hence, whitebox.

The point of variation is how the object is created from storage.

We will create the *get* method to be the template method in an abstract super-class *AbstractPersistenceMapper* that defines the template, and use a hook method in subclasses for the varying part. Figure 37.7 shows the essential design.

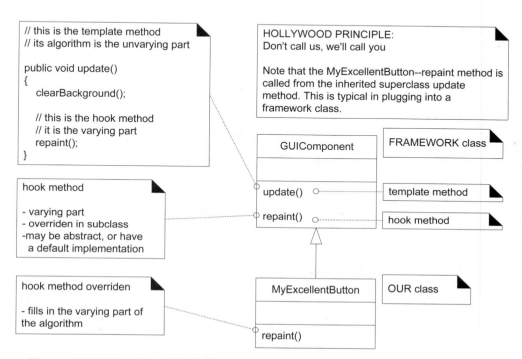

Figure 37.6 Template Method pattern in a GUI framework.

As shown in this example, it is common for the template method to be *public*, and the hook method to be *protected*. *AbstractPersistenceMapper* and *IMapper* are part of the PFW. Now, an application programmer can plug into this framework by adding a subclass, and overriding or implementing the *getObject-FromStorage* hook method. Figure 37.8 shows an example.

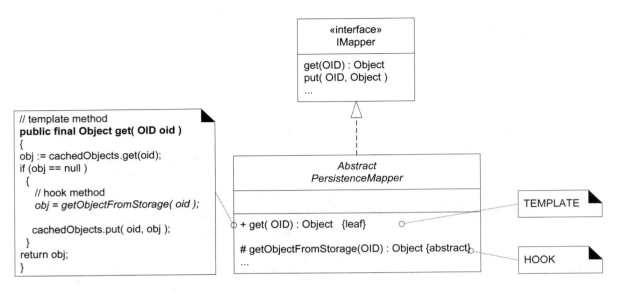

Figure 37.7 Template Method for mapper objects.

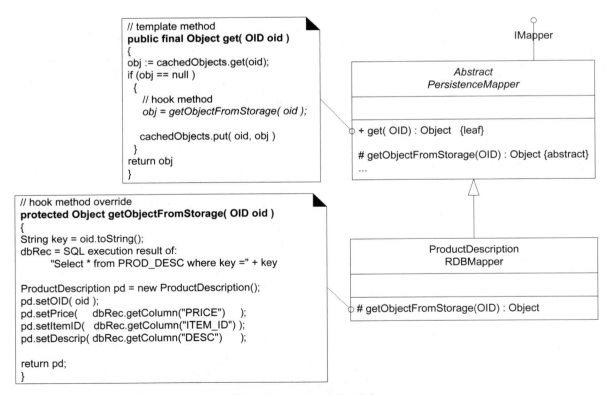

Figure 37.8 Overriding the hook method.[4]

Assume in the hook method implementation of Figure 37.8 that the beginning part of the algorithm—doing a SQL SELECT—is the same for all objects, only the database table name varies.[5] If that assumption held, then once again, the Template Method pattern could be applied to factor out the varying and unvarying parts of the algorithm. In Figure 37.9, the tricky part is that *AbstractRDB-Mapper.getObjectFromStorage* is a hook method with respect to *AbstractPersistenceMapper.get*, but a template method with respect to the new hook method *getObjectFromRecord*.

UML—In Figure 37.9 observe how constructors can be declared in the UML. The stereotype is optional, and if the naming convention of constructor name equal to class name is used, probably unnecessary.

Now, *IMapper*, *AbstractPersistenceMapper*, and *AbstractRDBMapper* are part of the framework. The application programmer needs only to add his or her subclass, such as *ProductDescriptionRDBMapper*, and ensure it is created with the table name (to pass via constructor chaining up to the *AbstractRDBMapper*).

The Database Mapper class hierarchy is an essential part of the framework; new subclasses may be added by the application programmer to customize it for new kinds of persistent storage mechanisms or for new particular tables or files within an existing storage mechanism. Figure 37.10 shows some of the package and class structure. Notice that the NextGen-specific classes do not belong in the general technical services *Persistence* package. I think this diagram, combined with Figure 37.9, illustrates the value of a visual language like the UML to describe parts of software; this succinctly conveys much information.

In Figure 37.10 notice the class *ProductDescriptionInMemoryTestDataMapper*. Such classes can be used to serve up hard-coded objects for testing, without accessing any external persistent store.

---

4. In Java as an example, the *dbRec* that is returned from executing a SQL query will be a JDBC *ResultSet*.

5. In many cases, the situation is not so simple. An object may be derived from data from two or more tables or from multiple databases, in which case, the first version of the Template Method design offers more flexibility.

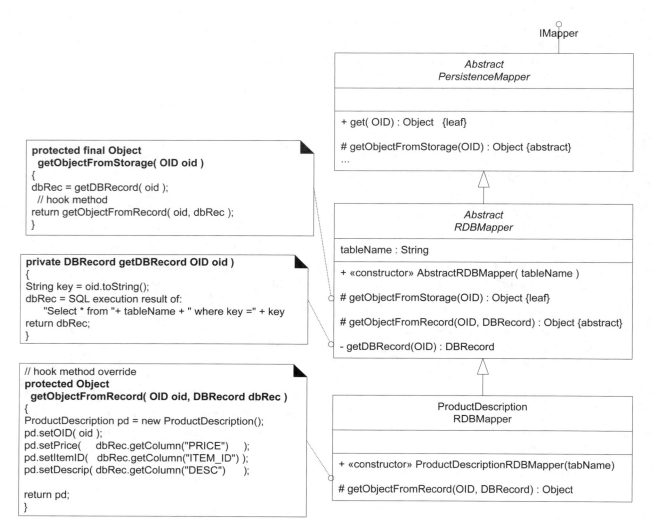

Figure 37.9 Tightening up the code with the Template Method again.

The UP and the Software Architecture Document

In terms of the UP and documentation, recall that the SAD is a learning aid for future developers, which contains architectural views of key noteworthy ideas. Including diagrams such as Figure 37.9 and Figure 37.10 in the SAD for the NextGen project is very much in the spirit of the kind of information an SAD should contain.

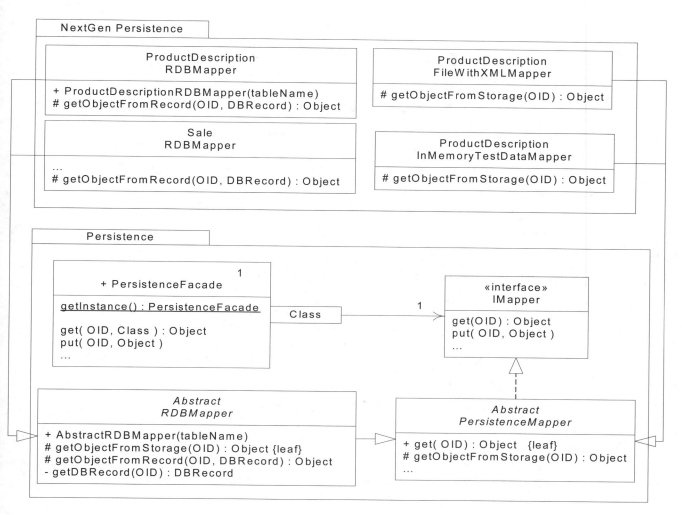

Figure 37.10 The persistence framework.

Synchronized or Guarded Methods in the UML

The *AbstractPersistenceMapper.get* method contains critical section code that is not thread safe—the same object could be materializing concurrently on different threads. As a technical service subsystem, the persistence service needs to be designed with thread safety in mind. Indeed, the entire subsystem may be distributed to a separate process on another computer, with the *Persistence-Facade* transformed into a remote server object, and with many threads simultaneously running in the subsystem, serving multiple clients.

The method should therefore have thread concurrency control—if using Java, add the *synchronized* keyword. Figure 37.11 illustrates a synchronized method in a class diagram.

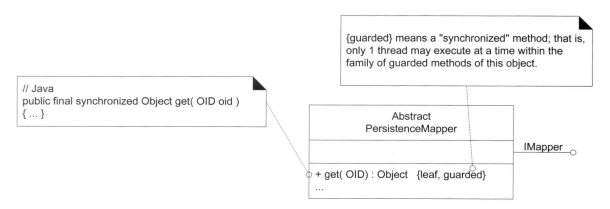

Figure 37.11 Guarded methods in the UML.

37.13 Configuring Mappers with a MapperFactory

Similar to previous examples of factories in the case study, the configuration of the *PersistenceFacade* with a set of *IMapper* objects can be achieved with a factory object, *MapperFactory*. However, as a slight twist, it is desirable to not name each mapper with a different operation. For example, this is not desirable:

```
class MapperFactory
{
public IMapper getProductDescriptionMapper() {...}
public IMapper getSaleMapper() {...}
...
}
```

This does not support Protected Variations with respect to a growing list of mappers—and it will grow. Consequently, the following is preferred:

```
class MapperFactory
{
public Map getAllMappers() {...}
...
}
```

where the *java.util.Map* (probably implemented with a *HashMap*) keys are the *Class* objects (the persistent types), and the *IMappers* are the values.

Then, the facade can initialize its collection of *IMappers* as follows:

```
class PersistenceFacade
{
private java.util.Map mappers =
    MapperFactory.getInstance().getAllMappers();
...
}
```

The factory can assign a set of *IMappers* using a data-driven design. That is, the factory can read system properties to discover which *IMapper* classes to instantiate. If a language with reflective programming capabilities is used, such as Java, then the instantiation can be based on reading in the class names as strings, and using something like a *Class.newInstance* operation for instantiation. Thus, the mapper set can be reconfigured without changing the source code.

37.14 Pattern: Cache Management

It is desirable to maintain materialized objects in a local cache to improve performance (materialization is relatively slow) and support transaction management operations such as a commit.

The **Cache Management** pattern [BW96] proposes making the Database Mappers responsible for maintaining its cache. If a different mapper is used for each class of persistent object, each mapper can maintain its own cache.

When objects are materialized, they are placed in the cache, with their OID as the key. Subsequent requests to the mapper for an object will cause the mapper to first search the cache, thus avoiding unnecessary materialization.

37.15 Consolidating and Hiding SQL Statements in One Class

Hard-coding SQL statements into different RDB mapper classes is not a terrible sin, but it can be improved upon. Suppose instead:

- There is a single Pure Fabrication class (and it's a singleton) *RDBOperations* where all SQL operations (SELECT, INSERT, ...) are consolidated.

- The RDB mapper classes collaborate with it to obtain a DB record or record set (for example, *ResultSet*).

- Its interface looks something like this:

```
class RDBOperations
{
public ResultSet getProductDescriptionData( OID oid ) {...}
public ResultSet getSaleData( OID oid ) {...}
...
}
```

So that, for example, a mapper has code like this:

```
class ProductDescriptionRDBMapper extends AbstractPersistenceMapper
{
protected Object getObjectFromStorage( OID oid )
{
ResultSet rs =
   RDBOperations.getInstance().getProductDescriptionData( oid );

ProductDescription ps = new ProductDescription();
```

```
ps.setPrice( rs.getDouble( "PRICE" ) );
ps.setOID( oid );
return ps;
}
```

The following benefits accrue from this Pure Fabrication:

- Ease of maintenance and performance tuning by an expert. SQL optimization requires a SQL aficionado, rather than an object programmer. With all the SQL embedded in this one class, it is easy for the SQL expert to find and work on it.

- Encapsulation of the access method and details. For example, hard-coded SQL could be replaced by a call to a stored procedure in the RDB in order to obtain the data. Or a more sophisticated **metadata**-based approach to generating the SQL could be inserted, in which SQL is dynamically generated from a metadata schema description read from an external source.

As an architect, the interesting aspect of this design decision is that it is influenced by developer skills. A trade-off between high cohesion and convenience for a specialist was made. Not all design decisions are motivated by "pure" software engineering concerns such as coupling and cohesion.

37.16 Transactional States and the State Pattern

Transactional support issues can get complex, but to keep things simple for the present—to focus on the GoF State pattern—assume the following:

- Persistent objects can be inserted, deleted, or modified.

- Operating on a persistent object (for example, modifying it) does not cause an immediate database update; rather, an explicit *commit* operation must be performed.

In addition, the response to an operation depends on the transactional state of the object. As an example, responses may be as shown in the statechart of Figure 37.12.

For example, an "old dirty" object is one retrieved from the database and then modified. On a commit operation, it should be updated to the database—in contrast to one in the "old clean" state, which should do nothing (because it hasn't changed). Within the object-oriented PFW, when a delete or save operation is performed, it does not immediately cause a database delete or save; rather, the persistent object transitions to the appropriate state, awaiting a commit or rollback to really do something.

As a UML comment, this is a good example of where a statechart is helpful in succinctly communicating information that is otherwise awkward to express.

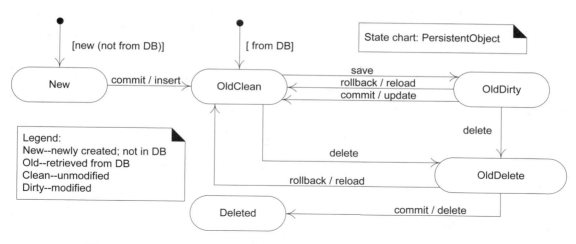

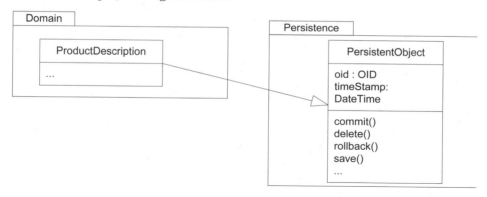

Figure 37.12 Statechart for PersistentObject.

In this design, assume that we will make all persistent object classes extend a *PersistentObject* class,[6] that provides common technical services for persistence.[7] For example, see Figure 37.13.

Figure 37.13 Persistent objects.

Now—and this is the issue that will be resolved with the State pattern—notice that *commit* and *rollback* methods require similar structures of case logic, based

---

6. [Ambler00b] is a good reference on a *PersistentObject* class and persistence layers, although the idea is older.

7. Some issues with extending a *PersistentObject* class are discussed later. Whenever a domain object class extends a technical services class, it should be pause for reflection, as it mixes architectural concerns (persistence and application logic).

on a transactional state code. *commit* and *rollback* perform different actions in their cases, but they have similar logic structures.

```
public void commit()              public void rollback()
{                                 {
switch ( state )                  switch ( state )
{                                 {
case OLD_DIRTY:                   case OLD_DIRTY:
    // ...                            // ...
    break;                           break;
case OLD_CLEAN:                   case OLD_CLEAN:
    //...                             //...
    break;                           break;
...                               ...
}                                 }
```

An alternative to this repeating case logic structure is the GoF State pattern.

State

Context / Problem

An object's behavior is dependent on its state, and its methods contain case logic reflecting conditional state-dependent actions. Is there an alternative to conditional logic?

Solution

Create state classes for each state, implementing a common interface. Delegate state-dependent operations from the context object to its current state object. Ensure the context object always points to a state object reflecting its current state.

Figure 37.14 illustrates its application in the persistence subsystem.

State-dependent methods in *PersistentObject* delegate their execution to an associated state object. If the context object is referencing the *OldDirtyState*, then 1) the *commit* method will cause a database update, and 2) the context object will be reassigned to reference the *OldCleanState*. On the other hand, if the context object is referencing the *OldCleanState*, the inherited do-nothing *commit* method executes and does nothing (as to be expected, since the object is clean).

Observe in Figure 37.14 that the state classes and their behavior correspond to the state chart of Figure 37.12. The State pattern is one mechanism to implement a state transition model in software.[8] It causes an object to transition to different states in response to events.

As a performance comment, these state objects are—ironically—stateless (no attributes). Thus, there does not need to be multiple instances of a class—each is a singleton. Thousands of persistent objects can reference the same *OldDirtyState* instance, for example.

37.17 Designing a Transaction with the Command Pattern

The last section took a simplified view of transactions. This section extends the discussion, but does not cover all transaction design issues. Informally, a transaction is a unit of work—a set of tasks—whose tasks must all complete successfully, or none must be completed. That is, its completion is atomic.

In terms of the persistence service, the tasks of a transaction include inserting, updating, and deleting objects. One transaction could contain two inserts, one update, and three deletes, for example. To represent this, a *Transaction* class is added [Ambler00b].[9] As pointed out in [Fowler01], the order of database tasks within a transaction can influence its success (and performance).

For example:

1. Suppose the database has a referential integrity constraint such that when a record is updated in TableA that contains a foreign key to a record in TableB, the database requires that the record in TableB already exists.

2. Suppose a transaction contains an INSERT task to add the TableB record, and an UPDATE task to update the TableA record. If the UPDATE executes before the INSERT, a referential integrity error is raised.

Ordering the database tasks can help. Some ordering issues are schema-specific, but a general strategy is to first do inserts, then updates, and then deletes.

Mind that the order in which tasks are added to a transaction by an application may not reflect their best execution order. The tasks need to be sorted just before their execution.

---

8. There are others, including hard-coded conditional logic, state machine interpreters, and code generators driven by state tables.

9. This is called a UnitOfWork in [Fowler02].

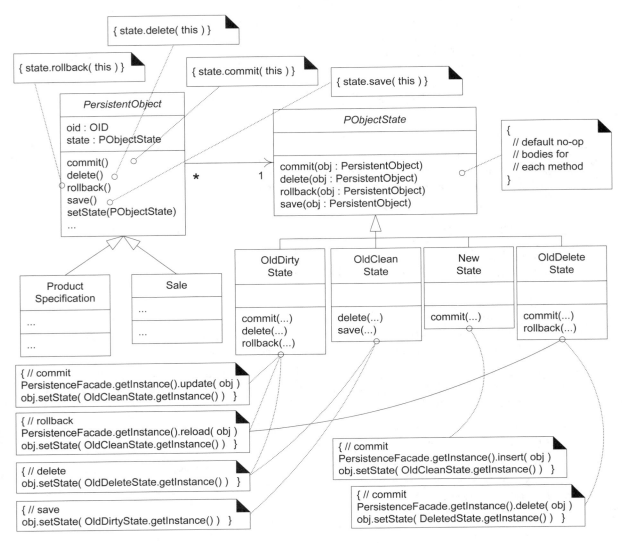

Figure 37.14 Applying the State pattern.[10]

---

10. The *Deleted* class is omitted due to space constraints in the diagram.

This leads to another GoF pattern: Command.

> ### Command
>
> *Context/Problem*
>
> How to handle requests or tasks that need functions such as sorting (prioritizing), queueing, delaying, logging, or undoing?
>
> *Solution*
>
> Make each task a class that implements a common interface.

This is a simple pattern with many useful applications; actions become objects, and thus can be sorted, logged, queued, and so forth. For example, in the PFW, Figure 37.15 shows Command (or task) classes for the database operations.

There is much more to completing a transaction solution, but the key idea of this section is to represent each task or action in the transaction as an object with a polymorphic *execute* method; this opens up a world of flexibility by treating the request as an object itself.

The quintessential example of Command is for GUI actions, such as cut and paste. For example, the *CutCommand's execute* method does a cut, and its *undo* method reverses the cut. The *CutCommand* will also retain the data necessary to perform the undo. All the GUI commands can be kept in a history stack, so that they can be popped in turn, and each undone.

Another common use of Command is for server-side request handling. When a server object receives a (remote) message, it creates a Command object for that request, and hands it off to a *CommandProcesser* [BMRSS96], which can queue, log, prioritize, and execute the commands.

37.18 Lazy Materialization with a Virtual Proxy

It is sometimes desirable to defer the materialization of an object until it is absolutely required, usually for performance reasons. For example, suppose that *ProductDescription* objects reference a *Manufacturer* object, but only very rarely does it need to be materialized from the database. Only rare scenarios cause a request for manufacturer information, such as manufacturer rebate scenarios in which the company name and address are required.

The deferred materialization of "children" objects is known as **lazy materialization**. Lazy materialization can be implemented using the Virtual Proxy GoF pattern—one of many variations of Proxy.

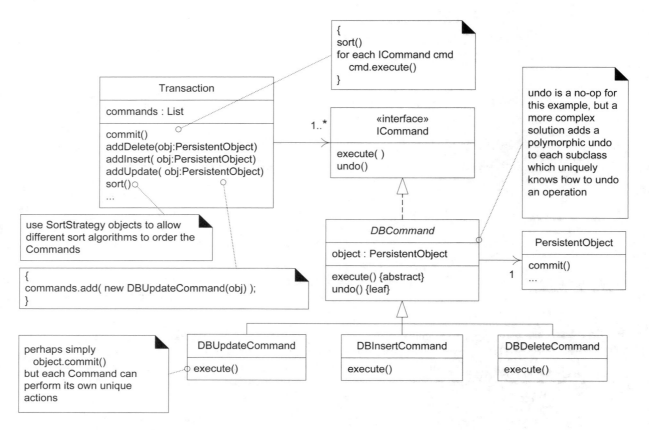

Figure 37.15 Commands for database operations.

A **Virtual Proxy** is a proxy for another object (the *real subject*) that materializes the real subject when it is first referenced; therefore, it implements lazy materialization. It is a lightweight object that stands for a "real" object that may or may not be materialized.

A concrete example of the Virtual Proxy pattern with *ProductDescription* and *Manufacturer* is shown in Figure 37.16. This design is based on the assumption that proxies know the OID of their real subject, and when materialization is required, the OID is used to help identify and retrieve the real subject.

Note that the *ProductDescription* has attribute visibility to an *IManufacturer* instance. The *Manufacturer* for this *ProductDescription* may not yet be materialized in memory. When the *ProductDescription* sends a *getAddress* message to the *ManufacturerProxy* (as though it were the materialized manufacturer object), the proxy materializes the real *Manufacturer*, using the OID of the *Manufacturer* to retrieve and materialize it.

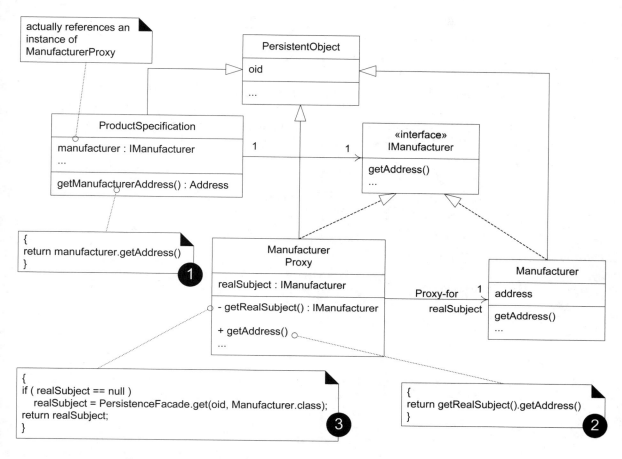

Figure 37.16 Manufacturer Virtual Proxy.

Who Creates the Virtual Proxy?

Observe in Figure 37.16 that the *ManufacturerProxy* collaborates with the *PersistenceFacade* in order to materialize its real subject. But who creates the *ManufacturerProxy*? Answer: The database mapper class for *ProductDescription*. The mapper class is responsible for deciding, when it materializes an object, which of its "child" objects should also be eagerly materialized, and which should be lazily materialized with a proxy.

Consider these alternative solutions: one uses eager materialization, the other lazy materialization.

```
// EAGER MATERIALIZATION OF MANUFACTURER

class ProductDescriptionRDBMapper extends AbstractPersistenceMapper
{
protected Object getObjectFromStorage( OID oid )
{
ResultSet rs =
    RDBOperations.getInstance().getProductDescriptionData( oid );


ProductDescription ps = new ProductDescription();
ps.setPrice( rs.getDouble( "PRICE" ) );


    // here's the essence of it

String manufacturerForeignKey = rs.getString( "MANU_OID" );
OID manuOID = new OID( manufacturerForeignKey );
ps.setManufacturer( (IManufacturer)
    PersistenceFacade.getInstance().get(manuOID,Manufacturer.class);
...
}
```

Here is the lazy materialization solution:

```
// LAZY MATERIALIZATION OF MANUFACTURER

class ProductDescriptionRDBMapper extends AbstractPersistenceMapper
{
protected Object getObjectFromStorage( OID oid )
{
ResultSet rs =
    RDBOperations.getInstance().getProductDescriptionData( oid );

ProductDescription ps = new ProductDescription();
ps.setPrice( rs.getDouble( "PRICE" ) );


    // here's the essence of it

String manufacturerForeignKey = rs.getString( "MANU_OID" );
OID manuOID = new OID( manufacturerForeignKey );
ps.setManufacturer( new ManufacturerProxy( manuOID ) );
...
}
```

Implementation of a Virtual Proxy

The implementation of a Virtual Proxy varies by language. The details are outside the scope of this chapter, but here is a synopsis:

Language	Virtual Proxy Implementation
C++	Define a templatized smart pointer class. No *IManufacturer* interface definition is actually needed.
Java	The *ManufacturerProxy* class is implemented. The *IManufacturer* interface is defined. However, these are not normally manually coded. Rather, one creates a code generator that analyzes the subject classes (e.g., *Manufacturer*) and generates *IManufacturer* and *ProxyManufacturer*. Another Java alternative is the Dynamic Proxy API.
Smalltalk	Define a Virtual Morphing Proxy (or Ghost Proxy), which uses *#doesNotUnderstand:* and *#become:* to morph into the real subject. No *IManufacturer* definition is needed.

37.19 How to Represent Relationships in Tables

The code in the prior section relies on a MANU_OID foreign key in the PRODUCT_SPEC table to link to a record in the MANUFACTURER table. This highlights the question: How are object relationships represented in the relational model?

The answer is given in the **Representing Object Relationships as Tables** pattern {BW96}, which proposes the following:

- **one-to-one** associations

    ○ Place an OID foreign key in one or both tables representing the objects in relationship.

    ○ Or, create an associative table that records the OIDs of each object in relationship.

- **one-to-many** associations, such as a collection

    ○ Create an associative table that records the OIDs of each object in relationship.

- **many-to-many** associations

    ○ Create an associative table that records the OIDs of each object in relationship.

37.20   PersistentObject Superclass and Separation of Concerns

A common partial design solution to providing persistence for objects is to create an abstract technical services superclass *PersistentObject* that all persistence objects inherit from (see Figure 37.17). Such a class usually defines attributes for persistence, such as a unique OID, and methods for saving to a database.

This is not wrong, but it suffers from the weakness of coupling the class to the *PersistentObject* class—domain classes end up extending a technical services class.

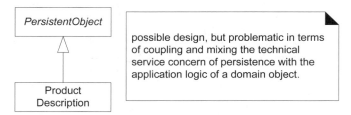

Figure 37.17 Problems with a PersistentObject superclass.

This design does not illustrate a clear separation of concerns. Rather, technical services concerns are mixed with domain layer business logic concerns by virtue of this extension.

On the other hand, "separation of concerns" is not an absolute virtue that must be followed at all costs. As discussed in the Protected Variations introduction, designers need to pick their battles at the truly likely points of expensive insta-bility. If in a particular application making the classes extend from *Persistent-Object* leads to a neat and easy solution and does not create longer-term design or maintenance problems, why not? The answer lies in understanding the evolu-tion of the requirements and design for the application. It is also influenced by the language: Those with single inheritance (such as Java) have had their single precious superclass *consumed*.

37.21   Unresolved Issues

This has been a very brief introduction to the problems and design solutions in a persistence framework and service. Many important issues have been glossed over, including:

- dematerializing objects
    - ○ Briefly, the mappers must define *putObjectToStorage* methods. Dematerializing composition hierarchies requires collaboration between multiple mappers and the maintenance of associative tables (if an RDB is used).

- materialization and dematerialization of collections
- queries for groups of objects
- thorough transaction handling
- error handling when a database operation fails
- multiuser access and locking strategies
- security—controlling access to the database

UML DEPLOYMENT AND COMPONENT DIAGRAMS

Call me paranoid but finding '/' inside this
comment makes me suspicious.*

—An MPW C compiler warning

Objectives

■ Summarize UML deployment and component diagram notation.

What's Next?   Having applied GoF patterns to the design of a framework, this chapter
summarizes UML notation useful in architecture documentation. The next
concludes this iteration, an introduction to documenting an architecture with
UML and the well-known N+1 view model.

More Object Design with GoF Patterns	Designing a Framework with Patterns	UML Deployment & Component Diagrams	Documenting Architecture: The N+1 View Model	Iterative and Agile Project Management

38.1   Deployment Diagrams

A deployment diagram shows the assignment of concrete software artifacts
(such as executable files) to computational nodes (something with processing
services). It shows the deployment of software elements to the **physical architecture** and the communication (usually on a network) between physical elements. See Figure 38.1. Deployment diagrams are useful to communicate the
physical or deployment architecture, for example, in the UP Software Architecture Document, discussed starting on p. 656.

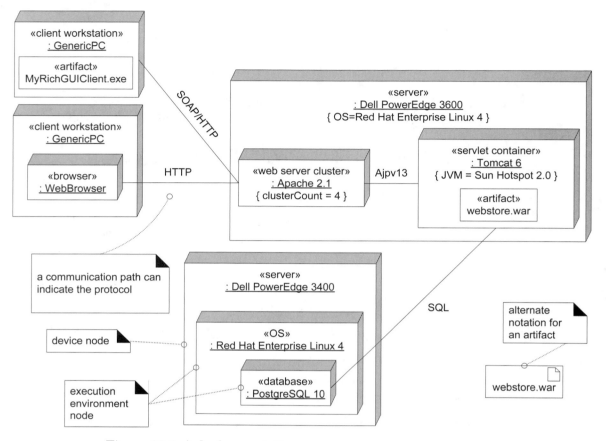

Figure 38.1 A deployment diagram.

The basic element of a deployment diagram is a **node**, of two types:

- **device node** (or **device**)—A physical (e.g., digital electronic) computing resource with processing and memory services to execute software, such as a typical computer or a mobile phone.

- **execution environment node** (EEN)—This is a *software* computing resource that runs within an outer node (such as a computer) and which itself provides a service to host and execute other executable software elements. For example:

    - an *operating system* (OS) is software that hosts and executes programs

    - a *virtual machine* (VM, such as the Java or .NET VM) hosts and executes programs

    - a *database engine* (such as PostgreSQL) receives SQL program requests and executes them, and hosts/executes internal stored procedures (written in Java or a proprietary language)

○ a *Web browser* hosts and executes JavaScript, Java applets, Flash, and other executable technologies

○ a *workflow engine*

○ a *servlet container* or *EJB container*

As the UML specification suggests, many node types may show stereotypes, such as «server», «OS», «database», or «browser», but these are not official predefined UML stereotypes.

Note that a device node or EEN may contain another EEN. For example, a virtual machine within an OS within a computer.

A particular EEN can be implied, or not shown, or indicated informally with a UML property string; for example, {OS=Linux}. For example, there may not be value in showing the OS EEN as an explicit node. Figure 38.1 shows alternate styles, using the OS as an example.

The normal connection between nodes is a **communication path**, which may be labeled with the protocol. These usually indicate the network connections.

A node may contain and show an **artifact**—a concrete physical element, usually a file. This includes executables such as JARs, assemblies, .exe files, and scripts. It also includes data files such as XML, HTML, and so forth.

A deployment diagram usually shows an example set of *instances* (rather than classes). For example, an instance of a server computer running an instance of the Linux OS. Generally in the UML, concrete **instances** are shown with an underline under their name, and the absence of an underline signifies a class rather than an instance. Note that a major exception to this rule is instances in interaction diagrams—there, the names of things signifying instances in lifeline boxes are not underlined.

In any event, in deployment diagrams, you will usually see the objects with their name underlined, to indicate instances. However, the UML specification states that for deployment diagrams, the underlining may be omitted and assumed. Therefore, you can see examples in both styles.

38.2   Component Diagrams

Components are a slightly fuzzy concept in the UML, because both classes and components can be used to model the same thing. For example, to quote Rumbaugh (one of the UML founders):

> *The distinction between a structured class and a component is somewhat vague and more a matter of intent than firm semantics. [RJB04]*

And to quote the UML specification [OMG03b]:

> *A* **component** *represents a modular part of a system that encapsulates its contents and whose manifestation is replaceable within its environment. A component defines its behavior in terms of provided and required interfaces. As such, a component serves as a type, whose conformance is defined by these provided and required interfaces.*

Again, this idea can be modeled with a regular UML class and its provided and required interfaces. Recall that a UML class can be used to model any level of software element, from an entire system to subsystem to small utility object.

But when one uses a UML component, the modeling and design intent is to emphasize 1) that the *interfaces* are important, and 2) it is *modular, self-contained* and *replaceable*. The second point implies that a component tends to have little or no dependency on other external elements (except perhaps standard core libraries); it is a relatively stand-alone module.

UML components are a design-level perspective; they don't exist in the concrete software perspective, but map to concrete artifacts such as a set of files.

A good analogy for software component modeling is a home entertainment system; we expect to be able to easily replace the DVD player or speakers. They are modular, self-contained, replaceable, and work via standard interfaces.

For example, at a large-grained level, a SQL database engine can be modeled as a component; any database that understands the same version of SQL and supports the same transaction semantics can be substituted. At a finer level, any solution that implements the standard Java Message Service API can be used or replaced in a system.

Since the emphasis of component-based modeling is replaceable parts (perhaps to upgrade for better non-functional qualities, such as performance), it's a general guideline to do component modeling for relatively large-scale elements, because it is difficult to think about or design for many small, fine-grained replaceable parts. Figure 38.2 illustrates the essential notation.

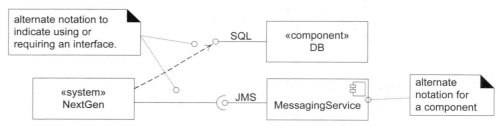

Figure 38.2 UML components.

The topic of dedicated component-based modeling and development is a large, specialized subject, outside of the scope of this introduction to OOA/D.

DOCUMENTING ARCHITECTURE: UML & THE N+1 VIEW MODEL

They have computers, and they may have other weapons of mass destruction.

—USA government official

Objectives

- Create useful architecture documentation based on the N+1 (or 4+1) view model.

- Apply various UML diagram types.

Introduction

Once an architecture takes shape, it may be useful to describe it, so that new developers can learn the big ideas of the system, or so that there is a common view from which to discuss changes. In the UP, the artifact that describes this is the **Software Architecture Document** (SAD). The chapter introduces the SAD and its contents.

What's Next?   Having summarized relevant UML notation, this chapter is an introduction to documenting an architecture with UML and the well-known N+1 view model. The next explores more issues in iterative development, and managing an iterative project with agile practices.

| Designing a Framework with Patterns | UML Deployment & Component Diagrams | Documenting Architecture: The N+1 View Model | Iterative and Agile Project Management |

39.1   The SAD and Its Architectural Views

The Software Architect Document

In addition to the UML package, class, and interaction diagrams, another key artifact in the UP Design Model is the SAD. It describes the big ideas in the architecture, including the decisions of architectural analysis. Practically, it is a *learning aid* for developers who need to understand the essential ideas of the system.

The essence of the SAD is a summary of the architectural decisions (such as with technical memos) and the N+1 architectural views.

Motivation: Why Create a SAD?

When someone joins the development team, it's useful if the project coach can say, "Welcome to the NextGen project! Please go to the project website and read the ten page SAD in order to get an introduction to the big ideas." And later, during a subsequent release, when new people work on the system, a SAD can be a learning aid to speed their comprehension.

Therefore, it should be written with this audience and goal in mind: What do I need to say (and draw in the UML) that will quickly help someone understand the major ideas in this system?

Architectural Views

Having an architecture is one thing; a useful description is something else.

In [Kruchten95], the influential and widely adopted idea of describing an architecture with multiple views was promoted; its multiple-view model is now considered the state of the practice. The essence idea of an **architectural view** is this:

Definition: Architectural View

A view of the system architecture from a given perspective; it focuses primarily on structure, modularity, essential components, and the main control flows. [RUP].

An important aspect of the view missing from this RUP definition is the *motivation*. That is, an architectural view should explain why the architecture is the way it is.

An architectural view is a window onto the system from a particular perspective that emphasizes the key noteworthy information or ideas, and ignores the rest.

An architectural view is a tool of communication, education, or thought; it is expressed in text and UML diagrams.

For example, the NextGen package and interaction diagrams shown in Chapter 34 on layering and logical architecture show the big ideas of the logical structure of the software architecture. In the SAD, the architect will create a section called *Logical View*, insert those UML diagrams, and add some written commentary on what each package and layer is for, and the motivation behind the logical design.

A key idea of the architectural views—which concretely are text and diagrams—is that they do *not* describe *all* of the system from some perspective, but only outstanding ideas from that perspective. A view is, if you will, the "one-minute elevator" description: What are the most important things you would say in one minute in an elevator to a colleague on this perspective?

Architectural views may be created:

- after the system is built, as a summary and learning aid for future developers

- at the end of certain iteration milestones (such as the end of elaboration) to serve as a learning aid for the current development team, and new members

- speculatively, during early iterations, as an aid in creative design work, recognizing that the original view will change as design and implementation proceeds

The N+1 (or 4+1) View Model

In his seminal paper, Kruchten not only promoted documenting an architecture from different views, but more specifically, showing the **4+1** views, which today has expanded more generally to the **N+1** views, reflecting the myriad concerns in a system.

Briefly, the 4 views described in the paper are: logical, process, deployment, and data. These are described in a following section. The '+1' view is the **use case view**, a summary of the most architecturally significant use cases or scenarios, and perhaps a summary of use-case realizations for these. The use case view pulls together a common story that ties together an understanding of the other views and how they interrelate.

Architectural Views in More Detail

Myriad views are possible, each reflecting a major architectural viewpoint on to a system; here is a list of common views:

1. **Logical**

    ○ Conceptual organization of the software in terms of the most important layers, subsystems, packages, frameworks, classes, and interfaces. Also summarizes the functionality of the major software elements, such as each subsystem.

○ Shows outstanding use-case realization scenarios (as interaction diagrams) that illustrate key aspects of the system.

○ A view onto the UP Design Model, visualized with UML package, class, and interaction diagrams.

2. **Process**

○ Processes and threads. Their responsibilities, collaborations, and the allocation of logical elements (layers, subsystems, classes, ...) to them.

○ A view onto the UP Design Model, visualized with UML class and interaction diagrams, using the UML process and thread notation.

3. **Deployment**

○ Physical deployment of processes and components to processing nodes, and the physical network configuration between nodes.

○ A view onto the UP Deployment Model, visualized with UML deployment diagrams. Normally, the "view" is simply the entire model rather than a subset, as all of it is noteworthy. See Chapter 38 for the UML deployment diagram notation.

4. **Data**

○ Overview of the data flows, persistent data schema, the schema mapping from objects to persistent data (usually in a relational database), the mechanism of mapping from objects to a database, database stored procedures and triggers.

○ In part, a view onto the UP Data Model, visualized with UML class diagrams used to describe a data model.

○ Data flows can be shown with UML activity diagrams.

5. **Security**

○ Overview of the security schemes, and points within the architecture that security is applied, such as HTTP authentication, database authentication, and so forth.

○ Could be a view onto the UP Deployment Model, visualized with UML deployment diagrams that highlight the key points of security, and related files.

6. **Implementation**

○ First, a definition of the **Implementation Model**: In contrast to the other UP models, which are text and diagrams, this "model" *is* the actual source code, executables, and so forth. It has two parts: 1) deliverables, and 2) things that create deliverables (such as source code and graphics). The Implementation Model is all of this stuff, including Web pages, DLLs, executables, source code, and so forth, and their organization—such as source code in Java packages, and bytecode organized into JAR files.

     ○ The implementation view is a summary description of the noteworthy organization of deliverables and the things that create deliverables (such as the source code).

     ○ A view onto the UP Implementation Model, expressed in text and visualized with UML package and component diagrams.

7. **Development**

     ○ This view summarizes information developers need to know about the setup of the development environment. For example, how are all the files organized in terms of directories, and why? How does a build and smoke test run? How is version control used?

8. **Use case**

     ○ Summary of the most architecturally significant use cases and their non-functional requirements. That is, those use cases that, by their implementation, illustrate significant architectural coverage or that exercise many architectural elements. For example, the *Process Sale* use case, when fully implemented, has these qualities.

     ○ A view onto the UP Use-Case Model, expressed in text and visualized with UML use case diagrams and perhaps with use-case realizations in UML interaction diagrams.

Guideline: Don't Forget the Motivation!

Each view includes not only diagrams, but text that expands and clarifies. In this prose section, an often forgotten but tremendously important section is to discuss the *motivation*. *Why* is the security the way it is? *Why* are the three major software components deployed on two computers rather than three? Indeed, this section often becomes more important than any other when it comes time to make significant changes to the architecture.

39.2   Notation: The Structure of a SAD

The following SAD structure is essentially the format used in the UP:

Software Architecture Document

Architectural Representation

(Summary of how the architecture will be described in this document, such as using by technical memos and the architectural views. This is useful for someone unfamiliar with the idea of technical memos or views. Note that not all views are necessary.)

Architectural Factors

(Reference to the Supplementary Specification to view the Factor Table.)

Architectural Decisions

(The set of technical memos that summarize the decisions.)

Logical View

(UML package diagrams, and class diagrams of major elements. Commentary on the large scale structure and functionality of major components.)

Deployment View

(UML deployment diagrams showing the nodes and allocation of processes and components. Commentary on the networking.)

Process View

(UML class and interaction diagrams illustrating the processes and threads of the system. Group this by threads and processes that interact. Comment on how the interprocess communication works (e.g., by Java RMI).

Use-Case View

(Brief summary of the most architecturally significant use cases. UML interaction diagrams for some architectural significant use-case realizations, or scenarios, with commentary on the diagrams explaining how they illustrate the major architectural elements.)

Other Views...

39.3 Example: A NextGen POS SAD

In this and subsequent examples, my goal is not to exhaustively show a thorough 10+ page SAD with fully descriptive text and detailed diagrams, but to give a flavor of what may be included.

Software Architecture Document
NextGen POS Project

Introduction: Architectural Representation

This SAD summarizes the architecture from multiple views. These include:

- logical view: ...brief definition
- data view: ...
- process view: ...

- ...

In addition, this SAD references the Supplementary Specification where you will find the architecturally-significant requirements recorded in a factor table. It also summarizes the key architectural decisions in a format called a technical memo—a short one-page description of a decision and its motivation.

Note that each view includes a discussion of motivation, which may help you when you need to modify the architecture.

Architectural Factors

See the Supplementary Specification factor table of architecturally-significant requirements starting on p. 548.

Architectural Decisions (Technical Memos)

Technical Memo
Issue: Reliability—Recovery from Remote Service Failure

Solution Summary: Location transparency using service lookup, failover from remote to local, and local service partial replication.

Factors

- Robust recovery from remote service failure (e.g., tax calculator, inventory)
- Robust recovery from remote product (e.g., descriptions and prices) database failure

Solution

Achieve protected variation with respect to location of services using an Adapter created in a Services-Factory. Where possible, offer local implementations of remote services, usually with simplified or constrained behavior. For example, the local tax calculator will use constant tax rates. The local product information database will be a small cache of the most common products. Inventory updates will be stored and forwarded at reconnection.

See also the *Adaptability—Third-Party Services* technical memo for the adaptability aspects of this solutions, because remote service implementations will vary at each installation.

To satisfy the quality scenarios of reconnection with the remote services ASAP, use smart Proxy objects for the services, that on each service call test for remote service reactivation, and redirect to them when possible.

Motivation

Retailers really don't want to stop making sales! Therefore, if the NextGen POS offers this level of reliability and recovery, it will be a very attractive product, as none of our competitors provide this capability. The small product cache is motivated by very limited client-side resources. The real third-party tax calculator is not replicated on the client primarily because of the higher licensing costs, and configuration efforts (as each calculator installation requires almost weekly adjustments). This design also supports the evolution point of future customers willing and able to permanently replicate services such as the tax calculator to each client terminal.

Unresolved Issues—none

Alternatives Considered

A "gold level" quality of service agreement with remote credit authorization services to improve reliability. It was available, but much too expensive.

Technical Memo

Issue: Legal—Tax Rule Compliance

Solution Summary: Purchase a tax calculator component.

Factors ...

... other technical memos ...

Logical View

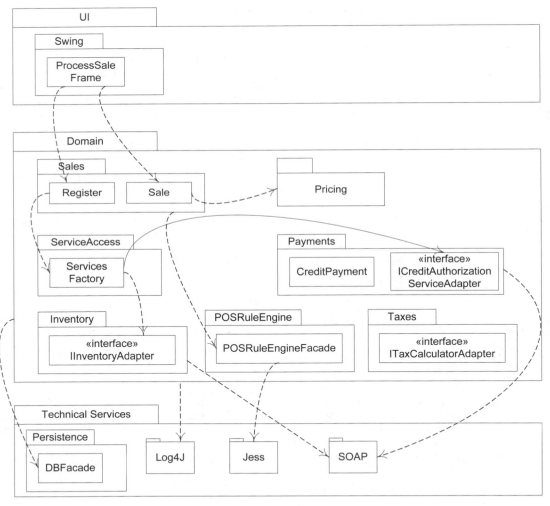

Figure 1. Package diagram of the logical view.

Discussion and Motivation

A classic layered architecture is used. No application layer of sessions objects was inserted between the UI and Domain layers, as the system operations are simple, without much workflow coordination. The primary controller receiving the system operation requests from the UI layer is the *Register* class. Note that a facade is placed in front of access to the Jess rule engine as we may wish to use an alternative in the future.

Deployment View

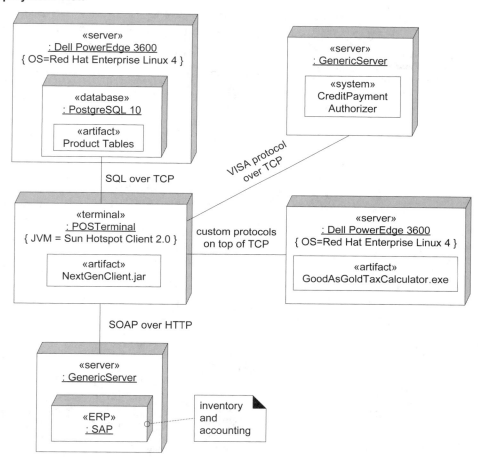

Figure 2. Deployment view.

Discussion and Motivation

The product database, inventory system, and tax calculator are deployed to different computers for performance and reliability goals. The tax calculator is centralized, rather than replicated on each POS terminal, because of its high licensing cost; there is a chance that in the future it will be inexpensive enough to replicate locally on each POS terminal.

Data View

Discussion and Motivation

A *Process Sale* use case scenario is a good example to understand the major data flows. A UML activity diagram is applied in a data-flow flavor to illustrate the major flows and data stores. See Figure 3.

Transformation of data read from the Products database into Java objects is done with the *Hibernate* O-R mapping system.

Transformation of sale data written to the ERP databases (inventory and accounting) is done by a custom NextGen adapter, usually into an XML format required by the ERP system.

Transformation of the payment request data sent to the external payment authorization service is done by a custom NextGen adapter, usually into the well-known VISA format (and protocol).

Motivation? These external systems and databases were a hard constraint that we had to conform to.

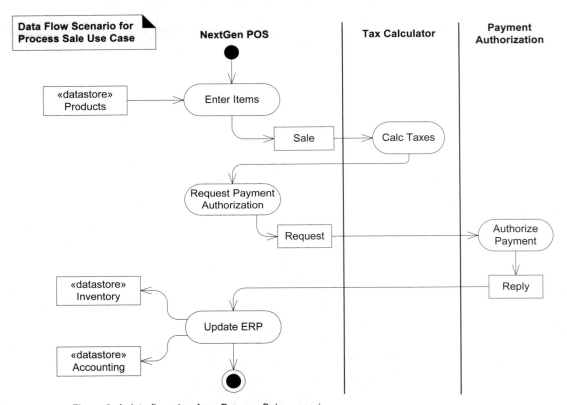

Figure 3. A data flow view for a Process Sale scenario.

Use-Case View

The most architecturally significant use case is *Process Sale*. See the use-case text starting on p. 67. By implementing this use case, most of the key architectural issues were confronted and resolved. A key system operation is *enterItem*; see Figure 4 for a partial interaction scenario across some noteworthy logical boundaries.

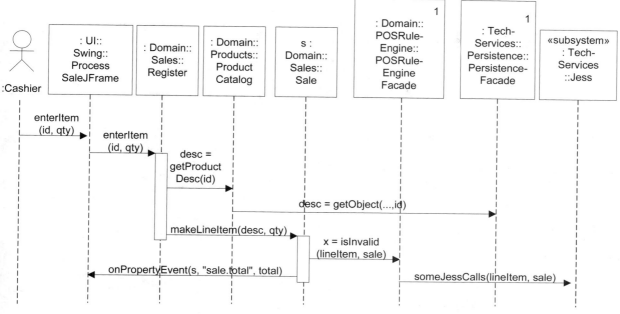

Figure 3. A partial use-case realization in a Process Sale scenario.

Other Views...

39.4　Example: A Jakarta Struts SAD

Struts is a popular open source Java technology framework for handling Web requests and page-flow coordination. In this example, partial SAD, I wish to illustrate a logical view in more detail.

Software Architecture Document
Jakarta Struts Framework

Architectural Representation

...

Architectural Factors

...

Architectural Decisions

...

Logical View

The Struts framework—and subsystems built with it—reside primarily in the UI layer of a web application. Figure 1 illustrates noteworthy layers and packages with a UML package diagram.

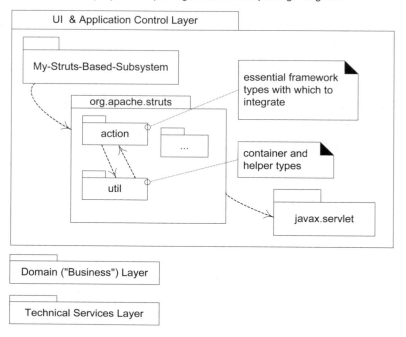

Figure 1. Noteworthy layers and packages related to Struts.

There is a distinction between pure UI layer responsibilities, that encompass creating the content and pages for display, vs. what is sometimes called the application control layer—the layer of components that is responsible for deciding the flow of control, and directing the presentation layer to display something. In common use, web presentation frameworks usually imply the inclusion of application control responsibilities, which is also true of Struts, as it requires developers to create subclasses of the Struts Action class that are responsible for flow control decisions.

Architectural Patterns

The Struts architecture is based on the Model-View-Controller (MVC) pattern; specifically, the web systems variant where the component roles are:

Controller—a multithreaded singleton Facade-like object responsible for receiving and delegating HTTP requests, and by collaboration with other objects, controlling the flow of the application.

View—components responsible for generating display content (e.g., HTML).

Model—components responsible for domain logic and state.

Struts adoption of MVC provides the architectural foundation to achieve a separation of concerns related to flow control, display content generation (and formatting), and application logic—in this case through modularization into separate component groups that specialize by cohesively related responsibilities.

The specific MVC roles mapped to Struts components is illustrated in the UML class diagram in Figure 2.

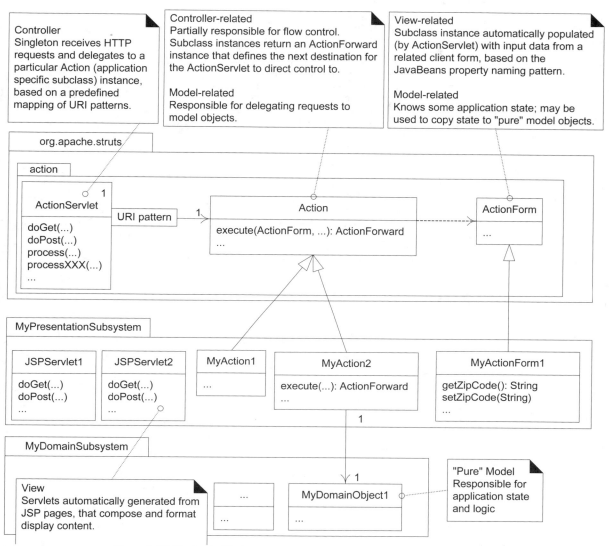

Controller
Singleton receives HTTP requests and delegates to a particular Action (application specific subclass) instance, based on a predefined mapping of URI patterns.

Controller-related
Partially responsible for flow control. Subclass instances return an ActionForward instance that defines the next destination for the ActionServlet to direct control to.

Model-related
Responsible for delegating requests to model objects.

View-related
Subclass instance automatically populated (by ActionServlet) with input data from a related client form, based on the JavaBeans property naming pattern.

Model-related
Knows some application state; may be used to copy state to "pure" model objects.

"Pure" Model
Responsible for application state and logic

View
Servlets automatically generated from JSP pages, that compose and format display content.

Figure 2. MVC roles in Struts.

Related Patterns

The ActionServlet acts as a Facade onto the presentation layer. And although not a classic Mediator that receives and mediates messaging between other decoupled objects, it is similar, because an Action object returns an ActionForward object to the ActionServlet, which is used to direct the next step.

The Struts ActionServlet and Action design also illustrates the Command Processor pattern, a variant of the GoF Command design pattern. The ActionServlet plays the role of Command Processor, receiving requests and mapping them to Action (Command) objects that execute requests.

Struts demonstrates the Front Controller and Business Delegate patterns. The ActionServlet is the Front Controller, or initial point of contact for handling requests. The Action objects are Business Delegates-abstractions that delegate to the "business" or domain layer of services.

The Action objects also play the role of Adapters, adapting the framework calls to the interface of the

667

domain layer objects.

As illustrated in the Figure 3, the ActionServlet implements the Template Method pattern: process is the template, and the processXXX are the hook methods.

Framework Hotspots

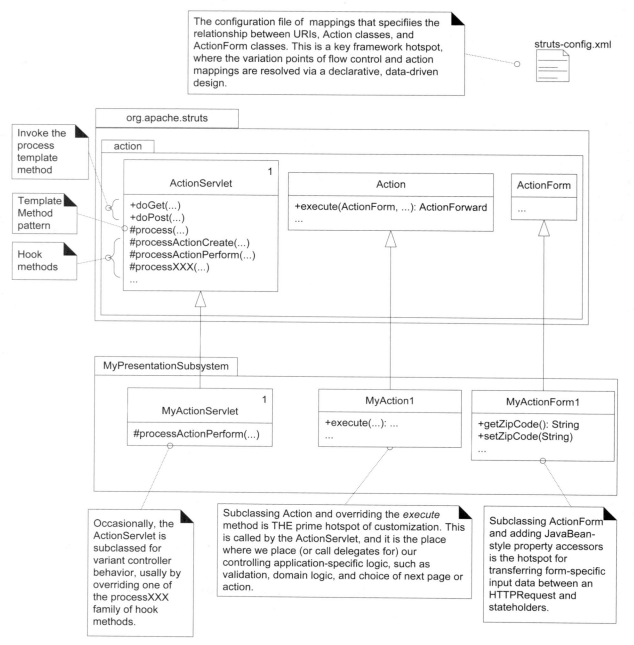

Figure 3. Struts framework hotspots.

Key to using a framework is knowing its hotspots—the variation points in the framework where the developer can parameterize or "plug in" applications-specific varying behavior, through techniques such as subclassing, composition based on interfaces, and declarative constraints or mappings usually externalized in configuration files. Figure 3 illustrates key Struts hotspots, which use subclassing and declarative mappings, typical of whitebox framework designs.

Other Views...

39.5   Process: Iterative Architectural Documentation

UP and the SAD

Inception—If it is unclear whether it is technically possible to satisfy the architecturally significant requirements, the team may implement an **architectural proof-of-concept** (POC) to determine feasibility. In the UP, its creation and assessment is called **Architectural Synthesis**. This is distinct from plain old small POC programming experiments for isolated technical questions. An architectural POC lightly covers *many* of the architecturally significant requirements to assess their *combined* feasibility.

Elaboration—A major goal of this phase is to implement the core risky architectural elements, thus most architectural analysis is completed during elaboration. It is normally expected that the majority of factor table, technical memo, and SAD content can be completed by the end of elaboration.

Transition—Although ideally the architecturally significant factors and decisions were resolved long before transition, the SAD will need a review and possible revision at the end of this phase to ensure it accurately describes the final deployed system.

Subsequent evolution cycles—Before the design of new versions, it is common to revisit architectural factors and decisions. For example, the decision in version 1.0 to create a single remote tax calculator service, rather than one duplicated on each POS node, could have been motivated by cost (to avoid multiple licenses). But perhaps in the future the cost of tax calculators is reduced, and thus, for fault tolerance or performance reasons, the architecture is changed to use multiple local tax calculators.

39.6   Recommended Resources

In addition to the original paper [Kruchten95], *Documenting Software Architectures: Views and Beyond* by Clements, et al. is a useful resource.

PART 6 SPECIAL TOPICS

MORE ON ITERATIVE DEVELOPMENT AND AGILE PROJECT MANAGEMENT

Prediction is very difficult, especially if it's about the future.

—anonymous

Objectives

- Rank requirements and risks.
- Compare and contrast adaptive and predictive planning.

Introduction

Iterative and agile project planning and management issues are large topics, but a brief exploration of some key questions related to iterative development and the UP is helpful, such as: What to do in the next iteration? How to track requirements in iterative development? How to organize project artifacts?

What's Next?

Having introduced architecture documentation, this chapter explores more issues in iterative development, and managing an iterative project with agile practices.

UML Deployment & Component Diagrams	Documenting Architecture: The N+1 View Model	Iterative and Agile Project Management		
○	○	●	○	○

40.1   How to Plan an Iteration?

There are many approaches, but the following is relatively typical:

1. Step one is to decide the length of the iteration; 2–6 weeks is the common range. In general, shorter is better. Factors that lengthen an iteration include early work with high degrees of discovery and change, large teams, and distributed teams. Recall that once the end date is chosen, it must remained fixed—that's the practice of timeboxing. However, the scope of work for the iteration can be reduced to meet the end date.

2. Step two is to convene an iteration planning meeting. This is usually done at the end of the current iteration, such as on the final Friday, before work starts on the next iteration on Monday. Ideally at the meeting are present most of the stakeholders: customers (marketing, users, …), developers, chief architect, project manager.

3. A list of potential goals (new features or use cases, defects, …) for the iteration is presented, ranked by some priority scheme (see p. 130). The goal list usually comes from both the customer (business goals) and the chief architect (technical goals).

4. Each member of the team is asked for their individual resource budget (in hours or days) for the iteration; for example, people know they will be away on vacation certain days, and so on. All the resource budgets are summed.

5. For one goal (such as a use case), it is described in some detail, and questions are resolved. Then, the meeting members (especially the developers) are asked to brainstorm the set of more detailed tasks for the goal, with some vague estimates. For example, UI tasks, database tasks, domain layer OO development tasks, external systems integration tasks, and so forth.

    ○   All the task estimates are summed into a running total.

6. Step #5 repeats until enough work has been chosen: The iteration task total is divided by the resource budget total. If the work closely fits given the available resources and the timebox deadline date for the iteration, the meeting is finished.

Notice in this "agile project management" approach that the developers are activity involved in the planning and estimating process, rather than being handed by the project manager an arbitrary set of goals, estimates, and deadlines.

40.2   Adaptive versus Predictive Planning

One of the big ideas of iterative development is to adapt based on feedback, rather than to attempt to predict and plan *in detail* the entire project. Consequently, in the UP, one creates an Iteration Plan for only the *next* iteration.

Beyond the next iteration the detailed plan is left open, to adaptively adjust as the future unfolds (see Figure 40.1). In addition to encouraging flexible, opportunistic behavior, one simple reason for not planning the entire project in detail is that in iterative development not all the requirements, design details, and thus steps are known near the start of the project.[1] Another is the preference to trust the planning judgement of the team as they proceed. Finally, suppose there was a fine-grained detailed plan laid out at the start of the project, and the team "deviates" from it to exploit better insight in how to best run the project. From the outside, this might be viewed as some kind of failure, when it in fact it is just the opposite.

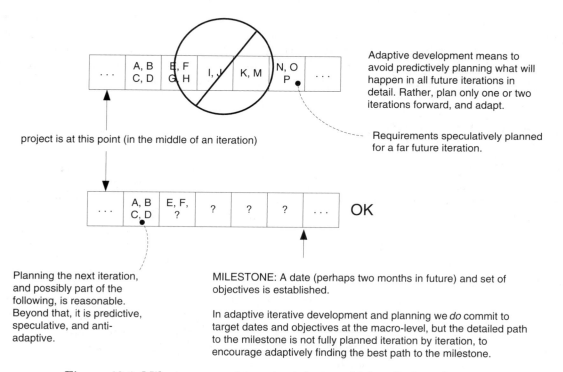

Adaptive development means to avoid predictively planning what will happen in all future iterations in detail. Rather, plan only one or two iterations forward, and adapt.

project is at this point (in the middle of an iteration)

Requirements speculatively planned for a far future iteration.

OK

Planning the next iteration, and possibly part of the following, is reasonable. Beyond that, it is predictive, speculative, and anti-adaptive.

MILESTONE: A date (perhaps two months in future) and set of objectives is established.

In adaptive iterative development and planning we *do* commit to target dates and objectives at the macro-level, but the detailed path to the milestone is not fully planned iteration by iteration, to encourage adaptively finding the best path to the milestone.

Figure 40.1 Milestones are important, but avoid detailed predictive planning into the far future.

However, there *are* still goals and milestones; adaptive development doesn't mean the team doesn't know where they are going, or the milestone dates and objectives. In iterative development, the team still does commit to dates and objectives, but the detailed path to these is flexible. For example, the NextGen team may set a milestone that in three months, use cases *Process Sale, Handle Returns*, and *Authenticate User*, and the logging and pluggable rules features will be completed. But—and this is the key point—the fine-grained plan or path

---

1. They aren't really or reliably known on a "waterfall" project either, although detailed planning for the entire project may occur as though they were.

of two-week timeboxed iterations to that milestone is not defined in detail. The order of steps, or what to do in each iteration over the following three months, is not fixed. Rather, just the next two-week iteration is planned, and the team adapts step by step, working to fulfill the objectives by the milestone date. Of course, dependencies in components and resources naturally constrain some ordering of the work, but not all activities need to be planned and scheduled in fine-grained detail.

External stakeholders see a macro-level plan (such as at the three-month level) to which the team makes some commitment. But the micro-level organization is left up to the best—and adaptive—judgment of the team, as it takes advantage of new insights (see Figure 40.1).

Finally, although adaptive fine-grained planning is preferred in the UP, it *is* increasingly possible to successfully plan forward two or three iterations (with increasingly levels of unreliability) as the requirements and architecture stabilize, the team matures, and data is collected on the speed of development.

40.3   Phase and Iteration Plans

At a macro level, it is possible to establish milestone dates and objectives, but at the micro level, the plan to the milestone is left flexible except for the near future (for example, the next four weeks). These two levels are reflected in the UP **Phase Plan** and **Iteration Plan**, both of which are part of the composite Software Development Plan. The Phase Plan lays out the macro-level milestone dates and objectives, such as the end of phases and mid-phase pilot test milestones. The Iteration Plan defines the work for the current and next iteration—not all iterations (see Figure 40.2).

During inception, the milestone estimates in the Phase Plan are vague "guesstimates." As elaboration progresses, the estimates improve. One goal of the elaboration phase is, at its completion, to have enough realistic information for the team to commit to major milestone dates and objectives for the end of construction and transition (that is, project delivery).

40.4   How to Plan Iterations with Use Cases and Scenarios?

The UP is use-case driven, which in part implies that work is organized around use-case completion. That is to say, an iteration is assigned to implement one or more use cases, or scenarios of use cases in the case that the complete use case is too complex to complete in one iteration.

This last point is important: It is common that a use case has too many varying scenarios to complete all in one short iteration. Thus typically the unit of work is a scenario, rather than a complete use case.

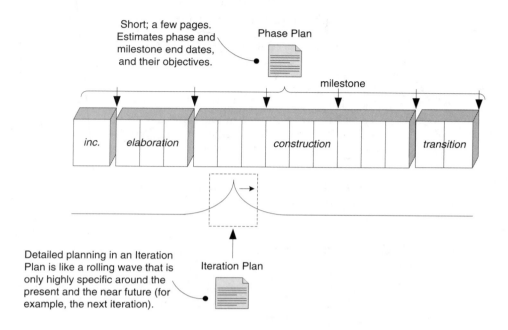

Figure 40.2 Phase and Iteration Plans.

Since the unit of work may be a scenario rather than an entire use case, requirements ranking (see p. 130) may be done with scenarios. This raises a common
question in use-case driven iterative development: How to label scenarios?
Answer: Use the Cockburn-format coding scheme in the fully-dressed format.

For example, consider the following use case fragment:

Use Case: **Process Sale**
Main Success Scenario:
1. Customer arrives at POS checkout with goods and/or services to purchase.
2. Cashier starts a new sale.
3. Cashier enters item identifier.
4. System records sale line item and presents item description, price, and running total.
    Price calculated from a set of price rules.
Cashier repeats steps 3-4 until indicates done.
5. System presents total with taxes calculated.
6. Cashier tells Customer the total, and asks for payment.
7. Customer pays and System handles payment.
8. ...
Extensions (or Alternative Flows):

7a. Paying by cash:
    1. Cashier enters the cash amount tendered.
    2. System presents the balance due, and releases the cash drawer.
    3. Cashier deposits cash tendered and returns balance in cash to Customer.

> 4. System records the cash payment.
> 7b. Paying by credit:
>   1. Customer enters their credit account information.
>   2. ...
> 7c. Paying by check...
> 7d. Paying by debit...

The scenario of *Process Sale* that includes "paying by credit" can be labeled "Process Sale-7b." This scenario label can be used in ranking, tracking, and reporting as a unit of work.

The ranking of requirements guides the choice of early work. For example, the *Process Sale* use case is clearly important. Therefore, we start to tackle it in the first iteration. Yet, not all scenarios of *Process Sale* are implemented in the first iteration. Rather, some simple, happy path scenario, such as "Process Sale-7a" is chosen. Although the scenario is simple, its implementation starts to develop some core elements of the design.

Since some requirements are not expressed as use cases, but rather as defect-fixes or features—such as logging or pluggable business rules—these too are allocated to one or more iterations. Thus, development of scenarios, use cases, defect-fixes, and features proceeds as in Figure 40.3.

Different architecturally significant requirements related to this use case will be tackled during the elaboration iterations, forcing the team to touch on many aspects of the architecture: the major layers, the database, the user interface, the interfaces between major subsystems, and so forth. This leads to the early creation of a "wide and shallow" implementation across many parts of the system—a common goal in the elaboration phase.

40.5   The (In)Validity of Early Estimates

Garbage in, garbage out. Estimates done with unreliable and fuzzy information are unreliable and fuzzy. In the UP it is understood that estimates done during inception are not dependable (this is true of all methods, but the UP acknowledges it). Early inception estimates merely provide guidance if the project is worthy of some real investigation in elaboration, to generate a good estimate. After the first elaboration iteration there is some realistic information to produce a rough estimate. After the second iteration, the estimate starts to develop credibility (see Figure 40.4).

> Useful estimates require investment in some elaboration iterations.

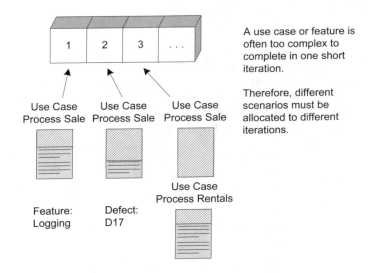

Figure 40.3 Work allocated to an iteration.

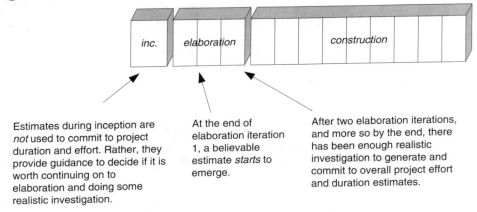

Figure 40.4 Estimation and project phases.

This is not to imply that it is impossible or worthless to attempt early, accurate estimates. If possible, very good. However, most organizations do not find this to be the case, for reasons that include continuous introduction of new technologies, novel applications, and many other complications. Thus, the UP advocates some realistic work in elaboration before generating estimates used for project planning and budgeting.

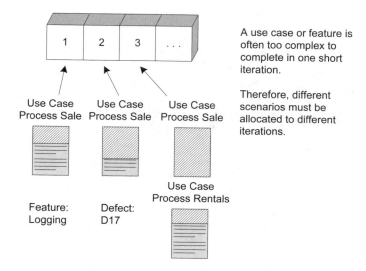

A use case or feature is often too complex to complete in one short iteration.

Therefore, different scenarios must be allocated to different iterations.

Figure 40.3 Work allocated to an iteration.

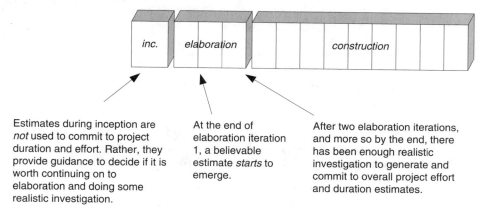

Estimates during inception are *not* used to commit to project duration and effort. Rather, they provide guidance to decide if it is worth continuing on to elaboration and doing some realistic investigation.

At the end of elaboration iteration 1, a believable estimate *starts* to emerge.

After two elaboration iterations, and more so by the end, there has been enough realistic investigation to generate and commit to overall project effort and duration estimates.

Figure 40.4 Estimation and project phases.

This is not to imply that it is impossible or worthless to attempt early, accurate estimates. If possible, very good. However, most organizations do not find this to be the case, for reasons that include continuous introduction of new technologies, novel applications, and many other complications. Thus, the UP advocates some realistic work in elaboration before generating estimates used for project planning and budgeting.

40.6   Organizing Project Artifacts

The UP organizes artifacts in terms of disciplines. The Use-Case Model and Supplementary Specifications are in the Requirements discipline. The Software Development Plan is part of the Project Management discipline, and so forth. Therefore, organize folders in your version control and directory system to reflect the disciplines, and place the artifacts of a discipline within the related discipline folder (see Figure 40.5).

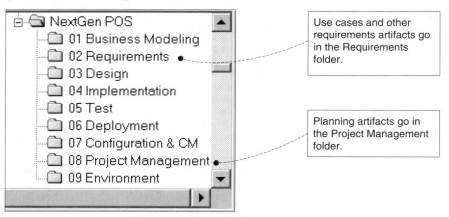

Figure 40.5 Organize UP artifacts into folders corresponding to their disciplines.

This organization works for most non-implementation elements. Some implementation artifacts, such as the actual database or executable files, are commonly found in different locations for a variety of implementation reasons.

Guideline

After each iteration, use the version control tool to create a labeled and frozen checkpoint of all the elements in these folders (including source code). There will be an "iteration-1," "iteration-2," and so on, version of each artifact. For later estimation of team velocity (on this or other projects), these checkpoints provide raw data of how much work got done per iteration.

40.7   You Know You Didn't Understand Iterative Planning When...

- All the iterations are speculatively planned in detail, with the work and objectives for each iteration predicted.

- Early estimates in inception or the first iteration of elaboration are expected to be reliable, and are used to make long-term project commitments; to generalize, reliable estimates are expected with trivial or light-weight investigation.

- Easy problems or low-risk issues are tackled in early iterations.

If an organization's estimation and planning process looks something like the following, planning in the UP was not understood:

1. At the start of an annual planning phase, new systems or features are identified at a high level; for instance, "Web system for account management."

2. Technical managers are given a short period to speculatively estimate the effort and duration for large, expensive, or risky projects, often involving new technologies.

3. The plan and budget of projects are established for the year.

4. Stakeholders are concerned when actual projects do not match original estimates. Go to Step 1.

This approach lacks realistic and iteratively refined estimation based upon serious investigation as promoted by the UP.

40.8   Recommended Resources

Agile and Iterative Development: A Manager's Guide by Larman provides many practice tips, in addition to the wide-spread evidence of the failure of the waterfall, and the advantage of iterative methods.

Organizational Patterns of Agile Software Development by Coplien and Harrison summarizes many successful iterative and agile process and project management tips.

Software Project Management: A Unified Framework by Royce provides an iterative and UP perspective on project planning and management.

Cockburn's *Surviving Object-Oriented Projects: A Manager's Guide* contains more useful information on iterative planning, and the transition to iterative and object technology projects.

Planning Extreme Programming by Beck and Fowler is another good resource.

Kruchten's *The Rational Unified Process: An Introduction* contains useful chapters specifically on planning and project management in the UP.

As a caution, there are some books that purport to discuss planning for "iterative development" or the "Unified Process" that actually belie a waterfall or predictive approach to planning.

Rapid Development [McConnell96] is an excellent overview of many practices and issues in planning and project management, and project risks.

BIBLIOGRAPHY

Abbot83   Abbott, R. 1983. Program Design by Informal English Descriptions. *Communications of the ACM* vol. 26(11).

AIS77   Alexander, C., Ishikawa, S., and Silverstein, M. 1977. *A Pattern Language—Towns-Building-Construction.* Oxford University Press.

Ambler00   Ambler, S. 2000. *The Unified Process—Elaboration Phase.* Lawrence, KA.: R&D Books.

Ambler00a   Ambler, S., Constantine, L. 2000. Enterprise-Ready Object IDs. *The Unified Process—Construction Phase.* Lawrence, KA.: R&D Books

Ambler00b   Ambler, S. 2000. Whitepaper: *The Design of a Robust Persistence Layer For Relational Databases.* www.ambysoft.com.

Ambler02   Ambler, S. 2002. *Agile Modeling,* John Wiley & Sons.

BDSSS00   Beedle, M., Devos, M., Sharon, Y., Schwaber, K., and Sutherland, J. 2000. SCRUM: A Pattern Language for Hyperproductive Software Development. *Pattern Languages of Program Design* vol. 4. Reading, MA.: Addison-Wesley.

BC87   Beck, K., and Cunningham, W. 1987. *Using Pattern Languages for Object-Oriented Programs.* Tektronix Technical Report No. CR-87-43.

BC89   Beck, K., and Cunningham, W. 1989. A Laboratory for Object-oriented Thinking. *Proceedings of OOPSLA 89.* SIGPLAN Notices, Vol. 24, No. 10.

BCK98   Bass, L., Clements, P., and Kazman, R. 1998. *Software Architecture in Practice.* Reading, MA.: Addison-Wesley.

Beck94   Beck, K. 1994. Patterns and Software Development. *Dr. Dobbs Journal.* Feb 1994.

Beck00   Beck, K. 2000. *Extreme Programming Explained—Embrace Change.* Reading, MA.: Addison-Wesley.

Bell04   Bell, A. 2004. Death by UML Fever. *ACM Queue.* March 2004.

BF00   Beck, K., Fowler, M., 2000. *Planning Extreme Programming.* Reading, MA.: Addison-Wesley.

BJ78   Bjørner, D., and Jones, C. editors. 1978. The Vienna Development Method: The Meta-Language, *Lecture Notes in Computer Science.* vol. 61. Springer-Verlag.

BJR97   Booch, G., Jacobson, I., and Rumbaugh, J. 1997. The UML specification documents. Santa Clara, CA.: Rational Software Corp. See documents at www.rational.com.

BMRSS96   Buschmann, F., Meunier, R., Rohnert, H., Sommerlad, P., and Stal, M. 1996. *Pattern-Oriented Software Architecture: A System of Patterns*. West Sussex, England: Wiley.

Boehm88   Boehm. B. 1988. A Spiral Model of Software Development and Enhancement. *IEEE Computer*. May 1988.

Boehm00+   Boehm, B., et al. 2000. *Software Cost Estimation with COCOMO II*. Englewood Cliffs, NJ.: Prentice-Hall.

Booch82   Booch, G. 1982. Object-Oriented Design. *Ada Letters* vol. 1(3).

Booch94   Booch, G. 1994. *Object-Oriented Analysis and Design*. Redwood City, CA.: Benjamin/Cummings.

Booch96   Booch, G. 1996. *Object Solutions: Managing the Object-Oriented Project*. Menlo Park, CA.: Addison-Wesley.

BP88   Boehm, B., and Papaccio, P. 1988. Understanding and Controlling Software Costs. *IEEE Transactions on Software Engineering*. Oct 1988.

BRJ99   Booch, G., Rumbaugh, J, and Jacobson, I., . 1999. *The Unified Modeling Language User Guide*. Reading, MA.: Addison-Wesley.

Brooks75   Brooks, F. 1975. *The Mythical Man-Month*. Reading, MA.: Addison-Wesley.

Brown01   Brown, K., 2001. The *Convert Exception* pattern is found online at the Portland Pattern Reposity, http://c2.com.

BW95   Brown, K., and Whitenack, B. 1995. *Crossing Chasms, A Pattern Language for Object-RDBMS Integration*, White Paper, Knowledge Systems Corp.

BW96   Brown, K., and Whitenack, B. 1996. Crossing Chasms. *Pattern Languages of Program Design* vol. 2. Reading, MA.: Addison-Wesley.

CD94   Cook, S., and Daniels, J. 1994. *Designing Object Systems*. Englewood Cliffs, NJ.: Prentice-Hall.

CDL99   Coad, P., De Luca, J., Lefebvre, E. 1999. *Java Modeling in Color with UML*. Englewood Cliffs, NJ.: Prentice-Hall.

CL99   Constantine, L, and Lockwood, L. 1999. *Software for Use: A Practical Guide to the Models and Methods of Usage-Centered Design*. Reading, MA.: Addison-Wesley.

CMS74   Constantine, L., Myers, G., and Stevens, W. 1974. Structured Design. *IBM Systems Journal*, vol. 13 (No. 2, 1974), pp. 115-139.

Coad92   Coad, P. 1992. Object-oriented Patterns. *Communications of the ACM*, Sept. 1992.

Coad95   Coad, P. 1995. *Object Models: Stategies, Patterns and Applications*. Englewood Cliffs, NJ.: Prentice-Hall.

Cockburn92   Cockburn, A. 1992. Using Natural Language as a Metaphoric Basis for Object-Oriented Modeling and Programming. *IBM Technical Report TR-36.0002*, 1992.

Cockburn97   Cockburn, A. 1997. Structuring Use Cases with Goals. *Journal of Object-Oriented Programming*, Sep-Oct, and Nov-Dec. SIGS Publications.

Cockburn01   Cockburn, A. 2001. *Writing Effective Use Cases*. Reading, MA.: Addison-Wesley.

Coleman+94   Coleman, D., et al. 1994. *Object-Oriented Development: The Fusion Method*. Englewood Cliffs, NJ.: Prentice-Hall.

Constantine68   Constantine. L. 1968. Segmentation and Design Strategies for Modular Programming. In Barnett and Constantine (eds.), *Modular Programming: Proceedings of a National Symposium*. Cambridge, MA.: Information & Systems Press.

Constantine94   Constantine, L. 1994. Essentially Speaking. *Software Development* May. CMP Media.

Conway58   Conway, M. 1958. Proposal for a Universal Computer-Oriented Language. *Communications of the ACM*. 5-8 Volume 1, Number 10, October.

Coplien95   Coplien, J. 1995. *The History of Patterns.* See http://c2.com/cgi/wiki?HistoryOfPatterns.

Coplien95a   Coplien, J. 1995. A Generative Development-Process Pattern Language. *Pattern Languages of Program Design* vol. 1. Reading, MA.: Addison-Wesley.

CS95   Coplien, J., and Schmidt, D., eds. 1995. *Pattern Languages of Program Design* vol. 1. Reading, MA.: Addison-Wesley.

Cunningham96   Cunningham, W. 1996. EPISODES: A Pattern Language of Competitive Development. *Pattern Languages of Program Design* vol. 2. Reading, MA.: Addison-Wesley.

Cutter97   Cutter Group. 1997. *Report: The Corporate Use of Object Technology.*

CV65   Corbato, F., and Vyssotsky, V. 1965. Introduction and overview of the Multics system. *AFIPS Conference Proceedings 27*, 185-196.

Dijkstra68   Dijkstra, E. 1968. The Structure of the THE-Multiprogramming System. *Communications of the ACM*, 11(5).

Eck95   Eck, D. 1995. *The Most Complex Machine.* A K Paters Ltd.

Fowler96   Fowler, M. 1996. *Analysis Patterns: Reusable Object Models.* Reading, MA.: Addison-Wesley.

Fowler99   Fowler, M. 1999. *Refactoring: Improving the Design of Existing Code.* Reading, MA.: Addison-Wesley.

Fowler00   Fowler, M. 2000. Put Your Process on a Diet. *Software Development.* December. CMP Media.

Fowler01   Fowler, M. 2001. Draft patterns on object-relational persistence services. www.martinfowler.com.

Fowler02   Fowler, M. 2002. *Patterns of Enterprise Application Architecture.* Reading, MA.: Addison-Wesley.

Fowler03   Fowler, M. 2003. *UML Distilled*, 3rd edition. Reading, MA.: Addison-Wesley.

Gartner95   Schulte, R., 1995. *Three-Tier Computing Architectures and Beyond.* Published Report Note R-401-134. Gartner Group.

Gemstone00   Gemstone Corp., 2000. A set of architectural patterns at www.javasuccess.com.

GHJV95   Gamma, E., Helm, R., Johnson, R., and Vlissides, J. 1995. *Design Patterns.* Reading, MA.: Addison-Wesley.

Gilb88   Gilb, T. 1988. *Principles of Software Engineering Management.* Reading, MA.: Addison-Wesley.

GK00   Guiney, E., and Kulak, D. 2000. *Use Cases: Requirements in Context.* Reading, MA.: Addison-Wesley.

GK76   Goldberg, A., and Kay, A. 1976. *Smalltalk-72 Instruction Manual.* Xerox Palo Alto Research Center.

GL00   Guthrie, R., and Larman, C. 2000. *Java 2 Performance and Idiom Guide*. Englewood Cliffs, NJ.: Prentice-Hall.

Grady92   Grady, R. 1992. *Practical Software Metrics for Project Management and Process Improvement*. Englewood Cliffs, NJ.: Prentice-Hall.

Groso00   Grosso, W. 2000. *The Name The Problem Not The Thrower* exceptions pattern is found online at the Portland Pattern Repository, http://c2.com.

GW89   Gause, D., and Weinberg, G. 1989. *Exploring Requirements*. NY, NY.: Dorset House.

Harrison98   Harrison, N. 1998. Patterns for Logging Diagnostic Messages. *Pattern Languages of Program Design* vol. 3. Reading, MA.: Addison-Wesley.

Hay96   Hay, D. 1996. *Data Model Patterns: Conventions of Thought*. NY, NY.: Dorset House.

Highsmith00   Highsmith, J. 2000. *Adaptive Software Development: A Collaborative Approach to Managing Complex Systems*. NY, NY.: Dorset House.

Hohman03   Hohman, L. 2003. *Beyond Software Architecture: Creating and Sustaining Winning Solutions*. Reading, MA.: Addison-Wesley.

HNS00   Hofmeister, C., Nord, R., and Soni, D. 2000. *Applied Software Architecture*. Reading, MA.: Addison-Wesley.

Jackson95   Jackson, M. 1995. *Software Requirements and Specification*. NY, NY.: ACM Press.

Jacobson92   Jacobson, I., *et al.* 1992. *Object-Oriented Software Engineering: A Use Case Driven Approach*. Reading, MA.: Addison-Wesley.

JAH00   Jeffries, R., Anderson, A., Hendrickson, C. 2000. *Extreme Programming Installed*. Reading, MA.: Addison-Wesley.

JBR99   Jacobson, I., Booch, G., and Rumbaugh, J. 1999. *The Unified Software Development Process*. Reading, MA.: Addison-Wesley.

Johnson02   Johnson, J. 2002. ROI—It's Your Job, XP 2002, Sardinia, Italy.

Jones97   Jones, C., 1997. *Applied Software Measurement*. NY, NY.: McGraw-Hill.

Jones98   Jones, C. 1998. *Estimating Software Costs*. NY, NY.: McGraw-Hill.

Kay68   Kay, A. 1968. *FLEX, a flexible extensible language*. M.Sc. thesis, Electrical Engineering, University of Utah. May. (Univ. Microfilms).

KL01   Kruchten, P, and Larman, C. How to Fail with the Rational Unified Process: 7 Steps to Pain and Suffering. (in German) *Objekt Spektrum*. June 2001.

Kovitz99   Kovitz, B. 1999. *Practical Software Requirements*. Greenwich, CT.: Manning.

Kruchten00   Kruchten, P. 2000. *The Rational Unified Process—An Introduction*, 2nd edition. Reading, MA.: Addison-Wesley.

Kruchten95   Kruchten, P. 1995. The 4+1 View Model of Architecture. *IEEE Software* 12(6).

Lakos96   Lakos, J. 1996. *Large-Scale C++ Software Design*. Reading, MA.: Addison-Wesley.

Larman03   Larman, C. 2003. *Agile and Iterative Development: A Manager's Guide*. Reading, MA.: Addison-Wesley.

Larman04   Larman, C. 2004. What UML Is and Isn't. *JavaPro Magazine*. March 2004.

LB03   Larman, C., and Basili, V. Iterative and Incremental Development: A Brief History, *IEEE Computer*, June 2003.

Lieberherr88   Lieberherr, K., Holland, I, and Riel, A. 1988. Object-Oriented Programming: An Objective Sense of Style. *OOPSLA 88 Conference Proceedings*. NY, NY.: ACM SIGPLAN.

Liskov88   Liskov, B. 1988. Data Abstraction and Hierarchy, *SIGPLAN Notices*, 23,5 (May, 1988).

LW00   Leffingwell, D., and Widrig, D. 2000. *Managing Software Requirements: A Unified Approach*. Reading, MA.: Addison-Wesley.

MacCormack01   MacCormack, A. 2001. Product-Development Practices That Work. *MIT Sloan Management Review*. Volume 42, Number 2.

Martin95   Martin, R. 1995. *Designing Object-Oriented C++ Applications Using the Booch Method*. Englewood Cliffs, NJ.: Prentice-Hall.

McConnell96   McConnell, S. 1996. *Rapid Development*. Redmond, WA.: Microsoft Press.

Meyer88   Meyer, B. 1988. *Object-Oriented Software Construction*, first edition. Englewood Cliffs, NJ.: Prentice-Hall.

MO95   Martin, J., and Odell, J. 1995. *Object-Oriented Methods: A Foundation*. Englewood Cliffs, NJ.: Prentice-Hall.

Moreno97   Moreno, A.M. Object Oriented Analysis from Textual Specifications. *Proceedings of the 9th International Conference on Software Engineering and Knowledge Engineering*, Madrid, June 17-20 (1997).

MP84   McMenamin, S., and Palmer, J. 1984. *Essential Systems Analysis*. Englewood Cliffs, NJ.: Prentice-Hall.

MW89   1989. *The Merriam-Webster Dictionary*. Springfield, MA.: Merriam-Webster.

Nixon90   Nixon, R. 1990. *Six Crises*. NY, NY.: Touchstone Press.

OMG03a   Object Management Group, 2003. UML 2.0 Infrastructure Specification. www.omg.org.

OMG03b   Object Management Group, 2003. UML 2.0 Superstructure Specification. www.omg.org.

Parkinson58   Parkinson, N. 1958. *Parkinson's Law: The Pursuit of Progress*, London, John Murray.

Parnas72   Parnas, D. 1972. On the Criteria To Be Used in Decomposing Systems Into Modules, *Communications of the ACM*, Vol. 5, No. 12, December 1972. ACM.

PM92   Putnam, L., and Myers, W. 1992. *Measures for Excellence: Reliable Software on Time, Within Budget*. Yourdon Press.

Pree95   Pree, W. 1995. *Design Patterns for Object-Oriented Software Development*. Reading, MA.: Addison-Wesley.

Renzel97   Renzel, K. 1997. *Error Handling for Business Information Systems: A Pattern Language*. Online at http://www.objectarchitects.de/arcus/cookbook/exhandling/.

Rising00   Rising, L. 2000. *Pattern Almanac 2000*. Reading, MA.: Addison-Wesley.

RJB99   Rumbaugh, J., Jacobson, I., and Booch, G. 1999. *The Unified Modeling Language Reference Manual*. Reading, MA.: Addison-Wesley.

RJB04   Rumbaugh, J., Jacobson, I., and Booch, G. 2004. *The Unified Modeling Language Reference Manual, 2e*. Reading, MA.: Addison-Wesley.

Ross97   Ross, R. 1997. *The Business Rule Book: Classifying, Defining and Modeling Rules*. Business Rule Solutions Inc.

Royce70   Royce, W. 1970. Managing the Development of Large Software Systems. *Proceedings of IEEE WESCON*. Aug 1970.

Rumbaugh91   Rumbaugh, J., *et al*. 1991. *Object-Oriented Modelling and Design*. Englewood Cliffs, NJ.: Prentice-Hall.

RUP   The Rational Unified Process Product. The browser-based online documentation for the RUP, sold by IBM, and previously by Rational Corp.

Rumbaugh97   Rumbaugh, J. 1997. Models Through the Development Process. *Journal of Object-Oriented Programming* May 1997. NY, NY: SIGS Publications.

Shaw96   Shaw, M. 1996. Some Patterns for Software Architectures. *Pattern Languages of Program Design* vol. 2. Reading, MA.: Addison-Wesley.

Standish94   Jim Johnson. 1994. *Chaos: Charting the Seas of Information Technology*. Published Report. The Standish Group

SW98   Schneider, G., and Winters, J. 1998. *Applying Use Cases: A Practical Guide*. Reading, MA.: Addison-Wesley.

Thomas01   Thomas, M. 2001. IT Projects Sink or Swim. *British Computer Society Review*.

TK78   Tsichiritzis, D., and Klug, A. The ANSI/X3/SPARC DBMS framework: Report of the study group on database management systems. *Information Systems*, 3 1978.

Tufte92   Tufte, E. 1992. *The Visual Display of Quantitative Information*. Graphics Press.

VCK96   Vlissides, J., et al. 1996. *Patterns Languages of Program Design* vol. 2. Reading, MA.: Addison-Wesley.

Wirfs-Brock93   Wirfs-Brock, R. 1993. Designing Scenarios: Making the Case for a Use Case Framework. *Smalltalk Report* Nov-Dec 1993. NY, NY: SIGS Publications.

WK99   Warmer, J., and Kleppe, A. 1999. *The Object Constraint Language: Precise Modeling With UML*. Reading, MA.: Addison-Wesley.

WM02   Wirfs-Brock, R., and McKean, A. 2002. *Object Design: Roles, Responsibilities, and Collaborations*. Reading, MA.: Addison-Wesley.

WWW90   Wirfs-Brock, R., Wilkerson, B., and Wiener, L. 1990. *Designing Object-Oriented Software*. Englewood Cliffs, NJ.: Prentice-Hall.

GLOSSARY

abstract class A class that can be used only as a superclass of some other class; no objects of an abstract class may be created except as instances of a subclass.

abstraction The act of concentrating the essential or general qualities of similar things. Also, the resulting essential characteristics of a thing.

active object An object with its own thread of control.

aggregation A property of an association representing a whole-part relationship and (usually) lifetime containment.

analysis An investigation of a domain that results in models describing its static and dynamic characteristics. It emphasizes questions of "what," rather than "how."

architecture Informally, a description of the organization, motivation, and structure of a system. Many different levels of architectures are involved in developing software systems, from physical hardware architecture to the logical architecture of an application framework.

association A description of a related set of links between objects of two classes.

attribute A named characteristic or property of a class.

class In the UML, "The descriptor of a set of objects that share the same attributes, operations, methods, relationships, and behavior" [RJB99]. May be used to represent software or conceptual elements.

class attribute A characteristic or property that is the same for all instances of a class. This information is usually stored in the class definition.

class hierarchy A description of the inheritance relations between classes.

class method A method that defines the behavior of the class itself, as opposed to the behavior of its instances.

classification Defines a relation between a class and its instances. The classification mapping identifies the extension of a class.

collaboration Two or more objects that participate in a client/server relationship in order to provide a service.

composition   The definition of a class in which each instance is comprised of other objects.

concept   A category of ideas or things. In this book, used to designate real-world things rather than software entities. A concept's intension is a description of its attributes, operations and semantics. A concept's extension is the set of instances or example objects that are members of the concept. Often defined as a synonym for domain class.

concrete class   A class that can have instances.

constraint   A restriction or condition on an element.

constructor   A special method called whenever an instance of a class is created in C++ or Java. The constructor often performs initialization actions.

container class   A class designed to hold and manipulate a collection of objects.

contract   Defines the responsibilities and postconditions that apply to the use of an operation or method. Also used to refer to the set of all conditions related to an interface.

coupling   A dependency between elements (such as classes, packages, subsystems), typically resulting from collaboration between the elements to provide a service.

delegation   The notion that an object can issue a message to another object in response to a message. The first object therefore delegates the responsibility to the second object.

derivation   The process of defining a new class by reference to an existing class and then adding attributes and methods The existing class is the superclass; the new class is referred to as the subclass or derived class.

design   A process that uses the products of analysis to produce a specification for implementing a system. A logical description of how a system will work.

domain   A formal boundary that defines a particular subject or area of interest.

encapsulation   A mechanism used to hide the data, internal structure, and implementation details of some element, such as an object or subsystem. All interaction with an object is through a public interface of operations.

event   A noteworthy occurrence.

extension   The set of objects to which a concept applies. The objects in the extension are the examples or instances of the concept.

framework   A set of collaborating abstract and concrete classes that may be used as a template to solve a related family of problems. It is usually extended via subclassing for application-specific behavior.

generalization   The activity of identifying commonality among concepts and defining a superclass (general concept) and subclass (specialized concept) relationships. It is a way to construct taxonomic classifications among concepts, which are then illustrated in class hierarchies. Conceptual subclasses conform to conceptual superclasses in terms of intension and extension.

inheritance	A feature of object-oriented programming languages by which classes may be specialized from more general superclasses. Attributes and method definitions from superclasses are automatically acquired by the subclass.
instance	An individual member of a class. In the UML, called an object.
instance method	A method whose scope is an instance. Invoked by sending a message to an instance.
instance variable	As used in Java and Smalltalk, an attribute of an instance.
instantiation	The creation of an instance of a class.
intension	The definition of a concept.
interface	A set of signatures of public operations.
link	A connection between two objects; an instance of an association.
message	The mechanism by which objects communicate; usually a request to execute a method.
metamodel	A model that defines other models. The UML metamodel defines the element types of the UML, such as Classifier.
method	In the UML, the specific implementation or algorithm of an operation for a class. Informally, the software procedure that can be executed in response to a message.
model	A description of static and/or dynamic characteristics of a subject area, portrayed through a number of views (usually diagrammatic or textual).
multiplicity	The number of objects permitted to participate in an association.
object	In the UML, an instance of a class that encapsulates state and behavior. More informally, an example of a thing.
object identity	The feature that the existence of an object is independent of any values associated with the object.
object-oriented analysis	The investigation of a problem domain or system in terms of domain concepts, such as conceptual classes, associations, and state changes.
object-oriented design	The specification of a logical software solution in terms of software objects, such as their classes, attributes, methods, and collaborations.
object-oriented programming language	A programming language that supports the concepts of encapsulation, inheritance, and polymorphism.
OID	Object Identifier.
operation	In the UML, "a specification of a transformation or query that an object may be called to execute" [RJB99]. An operation has a signature, specified by its name and parameters, and it is invoked via a message. A method is an implementation of an operation with a specific algorithm.

pattern A named description of a problem, solution, when to apply the solution, and how to apply the solution in new contexts.

persistence The enduring storage of the state of an object.

persistent object An object that can survive the process or thread that created it. A persistent object exists until it is explicitly deleted.

polymorphic operation The same operation implemented differently by two or more classes.

polymorphism The concept that two or more classes of objects can respond to the same message in different ways, using polymorphic operations. Also, the ability to define polymorphic operations.

postcondition A constraint that must hold true after the completion of an operation.

precondition A constraint that must hold true before an operation is requested.

private A scoping mechanism used to restrict access to class members so that other objects cannot see them. Normally applied to all attributes, and to some methods.

public A scoping mechanism used to make members accessible to other objects. Normally applied to some methods, but not to attributes, since public attributes violate encapsulation.

pure data values Data types for which unique instance identity is not meaningful, such as numbers, booleans, and strings.

qualified association An association whose membership is partitioned by the value of a qualifier.

receiver The object to which a message is sent.

recursive association An association where the source and the destination are the same object class.

responsibility A knowing or doing service or group of services provided by an element (such as a class or subsystem); a responsibility embodies one or more of the purposes or obligations of an element.

role A named end of an association to indicate its purpose.

state The condition of an object between events.

state transition A change of state for an object; something that can be signaled by an event.

subclass A specialization of another class (the superclass). A subclass inherits the attributes and methods of the superclass.

subtype A conceptual superclass. A specialization of another type (the supertype) that conforms to the intension and extension of the supertype.

superclass A class from which another class inherits attributes and methods.

supertype A conceptual superclass. In a generalization-specialization relation, the more general type; an object that has subtypes.

transition A relationship between states that is traversed if the specified event occurs and the guard condition met.

visibility The ability to see or have reference to an object.

INDEX

Symbols

.NET 307, 309

Numerics

4+1 view model 655, 656

A

abstract class 260, 514
   in UML 250, 260
abstract conceptual class 513
Abstract Factory 605
abstract operation 260
   in UML 250, 260
abstract use case 497
action 477
activation bar 228
active class 239, 269
active object 239, 269, 592
activity diagram 477, 478
actor 63, 80
   in use case 66
   offstage 66
   primary 66
   supporting 66
Adapter 436
adaptive development 21
adaptive vs. predictive planning 674
addition use case 497
aggregation 264
agile methods 17, 27, 28, 326, 673
agile modeling 14, 30
agile UP 31
analysis 6
analysis and design
   definition 6
analysis object models 134
architectural
   analysis 543, 544
   baseline 128
   decisions 544
   design principles 553
   factors 544
   patterns-promotion of 555
   proof-of-concept 557, 669
   prototype 128
   synthesis 557, 669
   view
      data 658
      deployment 658
      implementation 658
      logical 657
      process 658
      security 658
      use case 659
architectural approach documents 550
architectural factors 545
architectural view 656
architecturally significant requirements 545
architecture 200, 559
   cross-cutting concerns 554
   documenting 655
   factor table 546
   issue cards 550
   layered 202
   logical 197
   separation of concerns 554
   technical memos 550
artifact
   UML deployment diagrams 653
artifacts 34
   organizing 680
ASP.NET 307
aspect-oriented programming 555
association 150
   criteria for useful 150
   end name 255
   finding with list 155
   for UML properties 252
   link 240
   multiple between types 155
   multiplicity 153
   naming 152
   qualified 525
   reflexive 526
   role names 522
   UML notation 151
association class 266, 517
asynchronous message 596
   in communication diagrams 246
   in sequence diagrams 238
attribute 158
   and quantities 165
   data type 162
   derived 160, 524
   for UML properties 252
   in UML 250
   no foreign keys 165
   non-primitive types 163
   UML notation 159
   valid types 160

Q

R

S

X

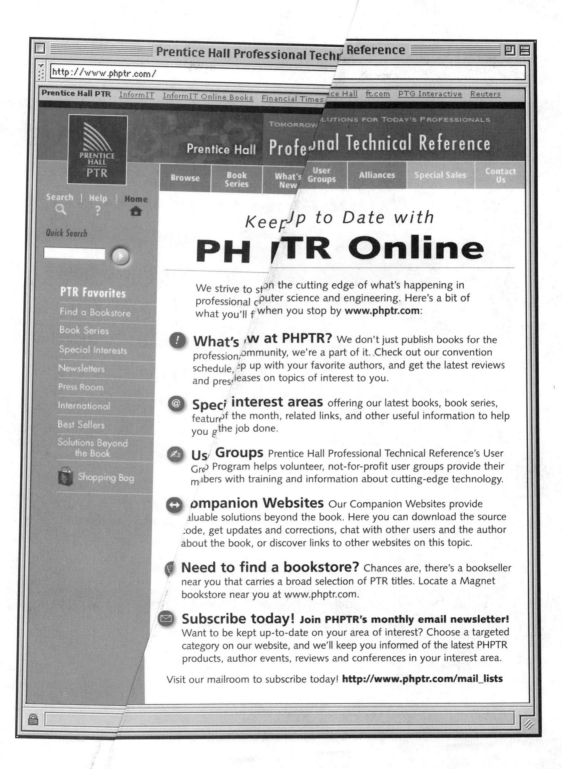

Also from Craig Larman

The Definitive
Guide for
Managers,
Practitioners,
and Students
of Agile and
Iterative
Development
Methods

In this book you will also find

- Compelling evidence that iterative methods reduce project risk
- Agile and iterative values and practices, as well as an FAQ
- Dozens of extremely useful iterative and agile practice tips
- New management skills for agile and iterative project leaders

Addison
Wesley

If you need to learn what agile and iterative development methods are, *the evidence,* how they work, and how to implement them, this is the book for you! Craig Larman offers a concise, information-packed summary of the key ideas that drive all agile and iterative processes, along with detailed comparisons of four distinct iterative methods: Scrum, XP, RUP, and Evo.

This book is the most convincing case ever made for iterative development. Craig Larman backs up his analysis with statistically significant research and large-scale case studies.

To learn more about this book and read a sample chapter, go to: www.awprofessional.com/titles/0131111558

Sample UML Notation

Class Diagram

AlternateUMLFor AbstractClass {abstract}
...

Abstract ClassX
...

«interface» InterfaceX
operation1()

ClassX
- classOrStaticAttribute : Int + publicAttribute : String - privateAttribute assumedPrivateAttribute isInitializedAttribute : Bool = true burgerCollection : VeggieBurger [*] attributeMayLegallyBeNull : String [0..1] finalConstantAttribute : Int = 5 { readOnly } /derivedAttribute

+ classOrStaticMethod()
+ publicMethod()
assumedPublicMethod()
- privateMethod()
# protectedMethod() 	
~ packageVisibleMethod()
«constructor» SuperclassFoo(Long)
methodWithParms(parm1 : String, parm2 : Float)
methodReturnsSomething() : VeggieBurger
methodThrowsException() {exception IOException}
abstractMethod()
abstractMethod2() { abstract }   // alternate
finalMethod() { leaf } // no override in subclass
synchronizedMethod() { guarded }

FinalClass {leaf}
...

1 Singleton
...

generalization

interface implementation

ClassY
operation1() ...

AlternateUMLFor ImplOfInterfaceX
operation1()

InterfaceX

Whole

1

Composition

*

Part

Associations:

ClassA	1 Association-name ▸ 1	ClassB
	role-1 role-2	

AssociationClass

Multiplicity:

*	Class	zero or more; "many"
1..40	Class	one to forty
1..*	Class	one or more
5	Class	exactly five

Domain::ClassX
myClock : Runnable
...
...

home package of class

1

myClock

navigability

Clock
myThread : Thread ...
run() ...

Runnable

active class

Use Case Diagram

NextGen POS

Cashier

Process Sale

Extension Points:
Payment
VIP Customer

«actor»
CreditAuthorization
Service

«extend»
Payment, if Customer
presents a gift certificate

«include»

Handle Gift Certificate
Payment

Handle Credit
Payment